introduction to
FORENSIC
SCIENCE
& Criminalistics

R. E. Gaensslen
University of Illinois at Chicago

Howard A. Harris
University of New Haven

Henry C. Lee
University of New Haven

introduction to
FORENSIC
SCIENCE
& Criminalistics

Boston   Burr Ridge, IL   Dubuque, IA   Madison, WI   New York   San Francisco   St. Louis
Bangkok   Bogotá   Caracas   Kuala Lumpur   Lisbon   London   Madrid   Mexico City
Milan   Montreal   New Delhi   Santiago   Seoul   Singapore   Sydney   Taipei   Toronto

Higher Education

Published by McGraw-Hill, a business unit of The McGraw-Hill Companies, Inc., 1221 Avenue of the Americas, New York, NY, 10020. Copyright © 2008 by The McGraw-Hill Companies, Inc. All rights reserved. No part of this publication may be reproduced or distributed in any form or by any means, or stored in a database or retrieval system, without the prior written consent of The McGraw-Hill Companies, Inc., including, but not limited to, in any network or other electronic storage or transmission, or broadcast for distance learning.

Some ancillaries, including electronic and print components, may not be available to customers outside the United States.

This book is printed on acid-free paper.

Printed in China

7 8 9 0 CTP/CTP 12

ISBN: 978-0-07-298848-2

MHID: 0-07-298848-7

Publisher: *Frank Mortimer*
Sponsoring Editor: *Katie Stevens*
Freelance Developmental Editor: *Craig S. Leonard*
Senior Marketing Manager: *Daniel M. Loch*
Senior Project Manager: *Christina Thornton-Villagomez*
Art Editor: *Robin Mouat/Rennie Evans*
Design Manager: *Laurie J. Entringer*
Senior Photo Research Coordinator: *Alexandra Ambrose*
Photo Researcher: *Christine Pullo*
Media Producer: *Christie Ling*
Production Supervisor: *Janean A. Utley*
Composition: *Techbooks*
Printing: *CTPS*

Credits: The credits section for this book begins on page 405 and is considered an extension of the copyright page.

Cover: © Photo Disc/Getty Images

Library of Congress Cataloging-in-Publication Data

Gaensslen, R. E. (Robert E.)
 Introduction to forensics and criminalistics / R.E. Gaensslen, Howard A. Harris, Henry C. Lee.
     p. cm.
 Includes bibliographical references and index.
 ISBN-13: 978-0-07-298848-2 (hardcover : alk. paper)
 ISBN-10: 0-07-298848-7 (hardcover : alk. paper)
 1. Criminal investigation. 2. Crime scenes. 3. Forensic sciences. 4. Evidence, Criminal. I. Harris, Howard A. II. Lee, Henry C. III. Title.
HV8073.G274 2008
363.25—dc22

                                                                    2006021412

The Internet addresses listed in the text were accurate at the time of publication. The inclusion of a Web site does not indicate an endorsement by the authors or McGraw-Hill, and McGraw-Hill does not guarantee the accuracy of the information presented at these sites.

www.mhhe.com

To all the highly committed and largely unrecognized professionals who labor in forensic science laboratories throughout the nation. Former Attorney General John Ashcroft stated the case for their importance well in remarks made at the 2004 Plenary Session of the American Academy of Forensic Sciences annual meeting.

Excerpts from the Remarks of Hon. John Ashcroft, Attorney General of the United States, to the American Academy of Forensic Sciences, Dallas, Texas, February 18, 2004

We have the privilege, the opportunity, and the responsibility to protect the lives and liberty of the American people. This means preventing and punishing the predatory and lawless; detecting, disrupting and deterring those who would harm Americans; and, all the while, honoring the Constitution and the rule of law. . . .

The American Academy of Forensic Sciences has become a critical part of our nation's effort to provide equal protection under the law for every citizen.

Few groups have had as profound an impact on justice as the forensic science community.

The men and women in this room save lives. Your knowledge, your expertise, and your dedication to the truth bring justice to the guilty and a measure of peace to victims.

Forensic science is no longer on the fringes of criminal investigations. Science is solving cases that would otherwise remain unsolved. Science is identifying the guilty with a certainty that protects the innocent at the same time.

Forensic science plays no favorites. It cuts through prejudice. It validates truth. And to the extent that it speeds the arrest of criminals, it helps prevent crime, cutting short the careers of habitual offenders. . . .

A free nation is built on a fundamental trust in the citizen. And our free institutions, in turn, depend on the public's trust in the justice system. Thanks in part to advances in technology, Americans have grown more confident in law enforcement and more cooperative in the battle against crime. That is why the Department of Justice has been so supportive of proven forensic science and seeks to push forward new forensic advances. . . .

The war against terror reminds us all what an extraordinary vision founded this nation.

The war on terror has reminded us that there are those who oppose freedom, who abhor tolerance and new ideas, and who distrust this nation's fundamental belief that every life has potential and every life is precious. This shared vision is why we defend the rule of law. It is why we seek to punish the guilty. It is why we wish to take heart when the innocent are exonerated.

Your towering accomplishments—often beginning with the tiniest molecules of evidence—have had a profoundly powerful effect: protecting the integrity of the law and vindicating the suffering of victims.

dedication

R. E. GAENSSLEN

Dr. Gaensslen received his bachelor's degree from the University of Notre Dame and a Ph.D. in biochemistry from Cornell University. He was a professor at John Jay College in New York for eight years, and a Visiting Fellow to the National Institute of Law Enforcement and Criminal Justice of the Law Enforcement Assistance Administration, U.S. Dept of Justice, for two years. For 18 years, he was a professor at the University of New Haven and director of the forensic science program for most of those years. Since the mid-1990s he has been a professor at the University of Illinois at Chicago and head of its forensic science graduate program.

Dr. Gaensslen has published numerous scientific papers and authored or co-authored a number of books. He was editor of the *Journal of Forensic Sciences* for nine years and continues to be an associate editor of that journal. He has received numerous awards and recognitions from professional organizations. He has also participated in many crime scene training programs for police personnel.

Howard A. HARRIS

Dr. Harris received his bachelor's degree in chemistry from Western Reserve University and his master's degree and Ph.D. in chemistry from Yale University. Dr. Harris also has a law degree from St. Louis University and was admitted to the Missouri Bar.

Dr. Harris was a research chemist for seven years for the Shell Oil Company before entering the forensic field as the director of the New York City Police Department Police Laboratory, where he served for 12 years. He moved upstate to become the director of the Monroe County Public Safety Laboratory in Rochester, New York, and continued there for 11 years until he took early retirement and joined the University of New Haven as the director of the forensic science program. He is currently a full-time faculty member in the forensic science program at the University of New Haven.

He has been active in the field, holding leadership positions in several national organizations such as the American Academy of Forensic Sciences and the American Society of Crime Laboratory Directors, and he has presented and published technical papers in the field of forensic science.

Henry C. LEE

Dr. Lee began his law enforcement career in Taiwan, reaching the rank of police captain, before coming to the United States. He earned a second bachelor's degree from John Jay College in New York City and a Ph.D. in biochemistry from New York University. He was a full-time professor at the University of New Haven for several years and is responsible for building the forensic science academic program there, while acting as a consultant to the Connecticut State Police. In 1979, Dr. Lee became the laboratory director and chief criminalist of the state police forensic science laboratory, a position he held for 20 years. He served for several years as Commissioner of Public Safety of the State of Connecticut, prior to retiring from government. He is now director of the Henry C. Lee Institute of Forensic Sciences at the University of New Haven.

Dr. Lee is an internationally recognized authority in forensic science. He has worked on thousands of cases and testified at thousands of trials in his career. He is a regular guest on television shows. He has written hundreds of scientific papers and numerous books. In addition, Dr. Lee has many honorary doctoral degrees from numerous institutions and has lectured widely for colleges, universities, and law enforcement organizations. He also has received numerous awards from professional organizations and law enforcement agencies, as well as from state governments.

Brief Contents

Contents

Part 3   Physical Pattern Evidence and Technological Examinations   105

CHAPTER 5
Examination of Physical Pattern Evidence   107

CHAPTER 6
Fingerprints and Other Personal Identification Patterns   123

Part 4 Biological Evidence 209

Forensic science has become something of a household word in the past decade or so. Forensic DNA analysis, perhaps the most important development in forensic science ever, regularly makes the news now. For a number of years, probably beginning with cable television's interest in covering high-profile criminal trials, and the O.J. Simpson trial in particular, forensic science has become a regular feature on documentary as well as on news programs. And, in recent years, network television has featured prime-time programming that has forensic science as a focus; the *CSI* series is no doubt the most widely recognized.

The mass exposure to forensic science through media creates a danger of incorrect or misleading impressions and information through sensationalism and "artistic license." Under these circumstances, there is a need to provide good, reliable sources of information on the subject. Many college and university students throughout the country take introductory forensic science courses. The majority of them want to learn something about the subject, and perhaps how investigators, police, and attorneys make use of the information it can provide. They do not intend to be forensic scientists. There has never been a forensic science textbook directly aimed at these students, who are our citizens future, jurors, police officers, investigators, and lawyers. This is that book. It has a structure reflecting an underlying philosophy about forensic science as a science and as a profession. Appropriate pedagogic features have been incorporated. And the authors have vast and varied experience as forensic scientists and teachers.

The book was written for students to use in an undergraduate college or university course for nonmajors. It comfortably fits into a one-semester schedule. The book is primarily an introduction to what is often called "criminalistics." Think of criminalistics as comprising the activities and specialty areas found in a modern, full-service forensic science laboratory.

Organization

The whole book is organized along the lines of the criminalistics concepts of identification, individualization, and reconstruction. After introductory material and orientation to the subject, we move from crime scene investigation and reconstruction pattern analysis to categories of evidence for which individualization is the goal. Finally, types of evidence having identification as the primary goal of laboratory analysis are treated.

Following the introductory material in Part One, the book is divided into four more parts, each with two or more chapters. Those parts reflect the underlying philosophy of the book's order and organization. Part Two covers crime scene analysis and reconstruction patterns. Part Three treats another kind of pattern evidence; namely, pattern evidence, the primary goal of which is often individualization. Part Four covers biological evidence analysis and forensic DNA typing. Although biological evidence fits into the category of "evidence for individualization," the subject has become so important that it warrants separate treatment. Part Five involves evidence often called "chemical" and "trace." With these classes, identification and possibly quantitation is all that the lab is generally required to do.

The chapters on particular types of evidence (such as blood, drugs, etc.) all have an internal organization: the subject matter and background are introduced and explained; strategies and methods for collecting and packaging that type of evidence are enumerated and explained; and finally, the methods used for the forensic examination of that type of evidence, results that can be expected, and the strengths and limitations of the tests are presented and discussed.

Pedagogy

Even though the book was written for students who have little or no science or chemistry background, some basic concepts in scientific measurement and methods are necessary to fully understand all the material. Understanding the basic concepts will help students understand the science behind forensic science. Each chapter contains *More on the Science* boxes that take the students further into the methods or techniques that are described and may enrich the reading of the text for students who have more science background. We have tried to arrange the boxes so that a basic understanding of the subject does not require them.

In addition, there is an appendix called "Scientific Tools of the Trade—Methods of Forensic Science," which provides students with brief introductions to metric system measurement, the basic concepts of physical properties, and the chemical makeup of matter, elements, molecules, light and its interactions with matter, and an introduction to various instrumental methods.

Real-world forensic cases from our collective experience, and from the experience of other forensic scientists, are presented at the beginning of each chapter. Each case contains some of the basic topics covered in the chapter, so that students can see how the concepts are applied to real-world forensic investigation. The cases are designed to illustrate how the evidence discussed in that chapter can figure importantly in sorting out a real case. In addition, we have placed short case studies throughout the chapters of the book to help illustrate specific points and reinforce the potential utility of the evidence.

Each chapter is well illustrated with photographs and figures from the case files of the authors. This way, students can actually see how to dust for fingerprints or what the different types of bloodstain patterns look like.

Collectively, we have spent nearly 100 years practicing and teaching forensic science, and we do hope that the book manages to convey some of the sense of excitement and commitment that we still feel about our work!

Supplements

As a full-service publisher of quality educational products, McGraw-Hill does much more than just sell textbooks. The company creates and publishes an extensive array of print, video, and digital supplements for students and instructors.

For the Student

Online Learning Center Web site—A great source for self-quizzes and additional information on forensic science.

For the Instructor

- *Instructor's Manual*—detailed chapter outlines, lecture notes, and teaching tips.
- *Test Bank*—a complete source of questions for each chapter of the text.
- *PowerPoint Slides*—chapter-specific slide shows featuring many of the illustrations from the text.
- *Online Learning Center Web site*—password-protected access to downloadable supplements and other important instructor support materials and additional resources.
- *Course Management Systems*—whether you use WebCT, Blackboard, e-College, or another course management system, McGraw-Hill will provide you with a cartridge that enables you either to conduct your course entirely online or to supplement your lectures with online material. And if your school does not yet have one of these course management systems, we can provide you with PageOut, an

easy-to-use tool that allows you to create your own course Web page and access all material on the Online Learning Center.
- *Primis Online*—a unique database publishing system that allows instructors to create a customized text from material in this text or elsewhere and deliver that text to students electronically as an e-book or in print format via the bookstore.

Acknowledgements

The authors would like to thank the following reviewers for lending their valuable experience and knowledge to this text.

John Boal
University of Akron

David Collins
Colorado State University–Pueblo

Charles Cornett
University of Wisconsin-Platteville

Cindy DeForest Hauser
Davidson College

Wavell Fogleman
Plymouth State University

J. Brent Friesen
Dominican University

David Fruchtman
Chaparral College

Joanna Haan
Parkland College

Julie Jervis, M.D.
Chief Medical Examiner, Mohave County, Arizona

Frank Keegan
Guilford College

Craig Laker
Tri-State University

Lakshmaiah Sreerama
St Cloud State University

William Lavell
Camden County College

Matthew J. Mio
University of Detroit Mercy

Disa Padgett
Texas Wesleyan University

Corey Stilts
Chatham College

Kenneth Traxler
Bemidji State University

Dawnie Wolfe Steadman
Binghamton University

We also thank Jacqueline Gaensslen and Carolyn Sher Harris for many years of patience and tolerance, and Sara Melton, a one-time graduate student at UIC, for assistance with the pictures and artwork; Margaret Lee, An Fu Lee, and colleagues at the Connecticut Forensic Science Laboratory, Connecticut State Police and University of New Haven; and finally, generations of students for "beta testing" the material in this book.

walkthrough

Learning Objectives

Learning Objectives provide students with learning goals for mastering the content in each chapter.

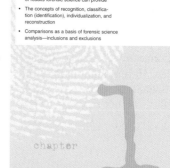

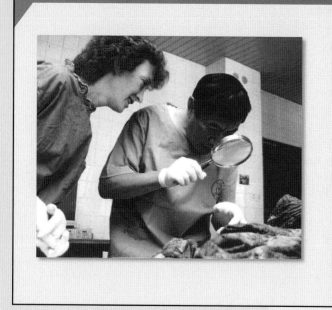

Introduction to Forensic Science

Learning Objectives

- The nature and role of forensic science
- The value of forensic science to the society
- The historical development of forensic science
- Development of forensic science and laboratories in the United States
- Forensic science laboratory operations
- The importance of anthropometry and fingerprint identification to the development of forensic science
- Nature of the scientific method and how it might operate in everyday situations
- The key role that scientific method plays in all aspects of forensic science and investigation
- The main specialty areas of forensic science and the scope of each of them
- Elements of forensic analysis and the types of results forensic science can provide
- The concepts of recognition, classification (identification), individualization, and reconstruction
- Comparisons as a basis of forensic science analysis—inclusions and exclusions

Outline

What Is Forensic Science?
Science in the Service of the Law
Value of Forensic Science
A Brief History of Forensic Science
Development of Forensic Science
    Laboratories and Professional
    Organizations
Nature of Science and the Scientific Method
The Scientific Method and Its Applicability to
    Forensic Science and to Investigation
Forensic Science Specialties
Elements of Forensic Evidence Analysis—
    The Types of Results Forensic
    Scientists Produce

chapter 1

Chapter Outlines

The Chapter Outlines provide an overview of the major sections in each chapter.

Lead Case

State V. Richard Crafts
(This case has sometimes been called the "Wood Chipper Case")

In November of 1986, a flight attendant for Pan American World Airways named Helle Crafts returned to New York's John F. Kennedy International Airport from a routine international flight. She and another flight attendant, who both lived in Newtown, Connecticut, and were friends, took a limousine ride home. The limousine dropped Mrs. Crafts off at her home, and she and her flight attendant friend agreed to call one another later. Helle Crafts was never seen again.

Later, and into early December, the flight attendant friend tried to contact Helle without success. A private investigator named Oliver Mayo, who had been hired by Mrs. Crafts to investigate the possible extramarital activities of her husband, Richard, was also trying to find Helle. He had gathered unequivocal incriminating evidence of an extramarital affair against her husband, Richard, and Mayo wanted to give the information to Mrs. Crafts and collect his fee. When the local police were contacted, they did not show much interest in the case, indicating that Mrs. Crafts was an adult, that she hadn't been missing that long, and that she would probably turn up. Ultimately, the state attorney's office was contacted and an investigation by the state police was initiated.

Richard Crafts was a pilot for Eastern Airlines and flew a regular New York to Miami run. He was also a part-time officer in the local police department. The couple had three children, and

because they were in the airline industry and required to travel so much, they had a live-in nanny.

Investigation by the state police showed that the morning after Helle returned from the international trip, Richard had risen early and told the nanny to take the children to the grandparents. Further investigation revealed that he had rented a large, diesel-powered wood chipper from a dealership a week earlier. (See Figure 1.1.) This large model wood chipper was one of only two in the state, and the only one in the southwestern area. The rental agent remembered Richard, because he had come to rent the machine driving a small passenger vehicle. The agent had told him the car was not powerful enough to pull the wood chipper, so Richard had then gone out and rented a U-Haul truck to pull the wood chipper. The agent also remembered that the wood chipper had been returned in the cleanest condition that he could ever remember.

Richard did own a wooded lot in Newtown. It was not, therefore, illogical for him to go and rent the chipper, except that all this activity was taking place during a major snowstorm in that part of the state. The storm had most people off the roads and at home, and many institutions were temporarily closed. A state snowplow driver reported seeing a U-Haul truck towing a large wood chipper headed toward Lake Zoar, a man-made lake (reservoir)—but he could not see who was driving. This activity took place the next night after Helle Crafts had returned home and gone missing.

The state police were suspicious that Helle might have met with foul play, and that Richard might be involved, but the evidence

Richard Crafts.

Figure 1.1 The diesel-powered wood chipper believed to have been used by Richard Crafts to dispose of portions of his wife's body following her murder.

was sketchy. Thinking the wood chipper might somehow be involved, an extensive search of the area along Lake Zoar was conducted. Thinking the worst—that maybe Helle had been killed and the wood chipper used to dispose of her remains—the state police, with the help of criminalists and a forensic odontologist from the forensic laboratory, searched for skeletal or other remains. With winter arriving, heavy snow covered the leaves that had fallen to the ground. The investigators and forensic scientists melted away the snow inch by inch as they searched, because the leaves and debris had to be separated from things underneath them. Large quantities of leaves, debris, and anything else on the ground were placed in oil drums filled with water to float off the leaves and light plant material. The water was then emptied through narrow mesh sieves to capture any small items that might have been present on the ground.

After some days searching, the forensic investigation team recovered the following (Figure 1.2):

- A human tooth
- A dental restoration
- 56 small pieces of bone, and 2,660 strands of human hair
- A portion of a human finger with some friction ridge skin
- A toenail painted with red nail polish

Now convinced they were handling a [...]
the state police and the forensic laborato [...]
forensic team to try and establish what h [...]

A state police dive team search in [...]
resulted in the recovery of a gasoline-pow [...]
not very old, and its fuel tank was still hal [...]
number had been filed down to prevent re [...]
number restoration in the laboratory reve [...]
records showed that this chain saw had be [...]
Crafts a few years previous. He had use [...]
purchase record was still available. The [...]
Richard had rented the U-Haul truck and [...]
were extensively searched for evidence.

Wood chips were recovered from the [...]
truck. The chain saw blade was carefully [...]

Figure 1.2
Some of the numerous human bone fragments recovered in and near the wooded lot owned by Crafts on the shore of Lake Zoar; all the recovered fragments were human, and originated from the head, hands, or the feet.

bits of blood, tissue, fragments of head hair, and some bluish-green fibers. There was blood on some of the fibers.

The forensic issues in the case can be summarized as follows:

- Were the skeletal remains recovered those of Helle Crafts?
- Could a cause and manner of death be established? Was this a homicidal death?
- If the remains were of Helle Crafts, and if the death was homicidal, could Richard be implicated?

The forensic aspects of the investigation of this case involved many specialties: pathology, odontology, bone identification (physical anthropology), criminalistics, trace and materials evidence comparisons (such as the nail polish), wood chip comparisons, biological evidence, hair and fiber, toolmarks, and handwriting comparisons.

The evidence gathered is shown in the table on the next page, along with the forensic testing used for its examination, and the conclusions reached. Note that some of the findings are conclusive, but others are circumstantial.

The tooth and restoration identity were definite, so the remains recovered on the shoreline were those of Helle. The pathologist ultimately ruled the death a homicide based in part on

Lead Case

Hit-and-Run Death
of a State Police Lieutenant

One morning early, a Connecticut state police lieutenant, commander of the Troop A barracks, was driving to work along Interstate 84 between Hartford and Waterbury. He noticed a disabled motorist pulled over on the shoulder of the road. Although he was not a patrol officer, and had no obligation to stop, he pulled over to assist the motorist. In accordance with protocol, he pulled the police cruiser up behind the disabled vehicle, engaged the emergency light bar, and exited the car. According to the motorist, his vehicle, the lieutenant's vehicle, and the lieutenant, were off the roadway and on the shoulder.

While the lieutenant was out of his vehicle, he was struck by a passing tractor-trailer rig, thrown a considerable distance, and probably died almost immediately. The tractor-trailer rig did not stop.

Word of the mishap was quickly relayed to state police who rushed to the scene of the hit-and-run and deployed considerable manpower to locate and stop the truck. The major crime squad and a team from the laboratory also helped in the hit-and-run scene investigation.

State police located and stopped a tractor-trailer rig that fit the description that had been given by the motorist. They were able to stop the rig before it could cross the bridge into New York State.

The major crime squad and laboratory team carefully examined the tractor-trailer for evidence. On the front portion of the trailer at what would be just about shoulder height for the state police lieutenant, the lab investigators found a nearly perfect mirror-image dust impression of the Connecticut state police shoulder patch worn on both shoulders of the uniform (see photos below).

The dust impression sealed the case from both criminal and civil points of view. The truck driver was convicted of hit-and-run manslaughter and sentenced to prison time. The company that owned the truck was sued civilly on behalf of the state police lieutenant's family, and the jury came back with a multimillion-dollar award for the lieutenant's wife and young family.

This case starkly illustrates the extraordinary value that physical pattern evidence can have sometimes, because it can be so clear, intuitive, and correspondingly convincing.

(a) (b) (c)

(A) The trailer (number 160) thought to be involved in the hit-and-run showed a dust-like smudge near the corner of the trailer. (B) Closer inspection revealed a near perfect mirror image of the Connecticut State Police shoulder patch that resulted from the trailer hitting the lieutenant. (C) The uniform shirt with the actual shoulder patch worn by the lieutenant on the morning of his untimely death.

Lead Cases

Lead Cases are presented at the beginning of each chapter and offer *Real-world forensic cases* from the authors' collective experience, and from the experience of other forensic scientists. Each case contains some of the basic topics covered in the chapter, so that students can see how the concepts are applied to real-world forensic investigation.

Case Study Boxes

Case Study Boxes provide short cases and appear throughout each chapter to help illustrate specific points and reinforce the potential utility of the evidence.

Case Study 5.1

Imprint Evidence Associates a Suspect with a Multiple Murder Scene

Several years ago, people in Warwick, Rhode Island, were shocked by the finding of all three members of one family—a mother and her two daughters—brutally stabbed to death in their home. The mother was raising her daughters by herself, had no known enemies, and was not involved in any kind of criminal activity. There was no obvious motive for the homicide.

Forensic experts from the FBI and the Connecticut state police were asked to assist in the investigation. The youngest daughter's body was found in the kitchen; the oldest daughter's body, in the hallway; and the mother's body, in the bedroom. The clothing on all three was intact, and there were no signs of sexual attack. It did not appear that rape was the motive.

A kitchen window at the back of the house had been pried open and appeared to be the point of entry. The window was high off the ground, suggesting that the perpetrator, who more than likely climbed in the window, would have to be of above average height and strength. Inside the house, directly below the window, a small kitchen table appeared to have just been broken, as if someone heavy had stepped on the table while coming through the window. A reddish footwear imprint pattern was observed on the tabletop. In addition, a partial palm print was also found.

There was a large amount of blood in the kitchen, hallway, and bedroom. Bloody footwear-like prints were observed leading from the kitchen to the living room window, then toward the hallway. Upon closer examination, it was found that the prints were made by socks, not shoes. The sock prints were found throughout the house, as if someone, one person only, searched every room, looking for something.

It was also discovered that bloodstains were in different stages of coagulation. The youngest daughter's blood was clearly dry. The mother's blood was in an advanced stage of coagulation. But other drops of blood definitely were fresher and in semiliquid stage. These blood drops were consistent with low-velocity passive dripping from a height of approximately 3 to 4 feet. The fresh blood drops were consistent with someone bleeding from a serious cut of the hand or finger.

A crime scene profile indicated that the house was the primary scene, and sex was not the motive. The suspect was more than likely a strong young man, perhaps a teenager, of above average height, overweight, and with a serious cut on one hand or arm.

Police put out the word, and, in one of those examples of keen observation that would bring a pat on the back from every law enforcement officer, a Warwick detective noticed a teenager working on a car. What caught the officer's attention was the bandage the boy wore on his hand. The officer stopped to chat and asked the boy about the bandage. Craig Price said he had cut his hand. The police officer asked Price to come to the station.

A court order was obtained for blood, hair, fingerprints, footprint, and shoe exemplars. Laboratory testing showed the following results:

1. The partial handprint on the kitchen tabletop matched the right hand of the suspect.
2. The footwear imprint on the kitchen tabletop was similar in size, shape, sole pattern, and other class characteristics to the suspect's shoe.
3. Several latent fingerprints were found inside the house that matched the known fingerprints of the suspect.
4. DNA profiling showed that several blood drops matched the known DNA from the suspect.

The evidence was sufficient to allow the prosecution to proceed and for a trial jury to convict this suspect of three counts of murder.

techniques can be used to address such problems and make pattern information more useful.

Several photographic techniques such as side lighting, and use of special illumination such as UV, laser, or alternate light source, have been mentioned. In addition, filters can be used to increase contrast where background and pattern are of different colors. Special films and high-contrast printing papers can also help in some situations.

A number of physical and chemical techniques are also used to clarify or enhance contrast. As mentioned, chemical blood test reagents can be used to make very subtle blood patterns visible through color change or added image intensity of even very weak patterns. Fingerprint powders and a variety of lifters can help isolate the imprint from the background or enhance contrast.

Finally, many of the preceding enhancements can be done more quickly and more effectively using digital imaging techniques. A number of programs, such as Photoshop and Image Pro, have tremendous power to improve the clarity and contrast of images. They work well on digital images captured either photographically or scanned on a flat-bed scanner. Once the image information is digitized, the variety of techniques available is extensive. They must be done in a well-documented way if such improved images are to be used in court. The Scientific Working Group on Imaging Technology (SWGIT) established proposed guidelines for image acquisition, handling, documentation, and enhancement in 2005.

With all the mentioned clarification techniques, it is critical that the original image be well documented before any of the techniques are used, since some may degrade or destroy the image rather than clarify it.

Weapon, Tool, and Object M

Many types of patterns crime scene or be left object. Those patterns direct contact of two earprints, button prints, or they can be produce cuts, wounds, or patter

---

Classification (Identification)

The next step in almost any examination of evidence is **classification (identification).** Whatever is being examined—a glassine envelope containing white powder, a hair, a fiber, a paint chip, a bloodstain—it must first be classified; that is, identified. Classification is the process of placing that object within a group of similar objects. For example, we can recognize many different objects, with quite different appearance, and still classify them all as chairs. It might be a very broad group or a highly specific group. Classifying things is not "individualizing" them.

With some types of evidence, generally the ones we will group under the heading of "chemical evidence" (illicit drugs, gunshot residue, etc.), examination in the forensic lab consists exclusively of classification. Chemical or instrumental techniques are required to establish these classifications, and the courts require that this be done to sustain a prosecution. Note that sometimes, items are classified in the laboratory as a means of establishing the corpus delicti of a crime (see earlier). Demonstrating that fire debris contains an ignitable liquid residue that could be an accelerant material helps establish that arson may have been committed. Demonstrating that semen is present on a vaginal swab taken from a sexual assault complainant corroborates that penetration occurred. The laboratory must establish these crucial facts if cases are going to be properly proven.

An important result of the classification, or the association, process is exclusion from the class, or disassociation. The "negative association" has the advantage of being an absolute in most instances. When significant differences from other items in the class are found, the object is excluded and is clearly not in the class. As one compares two objects and tries to see if they are in the same very small class, one can never be sure that one more comparison might not remove them from the same class. The same problem does not exist with elimination or disassociation (also see later under Individualization).

One common problem in understanding forensic results is that the word *identification* can mean *classification* in one context, but it is also used to mean *individualization* in another context. Identifying a small piece of material, such as a paint chip, is a classification. Identifying a fingerprint, or a person, is an individualization. We will use the term "identification" to mean individualization in the pattern evidence chapters and in discussing the identification of persons, because that is the terminology that those specialists regularly use. We will use "classification" or "classification (identification)" to mean placing an item or person into a group when dealing with other items of physical evidence.

Case Study 1.2

Simple Classification of a Common Object Can Be an Important First Step in Formulating a Hypothesis about a Case

A knife is found near the victim at the scene of a homicide. The first thing that the investigator does, sometimes largely unconsciously, is classifying that knife. It appears to be a kitchen knife with a 7-inch blade and a 3-inch handle. The blade is pointed and is narrow and not tapered. The handle is wood and fastened with two rivets, where the shaft of the blade is fastened into the wood of the handle. If the investigator is familiar with kitchen knives he/she may further categorize (classify) it as a "boning knife." Collecting this knife and sending it to a crime laboratory will result in more detailed measurements of width and length and perhaps description of the metal of the blade and the wood of the handle.

The initial description (classification/identification) alone may be useful to the medical examiner in determining if the knife was the weapon used in the crime. If, however, the investigator moves into the kitchen and discovers that there is a knife block with six slits and five knives and that the empty slit is a narrow one, the classification of the knife becomes more investigatively important. If the knife found near the victim is indeed the missing knife from the block, the hypothesis is that this is not a premeditated crime, but one of opportunity. This is all done just from a careful classification of the knife. An individualization that this is the one and only knife from this set is likely to be impossible, since the manufacturer probably made tens of thousands of these sets. The block and its knives are packaged separately and sent to the forensic science laboratory for further examination.

Careful measurement of the knife and comparison to the other knives of the set may disclose that they are not consistent (disassociation). The knife is a few millimeters wider than the slot, and the rivets in the handle are steel, not brass as in the rest of the set. The hypothesis must be reevaluated. It is not necessarily false. Perhaps the original knife was lost or broken and someone in the household purchased a replacement knife of similar type and discovered it would not fit in the slit. It was, therefore, kept in a nearby drawer. On the other hand, perhaps the killer brought a knife along to commit the murder. The important point is that a careful and complete classification of the evidence is critical to the investigation of the case, and jumping to conclusions may cause serious detours on the road to a solution of the case.

Marginal Glossary Terms

Marginal Glossary Terms highlight important terms for students to remember.

classification (identification)

To place things into groups according to their basic characteristics.

More on the Science

Everyday Examples of Applying the Scientific Method

Many applications of scientific method are quite mundane. If you were to spill some water on the ground, when you returned a couple of hours later you would probably observe that the water had disappeared. The first person who made that observation didn't understand the concept of evaporation but knew there was a puddle there and then some time later there was no puddle there. Something had happened. We know that the water passed from the liquid phase to the gas phase and as the air circulated the water dissipated. You might also observe that on a hot day it tends to disappear a little faster than on a cold day. Perhaps there is a correlation between temperature and the rate in which things pass from the liquid phase to the gas phase.

Let's say we never had high school science so we propose a simple set of experiments to test our hypothesis that when water evaporates, heat seems to be involved. How could you test this? Start with the hypothesis that heat has something to do with water passing from liquid phase to gas phase and dissipating. Go to the kitchen and measure out one cup of water and place it in a pot. Place the pot on a burner and turn on the burner. If you have an electric stove, you have numbered positions, so you can turn it to position two, for example. Measure how long it takes for the water to evaporate. Let's say it takes 15 minutes for the water to disappear. Next measure another cup of water and place it in the cooled pot, put it on the burner, and set the burner at position five (a higher heat setting). Measure the time until the water is gone; you may notice that instead of taking 15 minutes, it takes only 11 minutes. This is one simple test of the hypothesis that the more heat one puts into the water, the faster it disappears.

Another example that virtually everyone who drives has experienced at one time or another is the timing of traffic lights on a stretch of road with many intersections. We've all driven late at night when traffic is light and we've been anxious to get home. What's going to happen if you're in a big hurry and try to drive 70 mph? Besides risking being arrested, you will be stopped by virtually every traffic light. It will seem as if there is a traffic light every 15 feet and the trip will seem to take forever. It is common knowledge that some great force—actually the traffic department—regulates traffic lights.

In the past, clocks were located in the poles of traffic lights to control the action of the lights; however, today they are controlled by computers. The point is that there should be some speed at which you can travel that will allow you to go through a series of lights, maybe 10 or 15 lights, and make them all. You can guess that that speed is not going to be 70 mph because the traffic department does not want you to go 70 mph. The magic speed is probably not going to be 15 mph, either, because the traffic department gets judged on how well it moves traffic along.

How do we use scientific method to answer this question? The hypothesis is that these lights are timed for a particular speed. Therefore, you can try to travel the course at a steady speed. For example, you can try 42 mph and see what happens. You will probably make three or four lights and then get stopped, make a few more and get stopped again. The next experiment is perhaps at 37 mph. Carefully observe the results and try to see if you miss fewer lights. Try a series of speeds based on how well you seem to be avoiding red lights. You will probably find that the lights are timed fairly close to the speed limit. It will not necessarily be the speed limit, and it may change with the time of day.

Here is one last illustration, which you might call the "shower caper." Let's say a family moved into their first house and within the first two weeks, much of the kitchen ceiling fell on their heads while they were eating breakfast in the kitchen. The preteen daughter was taking a shower upstairs in the hall bathroom, which was right over the kitchen. As it turned out, it wasn't really her

Careful Observation

The importance of the words *careful observation* cannot be overemphasized. The first step in the scientific method is being receptive and inquisitive. Anyone can be a careful observer. Observations of events and phenomena in the natural world and curiosity about what is behind them have been the driving force behind the development of science.

Make Logical Suppositions to Explain the Ob[...]

The point of scientific inquiry is to try to understand natural [...] natural world. So, the second step is to take an "educated guess" [...] The educated guess is usually called a **hypothesis**. The essent[...] hypothesis is that it must be composed of *experimentally testab[...] dictions can be made based on the truth of the hypothesis. If the[...] certain things that follow from it must be true, and experiments [...] the predictions.

hypothesis

An as yet unproven attempt to develop an explanation for an observation or series of related observations.

More on the Science

Each chapter contains *More on the Science* boxes that take the students further into the methods or techniques that are described and may enrich the reading of the text for students who have more science background.

---

existing bloody surface with motion. A swipe pattern is created by a bloody object contacting another surface with motion (Figures 4.4C).

An *arterial spurt* pattern results when an artery is cut or severed, and blood is literally pumped out of the body by the beating heart and onto a nearby surface. The repeated spurts cause a rather characteristic pattern. These patterns generally contain quite a bit of blood. In addition, an individual with a seriously severed artery is losing blood at such a rate that he or she will not be able to move too far and, without immediate and extreme medical intervention, will die fairly quickly.

Cast-off (also called *arc swing*) patterns result when a bloody object is swung through space and throws off droplets onto a nearby surface (Figure 4.4D). These patterns may be seen on ceilings or walls, even occasionally on floors. The most common action causing such a pattern is repeated use of blunt force on a person who is bleeding. This pattern was noted on the ceiling of the van in the lead case for this chapter.

Running patterns are just what the name says. Blood hits a vertical surface, but the volume is sufficiently high that gravity causes the droplet to run. Note that blood can only run down. As obvious as that statement is, it is sometimes quite helpful in reconstructing events from blood patterns.

Secondary spatter patterns result when blood drops fall into a preexisting pool of blood. As each drop hits the liquid surface, it can cause small droplets to splash upward, and some of these may hit a nearby vertical surface (Figure 4.4E). The

Figure 4.3

A straight-line reconstruction from a high/medium velocity blood spatter pattern. The straight lines formed by string are arranged at the angles of incidence calculated for selected droplets in the pattern. These lines converge approximately to a point. In this case, a person committed suicide in a bathroom by placing the muzzle of a shotgun in his mouth and firing. The blood pattern reconstruction confirms that the source of the blood was approximately in the position of the victim's head. The strings project outward from the wall into the room. (Courtesy of Timothy Palmbach, University of New Haven)

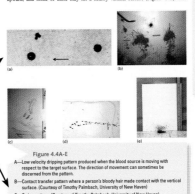

(a) (b) (c) (d) (e)

Figure 4.4A-E

A—Low velocity dripping pattern produced when the blood source is moving with respect to the target surface. The direction of movement can sometimes be discerned from the pattern.

B—Contact transfer pattern where a person's bloody hair made contact with the vertical surface. (Courtesy of Timothy Palmbach, University of New Haven)

C—Swipe pattern. (Courtesy of Timothy Palmbach, University of New Haven)

D—Cast off pattern. (Courtesy of Timothy Palmbach, University of New Haven)

E—Secondary spatter pattern. Blood dripping onto a hard floor surface causes a secondary spatter pattern on the nearby vertical surface. In this controlled setup, blood was dripping from 4 feet above the floor. The scale on the right side of the target is marked off in centimeters.

Photographs and Figures

Each chapter is well illustrated with photographs and figures from the case files of the authors. This way, students can actually see how to dust for fingerprints or what the different types of bloodstain patterns look like.

End of Chapter Elements

Each chapter closes with a summary, list of key terms, review questions, and further references.

Summary

Fingerprints comprise one of the oldest kinds of forensic evidence. Their individuality has been recognized for hundreds of years, and they have been used in criminal identification for most of the 20th century. Fingerprints are formed before birth and are permanent and unchanging throughout life. The patterns are not completely explainable through genetics, because identical twins have distinguishable fingerprints. The basic fingerprint patterns are arches, loops, and whorls. There are variations within these basic patterns. Individual characteristics within the friction ridge skin that makes up fingerprints are called minutiae; the most common are ridge endings and bifurcations.

The use of fingerprints for personal identification was developed in Europe and by Europeans working in India and Asia. The first systematic biometric system for criminal identification was called anthropometry and was developed by Bertillon in France. It consisted of a set of body measurements. Bertillon's system was supplanted by fingerprints when it was realized that there could be duplicate Bertillon measurements in different individuals. Fingerprints as a means of criminal identification were adopted by the London Metropolitan Police and by the police in Argentina, after which their use in criminal investigations spread all over the world. Classification systems for 10-print cards were devised by Vucetich and by Henry and were used for decades until Automated Fingerprint Identification Systems (AFISs) were developed. AFISs enabled searching large files for single prints and revolutionized the use of fingerprints for criminal identification. AFIS databases also enabled the use of fingerprints for verification of identity—this is an example of fingerprints as biometrics. Law enforcement AFISs contain fingerprints of known persons and fingerprints of unknown origin from unsolved cases (forensic file).

Evidentiary prints may be visible, plastic, or latent. Enhancement, or visualization, procedures are used to make latent prints visible and suitable for comparisons. They include physical methods (such as powder or SPR), chemical methods (such as ninhydrin or iodine fuming or Super Glue), and special illumination techniques (such as alternate light sources and lasers) and combination methods. Bloody fingerprints may require special techniques of enhancement. It may also be important to decide on the relative importance of the blood (for DNA typing) and the fingerprint. Fingerprints on sticky tape also require special

techniques. Systematic approaches involve using a series of enhancement methods serially, such that the least destructive techniques are used first.

Fingerprint identification is based on fingerprints being unchangeable throughout life, and being individual. The entire process involved is termed ACE-V, for analysis, comparison, evaluation, and verification. The overall patterns and ridge flow of a fingerprint are known as "level I" features, minutiae are known as "level II," and ridge relationships and pore sizes and distributions are known as "level III." Fingerprints can often be matched to an individual using level I and level II detail. An examiner can also exclude someone as the depositor of a fingerprint. Of course, sometimes evidence fingerprints are of poor quality and therefore unsuitable for comparison.

The primary professional organization for fingerprint examiners is the International Association for Identification, which publishes the *Journal of Forensic Identification*. More recently, there has been a Scientific Working Group on friction ridge pattern comparisons. Research is ongoing to try and systematically establish fingerprint individuality.

Other patterns for personal identification include palm and sole prints. They are examined like fingerprints. Bite marks may contain individuality as well, reflecting the individual characteristics of the teeth that made them. They are compared by forensic dentists. Skeletal patterns that are examined by forensic anthropologists can help narrow down the identity of skeletal remains. Forensic radiologists can sometimes identify people from a comparison of pre- and postmortem X-rays. Occasionally, lip or ear prints have been examined in criminal cases, and voice patterns have considerable individual character as well.

Fingerprints (and Bertillon's system of measurements) are examples of biometrics. Today, biometrics also includes eye (iris or retinal) patterns and various facial patterns. Biometrics is coming into use more and more as a method of verification of identity. These methods are considered superior to "paper" forms of identification and less subject to loss and forgery.

In mass disasters, where identification of remains cannot be done by direct viewing, fingerprints and dental identification are the preferred methods. DNA typing may also be used, but it is more complicated and time-consuming.

Key Terms

friction ridge skin (p. 126)
basic fingerprint patterns: arches, loops, and whorls (p. 126)
minutiae (p. 126)
anthropometry (bertillonage) (p. 127)
classification system (p. 129)
AFISs (p. 130)
visible (patent) print (p. 132)
plastic (impression) print (p. 132)
latent print (p. 132)

development (enhancement, visualization) (p. 132)
powder dusting (p. 134)
magnetic brush technique (p. 134)
small particle reagent (SPR) (p. 134)
iodine fuming (p. 135)
ninhydrin (p. 135)
Super Glue (cyanoacrylate) (p. 137)
dye stains (p. 137)
physical developer (p. 137)

alternate light source (p. 138)
laser (p. 138)
suitability for examination (p. 142)
ACE-V method (p. 142)
level I, level II, and level III detail (p. 142)
biometrics (p. 146)

Review Questions—Short Answer

1. What are fingerprints? Why are they useful in criminal investigation?
2. What is an AFIS? Why is it valuable?
3. What are the main types of evidentiary prints that might be found at scenes?
4. What are some physical methods for enhancing latent fingerprints?
5. What are some chemical methods for enhancing latent fingerprints?
6. What are some special illumination methods for enhancing latent fingerprints?
7. How might bloody fingerprints be enhanced?
8. What is the basis for fingerprint identification? What are the main principles?
9. What are some other patterns useful in person identification?
10. What are the major methods of identifying human remains in mass disasters?

Fill-in-the-Blank & Multiple Choice

1. One important characteristic of friction ridge patterns is that they _____ between birth and death.
2. The three basic fingerprint patterns are (1) arch, (2) _____, and (3) _____.
3. Fingerprints found at crime scenes or on evidence can be divided into three broad categories (not classifications) based on their appearance and physical makeup: (1) _____, (2) patent (visible), and (3) _____.
4. When a latent fingerprint is compared with a known inked print, and according to the numerical rule, the number of points of comparison required to correspond before a positive identification can be declared is
   a. enough to satisfy the expert latent examiner.
   b. at least eight.
   c. at least twelve.
   d. the pattern and 10 minutiae.
5. Computerized fingerprint search systems match fingerprints by comparing the relative positions of
   a. core and delta.
   b. pattern center and all bifurcations.
   c. all individualizable minutiae.
   d. bifurcations and ridge endings.

Further References

Ashbaugh, D. R. *Quantitative-Qualitative Friction Ridge Analysis: An Introduction to Basic and Advanced Ridgeology.* Boca Raton, FL: CRC Press, 1999.

Champod, C., C. J. Lennard, P. Margot, and M. Stoilovic. *Fingerprints and Other Ridge Skin Impressions.* Boca Raton, FL: CRC Press, 2004.

Federal Bureau of Investigation. *The Science of Fingerprints: Classification and Uses.* Washington, DC: U.S. Department of Justice, 1993.

Gaensslen, R. E., and K. Young. "Fingerprints." In *Forensic Science: An Introduction to Scientific and Investigative Techniques,* 2nd ed., ed. S. James and J. J. Nordby. Boca Raton, FL: CRC Press, 2005.

Lee, H. C., and R. E. Gaensslen. *Advances in Fingerprint Technology.* 2nd ed. Boca Raton, FL: CRC Press, 2001.

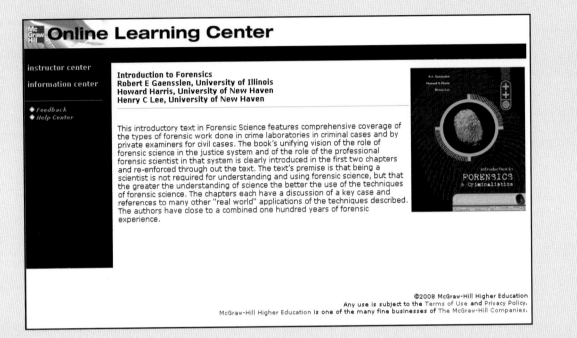

Online Learning Center Web site

Book-specific Web site features chapter quizzes to help students prepare for exams, flashcards to help students master vocabulary, and an interactive glossary.

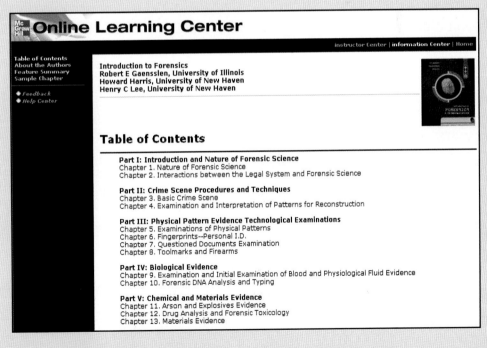

Part ONE

Introduction

This book is divided into several parts. Each part has chapters representing conceptually related material. Part Two is about crime scene procedures and reconstruction. Part Three is about physical pattern evidence that is individualizable through comparison. Parts Four and Five have to do with specific biological and chemical categories of physical evidence. The book is divided into various parts to relate different subjects and categories of evidence to the fundamental concepts of classification (identification), individualization, and reconstruction.

In this Part One, forensic science is introduced along with some of the fundamental concepts of criminalistics. Chapter 1 provides a broad overview of the forensic sciences, including a discussion of the relationship of forensic science to science as an enterprise, a brief history of the origins of forensic science, and the basic ideas of criminalistics. In Chapter 2, we look at how physical evidence can be produced, how it can be used in investigations, and the processes by which it is recognized, collected, and analyzed. The "forensic" aspect of forensic science is also treated—that is, how scientific examinations relate to the justice system and to the law.

Introduction to Forensic Science

Learning Objectives

- The nature and role of forensic science
- The value of forensic science to the society
- The historical development of forensic science
- Development of forensic science and laboratories in the United States
- Forensic science laboratory operations
- The importance of anthropometry and fingerprint identification to the development of forensic science
- Nature of the scientific method and how it might operate in everyday situations
- The key role that scientific method plays in all aspects of forensic science and investigation
- The main specialty areas of forensic science and the scope of each of them
- Elements of forensic analysis and the types of results forensic science can provide
- The concepts of recognition, classification (identification), individualization, and reconstruction
- Comparisons as a basis of forensic science analysis—inclusions and exclusions

Outline

chapter

Lead Case

State v. Richard Crafts
(This case has sometimes been called the "Wood Chipper Case")

In November of 1986, a flight attendant for Pan American World Airways named Helle Crafts returned to New York's John F. Kennedy International Airport from a routine international flight. She and another flight attendant, who both lived in Newtown, Connecticut, and were friends, took a limousine ride home. The limousine dropped Mrs. Crafts off at her home, and she and her flight attendant friend agreed to call one another later. Helle Crafts was never seen again.

Later, and into early December, the flight attendant friend tried to contact Helle without success. A private investigator named Oliver Mayo, who had been hired by Mrs. Crafts to investigate the possible extramarital activities of her husband, Richard, was also trying to find Helle. He had gathered unequivocal incriminating evidence of an extramarital affair against her husband, Richard, and Mayo wanted to give the information to Mrs. Crafts and collect his fee. When the local police were contacted, they did not show much interest in the case, indicating that Mrs. Crafts was an adult, that she hadn't been missing that long, and that she would probably turn up. Ultimately, the state attorney's office was contacted and an investigation by the state police was initiated.

Richard Crafts was a pilot for Eastern Airlines and flew a regular New York to Miami run. He was also a part-time officer in the local police department. The couple had three children, and because they were in the airline industry and required to travel so much, they had a live-in nanny.

Investigation by the state police showed that the morning after Helle returned from the international trip, Richard had risen early and told the nanny to take the children to the grandparents. Further investigation revealed that he had rented a large, diesel-powered wood chipper from a dealership a week earlier. (See Figure 1.1.) This large model wood chipper was one of only two in the state, and the only one in the southwestern area. The rental agent remembered Richard, because he had come to rent the machine driving a small passenger vehicle. The agent had told him the car was not powerful enough to pull the wood chipper, so Richard had then gone out and rented a U-Haul truck to use to pull the wood chipper. The agent also remembered that the wood chipper had been returned in the cleanest condition that he could ever remember.

Richard did own a wooded lot in Newtown. It was not, therefore, illogical for him to go and rent the chipper, except that all this activity was taking place during a major snowstorm in that part of the state. The storm had most people off the roads and at home, and many institutions were temporarily closed. A state snowplow driver reported seeing a U-Haul truck towing a large wood chipper headed toward Lake Zoar, a man-made lake (reservoir)—but he could not see who was driving. This activity took place the next night after Helle Crafts had returned home and gone missing.

The state police were suspicious that Helle might have met with foul play, and that Richard might be involved, but the evidence

Richard Crafts.

Figure 1.1 The diesel-powered wood chipper believed to have been used by Richard Crafts to dispose of portions of his wife's body following her murder.

Figure 1.2

Some of the numerous human bone fragments recovered in and near the wooded lot owned by Crafts on the shore of Lake Zoar; all the recovered fragments were human, and originated from the head, hands, or the feet.

was sketchy. Thinking the wood chipper might somehow be involved, an extensive search of the area along Lake Zoar was conducted. Thinking the worst—that maybe Helle had been killed and the wood chipper used to dispose of her remains—the state police, with the help of criminalists and a forensic odontologist from the forensic laboratory, searched for skeletal or other remains. With winter arriving, heavy snow covered the leaves that had fallen to the ground. The investigators and forensic scientists melted away the snow inch by inch as they searched, because the leaves and debris had to be separated from things underneath them. Large quantities of leaves, debris, and anything else on the ground were placed in oil drums filled with water to float off the leaves and light plant material. The water was then emptied through narrow mesh sieves to capture any small items that might have been present on the ground.

After some days searching, the forensic investigation team recovered the following (Figure 1.2):

- A human tooth
- A dental restoration
- 56 small pieces of bone, and 2,660 strands of human hair
- A portion of a human finger with some friction ridge skin
- A toenail painted with red nail polish

Now convinced they were handling a probable homicide case, the state police and the forensic laboratory set out to assemble a forensic team to try and establish what had happened.

A state police dive team search in the waters of Lake Zoar resulted in the recovery of a gasoline-powered chain saw. It was not very old, and its fuel tank was still half full. However, the serial number had been filed down to prevent ready identification. Serial number restoration in the laboratory revealed "E59266." Company records showed that this chain saw had been purchased by Richard Crafts a few years previous. He had used a Visa card, and the purchase record was still available. There was no question that Richard had rented the U-Haul truck and the wood chipper. Both were extensively searched for evidence.

Wood chips were recovered from the back end of the U-Haul truck. The chain saw blade was carefully examined and yielded bits of blood, tissue, fragments of head hair, and some bluish-green fibers. There was blood on some of the fibers.

The forensic issues in the case can be summarized as follows:

- Were the skeletal remains recovered those of Helle Crafts?
- Could a cause and manner of death be established? Was this a homicidal death?
- If the remains were of Helle Crafts, and if the death was homicidal, could Richard be implicated?

The forensic aspects of the investigation of this case involved many specialties: pathology, odontology, bone identification (physical anthropology), criminalistics, trace and materials evidence comparisons (such as the nail polish), wood chip comparisons, biological evidence, hair and fiber, toolmarks, and handwriting comparisons.

The evidence gathered is shown in the table on the next page, along with the forensic testing used for its examination, and the conclusions reached. Note that some of the findings are conclusive, but others are circumstantial.

The tooth and restoration identity were definite, so the remains recovered on the shoreline were those of Helle. The pathologist ultimately ruled the death a homicide based in part on the considerable fragmentation of the body, but there was no way to ascertain a cause of death. The bone chips and wood chips had consistent toolmarks. The wood chipper in the case had a single cutting blade, but it had been discarded before anyone knew it might be useful. The hairs were consistent with having come from the same person, and with hairs from Helle's hairbrush. Hair comparison is not a means of positive identification, and the defense could and did argue that the hairbrush was not a true "known," because its use by someone else could not be rigorously excluded. The nanny, the children, and Richard were all excluded as sources of the questioned hairs. The fibers were consistent with a nightgown Helle had owned and worn, but no "known" was recovered or available. The polish on the recovered toenail was consistent with fingernail polish Helle owned, but it could not be proven to be the only possible source.

—cont.

Evidence table

Item	Examination	Findings/Conclusion
Tooth—Lake Zoar shoreline	Odontological and radiological: identified as Helle Crafts by comparison with premortem dental X-rays	Tooth belonged to Helle Crafts
Dental crown—Lake Zoar shoreline	Odontological: identification Criminalistics: trace metal analysis	Identified as belonging to Helle Crafts by the dentist; trace metals linked to the laboratory that made the crown
Bone chips—Lake Zoar shoreline	Anthropological and biological	Human, from the head, hands and feet only; blood type O
Sum of human remains—Lake Zoar shoreline	Pathology—Medical Examiner: cause and manner of death	Homicidal death based on the recovered bone chips; cause could not be determined
Wood chips—Lake Zoar shoreline	Toolmark: compare with U-Haul wood chips and bone chips Wood identification: link type of wood	Chips consistent with one another (as having been made by the same cutting blade); consistent with having been made by the wood chipper; linked type of wood to the wooded lot (scene)
Wood chips—U-Haul truck bed	Toolmark: compare with Lake Zoar wood chips and bone chips Wood identification: link type of wood	
Hairs—Lake Zoar shoreline	Hair comparison: compare with hairs from chain saw and hairbrush	Hairs consistent with one another, and inconsistent with Richard, the nanny, or any of the children
Hairs—chain saw	Hair comparison: compare with hairs from chain saw and hair brush	
Hairs—hairbrush from Helle Crafts's dressing table	Hair comparison: compare with hairs from chain saw and Lake Zoar shoreline	
Tissue—chain saw	Biological	Human, blood type O, PGM 1-1
Blood—chain saw	Biological	Human, blood type O
Blood—medium-velocity spatter, from box spring in bedroom	Biological	Human, blood type O, and yielded a PGM isoenzyme type 1-1, same as the tissue
Blue-green fibers—chain saw	Fiber analysis: classify and characterize	Consistent with fibers from a nightgown Helle was known to have owned and worn
Chain saw serial number	Restoration: render readable	Traced through manufacturer to a dealer to Richard Crafts
Chain saw credit card receipt	Questioned documents: compared signature with authentic Richard Crafts signature	Signature on credit card receipt was Richard's
Partial finger with friction ridge skin	Fingerprints: compare with known fingerprints of Helle Crafts Biology/Serology and DNA	Consistent with the known prints, but inked knowns lacked detail; blood type O and female (X chromosome)
Partial toenail with toenail polish	Trace evidence: compare nail polish with known nail polish seized from Helle Crafts's dressing table	Chemical composition and color consistent with one another
Yellow paint sample from the U-Haul truck bed	Trace evidence: instrumental analysis comparison	Similar to yellow paint from the chain saw

This is one of the most interesting cases from a forensic science point of view, not only because so many different specialty areas and experts were involved, but also because forensic scientists were directly involved in the crime scene search and in the subsequent investigation.

The case came to trial in 1987 in New London (the defense had asked that the venue be changed because of extensive pretrial publicity). The trial lasted several months, and there was extensive testimony by forensic experts for both the state and for the defendant. Every finding and conclusion was challenged. The jury finally got the case in early 1988, but after many days of deliberations, one jury member bolted and refused to deliberate further. The judge declared a mistrial.

The state retried the case in 1989, this time in Norwalk, and that trial was much shorter. Richard was convicted by the second trial jury and sentenced to a long prison term. The conviction was ultimately upheld by the Connecticut Supreme Court.

What Is Forensic Science?

What would be a better way to start a book about **forensic science** than with a definition of forensic science in its broadest sense? A very simple, working definition is forensic science is science in the service of the law. **Forensic** means "having to do with the law." The word comes from a Latin root that means "having to do with argumentation and debating." Science is a way of studying questions about the natural world in a systematic way that will be discussed shortly. Thus "science in the service of the law" is a concise description of what forensic science is all about. There is a narrower sense of "forensic science" encompassed by the term "criminalistics." *Criminalistics* is usually used to refer to the activities of a full-service forensic science laboratory. We will develop this concept more later. Most of this book is about criminalistics.

The word *forensics* means "debating" and, in spite of popular media use, is not the same as forensic science. Forensic science is a very broad subject that people now use to cover virtually any scientific and even some technical endeavors that have applications to the law.

forensic science
Science applied to legal problems.

forensic
Having to do with the law.

forensics
The art of argumentative discourse, debate.

Science in the Service of the Law

This book concentrates, primarily, on forensic science in the service of criminal law; that is, science applied to criminal cases. Besides criminal matters, however, there are numerous civil and administrative matters that can sometimes benefit from scientific and technical analyses. More and more forensic scientists are now involved in such civil, national security, and other administrative matters. Although most governmental crime laboratories work primarily on criminal cases, considerable forensic science effort is applied to civil matters, such as product failure liability, disputed paternity resolution, and so on. More "expert witnesses" actually work on civil and administrative matters than on criminal ones. This book emphasizes applications to criminal cases. The application of science to other types of cases is largely analogous. In the following, we will briefly describe and discuss some of the non-criminalistics specialty areas of forensic science. They are complex enough to require special treatment, and entire books are written on each of them.

Value of Forensic Science

One way of thinking about the "value" of forensic science is to ask: How does it serve the community? Another is to consider whether the benefits exceed the costs. Another way of thinking about it is to ask: What are the uses of physical evidence and physical evidence analysis in our legal system? We will discuss a number of these uses in the following sections.

Most public forensic science laboratories are supported by municipal, county, state, or federal governments. Municipal and county labs with a dozen employees can have operating budgets of 1–2 million dollars per year. Large laboratories serving major cities and laboratories serving larger states have multimillion-dollar annual budgets. To put the costs of forensic science in some perspective, it must be realized that they are only a minuscule fraction of the total costs of our justice system. For governments to continue to be willing to fund forensic science laboratories there must be a belief that society significantly benefits from their work.

Looking into the type of information one can get from physical evidence helps clarify its value in investigations and prosecutions. The following are the major contributions that forensic laboratories provide to the criminal justice system, some of which are pretty obvious, while others are not (see Table 1.1).

Corpus Delicti—Elements of a Crime

In law, **corpus delicti** refers to the body or "elements" of the crime. The elements are the things that the prosecutor is obligated to prove "beyond a reasonable doubt"

corpus delicti
Latin term for the facts necessary to prove a particular crime.

Case Study 1.1

Forensic Analysis Can Test Witness Credibility

We have two middle-aged gentleman who look much older because they drink much too much. They have been alcoholics for years, living off odd jobs and welfare. Whenever the check comes, they go out and buy their bottles of wine and they get completely drunk. In between checks they live a classic homeless existence. So they are not exactly what we would call model citizens, but they are not really dangerous criminals, either. One night these two gentlemen are sitting in a cabin out in the woods. They are old friends—sort of friends and enemies—who do not trust anybody else and so they support each other. They are sitting in this cabin, rapidly approaching oblivion, when all of a sudden a shot rings out, the window in the cabin breaks, and a bullet zips by the head of one of them, misses, and buries itself in the wall. Both of them are startled, and about a minute later someone smashes in the door with his or her foot, comes in, shoots one of the two gentlemen in the head, and then runs out the door.

Do you believe this story, or does it seem a little self-serving? We have a likely homicide, and one of only two witnesses is dead. The survivor doesn't want to be in the position of facing a murder charge.

Has he made up this nice self-serving story after he and his buddy argued and he shot him in a drunken rage? That's the question a jury must ultimately decide. If you are his defense lawyer, you are going to clean him up a little bit and keep him sober for a while so that he makes a decent appearance. But no matter what you do, when he gets up on the stand, he is not going to be one of the world's most believable witnesses. He may be a perfectly honest individual, but once his history comes out, he is just not going to play well in front of the jury.

How can we assist the jury in making the correct decision? If we want to decide whether he is telling the truth or whether he's made this story up to cover the fact that he murdered his friend, how can we tell? Well, physical evidence, if it's collected properly and the scene is carefully processed, can tell us a lot about what might have actually happened. Here are a few examples.

The first thing the defendant said, in his description of the events, was that a shot rang out, the window broke, and the bullet just missed his buddy. What can we look for to corroborate his account? First, we can look at the glass that's lying on the floor. In Chapter 4 on pattern evidence, we will discuss the fact that it is often possible to tell from which direction a window was broken. Did the bullet come from the outside in, or did it go from the inside out? Anyone who has watched

---

to gain a conviction. Some of the analyses done in forensic laboratories serve primarily to establish elements of a crime. For example, in an illegal drug possession case, the laboratory must establish that the white powder seized is cocaine, or that those funny-looking cigarettes contain *Cannabis sativa* (marijuana). In a potential "drunk-driving" case, the laboratory has to show that the person charged had a blood alcohol content above the legally allowed limit. Identifying that semen is present on a vaginal swab from an alleged sexual assault victim corroborates a crucial element of a sexual assault, or rape, charge, namely penetration. Proving these elements of the crimes is required for successful prosecution, and prosecutors cannot convict someone without proving *all* the elements of the crime.

Support or Disprove Statements by Witnesses, Victims, or Suspects

The outcome of many investigations relies heavily on things people say about the case. In many instances, these things can become formal statements. For a host of reasons, eyewitness testimony is known to often be unreliable. For example, witnesses are often influenced by their perspectives, prejudices, memory flaws, and other things. In addition, suspects and sometimes even victims may have reasons not to be completely truthful in their statements.

Table 1.1
Information obtainable from physical evidence

Corpus delicti—elements of a crime
Support or disprove statements by witnesses, victims, or suspects
Identify substances or materials
Identify persons
Provide investigative leads
Establish linkages or exclusions

Murder She Wrote or other crime shows on television is aware of a common scenario. Jessica Fletcher, or another investigator, would often say; "Aha, this was staged. They really didn't break in through the French door because the glass is on the wrong side." When we look at the physical evidence, we can probably tell that that window was broken from the outside in. Does that prove the defendant is telling the truth? It really does not, but it doesn't hurt.

Second, we should look for a bullet or bullets. If our defendant is telling the truth, we should find two bullets or a bullet in the body and a second bullet or hole in the cabin. When we determine where they are, we should be able do a little bit of trajectory reconstruction, as will be discussed in Chapter 4. We should be able to tell whether one of those bullets at least came through that window. This also provides possible corroboration for the defendant's story.

Third, we can look at the door. Forensic labs get a lot of interesting things from doors all the time. What is on the door? We might find a dust print from somebody's foot having kicked that door in. Now if that somebody was wearing any kind of a patterned shoe, it will leave an image of its pattern on the door. If we look at a cross section of our society today, we find a high percentage of people wearing patterned shoes. There are hiking boots, waffle stompers, lots of sneakers, and a variety of other patterned soles. Even some shoes that look like dress shoes can have patterned soles. The point is, we can look at the defendant and reason that he may have probably one or two pair of shoes. We can examine them to see if they are patterned shoes, and whether any match the pattern on the door. If there is no match, then the defendant probably isn't the one who kicked in the door.

None of the evidence mentioned so far actually can tell us much about who committed the crime. But the physical evidence does tell us that if all these things check out, the defendant may be telling the truth. He probably is not knowledgeable enough to fool the experts, who look at these things. The net result is that his credibility is enormously improved. This is a key role that forensic science can play in making the justice system work better. It is the most subtle role, because people going to the scene have no idea who is going to turn out to be a creditable witness and who is going to turn out to be an abysmal witness and therefore what they ought to collect. That's why it's very important to treat each scene as important, even when the case seems simple and straightforward. The investigators may not be able to see any obvious probative value in collecting all the available physical evidence. However, in a particular case nonprobative evidence may say a lot about who is telling the truth and who is not.

Physical evidence and its analysis can play an important role as an "objective" reporter in a case, against which statements can be evaluated. Nothing is more important in gaining a proper result in our system of justice than judging the credibility of witnesses. The entire trial process depends on the **trier of fact** (judge, jury, or administrative officer) being able to accurately evaluate what is heard. Forensic science can play an important role in this regard. If physical evidence and its analysis objectively demonstrate something that contradicts a statement by someone in a case, it means that the statement is incorrect. Similarly, physical evidence can support a statement by a witness, victim, or suspect.

trier of fact

The person or persons charged with critically evaluating the facts as presented in a legal case. The judge or the jury.

Identify Substances or Materials

In many cases, the scientific examination of physical evidence provides an identification of a substance or material. Two obvious examples are a controlled substance possession case and a counterfeiting case. Further, identifying a probable accelerant material in debris from an arson case (an accelerant is a fuel, such as gasoline, that can be used to start a fire) or finding gunshot residue on the hands of an individual suspected of firing a weapon in a shooting case are other examples.

Identify Persons

Reliable identification of individuals is critical to the proper operation of our justice system. Biological evidence (Part Four) and fingerprints (Chapter 6) are routinely used to identify persons in criminal cases. Fingerprints have served the justice system well for over 100 years. As we will also see in Chapter 6, the identification of human remains is an important activity in cases of individual death and of mass disasters.

Provide Investigative Leads

A considerable proportion of the work submitted to, and done in, forensic science laboratories is *post facto;* that is, not only after a crime has been committed, but also only after someone has been arrested. Traditionally, laboratory services and findings have not been maximally utilized during the critical investigative period before arrest. Laboratories are typically overloaded with casework, and sometimes severely backlogged, which can prevent prompt analysis. But physical evidence analysis can help provide investigative leads, or keep an investigation from going down an unproductive path.

Recently, national databases have been developed that have made forensic science much more helpful during the investigative phase. We will discuss them in detail in the appropriate chapters. The Combined DNA Indexing System (**CODIS**) contains DNA profiles of convicted offenders and unidentified suspects in unsolved cases. Automated Fingerprint Identification Systems (**AFIS**) contains many known fingerprints, and evidentiary fingerprints not yet identified. The National Integrated Ballistic Identification Network (**NIBIN**) contains image data from bullets and cartridge cases from known weapons seized in cases and also from unsolved cases.

The database files with the profiles or images from unsolved cases are often called "forensic" files. A DNA profile, fingerprint, bullet, or cartridge case from a newly submitted case can be searched for against the known database files (to try to identify the person or weapon), but also against the forensic files to see if it matches evidence in other cases. Matches in the forensic file help investigators connect cases that they may not have known were connected.

Establish Linkages or Exclusions

This use of physical evidence is extremely important in cases where there are no reliable witnesses or useful testimony. As we will see, some categories of evidence are "individualizable"; that is, a common origin between a questioned and known specimen can be established. With other categories of evidence, associations may be established, but they are not sufficiently strong to establish individuality or common origin. In any event, these linkages provide strong circumstantial evidence in cases where they can be established. They may connect a suspect with a victim, a suspect with a scene, an instrumentality (weapon, automobile) with a suspect or victim, or even a victim with a primary scene (if there are several scenes).

Similarly, and just as important, exclusions prove disassociation between questioned and known specimens. Exclusions can help guide an investigation, eliminate potential suspects, and help get investigators focused on the proper individuals.

A Brief History of Forensic Science

To understand forensic science as it is today, it is helpful to take a brief look at its evolution. Some very early work on forensic medicine was published in China in AD 1250. Although many of the concepts that we think of as belonging to forensic science have been around much longer, one can argue that the formal beginnings of modern forensic science in the Western world fall in the period between about 1800 and 1850.

Around that time, the formal scientific approach was developing. The beginnings of chemistry as an empirical science were evident, and medicine was becoming more fact based. Doctors were carefully dissecting bodies, and the microscope became available to help develop a better understanding of anatomy and body functions. In ancient and medieval times, there are accounts of alleged homicidal poisonings. For example, the Medicis are thought to have poisoned people in the 1600s, and Socrates was killed by being forced to drink hemlock (which has nothing to do with hemlock trees, but contained a toxic substance later identified as coniine).

Many forensic science specialties we recognize today can be traced back to **medicolegal** institutes (Figure 1.3) in Europe.

Although these institutes concentrated on investigating death cases, some of the early medicolegalists did work on the identification of poisons, blood, and semen stains (Figure 1.4) as well. One of the most renowned figures of this period was Mathieu J. B. Orfila (1787–1853). Born in Majorca, Spain, he went to Paris as a young man, became a physician, and rose to be the best-known medicolegalist in France. He is sometimes called the "father of forensic toxicology" (Figure 1.5).

CODIS, AFIS, and NIBIN

The acronyms given to databases of DNA profiles, fingerprints, and firearms evidence images, respectively, maintained for investigative purposes and used to search evidence patterns against previously existing patterns.

---

medicolegal

A reference to forensic or legal medicine; in the past, the term could encompass many activities that would be called "criminalistics" today.

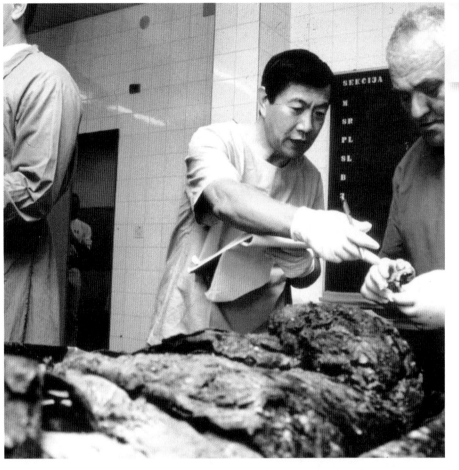

Figure 1.3
Forensic scientists examining highly decomposed medicolegal evidence.

Figure 1.4   In this 19th century Flemish painting, a chemist observes a test tube in a scene characteristic of the early development of chemistry.

Figure 1.5
Mathieu J. B. Orfila (1787–1853), a French medicolegalist, is sometimes called the father of forensic toxicology.

(Courtesy National Library of Science.)

Figure 1.6

A New York City Police Department Bertillon card.

JUNE 1894

"Mr. Francis Galton affirms that 'the patterns of the papillary ridges upon the bulbous palmar surfaces of the terminal phalanges of the fingers and thumbs are absolutely unchangeable throughout life, and show in different individuals an infinite variety of forms and peculiarities. The chance of two finger-prints being identical is less than one in sixty-four thousand millions. If, therefore, two finger-prints are compared and found to coincide exactly, it is practically certain that they are prints of the same finger of the same person; if they differ, they are made by different fingers.'—*Lancet.*"

Figure 1.8

Reproduction of Galton article 100 years later in *Scientific American*.

Figure 1.7 Fingerprints from the same fingers of identical twins.

Reprinted from *Pattern Recognition,* volume 35, No. 11, Page 2660, "On the Similarity of identical twin fingerprints," by A. Jain, S. Prabhakar and S. Pankanti, Copyright 2002, with permission of Elsevier.

The recognition of the potential value of forensic science, particularly criminalistics, took a giant stride with the writings of Hans Gross. He published a book entitled *Handbuch für Untersuchungsrichter* (literally, *Handbook for Magistrates,* sometimes translated as *Criminal Investigation: Application of Scientific Techniques*) in 1893 that greatly influenced the practice of criminal investigation. Gross was not a scientist, but rather a magistrate and law professor, in Austria. His championing of the utility of the developing forensic science was very important to its acceptance by many rather skeptical police agencies. Gross is responsible for the word *criminalistics* and was one of the first persons to carefully consider the value of physical evidence in investigations. In European justice systems, the magistrate had a role both as judge and the primary investigator in a case. In that primary investigator role, Gross could call on the services of forensic experts, and that is what prompted his interest in what we now call forensic science.

Overlapping with this period and continuing until about 1900 was the major period of development of more scientific methods for human identification. In the 1890s, Alphonse Bertillon developed a method for criminal identification for the metropolitan police agency in Paris based on a series of body measurements (Figure 1.6).

The measurements of people arrested or incarcerated were classified and kept on file. Since many people apparently misrepresented their identities to the police, this proved a valuable way to see if an arrested individual might be a person wanted by the police for another crime, perhaps under a different name.

After a time it became clear that there could be duplicates in these files because of measurement error and because there were not enough independent measurements to truly distinguish everyone. In the early years of the 20th century at the U.S. Penitentiary at Leavenworth, Kansas, two men named Will West and William West who were unrelated, were found to have identical Bertillon measurements, but their fingerprints easily distinguished them. Even the fingerprints of identical twins are different (Figure 1.7).

At about the same time Francis Galton (Figure 1.8), William Herschel, Edward Henry, and others in England were studying and trying to apply fingerprints to identification. This resulted in the newly developing science of fingerprints becoming the method of choice for routinely identifying people, and this is still true today (Figure 1.9). These developments are described more fully in Chapter 6.

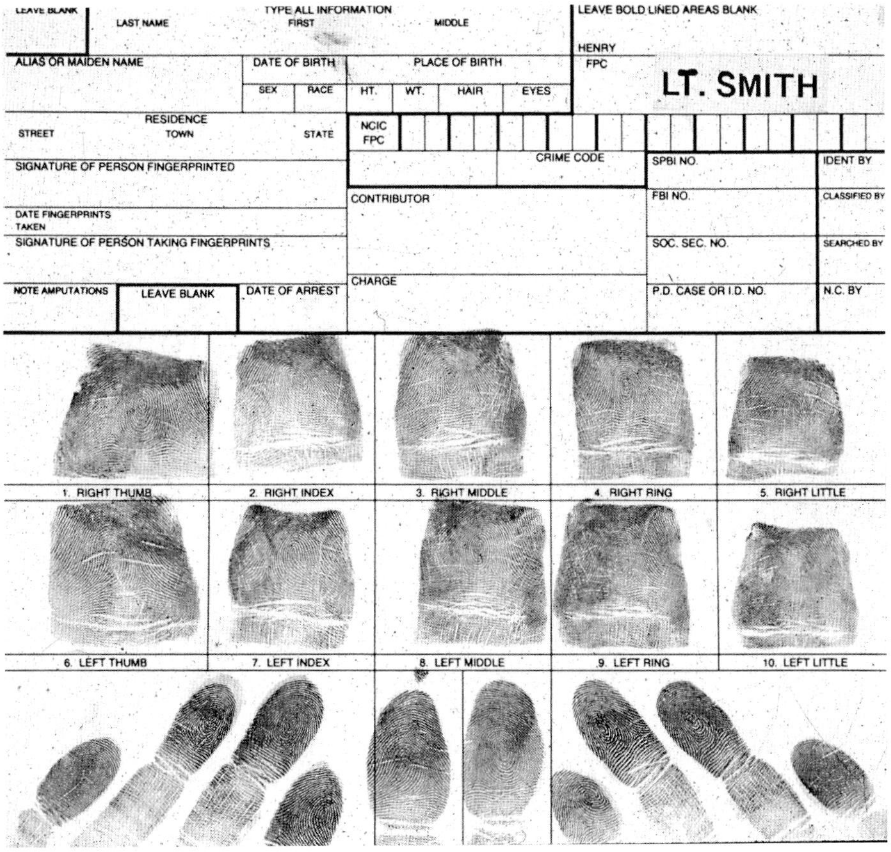

The fingerprint card image shows a ten-print card with the following field labels:

LEAVE BLANK | LAST NAME | TYPE ALL INFORMATION FIRST | MIDDLE | LEAVE BOLD LINED AREAS BLANK

HENRY FPC

LT. SMITH

ALIAS OR MAIDEN NAME | DATE OF BIRTH | PLACE OF BIRTH | SEX | RACE | HT. | WT. | HAIR | EYES

SIGNATURE OF PERSON FINGERPRINTED

RESIDENCE | STREET | TOWN | STATE | NCIC FPC

CRIME CODE | SPBI NO. | IDENT BY

CONTRIBUTOR | FBI NO. | CLASSIFIED BY

DATE FINGERPRINTS TAKEN

SIGNATURE OF PERSON TAKING FINGERPRINTS | SOC. SEC. NO. | SEARCHED BY

NOTE AMPUTATIONS | LEAVE BLANK | DATE OF ARREST | CHARGE | P.D. CASE OR I.D. NO. | N.C. BY

1. RIGHT THUMB | 2. RIGHT INDEX | 3. RIGHT MIDDLE | 4. RIGHT RING | 5. RIGHT LITTLE

6. LEFT THUMB | 7. LEFT INDEX | 8. LEFT MIDDLE | 9. LEFT RING | 10. LEFT LITTLE

Figure 1.9
A typical ten-print card of the type taken upon arrest.

Development of Forensic Science Laboratories and Professional Organizations

Forensic science laboratories as we know them today began to emerge during the 20th century. In Europe, they tended to grow out of the medicolegal institutes, which performed what we now think of as forensic pathology functions. The English developed a system of coroner's juries, which heard testimony on suspicious deaths. The coroner was not the expert, but rather the individual who brought together the necessary witnesses and experts to allow the jury to make an informed decision. In the United States, there were a few medicolegal institutes in large eastern cities, but as medical examiners' offices developed in larger cities, the coroner system dominated in most states.

In 1909, a professor named R. A. Riess started a forensic photography laboratory at the University of Lausanne in Switzerland, and in 1910, Edmond Locard (Figure 1.10) started the first crime laboratory in France, in Lyons. Locard is particularly important in the history of forensic science, because of the Locard Exchange Principle, which will be discussed in some detail in Chapter 13. In Europe many forensic science laboratories were affiliated with universities. Often medicolegal institutes in Europe are associated with university medical schools. In the United States most forensic science laboratories initially emerged in police agencies.

The laboratory in Lyons, France, was among the first in the Europe (and the world). The development of crime laboratories in the United States came a little later. August Vollmer was the police chief in Berkeley, California, in 1928. Vollmer became interested in the use of scientific evidence in police investigations and was responsible for starting the crime laboratory of the Los Angeles Police Department while he was chief there. It is interesting that many of the pioneers in forensic science were medical doctors. An important person in the development of firearms examination, Calvin Goddard, was a military physician. He was involved in several

Figure 1.10
Edmond Locard started the first crime laboratory in Lyons, France, in 1910.

American Society of
Crime Laboratory Directors

Laboratory Accreditation
Board Manual

Figure 1.11

Cover page of the Laboratory
Accreditation Manual developed
by ASCLD/LAB for Crime
Laboratory Accreditation.

accreditation

Recognition by a body or organization
external to a lab that inspection and
evaluation of the laboratory have
determined that its work meets high
professional, predefined standards.

TWG and SWG

Working groups made up of highly
experienced individuals with technical
or scientific expertise in a particular
subject, who meet to develop standard
procedures to be used in their area of
expertise.

pioneering studies that demonstrated the value of firearms identification to a skeptical law enforcement community. Following the St. Valentine's Day massacre in Chicago, Goddard was called in as a consultant and demonstrated the usefulness of examining bullet and cartridge case evidence. That led to his starting a crime laboratory in 1929 in Chicago. It was originally a privately funded laboratory housed at Northwestern University, but subsequently became the Chicago Police Department Laboratory. The Federal Bureau of Investigation (FBI) started its lab in 1932, and the New York City Police Laboratory can trace its origin to around 1934. Originally two detectives were assigned to the New York City Police Department crime laboratory. In the next few years many other crime laboratories were started.

Between 1940 and 1970 the governmental responsibility to provide crime laboratory services to law enforcement became fully recognized. Between 1970 and 1980, the growth in the number and scope of crime laboratories was rapid. The Law Enforcement Assistance Administration, set up by the federal government as a result of the Safe Streets Act of 1968, provided considerable funding to state and local jurisdictions to start new laboratories or expand and improve existing ones.

The American Academy of Forensic Sciences (AAFS) was formed by a small group of interested pathologists, psychiatrists, criminalists, and attorneys led by Dr. R. B. H. Gradwohl of St. Louis in 1948. Today, AAFS has sections representing all the forensic disciplines and specialties, and there are about 5,000 members. In 1956, AAFS started its peer-review journal, the *Journal of Forensic Sciences,* which most professionals feel has become the premier journal in the field. Besides the Academy, six regional associations of forensic scientists, primarily criminalists, have grown up across the country. The oldest is the California Association of Criminalists, founded in 1954. The International Association for Identification (IAI) was formally incorporated in 1919 but had begun to form in 1915. Many fingerprint examiners, and other pattern evidence specialists belong to the IAI. Today, there are professional organizations of firearms and toolmarks examiners and documents examiners as well. Some of them are discussed further in the chapters on those topics.

In the early seventies, the American Society of Crime Laboratory Directors (ASCLD) was formed by a sizable group of crime laboratory directors with a strong assist from the FBI. One of ASCLD's first projects was development of a system of voluntary laboratory accreditation. It took 10 years to develop a workable scheme, but they created the ASCLD Laboratory Accreditation Board and began laboratory accreditation (Figure 1.11) in 1982. ASCLD/LAB has since become a separate organization from its parent, ASCLD, and functions independently.

This has proven to be a highly successful venture, and most crime laboratories have become accredited or are actively working toward that goal. **Accreditation** is generally a voluntary process sought by the laboratories themselves to validate the quality of their work. Initially, only the State of New York has made accreditation mandatory for its laboratories through legislation. This initial bill accepted ASCLD/Lab accreditation as the primary mechanism for accreditation, but New York has considered developing its own inspection system. More recently, some forensic laboratories have started to become accredited under the Internation Standards Organization (ISO) 17025 standards. These standards are applicable primarily to analytical testing aspects of the laboratory's operations.

In 1994, Congress passed what is often called the "DNA Identification Act" as part of a larger bill devoted to criminal justice and crime control. The law created a DNA Advisory Board to set policy for the nation's forensic science laboratories engaged in DNA typing. Even before this legislation, the FBI Laboratory, along with a group of representatives of state and local laboratories, had developed standards for DNA analysis and for participation in the national data bank of DNA profiles of convicted felons (CODIS). The original group was called a Technical Working Group (or **TWG**). It later evolved into a Scientific Working Group (**SWG**). Development of this consensus standardization group for DNA analysis provided impetus for the formation of TWGs and SWGs in other specialty areas. There is no doubt that forensic science is evolving in a direction characterized by consensus standards.

Besides accreditation, which applies to laboratories, there has been the development of **certification** programs, which apply to individuals. The American Board of Criminalists (ABC) has the most extensive program for criminalists. There are specialty certification boards for forensic pathologists, forensic dentists, forensic anthropologists, forensic entomologists, forensic document examiners, and some other specialties. The IAI has certification programs for latent fingerprint examiners and crime scene investigators.

This book is mainly about criminalistics—things that are done in forensic science laboratories (see later discussion). Most of the forensic scientists who work in public agencies are employed in governmental forensic science laboratories. Most of the analyses in criminal cases are done in those laboratories.

There are over 300 governmental crime laboratories in the United States. They are maintained by agencies of the federal government (such as the FBI, Bureau of Alcohol, Tobacco, Firearms and Explosives [ATFE], Secret Service, Drug Enforcement Administration [DEA], etc.), or by units of local government (state, county or city). Some states have multiple laboratories organized into a central laboratory and satellite laboratories around the state. Some states have systems of multiple full-service laboratories as well. Many labs are located within a law enforcement agency, but they can be found in prosecutors' offices, medical examiners' offices, and in departments of health. Some laboratories are very small, and others have hundreds of personnel. The majority of labs tend to be smaller. There is a great deal of local variation in the level of services provided. Some labs provide a wide variety of criminalistics service and are called "full service"; other laboratories specialize in controlled substance identification, or provide just a few services. A number of forensic laboratories are privately operated, but most of them specialize in DNA analysis or toxicology.

Most full-service labs spend an enormous percentage of their analytical resources on controlled substance identification. For example, in the calendar year 2002, the Illinois State Police Forensic Science Center at Chicago, a large, full-service forensic science laboratory that primarily serves the City of Chicago, received about 56,100 new cases, and over 83 percent of them were drug analysis cases. The nation's ongoing battle with illicit drugs consumes a lion's share of forensic science laboratory resources. Another point worth noting is that many laboratories have unacceptable backlogs. Evidence is submitted faster than it can be analyzed and returned. As a result, it is necessary for most labs to develop some kind of "triage" system for handling the backlogs. Cases viewed as more "serious," like murder and sexual assault, move to the head of the queue, and cases that are called for court proceedings also require immediate attention. If the potential of forensic science is ever to be fully realized in the justice system, significant additional resources will be required so that important physical evidence can be analyzed in a timely manner.

Nature of Science and the Scientific Method

Forensic science is, first and foremost, *science*. It is important, therefore, to describe briefly how science differs from other areas of human inquiry, and how the **scientific method** works. Most scientists, who use the scientific method in their work all the time, don't consciously think about using it. The scientific method is more a way of approaching problems than a detailed recipe. It is that particular approach, the scientific approach, which distinguishes between scientists and others.

In forensic science, the scientific method is extremely valuable in many different ways. First, as noted, forensic science is science, but the importance of the scientific method in forensic science is not limited to scientific analysis tasks. It has major applications in doing investigations, reconstructions, and many other important tasks. We will illustrate as we go along that there is a distinct parallel between the scientific method and *reconstruction* (this will be discussed in more detail in Chapters 3 and 4).

The scientific method is not esoteric, and you don't have to be a professionally trained scientist to use it. Many people use it every day without even thinking about it. There are various "formulations" of the scientific method, but it can be viewed as a four-step process.

certification

The determination by an appropriate organization, after an application that includes qualifications, experience, and an examination, that an individual meets a high level of skill in the area of expertise in which he or she works.

scientific method

The multistep method by which scientists approach problems, formulate them for experimental inquiry, and validate their conclusions.

Everyday Examples of Applying the Scientific Method

Many applications of scientific method are quite mundane. If you were to spill some water on the ground, when you returned a couple of hours later you would probably observe that the water had disappeared. The first person who made that observation didn't understand the concept of evaporation but knew there was a puddle there and then some time later there was no puddle there. Something had happened. We know that the water passed from the liquid phase to the gas phase and as the air circulated the water dissipated. You might also observe that on a hot day it tends to disappear a little faster than on a cold day. Perhaps there is a correlation between temperature and the rate in which things pass from the liquid phase to the gas phase.

Let's say we never had high school science so we propose a simple set of experiments to test our hypothesis that when water evaporates, heat seems to be involved. How could you test this? Start with the hypothesis that heat has something to do with water passing from liquid phase to gas phase and dissipating. Go to the kitchen and measure out one cup of water and place it in a pot. Place the pot on a burner and turn on the burner. If you have an electric stove, you have numbered positions, so you can turn it to position two, for example. Measure how long it takes for the water to evaporate. Let's say it takes 15 minutes for the water to disappear. Next measure another cup of water and place it in the cooled pot, put it on the burner, and set the burner at position five (a higher heat setting). Measure the time until the water is gone; you may notice that instead of taking 15 minutes, it takes only 11 minutes. This is one simple test of the hypothesis that the more heat one puts into the water, the faster it disappears.

Another example that virtually everyone who drives has experienced at one time or another is the timing of traffic lights on a stretch of road with many intersections. We've all driven late at night when traffic is light and we've been anxious to get home. What's going to happen if you're in a big hurry and try to drive 70 mph? Besides risking being arrested, you will be stopped by virtually every traffic light. It will seem as if there is a traffic light every 15 feet and the trip will seem to take forever. It is common knowledge that some great force—actually the traffic department—regulates traffic lights.

In the past, clocks were located in the poles of traffic lights to control the action of the lights; however, today they are controlled by computers. The point is that there should be some speed at which you can travel that will allow you to go through a series of lights, maybe 10 or 15 lights, and make them all. You can guess that that speed is not going to be 70 mph because the traffic department does not want you to go 70 mph. The magic speed is probably not going to be 15 mph, either, because the traffic department gets judged on how well it moves traffic along.

How do we use scientific method to answer this question? The hypothesis is that these lights are timed for a particular speed. Therefore, you can try to travel the course at a steady speed. For example, you can try 42 mph and see what happens. You will probably make three or four lights and then get stopped; make a few more and get stopped again. The next experiment is perhaps at 37 mph. Carefully observe the results and try to see if you miss fewer lights. Try a series of speeds based on how well you seem to be avoiding red lights. You will probably find that the lights are timed fairly close to the speed limit. It will not necessarily be the speed limit, and it may change with the time of day.

Here is one last illustration, which you might call the "shower caper." Let's say a family moved into their first house and within the first two weeks, much of the kitchen ceiling fell on their heads while they were eating breakfast in the kitchen. The preteen daughter was taking a shower upstairs in the hall bathroom, which was right over the kitchen. As it turned out, it wasn't really her

Careful Observation

The importance of the words *careful observation* cannot be overemphasized. The first step in the scientific method is being receptive and inquisitive. Anyone can be a careful observer. Observations of events and phenomena in the natural world and curiosity about what is behind them have been the driving force behind the development of science.

Make Logical Suppositions to Explain the Observations

The point of scientific inquiry is to try to understand natural phenomena and the natural world. So, the second step is to take an "educated guess" as to an explanation. The educated guess is usually called a **hypothesis.** The essential thing about the hypothesis is that it must be composed of *experimentally testable* propositions. Predictions can be made based on the truth of the hypothesis. If the hypothesis is true, certain things that follow from it must be true, and experiments are designed to test the predictions.

Hypothesis Testing—Controlled Experiments

Developing ways to test the hypothesis is the heart of experimental science [and scientific method]. The experiments that are devised must be *controlled*, that is, designed so that only one thing varies at a time. If the experimental design is correct, it enables the experimenter to find out the effect of that variable alone.

hypothesis

An as yet unproven attempt to develop an explanation for an observation or series of related observations.

fault. This was a 25-year-old house when the people bought it, and it was discovered that in the hall bathroom a big area in the grout around the soap dish had largely disappeared. When someone took a shower, the shower spray would hit that part of the wall and go right through the area where the grout should have been. The water ran down the wall soaking the kitchen ceiling and making the plaster soggy enough that it fell into the kitchen.

A few years later the family moved to a different house in a different state. The teenage daughter was living at college but did occasionally come home for part of her summer vacation. The first or second time she came home, her mother was in the basement in the laundry room and all of a sudden water poured down through the ceiling. In the second house the hall bathroom was over the laundry room. Remembering the experience in the other house, the parents asked the daughter, what are you doing up there? "Just taking a shower," she replied. It was time to investigate. They poked at the grout surrounding the soap dish.

How would the family scientifically approach this problem? What is the first thing they must worry about? Is there a leak in the plumbing? If there is a leak in the plumbing, it is a potentially sizable, expensive problem. On the other hand, if it's leaky grout, they can buy some silicone sealant or regrout and the problem is solved. Fortunately the family had solved the earlier problem that easily, although it did cost quite a bit to repair the kitchen ceiling.

The first hypothesis is that the plumbing is leaking. The first test is to not turn on the shower but to turn on the water and let it run in the tub and observe the results. If it is the plumbing that is leaking, when they observe the area where it was leaking in the basement, it should still leak. Not a drop. Good, it is unlikely that they will have to tear the walls apart and put in new plumbing.

The second hypothesis is that the water is leaking through the walls in the shower enclosure. The second test is to turn on that shower blasting hard and point the showerhead to various areas in the enclosure, with somebody downstairs to look for water. Spraying the back wall, the sidewall, and every other possible area of leakage, no water is observed in the laundry room.

The third hypothesis is the water is coming through the floor somewhere just outside the shower enclosure. The third test is to put the shower curtain very carefully in the shower to make sure that water is confined to the shower enclosure. No water is observed in the laundry room.

The fourth hypothesis is that water is getting out of the enclosure onto the floor and leaking through the floor. The fourth test is to open the shower curtain, splash a little water along the edge of the tub, and look for leakage from below. There is no evidence of leakage. That is enough scientific method for now. Perhaps the problem mysteriously disappeared.

A few days later the family's daughter is again taking a shower and again water pours into the laundry room. The fifth and it turns out, final hypothesis is that, possibly, water is running across the floor from the shower to the toilet next to the shower and leaking though the area around the toilet bowl. The final test is to take several towels and put them around the base of the toilet bowl, splash a bunch of water on the floor, and look for leakage. Then repeat without the towels.

This test is a success in confirming the fifth hypothesis. The leak was around the toilet bowl and, best of all, the problem could be solved with a little more of the silicone sealant. This is not exactly an earth-shattering scientific breakthrough, but a clear demonstration of what can be accomplished through careful observation and reasoned testing of possible hypotheses.

The idea behind these everyday illustrations is that a systematic approach of selecting a hypothesis, testing it, and making adjustments based on the tests results is an efficient method to solve many problems. That is basically the scientific method. Most people use the scientific method and never think about it as being the scientific method.

As an example, a scientist might want to know how adult salmon can find their way from the Pacific ocean hundreds of miles up freshwater streams and tributaries to the place they were born in order to spawn. Do they do this visually, by smell, or some other way? A **controlled experiment** might be designed in which the fishes' sense of smell was disrupted to test whether the mechanism was olfactory. Suppose the fish whose olfactory faculties were disrupted found their way to their spawning ground just as well as control fish (whose sense of smell was not tampered with). The hypothesis being tested was: The fish use their olfactory sense to make the journey. The experimentally testable prediction was: If the hypothesis is true, disrupting the fishes' olfactory abilities will prevent them from migrating. The prediction was found to be false, invalidating the tested hypothesis.

controlled
experiments

Experiments carefully designed to test one variable of a hypothesis.

Refining the Hypothesis—Theories and Natural Laws

Hypotheses must be continually refined, that is, retested over and over. The reason is that while true hypotheses generate true predictions, false hypotheses can also generate true predictions in a particular test. It may take a long time to discover the proper tests to show that a hypothesis is false and has to be changed.

The "closed loop" of hypothesis testing continues forever. Some hypotheses that have been tested extensively by many different scientists and are found to be sound become established as *theories*.

Figure 1.12

The Scientific Method

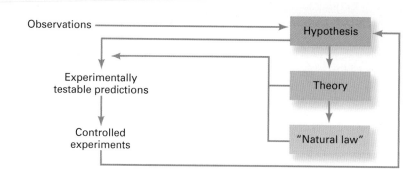

---

theory

A plausible explanation of a phenomenon or a series of phenomena that has gained some general acceptance; a well-tested hypothesis.

natural law

A generally accepted explanation of a phenomenon or a series of phenomena so thoroughly tested that it is regarded as highly reliable.

Think of a **theory** as a well-tested hypothesis. Occasionally, a well-tested theory may become known as a **natural law.** But no matter how well tested a theory is, it may still be shown to be wrong at some point. All good scientists recognize that no hypothesis, theory, or natural law is absolute. Someone may come up with another experiment that shows a flaw, which then requires modification of the original hypothesis or theory. That is what the scientific method is all about: the recognition that one is never finished, that each observation must be tested in new ways to ensure that the current theory keeps being refined. The process is diagrammed in Figure 1.12.

Science, because it follows the scientific method, does not deal with absolutes. Scientific "truth" is the current, best, most-refined hypothesis or theory. This concept is important, because forensic scientists work extensively in the legal system. References to "proof" and "truth" by lawyers do not have the same meaning as they do to scientists.

The Scientific Method and Its Applicability to Forensic Science and to Investigation

The essence of the scientific method is the combination of observation and "feedback" from testing predictions generated by the hypothesis. Careful testing of a false hypothesis will, sooner or later, reveal the flaws in the hypothesis.

The scientific method is an important component of forensic sciences and of investigation in three significant ways. First, as we have noted, forensic science is *science,* and therefore it follows the scientific method in building its knowledge foundation. Second, the scientific method forms the basis for event reconstruction. In the criminal case context, this may be called "crime scene reconstruction." This means using the physical evidence record, and all other available information, to determine the most likely explanation for past events, or sometimes to rule out a seemingly possible explanation. Reconstruction is discussed later in this chapter and in Chapters 3 and 4. Third, the scientific method provides a logical and productive basis for investigation. Investigators approaching a new case inevitably form a theory (hypothesis) about what might have happened. Use of a thoroughly scientific testing approach to building and correcting this theory will go a long ways toward ensuring a just outcome.

Investigators may narrow in on one suspect and look only for evidence that points to that suspect. This behavior is common in what people often call the "open and shut" case. The explanation for what happened appears so obvious in the first moments of the investigation that more thorough investigation seems unwarranted. The problem is, after further investigation and physical evidence analysis, things may appear quite different. If the investigators have locked on to a bad theory or wrong suspect, it will likely turn out to be impossible to proceed, and the case may go unsolved. In the extreme, the result is criticism in the newspapers or on TV when it is discovered that an innocent individual was convicted, or an obvious suspect was overlooked. Were the investigators to take a more scientific approach, they would look at all the evidence uncovered, and take time in forming and refining their hypothesis. The key to making this approach work is to let the data control the hypothesis or theory, not to ignore data or information that doesn't fit a preexisting theory.

Forensic Science Specialties

Forensic science, in the broad sense of the term, encompasses many different scientific and technological specialty areas. All or most of them can have applications in both the civil and criminal justice systems. Some of the specialty areas are described in the following sections, particularly those that are not discussed in detail in subsequent chapters. There are many others, such as forensic accounting, forensic meteorology, and forensic nursing (mentioned in Chapter 9) that are not discussed. Today, "forensic" is used as an adjective to describe many disciplines in the context of applying the methods of that discipline to legal matters and new forensic specialties are regularly being developed.

Forensic Pathology

Forensic pathology is another name for forensic medicine. Forensic pathologists are Doctors of Medicine (M.D.) who have first specialized in **pathology** (the study of the nature of disease and its causes, processes, development, and consequences), then taken further training in forensic pathology. Forensic pathologists are experts in determining the cause and manner of death. The *cause* of death is a medical determination—the medical explanation for why a person died. The *manner* (also called circumstances) of death is a medicolegal determination. Cause of death is a gunshot wound, asphyxiation, poisoning, and so on. Manner can be homicide (one person kills another), suicide (a person kills himself or herself), accidental, or natural. The media routinely confuse cause and manner of death. Either the cause or manner of death may sometimes be *undetermined*.

The United States has two "systems" of death investigation: the coroner system and the medical examiner system. A **coroner** is an elected official, and need not have any special medical knowledge or training, since he or she can call on specialists to assist in technical determinations. A coroner has the power to convene a *coroner's inquest* and take sworn testimony at a proceeding if necessary to assist in making determinations. A **medical examiner** system specifies by law that a forensic pathologist make appropriate determinations in cases of questioned, suspicious, or unattended deaths. Some bigger cities and some states use the medical examiner system, but most jurisdictions are under the coroner system. Some coroners are forensic pathologists; other coroners engage the services of a medical examiner or other pathologist.

A medical examiner's determinations are based on all available information about a death, including from the scene, results of the police investigation, results from the forensic science laboratory, and results from the **postmortem** toxicology, in addition to the findings at autopsy.

Forensic Entomology

Entomology is the branch of biology devoted to the study of insect species. When an animal or human dies, houseflies and some other insects are able to detect the location of the body quickly. The adult flies will lay their eggs on a corpse, if they have access to it. The life cycle of many insects consists of egg, larva (or maggot), pupa (or cocoon), and adult. In some insects, there can be multiple larval stages. Entomologists know the life cycles of the insects intimately, and they know how long each stage of the life cycle takes. The time is governed by temperature and by the length of daylight and darkness each day. Forensic entomologists can examine insect eggs, larvae, or pupae from a body to determine which species of insect produced them. Eggs and larvae must be collected and reared to the adult stage to identify the species. Then, using information about temperature, length of daylight hours, and other information from the scene, they can often "back calculate" to estimate the time of death.

Since determining exact time of death is often a problem, forensic entomologists can make important contributions to cases when insect evidence is found and when time-since-death is an issue.

---

pathology
The medical specialty that deals with disease and the bodily changes caused by disease.

coroner
An elected official whose responsibility is to look into suspicious or unattended deaths.

medical examiner
A medical doctor, usually a forensic pathologist, whose responsibility is to determine the cause and manner of suspicious or unattended deaths.

postmortem
Occurring after death.

entomology
The branch of zoology that deals with insects.

Forensic Odontology

Forensic odontologists are forensic dentists. They do two major types of analyses involving human dentition. One is identifying human remains that are so changed by decomposition, fire, or explosion that they cannot readily be identified by visual means. Typically, the odontologist looks at premortem and postmortem dental X-rays. The dentition is sufficiently individual to permit personal identification in this way. The X-rays of a decedent must be compared with premortem X-rays from one or more persons suspected of being the person. The use of dental identification in mass disaster situations is discussed further in Chapter 6.

The second major activity in forensic **odontology** is bite mark comparisons. There are several different techniques for actually doing the comparisons. Bite marks may be found on human bodies in cases of assault, sexual assault, and child abuse and occasionally on other objects that show an impression of the teeth. If the marks are recognized, properly documented, and examined by a forensic odontologist, they can be compared with known bite marks obtained from suspects. Suspects who did not make the bite mark can be readily excluded. Sometimes, a suspect who did make the bite mark can be identified.

Forensic Anthropology

Physical anthropology is the science of the human skeleton (Figure 1.13) and how it has evolved over time. Forensic anthropologists are physical anthropologists specialized in examining human skeletal remains. They can quickly determine if skeletal remains are human or animal and often can estimate approximately when they were deposited. If they are human, the remains can be "reconstructed" (laid out in proper orientation). Depending on the condition and amount of skeletal remains, forensic anthropologists can often provide estimates of the age, stature, and gender of the individual. They can also sometimes tell if the remains are "Caucasoid," "Negroid," or "Mongoloid." They can spot skeletal abnormalities and skeletal trauma that may be present. Traumatic injuries can provide information about cause of death (e.g., a knife blade cut on a bone supports a stabbing death), and sometimes help in identification based on comparison with **antemortem** X-rays.

As a rule, the information a forensic anthropologist provides consists of what we call "class characteristics." These provide descriptive general information about a person, but not enough to identify (individualize) the skeletal remains.

Although not a part of forensic anthropology per se, we should mention that there is a specialty sometimes called "forensic sculpture." Forensic sculptors need a skull to work with. From the skull, they attempt to reconstruct what the person's face may have looked like. The reconstruction is based on tissue thickness and other data that has been gathered from studies of populations. Eye color, hair color, and hairstyle are usually unknown, so it is often difficult for the sculptor to create a readily recognizable likeness of the person. But perhaps the biggest problem is trying to decide where to show the reconstruction. Many times, a missing person's remains can be found far away from where anyone might actually recognize the person. Today, computer technology can also be used to "age" a missing person's photograph, and this kind of information can sometimes be important in locating the individual.

Forensic Toxicology

Forensic **toxicology** is the study of the effects of extraneous materials such as poisons, toxins, and drugs in the body. Forensic toxicologists must determine both the presence and amounts of such materials in the body and also attempt to interpret the possible effects of these materials. They must be quite knowledgeable in analytical chemistry techniques as well as biology, physiology, and pharmacology. Toxicology is discussed in Chapter 12. Forensic toxicologists who work on postmortem specimens are often associated with medical examiners' offices. Many forensic toxicologists are also involved in testing specimens from living persons as well. Blood and breath alcohol determinations in the enforcement of "driving under the

odontology

The study of the physiology, anatomy, and pathology of teeth.

physical anthropology

The study of human evolution, as revealed by the skeleton or by evolutionary patterns in DNA.

antemortem

Occurring before death.

toxicology

The medical study of the chemistry, effects, and treatment of poisonous substances and drug action and detection in the body.

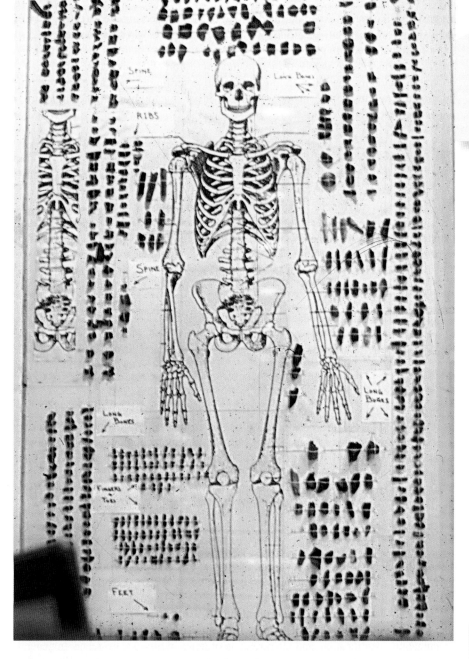

Figure 1.13

A depiction of the human skeleton showing the intact skeleton, and its many fragments and parts. A forensic anthropologist can readily recognize that a bone fragment is human or animal, and if human, the part of the skeleton from which it originated.

influence" laws, urine, or hair testing to enforce "drug free workplace" rules, and checking for "date rape" drugs in sexual assault complainants are examples.

Forensic Psychiatry and Psychology

Forensic psychiatrists and psychologists do similar work. The psychiatrists are medical doctors in **psychiatry,** while the psychologists are usually Ph.D.s in **psychology** who have obtained a license to have a clinical practice. Forensic psychiatrists and psychologists evaluate offenders for civil and criminal competence and may be involved in offender treatment programs. They may also evaluate juveniles to assist courts in determining the best placement for them. A few of these specialists "profile" criminal cases. Profilers can sometimes provide useful information about the characteristics of an unidentified offender based on his or her **modus operandi, (MO)** habits, and crime scene patterns. Profiling has concentrated primarily on serial murderers and serial rapists.

psychiatry

The branch of medicine concerning the diagnosis, treatment, and prevention of mental illness.

psychology

The scientific study of the mind and behavior of humans.

modus operandi (MO)

The habits of a criminal; actions a criminal repeats in different crimes that may help investigators recognize that the same person was responsible.

Forensic Engineering

Forensic engineers are experts trained in one of the engineering areas (often, but not exclusively, mechanical, electrical, or civil). Many are "professional engineers" (a professional licensure gained by applying and passing a challenging examination). Forensic engineers are involved in investigating automobile and some other transportation accidents, materials failure cases, and determining the causes of building or structure collapses. The majority of cases involving forensic engineers are civil rather than criminal.

Forensic Computer Science

There are two aspects to forensic computer science. You may hear this specialty called "computer forensics." This is misleading terminology since, as we have explained earlier, forensics is not forensic science. One aspect of computer forensic science is the investigative use of computer technologies and electronic records (sometimes called "digital evidence"). Investigators may make use of information on computer hard drives, in pagers or on answering machines, and other such technologies to help solve cases. Another aspect is more technical, where considerable knowledge of computer science and computer engineering may be needed to find hidden or deleted information on electronic media and to trace those who have committed computer crimes such as circulating pornography or unauthorized accessing of confidential information residing on computer networks. This work can include Internet-based child pornography investigations, tracing the origin of computer viruses and worms, and so forth.

Forensic/Investigative Technologies

Almost any kind of technology that has or could have any application to criminal or civil investigation can loosely be called "forensic." Often, products or technologies are called "forensic" for marketing purposes. Many technologies associated with scene investigation fall in this category. Use of various types of specialized light sources and specialized scene search techniques, like ground penetrating radar, are just two examples. Many advanced photographic and video techniques, especially digital, are coming into more frequent use in appropriate cases.

Criminalistics

Criminalistics has been saved for last, not because it is least important, but because it is the hardest to define in a few words, and because it is the primary subject of this book.

criminalistics

The recognition, classification (identification), individualization, and evaluation of physical evidence using the methods of science.

An easy way to think about **criminalistics** is that it encompasses all or most all of the specialty areas found in full-service forensic science laboratories. It involves the examination, identification, and interpretation of items of physical evidence. In general, criminalistics can be divided into four major categories of examinations: biological evidence analysis (Figure 1.14); analysis of materials evidence (Figure 1.15); forensic chemistry, including but not limited to fire debris and controlled substance identification (Figure 1.16); and pattern evidence, including documents, firearms, toolmarks, fingerprints, footwear (Figure 1.17), and other patterns, including scene reconstruction patterns. Most of the rest of the chapters in the book are devoted to these subjects.

Criminalistics is as much an approach to case and evidence analysis—a way of looking at it—as it is a collection of specialties. A criminalist is a person who thinks about a case and evidence in specific ways. Criminalists are usually specialists in one of the analysis areas, but that alone is not what makes them criminalists. It is possible to be a skilled chemist or molecular biologist and not be a criminalist at all. In the following, and at intervals as we go through the book looking at different categories of evidence and analyses, we hope to give you an appreciation for those elements of forensic thinking and analysis that define criminalistics.

Figure 1.14

A bloodstained shirt on the examination table in the laboratory, for initial evaluation, documentation, and presumptive testing.

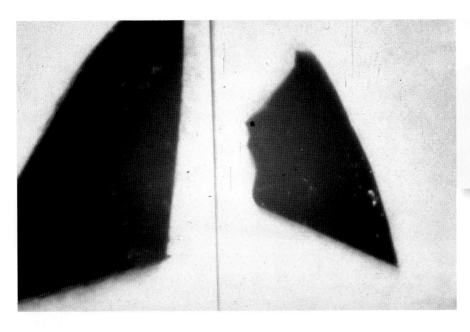

Figure 1.15

Automotive paint chips—one from the crime scene and a control chip from a suspected car. If the two are consistent in all the properties compared, the questioned chip could have come from the suspected car. If they differ in a compared property, the car is excluded as a source.

One way to start looking at this concept is to examine the elements of a forensic science investigation of evidence. What types of results do forensic scientists produce?

Elements of Forensic Evidence Analysis— The Types of Results Forensic Scientists Produce

The principal elements of an overall forensic investigation involving physical evidence are recognition, classification (identification), individualization, and reconstruction. These terms also describe the types of results forensic scientists can produce from an item of evidence. Indeed, one of the subliminal themes of this

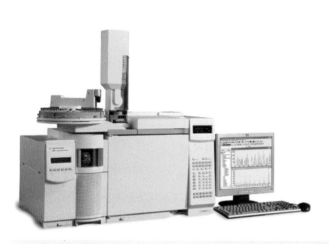

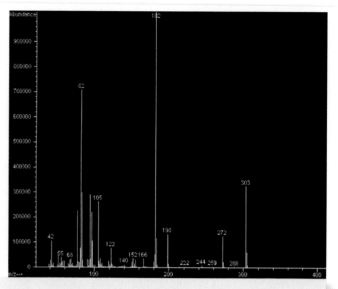

Figure 1.16

A gas chromatograph-mass spectrometer (GC-MS) instrument, and the mass spectrum of a drug of abuse typical of what the instrument produces. Drugs and controlled substances can be unequivocally identified by GC-MS.

Figure 1.17

An inked print of a pattern left by a sneaker. Such an inked print exemplar (known) can be compared with a sneaker imprint from a crime scene.

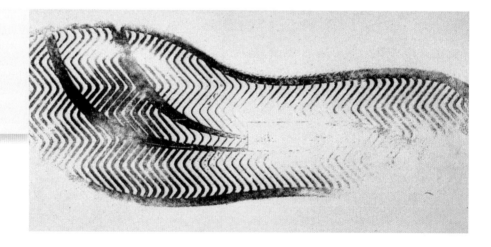

book is the arrangement of chapters into groups based on whether the types of evidence included are or can be used in reconstruction, individualization, or classification. Developing a clear understanding of the significance of the various results forensic scientists report is one of the primary goals of this book. Without some understanding of the basic concepts underlying criminalistics, it is difficult for nonspecialists to appreciate the results produced by forensic scientists.

Evidence Recognition

recognition

To know something because one has seen, heard, or experienced it before.

Recognition of physical objects as evidence or potential evidence is the first step in a forensic investigation. As we will discuss again in later chapters, physical evidence can be important in an investigation only if is recognized. One of the key skills an experienced crime scene investigator brings to a scene is the ability to recognize evidence (Chapter 3).

Classification (Identification)

The next step in almost any examination of evidence is **classification (identification).** Whatever is being examined—a glassine envelope containing white powder, a hair, a fiber, a paint chip, a bloodstain—it must first be classified; that is, identified. Classification is the process of placing that object within a group of similar objects. For example, we can recognize many different objects, with quite different appearance, and still classify them all as chairs. It might be a very broad group or a highly specific group. Classifying things is not "individualizing" them.

With some types of evidence, generally the ones we will group under the heading of "chemical evidence" (illicit drugs, gunshot residue, etc.), examination in the forensic lab consists exclusively of classification. Chemical or instrumental techniques are required to establish these classifications, and the courts require that this be done to sustain a prosecution. Note that sometimes, items are classified in the laboratory as a means of establishing the corpus delicti of a crime (see earlier). Demonstrating that fire debris contains an ignitable liquid residue that could be an accelerant material helps establish that arson may have been committed. Demonstrating that semen is present on a vaginal swab taken from a sexual assault complainant corroborates that penetration occurred. The laboratory must establish these crucial facts if cases are going to be properly proven.

An important result of the classification, or the association, process is exclusion from the class, or disassociation. The "negative association" has the advantage of being an absolute in most instances. When significant differences from other items in the class are found, the object is excluded and is clearly not in the class. As one compares two objects and tries to see if they are in the same very small class, one can never be sure that one more comparison might not remove them from the same class. The same problem does not exist with elimination or disassociation (also see later under Individualization).

One common problem in understanding forensic results is that the word *identification* can mean *classification* in one context, but it is also used to mean *individualization* in another context. Identifying a small piece of material, such as a paint chip, is a classification. Identifying a fingerprint, or a person, is an individualization. We will use the term "identification" to mean individualization in the pattern evidence chapters and in discussing the identification of persons, because that is the terminology that those specialists regularly use. We will use "classification" or "classification (identification)" to mean placing an item or person into a group when dealing with other items of physical evidence.

Case Study 1.2

Simple Classification of a Common Object Can Be an Important First Step in Formulating a Hypothesis about a Case

A knife is found near the victim at the scene of a homicide. The first thing that the investigator does, sometimes largely unconsciously, is classifying that knife. It appears to be a kitchen knife with a 7-inch blade and a 3-inch handle. The blade is pointed and is narrow and not tapered. The handle is wood and fastened with two rivets, where the shaft of the blade is fastened into the wood of the handle. If the investigator is familiar with kitchen knives he/she may further categorize (classify) it as a "boning knife." Collecting this knife and sending it to a crime laboratory will result in more detailed measurements of width and length and perhaps description of the metal of the blade and the wood of the handle.

The initial description (classification/identification) alone may be useful to the medical examiner in determining if the knife was the weapon used in the crime. If, however, the investigator moves into the kitchen and discovers that there is a knife block with six slits and five knives and that the empty slit is a narrow one, the classification of the knife becomes more investigatively important. If the knife found near the victim is indeed the missing knife from the block, the hypothesis is that this is not a premeditated crime, but one of opportunity. This is all done just from a careful classification of the knife. An individualization that this is the one and only knife from this set is likely to be impossible, since the manufacturer probably made tens of thousands of these sets. The block and its knives are packaged separately and sent to the forensic science laboratory for further examination.

Careful measurement of the knife and comparison to the other knives of the set may disclose that they are not consistent (disassociation). The knife is a few millimeters wider than the slot, and the rivets in the handle are steel, not brass as in the rest of the set. The hypothesis must be reevaluated. It is not necessarily false. Perhaps the original knife was lost or broken and someone in the household purchased a replacement knife of similar type and discovered it would not fit in the slit. It was, therefore, kept in a nearby drawer. On the other hand, perhaps the killer brought a knife along to commit the murder. The important point is that a careful and complete classification of the evidence is critical to the investigation of the case, and jumping to conclusions may cause serious detours on the road to a solution of the case.

---

classification (identification)

To place things into groups according to their basic characteristics.

It is important to realize that only pattern evidence (fingerprints, handwriting, firearms, toolmarks, tire tracks, footwear, bite marks) and some biological evidence (blood, physiological fluids and tissues) are commonly able to be individualized. Individualization means we can state there was a single origin and we know what it was (this person left that blood; this shoe made that impression; this tire made this track mark; etc.). We cannot individualize chemical and materials evidence, like paint, drugs, fibers, and so on. It may be possible to "associate" these items to such a small class that, in some cases, it may almost be an individualization. The discussion that follows clarifies these ideas.

Individualization

Individualization can mean either of two things: (1) that in some way, by examining the various characteristics of something, it can be recognized as unique—one of a kind—among members of its class; or (2) that when a "questioned" or unknown object or item is compared with a "known" or exemplar item, they are found to have a common origin. We discussed *class* characteristics in the last section. Class characteristics are those that enable us to classify something into a class of items (or people). Objects and individuals may also possess *individual* characteristics, features that are unique to them individually and distinguish them from all other members of the class. It is the use of individual characteristics that permits evidence or persons to be individualized.

In one sense, individualization is narrowing of classification until only one item remains in the class. Traditionally, in forensic science, this ability has generally been restricted to human identification, fingerprints, certain other patterns, and jigsaw fit matches (Figure 1.18). Recent advances in DNA technology have brought some DNA profiling into the group as well.

The word *individualization* implies uniqueness of an item or person among members of the class. In forensic science, one sometimes hears of "partial individualization." This sounds contradictory. What is meant is a narrowing of classification, but not to the point of exclusivity. We may know, for example, that a small fragment of glass recovered from a suspect's pants cuff has the same chemical composition and optical properties as the known glass that was broken at a scene. The forensic question is how to interpret these findings. The glass has been placed in a small class, and a lot of different types of glass and sources can be excluded, but we don't know, or have any way to evaluate, how many sources there could be other than the one at the scene. Forensic scientists often call this type of finding an "inclusion." The questioned item *could be* from the known. It *cannot be excluded* as having come from the known. Sometimes we say it is *consistent with* the known. We know that this sort of conclusion is not a satisfying one, or one that is easy to evaluate. But oftentimes it is the best that the science can do with this evidence.

Many of the examinations done in criminalistics, as we will see throughout the book, are *comparisons*. A known, or *exemplar,* specimen is compared with a questioned (usually evidentiary) specimen. Sometimes we know, and it is generally accepted, that if we can match enough specific characteristics during the comparison, we have *individualized* the evidence; that is, we can say that the questioned came from the known, to the exclusion of other members of the same class. However, sometimes, as in the preceding glass fragment example, we cannot get to complete individualization. Another complicating factor is that with some types of evidence, different examiners may compare more or fewer features. One examiner might compare 6 characteristics of known and questioned head hair under the microscope, for example, while another might compare 12. Suppose both find these hairs to be consistent in all those characteristics, that is, the hairs are consistent insofar as they have been compared. Intuitively, you feel that the

individualization

Demonstration that an object is unique, even among members of the same class, or that two separate objects were at one time a single object (had a common source or origin).

Figure 1.18

Broken plate and pieces for jigsaw fit match reconstruction. Showing that the pieces fit together perfectly demonstrates that all the pieces were originally part of the same item.

second person's evidence is stronger, but we don't have any way of evaluating how much stronger.

The opposite, but equally important, aspect of matching features in a comparison is *exclusion*. Exclusions are absolute. If there are unexplained differences in individual characteristics between questioned and known specimens, the known is excluded as a source of the questioned specimen. They could not have had a common origin. Exclusionary findings are as telling as a full or partial individualization. They can cause an investigation to be redirected or, in the extreme, demonstrate that an accused or even someone already convicted is innocent. The role that DNA exclusions have played in the review of cases of individuals wrongly convicted before DNA testing was available has received considerable publicity.

Reconstruction

Reconstruction is the use of physical evidence and its analysis to try to understand the events that produced that evidence. It is the result least discussed in forensic books and literature. Because reconstruction requires the integration of many different kinds of information, and is sometimes somewhat speculative in nature, it is not attempted in many instances. One of the interesting things about reconstruction is that although it can be extremely useful if one is correct, often there is no single clear interpretation of the available information. As a result, the possibility of an incorrect interpretation (reconstruction) is much higher than with most other types of forensic analysis. Therefore, as useful as a reconstruction may be, it must be viewed cautiously. Let's reexamine the illustration used earlier in Case Study 1.1. The ability to reconstruct where the gunshot came from, and some of the other characteristics of that particular incident, allowed us to say, "It looks like the survivor was telling the truth." Corroboration is certainly one important application of reconstruction

As we will try to develop throughout the book, and particularly in Chapter 3, the proper approach to reconstruction is developing it carefully using the scientific method. A forensic scientist should not just say: "Well, I think he walked over and he beat his wife on the head over there because there is some blood splattered there and then he dragged her body out and I see some stains going out that way and that is probably what happened." Forensic scientists must look at all the evidence, look at all the bloodstains, look at the patterns in the carpet, look at where the body was found, look at the nature of the wounds, and so forth. Each observation and possible scenario must be tested against the hypothesis (potential reconstruction). Criminalists must make observations, come up with a hypothesis, and then *thoroughly* "test" that hypothesis by making sure it accommodates all the available evidence and information. If it doesn't, the hypothesis has to be changed. Sometimes, as we will illustrate later, criminalists may even do experiments to show that certain physical events *could have* occurred in accordance with the hypothesis (reconstruction). There is a strong tendency for "experienced" investigators to feel they can look at a scene and know what happened, because they have been involved in many cases. Jumping to conclusions in a case too quickly is always a mistake. When there are no lab results, and not everyone involved has been questioned, it is too early to do a reconstruction. It's fine to have a "working" hypothesis, but investigators should be prepared to modify it as further information is gathered. It is critical to remember that a reconstruction is, and always will be, a hypothesis or theory of events. Forensic scientists can never prove that they are absolutely right. We discuss reconstruction more in Chapter 3.

reconstruction
The process of putting together the evidence available with the objective of understanding the nature and sequence of events that created it.

Summary

Forensic science is the application of science and technology to matters of law. More narrowly, forensic science is criminalistics—those activities that you find in a modern, full-service forensic science laboratory. Forensic science is used in criminal, civil, and regulatory matters. It is capable of contributing many elements to investigations, including establishing corpus delicti, supporting or disproving statements made to investigators, identifying substances or persons, providing leads, and establishing linkages between persons and things.

From mediaeval beginnings in China, the development of forensic science parallels the development of experimental science in Europe, then elsewhere, through the 18th, 19th, and 20th centuries. Major figures in the history of forensic science include Dr. M. J. B. Orfila, often called the father of toxicology, and Hans Gross, who wrote extensively about, and defined, criminalistics. Many late-19th- and early-20th-century developments in forensic science revolve around establishing fingerprints as means of criminal identification. Development of forensic science in the United States began in the early 20th century. Calvin Goddard, an early firearms examiner who helped sort out the St. Valentine's Day Massacre case, and established a laboratory in Chicago, was another pioneer. Today, there are many laboratories and many professional organizations in forensic science. Laboratory accreditation by peer organizations and certification of examiners have become important elements of modern forensic science, as has consensus standardization of methods and establishment of quality control measures in the different disciplines. Considerable forensic science laboratory effort is still expended on chemical identification of controlled substances.

Forensic science is science, which operates using the *scientific method:* observations leading to hypothesis, repetitive testing of hypothesis through controlled experiments, evolution of some hypotheses into theories and natural laws. There is a parallel relationship between the scientific method and crime scene reconstruction.

There are a number of specialties in forensic science in its broadest sense. The primary ones are pathology, odontology, entomology, anthropology, toxicology, psychiatry, psychology, engineering, and forensic computer science, in addition to criminalistics.

Elements of a forensic analysis include evidence recognition, classification (identification), individualization, and reconstruction. The latter three also describe the categories of results forensic scientists produce.

Key Terms

forensic science (p. 7)
forensic (p. 7)
forensics (p. 7)
corpus delicti (p. 7)
trier of fact (p. 8)
Combined DNA Indexing System (CODIS) (p. 9)
Automated Fingerprint Identification Systems (AFIS) (p. 9)
National Integrated Ballistic Identification Network (NIBIN) (p. 9)
medicolegal (p. 10)
accreditation (p. 14)

TWG and SWG (p. 14)
certification (p. 14)
scientific method (p. 15)
hypothesis (p. 15)
controlled experiment (p. 16)
theory (p. 17)
natural law (p. 17)
pathology (p. 19)
coroner (p. 19)
medical examiner (p. 19)
postmortem (p. 19)
entomology (p. 19)
odontology (p. 20)

physical anthropology (p. 20)
antemortem (p. 20)
toxicology (p. 20)
psychiatry (p. 21)
psychology (p. 21)
modus operandi (MO) (p. 21)
criminalistics (p. 22)
recognition (p. 24)
classification (identification) (p. 25)
individualization (p. 26)
reconstruction (p. 27)

Review Questions—Short Answer

1. What is forensic science?
2. What is corpus delicti? What role does forensic science play in establishing corpus delicti?
3. List and briefly discuss three uses of physical evidence in criminal investigation.
4. What roles did Orfila and Gross play in the development of forensic science?
5. What roles did anthropometry and fingerprints play in the development of forensic science?
6. Highlight major developments in forensic science and forensic laboratory development in the United States.
7. What is the scientific method? Why is it important in criminal investigation?
8. Briefly discuss forensic pathology, odontology, entomology, anthropology, psychiatry and psychology, engineering, and computer science.
9. List and discuss the elements of forensic evidence analysis.
10. Describe and discuss classification (identification), individualization, and reconstruction.

Fill-in-the-Blank & Multiple Choice

1. In forensic science the term "identification"
   a. refers to the placement of an inanimate object into its proper class.
   b. refers to individualization of an inanimate object.
   c. refers to establishing the identity of a person.
   d. refers only to class determinations involving quantitative comparison.
   e. a and c only.
   f. b and d only.

2. The two most common forensic activities performed by a forensic odontologist are _____ and _____.

3. Forensic science differs from the traditional natural sciences because the results are often used in _____.
   a. jury selection
   b. ex post facto cases
   c. jurisdictional hearings
   d. legal proceedings

4. The American Society of Crime Lab Directors (ASCLD) is associated with laboratory development primarily through its program of _____.

5. In a civil liability suit arising from a hit-and-run automobile incident, *physical evidence* examined at a forensic laboratory would *most likely* be used to help the jury to _____ _____ the incident.

Further References

Inman, K. and Rudin, N. *Principles and Practice of Criminalistics: The Profession of Forensic Science.* Boca Raton, FL: CRC Press, 2001.

Kearney, J. J. *Annual Report 2002.* Illinois State Police, Division of Forensic Services, Forensic Sciences Command, Forensic Science Center at Chicago.

Thornton, J. I. "Criminalistics: Past, Present and Future." *Lex et Scientia* 11, no. 1 (1974): 1–44.
———. "The General Assumptions and Rationale of Forensic Science." In *Modern Scientific Evidence,* ed. by Faigman, D. L., Kaye, D. H., Saks, M. J., and Sanders, J. St. Paul: West, 1997.

Thorwald, J. *Century of the Detective.* Orlando, FL: Harcourt, 1965.

Thorwald, J., Winston, R. and Winston, C.. *Crime and Science: The New Frontier in Criminology.* Orlando, FL: Harcourt, 1969.

www.ascld.org/. Web site of the American Society of Crime Laboratory Directors.

www.cstl.nist.gov/biotech/strbase/dabqas.htm. Web site of the National Institute of Standards and Technology.

www.criminalistics.com/ABC/A.php. Web site of the American Board of Criminalists.

www.theiai.org/. Web site of the International Association for Identification.

Physical Evidence and the Legal System

Learning Objectives

- How physical evidence is created during an incident
- The nature of impressions, imprints, indentations, and striations
- The Locard Exchange Principle and its centrality to forensic science
- How physical evidence might be classified in ways that are useful to investigators
- The major uses for physical evidence in cases
- The steps required for the effective discovery and use of physical evidence
- Basic practices of physical evidence labeling, packaging, and preservation
- Different types of laboratory analysis and their applicability to different types of evidence
- The importance of reporting and testimony to the forensic scientist's function
- How the need for social organization developed into the rule of law
- The complex pathways of the flow of evidence in the criminal justice system as an incident goes from initial report to final resolution
- Admissibility of evidence versus its weight in a legal context
- Rules for the admissibility of scientific and technical evidence—the *Frye* and *Daubert* cases and criteria

chapter

Lead Case

The LeGrand Case

Reverend Devernon LeGrand had organized St. John's Pentecostal Church of Our Lord in Brooklyn. When he was indicted, his headquarters—a four-story town house—was occupied by 11 "nuns" and their 47 children, many of them fathered by LeGrand. According to police, LeGrand did most of his recruiting by seducing and impregnating young women, then threatening them or their children if they refused to beg for money on the streets. His black-clad "nuns" were often seen around Grand Central Station, and even in New Jersey. It was inside this headquarters that LeGrand had raped his victim, during August 1974, and authorities suspected that sexual assault was only the tip of the iceberg. In 1975, LeGrand was convicted, along with his 20-year-old son, Noconda, of kidnapping and rape; he was sentenced to 5 to 15 years in prison. This was only one of several serious encounters with the law for Reverend LeGrand dating back over 10 years.

Church members Yvonne Rivera, 16, and her sister Gladys Rivera Stewart, 18, had testified for the prosecution in an earlier bribery trial, but they were missing when the district attorney (DA) sought to use their testimony in the later rape case. Informants said the girls were dead, dismembered in the Brooklyn "church." In an affidavit it was alleged that Mrs. LeGrand had told the DA's investigators that the two Rivera sisters were told to go with the reverend, and all the other members of the household were instructed to assemble in the downstairs front room to sing hymns. Two hours later, Mr. LeGrand's daughter, Teasiene, appeared in the room and told Mrs. LeGrand, "Daddy is stomping Gladys." Reverend LeGrand's son, 26-year-old Steven LeGrand, was also charged with murdering the Rivera sisters.

The four murders listed in Reverend LeGrand's May 1975 indictment were all said to have occurred in the four-story town house Mr. LeGrand maintained as a church and residence. According to the indictments, all the victims were "beaten, stomped and dismembered." Ann Sorise, one of the two wives Mr. LeGrand allegedly killed, was also shot. She was said to have been murdered in September 1963. The other wife he allegedly killed was identified as Ernestine Timmons. She was said to have been killed about May 1, 1970. Both women were in their 30s. The Rivera sisters, the indictment said, were stomped to death in October of 1975 by Devernon LeGrand and his son Steven, "acting in concert with another person." The third person was not identified. That third person was expected to testify against the two LeGrands under a grant of immunity.

Rev. Devernon LeGrand being arrested.

In an affidavit filed with the DA, a caretaker for the LeGrands, Frank Holman, said he helped transport the dismembered bodies of the two sisters from the house in Brooklyn to the Catskills for disposal near "LeGrand Acres," a large farm maintained by Mr. LeGrand for members of his church and their children in Liberty, New York. In 1966, LeGrand's "church" had purchased a 58-acre parcel in the Catskills and converted it to a summer retreat for the faithful. LeGrand's followers returned each summer, without fail. State police dug up the grounds of the ranch in mid-December 1975, but they came away empty-handed. Three months later, on March 6, 1976, assorted bones and bits of cartilage were found in Lake Briscoe, and a Brooklyn DA raiding party turned up human bloodstains in the Crown Heights town house.

Mr. Holman also said he had helped burn the bodies in a metal washtub and then had dumped the remains into Lake Briscoe, several miles away from the LeGrand farm. Indeed many small pieces of burned bone were found at the edge and further out in Lake Briscoe by divers and suction dredging.

The weakness in the case was the dependence on the testimony of informants who themselves were deeply involved in the crimes. The prosecution needed physical evidence to lend credibility to their testimony. Corroboration, particularly in the form of physical evidence, was deemed essential to the success of the case.

The anthropologist at the Office of the Chief Medical Examiner did an impressive job of building an exhibit to substantiate that the bone fragments might be from the two missing girls. A life-size construction was made with an outline of two female bodies. The anthropologist placed the bone fragments on the outline in areas corresponding to the location on the body from which that piece had come. When he was done, the two outlines were largely covered with bone fragments. This exhibit was presented in court and placed prominently where the jury could see it.

There was concern about further corroborating Mr. Holman's testimony. He had indicated that the chopped-up bodies were doused with solvent and burned to destroy most of the flesh. In his detailed testimony he had indicated the type of flammable liquid that had been used to burn the evidence. Some evidence samples of bone, bone burned with no added flammable liquid, and a sample of the same brand of flammable liquid were submitted to the forensic laboratory for examination. The bone samples were sealed in vials and warmed. It was discovered that traces of flammable liquid could be recovered from the headspace above the evidence bone samples and no trace of flammable liquid was found in the samples of bone that had been burned with a torch. Further, when the known flammable liquid was examined, it was found to contain each of the flammable chemicals already identified in the evidence sample. It certainly was not possible to say that the bone had been doused with that flammable liquid, but it was possible to say that the evidence samples appeared to have been doused with a flammable liquid that had many of the same chemical components as the liquid named by Mr. Holman.

Mr. Devernon LeGrand and his son Steven LeGrand were convicted of beating and stomping to death Yvonne Rivera, 16 years old, and her sister, Gladys Rivera Steward, 18, in the headquarters of the church at 222 Brooklyn Avenue in Brooklyn, and both drew prison terms of 25 years to life.

Source: www.crinezzz.net/serialkillers/L/LEGRAND_devernon_steven.php; *New York Times* articles from May 14, 1976; May 25, 1976; May 7, 1977; and September 1, 2002.

How Physical Evidence Is Produced

The nature of physical evidence and the mechanism of how it is generated are critical concerns of forensic scientists. Just finding or identifying physical evidence is not sufficient to allow them to make the best possible use of it. In many cases, knowing the process that produced it, the precise location where it was found, or observing change at an incident scene can all help with making the best use of the physical evidence.

Change Induced at a Scene

A common mechanism of producing physical evidence is some change induced at a crime scene. The change could take the form of depositing something not previously there, or an alteration of something that was there. For example, finding a blood spatter pattern (Figure 2.1) at a particular location will often reveal something important about what occurred there.

It cannot be overemphasized that virtually any object or observed condition may prove to be useful physical evidence. The finding of traces of broken glass, hairs, fibers, or paint chips, just to name a few examples, can often tell a story. Even something such as a necklace or a bracelet that is broken during a scuffle can yield valuable information through the location of a missing piece. Although there may be no additional information from examination of the object from the necklace or bracelet, the fact that it is found lying on the floor in a particular location may turn out to be an important piece of evidence. A body that was found dumped along the side of the highway a distance away may be associated to that scene by a charm or link broken from that bracelet (Figure 2.2). Further, finding something disturbed from its normal location can be an important piece of physical evidence.

Imprints or Indentations

Imprints and indentations are important types of physical evidence that can easily be overlooked. A footprint in dust or blood, or a clear three-dimensional footprint in mud or snow, is easily recognized. Unfortunately, some imprint and indentation evidence may be subtle or require enhancement to be visualizable as an evidential imprint, and therefore such evidence is often overlooked. A good illustration of the difficulties of recognizing pattern evidence can be found in the trial of O. J. Simpson for the murder of his ex-wife, Nicole, and Ron Goldman. There was a serious controversy over whether or not O. J. could have committed the crime alone. Dr. Henry Lee testified that when he visited the scene, he observed and took pictures of bloody footwear imprints (Figure 2.3) with a different sole pattern than those that had a pattern consistent with a style of Bruno Magley shoes that O. J. Simpson had purchased. Other experts denied that what Dr. Lee had observed were even footwear impressions.

Figure 2.1

Blood patterns on a ceramic tile wall at a crime scene.

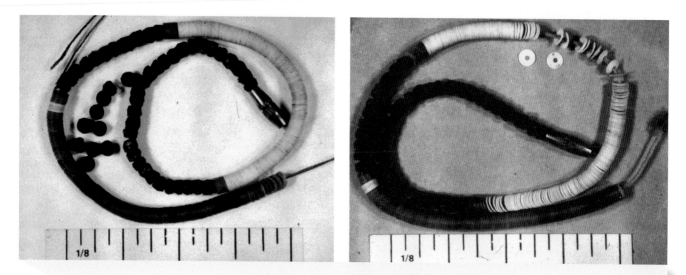

Figure 2.2   Beads or discs from separate victims' necklaces were found in a suspect's vehicle, providing a link between the car and the victims, and thus between the suspect and victims.

Figure 2.3
Markings on walk that appear to be a shoe print.

Because no one recognized that these might be shoe prints, the marks were never properly documented and photographed during the initial crime scene processing. One can see hints of them in other pictures taken at the scene. Were these actually shoe prints, and from a different shoe than the Bruno Magley, it could have significantly changed the theory of how the vicious murders were committed.

An **imprint** is produced when an object comes into contact with a hard surface and leaves a two-dimensional representation of itself on a floor or concrete surface in dirt, dust, blood, or some other medium. An **indentation** is produced by an object being impressed into a soft receiving surface, such as sand, snow, or mud, creating a three-dimensional mark. These markings are discussed further in Chapter 5. Footwear and other imprints can be a particular problem at crime scenes because, if the scene is not properly protected before and during processing, the footwear and other marks not associated with the incident can be confused with actual evidential material.

imprint

A mark (pattern) left by an object through contact with another object; an imprint has very little depth.

indentation

A three-dimensional mark (pattern) left in a deformable object through contact with another object.

Striations

Striation markings are the result of a hard (often metal or finished wood) surface being marked by another object in motion along its surface. Sliding toolmarks (see Chapter 8) are a classic form of striation markings. They can be important in reconstruction of events and association of a tool to a particular scene, and, in some cases, they can lead to individualization of a tool.

Striation is a more scientific way of referring to what are commonly thought of as scratches. Their individuality is caused by imperfections in the marking surface of a tool. In some cases, when large, striations can be seen with the unaided eye but may be much too fine to be seen without magnification. Most toolmarks are a combination of both macroscopic and microscopic striations (scratches). Perhaps the most important toolmark to forensic science is that left by the inside of a gun barrel on the bullet (Figure 2.4) as it travels down the barrel. These striations result from imperfections that have been left in the barrel as a result of the rifling (gouging out of helical grooves) in the barrel (Chapter 8) during the manufacturing process, which leaves the identifiable markings. Of course, other tools like pry bars, screwdrivers, and bolt cutters all have imperfections on their surfaces that could result in striation markings.

Damage

Physical evidence is also produced as a result of damage, tearing force, breakage, cuts, and many other processes. Many of these processes produce unique two- or three-dimensional surfaces, which, under the right conditions, may produce individualization and allow an examiner to say that these two (or sometimes more) pieces were at one time part of the same object (Figure 2.5).

Examples are broken auto headlights or parking lights, pieces of a knife blade, or parts of a license plate frame. Many things you might not think of can, under the right conditions, provide useful evidence. For example, a pocket torn from a piece of clothing can be compared to the color of the clothing, and the torn threads or cloth can be matched to the damaged area. Particularly if there is a ragged edge the two pieces can be matched against each other, and if every

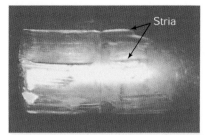

Figure 2.4

Fired bullet with lands and groove impressions visible. Stria can be seen within the facing land impression.

striation

A number of parallel or nearly parallel lines or scratches on a surface inscribed by another object passing over that surface.

Figure 2.5

Pieces of a torn American flag physically matched together. One portion was from a scene while the other was taken from a suspect. Physical matches of fabric materials like this flag may be less convincing than physical matches of fractured solid materials like glass or plastic.

thread has a corresponding thread, and the shape, size, and makeup conforms exactly, the result is individualization (Figure 2.6). An expert may be able to say "In my expert opinion, that piece of cloth, at one time, was a part of that jacket or pair of pants."

Exchange of Material Upon Contact

Another way that physical evidence is generated is through transfer of material between surfaces that come into contact. The first important statement concerning this type of evidence was formulated by Edmond Locard, who started one of the world's first forensic science laboratories in Lyons, France, in 1910. This is one of the guiding principles of forensic science and is called the **Locard Exchange Principle** in his honor. A commonly expressed version of this principle is "When two objects come into contact, there is an exchange of material across the contact boundary." Although his statement is probably essentially true, remember that an investigator or forensic scientist may not always be able to find the transferred material. For example, any material exchanged may fall off, or perhaps so little material was exchanged that it cannot be found. Logically, the likelihood of a transfer is increased if there is a violent contact.

An example of the Locard principle is the finding of animal hair on the clothing of a burglar. Anyone who has a dog or cat for a pet knows that when someone walks into the owner's home, pet hairs seem to jump up and attach themselves to the visitor's clothing. Often a pet has made a particular piece of furniture its own. Even diligent efforts to clean it using a vacuum cleaner, sticky tape, and anything the owner can think of will usually fail to remove all the pet hair. Should anyone brush against or sit on or, seemingly, even come near that piece of furniture there is a copious transfer of potential trace evidence. A great variety of materials can be transferred. It is difficult to conduct properly controlled studies on how frequently different materials are transferred from an individual to a chair, for example, or between two individuals who come into contact. The results of such studies have been found to be highly variable depending on the type of surfaces involved, the condition of the clothing, and many other factors. The reason it is important to try to study the frequency of chance transfers is that the information helps evaluate the significance of small traces of exchanged materials found on casework items.

Locard Exchange Principle

States that when two objects come into contact, there is a mutual exchange of material between the objects across the contact boundary.

Deposits

In addition to transfers resulting from direct contact (Locard Exchange Principle), one can find useful traces of evidence of many types that result from a **deposit** rather than a direct contact transfer. Deposits can be made up of large quantities of material, such as blood or paint traveling through air and splattering onto a surface, or they can be of smaller quantity, or of small particles, and thus much less obvious. Dust, for example, may settle on objects and then provide useful information about where that object has been.

An interesting example is the settling of pollen on an object that is outside during the season when a plant is releasing its pollen to the winds. Pollen is a biological material that is unique to the type of plant from which it comes. Because of its small size, it is readily transported through the air and deposited over a sizable area during a particular period of time. The presence of a particular type of pollen on an object or vehicle can provide information on where the object or vehicle has been, and perhaps that it has been moved to several different locations. For example, by examination of a marijuana brick, an expert might tell if the marijuana is of local origin and, if not, where it did originate and perhaps even several other locations where it was exposed to the atmosphere.

deposit

Material that is laid down or left behind by a physical process.

The finding of different types of pollen on the packaging material and the actual marijuana itself may convey information on when it was harvested and where the packaged bricks were stored. Several different countries produce marijuana around the world, and sometimes it is important to know where a particular seizure was actually grown. A pollen expert can easily determine whether marijuana was grown in India, the Middle East, the Far East, Australia, Africa, Hawaii, or the mainland USA. Because the local plant life is different in each major growing region, the mix of pollens will usually indicate to an expert where it was grown. Pollen is an interesting material because it is almost indestructible; it can be recovered intact even long after it was deposited.

Pollen is just one possible component of dust. That material that dulls the shiny coffee table is a complex mixture of many different types of tiny particles. It is different in each location depending on what type of material is suspended in the air at that location. Particularly where humans are, dust will contain materials characteristic of local activity. If you are near a power plant, the dust will have residues characteristic of the power plant's fuel. If you are near—and near is a broad term since fine particles can travel considerable distances before settling—a cement plant, calcined lime will be a sizable component of the dust.

Classification of Physical Evidence

Almost anything has the potential of becoming physical evidence. That fact makes it difficult to find only one way of classifying physical evidence.

There are some ways of thinking about physical evidence, however, that can be of assistance to investigators and crime scene personnel. As we noted in Chapter 1 and will discuss further in Chapter 3, cases should be approached scientifically. The first step is formulating a working hypothesis; this is an "educated guess" about what may have happened, based on the evidence available at the moment. Then, as the scene is searched and the investigation proceeds, other evidence is found that may reinforce or perhaps force a reevaluation of the first ideas. There are two potentially useful ways of thinking about physical evidence in this context. First, we can consider whether the evidence is going to be useful mainly for classification (identification) (what it is), for individualization (providing linkages between persons and things), or for reconstruction. Second, we can go back to the various uses of physical evidence discussed in Chapter 1. Searching for evidence at a scene or in an investigation with these concepts in mind will help investigators *recognize* potentially valuable evidence.

One way to classify physical evidence is according to whether it will be used primarily for identification, individualization, or reconstruction. Often identification (classification) of some critical component of materials or transfer evidence is all that is needed to provide useful information. Finding white powdery material on a suspect's clothing might not seem important. However, if the white powder is shown to be milk sugar (lactose), that could be very helpful in connecting someone to the cutting of drugs.

Many other types of evidence are valuable mainly in demonstrating or disproving linkages between or among people and scenes. The purpose of collecting this kind of evidence is to submit it to the laboratory

Case Study 2.1

Simple Identification of Transferred Evidence Can Provide Persuasive Association

A case a number of years ago involved a break-in at a machine shop, where some money had been stolen. Anyone who has visited a machine shop knows that the lathes produce little pieces of metal turnings, which will be all over the floor. These metallic spirals are quite characteristic, and finding a couple imbedded in the shoes of a suspect can prove to be excellent evidence. A forensic scientist can show that these turnings have the same shape, appearance, and type of material as the turnings collected from the scene. Further, it can be shown by instrumental analysis of the metals involved that the metallic composition is identical to a collected control sample. Metallic spirals are not the type of material that a worker at a fast-food restaurant, for example, would be likely to have in his or her shoes.

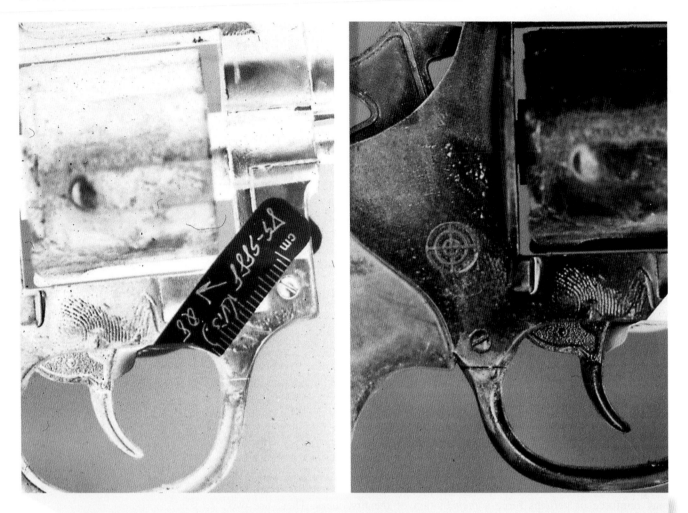

Figure 2.6   Handgun with a fingerprint developed on the surface.

for individualization testing. Biological evidence like blood or semen will be compared via DNA typing to particular people. Fingerprints (Figure 2.6) will also be compared with known prints from people.

Fired bullets or cartridge cases may be matched to a particular firearm. Footwear or tire impressions may be matched to a particular shoe or tire. Even when complete individualization is not possible, the evidence has value. Remember, often there is as much value in demonstrating an **exclusion** as there is in demonstrating an inclusion. Hair, fiber, glass, soil, and paint evidence all have exclusionary value, and they may at times have associative value in cases where they are consistent with known control samples.

Another important aspect of physical evidence would be to assist in reconstructing the crime or incident of interest. Many investigators take forensic science courses largely to become better at evaluating the scene and the physical evidence it produces and to develop skill in understanding what happened at a scene. There are well-known forensic experts who have visited thousands of crime scenes and are knowledgeable at evaluating crime laboratory reports. Often, they can look at all the evidence and give considerable insight into what actually happened. When there are no witnesses or when there are questions about the witnesses' truthfulness, such insight can be particularly useful. Therefore, helping to accurately reconstruct events using forensic evidence gathered at a scene is certainly an important application of physical evidence. An investigator should examine a scene for patterns that may be helpful in reconstruction. As we will discuss further in Chapters 3 and 4, certain patterns can be quite useful for reconstruction. Blood spatter, glass fracture, and trail patterns are three examples. Often, the patterns cannot be "collected" as such and must be "captured" by being documented. As we already noted, this is a second useful way to look and think about physical evidence, particularly during the course of an investigation or scene search.

Utilization of Physical Evidence

As just noted, physical evidence could be collected to be used primarily for identification, for individualization or for reconstruction. The following sections describe a different way of looking at how physical evidence can be used during the course of investigations.

Provide Investigative Leads— Helping Develop MO and Leads from Databases

Physical evidence can help investigators develop leads. For example, it can help in developing a **modus operandi (MO),** or the perpetrator's method of operation. Perpetrators of criminal acts follow behavioral patterns. One of the things that is used frequently in trying to develop these behavioral patterns is a careful examination of the physical evidence that is left behind. The key is often looking at the way the crime was committed, how the house was broken into if it's a burglary, how the victim was attacked if an assault. The physical evidence left behind will provide insight into many different aspects of how an incident unfolded. This is in many ways similar to reconstruction, but the emphasis is more on tying together different incidents that may have been committed by the same person or persons. Such information can be extremely important to an investigation. In many situations, ability to connect two or three seemingly unrelated incidents provides critical information to help the investigators to progress in their investigation. If several incidents appear to have been committed by the same individual, searching for a common thread may allow investigators to narrow down the suspect list significantly. This can be illustrated by the situation where a number of incidents appear connected by MO, physical evidence, or now, particularly, DNA results. If these incidents fall into two time groupings with a considerable period between the groups, it may be indicative of an individual who has been in jail or prison during that period of inactivity. This may provide a solid investigative lead by looking at prison or jail records for persons who were incarcerated during that period.

Although, traditionally, physical evidence has not been a major source of investigative leads, this situation has been changing in recent years. Three databases, AFIS, CODIS, and NIBIN (Figure 2.7), are the major causes of that change (see Chapter 1).

Each of those acronyms stands for a computerized database of information collected on physical evidence: AFIS stands for Automated Fingerprint Identification System(s); CODIS, the Combined DNA Indexing System; and NIBIN, the National Integrated Ballistics Information Network. These systems have in common the ability to store data in a readily available computer database and then compare newly collected evidence against that data. They allow an investigator, for example, to determine if a fingerprint found at a crime scene belongs to someone who has been previously fingerprinted. CODIS allows a DNA profile to be searched against individuals who have been convicted of a previous crime, or who have been involved in a previous crime but not yet identified. And NIBIN permits searches of the identification patterns on fired bullets or cartridge cases to be matched with other such evidence recovered previously. Importantly, the databases also allow cases to be connected even if the source of the evidence is still not known, that is, if the

modus operandi (MO)

The habits of a criminal; actions a criminal repeats in different crimes that may help investigators recognize that the same person was responsible.

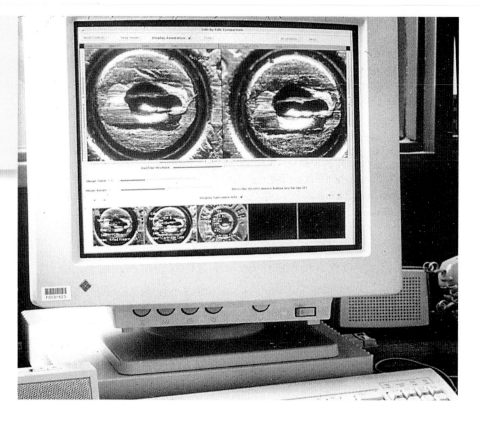

Figure 2.7

A NIBIN search result showing a cartridge case breach face image being compared with a previously recorded cartridge case image from the database. A match would show the cartridges were fired from the same weapon.

source of the fingerprint or DNA profile is unknown, or if the weapon has never been recovered. This can energize an investigation and give it direction. The systems now allow searching for matching data across state lines, and since they are all in their relatively early stages, they will grow and become even more useful with time.

Before AFIS, when an investigator found a fingerprint at a crime scene, it had limited value to the investigation unless the detective had a pretty good idea whose fingerprint it was. The shear volume of fingerprint cards, in even a medium-size jurisdiction, precluded searching an evidence print against all those ten-print cards. Even if sufficient time and energy are devoted to such a search, there is a real probability of missing the print of interest because searching a large file manually is such a mind-numbing activity. AFIS has more than a 10-year head start on CODIS and NIBIN, but as data are rapidly collected and incorporated into these databases, they are quickly becoming larger. With databases, larger is better, but investigators must have the ability to accurately search the mountain of data. Computerized systems, which bring that capability, have revolutionized the use of fingerprint evidence and will likely continue to improve its effectiveness.

Establish Linkages or Exclusions

Certainly the classic application of physical evidence is developing linkages. That is undoubtedly one of the most important uses of physical evidence during the investigation and particularly at the adjudication stage. **Linkage** of victims, suspects, scenes, and instrumentalities can apply at many levels, from a mere possibility that two items could have a common source to individualizations. For example, we may be able to say that a particular individual is the primary suspect in a sexual assault because we found seminal material in the 80-year-old victim's vaginal tract that came from the defendant. Should the victim indicate that she has not been sexually active in years, this becomes a compelling piece of evidence. These linkages can

linkage

A connection, relationship, or association between objects and/or persons.

and do take a wide variety of forms. Forensic scientists can find paint chips on a hit-and-run victim's clothing, fiber transfers from a struggle, or soil on a suspect's shoes consistent with that at an outdoor crime scene. It is useful to find fibers from the suspect on the victim, or fibers from the victim on the suspect's clothing, but if an expert finds transfers in both directions, the evidential value is more than twice as strong. Multiple linkages, even if individually fairly weak, combine to provide much stronger evidence.

Connection of a victim or suspect to a scene can be as important, in some cases, as a connection between victim and suspect. A simple illustration is the situation where someone is suspected of breaking into a bakery to commit a burglary or robbery. A possible suspect is stopped a few blocks away and upon being questioned he says, "No, I was never near that place"; yet the white powder all over his clothes is found to be flour. Certainly this does not prove he broke into the bakery, but it does provide a linkage, since it is observed that there are at least small amounts of flour on virtually every surface in the bakery. Another example might occur when a burglar is known to have broken in through the ceiling and a suspect is found to have some kind of insulation on his clothes that happens to be the same kind of insulation that is used in the ceiling of that particular place. Individuals who break into safes will usually be found to have safe insulation on their person. It requires considerable force to break into a safe, and it is a messy job. Most safes are primarily designed to keep important papers or money from being destroyed in a fire. To provide this protection, safes have a thick layer of insulation in the walls surrounding the safe compartment. There are a variety of things that have been used as safe insulation over the years. These are not materials that anyone is likely to have on his clothing if the person has not broken into a safe; even if the safe burglar has tried to clean himself off, sending the clothes to a competent crime laboratory will usually disclose traces of safe insulation.

Linkages between suspects or victims and weapons, such as the connection of a hammer used in an assault to the victim or suspect, are also frequently useful. A criminalist may find a fingerprint from the suspect on the hammer or perhaps a hammer is found in a suspect's possession and, even though it has been cleaned, the forensic scientist is able to find a couple of minuscule spots of blood remaining that can be shown to be consistent with the victim. It seems that in every crime show or movie the investigator finds something and says: "Aha! That little statue was the one that was used to bash the victim's head." This may seem a little too convenient in the fictional context, but in the real world the forensic scientist often can determine the nature of a weapon in just that way. You can think of a vehicle as an instrumentality as well. Hit-and-run cases often yield considerable evidence that helps establish linkages. In a surprisingly high percentage of such cases, it is possible to tie a particular car to an accident scene or victim using a multitude of different types of physical evidence. This ability increases the solvability of hit-and-run cases, but keep in mind that placing the vehicle at the scene does not establish who was driving.

Thus far in this section, we have talked about establishing linkages using physical evidence. However, as has been mentioned earlier, exclusions are equally important. An exclusion means that the forensic scientist establishes that the questioned specimen cannot have come from the known. Thus, for example, fragments from a vehicle at a hit-and-run scene do not match a suspect vehicle, thus excluding it. Or, a fingerprint found on a hammer used as a weapon in an assault case does not match the suspect's prints. This finding excludes the suspect as the depositor of the latent print, but does not necessarily exclude him as the perpetrator of the assault. Someone else may have innocently handled the hammer, then the suspect used it in the assault but wore gloves, for example. Exclusions are just as important as inclusions, though. Sometimes, they prevent unwarranted conclusions or even miscarriages of justice.

Corroboration—Credibility—Supporting or Disproving Statements

One of the most useful applications of physical evidence is to corroborate statements or testimony. Corroboration can be critical to the development of a case, yet it is frequently overlooked as a role for physical evidence. Case 1.1 in the last chapter and the Lead Case in this chapter were used to emphasize the potential importance of physical evidence that has no potential for proving who committed a particular crime. In such applications its role is only to enhance credibility. Most practitioners are well aware of the common uses of physical evidence to point the finger toward or help exonerate a defendant. However, long after the evidence has been collected, a scenario may develop where physical evidence may play a critical part in breaking or corroborating an alibi or in making a witness seem more believable. This application is underutilized, at least partially, because it requires insight and creativity to identify possible applications. The search for possible evidence must be done thoroughly because one cannot know in advance what may turn out to be a critical piece of corroborative evidence. The ability to spot something that is not obviously important, but collect it anyway just in case, can make a significant difference in the right case.

Identification of Persons

The role of physical evidence in helping to identify a victim or a suspect is central to forensic evidence. Fingerprints have been used for over 100 years, but nowadays we have come to depend on blood droplets, dental patterns (Figure 2.8), and a whole variety of other things to help to identify a victim, a suspect, or perhaps a witness.

Unambiguous identification is not restricted to homicide, or even to criminal cases. In criminal cases, we tend to concentrate on identifying victims and then trying to identify suspects and, ultimately, perpetrators. But in virtually every type of case, there is a need to unambiguously identify the individuals involved.

Figure 2.8

Dental records used in human identification. Premortem X-rays (top) can be compared with postmortem X-rays of the same dentition to make a positive identification of a person.

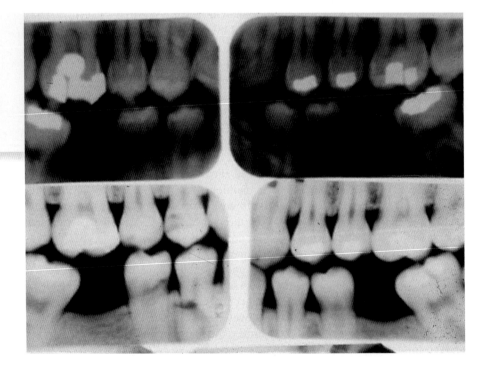

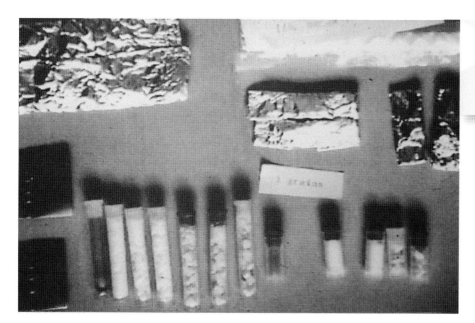

Figure 2.9
Different street forms of cocaine commonly encountered by the forensic laboratory.

In accident or disaster situations, victims have to be identified so the remains can be returned to families. In disputed parentage cases, the parent(s) of a particular child must be identified so the law can assign proper responsibility for the child's care and support.

Identification of Substances or Materials

The proof that an item of physical evidence falls into a class to support a particular legal action is one of the most important functions of forensic laboratories. Substances or materials that require chemical or instrumental testing to be identified must be subjected to these tests to prove an offense occurred. Thus, someone qualified must say that this sample of white powder seized by an officer from the defendant contains a particular controlled substance (such as heroin or cocaine) (Figure 2.9).

Similarly, the scientific determination that a sample of blood taken from a driver contains more alcohol than the law allows when a person is operating a motor vehicle is critical to the driving while intoxicated case. These identifications are not crucial to *solving* a crime, but they are critical to proving that a crime has been committed and perhaps who committed it. As mentioned earlier, forensic laboratory analysis has traditionally been reactive rather than proactive. This is partly because of the nature of forensic evidence and its examination in the laboratory. Identification testing is the easiest and least time-consuming. Examinations involving comparisons are more involved, in addition requiring an exemplar specimen. Another reason forensic labs are overwhelmed with this type of examination is the disproportionately large number of controlled substance possession cases that are submitted. And, as we have noted, the chemical identifications must be done to support the prosecutions.

Establishing a Basis for a Crime and Criminal Prosecution—Corpus Delicti

As noted in Chapter 1, some forensic testing, usually identification (classification) tests are required to establish that a crime has been committed—that the elements of the law defining the offense are present. Establishing that a seized substance is controlled, that fire debris contains ignitable liquid residue, or that semen is present on a vaginal swab taken from a sexual assault complainant are all examples of utilizing physical evidence to establish corpus delicti.

The Physical Evidence Process

Utilization of physical evidence in the justice system requires that a series of steps be taken in the proper sequence. This process of recognizing and handling physical evidence is outlined in the following sections.

Recognition—Most Critical and Requires a Trained Observer

Clearly the first step requires that one recognize that an object may be useful as physical evidence. We cannot overemphasize the fact that recognition of physical evidence is not always a routine, straightforward process. Some things that have evidentiary value are obvious, but many are not. What is or is not evidence in a particular case depends on the scene, location, context, type of case, and other factors. A good crime scene investigator is one who has the ability to recognize evidence. Education and training contribute to developing this ability, but experience also plays an important role. Obviously, if an item of evidence goes unrecognized, that is the end of any potential value it might have had in a case.

Documentation and Marking for Identification

After recognition comes documentation. Proper and complete documentation is critical to establish the legal and scientific requirements of the chain of custody. Prosecutors must be able to show that each particular item being offered as evidence in court is the exact same object that was collected from the victim, suspect, or crime scene. They must also be able to establish where it has been in the interim, and who handled it after it was collected. In some ways it is analogous to the provenance of an art object so necessary to establish its authenticity. Any break in that chain of evidence will likely destroy the item's value as evidence because the court will not permit it to be admitted as evidence. Documentation includes the markings used for identification. Documentation, as we will see in Chapter 3, is a crucial element of scene investigation. The exact location where an item was found can be very important in reconstruction of the incident. A reconstruction requires the synthesis of all the information available. Knowing where evidence was found is an essential part of that synthesis.

Documentation of a scene is as necessary as documentation of individual items of evidence. Many types of pattern evidence can only be recorded by proper documentation.

Recently, more attention has been paid to reinvestigating unsolved cold cases. Every sizable police agency now has a **cold case** unit. This new emphasis on re-investigating old cases illustrates the importance of good documentation. During the initial investigative process, a good investigator may depend on his or her memory. However, when reinvestigating a case that is 10, 15, or even 25 years old, memory is no longer a useful tool. Those directly involved in the initial investigation may be retired or even dead. Even if they are still available and they may think they remember the facts surrounding the incident and each piece of evidence quite clearly, their memory and recollections may well not be accurate. Those reviewing a case years later will need to look at photographs and read complete and accurate documentation to develop a solid understanding of what things were found and where to carry out a thorough reinvestigation.

Collection, Packaging, and Preservation

After recognition and documentation, the physical evidence must be collected, packaged, and properly preserved. Identifying potential physical evidence is of little use if it does not reach the persons who are to analyze or evaluate it in its original condition (Figure 2.10).

cold case

An investigation that has become inactive for a period of time, for a variety of reasons, although the case has not yet been solved.

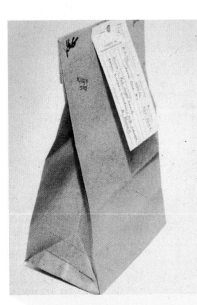

Figure 2.10

Sealed and labeled paper bag with evidence for submission. Different types of evidence require different packaging. The label and markings must be sufficient to be able to identify the item and packaging at a later time.

Biological evidence that is packaged inappropriately by untrained individuals can reach the laboratory in a condition unsuitable for analysis. A glaring example of this is how, for many years, evidence from violent crime scenes was packaged; it was placed in the most available container: plastic trash bags. If the body fluid evidence was still damp, as it usually is, it would deteriorate very rapidly. If moisture is present, bacteria are everywhere and will multiply and destroy most body fluid evidence. Inside a plastic bag, moisture is retained. Bacteria that destroy biological evidence prefer warm, moist, dark conditions. Placing this type of evidence in paper containers (Figure 2.11) that can "breathe," and ensuring the evidence is dry before packaging, avoids these problems. Different types of physical evidence have somewhat different requirements in terms of packaging and marking. These are discussed in each of the chapters devoted to particular types of evidence.

An essential consideration in the collection and preservation of physical evidence is **control** and **comparison specimens.** Remembering that many forensic examinations involve comparisons between evidentiary and known specimens, and that certain control or comparison specimens are required for some types of evidence to make sure the evidentiary findings are sound. There are three types of controls: blank, known, and alibi (or alternative) known. A substratum (background) comparison specimen is required for certain types of evidence. Control and comparison specimens are discussed in detail in Chapter 3 along with illustrations of the circumstances where they may be needed.

Case Study 2.2

The Importance of Properly Packaging Evidence

This case study discusses why drying and proper packaging of botanical evidence is absolutely critical.

At a large police department, a huge quantity of peyote buttons (a portion of a cactus that is abused as a hallucinogenic drug) was seized from a self-styled minister of the Native American Church. Two or three large garbage bags full of peyote buttons were submitted to the laboratory. As in most laboratories, unless there is an immediate need for a report, evidence is often put aside for a while before being examined. Because this was a major seizure and carried the potential for a very long sentence, it was only a week or two before the case was assigned to a chemist for analysis. When the evidence was removed from the evidence vault, the chemist discovered that instead of having bags full of cactus buttons, the bags were filled with foul-smelling greenish-brown slime. Sealing still moist vegetable matter in plastic bags was a big mistake. There were plenty of natural bacteria on the peyote buttons, which caused the material to rapidly rot, transforming it into the disgusting-smelling slime found in the bags. The material was so badly decomposed that it was difficult to find enough active ingredient to sustain even a minimum charge. So a major seizure of several hundred pounds of material dropped from a felony charge carrying 20 years or more in prison to a misdemeanor (less than 1 year) charge because the evidence had not been properly preserved.

control specimens

Separate specimens included in a test protocol to ensure that the test is performing properly.

comparison specimens

Separate specimens taken of a material for comparison purposes.

Laboratory Analysis

The next step in the physical evidence process is laboratory analysis. Some form of analysis is expected, or the item should not have been submitted to the laboratory in the first place. It may be as simple as an identification, or as complex as a reconstruction.

Many types of forensic analysis involve comparisons. Tests designed to individualize evidence commonly require comparison between an evidentiary specimen and a known specimen. An evidentiary specimen originating from scenes and unknown sources is often called a **questioned specimen** (or Q). Specimens from known sources or people are often called *known* (or K) specimens. This terminology may carry over into evidence labeling: Known specimens may be numbered with a "K" prefix, while evidentiary ones may be numbered with a "Q" prefix.

You can think of laboratory examinations as having one or more of three major objectives: identification (classification), individualization, or reconstruction. Keep in mind the types of the examinations that can be done for each particular type of physical evidence. Which have the potential for individualization, and what levels of subjectivity are there in the lab examination?

questioned specimen

A piece of potential evidentiary material that will be examined and may be compared to a control specimen.

Reporting and Testimony

Next, forensic scientists need to convey the results of the examination to those who must use this information. Laboratory scientists must be able not only to

Figure 2.11
Evidential clothing properly packaged in sealed paper bags.

master analytical skills but also to write clear and informative laboratory reports. The findings must be understandable to the investigators and lawyers as well as the jury or other fact finders if the information is to have an effect on the outcome of the case. An expert can be a brilliant scientist, but if others do not become aware of or cannot understand that person's findings, all that effort will be useless. Failure to effectively communicate with the officers involved in the investigation, those responsible for the prosecution or defense, and those ultimately responsible for determining guilt or innocence will negate the effect of the evidence analysis. Opposing counsel may use poorly written reports as a basis for discrediting a forensic scientist upon cross-examination. Recent emphasis on laboratory accreditation has helped to reduce the incidence of uninformative or sloppy laboratory reports. In most laboratories the reports must be read for technical content by a colleague and for other errors by a supervisor. Serious problems can often be avoided where the laboratory examiner improves communication through informal oral reporting to the submitter of the evidence.

Forensic laboratories can be more effective if they develop a rapport with their users. It helps the scientists understand what types of analysis will best suit the case. That rapport is not developed through formal written laboratory reports but through informal discussion with those involved. Such interaction is often an important component of true communication.

A final step in this multistep process necessary for full utilization of physical evidence can be court testimony. Each case must be treated as if it will have to be presented in court in a highly contested case. Most examiners do not have to testify too often, but it can never be known for certain in advance which cases or evidence will lead to testimony. Many cases go unsolved. Many solved cases never get to trial. Although most examiners actually testify on a very small percentage of their cases, testimony represents the capstone of their work and work product. It is essential to treat every item and every case as if it will go to trial.

Most forensic scientists testify in court as **expert witnesses.** An expert witness enjoys some special privileges in court, such as the ability to give his or her

expert witness

An individual who by training, knowledge, or experience is a specialist in a subject and therefore is qualified to give opinion testimony in legal settings.

opinion. An expert must be *qualified* as an expert in advance of any substantive testimony, and this process takes place at every single court appearance. Qualification as an expert takes into account education, training, experience, prior testimony, and other evidence of professional expertise such as publications and presentations at meetings.

Origin of Legal Systems

Before discussing an overview of the workings of the criminal justice system, it is appropriate to speak a little about the origins of legal systems. We may look at this as a short digression into sociology. The important question is: Why do we have social systems, or more specifically, legal systems? A simple answer to this question is the long recognized need of people to live in relatively close proximity for economic reasons, but also with relative harmony and safety. The operative concern is avoiding loss of property, serious injury, or death at the hands of neighbors because of disputes. It has been recognized for centuries that it is best to group certain tasks and provide them for the whole community rather than have each individual or family group work independently. A few highly skilled individuals might be able to live totally independent of others. However, for most, it is much more practical to take advantage of many services that can be more efficiently provided to those belonging to a social group. For such social living conditions, there must be rules of conduct to resolve differences and to maintain stability.

What has developed as a result of these fairly common, well-recognized needs is that we have social organizations that provide certain services. For such organizations to function the members must give up a certain amount of freedom of action. When people feel secure they are reluctant to give up their liberties. Although Western democracies are built on the recognition that the members are jealous of their liberty and reluctant to cede it to the central organization (government), when people feel physically threatened, they are more willing to give up some of that freedom. Thus, when crime rates are high, civil rights are ceded more readily, but when the crime rate declines, there is a desire to regain those civil rights. This is just a reflection of the initial social drive to organize to satisfy the need to resolve differences between individuals or groups to promote stability and safety. Social organizations (governments) provide a variety of different functions aimed at providing a safe and secure social environment. One could oversimplify this highly complex process by saying that society desires a mechanism to deal with disputes and settle them without bodily harm to the disputants.

In addition to the governmental function of trying to provide safety and security in individual dealings, certain services are better provided for the group than for individuals. The most important of these is defense. Societies need to be able to protect themselves from outside threats.

As potential dangers became more formidable, the citizen militia was no longer a viable force to repel invaders; therefore, an important role for government is delivery of defense to society. There are many other more mundane, but highly valuable group services, which are often taken for granted, such as public water. There are sizable parts of the world where there is no public water or sanitation, or it is of dangerously poor quality. Many other services are provided by government that one simply expects without realizing their importance, since their costs are minimized by being split over the entire society.

The governmental function most relevant to this text is the development and enforcement of rules of conduct, the rule of law. Development of rules of conduct is one of the most important functions of a society. Laws sometimes seem oppressive, but they prevent many problems. From economic issues to safety issues, our society functions fairly smoothly because we have a well-defined legal system with mechanisms for modification as new problems arise. Some might argue that we have developed an overly complex set of laws, but they do seem to work moderately well, if rather slowly, at resolving disputes and enforcing order.

Forensic science plays a small but significant role in the rule of law. Most important, it appears to be playing a considerably larger role than it did 50, 20, or even 10 years ago. Within the recent past, there has been a significant change in society's and the legal system's interest in and reliance on physical evidence and forensic science. Although forensic science and scientific examination of physical evidence have played a role for many years, that role has changed from a rare to a more familiar involvement, one that is almost expected. For most of its early history forensic science did not come into play in most criminal cases and was used in even fewer civil cases. Even as its use began to expand, the primary emphasis was on a few types of evidence: identification of street drugs, determination of alcohol level in body fluids of drivers, fingerprints, and firearms examination. There was a little materials ("trace") evidence work and some serology in sexual assault and violence cases, but they were central to only a small percentage of the criminal prosecutions.

In recent years, the use of forensic science has virtually exploded. Certainly part of that is attributable to the development of DNA technology. DNA has solved one of the longest-standing problems in forensic science: the desire to associate, unambiguously, a blood or body fluid stain with an individual. This level of individualization may not always be possible in every stain or in every laboratory. Many other areas of forensic science have also been making great strides, even though DNA has garnered most of the attention. These greatly improved capabilities, as well as the public's recognition of the value and reliability of forensic evidence, have moved the field into a much more prominent position in the justice system.

The Criminal Justice System and Process

The legal flowchart in Figure 2.12 presents a shorthand way to look at the importance of physical evidence in the legal process. Since the detailed operation of the legal system is different in every state and the federal system, the chart has been generalized to make it applicable to as many jurisdictions as possible. The flowchart format allows us to look at how physical evidence can be used at many different stages as an incident or case moves through the criminal justice system from beginning to end.

First, there is an incident, but at this stage it is premature to label it a crime. Perhaps someone has called a police dispatcher, a call has been made to 911, or an officer has observed suspicious activity.

Further investigation is undertaken to determine whether a crime has been committed. In many smaller jurisdictions the deputies or police officers are often not as busy as big-city police and have the luxury of looking into incidents that might not be examined in a high-crime area.

In the flowchart, the top line is quite straightforward. If one moves to the right, the box shows "Undetected or Unreported." Under such circumstances there can be no action taken and that is the end. Surprisingly, a great many incidents fall into this category, even some rather serious criminal incidents. As an example, an older person is found dead at home, with no indication of foul play. No autopsy is performed, and the incident is closed as death by natural causes. If that individual had been smothered with a pillow or poisoned, a homicide would have gone undetected.

Moving to the left, "Detected and Reported" is clearly more interesting. Could this incident be a crime? That is where the initial investigation has to be done and a decision made whether further investigation is warranted. Case Study 2.3 is a good example of such an incident.

If the initial investigation discloses a noncriminal explanation or there is no indication of criminal action, then the answer to the box question "Is it a crime?" is "No" and the investigation stops. There may still be civil action or someone

Figure 2.12

Criminal Justice System Flowchart.

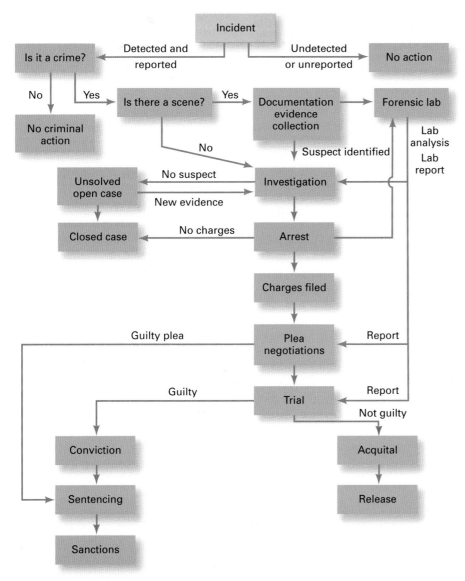

interested for other reasons, and evidence may even be collected and sent to a private laboratory. If, however, no violation of the criminal law has occurred, there will be no further involvement of the criminal justice system. If police determine that a crime has been committed, an investigation is opened. This is sometimes called "founding" the case. We can next ask: Is there a crime scene? This is a particularly important concern in terms of physical evidence and not quite as simple to answer as it sounds.

Is it clear that there is a location where at least part of this incident took place where physical evidence may be found or possible witnesses may be discovered? If one has a scene, even just a potential scene, then that is where the investigation is initiated. With modern techniques, careful processing is likely to uncover useful evidence that may further help to decide if this location is indeed a crime scene or not. Many crimes do not have scenes, or do not produce useful crime scenes. For example, someone reports she had a wallet stolen from her purse. The individual says that she had it in the morning when she left home, but when returning home, it was no longer there. That does not mean that the incident cannot be investigated, but there is probably not a scene to investigate, other than the pocketbook itself. Finding a crime scene is not only going to be quite difficult, but perhaps the wallet

Case Study 2.3

Physical Evidence Examination May Help Determine What Type of Incident or Crime Has Occurred

In a rural county in New York, someone noticed a considerable amount of what appeared to be bloody rags and papers in a dumpster and called the sheriff's department. The responding officers were concerned that this material might have resulted from a violent incident. It was collected and brought to a nearby crime laboratory. Forensic scientists were asked if the material could be examined to determine if it really was blood and, if so, whether it was human blood. It was quickly determined that the material tested positive for blood. However, the next test showed it was not human blood. Further testing established that it was consistent with deer blood. It became clear what had probably happened. Somebody had taken a deer out of season, gutting and cleaning it and trying to conceal the bloody residues to avoid being fined for taking a deer out of season. Thus, it was not a homicide, but a hunting violation incident, and the prompt use of physical evidence made what could have been a time-consuming criminal investigation unnecessary.

was lost and there was no crime at all. Even in a more serious case, a sexual assault, the victim may have been overcome, transported to an unknown location, assaulted, and then taken in a car to another location and dumped out. There certainly is a crime scene, but it may take a great deal of investigation before the scene is located, if it ever is.

There are two possibilities if a scene is established; the "Yes" arrow is followed to the important scene-processing block. This block symbolizes many activities, including a careful processing of the scene and full documentation of that process. This should include collecting possible physical evidence, packaging and properly identifying anything taken from that scene, and ensuring that any evidence that needs scientific examination reaches the forensic laboratory or other skilled examiner for analysis. The crime scene block is usually under the control of the investigators, but those carrying out the documentation and collection of evidence, fingerprinting, photography, and many other activities are usually technically trained individuals who are specialists in such matters. Much of the physical evidence collected will be processed at a forensic laboratory and any information gathered passed on to the investigators. This information will eventually be available for use at subsequent steps in the process. The forensic laboratory block at the far right may also receive physical evidence in several other ways, depending on the type of incident and how the investigation proceeds.

If there is no identification of a crime scene at this stage, all the responsibility falls on the investigators. It is clear that the key box, the one with the most arrows in and out of it, is the one marked "Investigation." That block symbolizes control over all that will be done to investigate that incident and determine if a crime has been committed. Whoever is assigned to investigate the incident is responsible for many key decisions. Depending on the nature of the incident, that control may rest with an individual or a large team led by a high-level police or prosecution official who is assigned the responsibilities of supervising a task force. The investigation block symbolizes the nerve center of the investigation. How effectively the investigation is run can make a tremendous difference in how likely it is to be successful and how well the criminal justice system works for this incident.

The investigation may disclose that no crime was committed after all and close down the investigation. More commonly a suspect is identified and if it is judged that there is enough evidence, an arrest will be made (downward arrow). If within a reasonable amount of time no suspect has been identified, the case may be transferred from an active investigation to an unsolved open case file (arrow to left). Depending on the nature of the incident, after a while the case may be closed (arrow down). Many incidents reside in the unsolved open case file for a considerable period of time. In most busy jurisdictions, after a legitimate effort has been made, and there are no further strong leads on which to work, the case will go to the cold case file.

Unfortunately, new incidents to investigate are coming in every day, demanding the attention of a limited pool of investigators. However, should some new evidence become available, a case with suspiciously similar circumstances, information from an informant, or perhaps a new witness suddenly appears, any of these can trigger a transfer back to active status (arrow to right, "New Evidence"). In the last few years, many jurisdictions have formed "cold case squads" to take a fresh look at unsolved cases and apply new technology or just revive the investigation. New investigators retrace what was done and perhaps realize that someone who should have been interviewed was missed or perhaps evidence was collected and unfortunately it went to a property room and somehow was never sent for scientific examination. These squads have in many cases been successful in developing suspects and moving the case back into the active stream. The arrow that says "New Evidence" extends back to investigation, but if there is physical evidence, it could also extend from the investigation block back to the forensic lab box. It can then produce information that can take the same three branches emanating from the "Lab Analysis Lab Report" block.

The "Investigation" block, as mentioned, represents the control center. If the investigators are successful, they will develop a possible suspect. If the investigators have developed enough believable evidence to convince the legal authorities that there is "probable cause" to believe that a particular person committed the crime, then that person will be arrested.

Probable cause is an important legal concept that says the evidence offered is sufficient to convince a reasonable person that a particular individual may be guilty. There are a lot of qualifiers in that description, and whole legal treatises have been written trying to define it, but for present purposes, this definition is adequate. The important distinction to grasp is that the amount of evidence needed to supply probable cause is considerably less than the amount needed for conviction at a trial. Juries are instructed that they must be convinced beyond a reasonable doubt that someone is guilty before they return a guilt verdict. A suspect may be arrested on the much lesser proof of probable cause. Some time between arrest and trial, sufficient evidence must be developed to meet the higher standard, if the suspect is to be convicted.

From the arrest block, arrows go in three different directions. The individual is interviewed and there may be some admissions made, or an **alibi** given. Sometimes when the alibi is checked, it is found not to be valid. Eventually, if enough information is gathered, and the court system believes there is enough evidence to charge the individual, charges are filed and the prosecution and defense processes are put into motion. If it is decided that the case is too weak to pursue, then no charges are filed and the case is closed. The third arrow is important to our interest in physical evidence. Once a suspect is identified, even before an arrest is made, it is possible to seek a court order to obtain evidence from that individual. This may be body fluid control samples, search of premises, taking of clothing for trace evidence, search of a vehicle, and many other possible evidence sources. These often are the samples that the forensic laboratory needs to compare with material gathered at the crime scene or from the victim.

Note that the arrow coming from the forensic block "Lab Analysis Lab Report" has three branches. The criminal justice system looks for a formal report when evidence is submitted to a forensic laboratory. That report can play an important role in several different aspects of a case. Whoever submitted the evidence, generally an investigator, gets a copy of the laboratory report. As indicated earlier, that report may help in the investigation and identification of a suspect. However, many laboratory reports are not issued until well after someone has been arrested. Evidence obtained from the individual arrested may have been critical to the laboratory examination. Therefore, a copy of the laboratory report will go to the prosecutor, in most cases, to help in developing the necessary evidence for trial, or it may be used in the **plea bargaining** process.

The block below "Charges Filed" is labeled "Plea Negotiations." In most busy jurisdictions, the majority of cases are settled at this stage by the charges being dropped or, more likely, the defendant pleading guilty to some lesser charge to avoid

probable cause

Sufficient reason based on known facts to believe a crime has been committed or that certain property is connected with a crime.

alibi

An innocent explanation of events used by a person accused or suspected of a crime.

plea bargaining

A negotiation between a defendant and his attorney on one side, and the prosecutor on the other, in which the defendant agrees to plead "guilty" or "no contest" to some crime, in return for reduction of the severity of the charges or a lighter sentence recommendation.

the perils, to both sides, of a trial. At this juncture the prosecution and the defense will have the laboratory reports available as part of the information that they will use in their plea negotiations. A laboratory report that tends to support the prosecution's case will be a strong bargaining chip for them. Conversely, a laboratory report that is weak may strengthen the hand of the defense in negotiations. Thus the presence of physical evidence may exert a significant effect even in cases where there is no trial.

The third arrow from the "Forensic Lab" block points to the "Trial" block. Should the case go to trial, the forensic expert from the laboratory will be called to present the findings for the jury to hear, and often the laboratory report itself will be offered into evidence.

Remember that although it is virtually always the prosecution that collects physical evidence for analysis, either side might use that evidence to advance its case. It is not uncommon for the defense to call for the presentation of physical evidence findings where the prosecution has decided that such presentation may not aid its case. Each side must at this stage weigh the evidence available and how well it will "play in court." Not every witness is highly believable and can express her- or himself clearly and in a convincing manner. Even though a witness is absolutely truthful, his or her evidence might not be well received by a jury. Conversely, some individuals are particularly talented liars and can provide convincing-sounding spurious opinions.

If plea bargaining produces a guilty plea, the arrow goes directly to the "Sentencing" block. The time and cost of a trial are avoided. Otherwise either the case is dropped or proceeds on to trial. The "Trial" block will eventually produce a verdict of guilty or not guilty. There is a third possibility of a mistrial, but that generally just results in another trial and is not indicated in the diagram. If the trial results in a not guilty verdict, the defendant is acquitted and released. In the criminal portion of our justice system, if there is a trial and the person is found not guilty, there is, for all practical purposes, no appeal. Once a defendant is found not guilty he or she is free. Should convincing evidence of guilt later be discovered, it does not matter, since the person cannot be tried again for the same crime.

If the trial results in a guilty verdict, the next step is sentencing, followed by some kind of sanction. If the defendant is convicted of a felony, it usually means confinement in a state or federal penitentiary. If the person is convicted of a misdemeanor, it usually means confinement in a local jail for a period of less than one year or perhaps a fine, a sentence of public service, or a number of different sanctions that can be applied. Sometimes a defendant who is charged with and tried for a felony may be convicted of a lesser crime that is a misdemeanor and therefore subject to the lesser sanctions associated with the misdemeanor.

Scientific and Technical Evidence Admissibility and the Expert Witness

Courts, through judges, control what evidence gets "admitted" in a case, that is, what evidence the trier of fact (judge or jury) can use in determining guilt or nonguilt. Once evidence has been "admitted," it is said to "go to the weight." That means the jury or, if the defendant waives a jury, the judge in the case can consider the evidence and accord it whatever amount of weight they think it deserves in the overall case. Forensic scientists get involved in admissibility issues when a new method or test is used in a case, or when an existing method or test is challenged. Over a long period of time, a body of law has developed around the issue of admitting scientific or technical evidence.

The most basic standard for admissibility is relevance, and this applies to technical and scientific evidence as well. The evidence has to be pertinent to the case and have the potential of helping the trier of fact reach a verdict. In the 1920s, a case called *Frye* v. *United States* came before the U.S. Circuit Court of Appeals for the District of Columbia. The case involved the use of a polygraph in determining whether the defendant was being truthful. The court would not allow the polygraph results, and most courts still will not, because it is simply not considered sufficiently reliable. The importance of the *Frye* case, however, was not the actual ruling, but the test the court laid out for determining whether "novel" scientific or technical evidence could be admitted. The court said that the principle governing admissibility was general acceptance of the test's underlying principles by the scientific community to which the test belongs. This language sounds straightforward, but often it is not when it comes to applying the principle to an individual case. What "scientific community" does polygraph testing belong to? Polygraph examiners? Neuroscientists? Electrophysiologists? All of them? What about forensic DNA testing? Is the scientific community forensic DNA analysts? Molecular biologists? Each court has to decide these issues for itself.

Some admissibility issues were clarified for the federal courts with the issuance of the *Federal Rules of Evidence*. These rules, strictly speaking, apply only to the federal courts for federal cases, and the individual states do not necessarily have to adopt the federal rules, though many have. Over the decades following *Frye,* many states adopted a **Frye rule,** either identical or similar to the federal rule. The *Federal Rules of Evidence* was amended several times over this period and came to emphasize the dual test of relevance and reliability as the appropriate standard for admissibility. There was still controversy on what exactly constituted a proper test for reliability and relevance.

In 1993, the U.S. Supreme Court (Figure 2.13) agreed to review a complicated epidemiology case called *William Daubert et ux., etc., et al.* v. *Merrell Dow Pharmaceuticals, Inc.* The case was about whether a drug called Bendectin caused birth defects in children whose mothers took the drug to control morning sickness during pregnancy. It is usually just called *Daubert,* for simplicity. The importance of the case is that the court took the occasion to issue guidelines for deciding the admissibility of scientific evidence.

This was significant because it was the first time the U.S. Supreme Court had ever considered this matter. The guidelines are called the Daubert criteria, and they outline several different approaches, or prongs, of the Daubert test. Strictly

Frye rule

The basic standard enunciated by the U.S. Circuit Court of Appeals in 1929 for admissibility of new technical evidence, which placed emphasis on general acceptance in the appropriate scientific community.

Figure 2.13
Members of the United States Supreme Court.

speaking, they only apply to the federal jurisdiction, but many states have adopted them either in detail or in spirit. The Daubert rules require that scientific tests on evidence be truly scientific. They must have been subjected to significant hypothesis testing of the underlying principles. Other criteria include whether the test is generally accepted (the Frye criterion), whether anything is known about its error rate, and whether there has been peer review, such as publication in a peer-review journal. Under Daubert, the judge is the "gatekeeper"; that is, he or she determines admissibility using the criteria. The Daubert criteria appear to create a stiffer test for admissibility than Frye did. Adoption of the **Daubert standard** by a jurisdiction also creates opportunities for attorneys to challenge admissibility of evidence long accepted under the Frye rule using the new criteria. The Supreme Court has made it clear in a subsequent case that its Daubert criteria apply equally to "technical examinations" as well as scientific evidence. Thus, the Daubert standard applies to handwriting examination, fingerprints, engineering, and many highly technical but not necessarily strictly scientific types of expert testimony.

Often, a judge determines admissibility of evidence following a hearing held specifically to determine admissibility. These hearings may be convened to consider whether the testing used by the laboratory conforms to Frye or to Daubert standards, depending on which one is applicable in the jurisdiction. Many other evidentiary hearings are held to determine, for example, whether the evidence chain of custody was properly intact or a search warrant was properly obtained.

Most forensic scientists and many other kinds of experts testify in courts as *expert* witnesses. Certainly, well-qualified scientists are expert witnesses, but our legal system considers someone an expert witness if he or she has knowledge or special training that would be beyond the scope of the average juror. An expert might be a forensic chemist or DNA analyst but could be a baker, a design engineer, a ship's captain, or a computer programmer, depending on the type of case. As noted, experts must be qualified each time they testify, and if found qualified, they are allowed to give opinion testimony. Other witnesses are normally allowed to testify only as to what they personally know, saw, or heard. Becoming a good expert witness and a good communicator in the courtroom is an important part of the training of a successful forensic scientist.

Daubert standard

A broad set of criteria laid out by the U.S. Supreme Court opinion in the *Daubert* case for the admissibility of scientific evidence, with the judge as the "gatekeeper" responsible for applying those criteria.

Summary

Physical evidence may be produced in a number of ways: changes induced at a scene, imprints, indentations, striations, damage, exchanges of material, and deposits. The principle that objects which contact one another exchange material across a contact boundary is called the *Locard Exchange Principle.*

Physical evidence can be classified in several ways. One useful way is for investigators to think about classifying evidence in terms of what forensic scientists will be asked to do with it: identification, individualization, or reconstruction.

There are a number of ways physical evidence can be used in investigations, including establishing leads, or developing MOs, establishing linkages or exclusions, providing corroboration or disproof of statements, identifying substances or persons, and establishing corpus delicti—that a crime has actually been committed.

The complete physical evidence process includes recognition, documentation, collection and packaging for preservation, laboratory analysis, reporting, and possibly testimony in court.

Law arises from a desire by societies to establish rules that enable people to live together in relative harmony. Law includes criminal codes, civil codes, and regulations. Forensic science plays a role in all of them, and its role has increased in the past several decades. The criminal justice process is complicated and involves many steps and branch points. Forensic science is involved in some of them, but not in others.

Both the U.S. and state constitutions form the basis for the admissibility of scientific and technical evidence into courts. Recently, a U.S. Supreme Court decision called *Daubert* has changed the rules of admissibility in important ways from what they were for many decades previously under a standard originating with the *Frye* case.

Key Terms

imprint (p. 34)
indentation (p. 34)
striation (p. 35)
Locard Exchange Principle (p. 36)
deposit (p. 36)
exclusion (p. 38)

modus operandi (MO) (p. 39)
linkage (p. 40)
cold case (p. 44)
control specimens (p. 45)
comparison specimens (p. 45)
questioned specimen (p. 45)

expert witness (p. 46)
probable cause (p. 51)
alibi (p. 51)
plea bargaining (p. 51)
Frye rule (p. 53)
Daubert standard (p. 54)

Review Questions—Short Answer

1   List and discuss the ways physical evidence is produced.
2. What is a useful way of classifying physical evidence?
3. List and discuss some of the uses of physical evidence in criminal investigations.
4. List and discuss the steps in physical evidence recognition and processing.
5. What is a "questioned" and a "known" specimen in forensic laboratory analysis?
6. What is an expert witness?
7. What role does forensic science play in the operation of the rule of law?
8. Describe the different possible steps in the "flow" of physical evidence in a criminal investigation and prosecution.
9. What is evidence admissibility?
10. What are and what have been the standards for the admissibility of forensic (scientific) evidence into court?

Fill-in-the-Blank & Multiple Choice

1. When two complex three-dimensional surfaces fit together perfectly, it is commonly referred to as a _____.
2. The results of examination of physical evidence can prove of considerable value to the operation of the criminal justice system even if a case never goes to trial by facilitating
    _____.
3. Physical evidence can be used in at least six different ways: (1) help reconstruct the occurrence, (2) _____, (3) provide linkages, (4) _____, (5) identify victims or suspects and (6) _____ to help the trier of fact (jury or judge) reach a just conclusion.
4. The ability to establish the exact whereabouts of an item of evidence and under whose control it was from its collection to the courtroom and everywhere in between is known as maintaining the
    a. chain of command
    b. continuity of investigation
    c. chain of custody
    d. business records circle
5. In the American legal system, whether or not a particular expert's testimony could be used during trial was, from about 1923 to the mid-1990s, determined by
    a. the standard laid down by the *Daubert* case.
    b. a "General Acceptance in the Community" standard.
    c. the Locard standard.
    d. a "Don't Ask Don't Tell" standard.

Further References

Dixon, L., and B. Gill. "Changes In The Standards For Admitting Expert Evidence In Federal Civil Cases Since The Daubert Decision" *Psychology, Public Policy and Law* 8 (2002): 251–308.

Horvath, F., and R. Meesig. "The Criminal Investigation Process and the Role of Forensic Evidence: A Review of Empirical Findings." *Journal of Forensic Science* 41 (1996): 963–969.

Peterson, J. L., J. P. Ryan, P. J. Houlden, and S. Mihajlovic. "Forensic Science and the Courts: The Uses and Effects of Scientific Evidence in Criminal Case Processing." Chicago: Chicago Center for Research in Law and Justice, University of Illinois at Chicago, 1986.

Osterburg, J. W. "The Scientific Method and Criminal Investigation." *Journal of Police Science and Administration* 9 (1981): 135–144.

Scientific Testimony—An online journal, www.scientific.org.

Swanson, C. R., N. C. Chamelin, L. Territo and R.W. Taylor. *Criminal Investigation.* 9th ed., Burr Ridge, IL: McGraw-Hill, 2006.

William Daubert, et ux., etc., et al., Petitioners v. Merrell Dow Pharmaceuticals, Inc., No. 92–102, 113 S. Ct. 2786 (1993); General Electric Company, et al., Petitioners v. Robert K. Joiner et ux., No. 96–188, 118 S. Ct. 512 (1997); Kumho Tire Company, Ltd., et al., Petitioners v. Patrick Carmichael, etc., et al., No. 97–1709, 119 S. Ct. 1167 (1999).

Part TWO

Crime Scene Procedures, Techniques, and Analysis

Crime scene investigation is an important part of overall forensic science and criminal investigation. You could say that there are two aspects of overall crime scene investigation: crime scene processing and crime scene analysis. We will talk about both of them in Chapter 3.

Crime scene analysis is more complicated than crime scene processing, though processing is also to some extent dependent on analysis. Analysis implies that the scientific method—hypothesis testing—is used to help understand the events that occurred at the crime scene, to figure out what the relevant evidence is, and to work toward some kind of reconstruction. Overall crime scene analysis requires assimilating the data at the scene, collecting physical evidence and awaiting the results of its analysis, and often analyzing patterns at the scene. The results obtained in the investigation must also be factored in.

Many of the patterns found at scenes cannot be "collected," in the sense that they cannot be packaged and labeled. They can only be documented. We call those types of patterns "reconstruction patterns," and they are the subject of Chapter 4.

In Part Three, we will examine various physical patterns, like handwriting, fingerprints, footwear impressions, and so on. We will call those "individualization patterns" because the goal is to try to "individualize" the pattern, that is, figure out who or what was responsible for making it. The individualization patterns—those that are seen in connection with scene investigations—are discussed in Chapter 5.

Crime Scene Processing and Analysis

- The steps in crime scene processing
- The process of evidence recognition based on hypothesis formulation
- The schemes for searching crime scenes
- The importance of and major methods for crime scene documentation
- Making notes
- Making sketches and types of sketches
- Technical and forensic guidelines for photography
- Videotaping crime scenes
- About the duty to preserve crime scene work product
- Different methods of collecting physical evidence and applicability to different categories of evidence
- Numbering and description of physical evidence from the scene
- Various types of packaging for different types of evidence
- Types of controls, and standards for each type of physical evidence
- Submission of physical evidence for laboratory analysis
- Crime scene analysis and crime scene reconstruction
- The difference between reconstruction and reenactment

Outline

Learning Objectives

- How crime scene processing is different from crime scene analysis
- The different types of crime scenes
- Initial actions at a crime scene
- Establishing crime scene security and reasons for maintaining security

chapter

3

Lead Case

State of Connecticut v. Duntz

In August 1985, the 234-year-old town hall in Salisbury, Connecticut, was burned down (see photo). The fire marshall searched the scene and determined that this fire was arson. Two local people, Earl Morey and Richard Duntz, were suspected of setting the fire. As the case developed, Morey decided to become a state witness and testify against Duntz on the arson charges. However, a day before Morey was set to testify, his body was found shot to death on the shores of a lake in the area called Long Pond.

The crime scene was investigated by the state police major crime squad and Dr. Henry Lee from the laboratory. A major storm was moving into the area from the west, and the investigators worked quickly to get to the crime scene and collect any available evidence before the rainstorm.

The physical evidence, laboratory and autopsy findings, and investigative information developed in the case included the following:

- Two sets of tire impressions were found at the scene. One set was consistent with a tire from Morey's car. A second set was on top of the first one, which was identified as having come from a tow truck. Service request records from the tow truck company showed that it was called to the scene to tow a disabled car at 7:30 A.M. This information indicated that the tire impressions of Morey's car were likely deposited the night before the tow truck was summoned.

- Two different types of shoe impressions were observed near the victim's body. One set of shoe prints had a parallel wave type of sole pattern that was identified as coming from the victim's own shoes. A second set of shoe prints had an unusual hexagonal sole pattern. A search of the laboratory footwear files showed that this pattern came from a FootJoy brand sneaker.

- A shoe print with the hexagonal design was found on the floor in the back of Duntz's van. The shoe imprint in the van had the same size and sole pattern as the shoe prints found at the crime scene. During a search of Richard Duntz's home, police were able to find a picture of Richard wearing the same brand of FootJoy shoes.

- Four spent cartridge cases were recovered from the scene. The head stamp showed that they were S&W (Smith & Wesson).

- Bullet holes and gunpowder residue were found in and on the victim's clothing. Green color paint deposits were found on his pants. A "nickel bag" of white powder was found in his shirt pocket. The white powder was identified as aspirin powder by Fourier transform infrared spectroscopy (FTIR) analysis.

Fall Of A Landmark

The distinctive pillars at the front of the Salisbury Town Hall collapsed after flames had engulfed the upper story and roof. The pillars did not support a load and were not an original feature of the Town Hall. They were added during an extensive remodeling and reconstruction in 1913-1914.

PHOTO BY ROBERT ESKAROOK

Salisbury, Connecticut, Town Hall ablazed.

- A Red Devil chewing gum wrapper was found in his pants packet. Similar chewing gum wrappers were found in Richard Duntz's van. However, no positive linkage between the gum wrappers could be made.

- No gun was found during the police search. However, they did find an elastic belt with an impression of a weapon and a gun-cleaning kit. Laboratory examination of this gun impression showed that it could have come from 9 mm caliber weapon.

- Earl Morey's car was found in a parking lot with a large, fresh blood smear on the back left side panel. Serological analysis (this case happened before DNA analysis was routine) showed these bloodstains had the same blood and isoenzyme types as Morey. This fact indicated that the car was at the crime scene when Morey was shot.

- Fifteen latent prints were developed inside Morey's vehicle. However, none of them matched Richard Duntz's prints.

- Police searched Duntz's home and van but did not find any of the clothes that he was reportedly seen wearing on the evening in question.

- The dome light of Morey's car was found to be not working. Examining the dome light, an investigator found that the lightbulb was missing. During the search of Duntz's van, a lightbulb was found near the driver's seat. Toolmarks were found on the metal ends of the lightbulb during laboratory examination. Microscopical examination of toolmarks indicated that those toolmarks could have come from the metal clip housing of the dome light.

Autopsy showed that Earl Morey was shot three times. Three 9 mm bullets were recovered from his body. The bullets had been fired from a weapon with a 5-right twist. The firearms examiner was able to say that these bullets were more than likely fired from a Smith & Wesson Model 55, 9 mm pistol.

Information was developed through witness interviews that Richard Duntz in fact owned a 9 mm pistol. He fired the weapon into a tree in his friend's backyard in upstate New York for target practice. Detectives went to New York and removed a section of tree from the yard. The firearms examiner was able to recover several 9 mm bullets from the tree. Those bullets exhibited identical class and individual characteristics to the 9 mm bullets from Earl Morey's body.

Duntz's brother, Ronald, was arrested on drug charges. He later admitted that he sold a stolen 9 mm S&W Model 55 pistol to his brother, Richard.

A weapon of the same type was used for test fires and reconstruction experiments. The cartridge case ejection pattern helped to reconstruct the shooter's and victim's position relative to the tire mark at the time of shooting. Muzzle to target distance was estimated by comparing the GSR (gunshot residue) pattern on the victim's clothing with the test firing results at measured distances.

Based on the forensic testing results and physical evidence, police arrested and charged Richard Duntz with the murder of Earl Morey. The case went to trial in 1990. The jury found him guilty of the murder of Earl Morey, and he was sentenced to 60 years in prison. However, in 1992, the Connecticut Supreme Court set aside the verdict, stating that the warrants used to search Richard's home and van were not valid. In 1994, a second trial began and within days, Richard accepted a plea bargain and was sentenced to prison for 15 years. He died from a heart attack a year before his scheduled release date.

Processing versus Analysis

You can think of crime scene investigation as having two aspects: processing and analysis. There is no way to set out a "formula" for crime scene investigation. It requires a scientific (logical and systematic) approach, forensic science knowledge, and experience. Processing has some common guidelines that we will discuss. However, there is almost always some variation in the processing depending on the individual scene and case. And some analysis is necessarily part of the evidence recognition process. A series of fairly standard steps can be followed in processing most scenes.

Analysis depends on detailed observation, proper processing, and making logical connections. It also depends on the results of the laboratory analysis of evidence, analysis of scene patterns, and integrating all the data available from the scene and the investigation. In death cases, the data will include the findings and opinions of the forensic pathologist. Crime scene analysis and reconstruction is a distinctly scientific activity; that is, proper crime scene analysis roughly follows the steps of the scientific method itself (Chapter 1). It requires scientific background, forensic knowledge, and experience. This is the main reason some people have argued that crime scene investigators should be trained in forensic science and criminalistics. Except in a handful of jurisdictions, however, crime scene investigators are not usually forensic scientists; they are police personnel. Most crime scene investigators have learned their specialty through a combination of training and experience.

Television programming about forensic science in recent years would have you believe that the same people who do crime scene processing also do the laboratory analysis, interview witnesses, and investigate the case. This is almost never true. Most of the time, police investigators—sometimes with special training in crime scene investigation—do the crime scene processing. Laboratory analysts generally go out to scenes only rarely. There are some laboratory analysts with crime scene skills and experience as well as some crime scene investigators with considerable knowledge and experience. Sometimes, working through a scene is a collaborative effort between laboratory analysts and crime scene investigators. This tends to happen more often in major cases that have complicated scenes or special requirements.

Types of Scenes

Crime scenes can be classified in many ways, but just a couple will help us organize our thinking about this. The point here is that each scene should be approached a little differently. Actions at scenes may be affected by where the scene is located, how much control we have over the scene, weather conditions, what equipment and personnel are available, what type of case it is, and other legal or scientific issues.

Scenes could be classified broadly according to the type of crime. Remember that not every crime has a crime scene. Crimes like extortion, various "white-collar" criminal activities, and crimes like driving under the influence, prostitution, illegal activities using the Internet, dealing in controlled substances, and even some simple larcenies may not have scenes as such. The two major categories of criminal activities that do have scenes are property crimes and crimes against persons. Property crimes are primarily larceny, burglary, and auto theft. Person crimes are primarily assault, battery, sexual assault, robbery, attempted murder, and murder. Virtually all death cases occurring outside a medical facility have a scene, regardless of whether they are homicides, suicides, or accidental or natural deaths. Generally, person crime gets higher priority from police investigators. To some extent, the type of crime suggests looking for certain types of evidence. For instance, we would tend to expect semen or other biological fluid evidence in connection with a sexual assault investigation or scene, but not in connection with a robbery or larceny. As we will note again later, however, it is important to try not to overlook anything at any crime scene.

Scenes could also be classified broadly according to whether they occurred indoors or outdoors, and whether they are on public or private property. Indoor scenes have built-in protection from the elements; outdoor scenes do not and may require special setups to try to protect evidence. Further, evidence can be compromised or destroyed, by rainfall for example, before investigators even have a chance to look. Whether a scene is on public or private property, and whether it is a private home or apartment, or a place with a lot of human traffic, all have implications for the way the scene is handled. A scene in a public area of any kind may have experienced a lot of human activity before police or investigators arrive. In addition, these areas may be difficult to secure.

Another important matter that will seriously affect any resulting legal case arising from the scene is how the evidence is acquired. Do the investigators have the right to be at the scene? Do they have the right to seize any physical evidence without a search warrant? Do they have the right to take pictures, or to ask people who belong there or who own the premises to stand back? These are all questions with potentially complex answers that revolve around search and seizure law. Moreover, these laws vary somewhat from state to state. Note that any evidence collected or seized that is later found to have been collected or seized illegally will be inadmissible—and that inadmissibility includes all the laboratory findings associated with it. A blood or semen stain that is matched to a suspect through DNA typing will be of no value to the prosecutor if the stain was seized illegally.

Initial Actions and Scene Security

Police personnel are generally trained to "render aid and assistance" at a crime scene as their initial step, if this is applicable. Sometimes, however, protecting a victim, a police officer's partner, or the officer him- or herself from harm, in case a dangerous perpetrator is still around at the scene, is an even higher priority. Once the scene is deemed secure and injured persons have been assisted, initial responders' attention can turn to scene security. Rendering assistance may involve an EMS response. While taking care of injured victims is clearly the first priority, both police and EMS personnel should make an effort to do as little damage to the scene as possible. This could involve such actions as taking a single straight pathway in and out, not throwing bandage wrappers around at the scene, not cutting through obvious stab or gunshot wound holes in clothing, and so on. These precautions do not waste any precious lifesaving time, and they can be very helpful in preserving scene integrity.

Establishing control and security at a scene may involve arresting suspects, detaining witnesses, removing people from the premises, maintaining crowd and vehicular traffic control, and so on, depending on the location and situation. **First responders** are generally on-site because they were called there, and their actions in establishing initial order and rendering aid and assistance are usually not legally questionable. As soon as the exigent emergency situation is resolved, however, police and investigators have to decide whether any subsequent activities are permissible without a warrant. The answer requires some knowledge of search and seizure law as applied to the particular situation.

First responders should notify their supervisors as soon as possible. Supervisors in turn must normally make the formal notification of the crime to the crime scene unit, the medical examiner, the prosecutor's office, and so on, in accordance with their training and the practices of the department.

If it is determined that investigators have the right to take control of the scene, a security perimeter should be established using tape, rope, or other barrier. The purpose of **crime scene security** is to keep out as many people as possible in order to preserve the integrity of the crime scene for detailed investigation. The extent to which a scene can be secured depends on where it is and the type of situation. In a residential setting, it should generally be possible to establish security. The more public an area is, the more difficult security may be. In some circumstances, such as on a busy street or highway, it may not actually be possible to truly secure an area, and investigators may have to work around the traffic and activity as best they can. It is well to remember that the initial security perimeter may have to be expanded, depending on what is found or what information is developed.

Figure 3.1 shows a mnemonic designed by a police agency to help remind first and subsequent responders of their duties and responsibilities at a crime scene. The order of actions on the list is not necessarily the order in which they would be done at a scene.

Over the years, different authors have discussed various strategies about the best ways to keep people out of crime scenes who have no appropriate role there, and whose presence might introduce unwanted contamination. Anyone who must obey police directions can generally be prevented from entering scene security perimeters. But police and/or political superiors may be a more difficult problem. Collecting **elimination fingerprints** from anyone who enters a scene has been suggested as a potential deterrent. The prospect of having to provide a set of fingerprints to investigators might discourage someone from actually going into the scene. Today, collecting a buccal (inner cheek) swab from anyone entering a scene as a DNA profile elimination standard could also be in order and might provide additional disincentive. Taking a few initial photos or shooting a few minutes of initial video by one investigator to bring out and show authorized people is another potential strategy.

first responder
The first police officer or investigator to arrive at and witness a crime scene, often a uniformed patrol officer.

crime scene security
Limiting and controlling access to a crime scene and maintaining records of who was present.

elimination fingerprints
A ten-print set of inked (or live-scanned) fingerprints from everyone who enters the secure crime scene area.

P roceed promptly and safely

R ender aid and assistance

E ffect preliminary notifications

L ocate witnesses

I nvestigate briefly and secure the scene

M aintain control

I nterview witnesses

N ote all conditions

A rrest suspects as appropriate

R eport fully and accurately

Y ield to continuing investigation

Figure 3.1
Mnemonic guide to preliminary steps at crime scenes.

First responders and/or follow-up investigators should gather the names and contact information of witnesses and others who may have information. They should also make notes about other potentially relevant matters, such as vehicles parked in the area, and so on.

It is worth noting here that some crimes can have more than one scene. For example, a victim might be assaulted at one location and forced into a vehicle, then taken to another location and assaulted further. In that event, there are scenes at both the locations, and the vehicle is another scene.

It is also worth distinguishing between a crime scene and what is often called a *dumpsite*. The crime scene is where the initial actions took place, and the majority of physical evidence is expected to be found there. A dumpsite usually refers to a secondary location where a body has been left, often well after and some distance from the criminal events. Less physical evidence may be expected at a dumpsite compared with that at an actual crime scene.

Steps in Scene Processing and Analysis

The steps in crime scene processing are briefly described here, then discussed in detail in separate sections, except for the final one which does not require further elaboration.

1. Scene Survey and Evidence Recognition

scene survey

A preliminary walk-through and look at the overall scene to try to establish the type of scene, note any transient physical evidence, and get a first impression of the relevant physical evidence.

Once the scene is under control (as much as it is going to be), any injured persons have been properly cared for, and the area is safe, the first action is to conduct a quick **scene survey** with special attention paid to potentially transient evidence. Transient evidence refers to evidence that is easily destroyed or compromised. A footwear or tire impression that could easily be inadvertently driven on with a vehicle or stepped on by someone is one example. Another example is a pattern of objects at the scene that may be destroyed if people start moving things around. The second aspect of this survey is recognition of the potential evidence. **Evidence recognition** is the hardest thing to teach because it depends so much on experience and is least amenable to any prescribed protocol. There are always a lot of things at crime scenes. The objective is to figure out what is relevant to the investigation and what is background.

evidence recognition

Determination of which physical evidence items and/or patterns are relevant to the case as opposed to being part of the scene background.

2. Scene Searches

scene search

A detailed, systematic search of a crime scene with the objective of noting every condition and every relevant item of physical evidence.

Several commonly used "formula" methods are used to conduct searches. They are discussed later. The **scene search** method chosen depends on the type of scene and how much area it covers. A large outdoor area thought to contain a shallow grave would not be searched the same way as a house, for example. The primary consideration is to be thorough. Crime scene processing is a onetime thing—many times there are no second chances. It is often said "two searches are better than one." The point is that investigators want to ensure that the scene has been completely searched before releasing it.

3. Documentation

documentation

Creation of a detailed, complete record of a crime scene, including notes, sketches, photographs, and possibly audio- or videotape.

The next step is **documentation.** Three or four different methods of documentation must be used to ensure a thorough record. The methods commonly used are notes, sketches, photographs, and video. Investigators should create a detailed record of the scene itself and of all relevant evidence that was recognized. A perfectly documented scene would enable someone to reconstruct (at least in their minds) every detail of the scene in proper perspective at some later time. One reason documentation is so important is that many patterns cannot be collected in the "bag and tag" sense but

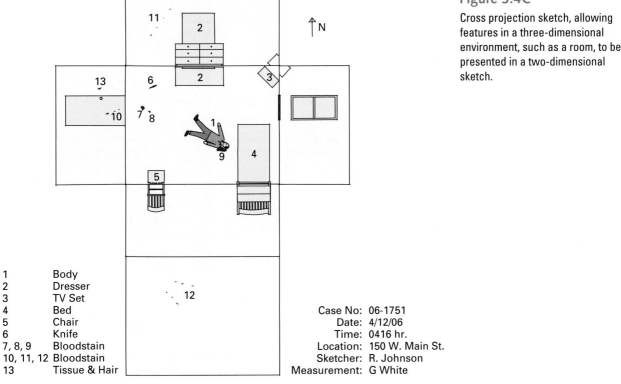

Figure 3.4C
Cross projection sketch, allowing features in a three-dimensional environment, such as a room, to be presented in a two-dimensional sketch.

1	Body
2	Dresser
3	TV Set
4	Bed
5	Chair
6	Knife
7, 8, 9	Bloodstain
10, 11, 12	Bloodstain
13	Tissue & Hair

Case No: 06-1751
Date: 4/12/06
Time: 0416 hr.
Location: 150 W. Main St.
Sketcher: R. Johnson
Measurement: G White

at the scene, during processing. They are usually not to scale and contain measurements within the sketch. A smooth sketch is prepared later from the data contained in the rough sketch. Smooth sketches are drawn to scale. The scale should be indicated on the sketch. There are no measurements shown in the smooth sketch, because it is drawn to scale, and items or objects that are not relevant to the case are usually omitted.

Although we talk about crime scene sketches as if there were one sketch, in fact there will probably be a whole set of sketches, showing different scales and perspectives. One sketch might show the location of a house in relation to the street, for example. The next might show the whole house floor plan. Another could show a second story or basement floor plan. Another might show a floor plan of the garage. And there will be sketches that show the details for the rooms or areas in which most of the action occurred and/or in which most of the evidence seems to be located.

The type of sketch that can be used to show three-dimensional character and features, if necessary, is called a **cross-projection sketch,** and it is most easily envisioned using a rectangular room as the scene. Think of the room as a box. Then think of slitting open the seams of the box at its edges and folding it open to make a pattern of flat rectangles, each representing a wall, the floor or the ceiling. Figure 3.4C shows an example. This type of sketch could be used to show the location of bullet holes or blood patterns on walls or a ceiling, for example. Although many sketches will be "floor plans," it is sometimes necessary to sketch and record a vertical dimension, that is, how far from the floor something is. A blood pattern on a wall is one example.

To make a sketch, the dimensions of the scene have to be measured. In addition, methods have to be used to determine the exact location of objects and evidence items. Taking measurements that provide an exact location for objects can be done in three ways: the triangulation on two fixed points method; the

cross-projection sketch

Sketch of a three-dimensional room or structure in two dimensions, by "collapsing" the walls and ceiling flat in the sketch.

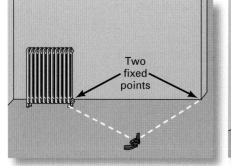

Figure 3.5A

Location of an item (gun) using fixed points in the scene (triangulation).

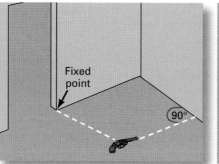

Figure 3.5B

Location of an item (gun) using a single fixed point and a 90-degree wall at the scene.

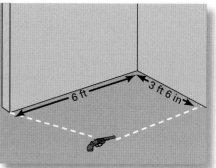

Figure 3.5C

Location of an item (gun) using measurements on an XY axis drawn in the scene sketch. This method depends on the presence of walls or other objects oriented 90 degrees to one another.

single fixed point with 90-degree walls method; and the XY axis method. Figure 3.5 shows how they all work.

The triangulation method may sometimes be the only useful method at an outdoor scene. The XY axis method requires that some fixed point be selected to represent the starting point (X = 0, Y = 0), and that the imaginary axes be oriented at 90 degrees to one another. Sketch preparers should be careful to select as fixed points objects or features that are not likely to move or disappear, in case reference has to be made to them later.

It isn't necessary to be an artist to make a good sketch. The point is to record the scene on a scale drawing. Various vendors sell templates to help sketch preparers draw objects, furniture, and so on into the sketch. When doing the finished sketch, the preparer should pick a scale that is logical for the area being sketched and for the level of detail that is necessary. The same scale will probably not be used for all the sketches in the series. For example, you might be able to show the street, the house and the driveway on one page with a scale like 1 inch = 25 feet. But in a sketch of a room whose real-life size is 8 × 12 feet containing a body and many items of evidence, you would be more likely to use a scale like 1 inch = 1 foot. Information that is not to scale may sometimes be included in a finished sketch if it is relevant.

Every sketch should show magnetic north on the drawing. A compass is an essential item in a crime scene processing kit. That way, all references to direction can be in absolute terms, rather than saying "left, right," and so on.

Some computer-based accident and crime scene sketch programs are now available to assist with producing accurate diagrams to scale. These require a bit of learning, but they can make sketching much easier. Hand notes should still be kept and used to verify the accuracy of the sketch produced. The cost of global positioning satellite (GPS) locators has also come down in recent years, and GPS could be useful in producing scene sketches with absolute location references.

Photography

crime scene photography

Technically proper photography of a crime scene for purposes of complete documentation.

Crime scene photography can be thought of as having two aspects: technical and forensic. The technical aspect has to do with a person's understanding of and skills in photography. The forensic aspect has to do with making good decisions about which pictures to take to accurately and appropriately capture the necessary details of the scene and physical evidence.

Technical Aspects Photographic equipment consists of **cameras, lenses,** and film. Today, the issue of digital versus analog cameras is also a factor. Digital photographic technology has improved so much in recent years that it may soon be the only type of photography commonly used. The strictly technical aspects of taking pictures can be divided into lighting, sharpness, and exposure.

Many different types of cameras have been used in crime scene photography. For practical purposes, cameras can be divided up into five categories: "point and shoot," instant Polaroid, 35 mm, 4 × 5, and digital. All of them except digital cameras use film as the recording medium.

Traditionally, the value of "point and shoot" and instant Polaroid cameras is ease of use. Anyone can take pictures with them with no training or photographic knowledge. An additional advantage of Polaroid cameras is the instant results. If the picture doesn't come out as expected, you know it immediately and can take another one. Digital cameras also offer the advantage of instant results. The 35 mm camera has been by far the most versatile available. The "35 mm" in the name refers to the size of image on the film. These cameras come in a wide range of models, with many lenses available, and a range of possible features. For years, the 35 mm was the camera of choice for general crime scene photography work. Most 35 mm cameras have microchips in them that allow them to be set fully automatic, shutter-preferred, f-stop preferred, or fully manual. Each operational mode has its value under different photographic conditions. The main point is that these cameras allow the photographer maximum control over the conditions. Some knowledge of photography—beyond the thumbnail sketch we are providing here—is necessary to make the most efficient use of any modern camera. A few scene photographers have used large format (4 × 5) cameras. Their advantage in crime scene photography is in photographing larger-size patterns or items of evidence. Because the film is larger, the image size on the film is larger, and there is less "compression" and loss of detail going from life-size to negative (and back again when the negative is printed). Better digital cameras resemble 35 mm cameras, although the image capture device is significantly smaller in most cases. Higher-end digital cameras, with interchangeable lenses, offer the greatest versatility, and their prices continue to come down. Many digital cameras offer significantly better performance than Polaroid or "point and shoot" cameras. In the last few years, digital photography has improved so dramatically that the choice between traditional film (analog) and digital cameras and images is now more a matter of preference.

Resolution is a major factor in digital photography. It is generally stated in megapixels. The higher the number, the higher the theoretical resolution (and probably, the more expensive the camera). Individual image resolution is generally stated in a "A × B" pixel format, where A and B are pixel numbers. The higher the numbers, the greater the resolution and the larger the image. Higher-resolution images can be printed in larger and larger sizes without loss of clarity. At the higher numbers there is less "compression." There are also various formats for digital images, such as .gif, .jpg, and .tif. Digital photographers need to understand these formats in terms of how much they "compress" the original image (with a potential for loss of detail), how large they are, and so on. Computer programs like Adobe Photoshop can convert digital images from one format to another, as well as adjusting many properties and parameters of the image.

Digital images are typically stored in the camera on some sort of card that slides into a slot. These cards come in different total capacities, usually stated in megabytes (mb). The more images or the larger the images one wants to store at a time, the larger the capacity of the card should be. Images from the card can be downloaded to a computer with a card reader or directly from the camera by way of a cable. Generally, digital images are fairly large and occupy quite a bit of disk or storage space. This factor has to be considered if many digital images must be stored for long periods. Another important consideration with crime scene images is backup provisions, in case something happens to the original images. Some people have suggested that the integrity of digital images will tend to be suspect because they

camera

An analog or digital device equipped with a lens and capable of recording images on film or an electronic storage medium.

lens

An optical component of a camera that focuses light onto the recording medium (film or digital recorder); "standard" lenses with a 50 mm focal length provide a "normal eyeball" view of the subject, "wide angle" lenses provide more peripheral views, and "telephoto" lenses provide closer but narrower views.

can be manipulated using computer programs such as Photoshop. However, digital image and photography experts have made great strides in developing methods to ensure that the images are original and to detect images that have been tampered with. Use of these strategies is very important in digital crime scene photography, because any manipulation of an image could potentially be viewed as an attempt to misrepresent evidence. There may be circumstances, however, where computer-based manipulation of an image—for example, to improve the contrast between a footwear impression and the background—would not really be any different from using traditional photographic techniques to do the same thing. The important factor in such a situation would be honesty about what was or was not done.

As noted earlier, lighting, sharpness, and exposure are the key technical elements in taking good photographs. They are equally important.

For crime scene photography, front lighting is virtually always preferred. Back and side lighting are generally reserved for special situations. That is one of the reasons we suggest using flash all the time. In low-light situations, the flash should provide adequate illumination for a good image. Even in daylight, shadows can be a problem (such as taking a picture of something in the shade under a tree). The flash tends to "fill" in the shadow and correctly illuminate the subject of the photo (hence the term "fill flash"). Backlighting is almost always a problem. In extreme situations, like having to try and take a photo looking into a setting sun, you may have to wait until the sun has set to get the picture. One important exception to the "front lighting is best" rule is in photographing three-dimensional impression markings (indentations), such as footwear or tire impressions in soft earth (Chapter 5). Here, side lighting (usually with a flash unit) provides the best image, because a slight amount of shadow illuminates the pattern detail. A series of exposures with the flash at different angles is generally recommended. Photographing reflective surfaces also requires special lighting techniques.

Sharpness of a photographic image is a function of two factors: having the camera properly focused, and holding the camera still while the lens is open. Many automatic cameras have autofocus; that is, with normal objects and conditions, they can focus without operator intervention. But if problems occur, the autofocus may have to be turned off, allowing manual focusing. The second factor is holding still. This factor becomes important when exposure times are slower. Under those circumstances, it is recommended to use a tripod.

Exposure is the most complicated element, because it is a function of two parameters that are separately adjustable on nonautomatic cameras: the f-stop, and the exposure time. The **f-stop**, or f-number, indicates the amount of light that will be allowed to reach the film or image capture device by controlling the **lens opening.** The exposure time is the amount of time the lens is open and is usually expressed in fractions of a second. The larger the lens opening, the smaller the exposure time can be to admit the same quantity of light. One other factor that has to be considered, however, is called **depth of field.** Depth of field is greater as the f-number is greater (i.e., as the lens is closed down more and more). You can think of depth of field as a range of distances from the lens where everything will be in focus. Narrow depth of field might mean that only objects between 6 and 12 feet will be focused, whereas wider depth of field might have almost everything in view in focus. How much depth of field is needed for a picture depends on what is being photographed and what needs to be in focus. A picture depicting an overall view of an outdoor crime scene should have a lot of depth of field—everything should be in focus. Depth of field may be less important in photographing a bloody footwear imprint on a flat surface. The photographer has to choose the f-number partly out of consideration for depth of field.

Forensic Aspects   The forensic aspects of crime scene photography have mainly to do with selecting the correct subjects and objects to photograph in order to do a good job of documenting the information contained in the scene. This will vary for different types of evidence and from scene to scene, but there are some guidelines to follow.

---

f-stop/lens opening

A selectable parameter on a camera that defines the amount of light entering the lens.

depth of field

A photographic term describing the distance behind and in front of the subject that is in focus; inversely related to lens opening.

Figure 3.6A

Highway crime scene showing a vehicle and a body (overall shot).

Figure 3.6B

Same scene as in figure 3.6A but closer to the vehicle and body (intermediate distance photo).

Figure 3.6C

Same scene as in figures 3.6A and B, but close-up to show auto license plate. Other close-up shots are also possible.

It is generally good practice to photograph the overall scene and subscenes proceeding from the bigger to the smaller—overall, midrange, close-up, as is often said (Figure 3.6). Sometimes, even aerial photos of an overall scene, taken from an aircraft or from atop a cherry picker, are needed. In some less extreme situations, use of a stepladder can improve the perspective.

Once the overall scene and subscenes (such as smaller areas, rooms, etc.) are photographed, the evidence must be photographed. First, the evidence items that have been identified for collection and packaging should be photographed in their original location (Figure 3.7). A label or number plates or markers may be placed next to an item at a scene.

The photographer should take a picture with and without this marker (the one without the marker is to document the item in place before any possible tampering takes place). These photographs, along with the sketches, should permit the original location of any seized item to be reconstructed accurately. It is very important to

Figure 3.7

Expended cartridge case in car on driver's side with evidence number marker.

videography

The use of a video recording device, in this context, to document a crime scene.

have good photographs of patterns that will not or cannot be collected or otherwise preserved. These may be "crime scene" patterns (Chapter 4), or they may be imprints or impressions that will not or cannot be actually collected. For patterns like tire tracks, footwear impressions, and so on, the photographer should take care that the film plane of the camera is parallel to the plane of the floor or ground. A tripod should be used for these kinds of shots. Multiple photos and bracketed shots are a good idea for these evidence items to ensure that there is a good picture.

There are a few other guidelines. For most evidence photos a scale (ruler) should be included in the picture—to show the size of the item and, in some cases, to show how far it is off the floor or ground (Figure 3.8). It is again good practice to take a photo of an item without the scale and another one with the scale. Using flash, which we recommend, tends to "wash out" the numbers and markings on white scales. Scales that are gray, yellow, and so on, are available to avoid this problem.

As we've already mentioned, the date, time, location, photographer, and so on should be noted, and, with film, investigators must keep track of the separate rolls. One strategy for "labeling" rolls of film is to use the first frame to take a picture of a paper or chalkboard containing the basic data and a label like "roll 1," "roll 2," and so on. This strategy could be followed with digital images, too, as long as all the images are ultimately kept in one "location," such as on one CD-ROM.

Video Recording

Video recording of crime scenes has been feasible for a number of years since the technology became affordable. Several different types of video cameras are available, mainly differing according to what type of media they use (VHS, 8 mm, etc., or digital).

Videography has several potential roles in crime scene documentation. It can be used as a stationary "monitor" of all the people and activities at the scene, acting as a sort of activity and security log. More often, a scene is video recorded as another means of documentation. This type of video can be used to show others who weren't there the overall layout of the scene, evidence locations, patterns, and so on. "Others" could be forensic scientists at the laboratory, pattern analysts, and sometimes the jury at a trial.

Some considerations in crime scene video recording include whether to narrate, whether to have the date/time stamp turned on in the image, and how much video to take.

Figure 3.8A

Fired bullet on ground near tire with evidence number marker.

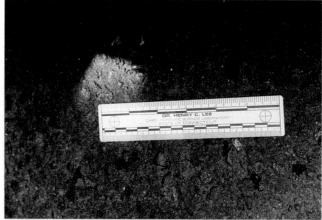

Figure 3.8B

Fired bullet on ground near tire with scale in place.

Some authorities suggest no narration and not having a live microphone during video recording. Their primary argument is that the microphones are too sensitive and pick up comments and remarks that may later seem inappropriate or insensitive. The argument for narration is that it orients the viewer and helps in understanding the video record. The narration should be slow and monotonic. References to direction should be absolute (north, south, etc.).

If the date/time stamp is on, it should be adjusted to be correct. The clock should also be synchronized with other watches at the scene so that all recorded times will be consistent.

How much video is taken depends on the primary purpose. If it is used as a silent "monitor," there may be many hours of tape. As a straight scene documentation device, one to several hours of tape may be shot. The longer the camera must be held, the more the videographer may need a tripod or monopod to help steady the camcorder.

Generally, the "overall, midrange, close-up" formula can be followed with video, just as it is with still photography. The videographer should avoid rapid camera movement and excessive zooming in and out, because these things detract from the quality and usefulness of the video record.

Rapidly advancing recording techniques may mean that "virtual reality" holographic scenes captured forever may become routine.

Duty to Preserve

In connection with the products of crime scene documentation (notes, audiotape, sketches, photographs, videotape, digital video or images, etc.), it is important for investigators to realize that there is generally a **duty to preserve** these materials and recordings for a long time. How long depends on the individual jurisdiction, but at a minimum most jurisdictions want the materials preserved until the "case has been adjudicated." If this means the first trial that yields a verdict, the time could amount to a few years. If it means until all the appeals in the case are exhausted, the time could exceed the investigator's life span. The courts have fairly consistently taken the position that the original documentation should be preserved for examination by defendant's counsel and/or experts, and for later reexaminations of the case on appeal. Another important reason for preserving documentation and records is the increasing revisitation and reinvestigation of cases by cold case units.

Thus, there must generally be arrangements for storage and archiving of various crime scene work products.

duty to preserve
An obligation imposed by courts on law enforcement agencies and personnel to preserve certain audio and video recordings for a specified length of time.

Evidence Collection and Preservation

After scene and evidence documentation is complete, **evidence collection and preservation** is the next step in crime scene processing.

Generally, physical evidence is collected and preserved because it will be submitted to a forensic science laboratory for analysis, but some physical items may be collected for other reasons. An example might be suspected stolen property. As noted elsewhere, some patterns may not be physically "collectible," so adequate documentation and/or preservation is particularly critical.

At death scenes, the medical examiner or coroner generally takes charge of bodies and some of the items associated with the body (clothing, etc.). Investigators should follow departmental procedures in notifying the medical examiner of a suspicious death and abide by accepted protocols in obtaining evidence associated with bodies. Often, detectives may attend the autopsy to see if the medical examiner can determine a tentative cause and manner of death, and to provide the medical examiner with additional information about the scene. Final determinations may require completion of the investigation, microscopic tissue examination, completion of toxicology tests, and so on. Clothing and other items associated with the body are generally turned over to investigators by the medical examiner for submission to a

evidence collection and preservation
The actual seizing and packaging of physical evidence items for submission to a forensic science laboratory in a manner that ensures integrity of the evidence, and/or documenting scene patterns that cannot be physically collected.

forensic science laboratory. In some cases, a sexual assault evidence kit may be taken postmortem, as well as trace evidence collected from the body and sent to a forensic science laboratory for analysis.

Collection Methods

Several methods can be used to collect physical evidence at scenes. The first, and the one that we recommend whenever possible, is to collect the evidentiary item intact. Collection of intact items is possible with many items and objects. Sometimes, such as with evidence on floors, walls, or other immovable things, it may not be realistic to collect the entire item intact. In those cases, investigators have to use sampling methods—that is, a sample of the evidence must be removed from the item on which it is located (often called the "substratum"; plural, "substrata"). These **evidence collection techniques** include:

- Use of forceps
- Tape lifting
- Shaking
- Scraping
- Vacuuming

Forceps and tape lifts, and occasionally, vacuuming may be used in the field (i.e., at a scene) under appropriate circumstances. But it is not advisable to shake or scrape items outside the laboratory, because traces of evidence could easily be lost. In connection with blood/physiological fluid stains, cutting, swabbing, or scraping can be used, as explained in detail in Chapter 9.

If investigators use forceps, they should be sure that the forceps are clean, and, if necessary, new forceps should be used for each evidence sampling to avoid any contamination. The word *sampling* implies that there are many items or a lot of evidence, and that the investigator is going to collect a representative sample. The key word is *representative,* and this activity may require some experience and judgment. Sometimes, all the evidence may be collected, as in the case of one or a few fibers or hairs. In other cases, sampling will be necessary, as in the case of a medium-velocity blood spatter pattern. The evidence pattern or deposit pattern may help guide investigators in their sampling.

Tape lifting can be a useful method for collecting evidence. It has the advantage of being thorough. But investigators should understand that the tape can sometimes cause problems for laboratory personnel trying to remove the evidence from the tape for examination.

Shaking and scraping are different versions of the same thing and generally apply to trace or materials evidence on clothing, or other similar items that can be processed in this way. This method should be used in the laboratory by forensic science personnel.

Vacuuming should be considered a last resort. Here, a vacuum cleaner hose is fitted with an in-line filter device in which the filter can be readily replaced and the system can be cleaned thoroughly in between uses. The principal drawback of vacuuming is that it collects every bit of trace and material ever deposited on the item, much of which probably has nothing to do with the case. A trace evidence examiner is then required to sort through hundreds of items on the vacuum filter to try and figure out what may be relevant.

It is good practice to thoroughly document the location of any evidence on an object or item before any collection technique is employed.

Numbering and Evidence Description Methods

Items collected at scenes or in the laboratory are generally given numbers and brief descriptions on the packaging and in the evidence log. There is no universal rule for numbering evidence. Each investigator or department should develop a thorough and

---

evidence collection techniques

Methods used to collect evidence when the intact item or item containing the evidence cannot be seized; usually includes using forceps or tape lifts at scenes; shaking, scraping, and vacuuming may be done in the laboratory or as last resorts.

consistent protocol, and stick with it. Obviously, the numbers and descriptions on the packaging should match those on the evidence log. It is best to use a numbering system acceptable to the forensic laboratory that will receive the evidence, thereby avoiding the lab having to renumber the items.

Signs or markers may be placed next to evidence items at scenes to help document their original locations. The number on the sign or marker must also match the number used on the packaging and in the log.

The identity of many items being collected at scenes is obvious, such as "beer bottle," "knife," "pair of shorts," and so on. In those cases, investigators should just use the name of the item as a description. It is wise to avoid adjectives that impugn value to an item in an evidence description—thus, "yellow metal ring" rather than "gold ring." With some items, investigators may not actually know the identity, such as with a suspected dried bloodstain. In those cases, descriptions like "bloodlike substance" or "reddish-brown stains" can be used to avoid being challenged in court about how the investigator "identified" the material or substance.

Evidence packaging should include the number and description of the item, as well as the case number, date, time, and name of the collector.

Packaging Options

Most evidence packaging is common sense, but there are a few principles to be followed. The majority of evidence items will be packaged in paper containers or evidence bags. The size of the container should be proportional to the size of the evidentiary item.

For most small items, particles, and objects, we recommend a "druggist fold" package as the primary container. A *druggist fold* is nothing more than a way to fold a piece of square or rectangular paper, so that it forms a leakproof container for particle- or powder-type material. It can also be used as a primary container for fibers or hairs. Figure 3.9 shows the making of druggist fold step-by-step.

Any piece of paper can be used for a druggist fold, and the size should be determined by the quantity of evidentiary material to be packaged. The use of

Figure 3.9   The Steps in the Preparation of a Druggist Fold to Contain Loose Trace Evidence.

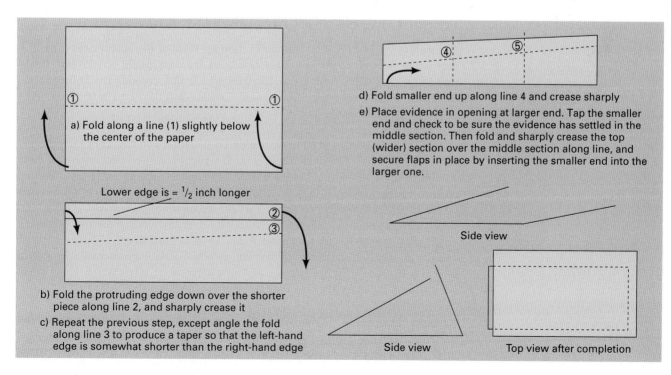

laboratory weighing paper for evidence collection is recommended, however, if it is available and the right size. This paper tends to resist having particles and powders stick to it or absorb into it. Otherwise, any clean white paper can be used. Although the druggist fold is intended not to leak, small evidentiary items like powders, particles, or fibers may work their way out as the package is handled and transported. Accordingly, the druggist fold should not be used as the *only* container of the evidence. The druggist fold containing the evidence should be placed in an appropriate *secondary* container to ensure that the evidence will not be lost. For blood or physiological fluid evidence, the secondary container must be paper and must not be airtight (see Chapter 9). For nonbiological evidence (see Chapter 13), the secondary container could be a plastic Ziploc bag.

Plastic Ziploc bags are suitable for many types of solid evidence items. The only major exception is biological evidence, which should be packaged in paper containers after thorough drying to avoid putrefaction and degradation. Plastic containers have the advantage that the contents can be seen without opening the container. Packaging is usually sealed at the scene with tamperproof evidence tape and not opened again until a laboratory examiner does so. We suggest that lab examiners open the package at a different location, preserving the original seal, if possible. The lab examiner can then reseal the package with tamperproof tape. This way, both seals are intact when the packaged item is presented in court.

Paper containers do have the disadvantage that you can't see into the container. There are paper containers on the market that have cellophane "windows." Paper containers must always be used with biological evidence.

A few other types of containers are used in special situations. With fire debris thought to contain ignitable liquid residues (see Chapter 11), clean paint cans with tight-sealing lids are used as containers. Liquids should be packaged in glass vials of appropriate size. Sometimes, boxes are used to contain weapons, multiple fragments of broken glass, and so on. Investigators should be certain that firearms are rendered safe before packaging. If a firearm or other weapon is found in water, it is recommended that it be left in the same water, that is, placed in a suitable container and covered with the water, for transport and submission to the lab. If items are fragile, steps should be taken to ensure that additional breakage does not occur during handling and transport.

Proper Controls and Comparison Standards

controls

In general, required to ensure that a laboratory test is working properly or to permit a proper comparison; the major types important in forensic investigations are blank, known, and alibi known.

Controls are very important in forensic testing. Without the appropriate control, it may not be possible to do an examination or to draw any useful conclusions. Investigators are generally responsible for seeing to it that controls are collected and submitted to the laboratory. The required controls differ to some extent depending on the type of evidence.

There are generally four different types of control and comparison standards that might be important in forensic testing of evidence: knowns, alibi knowns, and blank controls, and substratum (background) comparison specimens. Some of these specimens must be collected at the scene or in connection with evidence collection and processing. Investigators need to know which ones are required for which types of evidence. Traditionally, the substratum (or background) comparison standard has been called a "control." Strictly speaking, however, it is not a control, because a control is a specimen with a completely known or defined history. Thus, it is better called a comparison specimen. Remember, as noted earlier, one may not be able to return to a scene after its release, so the collection of all required control and comparison specimens the first time through is critical.

Known (Exemplar, Reference) Controls   Many types of forensic tests discussed in this book involve comparisons between a questioned (evidentiary) specimen and a known specimen (whose origin is known with certainty). The known (which may also be called the exemplar, or the reference) is essential for the comparison. Examples are known blood (or a buccal swabbing) from a person (for comparison with DNA types from evidentiary blood or body fluid specimens), known fibers from a carpet (for comparison with evidentiary fibers from a suspect's clothes), and known paint from an automobile suspected in a hit-and-run case (for comparison with a paint smear transferred onto a bicycle). Depending on the type of case and type of evidence, the known may be submitted along with the questioned specimen, or at a different time.

Alibi (Alternative) Known Control

An alibi (alternative) known is the same as a known control, but from a different source. Police might suspect, for example, that soil on a suspect's shoes is from an assault scene. Soil from that scene would therefore be the known control. But the suspect says the soil came from cutting through a muddy field nearby. Soil from that field would then be an alibi known in the case.

Blank Control

A blank control refers to a specimen known to be free of the item or substance being tested. Scientists use blank controls as negative controls (generally along with positive controls) to be sure tests and test chemicals are working properly. Investigators usually do not have to worry about blank controls.

Substratum Comparison Specimen

The term *substratum* refers to the underlying material or surface on which evidence is found or has been deposited. The term *substrate* is sometimes used for the same purpose, but for technical reasons is less desirable.

As noted earlier, this specimen has in the past been termed a "control." But strictly speaking, it is not a control, because its history is not known. With most blood and physiological fluid evidence (Chapter 9), arson accelerants (Chapter 11), and various types of materials or "trace" evidence (Chapter 13), investigators must remember to collect a sample of the substratum separately from the evidence in order to permit the analyst to interpret the scientific tests and make comparisons properly.

Typically, the substratum comparison specimen is subjected to the same testing as the evidence (which is on the substratum already) to make sure it is the evidence giving the test result, and not the underlying surface material.

Generally speaking, when intact items that have blood or other biological stains on them are collected, an unstained portion of the item can be used as a substratum comparison specimen. If investigators cannot submit an item with biological stains intact, and must use one of the sampling methods discussed previously, then they must take care to collect substratum comparison specimens.

> **comparison specimens**
>
> In general, required to ensure that laboratory test results will permit a proper comparison; for certain evidence, substratum comparison specimens are necessary.

Laboratory Submission

For evidence items that are to be submitted to a forensic laboratory, generally a specified "evidence submission request form" of some kind must be completed. The form has basic case information, date and time of incident, name(s) of victim(s) and suspect(s), type of incident, name and contact information for the submitting agency and investigator(s), and a list of items submitted. There may be space for a brief description of the case facts. Investigators are often required to specify what examinations or tests they want done on each submitted item.

If investigators and the laboratory that receives the evidence can agree on a numbering system, the lab submission sheet may become a de facto "evidence log." This saves the lab from having to renumber all the items and reduces the possibility of clerical errors when many items are submitted.

In major cases involving many seized items that require laboratory analysis, meetings between the investigative team and the laboratory team are recommended.

Crime Scene Analysis and Reconstructions

As discussed, crime scene analysis involves theory building and ultimately reconciling all the scene and investigative information to attempt to arrive at a "best theory" or reconstruction of what happened in the case.

Laboratory Analysis and Comparisons of Evidence

Laboratory personnel conduct analysis and comparisons of all the relevant evidence submitted in cases. This analysis can take considerable time and can involve multiple sections of the laboratory. Analysis of specific types of evidence is discussed in the chapters that follow.

Investigators should appreciate that many laboratories are underresourced for their caseloads and, as a result, have backlogs. It may be useful to discuss the facts of the case with a criminalist. This strategy can help focus on the most important items of evidence, and on the most relevant testing, and help avoid testing and analysis that has no clear purpose in the specific case. Good judgments, good choices, and good decisions in the examination of evidence from cases are key features of good criminalistics. The ability to make these choices and decisions wisely usually requires experience and insight, but it distinguishes forensic scientists from other laboratory scientists. Effective communication between crime scene and laboratory personnel is also an important factor in the process.

Medical Examiner's Reports in Death Cases

In death cases, there will be a report from the medical examiner, often detailing the findings at an autopsy. Toxicological analysis of blood and possibly organs and other fluids from the decedent are typically incorporated into the pathologist's report.

The medical examiner or coroner has the legal authority to rule the circumstances of a death: homicide, suicide, accidental, natural, undetermined. A cause of death is also stated when it can be determined. Final determinations may be delayed until the results of the investigation are complete and the toxicology is complete.

Reconstruction: Putting It All Together

reconstruction

Formulation of a "best theory" of a set of events in a case based on consideration of all the available evidence and information.

Conducting a **reconstruction** requires that all the data in the case be available. Thus, the final reconstruction cannot be completed until the laboratory report, the medical examiner's report, and all the investigative reports have been completed.

You can think of a reconstruction as forming the "best theory" of events in the case. This best theory will derive from hypotheses that have been formulated along the way and refined as more data become available. Remember that the best theory has to be able to explain all the data. If a theory is developed too quickly, later facts can make it look untenable.

In these times, especially if a case is even potentially high profile or "media worthy," there is often considerable pressure on investigators, police officials, and prosecutors to offer too much speculation too early in the case. It is generally better to wait for all the data before formulating a final theory of the case.

It is also important to realize that there are three types of reconstructions: complete, partial, and limited. There is rarely enough reliable data to actually discover every detail about what happened. Thus, reconstructions must be restricted to those facts that the data support, and scientists and others must understand the limitations of any reconstruction.

As noted earlier, experiments are sometimes done to try to duplicate some event that is hypothesized as part of a case reconstruction. Experiments are perhaps most common in cases involving blood spatter patterns or distance determinations from gunshot residue patterns. It is important to understand, though, that experimental duplication of a scene pattern does *not* prove that events at the scene happened exactly as in the experiment. It only shows that the theory is scientifically reasonable and that events *could have* happened in that way.

Finally, reconstructions do not always have to involve a big series of events or a lot of complexity. Some reconstructions are quite simple and have to do with one item or one event in a case. For instance, a contact transfer blood pattern on the knee of a pair of pants shows that the wearer knelt in blood (we might even know whose blood, based on DNA testing). That might be an important factor in the overall case.

Reconstruction versus Reenactment

Sometimes, efforts are made to reenact the events of a case after the fact. This exercise can involve computer animations, or even go so far as to employ actual actors and videotape or film.

It is important to understand, as we have tried to make clear in the foregoing section, that reconstructions are almost never complete in space and time and detail. Thus, a **reenactment** is by definition speculative and usually only partially supported by reliable physical evidence analysis.

Scientific criminal investigators should be appropriately cynical about reenactments of past events supposedly based on witness statements, and they should not be drawn into participating in this kind of activity without a full understanding of the limitations and potential to mislead. It is critical to consider *all* the available evidence, including the results from the forensic laboratory, in developing any reconstruction or reenactment.

reenactment

A hypothetical rendition of a set of events at a crime scene partially based on a reconstruction theory, but with all the "blanks" filled in to make a smooth, continuous story.

Digital Evidence and Forensic Computer Science

A rapidly emerging subdiscipline in the forensic sciences has to do with "digital evidence" and the valuable information it can provide to investigations. Digital evidence includes computers of any type (desktop, laptop, palmtop, handheld, etc.), phone answering devices, cell phone logs within the device, pagers, and so on. Many devices in our everyday lives record and retain digital records of various types, and these can be valuable in many investigations. More and more, larger departments are training investigators to be specialists in recognizing, handling, and deciphering the information on computers and digital devices. The digital devices must be looked upon as part of the crime scene, or as valuable separate evidence, and must be processed with the same care.

Gleaning investigative information from computers can be looked at as a sort of two-tier process. Investigators can be trained to extract readily decipherable information from someone's computer, such as looking at their files or their browser history of Web sites visited. If information is password protected, or has been "deleted," it may still be extractable, but the knowledge and techniques required are more complicated and require computer scientists.

Still another aspect of this area involves criminals who use computers and the Internet to commit various crimes, ranging from trying to lure children into chat rooms or even to actual face-to-face meetings, to every imaginable sort of financial fraud and victimization. Some larger departments, and some federal agencies, have trained special investigators to actively pursue the perpetrators of these activities. There is also no doubt that computers, the Web, and cellular devices can and have figured in terrorist activities.

Summary

Crime scene investigation includes processing and analysis. They are not the same thing. There are guidelines for processing, but they must be adapted to different scenes. Analysis follows the scientific method: formulating a hypothesis, and using data from the scene, lab, medical examiner, and investigation to refine it.

Scenes can be classified in various ways, but none is perfect. It is important whether a scene is on public or private property, and it is essential for investigators to know whether they have a right to be at a scene and process it without obtaining a search warrant.

First responders should protect themselves from harm, render aid and assistance as necessary, and then establish security. The initial perimeter of a scene may have to be extended as new information becomes available. A crime scene is a location at which a criminal event happened. A dumpsite is the location of a body, or perhaps a vehicle. Dumpsites typically have less evidence.

Steps in crime scene processing include an initial survey, thorough search, documentation, evidence collection, evidence submittal to a laboratory as appropriate, and release of the scene. During the initial survey, hypothesis formulation should begin. The hypothesis will help guide further steps. There are systematic methods for searching scenes, but the most important thing is to be thorough. Documentation of a scene is accomplished by notes, sketches, photography, and sometimes video. All are necessary. There should also be security logs, photo logs, and evidence logs. Sketches made at a scene are "rough." They are later revised to scale as "smooth." Several techniques are available for locating the position of evidence within a sketch. Crime scene photographers must be technically competent. The most important technical things to consider are lighting, sharpness, and exposure and depth of field. But crime scene photography is primarily documentation. Overall, mid-range, and close-up is the usual order of taking photos. Taking photos with and without scales or evidence markers is recommended. Scales must be readable. Video can act as a security log. It can also provide a method for documenting scene patterns for experts to examine later. And it may be played in court if there is a trial. Courts in many jurisdictions have specified that law enforcement must preserve audio- and videotapes until cases are fully adjudicated, including appeals.

There are several methods of collecting evidence. The best one is collecting the intact item with no tampering or sampling. If that is not possible, sampling with forceps or sticky tape may be considered. Vacuuming is a last resort method, and scraping should not generally be done in the field. Evidence items must be named and numbered in a consistent way. Biological and trace items can often be collected in a druggist fold. Biological evidence must be packaged in paper containers (nonairtight). Evidence should be sealed by the collector and be marked with the date, case number, name of collector, and name and number of the item.

Important control and comparison specimens for evidence items are known, alibi known, blank, and substratum. Investigators must be aware of what these are and when they need to be collected and submitted along with the evidence.

Major cases can involve evidence that is not submitted to the lab, laboratory analysis of submitted items, medical examiner's reports on victims in death cases, and all the scene documentation and investigative information. It may be possible to partially reconstruct the events from all this information. Reconstruction is the "best theory" of what happened. It is often incomplete, and because it is a theory, cannot be proven. Reconstruction is not the same as reenactment.

Digital and computer evidence has become more important in investigations in recent years. This may involve extracting data from actual computers, but it can also involve pagers, cell phones, PDAs, phone answering devices, and other appliances that record information.

Key Terms

first responders (p. 63)
crime scene security (p. 63)
elimination fingerprints (p. 63)
scene survey (p. 64)
evidence recognition (p. 64)
scene search (p. 64)
documentation (p. 64)
working hypothesis (p. 66)
notes (p. 67)

sketches (p. 67)
cross-projection sketch (p. 69)
crime scene photography (p. 70)
camera (p. 71)
lens (p. 71)
f-stop/lens opening (p. 72)
depth of field (p. 72)
videography (p. 74)
duty to preserve (p. 75)

evidence collection and preservation (p. 75)
evidence collection techniques (p. 76)
controls (p. 78)
comparison specimens (p. 79)
reconstruction (p. 80)
reenactment (p. 81)

Review Questions—Short Answer

1. What is crime scene processing versus crime scene analysis?
2. What are some types of crime scenes? What are the implications of the different types of scenes for crime scene investigators?
3. Describe the steps in crime scene processing and analysis.
4. What are the purposes of the initial scene survey?

5. What are some types of scene searches and to what kinds of scenes are they applicable?
6. What are the main kinds of scene documentation, and why is each necessary?
7. What are some ways of locating evidence items on a sketch?
8. What are the important principles of crime scene photography?
9. List and briefly discuss some methods for collecting physical evidence from scenes.
10. What are the main types of controls that must be available and/or used for the lab to be able to properly test physical evidence?

Fill-in-the-Blank & Multiple Choice

1. Photographs of crime scenes must include overall views, midrange shots, and _____, to properly record the details of the scene and object.
2. The rough sketch that is usually prepared at a crime scene is used to
   a. help identify the victim.
   b. reduce the number of photos.
   c. precisely locate evidence.
   d. help visualize the scene.
3. All unauthorized individuals should be _____ a crime scene during its processing.
4. The three most common, and classical, methods for documenting a crime scene are (1) _____, (2) _____, and (3) _____.
5. The best method for collecting evidence items from a scene is
   a. tape lifting
   b. submit intact the item that contains the evidence
   c. vacuuming
   d. using sterile forceps

Further References

Duerr, T. E., N. D. Beser, and G. P. Staisiuas. "Information Assurance Applied to Authentication of Digital Evidence." *Forensic Science Communications* 5, no. 4 (October 2004). (*Forensic Science Communications* is a Web-based scientific publication of the FBI, accessible through www.fbi.gov.)

Fisher, B. A. J. *Techniques of Crime Scene Investigation.* 7th ed. Boca Raton: CRC Press, 2003.

International Journal of Digital Evidence (IJDE), www.ijde.org.

Kessler, G. C. "An Overview of Steganography for the Computer Forensics Examiner." *Forensic Science Communications* 6, no. 3 (July 2004).

Lee, H. C., T. Palmbach, and M. Miller. *Henry Lee's Crime Scene Handbook.* New York: Academic Press, 2001.

Noblett, M. G., M. M. Pollitt, and L. A. Presley. "Recovering and Examining Computer Forensic Evidence." *Forensic Science Communications* 2, no. 4 (October 2000).

Scientific Working Group on Digital Evidence (SWGDE). "International Organization on Digital Evidence (IOCE), October 1999, Digital Evidence: Standards and Principles." *Forensic Science Communications* 2, no. 2 (April 2000).

Examination and Interpretation of Patterns for Reconstruction

- Some reconstruction patterns must be compared with experimentally produced patterns for interpretation
- Reconstruction patterns are generally intrinsic to scenes
- Reconstruction patterns must be documented
- Reconstruction patterns usually cannot be "collected" as such
- Blood droplets moving through air behave predictably according to physical laws
- Reconstruction from blood patterns is partially based on knowing the number of blood sources at a scene
- The side of broken glass from which force was applied to cause the breakage can be determined
- The order of gunshots or other impact points can sometimes be determined in glass that is broken but still essentially in one piece
- Foot, footwear, tire, or blood trail patterns can help reconstruct the number of persons at a scene and their movements
- Tire and skid mark patterns are used by traffic accident reconstruction experts to estimate position and speed of vehicles
- Clothing, article, or object patterns are based on looking for unusual or unexpected arrangements or disorder in a scene
- Tears, cuts, or damage to clothing or other objects can provide information for reconstruction
- Gunshot residue patterns on target surfaces can be used to estimate muzzle to target distances
- Trajectory analysis (ballistics) can help establish the positions and orientations of shooters and victims in shooting cases
- Ballistics should not be confused or equated with firearms identification
- Burn patterns at suspicious fire scenes can help establish origin and cause of fires
- Burn patterns are used by fire investigators along with analysis of the overall scene and investigation of mechanical and electrical equipment to help determine origin and cause
- MO refers to a repeat offender's habits and can be used to help connect related cases
- Criminal profiling involves statistical and psychological analysis to give insight in unsolved cases and on previous offenders

Outline

Learning Objectives

- The difference between reconstruction and individualization patterns
- Evidence patterns that can be collected, primarily for individualization, are called individualization patterns (Chapter 5)
- There are 10 major patterns for reconstruction: blood spatter, glass fractures, track and trail, tire and skid marks, clothing and article or object, gunshot residue, projectile trajectory, fire burn, MO and profiling, and wound, injury, and damage

chapter 4

Lead Case

State of Hawaii v. Mathison

At midnight on November 30, 1992, the Hawaii police in Hilo (Hawaii is the name of the largest Hawaiian island as well as the name of the state) received a call from a motorist reporting a traffic accident. Yvonne Mathison was dead on a roadside near Hilo. Her husband, Ken, a police sergeant, claimed Yvonne's death was a tragic accident. He said she jumped out of their moving van while they were having an argument. When he backed the van up to find her, he accidentally ran over her. He said he picked up her bloody body and put her inside the van while waiting for help.

A number of witnesses drove by the van that night and reported seeing suspicious behavior. Some police investigators believed that Ken Mathison had intentionally killed his own wife, but others in the department believed his version of events. The chief and deputy chief of police went to the hospital to console Mathison on the night of the incident. And, at the suggestion of Mathison himself, the police classified the incident as a negligent homicide. But several things in the van caught the investigators' eye, including physical evidence in unexpected locations, a rope with hair on it, broken glasses, and a shoe with drops of blood.

The local pathologist performed a thorough autopsy. The manner of the death was ruled homicide, and the cause of death was multiple head injuries. The file was reviewed by a forensic pathologist, who concluded that the injuries that killed Yvonne were not caused by the van. Because of the questions surrounding the evidence, the prosecutor asked for another autopsy by the chief medical examiner in Honolulu, and reexamination of the van. He was told that the van had been returned to the owner, and the body had been cremated on the orders of Ken Mathison.

With no body, and possibly no more evidence from the van, the prosecutor feared he could go no further in the case. At this point, he sought the assistance of Dr. Henry Lee. Fortunately, Mathison hadn't picked up his van from the towing company, because he didn't want to pay the $335 towing charge. The van was seized as evidence and secured by investigators.

The reconstruction based on pattern evidence found inside the van enabled forensic scientists to determine the following facts and help establish the sequence of events.

1. Approximately 200 hundred bloodstains were found on the instrument panel. These bloodstains were consistent with medium-velocity impact spatters. Reconstruction showed those blood droplets traveled from left to right downward and were deposited on the instrument panel at approximately a 45-degree angle. These spatters resulted from the impact force of a beating. It is more likely the bloodstains were caused by blows to the victim's head when she was in the front seat.

Ken Mathison being sworn in at his trial.

2. Approximately 50 small bloodstains (2–4 mm in size) were found on the driver's side window and door. These bloodstains were likely produced by medium-velocity impact force and could not have resulted from Mathison putting his wife in the back of the van.

3. Medium-velocity blood spatters found in the cargo bay suggested that the victim received additional blows in the back of the van as well.

4. A blood smear pattern was noticed on the van's cargo door. Enhancement of the pattern with tetramethylbenzidine (see Chapter 9) revealed a set of imprints consistent with a fist and hand moving from the top downward. This pattern indicated that the victim's bloody hands were against the cargo wall and subsequently slid down the wall onto the floor.

5. A mixture of soil and blood was found on a piece of sheetrock in the cargo bay floor area. Through detailed examination, it was determined that the blood was deposited before the soil, further undermining Mathison's story that he put his wife in the van after she was run over.

6. Bloodstains found on the floor of the van were whole blood with no indication of any dilution by water, as would have been expected if Yvonne had been outside the van in the middle of a rainstorm.

7. Three blood trail-like patterns were found on the roof of the van over the cargo bay. These blood spatters were consistent with an overhead cast-off pattern. This fact suggests that the victim was hit repeatedly while she was on the floor.

8. A bloodstain, 4 × 6 inches, was found on the driver's side sun visor and was consistent with a contact transfer pattern.

9. A large amount of bloodstains and head hair were observed on the roof over the driver's seat. These bloodstains were similar to a combination of multiple swipes and wipe patterns. Head hairs were found imbedded in blood. These patterns were the result of multiple contacts and hair swipes from a bleeding head.

10. Hairs were found on a piece of yellow rope and imbedded in blood. These hairs were microscopically similar to the victim's head hair.

These and some observations and interpretations were used to formulate a comprehensive reconstruction of events. Investigation of the exterior and interior of the van for damage patterns also showed no indication of a typical vehicle-pedestrian impact. Overall, the pattern evidence in the van did not match up with Mathison's story about what happened that night. Mathison was arrested and charged with murder. In 1995, a trial jury found him guilty of murdering his wife. He is now serving a long prison sentence.

Pattern Evidence: Reconstruction Patterns and Individualization Patterns

As we discussed in the previous chapter, many patterns that appear at crime scenes are useful for reconstruction. In some of the cases, these patterns can be "collected" only by documentation; that is, they cannot be "packaged." Ten major types of these patterns, which we call **reconstruction patterns,** are discussed in this chapter—as an extension of the discussion of crime scene investigation in the previous chapter.

Several categories of pattern evidence have the possibility of "individualization" as the primary goal. The major **individualization patterns** are fingerprints, palm prints, bare footprints, handwriting and other document patterns, and toolmarks and striae associated with firearms. They are discussed in Part Three (Chapters 5–8). This type of pattern evidence generally can be collected and brought to the laboratory for examination.

Most Reconstruction Patterns Are Crime Scene Patterns

The patterns discussed in this chapter are mainly found at scenes. If interpreted properly, they can provide information about the events—often, more reliable information than witnesses provide.

Ten common reconstruction patterns are discussed in some detail. These are the most common patterns seen in investigations, but there are other patterns that could fall into this class.

Importance of Documentation of Reconstruction Patterns

Many of the reconstruction patterns cannot be "collected" or transported to the laboratory. They have to be carefully documented by one or more of the methods mentioned in Chapter 3. At times, someone from the laboratory who is skilled in interpreting one or more of these patterns might be called to a scene to assist the investigation. More often, an expert in pattern interpretation will view photographs or videotape that investigators have made at the scene or examine the actual evidence that contains the pattern collected from the scene. Today, through technology, video from a scene can be made available to an expert at a laboratory or different site in real time. However, this tele-forensic technology has not as yet been widely exploited by investigative agencies.

Since many of the patterns are a part of the scene itself—in some cases, the integrity of the pattern is a function of the scene being undisturbed—the patterns will no longer be available—some may no longer exist—once the scene has been

reconstruction pattern

Pattern evidence that is principally useful to help reconstruct past events; blood spatter, glass fractures, fire burn, and track and trail patterns are examples.

individualization pattern

Pattern evidence that can potentially uniquely associate the pattern with the item or author responsible for it; fingerprints, handwriting, bullet striations, and footwear and tire impressions are examples.

processed and released. That is why thorough documentation is so important. The 10 major reconstruction patterns we will discuss are as follows:

- Blood spatter
- Glass fracture
- Track and trail
- Tire and skid mark
- Clothing and article
- Gunshot residue
- Projectile trajectory
- Fire burn
- Modus operandi (MO)
- Wound, injury, and damage

Blood Spatter Patterns

Blood spatter is probably the most common type of reconstruction pattern. **Blood spatter pattern** interpretation is something of a subspecialty in forensic science. There are laboratory examiners as well as investigators who specialize in blood pattern interpretation as a result of training and experience.

Basis of Blood Pattern Interpretation

Droplets of blood falling or projected through space follow standard physical laws. Those laws provide the scientific basis for understanding blood patterns.

By virtue of its makeup, viscosity, density, and other physical properties, blood forms predictable patterns when it falls, or is projected, through air and impacts a target surface.

Most of the time the blood forming a pattern of interest at a scene has already dried. But occasionally, it can still be in a liquid or semicongealed state. Blood deposited outside the body onto a surface will clot within a matter of minutes. Then it will dry. The larger the quantity of liquid in a blood deposit, the longer it will take to dry. Investigators sometimes use the state of the partially dried blood to draw inferences about how much time has elapsed since the blood was shed. Blood drying time will also be influenced by heat, humidity, air circulation, and the target surface. Such information must be taken into account in any attempt to predict time since deposit.

Velocity and Impact Angle

Blood spatter is often classified as *low, medium,* and *high* velocity. A **low-velocity blood spatter pattern** is any pattern formed where gravity is the only force acting on the blood. These are typically dripping patterns (Figure 4.1A). According to the laws of physics, any body falling through space (including blood droplets) will reach terminal velocity (32 ft/sec.) after a certain distance of fall. Once a droplet reaches terminal velocity, the pattern it makes will not be different no matter how far it fell (although there might be air resistance or air current effects). Most dripping blood only falls a

---

bleed spatter pattern

A pattern of dried blood on a surface resulting from an event that caused blood to exit the body and/or be broken into particles and distributed by force.

---

low-velocity bleed pattern

A pattern caused by blood falling onto a surface, influenced only by the force of gravity.

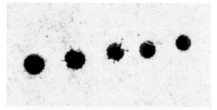

Figure 4.1A
Low-velocity blood spatter pattern.

Figure 4.1B
Medium-velocity blood spatter pattern.

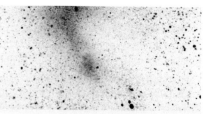

Figure 4.1C
High-velocity blood spatter pattern.

few feet—not far enough to reach terminal velocity. The force with which a droplet hits a nonabsorbent target surface affects whether "satellite" droplets are formed.

A **medium-velocity blood spatter pattern** is formed when moderate force from some object causes pooled blood to "scatter" in all directions surrounding the contact. The force causes the droplets produced to be smaller, so the resulting pattern consists of more and smaller droplets than are seen in typical low-velocity patterns (Figure 4.1B). These patterns are typically produced by an external force such as the use of blunt force to a bleeding source (such as a head), or someone stomping his foot or shoe into pooled blood. Medium-velocity spatter could also be produced by an arterial spurt.

A **high-velocity blood spatter pattern** is the result of extreme force acting on a blood source (Figure 4.1C). As a rule, such patterns are seen only in connection with gunshots, explosions, or the high-impact forces of a vehicle crash.

The shape of a blood spatter droplet indicates the angle from which it impacted the surface. A blood droplet hitting a nonabsorbent surface at a 90-degree angle (perpendicular to the surface) results in a circular stain. As the angle changes, the resulting stain becomes more elliptical (Figure 4.2A). In fact, using simple

medium-velocity blood pattern

A pattern caused by blood spattering in all possible directions from moderate force; many of the droplet stains are smaller than low-velocity pattern droplets and more numerous.

high-velocity blood pattern

A pattern caused by blood spattering in all possible directions from extreme force, such as might happen with a gunshot or explosion; many of the droplet stains are very small (aerosol spray size) and often more numerous than in a medium-velocity pattern.

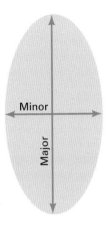

Figure 4.2A

Diagram of major and minor axis of an ellipse.

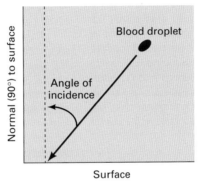

Figure 4.2B

Diagram showing the angle of incidence of a blood drop on a surface measured from the normal to the surface.

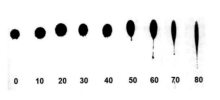

Figure 4.2C

Effect of angle of incidence on the shape of blood spatter dropped on a surface.

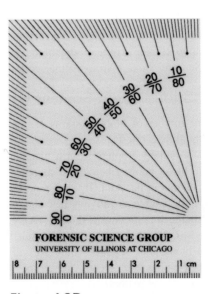

Figure 4.2D

A special angle scale measurement device.

Calculation of Blood Spatter Angle

A blood droplet impacting a nonabsorbent surface at exactly a 90-degree angle (exactly perpendicular to the surface) forms a circle pattern. Depending on the impact velocity, there can be satellite droplets around the outside of the circle, but the main pattern is a circle.

As the angle of the surface relative to the direction of the falling droplet changes from 90 degrees, the pattern becomes increasingly elliptical. Note that an ellipse is an "egg-shaped" two-dimensional figure that has a long diameter and a short diameter (Figure 4.3A).

There is a simple mathematical relationship between the properties of the ellipse and the angle of impact. The relationship is based on a trigonometric function known as the cosine. The cosine tables in various scientific and mathematical books and handbooks can be used to relate cosine values to angles. The cosine value is always a number between zero and one.

To figure the angle of impact for a blood droplet from its pattern, the major (long) and minor (short) diameters of the ellipse are measured as accurately as possible. Then the ratio of minor to major (width to length) is calculated. Because the measurements are used to compute a ratio, the units of measurement don't matter; that is, the measurements can be in inches, millimeters, and so on. Since the ratio is always that of a smaller to a larger number, the value will lie between zero and one. This ratio value is the cosine of the angle of incidence.

Expressed mathematically,

$$\cos \theta = \frac{\text{minor diameter}}{\text{major diameter}}$$

where we are designating the angle of incidence by the Greek letter θ (theta).

If you calculate the ratio of the two diameters in an elliptical blood pattern and then look up the angle corresponding to that ratio (cosine) in a cosine table, you get the angle of incidence.

It is important to note that the angle of incidence calculated using this formula is the angle of incidence of the blood droplet *with respect to a line perpendicular to the surface, not the angle with respect to the surface itself* (Figure 4.3C). Scales are available to make the angle estimation measurement easier (Figure 4.3D).

In a more complex pattern, such as a medium-velocity or cast-off pattern with numerous blood spatters, a selection of the droplet patterns can be measured and the angle calculations done. Then, straight lines (string, wires, etc.) can be drawn out from the droplet patterns at the estimated angles. The straight lines will tend to converge at a point that was the source of the blood pattern.

Note that the measurements generally cannot be that exact, so the resulting angles obtained are estimates. Although the straight lines will not converge to an exact point for that reason, they will usually converge to an area. These pattern reconstructions can tell an investigator approximately where the blood source (say, someone's head) was located at the time the pattern was formed. Experts may be able to tell, for example, whether a person was standing or lying down when a pattern was formed on a nearby wall, or whether a pattern in a vehicle is consistent with having originated from a person seated on the driver or passenger side.

---

angle of incidence

The angle at which a blood droplet impacts a surface, measured with respect to an imaginary line perpendicular to that surface.

measurements and some elementary trigonometry, the **angle of incidence** of a bloodstain can be estimated from the shape of the drop. See the "More on Science: Calculation of Blood Spatter Angle" box for a description of how this is done.

In a medium-velocity pattern, or a pattern that is partially medium and partially high velocity, the angle calculations can be used along with a straight line projection backward to the point of conversion (using strings, probes, or wires) to estimate the approximate origin of the blood forming the pattern, as noted in the "More on Science" box. A straight-line reconstruction is illustrated in Figure 4.3.

Various Blood Spatter Patterns

A number of blood patterns are commonly observed at scenes. We will describe them here briefly.

Falling droplets from a bleeding source that is stationary will generally result in blood pooling below the source. It may be possible to discern separate "droplet" patterns in the pool. If a dripping blood source is moving, blood "trails" can result. If the source is moving fast enough, the droplets may show which direction the source was moving (Figure 4.4A).

Contact deposit patterns result from an object coming into direct contact with a blood pool or blood source (Figure 4.4B). These patterns can appear on clothing or on objects at scenes. Sometimes, it is important to try to determine what object caused the pattern.

Wipe and swipe patterns result when an object contacts or transfers wet blood and smears it on a surface. A wipe pattern is created by an object contacting an existing bloody surface with motion. A swipe pattern is created by a bloody object contacting another surface with motion (Figures 4.4C).

An *arterial spurt* pattern results when an artery is cut or severed, and blood is literally pumped out of the body by the beating heart and onto a nearby surface. The repeated spurts cause a rather characteristic pattern. These patterns generally contain quite a bit of blood. In addition, an individual with a seriously severed artery is losing blood at such a rate that he or she will not be able to move too far and, without immediate and extreme medical intervention, will die fairly quickly.

Cast-off (also called *arc swing*) patterns result when a bloody object is swung through space and throws off droplets onto a nearby surface (Figure 4.4D). These patterns may be seen on ceilings or walls, even occasionally on floors. The most common action causing such a pattern is repeated use of blunt force on a person who is bleeding. This pattern was noted on the ceiling of the van in the lead case for this chapter.

Running patterns are just what the name says. Blood hits a vertical surface, but the volume is sufficiently high that gravity causes the droplet to run. Note that blood can only run down. As obvious as that statement is, it is sometimes quite helpful in reconstructing events from blood patterns.

Secondary spatter patterns result when blood drops fall into a preexisting pool of blood. As each drop hits the liquid surface, it can cause small droplets to splash upward, and some of these may hit a nearby vertical surface (Figure 4.4E). The

Figure 4.3

A straight-line reconstruction from a high/medium velocity blood spatter pattern. The straight lines formed by string are arranged at the angles of incidence calculated for selected droplets in the pattern. These lines converge approximately to a point. In this case, a person committed suicide in a bathroom by placing the muzzle of a shotgun in his mouth and firing. The blood pattern reconstruction confirms that the source of the blood was approximately in the position of the victim's head. The strings project outward from the wall into the room. (Courtesy of Timothy Palmbach, University of New Haven)

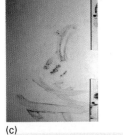

(a)

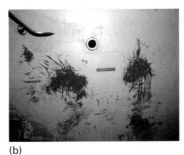

(b)

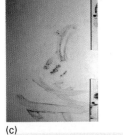

(c)

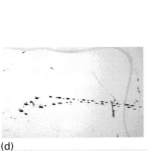

(d)

(e)

Figure 4.4A-E

A—Low velocity dripping pattern produced when the blood source is moving with respect to the target surface. The direction of movement can sometimes be discerned from the pattern.

B—Contact transfer pattern where a person's bloody hair made contact with the vertical surface. (Courtesy of Timothy Palmbach, University of New Haven)

C—Swipe pattern. (Courtesy of Timothy Palmbach, University of New Haven)

D—Cast off pattern. (Courtesy of Timothy Palmbach, University of New Haven)

E—Secondary spatter pattern. Blood dripping onto a hard floor surface causes a secondary spatter pattern on the nearby vertical surface. In this controlled setup, blood was dripping from 4 feet above the floor. The scale on the right side of the target is marked off in centimeters.

Case Study 4.1

Secondary Blood Spatter Patterns Help Solve a Homicide Case

Some years ago in a city in one of the mid-Atlantic states, a homicide occurred in which a man was thought to have murdered his estranged wife. There was enough evidence to arrest the suspect, but as prosecutors prepared their case, it became apparent that blood patterns on the suspect's clothing held the key to figuring out what had happened. Dr. Henry Lee was asked to look at the crime scene photographs, some of the physical evidence, and the suspect's clothing.

The victim lived in an apartment. On the date of the alleged murder, her estranged husband (who became the suspect and defendant) called the police to report that he had found her badly wounded and probably dying on the kitchen floor of her apartment. According to his account, she called him and said someone was trying to break in to her apartment. He lived a short distance away and said that he rushed to her apartment, only to find the front door locked. He broke a nearby window and climbed into the apartment. He then found the victim on the kitchen floor badly wounded and bleeding profusely. He said he knelt down, cradled her for a short time, then called the police.

Emergency responders arrived and removed the badly wounded victim. In doing so, blood pools and stains were stepped in, furniture was moved, and there were gurney wheel tracks in some of the kitchen floor bloodstains. Investigators took a number of color and black-and-white photographs at the scene. Two serrated-edge kitchen knives were recovered. Both belonged to the victim and were usually kept in kitchen drawers. One was on the living room

sofa, and the other was on the kitchen floor. There was an extensive blood pool in the living room area, a bloodlike trail leading to the kitchen, and extensive blood pools and some contact transfers on the kitchen floor and on appliances close to the floor.

The victim died in the emergency room a short time after being transported. She was autopsied by the state medical examiner, who reported that cause of death was a single stab wound to the heart. The knife track was slightly upward of horizontal from slightly left of the midline below the heart directly into the heart. She had other stab wounds, some of which were characterized as "defense" wounds. The death was ruled a homicide.

The estranged husband's story sounded suspicious to investigators, and he was questioned and later arrested for the murder of his wife. He had a small wound on his left elbow. Police documented the wound in a picture. The clothing he was wearing—primarily the trousers and a jacket, both khaki, both extensively bloodstained—were seized by investigators.

On the outside of the jacket and trousers were numerous low- and medium-velocity blood droplet spatter patterns and contact transfer stains. The stains were present on the back of the jacket and on the backs of the trouser legs as well as the fronts.

Samples of bloodstains from the living room, the kitchen, the suspect's clothing, and the knives were shown to be human blood, and analyzed for ABO and isoenzyme types. (This case happened before the DNA era.) The blood and enzyme types were consistent with those of the victim and excluded the suspect. All the bloodstains could be from her.

commonest example of this pattern may be on the cuffs of pants that were located for a time near a blood pool into which drops were falling. Since the secondary droplets splash upward, the direction of the blood spatter pattern on the pants cuff will indicate that the blood came from the floor. This sounds unlikely until you realize that it could be secondary spatter. Case Study 4.1 illustrates the importance of secondary spatter in reconstruction.

Imprint and impression patterns that we will talk about in Part Three (fingerprints, footprints, footwear impressions) are sometimes made with blood. In the sense that they are imprints made in blood, they are also considered blood patterns. But they would be handled like other fingerprints, footwear impressions, and so on, from the standpoint of analysis and comparison. One important difference is that there are some special techniques for "enhancing" bloody imprints (discussed in Chapter 6) that may help make such patterns clearer or more visible and thereby more suitable for comparison.

Factors Affecting Blood Patterns and Their Interpretation

Blood pattern interpretation can be a very helpful tool in crime scene reconstruction involving bloodshed. Several things about blood pattern interpretation should be kept in mind, however. Considerable training and experience is generally required to become skilled in this type of work. Many of the principles concerning blood patterns we have previously discussed and illustrated are most accurate as related to patterns on nonabsorbent surfaces. On absorbent surfaces, the patterns may not be as clear. Their

The suspect's account of events could explain some blood transfer, especially contact transfer patterns on his clothing. He could have knelt in a blood pool, explaining a large stain on one trouser knee. And some bloodstains on the front of the trousers and jacket could have transferred from cradling the bleeding victim. The story did not explain medium-velocity patterns on the front of his jacket and trousers. And perhaps most telling of all, there were medium-velocity droplet patterns on the pants cuffs, which had traveled upward from the floor at a steep angle. Secondary blood spatter could explain these patterns. At some point, the person wearing these clothes was standing in or near a pool of blood, and new blood was dripping down into the preexisting pooled blood, causing secondary upward spatter. Nothing in the suspect's account could explain this blood pattern. Experiments were conducted in Dr. Lee's laboratory by allowing blood to drip from measured heights into a pool of blood on a hard floor with a white target surface nearby. At heights around 3 to 4 feet from the floor, the secondary spatter pattern could be replicated.

Based on Dr. Lee's examination of crime scene photographs, and the bloodstain evidence, the state theorized that the suspect came to the apartment wanting the victim to open the door for him. When she refused, he broke the window inward, and climbed in. Frightened, the victim went to the kitchen and got one of the knives to defend herself. As she came back into the living room, a struggle ensued and she was cut and wounded. She bled for some time in one location, creating the pooled bloodstain. The knife was knocked from her hand and landed on the sofa nearby. Next, she either freed herself and got the second knife, or the suspect did, and another close-in struggle took place. Near the kitchen door, the fatal wound was administered. The victim could not have moved far on her own after that wound, and the wound caused substantial bleeding. At a location in the kitchen, she bled for a time in one place, the place where the pooled bloodstain was later seen.

The blood patterns on the suspect's jacket and trousers resulted in great part from the two struggles in which the victim was cut and bleeding. The secondary spatter on the cuffs resulted from his standing in or near the blood pools as fresh blood dripped from the victim.

The estranged husband was convicted by a trial jury and received a long prison sentence. It is important to point out here, as we have in the main body of the chapter, that the state's overall reconstruction is a theory. Although the physical evidence record is consistent with the theory, it does not necessarily support every element. The movements of the people are somewhat speculative, for example. However, it is not likely that the secondary spatter pattern observed on the trouser cuffs could have been made in a way other than blood dripping into a preexisting pool. And nothing in the suspect's account of the incident explained why he would have medium-velocity blood spatter on his trousers or jacket, especially on the back sides of those garments. It was also certain that the bloodstains which were typed could not have come from the defendant but could have come from the victim. In this case, even if DNA profiling had been available, putting the victim's blood on the suspect's clothing was not alone sufficient to cast doubt on his own account.

shapes and angles may not even be obvious. Target surface absorbency, texture of the surface, and volume of blood are important variables in blood pattern formation.

Other factors that can affect interpretation include ambient environment, which can affect the time it takes blood to clot and to dry, and wind or air currents, which could alter the resulting blood patterns. Activities of the victim, suspect, witnesses, medical personnel, and police officers can also change the appearance of a pattern and complicate its interpretation.

In some cases, experts may conduct experiments to try and replicate patterns observed at a scene. The experiments might involve varying the amount of force, distances, or motion of a source with respect to a target surface. As noted in the discussion of reconstruction in Chapter 3, successful experimental replication of a scene pattern does *not* prove that the experimental conditions are those that prevailed at the scene when the original pattern was formed. Rather, it shows that the *theory* concerning the formation of the pattern is scientifically sound. This logic applies in Case Study 4.1 above. Replicating the patterns did not prove how the blood got on the pants cuffs, but showed that the theory was scientifically sound and reasonable.

It should also be noted here that scene reconstructions involving blood patterns cannot be done accurately without knowing whose blood was shed. Generally, dried blood samples from the patterns will be DNA profiled in the laboratory (Chapter 10) to associate the bloodstain with a person. At times, it appears safe to assume that only one person (usually a victim) was bleeding at a scene; a blood pattern reconstruction based on such an assumption should be considered conditional until the DNA typing results confirm it. Should the blood be from more than one source, the interpretation of the pattern could be significantly affected.

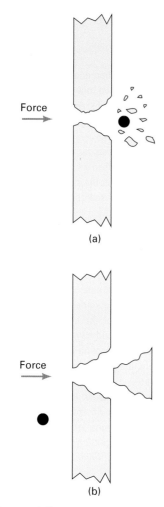

Force

(a)

Force

(b)

Figure 4.5

Drawing showing the cone-shaped hole on the far side of a piece of glass caused by a projectile striking or penetrating the glass.

tangential fracture lines

Fracture lines in glass that appear to encircle, or form a polyhedron, around the point of force.

radial fracture lines

Fracture lines in glass that appear to radiate outward from the center of the point of force.

Glass Fracture Patterns

There are different formulations of glass (Chapter 13), and the type of glass can affect the amount of information obtainable from a pattern of broken glass.

Determining the Side of the Glass Where Force Was Applied

Often, the side of the glass from which the force that caused its breakage was applied can be an issue in the investigation. Sometimes, glass can be fractured but remain essentially intact (i.e., not fall apart into pieces). Automobile windshield glass (called safety plate glass) and certain types of plate glass tend to behave in that way. It is much easier to derive information from a piece of fractured glass that remained intact. At a point of impact in an intact but fractured piece of glass, it is often possible to discern a cone-shaped pattern (Figure 4.5). The smaller end of the "cone" is on the side to which force was applied. The larger side of the cone is the side from which fragments were broken due to the force. If the force was a projectile, like a BB or a bullet, there will be a hole in the glass, where the projectile passed through, at the center of the cone. In the case where a projectile broke the glass, we would refer to surface corresponding to the smaller side of the cone as the "entry" and the other side as the "exit."

This same type of pattern can be formed in other objects such as walls, or even in people's skulls, as the result of being struck with extreme force by some object or a projectile.

If the glass did not remain intact and small pieces must be examined, the task is more difficult. With numerous small pieces, the examiner must first try to determine which side of the glass is which. In a case of an exterior window where one side of the glass was exposed to the outside, and the other side to the inside, the effects of weathering, dirt, and so on, may help in making this determination.

The broken edges of glass fragments have a pattern of marks, called *hackle marks,* which result from breakage by force. These patterns form in certain predictable ways depending on the side of the glass from which the force originated. There are "rules" to help determine the "force" side of glass fragments. The 3R's rule says that the force was applied from the *reverse* side to the side that shows *right angle* hackle marks when viewing the edge of a *radial* crack (Figure 4.6).

Determining the Order of Gunshots Fired Through Glass

Among glass types, the safety plate glass used for automobile windshields is unusual in that it is manufactured with two sheets of glass sandwiching a sheet of plastic material. This structure is intended to keep the windshield from fragmenting in a collision or accident. Side window glass, by contrast, is tempered glass, which pelletizes if fractured. As a result, windshields generally hold together even when fractured by intentional force or penetration by bullets or shotgun pellets or slugs. And, because they hold together, the resulting fracture patterns are easier to analyze. Side window glass is heat tempered, and it is very difficult to break. But when it does break, it forms square chunks of glass without sharp edges to reduce the possibility of injury. Because it is manufactured to disintegrate upon being forcefully impacted, its pieces are of little use in determining direction.

Glass breaks in a particular way under the stress of force, causing both *radial* and *tangential* fracture lines to form (Figure 4.7). Viewed at a 90-degree angle to the glass surface, the **tangential fracture lines** tend to encircle the projectile hole, while the **radial fracture lines** tend to appear to be radiating out from the center. Usually, a nascent tangential fracture line will not cross a preexisting fracture line. Both radial and tangential fracture lines that appear to stop at preexisting lines must belong to a breaking force that occurs *after* the preexisting lines were formed—and thus, to a hole formed later. If there are two holes, and they are

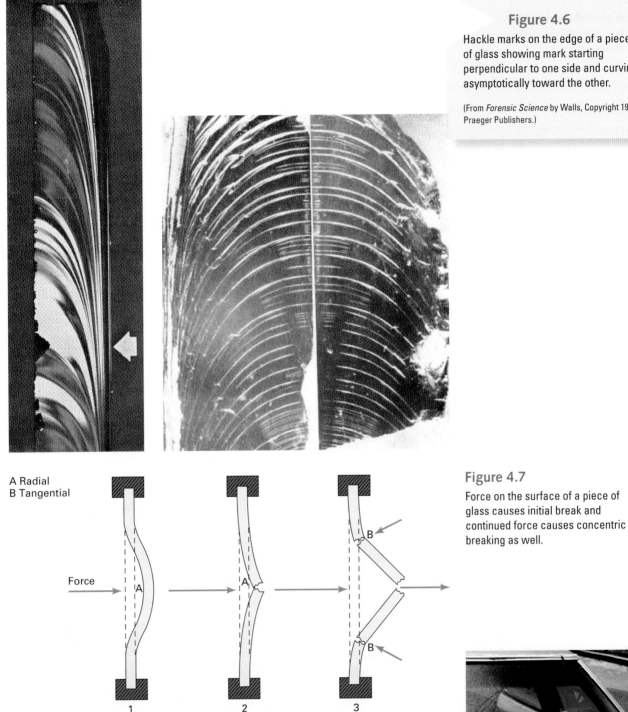

Figure 4.6

Hackle marks on the edge of a piece of glass showing mark starting perpendicular to one side and curving asymptotically toward the other.

(From *Forensic Science* by Walls, Copyright 1974, Praeger Publishers.)

A Radial
B Tangential

Force

1   2   3

Figure 4.7

Force on the surface of a piece of glass causes initial break and continued force causes concentric breaking as well.

reasonably nearby so that the interactions of the fracture lines can be observed, it is often possible to reconstruct the order in which they were made (Figure 4.8).

The amount of information available from glass fracture patterns thus depends on the type of glass, whether it holds together as a unit even though fractured, and what type of event caused the fractures. At times, this kind of information can be valuable in reconstructing events at a scene (Figure 4.9).

We will mention it again in Chapter 13, but it may be noted here that larger pieces of broken glass that can be physically fit back together in the manner of a jigsaw puzzle can thereby be shown to have had a common origin. With many small pieces, this activity is much more difficult or impossible.

Figure 4.8

Bullet holes in a windshield.

Figure 4.9

Diagram of radial and tangential fracture lines from two sequential holes in glass.

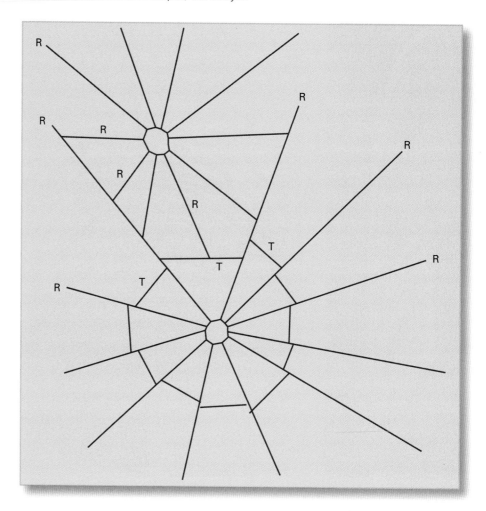

Track and Trail Patterns

As the name suggests, these patterns could be of footwear, socks or stockings, bare feet while walking, or other actions such as an object or body being dragged. These patterns often can exhibit a shape that indicates direction.

These patterns can help show how many people were present at a scene during the relevant activity, the direction(s) they were moving, and where they went.

Track or trail patterns can be fairly obvious, such as impressions in snow or soft earth, or made in blood or dirt. They can sometimes be subtle, too, such as a drag mark across grass. A bloody trail can often be made visible using special chemical techniques (discussed in Chapter 6 for bloody fingerprints) even after a fairly thorough cleanup. One presumptive test reagent for blood, called luminol (Chapter 9), can be useful in showing blood patterns after the blood has been cleaned up. Luminol with some other chemicals produces light under certain conditions if blood is present, and can "light up" blood patterns in a darkened room even if there is only a small quantity of blood remaining.

Case Study 4.2 emphasizes the importance trails (blood trails in this case) can have in reconstructing events.

Tire and Skid Mark Patterns

Tire and skid patterns are used in reconstructing vehicle accidents. Tire impressions that an expert might use to identify the tire that made the mark will be discussed in Chapter 5. The tire patterns discussed here refer to those that show the number, location, or direction of movement of a vehicle or vehicles at a scene.

Vehicle accident reconstruction is a specialized area of forensic science, often done by an accident reconstruction expert or forensic engineer (Chapter 1). Tire and skid mark patterns are only part of the data used in an overall vehicle accident reconstruction. The length of skid marks can help an expert determine the speed of the vehicle at the time the operator applied the brakes.

These patterns can also be helpful in reconstructing the presence, direction, and actions of a vehicle or vehicles at burglary, robbery, or carjacking scenes, too. Hit-and-run scenes and scenes where a body has been removed from a vehicle and dumped are also obvious examples.

Clothing and Article or Object Patterns

We include in this category the general state of things and clothing at a scene. These patterns must be looked at as a whole, and in the context of the scene location.

One "rule" often cited in looking for evidence at a crime scene is "Look for the unusual." In other words, look for things that seem out of place in the context of that location. You might expect a certain amount of disorder in a college dorm room, for example, that you would not expect in a private home managed by a scrupulous homemaker. Therefore, an area of considerable disarray in an otherwise very neat household will call for further investigation.

Clothing or objects scattered around at a crime scene, overturned furniture, and so on, can provide indications of struggles, of force being used, or of ransacking, among other things.

Clothing out of place or damaged on a victim may give indications of assault or sexual assault. It may also indicate that a body was hastily redressed after death. Cuts, tears, or damage to clothing articles may help to determine the type of force, weapon, or MO involved in the criminal activity.

Gunshot Residue Patterns

Gunshot residue, often abbreviated "GSR" and also called gunpowder residue, is produced when a firearm is discharged. Because the residue may be deposited on the hands of the shooter, testing may sometimes be done on hand swabbings or sticky tape lifts taken from people thought to be involved in shooting cases to detect any GSR. Rigorously identifying GSR is not a simple problem. Nor is interpreting the results of GSR testing on people's hands. Those matters are further discussed in Chapter 8. Gunshot residue comes up here, in the reconstruction patterns, because it can be deposited on a target surface, provided the target surface is not too far away from the muzzle of the weapon, when that weapon is fired. The pattern formed on a target surface, usually around a bullet hole, can help in estimating the muzzle to target distance at the time of firing.

Patterns of GSR may be deposited on target surfaces not too far from the weapon muzzle. The muzzle to target distance can be estimated by comparing these patterns with test fire patterns with the same weapon and ammunition.

The GSR that is propelled out of the muzzle of a fired weapon along with the projectile consists of powder particles (both burned and unburned), primer residue, traces of lead from the bullet (and copper or other metals from the bullet jacketing if present), and dirt, lubricants, and other debris from the barrel. On a white or light-colored surface, the GSR pattern may be visible without enhancement. The residue is dark gray to black. On colored surfaces, the pattern may require chemical treatment to enhance it or photographic enhancement using infrared photography. Objects or surfaces can be sprayed with sodium rhodizonate, a chemical that reacts with lead particles, or with Griess reagent that reacts with gunpowder residues. These chemical reactions produce strongly colored products that greatly enhance the visibility of the often small traces of material.

> **gunshot residue (GSR)**
>
> Materials created by the firing of a firearm that are dispersed by the force of the expanding gasses.

Case Study 4.2

Blood Trails Help in Reconstructing the Movements of a Murderer at a Scene

At 4:55 A.M. in July of 1983, a 911 operator received a phone call from John Hoeplinger. He was screaming on the phone that his wife had been seriously hurt. A police officer from the town police department was first on the scene, shortly after 5 A.M. He observed Mr. Hoeplinger emerge from the house distraught, sobbing and yelling, "She's all bloody." Hoeplinger led the officer into the bloody foyer, through a bloodstained trail and into the family room, where he found 33-year-old Mrs. Eileen Hoeplinger lying face up on a couch, wrapped in a sheet and blankets. Her skull appeared to be caved in, and there was blood around her head, on the couch, on a coffee table, and on the rug next to the couch.

Hoeplinger told the police that he had awakened during the night, realized that his wife was not beside him in bed, and proceeded to search the house for her. He then went outside to look for her and found her covered with blood in a wooded area near the entrance of the driveway. He said he returned to the house to get sheets and blankets, wrapped her up, and carried her into the house before calling the police.

Detectives from the town police department and state police major crime squad were called to the scene to conduct the crime scene investigation. While documenting the scene, detectives noticed a large quantity of blood droplets and bloodstains inside the house, inconsistent with the statement provided by Mr. Hoeplinger. Police contacted Dr. Henry Lee to come and assist with reconstruction at the crime scene. Dr. Lee arrived after the body had been removed for autopsy by the medical examiner. Physical evidence was collected by police. One detective found a long bloody trail along the circular gravel driveway, which matched with Hoeplinger's story of carrying his wife's body back to the house. However, Dr. Lee found that the blood trail actually consisted of *three separate* trails on the driveway. A detailed analysis showed that these three blood trails had the following patterns:

- The first bloody trail led from the foyer of the house to a wooded area approximately 50 yards from the house on the left side of the driveway. This trail consisted of largely vertical low-velocity blood drops from a moving blood source falling from approximately 4 feet high. A large bloodstain was found on the ground in the woods. This stain was the result of direct contact and deposit from a large wound.
- A second blood trail led from the first location in the woods to the second wooded area, where Mr. Hoeplinger said the body was found. This trail consisted of a combination of drips and smears. It appeared that a bloody object had been dragged along the driveway. The drag marks indicated that the direction of dragging was toward the driveway gate. A clump of clover growing between the gravel was bent toward the gate and had a blood smear on one side, indicating that something had been dragged over it. A large quantity of hairs and tissue was also found on the trap rocks along the driveway. There were also blood smears on the underside of the pachysandra plants. All these stains and trails indicated that the victim's bloody body had been dragged to the location where her husband reported the body was found.
- A third bloody trail led from the second wooded area, where the body was reportedly found, toward the house. This blood trail was a combination of blood drops mixed with a few bloody drag marks, showing the opposite direction—going into the house.

Large quantities of bloodstains were observed in the family room. Bloodstain patterns and trace evidence was noted as follows:

Figure 4.10 shows a series of GSR patterns at various muzzle to target distances. Usually, the "tight contact" or "loose contact" patterns, where the muzzle is essentially resting against the target surface, are quite distinctive. The patterns can be seen on clothing, or on other objects or surfaces that were in the path of a fired weapon. They can also sometimes be seen on human bodies, and pathologists use the patterns to estimate muzzle to body distances.

Gunshot residue particles are quite small and do not travel great distances. With all but the most powerful handguns, it would be unusual to see much GSR pattern beyond about 2 feet. With rifles, the distances are somewhat greater. With shotguns the pellet spread can be used similarly to measure muzzle to target distance. Since shotgun pellets travel much farther, pellet spread can also be used to estimate firing distance to a considerable distance.

Distance estimations (i.e., muzzle to target distances) using a GSR pattern cannot be done exactly just by looking at the pattern. There is too much variation between different weapons and different ammunition. To get a good estimate, an examiner does a series of test fires on the firing range using the same weapon and ammunition thought to have been used in the case itself. The test patterns are then compared to the scene pattern to make an estimate. As we have noted elsewhere in connection with reconstruction patterns,

- A large amount of heavy blood deposit was noted on the left end of the couch. Hairs, brain matter, and few small pieces of gray-colored trap rocks were found on the same side of the couch. The trap rocks had the same color and type as the trap rock from the driveway.
- Hundreds of medium-velocity blood spatters were found on the window adjacent to the couch, behind a pillow and the curtains. These bloodstains formed a medium-velocity impact pattern. Brainlike matter was also seen on the window. These observations indicated that blood and brain matter had been projected onto the window before the placement of the pillow and closing of the curtains.
- Two trails of bloodstains were observed on the ceiling and on the wall on the left end of couch. These bloodstains were consistent with a cast-off pattern. This observation indicated that the victim was more than likely hit three times while she was lying on the sofa with her head resting on the left end side of the sofa.
- Approximately 70 small bloodstains (2–5 mm in size) were located on one side of the coffee table. This medium-velocity impact blood pattern indicated that a portion of the table had been directly facing the source of the blood at the time the spatter was deposited.
- Hair fragments were found on the sofa and on the carpet next to the sofa. Microscopical examination of the hairs showed crushed ends and morphological similarity to the victim's known head hair.

The state medical examiner and investigators first believed the weapon was a golf club. However, crime scene patterns and the injury patterns indicated that the weapon was more consistent with a square-edge object. Subsequently, a brick with brownish-red stains was found in the pond behind the house by a police diving team. Hair and tissue were recovered from the brick. Blood group and isoenzyme typing showed the same profile as Mrs. Hoeplinger (this case happened before DNA was available). Hair and hair fragments were also recovered from the brick. They had been forcibly removed from the head and crushed into the brick. And they had microscopic characteristics similar to those of the known head hair from Mrs. Hoeplinger.

A damp T-shirt with a diluted bloodstain and algae on it was found hanging on the deck's railing. SEM (scanning electron microscope) examination of the algae from the T-shirt and comparison with a known algae sample from the pond showed similar microscopic patterns—a sausage-link type of structure. The algae on the T-shirt could have come from the pond. Diatoms found on both samples were also identical. These results indicated that Hoeplinger rinsed his bloody shirt in the pond. Bloodstains found on Mr. Hoeplinger's sneakers were a combination of blood drops, blood smears, and medium-velocity impact spatters, all of which was inconsistent with his account of events.

The physical evidence and crime scene patterns taken together were consistent with the following theory: Mrs. Hoeplinger was killed while sleeping on the couch, not by an intruder in the driveway. Mr. Hoeplinger struck his wife with the brick while she was sleeping in the family room, then moved her body 50 yards from the house into the woods. He washed up some of the blood and then apparently decided to move the body 200 yards away from the house into another location in the woods. He then decided to bring her back into the house and place her on the sofa to provide an explanation for the presence of the large amount of bloodstains on the couch. He then did some further cleaning up, washing his shirt, and tossing the murder weapon—the brick—into the pond.

The case went to trial in the Bridgeport, Connecticut, judicial district. John Hoeplinger claimed emotional distress and was convicted of manslaughter. His conviction was overturned because of improper police interview procedures. He was then retried and convicted again. He died of a heart attack in prison while playing basketball.

replicating the scene pattern on the firing range does not prove that the experimental muzzle to target distance is in fact the distance that prevailed at the scene. It does show, however, that the experimental distance is a reasonable estimate of the actual distance.

Distance determinations based on GSR patterns are commonly done in shooting cases in which the weapon to target distance may be in dispute. They may also be done to test the reliability of a victim, suspect, or witness statement concerning the actual distance. An allegation by a shooter that "we were struggling over the weapon and it went off" is rendered suspect when the muzzle to target (bullet hole in victim or victim clothing) distance is found to be more than 3 feet.

Projectile Trajectory Patterns

The physics of firearms projectile flight through the air is called **ballistics.** Laboratory activities done by firearms examiners (firearms identification work is discussed in Chapter 8) are often called "ballistics" in the popular media, but that is incorrect terminology. Ballistics has to do with projectile flight and path of travel. There is a subspecialty of forensic pathology called **wound ballistics** that has to do with the wounding and destructive power of firearms and ammunition to the body.

ballistics

The science of projectiles in flight; ballistics is not firearms identification.

wound ballistics

A subset of forensic pathology that examines the wounds and wound patterns made by various projectiles.

Figure 4.10

Gunshot residue patterns on a target surface from gun shots at various muzzle to target distances. As distance increases, the quantity of residue particles striking the target decreases.

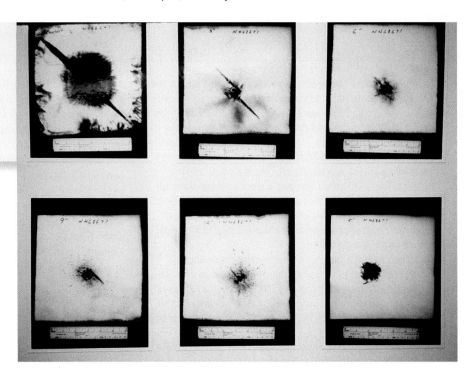

trajectory

The flight path from muzzle to target of a projectile fired by a firearm.

In some cases, an effort must be made to reconstruct **trajectory,** or path of flight, from the muzzle of the weapon to the target. Much of the time the distances involved are relatively short, and straight-line paths can be assumed (as long as there are no intermediate targets). Trajectory reconstruction is often used to estimate the position of the shooter from holes or impacts made by a bullet, particularly in "sniper"-type situations. In addition, movements of victim or shooter can sometimes be reconstructed (Figure 4.11).

Reconstructing trajectories, when a body was the target, require consultation with the pathologist, who makes the determinations of entry and exit wounds on the body and the direction of travel of the bullet in the body. These analyses can often help establish accurate enough theories of shootings to test the veracity of statements by witnesses, victims, or suspects.

Figure 4.11

Reconstruction of the trajectories of five shots into an automobile.

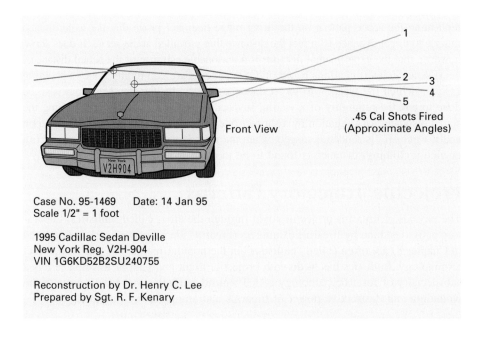

Figure 4.12
Burned building showing burn patterns.

Fire Burn Patterns

Fires and explosions are discussed in Chapter 11. An objective of a fire investigation is determination of the *cause* and the *origin* of the fire. Burn patterns can be helpful in reconstructing the point or points of origin of a fire, the pathway it followed, and provide estimates of the temperatures that may have been reached or the fuel that may have been available.

Figure 4.12 shows several burn patterns that may be visible at a fire scene. The classical "inverted cone" or "V pattern" often indicates the point of origin, since fire follows the pathway of available fuel (upward and outward). Multiple V patterns may indicate the possibility of arson. Smoke color can provide information about the nature of the fuel that is burning. For this reason, first responders are advised to take a picture of an active fire and the smoke if possible. Smoke stains can show the pathway traveled by the fire. Material melting patterns provide information about the temperature the fire reached.

Burn patterns are an important source of information for arson investigators. Along with the results of examining electrical and mechanical equipment and the scene generally, they can help reconstruct where the fire started and, in that way, help establish the cause and origin.

Fire patterns are discussed further in Chapter 11. Over the years, a number of myths about the meaning of certain burn patterns have developed and been perpetuated. It is important that the patterns be interpreted correctly.

Modus Operandi Patterns and Profiling

Long before anyone commonly used the term **criminal profiling,** police investigators were aware that repeat offender criminals develop habitual patterns. These habits, which can often be reconstructed from physical evidence, from a study of scenes, or from interviewing victims, are referred to as a criminal's **modus operandi (MO).** The MO can include language (words or phrases) used, methods of gaining entry to a scene, type of crime committed, use of or absence of weapons, use of or absence of force or threat of force, disguises used, and so forth. Such habit patterns are usually pieced together by investigators from a series of cases thought to have been committed by the same offender.

The development of criminal profiling took this basic reasoning a step further. Criminal profiling is based on the detailed analysis of numerous repeat offender cases. All the scene patterns resulting from the offender's activities are taken into account, along with the pathology and forensic science laboratory results from the scene and the evidence and a knowledge of human behavior and psychology.

criminal profiling

Application of psychology and of knowledge developed from past similar offenses and offenders to help create a hypothetical picture of an offender in an unsolved case.

modus operandi (MO)

The habits followed by a repeat-offender criminal in committing crimes, which may help police connect unsolved cases.

Profiling has been best developed for serial murderers and rapists, because these crimes are so serious and the offenders often difficult to apprehend. The idea is to use scenes, lab results, autopsy or medical findings, and information obtained from extensive interviews with known offenders, to construct a "profile" of an as yet unidentified serial offender. There has also been some work done on serial arsonists.

In general, profiling can occasionally be an aid for investigators. Other avenues of investigation are usually exhausted before those specializing in profiling are brought in. One reason is because there aren't too many trained criminal profilers available. Another factor is that a profile does not identify a specific person. Rather, it describes a category of person. The more information available, the better the profile and the narrower the category. Investigators can use the profile as an aid in focusing the direction of the investigation and eliminating possible suspects.

Some of the profiles that are developed turn out to be quite accurate, but a profile alone is not sufficient to identify and apprehend an offender. One of the major values of profiling on a national level by experts at the FBI is the ability to discern connections between cases from different jurisdictions. Many serial offenders tend to operate in different jurisdictions, even across different states. There would typically not be any way for investigators in any one jurisdiction to be aware of the similar cases in other jurisdictions without the connection via profiling.

Detailed interviews of serial offenders by profilers have also resulted in a more useful body of information concerning the psychology of those individuals.

Wound, Injury, or Damage Patterns

Wound and injury patterns generally refer to wounds or injuries on a human body. Forensic pathologists sometimes call these "patterns of injury." They tend to be characteristic of certain events, such as a walking pedestrian being hit by a motor vehicle. Similarly, certain kinds of industrial or farm accidents involving heavy equipment produce certain injury patterns. These can help the pathologist determine that injuries observed are consistent with having been caused by specific events. Wound patterns are similar. There are wound patterns consistent with gunshots, cutting (sharp force), blunt force, and so on. Gunshot wounds often show different characteristics depending on whether they are entrance or exit wounds. Bullet penetration wounds on uncovered skin can show GSR patterns if the muzzle was close enough at the time the weapon was fired. Knife wounds may show characteristics of the weapon, such as the presence of a serrated edge on one side. Blunt force injuries sometimes provide indications of the type of weapon that was used to administer them, such as a round shape, sharp corners, and so on. The wound and injury patterns on victims must be carefully considered in any reconstruction of a death case. In Case Study 4.2 earlier, the injury patterns on the victim's head led investigators to reassess their initial impression of the type of weapon used and prompted them to search further to find what was likely the actual weapon.

Damage patterns often refer to patterns seen on clothing. For example, clothing may be penetrated by a bullet, it may be cut, or it may be scraped on the hard surface of a road or the external surface of a brick or stone building. These patterns may also help in reconstructing events. In one sexual assault case, a complainant said that she had been assaulted while down on the ground on her back, still wearing a dress. The dress became bunched up under her, she said. The ground at the location consisted of dirt and small gravel. Later laboratory examination of the complainant's dress revealed no damage to the fibers of the dress, and no dirt or gravel particles. These findings cast doubt on her account of what had happened. In another case reported from Australia by criminalist Jane Taupin in 2000 in the *Journal of Forensic Sciences,* clothing damage analysis showed that a sexual assault complainant's account of events was highly suspicious. When confronted with the physical evidence analysis, the woman admitted that the report was an attention-getting incident, to try and get back in the good graces of her boyfriend. Clothing damage analysis can be and has been used to help corroborate the accounts of assault complainants as well.

Summary

Pattern evidence can be divided into two big categories: patterns for reconstruction and patterns for individualization. Most reconstruction patterns—the subject of this chapter—are crime scene patterns. Often, these patterns must be "collected" by documentation; they cannot be collected in containers. The main ones are blood spatter, glass fracture, track and trail, tire and skid mark, clothing and article, gunshot residue, projectile trajectory, fire burn, MO, and wound, injury, and damage patterns. Blood pattern analysis helps reconstruct the bloodshed events that caused them. Important blood spatter patterns include dripping, wipes, swipes, arterial spurts, contact transfers, cast-off, running, and secondary. The amount of force involved can be deduced from whether the blood patterns are low, medium, or high velocity. Glass fracture patterns help tell which side of the glass had force applied, and whether fracture was the result of force or heat. In safety plate glass, experts may be able to reconstruct the order of projectile (such as bullet) hits and from which side they came. Track and trail patterns can help show how many people were at a scene, and their movements. Drag marks may also be apparent. Tire and skid mark patterns are regularly used to help reconstruct vehicular accidents. Clothing, article, and object patterns at scenes help to show how much violent disruption may have taken place, and possibly something about the movements of the people. Gunshot residue patterns on target surfaces help reconstruct the distance from the muzzle of a weapon to the target. Projectile trajectory patterns are part of ballistics—the flight paths of projectiles. Wound ballistics is a branch of pathology and has to do with the injury patterns caused by various types of projectiles. Fire burn patterns help reconstruct the pathway of a fire and may also indicate how hot it got in various locations. They can help locate the point of origin. MO patterns are a criminal's habits and may be used as investigative aids. A sophisticated version of crime scene analysis to try and infer what type of individual may have committed the crime is called profiling. Wound and injury patterns help pathologists understand the events that may have caused those wounds or injuries. Many of the patterns are characteristic of certain types of events. Damage patterns, to vehicles or to clothing, for example, can help investigators eliminate certain theories of what may have happened. They can also corroborate or disprove statements by witnesses or persons involved in the case.

Reconstruction is theory based on all the available facts. It may also involve experiments—especially with GSR distance estimates and blood spatter patterns. The fact that the experiments can reproduce the scene patterns do *not* prove that the reconstruction is correct, only that it is consistent with physical reality and principles.

Key Terms

reconstruction pattern (p. 87)
individualization pattern (p. 87)
blood spatter pattern (p. 88)
low-velocity blood spatter pattern (p. 88)
medium-velocity blood spatter pattern
 (p. 89)

high-velocity blood spatter pattern (p. 89)
angle of incidence (p. 90)
tangential fracture lines (p. 94)
radial fracture lines (p. 94)
gunshot residue (p. 97)
ballistics (p. 99)

wound ballistics (p. 99)
trajectory (p. 100)
criminal profiling (p. 101)
modus operandi (MO) (p. 101)

Review Questions—Short Answer

1. What is the difference between individualization patterns and reconstruction patterns?
2. How are reconstruction patterns collected?
3. What are low-, medium-, and high-velocity blood patterns? What types of events are likely to produce them?
4. What can the shape of a dried blood droplet pattern tell you about the angle of impact?
5. List and briefly describe five blood patterns.
6. What can be learned from glass fracture patterns?
7. What can be learned from track and trail patterns?
8. Why are clothing and/or article patterns important at crime scenes?
9. What are gunshot residue patterns used for?
10. How can a wound or injury pattern help in reconstructing case events?

Fill-in-the-Blank & Multiple Choice

1. Radial and tangential fracture pattern lines in a broken but still largely intact piece of glass may enable the examiner to determine
   a. the direction from which the breaking force was applied.
   b. the refractive index of the glass.
   c. the order in which two or more distinct breaks occurred.
   d. only A and C.
   e. A, B, and C.

2. Examination of the blood spatter pattern flung from a weapon can help to determine
   a. the attacker.
   b. the shape of the weapon.
   c. where the attack took place.
   d. the time of the attack.

3. If suitable controls are available, examination of the distribution of gunpowder particles and other discharge residues around a bullet hole permits an approximate determination of the
   a. ammunition used.
   b. shot shell shot size.
   c. gun muzzle to target distance.
   d. condition of the weapon's barrel.

4. Ballistics is
   a. the path followed by a projectile from a firearm
   b. firearms identification
   c. NIBIN
   d. type of bullet

5. A blood spatter pattern consisting of well-formed individual separated droplets indicates that the stain that arose was from
   a. transfer.
   b. artery spurt.
   c. rapidly moving weapon.
   d. dripping from above the surface.

Further References

James, S. H., ed. *Scientific and Legal Applications of Bloodstain Pattern Interpretation*. Boca Raton: CRC Press, 1999.

James, S. H., P. E. Kish, and T. P. Sutton. *Principles of Bloodstain Pattern Analysis: Theory and Practice*. Boca Raton: CRC Press, 2005.

Lee, H. C., T. Palmbach, and M. Miller. *Henry Lee's Crime Scene Handbook*. New York: Academic Press, 2001.

Monahan, D. L., and H. W. J. Harding. "Damage to Clothing: Cuts and Tears." *Journal of Forensic Sciences* 35, no. 4 (July 1990): 901–912.

Taupin, J. M., "Clothing Damage Analysis and the Phenomenon of the False Sexual Assault," *Journal of Forensic Sciences* 45, no. 3 (May 2000): 568–572.

Part THREE

Physical Pattern Evidence and Technological Examinations

Reconstruction patterns are distinct from *individualization* patterns. With individualization patterns, the objective is to demonstrate individuality or common origin, if possible. Reconstruction patterns are often an intrinsic part of scenes, and many cannot be collected, preserved, and submitted to the laboratory as such. Individualization pattern evidence generally can be collected and preserved. Crime scene investigation and reconstruction patterns are connected, and were thus considered together in Part Two.

Part Three is about individualization patterns. Analysis of these patterns involves physical matching, or a comparison between an evidence (or questioned) specimen and a known (or exemplar). In some cases, the knowns can be produced in the laboratory; in other cases, investigators must provide the knowns or the suspected source of the knowns.

The term *individualization patterns* distinguishes them from *reconstruction patterns* and reinforces the symmetry between the different pattern types and the forensic-science concepts of classification (identification), individualization, and reconstruction (Chapter 1). Pattern evidence experts generally use the term "identification" to mean individualization. This terminology can sometimes be confusing, because strictly speaking, identification means classification, not individualization.

Individualization patterns can be divided into three categories according to comparison method: physical matching, comparisons of impression marks, and shape and form comparisons. The major categories of impression marks are fingerprints and toolmark and firearms evidence. Each is sufficiently complex and specialized to warrant separate chapters (6 and 8). The major categories of shape and form comparisons are handwriting (a subset of questioned documents, Chapter 7) and comparison of hairs (discussed in Chapter 13 because of its close relationship with fibers). In Chapter 5, we consider some basic principles of individualization pattern comparison and analysis, and describe physical matching, some impression patterns such as those made by footwear or tires, and shape and form comparisons.

In recent years, investigative techniques involving computers, computer components, and other digital devices containing memory chips have evolved. This area may be called digital evidence analysis, forensic computer science, or "computer forensics." The last term is popular, but incorrect ("forensics" is debating). Digital evidence is important in some cases. Because this area is more investigative than laboratory-based science, however, we have not devoted a separate chapter to it.

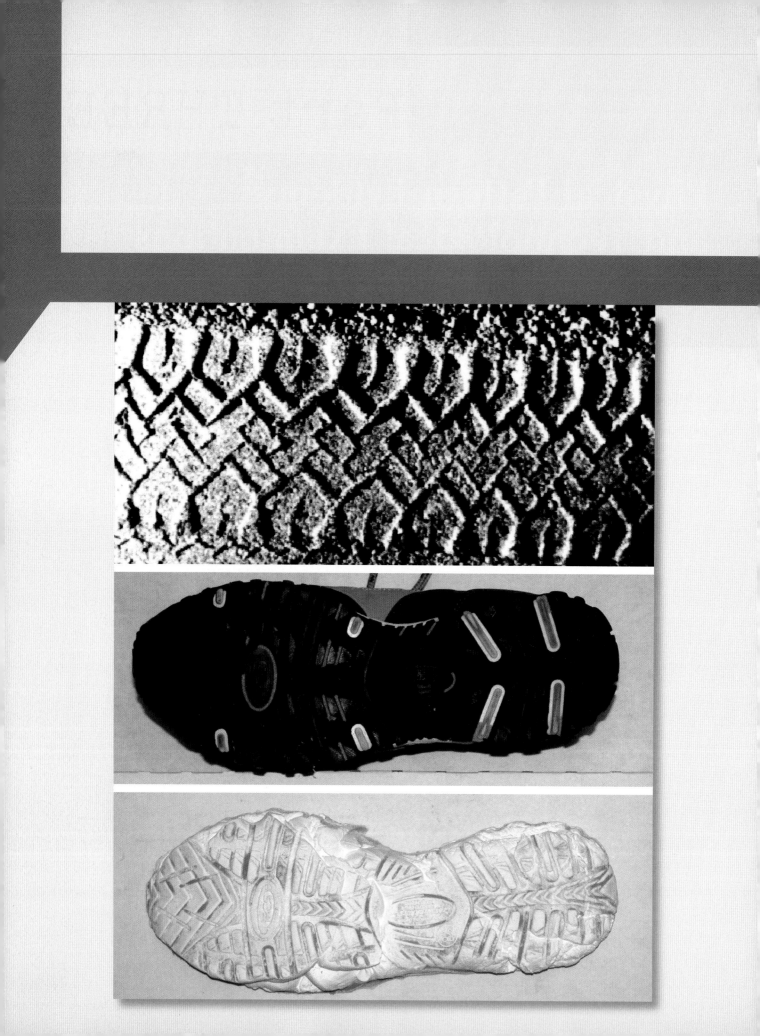

Examination of Physical Pattern Evidence

- Striation marks are characteristic of firearms, toolmark and some other evidence

- Using class and individual characteristics of patterns to compare for common origin is a multiple step process

- Comparisons between questioned and known patterns can lead to identification, exclusion, or they may be inconclusive

- Requirements for knowns (exemplars) differ according to the type of pattern

- The comparison process is similar with different pattern types

- The process involves pattern recognition, comparison, identification of class characteristics, then use of individual characteristics to try to achieve positive individualization

- The methods of pattern evidence comparison have come into question by a few courts as not sufficiently scientifically-based to meet the Daubert criteria for admissibility of scientific evidence into court

- Footwear and tire impressions are the most common individualization patterns, leaving aside fingerprints, firearms, and document evidence (such as handwriting)

- Shape and form patterns (such as handwriting and human hair shaft morphology) are compared in a manner similar to the way the human mind recognizes people and objects

- Several other individualization patterns include bite marks, certain skeletal features, and voice patterns

Learning Objectives

- The three types of forensic analysis of physical patterns

- Direct physical matching versus indirect physical matching

- Impression marks can be imprints (effectively two-dimensional) or indentations (three-dimensional)

- Striations are caused by a moving object making a dynamic impression

chapter 5

Lead Case

Hit-and-Run Death of a State Police Lieutenant

One morning early, a Connecticut state police lieutenant, commander of the Troop A barracks, was driving to work along Interstate 84 between Hartford and Waterbury. He noticed a disabled motorist pulled over on the shoulder of the road. Although he was not a patrol officer, and had no obligation to stop, he pulled over to assist the motorist. In accordance with protocol, he pulled the police cruiser up behind the disabled vehicle, engaged the emergency light bar, and exited the car. According to the motorist, his vehicle, the lieutenant's vehicle, and the lieutenant, were off the roadway and on the shoulder.

While the lieutenant was out of his vehicle, he was struck by a passing tractor-trailer rig, thrown a considerable distance, and probably died almost immediately. The tractor-trailer rig did not stop.

Word of the mishap was quickly relayed to state police who rushed to the scene of the hit-and-run and deployed considerable manpower to locate and stop the truck. The major crime squad and a team from the laboratory also helped in the hit-and-run scene investigation.

State police located and stopped a tractor-trailer rig that fit the description that had been given by the motorist. They were able to stop the rig before it could cross the bridge into New York State.

The major crime squad and laboratory team carefully examined the tractor-trailer for evidence. On the front portion of the trailer at what would be just about shoulder height for the state police lieutenant, the lab investigators found a nearly perfect mirror-image dust impression of the Connecticut state police shoulder patch worn on both shoulders of the uniform (see photos below).

The dust impression sealed the case from both criminal and civil points of view. The truck driver was convicted of hit-and-run manslaughter and sentenced to prison time. The company that owned the truck was sued civilly on behalf of the state police lieutenant's family, and the jury came back with a multimillion-dollar award for the lieutenant's wife and young family.

This case starkly illustrates the extraordinary value that physical pattern evidence can have sometimes, because it can be so clear, intuitive, and correspondingly convincing.

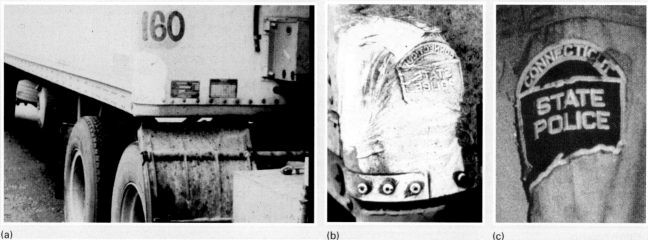

(a) (b) (c)

(A) The trailer (number 160) thought to be involved in the hit-and-run showed a dust-ike smudge near the corner of the trailer. (B) Closer inspection revealed a near perfect mirror image of the Connecticut State Police shoulder patch that resulted from the trailer hitting the lieutenant. (C) The uniform shirt with the actual shoulder patch worn by the lieutenant on the morning of his untimely death.

Classification/Types of Physical Patterns for Comparison

There are three categories of individualization pattern evidence commonly found at crime scenes, as noted in the Part Three introduction. Each of them has subcategories and classes of evidence.

Physical Matches

Physical matching is the simplest yet often one of the most persuasive types of evidence that can be obtained. **Physical matches** can be divided into *direct* (primary, first-order) and *indirect* (secondary, second-order). If the fractured or torn pieces are solid and from an item or object expected to fracture randomly, and if the pieces can be matched back together, a direct physical match is obtained. If some portions are missing, or if the item is not solid (like fabric) or has distorted or poorly defined edges, only a secondary match may be possible. In such cases the match is often the result of a complex pattern that carries across the boundaries of the two objects. A common example is the grain of a wood board that has been sawn. Although the saw has removed sufficient material to make a direct physical match impossible in most cases, the common pattern of the wood grain or growth patterns across the boundary allows a pattern match.

physical matches
Matches between or among pieces of a randomly fractured, torn, or cut objects that might show that the pieces were originally part of the same item.

Impression and Striation Marks

Impression marks result when a patterned object contacts a receiving surface and leaves a negative impression of itself. Among the most familiar examples are fingerprints and tire and footwear impressions. Striation marks result from a tool or object moving relative to a receiving surface. The most forensically important are the markings imposed by firearms' barrels onto bullets. In markings comparisons, a questioned mark from a scene is always compared with a known mark produced by the object suspected of being the source.

Shape and Form

Shape and form are terms we use to denote the extraordinary ability of the human mind to discern and discriminate patterns and subtle differences between them. A familiar example is recognizing a friend or acquaintance. You have no trouble doing this once you know the person. Yet if you tried to explain how you did it—in enough detail to allow someone else who did not know the person to recognize him or her—you probably couldn't do it. So, although we can't enumerate all the features and characteristics of the pattern in enough detail to make it uniquely recognizable to someone else, we are very good at pattern recognition and matching. Recognizing a friend's face involves comparing the visual data against an existing mental image and "making a match." Various patterns and impressions often found at a crime scene or left on clothing, vehicles, or other objects can be recognized because of features, shapes, or forms. The experienced criminalist can recognize certain objects, weapons, or shapes and know to preserve those marks.

shape and form
Refers to the ability of the human mind to recognize individual characteristics in complex shapes or forms, such as a human face; handwriting and morphological hair comparisons are examples.

This process is the same one forensic scientists use in comparing crystals under a microscope and in comparing handwriting. Later in the chapter, we will discuss why the inability to explain the comparison process in detail (i.e., the process is subjective) has created some problems when the Daubert admissibility standards are applied. Note that the subjectivity of a process does not make it intrinsically inaccurate; we recognize people we know very accurately.

General Principles
in Physical Pattern Comparisons

There are some general principles that apply to all types of individualization pattern evidence analysis, which are discussed in the following sections.

The Process of Identification

As we noted earlier, pattern evidence experts use the term **positive identification** to mean they have matched questioned (Q) and known (K) specimens well enough to say that they had the same origin.

The comparison process begins by ensuring that the proper specimens are being compared; that is, positives must be compared with positives, and negatives with negatives. A sneaker is a positive, for example. Its indentation in mud is a negative. The cast of that indentation is again a positive. The cast (the Q) would be compared with the shoe itself (the K). On the other hand, a grease-dirt impression of the sneaker on a linoleum floor is a negative. A tape lift or photograph of the impression is still a negative. These would be compared not with the sneaker, but with an inked impression made in the lab using the sneaker. In this way, a negative is compared with a negative. Table 5.1 summarizes some features of the pattern comparison process.

The next step is general orientation of the impressions to be compared. With footwear, left and right orientations can get confusing when you are working with lifts. Once the orientations of questioned and known impressions are the same, the class characteristics are compared.

Class characteristics are those that characterize the item as a member of a class. Brand, size, shape, and possibly the general pattern are class features. These must match if the Q and the K are really identical. Many times, forensic scientists will only be able to match class characteristics of an imprint or impression from the scene with a known object. The conclusion will be that the Q pattern is consistent

Table 5.1   Some features of individualization patterns and their comparison

Pattern		Examples	Comparison process	Known (exemplar) required
Physical match	Direct	Shredded paper; broken glass or plastic	Physical fit	No. Q and K specimens fitted
	Indirect	Wood grain; plastic bag sequence on roll	Juxtaposition and evaluation of continuities	No. Q and K specimens juxtaposed
Imprint		Footwear or tire impression on tile floor	Point by point; side by side or overlay	Yes. Produced from suspected object in the lab
Indentation		Footwear or tire impression in mud or snow	Point by point	Yes. Suspected object is K if Q is a cast of a marking
Striation		Rifled barrel markings on fired bullets; sliding tool marks	Continuity of marks in juxtaposed items	Yes. Produced from suspected firearm or tool in the lab
Shape and form		Hair comparisons; handwriting comparisons	Subjective pattern recognition	Yes. Multiple specimens required

with the K object. It is important to remember that the "class" can range from quite large to very small. Thus the evidentiary weight accorded the inclusion in the class will also vary.

Next, **individual characteristics** are compared. These are features that differ among individual members of the same class and thus have the ability to confer individuality. The specific individual features used in fingerprint and firearms identification comparisons will be discussed in subsequent chapters. With tire or footwear impressions, the individual characteristics are the result of wear. Besides modification of the pattern just due to wear on the surfaces, there can be cuts, tears, abrasions, and so on, that are random and accidental and would not be expected to be duplicated in another object from the same class. If a sufficient number of individual features are found to match in both the Q and K specimens, and there are no unexplained differences, the examiner makes a positive identification. That means the examiner is ready to give the opinion that Q and K came from the same source.

Physical Matching

Direct physical matching is *jigsaw fit* matching and is applicable to solid materials (typically glass, plastic, or metal) that break into pieces in a random way. A **direct physical match** shows unequivocally that the pieces were originally part of the same object or item (Figure 5.1). The value in a case is usually that some pieces have been recovered from a victim, a suspect, or a suspect vehicle while the others have been recovered at a scene. Match results thus place a suspect or a vehicle at the scene and link a victim and suspect. Hit-and-run scenes may have broken pieces of head lamp or parking lamp lenses, grill parts, or license plate frames. If the responsible vehicle can be found before any repairs are done, it can be placed at the hit-and-run scene by direct physical matching of objects still remaining on the vehicle to evidence recovered from the scene. Other solid physical items that fracture or separate in a random way may also sometimes be useful as objects for direct physical matches. Buttons, sometimes torn or cut paper or cardboard, and broken metal objects like knives, screws, or bolts may also be subject to direct physical matches.

---

individual characteristics

Accidental (unintentional) characteristics resulting from wear or random markings on items during manufacture; a sufficient number of matching individual characteristics between a known and questioned specimen can permit an examiner to make an identification.

direct physical match

A jigsaw fit match of pieces of a randomly fractured solid object that shows the pieces were originally part of the same item.

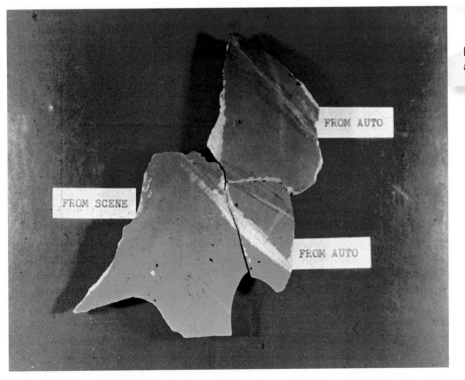

Figure 5.1
Direct physical match of pieces of auto body putty.

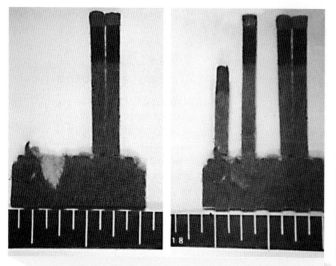

Figure 5.2A   A torn out match being directly physically matched back into the matchbook from which it came.

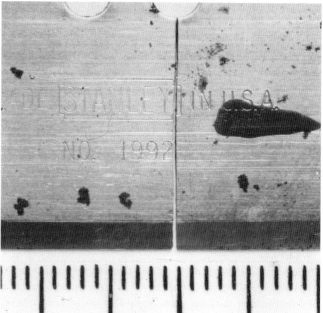

Figure 5.2B   Matching stria across a break in a utility knife blade.

There are a few requirements for direct physical matches—also sometimes called *fracture* matches. First, the object or item should have fractured or been severed in a way that produces a complex two- or three-dimensional surface. In other words, the object or item would not be expected to separate in exactly the same way twice. The pieces must be capable of being realigned. Physical matching is intuitive, and correspondingly persuasive. Another requirement is that the object is not too fragmented; otherwise reconstruction would be prohibitively difficult. For a complete *direct* physical match, all the major pieces must be available. If pieces are missing, the match becomes indirect.

With an **indirect physical match,** experts fit, or attempt to fit, severed, broken, or torn pieces of an item or object together in a way that convincingly demonstrates the pieces were once part of the same structure. If an object or item is solid and randomly fractured and would normally be amenable to direct physical match (Figure 5.2A) but there are significant missing pieces, any match becomes secondary (Figure 5.2B). Indirect matching also applies to items like fabric that are not solid, and therefore cannot be jigsaw fit matched, and whose edges may also be distorted during the cutting or tearing process, making matching more difficult. Other examples are matching broken pieces of certain wood, matching torn edges along perforated papers, and matching a torn-out match from a matchbook to the remaining stubs. Secondary physical matches are often less intrinsically convincing that primary matches, and examiners must convince themselves the match really exists before reporting it.

Exclusions, Inconclusives, and Insufficient Detail

If class characteristics do not match, or if there are unexplained differences between Q and K, the Q may be excluded as having come from the same source as K. An **exclusion**

indirect physical match

A secondary physical match between soft, pliable objects, such as torn fabric, between pieces of a randomly fractured object with some pieces missing, or between cross sections of a broken wooden object.

exclusion

A conclusion that a known and a questioned specimen do not match and could not have had a common origin.

is absolute. If should be remembered that sometimes an exclusion is just as crucial to an investigation or prosecution as an individualization.

Sometimes, an examiner may find that there is not enough individual marking detail to make a valid comparison. In that case, **insufficient detail for comparison** might be reported. Similarly, even if some details are present, there may be too few to make an identification. At the same time, what is present may match, so the examiner can't exclude. These comparisons may be reported **inconclusive.**

Physical Pattern Comparisons and the Daubert Criteria

The U.S. Supreme Court's *Daubert* v. *Merrell* decision (Chapter 2) set down new criteria for the admissibility of scientific evidence into court proceedings. In effect, the Court said that results intended to be introduced into court proceedings as scientific evidence, through expert witness testimony, must be based on a hypothesis-testing scientific method model. For evidence analysis that uses established methods of chemistry or biochemistry, and so on, like drug identification, toxicology, DNA typing, fiber identification, and so forth, it is almost self-evident that the conclusions are scientifically based, and thus admissible. With pattern evidence analysis, this is not so obvious.

Pattern evidence identification criteria rely on many decades of experience along with limited experimentation designed to show that trained, experienced examiners can in fact distinguish different individual patterns, even if they are expected to be quite similar, such as with bullets from consecutively manufactured gun barrels, or fingerprints from identical twins. There are any number of "experiments" of this kind in the open literature. You might call this "outcome research." That is, given a group of items of pattern evidence for comparison, do experienced examiners match the correct ones, and exclude the ones that don't match—do they obtain the correct outcome? You can also look at this sort of activity as proficiency testing. It can be voluntary, or it may be required by an accrediting or a certifying body. Generally, trained, experienced examiners do obtain the correct answer. However, while trained, experienced examiners nearly always get such exercises right, inexperienced and/or untrained individuals do not. Pattern evidence examiners are typically trained one-on-one by senior, experienced examiners in the same field. The training is long, and considerable proficiency testing and supervised casework is typically required before a new examiner is allowed to do casework alone.

Still, the collective body of experience and training over many decades does not constitute a systematic, hypothesis-driven, experimentally based test of pattern evidence individuality. Some courts, applying the Daubert standards, have found this situation troubling. At least one court has characterized handwriting comparison as a technical expertise (and admissible as such), but not reaching the threshold to be called "scientific."

There are approaches available to carry out experiments that will firmly establish on scientific grounds, once and for all, what most people already believe—namely, that individualization patterns are individualizable. The issues raised by Daubert are relatively new, however, and this process will take time to work through.

Impression and Striation Mark Comparisons

We use the term **impressions** here as the broader one, which includes imprints and indentations.

Impressions: Imprints and Indentations

The distinction between *imprints* and *indentations* is made because the two are generally found on different surfaces. An **imprint** is a mark that is effectively two-dimensional. By that we mean the mark has essentially no depth, no three-dimensional

insufficient detail for comparison

A conclusion by an examiner that a questioned specimen lacks enough class and/or individual characteristics to do a proper comparison with knowns.

inconclusive

A conclusion by an examiner that a comparison of known and questioned specimens permits neither an identification nor an exclusion.

impressions

Negative imprints or indentations of an object.

imprint

A mark (pattern) that is essentially two-dimensional left by an object on a hard receiving surface through contact with another object; an imprint has very little depth.

indentation

A three-dimensional mark (pattern) left in a deformable object through contact with another object.

character. Such marks are generally left on hard flat surfaces. An **indentation** is a mark that has distinct three-dimensional character. An object makes an imprint on a hard receiving surface, while it makes an indentation in a softer receiving surface.

The terminology describing marks with depth and marks without depth can vary with different kinds of evidence. For instance, fingerprints without depth are often called "residue" prints, while those in soft media (like silly putty or butter) are called "impression" or "plastic" prints. Similarly, the mark a firing pin makes on a cartridge primer is usually called a "firing pin impression" although it is an indentation.

Striations

striation

A number of parallel or nearly parallel lines or scratches on a surface inscribed by another object passing over that surface.

Striation marks are usually tool marks made by a tool sliding along a receiving surface. A special case of "tool marking" occurs with rifled barrels of firearms, which impart striation markings onto bullet surfaces as the bullet passes down the barrel. Striation marks can also be present on a tool or object and be impressed onto a receiving surface. These markings form the basis for firearms identification. This subject is discussed in Chapter 8.

Collection and Preservation of Impressions

Generally, both imprints and indentations should be documented by photography before collection. The photographs taken should show the location of the impression in the scene and the impression with an evidence number sign next to it. Depending on the impression and how it will be collected, a very good documentation photograph may be of nearly equal value as the collected mark for comparison purposes. Smaller impressions might be able to be photographed 1:1 (image at film plane is the same size as the actual object being imaged) with a Polaroid, 35 mm, or digital camera. If possible, such a photograph should be taken. With larger impressions, some reduction will inevitably occur to fit the image on to the film. However, the larger the negative, the less the loss of detail. That is the reason some crime scene photographers use 4 × 5 cameras for larger impressions, like footwear or tire tracks. Care should be taken to ensure that the plane of the film is parallel to the plane of the impression (to avoid distortion), and a tripod should be used. Bracketing the exposure is always a good idea, too. With indentations, use of the side light technique is recommended (Figure 5.3). If the indent is shallow, grazing illumination (lighting almost parallel to the surface) will help to make it more visible and therefore easier to record.

Figure 5.3

Photograph of tire track in snow, lighted so as to highlight the features of the indentation mark.

Following thorough photographic documentation, imprints are generally tape lifted or gel lifted or lifted with an electrostatic lifting device, and indentations are cast. As we stated in Chapter 3, the crime scene chapter, it is always best to collect the entire, intact object bearing the impression if possible. If that is not possible, investigators must think about lifts or casts.

Tape lifting is a classic method for collecting and preserving fingerprints, usually after they have been enhanced by powder dusting or other treatment (Chapter 6). But tape lifting can also be used for footwear or other imprints. There are larger lifting tapes and backings available. The technique involves overlaying the imprint with the sticky tape smoothly and avoiding air bubbles. Then the tape is lifted up in a single, continuous motion and transferred to a suitable backing surface that contrasts the color of the impression. In addition, there are commercial "gel lifters" available for this purpose. They are made of material that picks up the dirt, grease, oil, and so on, efficiently. For dust prints (Figure 5.4A), which are often subtle and would be destroyed by tape lifting, an electrostatic dust lifter device is available commercially (Figure 5.4B). It imposes a charge on a special film material (metalized Mylar sheet) laid over the imprint. The dust particles that

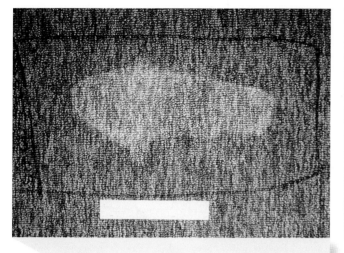

Figure 5.4A

Carpet with a barely visible footwear impression in dust. Electrostatic dust lifting is the only way this imprint can be collected.

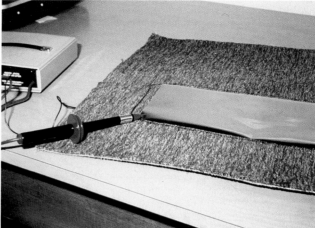

Figure 5.4B

Electrostatic lifting device in place on carpet, with the metalized film placed over the dust print.

Figure 5.4C

The same shoe impression in dust electrostatically lifted onto lifting film.

form the impression are attracted and transferred to the film and preserved (Figure 5.4C).

Indentation marks are generally cast using dental stone, a special form of plaster of paris. It comes in many grades and colors. Dentists use this material to make accurate casts of teeth so that inlays, crowns, or other restorations can be made. Generally, the impression is carefully sprayed with lacquer (the spray is deflected rather than being sprayed directly onto the mark itself to avoid damaging any detail) to preserve detail during addition of the plaster. Figure 5.5A shows an impression prepared for pouring the plaster. The dental stone is mixed so that it is about the consistency of pancake batter and is then poured into the impression using a spatula or stick as a pouring aid (Figure 5.5B). The mark is covered completely. The plaster is then allowed to set for a time, and a strengthening material (sticks, chicken wire, etc.) may be placed onto the cast before more dental stone is added and allowed to set. Once the cast is set up, it can be initialed or marked and then carefully collected. The cast should be packaged so

Figure 5.5A

Preparing an impression for casting with dental stone. Better: Preparing an impression for casting with dental stone. The marking is generally sprayed with lacquer, then "framed" to contain the dental stone.

Figure 5.5B

The casting of an impression with dental stone. Half the dental stone may be poured, then a solid support material such as chicken wire added to give the cast more strength, before pouring the last half. Identifying information such as case number, initials of person making the cast, etc., may be scratched into the dental stone surface before it completely hardens.

as to avoid breakage during transport. If the casting was done in soil, any soil clinging to the cast should be left in place, as a soil reference material (Chapter 13).

A special casting material called Snow Print Wax is used for indentation marks in snow. When plaster sets up, it releases heat. Heat would obviously destroy pattern detail in snow. The Snow Print Wax stabilizes the mark and insulates it from the heat of the setting dental stone (Figure 5.6). There are also some special casting materials like Mikrosil that may be used to capture fine detail in sliding tool marks. Many of these are silicone-rubber-type casting materials similar to those used in dental work.

Lifts and casts need to be properly labeled with the case number, date, investigator's initials, evidence number, and location. Some of the identifying information can be etched into the cast before the plaster is completely dry.

Footwear, Tire, and Other Impressions

We have mentioned footwear and tire impressions in the earlier discussion. Those are the most commonly encountered impression evidence other than fingerprints or firearms markings.

Footwear could be any shoe, slipper, sandal, sock, or stocking. Any of these can leave an impression. It is also possible to have a footprint, the impression of a bare

Figure 5.6

Spraying a shoe impression in snow with Snow Print Wax to stabilize it before casting.

foot. Since foot surfaces have friction ridge skin like that on the fingertips which forms fingerprints, footprints are compared by fingerprint examiners in the same manner as fingerprints.

Most footwear and tires are mass produced, so there are typically millions of pieces with the same class characteristics. Sufficient wear may introduce enough individual characteristics to make an identification possible. Keep in mind that an evidentiary impression may not reflect the whole shoe or tire, just a part of it. Further, the shoe or tire suspected of making the impression must be recovered before a known impression can be produced and a comparison done.

Known footwear impressions should be produced with someone wearing the footwear who is approximately the same weight as the suspected wearer. Similarly, known tire impressions should be produced with the suspected tire on the vehicle. And a mark must be made that covers a complete rotation of the tire, since there is no a priori way of knowing which part of the tire left the questioned impression at the scene.

Although footwear and tire impressions are the most common impression marks encountered as evidence other than fingerprints, footprints, or firearms markings, impressions could in theory be made by any object or material. In hit-and-run cases, there can sometimes be fabric impressions from the victim's clothing on the bumper. This type of impression may have been more common when automobile bumpers were bare metal. In Chapter 4, we mentioned "contact transfer" blood patterns. These are similar to the patterns we are discussing here, except they may not have much microstructure so that a point-by-point comparison could be done. But the contact transfer pattern might match an aspect of an object and enable an expert to say that the pattern is consistent with having been made by blood on that object.

Case Study 5.1 shows how important impression evidence can be in associating a person with a crime scene.

Clarification and Contrast Improvement Techniques

In many cases patterns are difficult to analyze or compare because of poor visibility. There can be lack of contrast between pattern and background, a very weak pattern, or interference between pattern and complex backgrounds. Three different types of

Case Study 5.1

Imprint Evidence Associates a Suspect with a Multiple Murder Scene

Several years ago, people in Warwick, Rhode Island, were shocked by the finding of all three members of one family—a mother and her two daughters—brutally stabbed to death in their home. The mother was raising her daughters by herself, had no known enemies, and was not involved in any kind of criminal activity. There was no obvious motive for the homicide.

Forensic experts from the FBI and the Connecticut state police were asked to assist in the investigation. The youngest daughter's body was found in the kitchen; the oldest daughter's body, in the hallway; and the mother's body, in the bedroom. The clothing on all three was intact, and there were no signs of sexual attack. It did not appear that rape was the motive.

A kitchen window at the back of the house had been pried open and appeared to be the point of entry. The window was high off the ground, suggesting that the perpetrator, who more than likely climbed in the window, would have to be of above average height and strength. Inside the house, directly below the window, a small kitchen table appeared to have just been broken, as if someone heavy had stepped on the table while coming through the window. A reddish footwear imprint pattern was observed on the tabletop. In addition, a partial palm print was also found.

There was a large amount of blood in the kitchen, hallway, and bedroom. Bloody footwear-like prints were observed leading from the kitchen to the living room window, then toward the hallway. Upon closer examination, it was found that the prints were made by socks, not shoes. The sock prints were found throughout the house, as if someone, one person only, searched every room, looking for something.

It was also discovered that bloodstains were in different stages of coagulation. The youngest daughter's blood was clearly dry. The mother's blood was in an advanced stage of coagulation. But other drops of blood definitely were fresher and in semiliquid stage. These blood drops were consistent with low-velocity passive dripping from a height of approximately 3 to 4 feet. The fresh blood drops were consistent with someone bleeding from a serious cut of the hand or finger.

A crime scene profile indicated that the house was the primary scene, and sex was not the motive. The suspect was more than likely a strong young man, perhaps a teenager, of above average height, overweight, and with a serious cut on one hand or arm.

Police put out the word, and, in one of those examples of keen observation that would bring a pat on the back from every law enforcement officer, a Warwick detective noticed a teenager working on a car. What caught the officer's attention was the bandage the boy wore on his hand. The officer stopped to chat and asked the boy about the bandage. Craig Price said he had cut his hand. The police officer asked Price to come to the station.

A court order was obtained for blood, hair, fingerprints, footprint, and shoe exemplars. Laboratory testing showed the following results:

1. The partial handprint on the kitchen tabletop matched the right hand of the suspect.
2. The footwear imprint on the kitchen tabletop was similar in size, shape, sole pattern, and other class characteristics to the suspect's shoe.
3. Several latent fingerprints were found inside the house that matched the known fingerprints of the suspect.
4. DNA profiling showed that several blood drops matched the known DNA from the suspect.

The evidence was sufficient to allow the prosecution to proceed and for a trial jury to convict this suspect of three counts of murder.

techniques can be used to address such problems and make pattern information more useful.

Several photographic techniques such as side lighting, and use of special illumination such as UV, laser, or alternate light source, have been mentioned. In addition, filters can be used to increase contrast where background and pattern are of different colors. Special films and high-contrast printing papers can also help in some situations.

A number of physical and chemical techniques are also used to clarify or enhance contrast. As mentioned, chemical blood test reagents can be used to make very subtle blood patterns visible through color change or added image intensity of even very weak patterns. Fingerprint powders and a variety of lifters can help isolate the imprint from the background or enhance contrast.

Finally, many of the preceding enhancements can be done more quickly and more effectively using digital imaging techniques. A number of programs, such as Photoshop and Image Pro, have tremendous power to improve the clarity and contrast of images. They work well on digital images captured either photographically or scanned on a flatbed scanner. Once the image information is digitized, the variety of techniques available is extensive. They must be done in a well-documented way if such improved images are to be used in court. The Scientific Working Group on Imaging Technology (SWGIT) established proposed guidelines for image acquisition, handling, documentation, and enhancement in 2005.

With all the mentioned clarification techniques, it is critical that the original image be well documented before any of the techniques are used, since some may degrade or destroy the image rather than clarify it.

Weapon, Tool, and Object Marks

Many types of patterns might appear at a crime scene or be left on a body or other object. Those patterns can be produced by direct contact of two surfaces, such as earprints, button prints, or belt buckle prints, or they can be produced by force, such as cuts, wounds, or pattern injuries.

Shape and Form Comparisons

As noted earlier, patterns called "shape and form" can be compared, but the comparison between Q and K is conducted looking at the overall pattern. There are individualizing features in the patterns, but the individuality of the pattern consists of more than a list of features that match. We likened this comparison to recognizing the face of a friend or acquaintance.

The most prominent examples of these patterns in forensic science are the microscopic structure of hair and handwriting. These are discussed in Chapters 13 and 7, respectively.

Other Patterns

A few other individualization patterns can be important in forensic science. Bite marks, certain individualizing features in the human skeleton, and voice patterns are all used to help identify individuals. They will be described in Chapter 6, along with fingerprints. Patterned injuries (Chapter 4) may also be of considerable forensic use, but are primarily the responsibility of the forensic pathologist. In jurisdictions where there is no forensic pathologist available, such patterns may be compared by forensic laboratory personnel.

Tear, cut, or damage patterns on clothing, furniture, or other objects can often provide evidence through pattern analysis. For example, was a window screen cut from the inside or outside? Was damage to a victim's clothing self-made or made by an assailant? Was a pattern found on carpet, a car seat, or floor consistent with a particular object?

Concluding Comments

Pattern evidence, as we have noted, can be seen as one of the four major categories of physical evidence in terms of the scope of criminalistics—the others are chemical, trace and materials, and biological evidence.

Pattern evidence is usually thought of as physical matching, imprints, striations, shapes and forms, and reconstruction patterns. Firearms, tool marks, fingerprints, questioned documents (especially handwriting), footwear, and tire tracks are the most common examples of pattern evidence.

It is useful to remember, however, that even in chemical and biological analysis, some of the analytical methods produce patterns that must be interpreted. Infrared spectra (Chapter 12), gas chromatographic patterns (Chapter 11), and DNA profiles (Chapter 10) are some examples.

Summary

This chapter begins the study of patterns for individualization. These patterns are physical patterns that can be examined visually. They can also be imprint, indentation, or striation patterns that can be reproduced by the suspected source, and the reproduced pattern then compared with the evidence one. Except for physical matches, all the pattern analyses are comparisons between a known specimen and a questioned (evidentiary) one. This chapter develops the general principles of pattern analysis and comparisons and discusses some patterns that do not have their own chapters. Fingerprints, firearms and tool mark patterns, and questioned document patterns fall into this category, but they all have their own chapters.

Individualization patterns may be direct or indirect physical matches, impressions—which can be imprints or indentations—striations, or general shape and form. Physical matches involve fractured or broken items or objects where the fragments are available. Impressions can be "imprints"—essentially no depth—or "indentations"—three-dimensional. Often, these may be tire or footwear impressions. Generally, imprint markings are tape lifted following photography, while indentations are cast following photography. Striations are commonly tool mark or fired bullet markings. General shape and form comparisons include morphological hair comparisons (Chapter 13) and handwriting comparisons (Chapter 7).

General principles of individualization pattern comparison include ensuring that the proper patterns are compared (such as positives vs. positives, and negatives vs. negatives), that the patterns are properly oriented (right, left, etc.), then comparison of class characteristics followed by that of individual characteristics. An examiner may reach a conclusion that there are sufficient matching individual characteristics between a questioned and known pattern to declare identification. Likewise, the examiner could conclude that the questioned pattern did not originate from the same source as the known. Sometimes, there is insufficient detail to even do a comparison, or an insufficient number of characteristics to form a conclusion. Although these analyses have been practiced for many decades, and it can be shown that properly trained examiners nearly always reach the correct conclusion, the Daubert admissibility standards have not been rigorously met.

Patterns that have been imaged or photographed can often be clarified or contrast enhanced by chemical, photographic, or digital methods. If the enhancement procedures are carefully documented, the enhanced images will likely be accepted in court as evidence. Cases can sometimes also involve unusual patterns or imprints, such as from a weapon or an object. Other patterns for individualization include human skeletal patterns, used by forensic anthropologists to narrow down whose remains the skeleton may be, bite marks, and voice patterns.

Key Terms

physical matches (p. 109)
shape and form (p. 109)
positive identification (p. 110)
class characteristics (p. 110)
individual characteristics (p. 111)

direct physical match (p. 111)
indirect physical match (p. 112)
exclusion (p. 112)
insufficient detail for comparison (p. 113)
inconclusive (p. 113)

impressions (p. 113)
imprint (p. 113)
indentation (p. 114)
striation (p. 114)

Review Questions—Short Answer

1. What are the three major types of patterns for individualization?
2. Discuss the general principles involved in pattern analysis and comparison. What is an "identification"?
3. What is the difference between imprints and indentations? What are examples of each?
4. What are the most common evidentiary striation markings?
5. What are class characteristics?
6. What are individual characteristics?
7. What are shape and form comparisons?
8. Why is pattern evidence identification an issue under the Daubert standard?
9. What are the main criteria for making a direct physical match?
10. What would cause an examiner to conclude that there was "insufficient detail for comparison" in a pattern evidence comparison case?

Fill-in-the-Blank & Multiple Choice

1. Whether a mark is three-dimensional or essentially two-dimensional determines if it is considered an imprint or an _____ marking.
2. A marking on a surface made by the movement of an object across the surface is referred to by the technical term _____.

3. Point-by-point matching of the jagged ends of two pieces of a wooden axe handle that had broken in an irregular way is known as
   a. comparison of markings.
   b. direct physical matching.
   c. general form recognition.
   d. indirect physical matching.
4. When shoe and tire marks are impressed in soft earth at a crime scene, their documentation and preservation are best accomplished by _____ and then _____.

Further References

Bodziak, W. J. *Footwear Impression Evidence: Detection, Recovery and Examination.* 2nd ed. Boca Raton: CRC Press, 1999.

Scientific Working Group on Imaging Technology (SWGIT). "Best Practices for Forensic Image Analysis, Version 1.5, 3/14/05." *Forensic Science Communications* 7, no. 4 (October 2005).

Fingerprints and Other Personal Identification Patterns

back to the 19th century in British India and the United Kingdom

- Fingerprints can be classified and the most useful system is the 10-print classification system developed by Henry
- Large files of 10-print cards cannot be searched for individual prints
- AFISs contain individual print images and can be searched for individual prints efficiently and quickly
- There are established procedures for collecting and preserving latent fingerprints and items from scenes suspected of having latents
- The three types of evidentiary fingerprints: visible, patent, and latent
- Methods for visualizing latent fingerprints
- Processing latent prints with maximum efficiency and results requires a systematic approach
- The approach commonly used in fingerprint comparisons and identification can be summarized "ACE-V" (Analysis, Comparison, Evaluation, and Verification)
- Fingerprint identification specialists belong to a professional organization that has its own professional journal and offers certification
- Other patterns for personal identification include palm and sole prints, bite marks, certain skeletal features, lip and ear prints, and voice identification
- Methods for the identification of human remains
- The method used to identify human remains depends on the circumstances, the condition of the remains, and the number of possible identities

Outline

Learning Objectives

- Fingerprints are an old and very valuable type of physical evidence
- What friction ridge skin is and how it makes up fingerprints
- Fingerprints for personal identification dates back to medieval times, but in the West, dates

chapter

Lead Case

California v. Gerald Mason:
Fingerprints Provide Solution to a Cold Police Killing Case

This case began in the 1950s but went unsolved and became a cold case. It was recently solved because a latent fingerprint taken from the scene decades ago could be subjected to a nationwide search, using AFIS technology that was unavailable when the crime occurred. The case—in which two young police officers on a routine traffic stop were gunned down in the Los Angeles suburb of El Segundo, California, in July 1957—was featured on the CBS newsmagazine program *48 Hours Mystery*.

On the night the crime occurred, four teenagers were coming home from a summer party when they decided to make a stop at Lover's Lane. "I rolled the window down. . . . And that's when the gun came through the window," recalled one of them. "[Somebody said,] 'This is a robbery.' I said, 'Gotta be somebody pulling a prank.'" But the gun was real. The gunman came prepared with surgical tape and a flashlight. He covered the teenagers' eyes with tape and ordered them to take off their clothes. They had little choice but to do what they were told. The perpetrator came around from the driver's side to the passenger side, opened the car door, and raped one of the girls. He told the four to get out of the car and said "I think I'm gonna kill you. I want you to march out into the field." Then, the car door closed and he drove away.

While making his getaway in the stolen 1949 Ford, the man stopped for a red light, and then, for no apparent reason, drove on through it. A police patrol car parked off the side of the road saw the stop light violation and proceeded to pull the violator over. El Segundo Officer Richard Phillips and rookie Officer Milton Curtis were in the police vehicle. A second patrol vehicle with Officers James Gilbert and Charlie Porter drove by shortly thereafter, but having no reason to be suspicious and still unaware of the events at Lover's Lane, drove on. Moments later, there was a radio call in which Phillips said that they'd been shot and needed an ambulance. Porter and his partner raced back to the scene. Phillips and Curtis were both dead, and the killer had simply disappeared. Hundreds of police from El Segundo and neighboring areas searched all night. They found the stolen Ford, but there was no sign of the suspect.

The crime became one of the oldest unsolved murder cases in Los Angeles County. At the time of the murders, the 1949 Ford hadn't yet been reported stolen, and the four teenagers had not yet told the police what happened to them.

Investigators arriving that morning to look at the stolen car noted bullet holes in the trunk and in the rear window. It appeared the car had been hit three times. Officer Phillips had fired six shots

Gerald Mason, (right), wipes away tears after pleading guilty to murder charges. To the left is his attorney Gaston Fairey. In March, 2003, Mason was sentenced to two consecutive life terms.

at the vehicle before he died and hit it three times. Two rounds were recovered from the vehicle's interior, but one was not. Police theorized that the killer might have been hit. Several latent prints were taken from the interior of the vehicle. At the time, however, automated fingerprint search systems didn't yet exist.

In 2002, a woman called the El Segundo police and said she had heard an uncle bragging about being responsible for the murders. A comparison of the latent prints from the vehicle with those of the uncle did not yield a match. The fingerprint examiners decided to take the search further, however. They cleaned up the latent a bit using modern digital imaging techniques and were eventually able to search for it in the nationwide IAFIS (Integrated Automated Fingerprint Identification System).

The print matched Gerald F. Mason, who had been arrested for burglary in 1956 in South Carolina. It was the only time he had ever been arrested, and it was the only record of his prints on file. Mason was easily located, still living in his hometown of Columbia, South Carolina. He wasn't a career criminal, but a retiree living with his family.

Looking through the boxes of evidence that had been collected in the case over the years, investigators turned up the actual murder weapon. It had been recovered in 1960 by a man digging weeds in a backyard not far from the original murder scene. The serial number allowed the gun to be traced to Shreveport, Louisiana. The gun was sold there in 1957 by Billy Gene Clark to someone who called himself G. D. Wilson. A "George D. Wilson" could be tracked to a nearby YMCA, but no one with the name could ever be found to match the latent print. The name was an alias. But a questioned document examiner was able to match the registration signature with the handwriting of Gerald F. Mason.

Mason was nearly 70 when El Segundo police arrested him at his home. There is no record of his ever having committed another crime. When he was examined, it was discovered that Mason had a bullet-shaped scar on his back, consistent with being hit by a bullet from Phillips's gun. After a hearing in South Carolina, Mason agreed to return to Los Angeles. He pleaded guilty to murdering Officers Phillips and Curtis, and he tried to make amends before being sentenced to life in prison: "It's impossible to express to so many people how sorry I am. I do not understand why I did this. It does not fit in my life. It is not the person I know. I detest these crimes."

Why did he do it? "I didn't have a family life. I didn't have any place to go, and things were not going well for me, so I took off to California," said Mason. "I bought a gun at Shreveport with the intention of using it simply as a deterrent insofar as I was hitchhiking." When asked why he attacked the teenagers and raped a 15-year-old girl, Mason said he really didn't remember. But as to why he killed two cops in cold blood, Mason's answer was: "I thought, 'If I don't get them, they're gonna get me.' So when the officer turned away from me, I shot both officers, got back in the car and drove away."

Gerald Mason will be eligible for parole in 2010, when he is 76 years old. The State of California has vowed that he will never be released.

Fingerprints—An Old and Traditionally Valuable Type of Evidence

Fingerprints are among the oldest and most important kinds of evidence used for human identification. The individuality of fingerprints is so impressed into the public consciousness that fingerprint analogies are regularly used in advertising interchangeably with "unique" or "specifically individual." Although the terms "DNA fingerprints" and "DNA fingerprinting" are often invoked by the popular press, and even some DNA scientists, to imply individuality, most forensic scientists feel it is not proper terminology.

The use of friction ridge skin patterns on fingertips as a means of personal identification dates back many centuries. A convincing fingerprint match is universally accepted as certain evidence that identifies a particular person.

As noted in the previous chapter, fingerprints belong to the individualization pattern category. Fingerprints are often essentially two-dimensional (residue prints), but they can be in soft receiving surfaces and be three-dimensional (plastic or impression prints).

We often think of fingerprints as being used primarily to help locate, identify, and eliminate suspects in criminal cases. The initial driving force behind the development of fingerprints was not solving crimes but unambiguous identification of individuals. Fingerprints, along with dentition patterns (see later in the chapter), are also important in making unequivocal identifications of human remains when more conventional methods of postmortem identification cannot be used. Fingerprints may also be thought of as one member of a class of biometric identifiers that includes retina or iris patterns of the eye, face thermography, hand geometry, and others. As the technology for rapid scanning and storage of these biometric patterns has developed, they have become more important as the basis for security systems, accessing information and secure areas, and to prevent incorrect identifications.

About Fingerprints—Their Nature and the History and Development of Their Use

It is important to understand something about the nature of fingerprints, and the properties that contribute to making them individual. We also look at how the use of fingerprints became so important in criminal records and investigations. The development of fingerprints as a means of personal identification is a major thread in the development of forensic sciences in the later 19th and earlier 20th centuries.

Nature of Fingerprints

Three features of fingerprints underlie their use as a means of personal identification: (1) every fingerprint is unique to an individual; (2) fingerprints do not change throughout life, unless there is some significant damage to the dermal layer of skin; and (3) they can be classified for convenient file searching.

It has been known for a long time that the fingertips, palms of the hands, and soles of the feet of humans and other primates have **friction ridge skin.** The skin on those areas forms a complicated pattern of "hills and valleys." The "hills" are called ridges, and the "valleys" furrows. This friction ridge skin on the fingertips form any one of a number of **basic fingerprint patterns—arches, loops, and whorls** (Figure 6.1). Within each basic pattern, there are a number of possible variations—such as plain and tented arches, and ulnar and radial loops. Loop and whorl patterns contain definable features called the *core* and the *delta* of the fingerprint (Figure 6.2). They are important in 10-print fingerprint classification, and in fingerprint comparison.

The patterns form early in embryonic development and remain constant throughout the embryonic life, birth, and life of the individual. A person's genetic composition almost certainly plays some part in determining the sizes and basic shapes of the patterns and ridges, but it cannot be the only factor. We know this because identical twins, who come from the same fertilized egg and thus have identical genetic makeup, have distinguishable fingerprints (see Figure 1.7 on page 12).

Within a fingerprint pattern are a number of features called **minutiae.** In fingerprint comparisons, these are the crucial features examiners use to actually compare the fingerprints to decide if they are or are not from the same source. Fingerprint ridges form the minutiae by (1) ending abruptly (forming an ending ridge), (2) splitting into two ridges (forming a bifurcation), or (3) being short, like the punctuation mark at the end of a sentence (forming a dot). The minutiae can combine to form

friction ridge skin

The skin on the fingertips, palms of hands, and soles of feet, characterized by patterns of hills and valleys.

basic fingerprint patterns: arches, loops, and whorls

The basic overall fingerprint patterns; variations and subcategories occur within these major classes.

minutiae

Features of the friction ridge skin pattern on fingertips that make the overall pattern individual; ending ridges, bifurcations, and dots are the primary minutiae.

Arch   Loop   Whorl

Figure 6.1   The three basic fingerprint patterns. From left to right: arch, loop, and whorl.

additional patterns. For example, two bifurcations facing each other form an island. Some fingerprint minutiae can be seen in Figure 6.3.

History and Development of the Use of Fingerprints

Archaeological excavations of old civilizations indicate that the use of fingerprint and handprint patterns as methods of personal identification dates back thousands of years in China and other early civilizations.

Methods for identifying fingerprints came to the United States from Europe, where their development dates back to the 17th and 18th centuries. The English plant morphologist Nehemiah Grew published accurate drawings of ridge patterns, and the Czech physiologist Johannes Purkinje wrote in detail about friction ridges and described some fingerprint patterns in 1823. Sir William Herschel is often credited as the first European to recognize the value of fingerprints as a means of personal identification. He was a British administrator who went to Bengal, India, to work in 1853. In his civil service work, Herschel developed the use of fingerprints as a means of controlling fraud in contracts, and false impersonations in government pension distributions and other matters. Attempts to convince others in the government to implement his practices were unsuccessful. He did demonstrate the persistence of the ridge patterns in his own fingerprints taken periodically over a period exceeding 50 years. Dr. Henry Faulds, a Scottish physician, went to India as a medical missionary in 1871. The following year he traveled to Japan. He was involved in studying fingerprints by 1879. Faulds wrote about his studies to Charles Darwin (famous for the theory of evolution). Darwin shared Faulds's letter with Sir Francis Galton, a renowned scientist and geneticist. Galton then did some fingerprint research of his own. His book *Finger Prints,* published in 1892, is regarded as a classic work. Fingerprint minutiae are sometimes called "Galton features" to recognize his contributions. Faulds noted that fingerprints could be classified, that ridge detail is unique, and that criminals might be apprehended by locating their fingerprints at scenes. Thomas Taylor, a microscopist for the U.S. Department of Agriculture, wrote in 1877 that fingerprints and palm prints might be used as identification features, especially in criminal matters.

The first scientific method of criminal identification—called **anthropometry**—was devised by Alphonse Bertillon—and is sometimes called **bertillonage.** Today, we could look at anthropometry as an older kind of biometry. Bertillon is always mentioned in discussions of the history of fingerprints, not because he contributed directly to fingerprints as an identification method, but because he laid a scientific foundation for personal identification. Ironically, the eventual acceptance of fingerprints as a scientific method for personal identification completely replaced Bertillon's method.

Bertillon worked in the Police Prefecture in Paris. He developed a system of identification based on head size, finger length, and so forth, ultimately choosing 11 measurements. The information was carefully recorded on file cards, and a system was devised for organizing the files. Eventually, the system proved its worth in identifying and helping to convict persons with prior arrest or conviction records. Bertillon went on to become director of the identification bureau of the Paris police, and police agencies in many places began using his system. Bertillonage was ultimately undone, however, when it was found that different individuals could have the same anthropometric measurements. One of the best-known examples of chance duplication came at the Leavenworth Prison. A new prisoner named Will West was having his measurements taken when a staff member began to suspect that he had encountered this profile before. Upon checking the files,

Figure 6.2
A fingerprint pattern showing the *core* and a *delta*.

anthropometry (bertillonage)

A system of bodily measurements devised by Alphonse Bertillon for personal identification of persons with criminal histories; eventually supplanted by fingerprints.

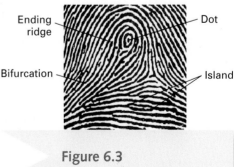

Figure 6.3
Some fingerprint minutiae: ending ridge, bifurcation, and dot. Also shown is an island, resulting from facing bifurcations.

Case Study 6.1

The First Fingerprint Identification in a Criminal Case

The illegitimate children of a woman named Rojas were murdered June 18, 1892. She acted distraught and accused a man called Velasquez, who she said committed the act because he wanted to marry her and she had refused. Velasquez maintained his innocence and had an alibi. An investigator assisting with the case from La Plata, the provincial capital, found out that another of Rojas's boyfriends had made statements about being willing to marry Rojas except for the children. The investigator, a man named Alvarez, who had been trained by Vucetich, found a bloody fingerprint at the scene and collected it. After comparison with Rojas's prints, the latent turned out to be of her right thumb. She confessed when confronted.

he discovered that the same measurements fit a William West who was already incarcerated at the prison (and unrelated to Will West though they looked a lot alike). The two did have different fingerprints. This incident, and probably others, came to convince police agency identification personnel that fingerprints represented the basis for a superior method of personal identification.

About 1893, the London Metropolitan Police ("Scotland Yard") added fingerprints to the Bertillon cards for criminals in the identification system. Soon the success of fingerprints overshadowed that of bertillonage in criminal identification, and anthropometry was abandoned in 1901.

Juan Vucetich is the Western Hemisphere's fingerprint pioneer. An employee of the police department in La Plata, Argentina, he became convinced of the value of fingerprints as a means of criminal identification and wrote a book on the subject in 1894. By 1896, the Argentine police were using fingerprints in criminal records. Vucetich devised a classification system for fingerprints that was used in Argentina and throughout South America. The first recorded case in which fingerprints were used to solve a crime took place in Argentina in 1892 (see Case 6.1).

Like William Herschel, Sir Edward Henry was also in the British Indian civil service in the late 19th century. He was interested in fingerprints and read Galton's book. He corresponded with and later visited Galton, who shared everything he had on the subject with Henry, including materials he had obtained from Herschel and Faulds. Henry worked out, and is widely known for, a fingerprint classification system that was adopted in British India, the United Kingdom, and in a modified form in the United States. Henry wrote a book entitled *Classification and Uses of Fingerprints*. In 1901, he became assistant commissioner of police for criminal identification for the London Metropolitan Police and he rose to commissioner in 1903.

In North America, the New York City civil service was using fingerprints by 1903 to prevent impersonations during examination, and fingerprints were introduced about the same time in the New York State prison system and at Leavenworth Penitentiary. A number of police departments began using fingerprints as identifiers in criminal records as well. The 1904 St. Louis World's Fair provided the venue for a chance meeting between Inspector Edward Foster of the Royal Canadian Mounted Police and Detective John Ferrier of Scotland Yard. As a result of what he learned in St. Louis, Foster convinced his superiors in the RCMP of the usefulness of fingerprints.

In 1910, a man called Thomas Jennings was arrested in Chicago and brought to trial for murder. The primary evidence against him was fingerprint evidence. The state, wanting to ensure that the fingerprint identification evidence would survive appeals to the Illinois Supreme Court, called Edward Foster of the RCMP as an expert witness. The defendant was convicted, the evidence did survive appeal, and the *Jennings* case is considered a landmark fingerprint case in American jurisprudence.

Fingerprint Classification, Management of Large Files, AFISs

Classification systems are based on ten-print sets from a person. Although very useful for managing large files of ten-print cards, the classification systems do not help in searching files for a single print. And, single prints (or partials of single prints) are generally what is recovered from crime scenes or evidence.

Classification and Large Files

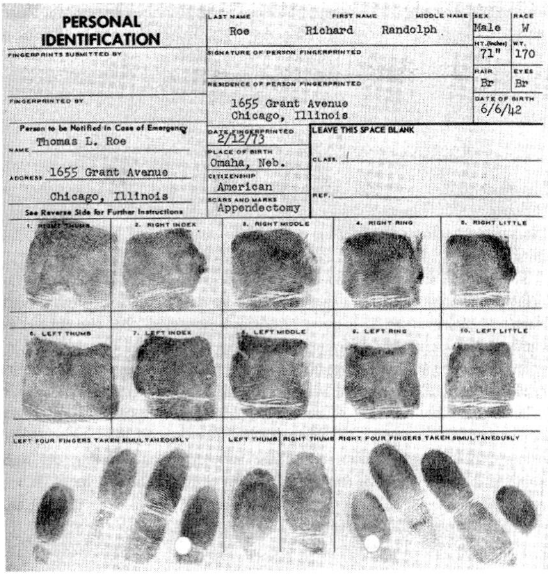

The early pioneers in the use of fingerprints for criminal identification realized that a manageable, consistent **classification system** was necessary to manage large sets of fingerprint files. In the United Kingdom and the United States, the classification systems are variants of the one Henry developed. In Argentina and other South American countries, a different system based on the one developed by Vucetich has been used. Until

Figure 6.4

A 10-print card.

fairly recently, when computer-based image file management was developed, fingerprint files consisted of 10-print cards (Figure 6.4). The modified Henry system as used in the United States is a scheme for the classification of 10-print sets, or a fingerprint card for one individual (Figure 6.5). Use of the classification system enabled efficient searching of large files of 10-print cards to see if a new 10-print set was there. The 10-print card files, especially the large ones, weren't much help in cold-searching for a single print. Of course, cards of suspects could be pulled to see if the single print belonged to any of them, but there had to be suspects. The development of computerized fingerprint search systems (see the next section) enabled cold searches (searches with no suspect) of large files for single prints or partials. For years, the fingerprint classification of wanted suspects was shown on wanted posters distributed to police agencies and displayed in public places such as post offices.

With the development and widespread adoption of computerized fingerprint storage and retrieval systems, searching large files for single and partial prints is now

classification system

A method of organizing large files of 10-print cards according to the features of the fingerprints; in the United States, a modified Henry system of classification was used.

Classification	Formula	Description
Primary	17 L **10** U 10M / **19** W 011 10	Obtained through the summation of the value of the whorls as they appear in the various fingers
Secondary	17 L10 **U** 10M / 19 **W** 011 10	The type of pattern appearing in the index fingers
Subsecondary	17 L10 U **10M** / 19 W **011** 10	The value of the ridge counts of loops or tracing of whorls of index, middle, and ring fingers
Final	17 L10 U 10M **▮** / 19 W 011 **10**	The ridge count of loops of little fingers
Major	17 **L** 10 U 10M / **▮** 19 W 011 10	The value of the ridge counts of loops or tracing of whorls of thumb
Key	**17** L10 U 10M / 19 W 011 10	The ridge count of the first loop appearing in fingers other than the little finger

Figure 6.5

Fingerprint classification by the modified Henry system.

routine. Classification is also largely unnecessary. At one time, not long ago, all fingerprint examiners and identification personnel were extensively trained in fingerprint classification using the modified Henry system, as were many police officers.

Automated Fingerprint Identification Systems (AFISs)

Computer storage and retrieval systems for fingerprints were originally developed for law enforcement applications. Efforts to develop the systems began in the early 1960s. In the United States, there was a collaboration between the FBI, which maintains the largest (and the only national) fingerprint database, and scientists at the National Bureau of Standards (which later became the National Institute of Standards and Technology, or NIST). The law-enforcement-based automated systems are commonly called Automated Fingerprint Identification Systems, or **AFISs.** There are two principal applications. The first is searching large files for the presence of a 10-print record (taken from a person). The second is searching large files for single prints, usually developed latent fingerprints (see later) from crime scenes. Fingerprint patterns are complex, and development of appropriate scanning and storage technologies and computer algorithms for efficient search and comparison was far from trivial.

By the late 1980s, there were at least five operational AFISs, four of which had been commercialized. Just about all larger jurisdictions had systems in place by the 1990s. Because different commercial vendors use different technologies, the systems are not intrinsically compatible with one another. Another important point about an AFIS is that a given person's fingerprints may be in one system, but not in others. For example, depending on the criteria for including a set of prints in the files, a large city system could have someone's prints, but the corresponding state system might not have them.

An AFIS is a complicated, expensive set of computer hardware and software for image processing and storage. A central mainframe or large server holds the database. There are multiple workstations for scanning, input, and searching. Large systems could have workstations distributed over dozens of locations in a state. Figure 6.6 shows some AFIS components.

AFISs can be viewed in perspective as one of the three types of major electronic databases for law enforcement purposes that are now available. The others are CODIS (Combined DNA Indexing System), which holds DNA profiles (Chapter 10), and NIBIN (National Integrated Ballistics Information Network), which holds searchable image information from fired bullets and cartridge cases (Chapter 8). Each of these databases holds two types of files or profiles. One is the knowns. In the AFIS, this file contains the prints of known individuals. Any questioned specimen, image, or profile can be searched for in the "known" file, and if it is found, its source is thereby identified. The other type is often called the "forensic" file. It consists of images or profiles from unsolved cases, the sources of which are not known. In the AFIS case, for example, the forensic file contains images of developed latent single fingerprints from unsolved cases. It contains evidence fingerprints that have not yet been associated with an individual. The file is valuable to investigators, however, in that it allows cases that are not obviously related to be connected because they have the same fingerprints. This kind of connection allows investigators to share information and leads, thus increasing the probability of apprehending a suspect.

The FBI criminal fingerprint database, called IAFIS for Integrated AFIS, is now available to law enforcement agencies nationally. It has been estimated that about 15 percent of latent prints entered into an AFIS result in identifications.

Another important application for AFISs is reexamination of unsolved older cases. Routine searching of latent or other single prints was not possible until fairly recently. Thus, there are many unsolved cases with fingerprints of a possible perpetrator in which it was not possible to search at the time. In addition, individuals whose prints were not in the file at the time of the crime and are later arrested can then be associated with the earlier crime. This chapter's lead case illustrates this point.

AFISs

Automated Fingerprint Identification Systems; several AFISs are commercially available for the imaging, storage, and rapid retrieval of single fingerprints; national system maintained by the FBI is called IAFIS (for Integrated AFIS).

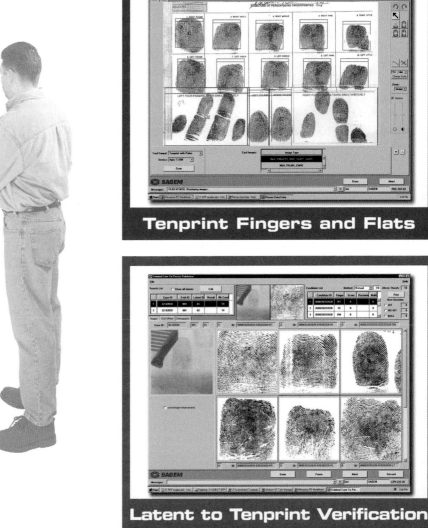

(a)   (b)

Figure 6.6   (A) A live-scan station for taking fingerprints without paper or ink directly into an AFIS.
(B) Two workscreens of an AFIS.

(Images courtesy of Sagem Morpho, Inc., Tacoma, WA)

As we noted earlier, an AFIS should be seen today as part of a larger picture that includes an array of automated systems for human biometrics—the use of some type of body metric for identification. It may be that the Bertillon system of anthropometry previously described was the first well-defined system of human biometry that made use of a database. Today, systems based on retinal scans, iris scans, and rapid fingerprint scanning, followed by quick comparison with database records, are available for security purposes. Criminal identification and related law enforcement applications of automated fingerprint systems remain very important, but AFISs and other biometric systems are rapidly finding their way into use as public and private security methods. These systems can help control entry and/or access into computers or structures, can identify persons for security purposes to prevent identity theft, and can help control welfare or social services fraud. Biometrics is further discussed later in the chapter.

Collection and Preservation of Fingerprint Evidence

Most of the time, collection of fingerprint evidence involves collecting and submitting the intact item that bears, or might bear, the fingerprint. At scenes, fingerprints are frequently not visible, but latent (see the next section). Latent prints must be developed using a physical or chemical technique to make the print clearly visible for comparison.

At a scene, logic may suggest collecting items for fingerprint processing at the laboratory. These items would be those that might have been touched or handled by people involved in the case. The purpose might be to try and identify fingerprints so a cold search can be done in AFIS to try and identify or eliminate possible suspects. Another purpose might be to find out who among several people involved in a case touched or handled an item.

At times, fingerprints may be on items that would be difficult or impractical to collect for processing at the laboratory. In addition, some crime scene investigators have knowledge and training in the development of latent fingerprints at the scene. Whether to attempt development of latent prints at a scene is a decision that has to be made in each case. It will be based on the practicality of submitting the intact item, on the latent print knowledge and skills of the investigators, and to some extent on which development technique is judged best in the circumstances.

Classically, powder-dusted fingerprints were collected by tape lifting. This is still a good technique. But powder dusting is no longer among the best choices as a technique for developing latent prints. Latent prints developed by other techniques at a scene should be carefully photographed, and the developed print then documented and collected if possible. The fingerprint should be documented by photography from a distance to show where the fingerprint lies in relationship to surrounding objects and up close to capture enough of the fine detail for comparison. With most techniques other than powder dusting, collection will involve submitting the intact item or object.

The principles of evidence documentation (Chapter 3) apply to fingerprint evidence. The location of prints at the scene and their orientation, or the location of objects or items that are later found to have prints, must be documented.

Latent Prints and Their Development

Developing latent fingerprints, to try and make them suitable for comparison, is an important aspect of crime scene and evidence processing.

Types of Evidentiary Fingerprints

Essentially, three types of prints may be encountered at crime scenes and/or on items of evidence: visible (patent), plastic (impression), and latent. A **visible (patent) print** is one that needs no "enhancement" or "development" to be clearly recognizable as a fingerprint. Such a print is often made from grease, dark oil, dirt, ink, blood, or other visible material. It may be suitable for comparison with no additional processing. A **plastic (impression) print** is a recognizable fingerprint indentation in a soft receiving surface, such as butter, Silly Putty, tar, drying paint, and so on. These prints have distinct three-dimensional character but are immediately recognizable and often require no further processing. A **latent print** is one that, by definition, requires additional processing to be rendered clearly visible, and thus potentially suitable for comparison. The processing of latent prints to render them visible, and hopefully suitable for comparison, is called **development** (or **enhancement** or **visualization**). Great progress has been made in this area by the clever applications of chemical and physical principles, coupled with a better understanding of the composition of latent fingerprint residues.

---

visible (patent) print

A fingerprint impression that is visible with no enhancement or any special illumination.

plastic (impression) print

A three-dimensional fingerprint indentation in a soft receiving surface, such as tar, margarine, or Silly Putty.

latent print

A fingerprint impression that requires development or special illumination to reveal the ridge detail in sufficient detail for comparison.

development (enhancement, visualization)

Physical or chemical treatment or special illumination, or a combination of both, that enhance the visibility of ridge detail of a latent fingerprint impression sufficiently to enable comparison.

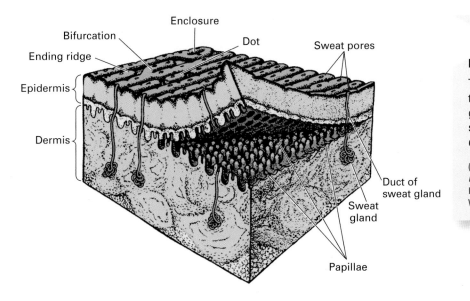

Figure 6.7

Friction Ridge Skin.

The diagram shows the epidermis and the dermis layers of skin, sweat glands and their ducts and pores, and several fingerprint minutiae on the epidermal surface.

(Modified from *The Science of Fingerprints: Classification and Uses,* Federal Bureau of Investigation, U.S. Government Printing Office, Washington, DC)

Development of Latent Fingerprints

Composition of Latent Print Residue   Latent print developing techniques are based on using physical or chemical methods to target one or more components of the latent fingerprint residue itself. Friction ridge skin (Figure 6.7) has pores through which small sweat glands can empty their contents onto the skin surface. These sweat glands make a watery type of sweat, the composition of which forms a basis for latent fingerprint residue. Another type of sweat gland in other parts of the body secretes a more oily sweat. The oily material could become part of the latent residue from a person touching portions of his or her or another person's body such as forehead and hair, which have that type of residue, thereby transferring it to their hands. In addition, an almost unlimited variety of substances from the environment can get on to the friction ridge skin and can then be deposited with the latent residue when the person touches a surface. Thus, there are a number of common constituents of most latent print residues based on the composition of sweat, but the proportions can vary, and many other compounds and materials from the environment could be present. Table 6.1 shows some of the common constituents of the sweat that make up fingerprint residue.

Methods for developing latent prints were devised based on knowledge of the latent print residue composition. A method known to be capable of visualizing one of the compounds or elements present in latent residue is applied to try and target that compound or element. For the application to be successful, investigators must be able to apply the method to evidentiary fingerprints on the variety of surfaces where they are found, and without destroying the integrity of the impression pattern. The methods commonly used fall broadly into three groups: physical, chemical, and combination or special illumination methods (which often involve laser or narrowband pass forensic light sources).

Scene or Laboratory   When potential latent prints are recognized at a scene, investigators and scene technicians have a choice: apply latent print development methods at the scene or collect the relevant item or object intact and submit it to the latent print section of the laboratory.

Any item, object, or surface at a scene thought to contain latent prints should be documented by photographs and sketches. Smaller objects or items that are easy to collect and submit should be taken to the laboratory. If it is impractical or impossible

Table 6.1

Some components of latent print residue originating from sweat

Ions: sodium, potassium, calcium, iron, chloride, fluoride, bromide, iodide, bicarbonate, phosphate, sulfate, ammonium and some magnesium, zinc, copper, cobalt, lead and manganese
Proteins
Amino acids (serine, glycine, ornithine, alanine, aspartic acid)
Glucose
Lactic acid
Urea
Pyruvic acid
Creatine
Creatinine
Glycogen
Uric acid
Fatty acids
Triglycerides
Sterols

to remove a surface or object, investigators may have to apply latent development techniques at the scene. Depending on their training and experience, they may want to call on latent print examiners from a forensic lab or identification unit for consultation or assistance. Any fingerprints developed at the scene must be thoroughly photographed and lifted if possible. If neither the developed print nor the object can be moved or collected, the photographs will be the only record of the fingerprint.

Physical Methods Physical methods do not involve any chemicals or reactions. They usually work by applying some type of fine particles to the fingerprint residue; these particles adhere better to the print residue than to the background material, creating a contrasting ridge pattern on the background.

The best-known physical method is **powder dusting**—a mainstay of latent fingerprint detection. The most common powders are inorganic and come in several colors. A variety of brushes is also available. The principle of powder dusting is simply that the powder particles adhere to the latent residue. Careful use of the proper brush and powder often reults in the development of excellent prints. Black or chemist's gray powders are generally superior to other colors. These powders are produced in a way that yields more uniform particle size and generally produces better contrast. Figure 6.8 illustrates the technique. Also shown is the tape lifting of the dusted latent impression. The tape lift is then mounted on a backing with a color that provides maximum contrast with the powder (e.g., white backing for black powder). One-piece lifters (so-called hinge lifters) are commercially available for this purpose. A powder-dusted, lifted latent fingerprint is also shown in Figure 6.9A.

The magnetic brush is a variant of the simple brush and powder combination. The original trademarked version is called the Magna Brush. Actually it contains a small retractable magnet and is not a real brush at all. The magnet protruding from its tube holder is placed close to the magnetic powder, which is attracted to the magnet (and the particles are attracted to one another), thus forming a loose aggregate that acts as the "brush." The magnetic brush uses special magnetic powders that can be obtained in several colors. The principle of magnetic powder enhancement is the same as for conventional powder; namely, adherence of the fine particles to moisture or fatty components of the residue (Figure 6.9B). The **magnetic brush technique** is applicable to a larger variety of surfaces (especially vertical surfaces) than conventional power dusting is. It is also a gentler technique, in the sense that there is no actual brush, and thus no bristles, so it is less possible to damage the latent pattern in the brushing process.

Another physical latent print developing procedure involves **small particle reagent (SPR).** Typically applied by spraying or dipping, the most common

`powder dusting`

An old but tried-and-true method for visualizing fingerprints on nonporous surfaces.

`magnetic brush technique`

A variant of powder dusting that uses a magnet and magnetic particles instead of a brush and powder.

`small particle reagent (SPR)`

A formulation of small inorganic particles in special suspension that can be applied to latent print impressions to enhance ridge pattern features; can be useful with weathered latents, especially those that have been exposed to moisture.

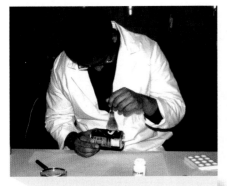

Figure 6.8A

Powder Dusting and Transparent Tape Lift Techniques.
(A) Dusting a soda can with black fingerprint powder.

Figure 6.8B

(B) Using fingerprint lifting tape to lift dusted print.

Figure 6.8C

(C) Lifted print placed on a card of contrasting color for easy viewing and preservation.

formulation of SPR is molybdenum disulfide (a heavy, black, very finely divided powder) suspended in a detergent solution. The particles adhere to the lipid components of the residue. SPR is most commonly used on evidence that has been wet or has been recovered from water.

Chemical Methods   Classically, the chemical techniques were treatment with silver nitrate, iodine, or ninhydrin. Silver nitrate is now only used as part of physical developers (see later). Elemental iodine, which is a deep purple solid, is one of the compounds in nature that *sublimes;* that is, it can pass from the solid to the vapor state without becoming a liquid. Solid iodine crystals sublime easily, with moderate warming producing a purple vapor that dissolves in oily materials to produce a deep brown coloration. The iodine vapor can be directed toward a latent fingerprint with an iodine fuming gun. Alternatively, an object to be "fumed" can be placed in a closed cabinet, which is then filled with iodine fumes by warming a small dish of iodine crystals in the bottom of the cabinet. Iodine treatment of latent prints is usually called **iodine fuming,** because the latent print residue is actually exposed to the iodine vapors (fumes). Even though it has long been placed under the "chemical methods" category of latent print development methods, the iodine probably doesn't react chemically with any of the components in the residue. It probably interacts with the lipid components in such a way that it is selectively dissolved by the lipid residue, giving the ridge features a dirty-brown colored appearance (Figure 6.9C). The iodine-developed color is not stable in the latent print and the iodine will soon re-vaporize to return the latent print to its original colorless condition. Therefore, iodine prints must be quickly photographed. There are also chemical methods for converting iodine prints to a permanent color that will not fade. The traditional method involved using starch solution for that purpose, but 7,8-benzoflavone (α-naphthoflavone) treatment is the preferred method today. Iodine fuming is used primarily on inherently valuable items precisely because of its impermanence or where one wants to visualize where a print is located before applying another visualization technique.

One of the oldest chemical procedures for visualizing latent prints makes use of **ninhydrin.** Ninhydrin reacts with compounds called amino acids—amino acids are the building blocks of proteins, and they are found in fingerprint residue—to form another compound called Ruhemann's purple Ninhydrin can be applied by spraying, painting, or dipping. It reacts slowly unless the process is accelerated by heat and humidity. Ninhydrin used to be made up in Freon 113 (a compound similar to the one used in air conditioners), but the concern over the effect of these compounds on the earth's ozone layer culminated in the signing of the Montreal Protocol in 1987, resulting in a ban on the Freon. Now, ninhydrin can be made up in several

iodine fuming

A latent print development technique in which solid iodine is sublimed to iodine vapor, which can then deposit on the ridge patterns of a latent print impression, especially on porous surfaces.

ninhydrin

A chemical for latent print impression enhancement especially on porous surfaces; postninhydrin treatments can further increase the value of this method.

Figure 6.9A
Latent fingerprint visualized by powder dusting.

Figure 6.9B
Latent fingerprint visualized by dusting with magnetic powder.

Figure 6.9C
Latent fingerprint visualized by iodine fuming.

Figure 6.9D
Latent fingerprint visualized by treatment with ninhydrin reagent.

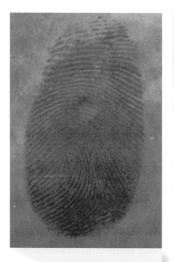

Figure 6.9E
Latent fingerprint visualized by treatment with ninhydrin, followed by zinc chloride, then viewed under a laser.

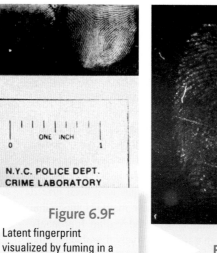

Figure 6.9F
Latent fingerprint visualized by fuming in a closed chamber with Super Glue (cyanoacrylate).

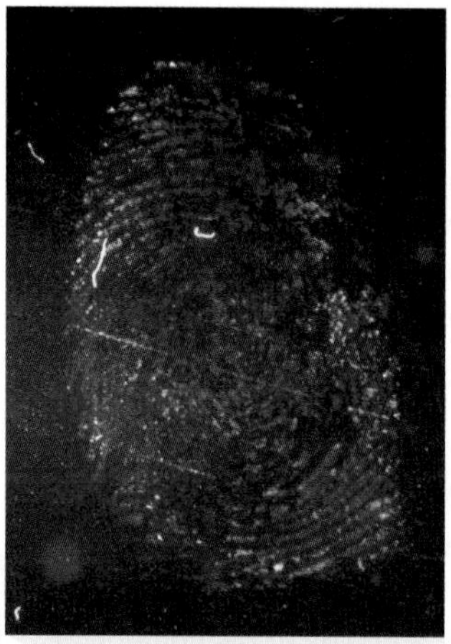

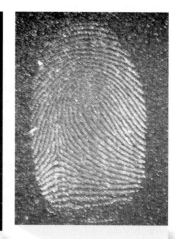

Figure 6.9G
Latent fingerprint visualized by Super Glue fuming and washing with laser dye Ardrox to produce a fluorescent print.

Figure 6.9H
Plastic fingerprint (impression) visualized by side (oblique) lighting.

different solvent systems. One selects the solvent system depending on the type of absorbent material to be processed and what else is present on the evidence.

Ninhydrin develops bluish-purple fingerprints (Figure 6.9D) and is extremely useful on porous surfaces (such as paper). Currently, ninhydrin is often used as a preliminary treatment in processing, followed by further treatment of the ninhydrin-developed prints with other chemicals, and subsequent viewing under laser or alternative light source illumination (see later). Figure 6.9E shows a ninhydrin-developed print, which has been treated with $ZnCl_2$, viewed under blue-green light.

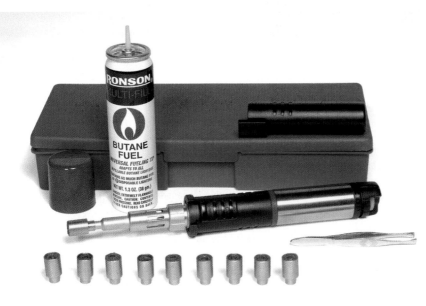

Figure 6.10
Small handheld device used to deliver Super Glue (cyanoacrylate) vapor to a latent print, usually at a crime scene.

The most important other chemical procedure is treatment with **Super Glue (cyanoacrylate).** Super Glue "enhancement" of latent print residue was first observed by scientists at the National Police Agency in Japan. The method quickly caught on and is now used by latent print examiners all over the world. In the early 1980s, fingerprint examiners in the U.S. Army Criminal Investigation Laboratory in Japan, and a little later in the U.S. Bureau of Alcohol, Tobacco and Firearms (ATF) Laboratory, introduced Super Glue fuming for latent print development in the United States. Super Glue will fume (vaporize) with gentle heating, and the fumes will interact with latent print residue by polymerizing and yielding a stable friction ridge impression pattern off-white in color (Figure 6.9F). Items to be processed with Super Glue are usually placed into fuming cabinets where the glue is induced to fill the cabinet with vapors. Glue vaporization is very slow by itself, so it is usually accelerated with strong alkali or heating. Handheld devices have been designed to vaporize Super Glue for fingerprint work (Figure 6.10). Super Glue is an excellent method of developing latent fingerprints on many surfaces. Super Glue–developed prints, like ninhydrin-developed ones, can be further treated before examination. The simplest enhancement of a glue-developed print is powder dusting. Other posttreatments of Super Glue prints include **dye stains.** Because the Super Glue ridges will selectively absorb certain dyes, they can be "dye stained" to make them luminescent or fluorescent. Illumination with a laser or alternate light sources at the appropriate wavelengths for the particular dye used produces greatly enhanced visibility of the print. Gentian violet, coumarin 540 laser dye, Ardrox (Figure 6.9G), rhodamine-6G, and other chemical treatments have been used to produce Super Glue–developed print luminescence under alternate light or laser illumination.

Another chemical method is the use of **physical developer.** The process is obviously misnamed, because it involves chemical reactions. Physical developer enhancement is essentially a photographic process, based on the production of metallic silver on a latent fingerprint image by means of a reaction involving silver ions and an oxidation/reduction reaction involving iron salts. It is thought that physical developer reacts with lipid (fatty) material in the fingerprint residue. The procedure can be used for latent prints on paper, nonabsorbent surfaces, and pressure-sensitive tapes. It has been reported that physical developer sometimes works on latent prints that did not develop with ninhydrin. This result makes sense considering that this procedure is based on reactions with lipid components rather than the soluble amino acids.

Special Types of Illumination and Combination Methods

Sometimes, a latent fingerprint can be visualized simply by illuminating it from an oblique angle (Figure 6.9H). This technique may work with white light or with what is often called

Super Glue (cyanoacrylate)

An adhesive material that polymerizes (the chemicals in it react to form a solid matrix) in place when applied to surfaces; Super Glue vapors, produced by heating it, interact with latent fingerprint residue and produce the solid matrix polymer on the ridges.

dye stains

Chemicals that stain cyanoacrylate polymer and can thus be used to further enhance the visibility of Super Glue–developed latent prints; some of the chemicals require the use of alternate light or laser illumination.

physical developer

A special silver-based solution for enhancing latent print impressions by reacting with the fatty (lipid) components; a chemical method.

Postninhydrin and Post-Super-Glue Treatments

In the book's Appendix *Scientific Tools of the Trade—Methods of Forensic Science,* the interactions of light with materials are discussed. Light impinging on a material may be reflected, transmitted, or absorbed. When light is absorbed, it brings about changes in the electronic structure of the material absorbing it. One potential change in the material is a state of temporary excitation. This excited state is not stable, and the material tends to relax back to the original state fairly quickly. In the process of relaxing, energy may be given off in the form of fluorescence or of phosphorescence. Fluoresced or phosphoresced light is always of lower energy (longer wavelength) than the light causing excitation of the material, because some energy is lost during the process of excitation and relaxation.

Different wavelengths of light are absorbed differently by different classes of chemicals. This behavior is the basis of spectrophotometry. A spectrophotometer is essentially an instrument that exposes a chemical or material to a range of wavelengths or light and can detect whether the material absorbs a particular wavelength or not. The result is plotted out pictorially on paper, or on a computer monitor, and is called a spectrum. There are also instruments called spectrofluorometers that can monitor fluoresced light as a function of excitation light wavelength.

Latent fingerprints treated with ninhydrin have formed Ruhemann's purple. Ruhemann's purple can, in turn, be treated with chemicals that form chemical complexes with it. These complexes have particular light absorption-emission characteristics. In the same way, Super Glue–treated fingerprints can be treated with dyes that have particular light absorption-emission characteristics. These characteristics can be exploited to help better visualize treated latent prints.

In the simplest case, suppose one of the complexes or dyes absorbs red light of the visible part of the spectrum and reflects green light. We could then use an instrument or device to impinge light onto the material and look for green reflectance. The easiest way to do this might involve using a viewing filter that transmits the green light. In this kind of situation, a so-called alternate light source and viewing filter could be used. An alternate light source is really just a high-intensity white light source. Filters can be used to select a particular output color of light. Similarly, filtered viewers can be used to enable the observer to see particular wavelengths of light (that are reflected by the material).

Intense white light sources can also cause fluorescence or phosphorescence in some chemicals. From what has been said above, it should be clear that a particular wavelength of the "white" light is being absorbed, and thus giving rise to the fluorescence or phosphorescence. Alternate light source outputs can be filtered to select a narrowband of wavelengths containing the wavelength that is absorbed by the material of interest. Lasers are extremely intense light sources whose beams have particular vibrational characteristics while traveling through space and are of a single wavelength. For a laser to be useful as an excitation source, the material of interest (like the complex or the dye in the latent print cases) must absorb that wavelength of light. Thus, chemicals capable of being excited by certain wavelengths of light can be formed by appropriate latent print treatments. Then, lasers or alternate light sources can be used to produce reflected light, or fluoresced emissions, that can be visualized, and make the ridge characteristics of the fingerprint that much clearer. Certain lasers can be used to help visualize untreated latent prints. That fact means that there is something in the latent print residue that can absorb the laser light wavelength, and then give off phosphorescence. The Argon laser, with an output wavelength of 488 nm, has been used quite a bit in latent fingerprint enhancement techniques.

---

alternate light source

A high-intensity white light source filtered to emit only a limited range of wavelengths of visible light.

laser

A special light source that emits light that is of a single wavelength (monochromatic light) and, further, vibrates in a single plane; extremely efficient at exciting chemicals that absorb its wavelength, and can then fluoresce or phosphoresce as the molecules relax.

an **alternate light source,** or "alternative" light source. These are special, high-intensity light sources that often have filters to control wavelength (see the "More on Science" box). Sometimes, latent fingerprints show up better under illumination by certain wavelengths of light.

Alternative light sources are also regularly used in connection with some of the various chemical treatment methods discussed earlier. Often, the chemical treatments result in producing a compound that has a specific fluorescence when illuminated with light of a particular wavelength. This principle is the basis for using alternative light sources and lasers to visualize latent fingerprints. A **laser** emits high-intensity light beams of a single wavelength. Several methods have been developed to take advantage of the excitation wavelengths afforded by the lasers available. The undisputed pioneer in this field was the late Dr. E. Roland Menzel of Texas Tech University. The most recent development in this context has been the development of luminescent nanoparticles for latent fingerprint enhancement.

Bloody Fingerprints and Other Special Conditions
Bloody fingerprints have a special value because they often allow experts to put a time on when a fingerprint print was made. One of the limitations on latent fingerprints is that when an individual has normal access to the crime scene it is not possible to say that a print was made at the time of a crime or had been made some time before or even shortly after the incident. Bloody prints must have been made at the time of bleeding and before the blood dries (Case 6.2).

Bloody fingerprints are not really "latent," in the sense that there is at least some faint visibility from the blood, and investigators may recognize that even a very faint pattern in blood could be a fingerprint (or palm print or footprint). However, the ridge characteristics may not be sufficiently defined to make the print suitable for comparison, or an area may have so little residual blood that prints are not visible at all. Under these conditions, use of a blood enhancement reagent might be considered. In this situation, investigators need to think about whether they should try DNA profiling of the blood that is forming the apparent ridge patterns. Substantial published evidence indicates that most latent fingerprint enhancement procedures, including those designed for bloody prints, do not interfere with subsequent DNA profiling. But this situation is one where discussion among latent print examiners, DNA analysts, and investigators is important. Bloody fingerprint enhancement reagents are usually applied as a very fine spray to keep from washing the print away. Some of the recipes produce a reagent that is not very stable in solution and thus has a short shelf life. These need to be prepared shortly before use. Further, there are potentially serious chemical hazards associated with some of the ingredients, so some training and experience are required to prepare and use these reagents. Many bloody fingerprint enhancement reagents are based on the "peroxidase reaction" chemicals (phenolphthalin, leucomalachite green, tetramethylbenzidine, etc.) that we talk about in connection with presumptive blood testing (Chapter 9). These interact with the hemoglobin portion of the blood. There are also some recipes and techniques based on general protein staining dyes like Amido Black and Coomassie Blue. They are generally less hazardous and easier to use than the peroxidase reaction chemicals.

Fingerprints deposited on tape, especially on the sticky surface, present another special situation. Techniques for visualization include staining with crystal violet and a material called "sticky side powder." Crystal violet stains skin cells trapped by the adhesive a deep violet. Sticky side powder is actually composed of lycopodium (a plant) pollen mixed with a detergent and water. The sticky side powder slurry is painted onto the sticky side of the tape with a brush, and the tape is then rinsed off with water. The tiny, brightly colored pollen grains preferentially adhere to the skin cells, making them visible. The process can be repeated until the desired contrast has been achieved.

Another special situation is the development of latent prints on human skin, almost always on a decedent's body. The idea is to bring up the fingerprints of those who have touched the person. In murder cases, especially involving manual strangulations, the murderer's fingerprints might be on the victim's skin. A variety of different techniques have been tried for this purpose over many years, but the success stories are few and far between. Although a generally useful, robust procedure has not yet been devised, tenting the area of suspected fingerprints and applying Super Glue vapors will occasionally work under ideal conditions.

Systematic Approaches   Most latent fingerprint examiners probably use a "systematic approach" even if they don't say it quite that way. The idea is to apply latent development techniques in a way that maximizes the number of identifiable prints. The least destructive technique is applied first, and techniques are generally

Case Study 6.2

Bloody Fingerprint Helps Place a Suspect at a Homicide Scene at the Time of the Homicide

An elderly man was found dead in a pool of blood in his bed. He had few if any valuable possessions and lived on Social Security. Nevertheless, he was admired in the neighborhood for helping others in time of need. He had become close to a troubled youth who ran errands for him and came to see him and talk frequently. When the man's modest house was processed after the murder, the young man's prints were found everywhere. This had limited significance since he was known to be a frequent visitor. During the careful processing of the scene, however, a small patent print in blood was found on the back of the victim's headboard in a position consistent with where one would place one's hand to hold onto the headboard while attacking the man in the bed. Experts found that this print also belonged to the youth, and the blood was consistent with the victim. This established the youth's presence during the attack on the victim and proved to be a major piece of physical evidence in bringing him to justice.

Figure 6.11A

Flowchart for sequence of reagents to use to develop a latent print on a nonporous surface.

Figure 6.11B

Flowchart for sequence of reagents to use to develop latent prints on a porous surface.

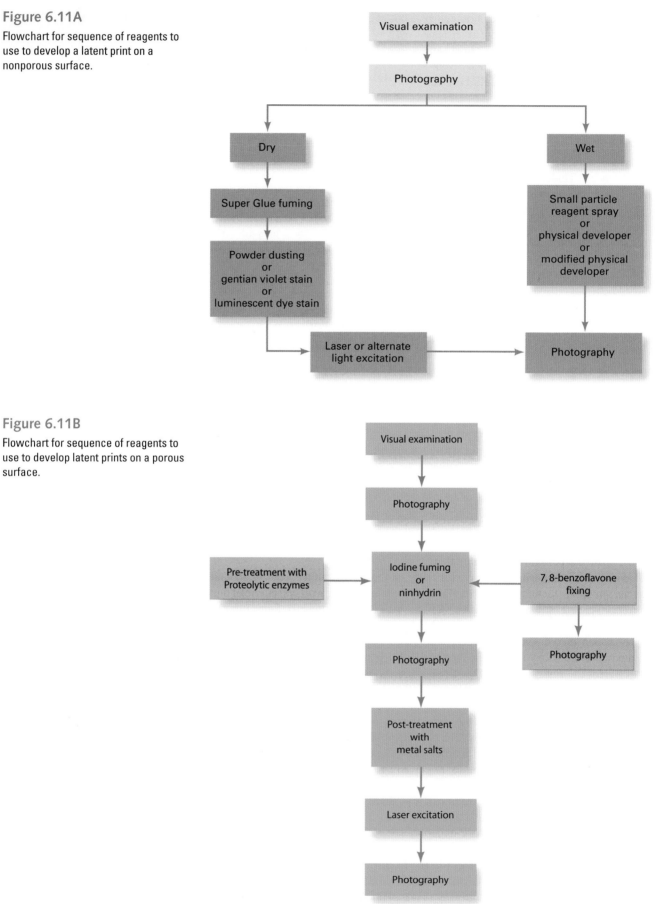

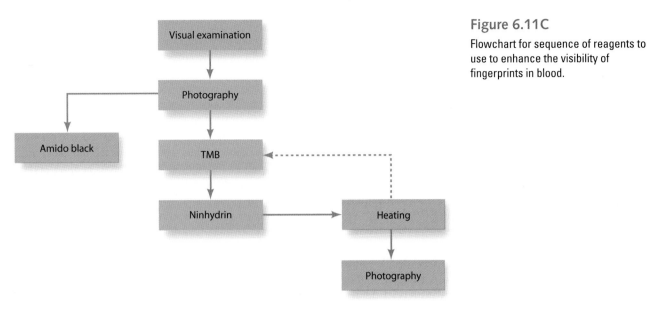

Figure 6.11C

Flowchart for sequence of reagents to use to enhance the visibility of fingerprints in blood.

applied in an order that allows the maximum number to be used until a "suitable" latent (one deemed suitable for comparison) is obtained.

Systematic approaches vary according to the surface (or substratum) on which the latent is located. Porous surfaces, such as paper, for example, call for a different set of techniques applied in a different order than nonporous surfaces. Flowcharts illustrating these approaches are shown in Figure 6.11.

Fingerprint Comparison and Identification

Everything we have talked about in this chapter—indeed, the reason there is a chapter on fingerprints at all—comes down to the use of fingerprints to identify persons. As noted earlier, the uniqueness of fingerprints is a matter of common knowledge. Ads and commercials commonly use phrases like ". . . as unique as a fingerprint," and so on. Even the term "DNA fingerprints," as undesirable and sometimes misleading as it is, was coined to reflect the notion that a DNA profile might be as "individual" as a fingerprint. And infrared spectra of pure compounds are sometimes called "chemical fingerprints."

David Ashbaugh, among others, has noted that fingerprint individuality, and therefore fingerprint identification, is based on four premises:

1. Friction ridges develop in fetuses before birth in their definitive form.
2. Friction ridges remain unchanged throughout life with the exception of permanent scars.
3. The friction ridge patterns and their details are unique and not repeated.
4. The ridge patterns vary within certain boundaries and allow the patterns to be classified.

Fingerprint examiners are generally extensively trained and required to accumulate significant experience before they are given the responsibility of making identifications in cases. Thus, in addition to the general principles and approaches used to make identifications, the knowledge, training, and experience of the individual examiner is an important factor. In law enforcement situations, identifications are always made by trained, often certified, examiners. Where unambiguous identification of someone arrested is the goal, inked prints from a person may be compared with a set of inked prints on file to determine if they came from the same individual. The more complex problem is where the examiner will be comparing a developed latent print, from a crime scene or a piece of evidence, with inked prints from a known person or persons. Evidence fingerprints may not be clear and/or may represent only a small

suitability for examination

A latent print impression that has sufficient ridge detail for an examiner to determine it to be suitable for comparison with known print impressions.

ACE-V method

An acronym that stands for analysis, comparison, evaluation, verification, which are the four steps in the analysis and comparison of a latent print impression with a known.

level I, level II, and level III detail

Terms used to describe the overall fingerprint pattern, such as loop, whorl, arch (level I), the minutiae (level II), and pore numbers, locations and relationships, and the shape and size of ridge features (level III).

portion of the finger; therefore, the quality and amount of fingerprint ridge detail will seldom be ideal in evidence prints. If someone's fingerprints are in an AFIS, searches can quickly whittle down the number of possible suspects to a manageable size, but an examiner, not a computer, actually makes the final identification.

In examinations of latents, the first issue is determining what is called **suitability for examination.** Here, the examiner must decide if sufficient quality and quantity of the ridge detail is present in the latent fingerprint to make it possible to do a comparison with a known. This determination also requires training and experience. Once a latent is judged suitable for comparison, known prints that might match the latent must be sought. Such knowns might be obtained through an AFIS search, or from certain persons who are suspected—their prints might be taken or may already be on file.

The overall process an examiner uses has been described by Ashbaugh as the **ACE-V method,** for "analysis," "comparison," "evaluation," that comprise the formal process, then "verification." The examiner must first analyze the latent, figure out its proper orientation, decide if there are any color reversals or other unusual circumstances, decide suitability, then proceed to the comparison. Comparison with the known fingerprints takes place at several levels. The overall pattern and ridge flow (called **level I detail**) must be examined. Next, the minutiae (called **level II detail**) are compared, point by point, as to type and location. Finally, another level of detail (called **level III detail**), consisting of pore shape, locations, numbers, and relationships, and the shape and size of ridge features, is compared. Any unexplained difference between known and latent during this process would result in the conclusion that the known is *excluded* as a source of the latent. This is one possible outcome of the evaluation decision. If every compared feature is consistent with the known, and enough features are sufficiently unique when considered as a whole, the examiner may make an identification. This is the other possible evaluation decision outcome. Since peer review is a feature of most scientific endeavors, Ashbaugh notes that verification of conclusions by an independent examiner is a necessary practice.

Thus, submitting a latent or an item bearing latents to a fingerprint examiner—assuming there is a suspect—could result in several possible outcomes: identification (the latent was made by the suspect); exclusion (the latent was not made by the suspect); the latent is unsuitable for comparison; or inconclusive (the latent is suitable, but there are not enough features to form a definite conclusion).

There has been considerable discussion in the identification literature about defining the criteria for making a fingerprint identification. For many years in some jurisdictions, a "minimum number of points" rule was followed. During that time, if the rule was "12 points to make an identification," the examiner had to find that many or more points of comparison or could not make the identification. Over time, it became clear that such an absolute rule was not a proper basis for making decisions in every situation. The International Association for Identification (IAI), the organization that, by and large, sets peer standards for the fingerprint community, adopted a resolution in 1973 that no minimum number of features is required for making a fingerprint identification. This position was reiterated in a slightly modified form in 1995. Most fingerprint examiners subscribe to this principle. Discussions of the criteria for making a fingerprint identification lead naturally into discussions of the basis for fingerprint uniqueness. Although the subject has been discussed in the literature, it is beyond the scope of this chapter.

The Fingerprint Identification Profession

We noted earlier that identification of persons by fingerprints was primarily a law enforcement function for a long time. So the "fingerprint identification" profession is primarily within the law enforcement community. Now, however, with live-scan and AFIS technologies working together to bring fingerprint identification onboard as a security strategy, many of the fingerprint and other "biometric" identification technology specialists might be seen as part of the "identification" profession.

In the past several decades, a number of trends have worked to further professionalize fingerprint examiners in law enforcement. People entering the profession today have more formal education than was once true. The extraordinary progress in latent development methods previously noted has demanded that fingerprint examiners understand much more chemistry and physics than ever before. The IAI has been a positive force, through facilitation of discussions, encouragement of research and scientific approaches, and through its professional journal, the *Journal of Forensic Identification*. Journals are commonly and routinely the primary, peer-reviewed source of original research in scientific fields, and the IAI journal rose to fulfill that role for the fingerprint and identification sciences. The IAI has also been the primary peer standard-setting group in the identification sciences. And the latent fingerprint certification program is operated by IAI. Today, there is a so-called SWG (Scientific Working Group) on friction ridge analysis, study, and technology (SWGFAST) that started in 1995. Like all TWGs (Technical Working Groups) and SWGs, its purpose is to arrive at consensus standards for the professional area. In the 1990s, DNA typing and profiling became a major feature of forensic science. That, coupled with the Supreme Court's *Daubert* decision, has forced many forensic disciplines besides DNA to take a careful look at their underlying assumptions and criteria for evaluating matches and identifications. These trends are likely to continue.

Fingerprint examiners today have a wide range of educational backgrounds, but as we have noted, the trend is in the direction of more education. The SWGFAST recommends that trainees hired after 2005 should have a four-year college degree. In addition, a considerable period of training is involved in learning the fingerprint specialty. Individuals may be hired in some agencies primarily as AFIS technicians, to maintain systems, scan images into the system, and so forth. They do not need the level of training required for someone who wants to be an independent latent print examiner. More and more employers are requiring the IAI latent print certification as a condition of continued employment. The certification requires passing a challenging written test, demonstrating competency in comparisons, and then maintaining a record of activity and continuing education during the certification period.

Although fingerprint examination may be the oldest of the forensic science disciplines, it is still one of the most interesting and exciting. The development and widespread use of AFIS has reenergized this field by making it a valuable investigative tool rather than just a confirmatory one. More cases may be solved by fingerprints than by any other single type of physical evidence.

Other Patterns for Person Identification

In Chapter 1 we talked about the concepts of identification, individualization, and reconstruction, noting that these three are often cited as the key ingredients of a forensic investigation. In that context, identification meant classification. We noted that pattern evidence analysts (document, fingerprint, and firearms examiners) use the term "identification" to mean individualization, just as we usually do in the common language. In this section, we are really talking about some types of patterns other than fingerprints that can be used to "identify" specific people.

Palm and Sole Prints

The palms of the hands and soles of the feet have friction ridge skin just like the fingertips. As a result, these surfaces have "fingerprint-like" patterns on them that can be used for identification just like fingerprints. Palm and sole prints are handled exactly like fingerprints in terms of recognition, enhancement, collection, documentation, and comparison.

These impressions are not seen as often at scenes as fingerprints. In addition, there are no standardized classification systems for palm or sole prints in widespread use, and these impressions are not organized and stored in databases like an AFIS. Thus,

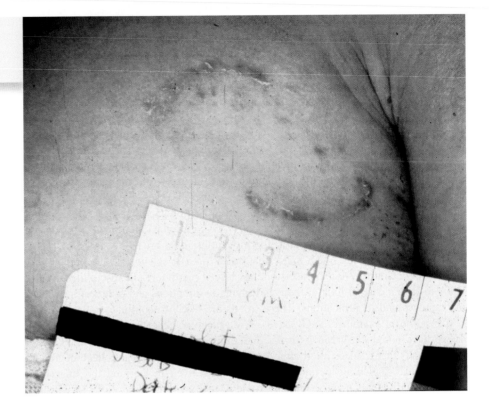

Figure 6.12

Bite mark on the breast of a victim.

an examiner can't look for a palm or sole pattern in a file. There must be a suspect or a limited group of suspects to provide known impressions for comparison.

Bite Marks

Bite marks are produced by human teeth into skin and flesh or into food items such as an apple or a piece of cheese. Human dentition develops differently in every person, and when dental work like caps and fillings is also considered, the dentition has considerable individuality.

Bite marks are seen in assault and sexual assault cases, often on limbs, buttocks, or female breasts, and they are also seen in abused children. Sometimes, children bite other children, and sometimes an adult bites a child. Forensic pathologists ordinarily look for bite marks on bodies during the examination and autopsy. An example of a bite mark is shown in Figure 6.12.

Forensic odontologists (forensic dentists) compare bite marks and arrive at conclusions as to whether a suspected biter is excluded or included, and sometimes even identified. Bite mark identifications (using a bite mark comparison to actually identify someone as the biter) have become somewhat more controversial lately, because a few cases have surfaced in which odontologists identified a suspect as the biter, but later DNA testing of the saliva surrounding the bite mark excluded the person. What can be done depends on the size and quality of the questioned bite mark and how well that mark has been recorded. A forensic dentist first usually casts the teeth of the suspected biter, much as would be done if a dental restoration were being made. The negative impression of the teeth is then used to produce a positive model of the upper and lower dentition. These may be made from dental stone plaster and can be placed in an articulator device (sort of a synthetic jaw) so they are oriented just as the teeth are in the person's mouth. The model can then be used to produce known marks for comparison with the questioned bite mark. Point-by-point, overlay, and photographic techniques can be used. Forensic dentists can also cast known bite marks from suspects in high-resolution casting material for use in subsequent comparisons.

Bite marks should be documented as quickly as possible once they are recognized, and a forensic odontologist should be consulted. Photography is probably the best single method of documentation, but photographing bite marks is complicated because they are often on curved surfaces, and strategies must be used to avoid distortion. Since bite marks are actually bruises, in living victims, the marks change with time as healing occurs, and the changes can affect their appearance and value as individualizing marks. Sometimes it is necessary to document the marks more than once, as healing is occurring.

Skeletal Features

Forensic (physical) anthropologists and forensic radiologists are sometimes able to identify people from premortem and postmortem X-ray comparisons. Usually, this is done to identify skeletal remains. There are features of the sinus cavities in skull X-rays, and sometimes of spongy long bone tissue, that are individualizing. If these features are adequately visible in both X-rays, an expert may be able to identify the remains as those of the person who was x-rayed while alive. Fractured and healed factures and other injuries can also have strong identification potential.

Dental X-rays make up a special subcategory of skeletal features and are extremely valuable in identifying bodies in mass disasters. The forensic odontologist looks not only at restoration and other dental work done on the individual, but also the shape of root channels and other bony characteristics of the teeth and jaw in making identifications.

This type of analysis is different from the more usual examination of actual skeletal remains by forensic anthropologists. With skeletal remains alone, usually only class characteristics can be discerned, not identity. With advances in DNA typing of bone, identification of skeletal remains as those of a particular individual is becoming more practical.

Lip and Ear Prints

For many years, occasional discussions have occurred in the forensic science literature about lip and ear prints. Both lips and ears are capable of producing impression patterns that can then be compared with knowns obtained from suspected depositors. Cases involving these impressions are unusual, and not too many examiners have sufficient experience with this type of marking.

There is a sense among pattern evidence examiners that these markings possess considerable individuality. It would be up to an individual examiner in a particular case to decide what could be said in a nonexclusion case comparison. The courts in individual jurisdiction have accepted such identifications in a number of cases.

Voice Identification

Voice prints represent a record of a person's speech patterns. Voice analysts use a combination of aural (listening) and sound spectrograph records to make comparisons between questioned and known voice patterns. The sound spectrograms might be called "voice prints" (Figure 6.13). This area is highly specialized, and comparisons are done by examiners having specific training and experience. A high degree of reliability is reported when the comparisons are done by appropriately trained and experienced examiners on high-quality evidence recordings. With more limited quality evidence, such as that from most telephone lines, the results are rarely conclusive. This is an evolving area. Computer technology for decoding voice messages has developed better ways of comparing voices, and this has become an area of considerable research, particularly in the intelligence community.

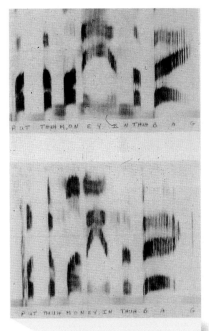

Figure 6.13

A voice spectrogram, showing the frequency distribution of a short segment of speech. Two examples of the same speech segment could be compared to see if they were spoken by the same person.

Biometrics

biometrics

Abstraction of measurements or portions of complex patterns from the human body to build a database that can then be used to "verify" the "identity" of person within that database.

The term **biometrics** means measurements of some part or feature of the human body for purposes of verification or identification. The availability of imaging acquisition, storage, and rapid retrieval has made some biometrics methods cost-effective.

We have talked about "identification" in this chapter as meaning "individualization." In forensic cases, we are trying to identify someone (i.e., to say who it is) from a fingerprint, or sometimes from a skeletal or dental X-ray, or from a bite impression. Fingerprints and the other methods of personal identification we have discussed are all different examples of biometrics. Bertillon's anthropometric measurements, discussed at the beginning of the chapter, might be the original example of a biometric method for human identification.

For some purposes, however, it may not be necessary for a biometric method to yield individuality among everyone in the country or the world. It may be enough to distinguish several hundred, or several thousand, or several hundred thousand people, from one another. Applications like this are called "verification" techniques. You are familiar with dozens of examples of verification in daily life: computer passwords, magnetic strips on your credit cards containing "identifying" information, photo identification cards, even fingerprints on some types of identification. In a verification system, it is not necessary to distinguish everyone, just a subpopulation. On a college or university campus, for example, a verification system for gaining building entry need only distinguish people who would need or might try to gain entry.

Everyone is familiar with the problems associated with paper and plastic card identification (verification) systems. The biggest problems are potential loss by the owner, and fraud and forgery by others. To avoid these problems, biometric verification methods are an attractive alternative. Biometric methods include fingerprints, iris scans, retinal scans, and various types of facial scans. In each case, a system must be able to rapidly extract a limited number of features from a complex pattern and compare the nature and location of those features with previously recorded ones in a database. A "match" provides a verification of "identity." As we have noted, these systems don't have to be designed to identify a person to the exclusion of every other person—only to "verify" that person's identity among a subpopulation of people who do or may seek verification. Thus, one could design a fingerprint abstracting or other biometric system to distinguish every United Airlines frequent flyer who boards airplanes at Chicago O'Hare international airport, or every student on a large campus who has a meal plan, or every employee of a large company doing classified research. We will be seeing more and more of these systems as the technology improves and people become more convinced of their value. Bertillonage was a biometric system of exactly this kind. It worked until it got too big; that is, until there were too many people in the database. At that point, the number of parameters (features) being abstracted was insufficient to distinguish everyone in the database, and duplicates arose.

Identification of Human Remains— Handling of Mass Disasters

Under this topic of personal identification patterns, we briefly consider the methods used for identifying human remains. Most of the time, identifying human remains is straightforward. It becomes a problem when there is destruction of the body, or when the body is fragmented. Both destruction and fragmentation can be issues in mass disaster situations.

As a society, we have traditionally placed considerable value on positively identifying the remains of the dead and providing those remains to decedents' families for interment or cremation in accordance with their traditions and beliefs. As a result, governmental agencies expend considerable effort to achieve reliable identifications of remains. It is often the duty of the medical examiner or coroner to positively identify human remains. In doing so, these officials may at times rely on various other specialists.

Usually, human remains consist of an intact body, and identification is achieved by having a relative, friend, or acquaintance of the deceased identify the person by direct viewing. If there is destruction or fragmentation of a body because of fire or traumatic events, viewing may not be possible. Next to be used are dental and fingerprint identifications. As mentioned, forensic odontologists can make positive identifications of persons from X-rays of their dentition, provided premortem X-rays are available. That means there must be suspected identities, because there are no files of dental X-rays. Fingerprint specialists can make identifications using fingerprints obtained postmortem, again provided there is a premortem record of the person's fingerprints on a card in a file or in an AFIS system. Dental and fingerprint identifications are considered definitive. They leave no doubt as to the decedent's identity. Use of dental records assumes that the remains have the jaws (with the teeth). Use of fingerprints is possible only with relatively recent remains. If neither of these techniques can be used, other less direct methods can be tried.

The less direct methods consist of using clothing; personal items (such as jewelry); marks, scars, or tattoos; or artificial body parts or limbs. Because there is the possibility of chance duplication of scars, marks, or tattoos and of mix-ups involving belongings, many authorities would not rely on these methods alone for definitive identification. However, the conclusions that can be reached have to be considered in context. If the universe of possible identities is small—say a plane with 50 passengers has crashed—and if an item is expected to be unique in that small universe (such as a wedding ring engraved with initials and marriage date), an identification might be made.

Skeletal remains are normally examined by a forensic anthropologist. Depending on what bones are recovered, an anthropologist can provide estimates of race, sex, age, stature, and other features that may ultimately aid in making an identification. Anthropological features alone will not yield an identification in the absence of highly individual injuries or medical interventions. In this day of transplants and other repair procedures, a whole new type of material for identification is available in such cases. These "repair" materials are often serialized and therefore readily identifiable. For example, a pacemaker has a serial number that should be traceable to the person into whom it was installed.

Occasionally, when skeletal remains cannot be identified but a skull is recovered with the remains, a forensic sculptor may be called upon to "reconstruct" the person's face. The reconstruction is based on data provided by the anthropologist as to gender, race, and approximate age, and upon a database of tissue thickness measurements. Unless hair was recovered, hair color is unknown to the sculptor, as are hairstyle and eye color. Different eye colors and wigs may be used to provide different possible images of the face. Typically, these images are circulated in the hope that someone might recognize the person. The Michigan State Police and Louisiana State University, for example, maintain Web sites showing facial reconstruction images of unidentified persons.

In Chapter 10, we discuss the use of both nuclear and mitochondrial DNA in human identification from tissue or bone specimens. DNA profiling has been used extensively in several recent mass disaster situations, including the World Trade Center terrorist attacks on September 11, 2001. Nuclear DNA identifications are definitive. Mitochondrial DNA identifications are probably not definitive alone, but with other circumstantial evidence and a limited universe of possible identities, identifications can be made. It should be noted that DNA profiling is the most expensive and labor intensive of all the methods of identification available. Its success relies on an accurate universe of possible identities; that is, there has to be an accurate list of who may have been involved in the event. Without such a list, appropriate reference specimens cannot be sought or obtained.

Summary

Fingerprints comprise one of the oldest kinds of forensic evidence. Their individuality has been recognized for hundreds of years, and they have been used in criminal identification for most of the 20th century. Fingerprints are formed before birth and are permanent and unchanging throughout life. The patterns are not completely explainable through genetics, because identical twins have distinguishable fingerprints. The basic fingerprint patterns are arches, loops, and whorls. There are variations within these basic patterns. Individual characteristics within the friction ridge skin that makes up fingerprints are called minutiae; the most common are ridge endings and bifurcations.

The use of fingerprints for personal identification was developed in Europe and by Europeans working in India and Asia. The first systematic biometric system for criminal identification was called anthropometry and was developed by Bertillon in France. It consisted of a set of body measurements. Bertillon's system was supplanted by fingerprints when it was realized that there could be duplicate Bertillon measurements in different individuals. Fingerprints as a means of criminal identification were adopted by the London Metropolitan Police and by the police in Argentina, after which their use in criminal investigations spread all over the world. Classification systems for 10-print cards were devised by Vucetich and by Henry and were used for decades until Automated Fingerprint Identification Systems (AFISs) were developed. AFISs enabled searching large files for single prints and revolutionized the use of fingerprints for criminal identification. AFIS databases also enabled the use of fingerprints for verification of identity—this is an example of fingerprints as biometrics. Law enforcement AFISs contain fingerprints of known persons and fingerprints of unknown origin from unsolved cases (forensic file).

Evidentiary prints may be visible, plastic, or latent. Enhancement, or visualization, procedures are used to make latent prints visible and suitable for comparisons. They include physical methods (such as powder or SPR), chemical methods (such as ninhydrin or iodine fuming or Super Glue), and special illumination techniques (such as alternate light sources and lasers) and combination methods. Bloody fingerprints can require special techniques of enhancement. It may also be important to decide on the relative importance of the blood (for DNA typing) and the fingerprint. Fingerprints on sticky tape also require special techniques. Systematic approaches involve using a series of enhancement methods serially, such that the least destructive techniques are used first.

Fingerprint identification is based on fingerprints being unchangeable throughout life, and being individual. The entire process involved is termed ACE-V, for analysis, comparison, evaluation, and verification. The overall patterns and ridge flow of a fingerprint are known as "level I" features, minutiae are known as "level II," and ridge relationships and pore sizes and distributions are known as "level III." Fingerprints can often be matched to an individual using level I and level II detail. An examiner can also exclude someone as the depositor of a fingerprint. Of course, sometimes evidence fingerprints are of poor quality and therefore unsuitable for comparison.

The primary professional organization for fingerprint examiners is the International Association for Identification, which publishes the *Journal of Forensic Identification*. More recently, there has been a Scientific Working Group on friction ridge pattern comparisons. Research is ongoing to try and systematically establish fingerprint individuality.

Other patterns for personal identification include palm and sole prints. They are examined like fingerprints. Bite marks may contain individuality as well, reflecting the individual characteristics of the teeth that made them. They are compared by forensic dentists. Skeletal patterns that are examined by forensic anthropologists can help narrow down the identity of skeletal remains. Forensic radiologists can sometimes identify people from a comparison of pre- and postmortem X-rays. Occasionally, lip or ear prints have been examined in criminal cases, and voice patterns have considerable individual character as well.

Fingerprints (and Bertillon's system of measurements) are examples of biometrics. Today, biometrics also includes eye (iris or retinal) patterns and various facial patterns. Biometrics is coming into use more and more as a method of verification of identity. These methods are considered superior to "paper" forms of identification and less subject to loss and forgery.

In mass disasters, where identification of remains cannot be done by direct viewing, fingerprints and dental identification are the preferred methods. DNA typing may also be used, but it is more complicated and time-consuming.

Key Terms

friction ridge skin (p. 126)

basic fingerprint patterns: arches, loops, and whorls (p. 126)

minutiae (p. 126)

anthropometry (bertillonage) (p. 127)

classification system (p. 129)

AFISs (p. 130)

visible (patent) print (p. 132)

plastic (impression) print (p. 132)

latent print (p. 132)

development (enhancement, visualization) (p. 132)

powder dusting (p. 134)

magnetic brush technique (p. 134)

small particle reagent (SPR) (p. 134)

iodine fuming (p. 135)

ninhydrin (p. 135)

Super Glue (cyanoacrylate) (p. 137)

dye stains (p. 137)

physical developer (p. 137)

alternate light source (p. 138)

laser (p. 138)

suitability for examination (p. 142)

ACE-V method (p. 142)

level I, level II, and level III detail (p. 142)

biometrics (p. 146)

Review Questions—Short Answer

1. What are fingerprints? Why are they useful in criminal investigation?
2. What is an AFIS? Why is it valuable?
3. What are the main types of evidentiary prints that might be found at scenes?
4. What are some physical methods for enhancing latent fingerprints?
5. What are some chemical methods for enhancing latent fingerprints?
6. What are some special illumination methods for enhancing latent fingerprints?
7. How might bloody fingerprints be enhanced?
8. What is the basis for fingerprint identification? What are the main principles?
9. What are some other patterns useful in person identification?
10. What are the major methods of identifying human remains in mass disasters?

Fill-in-the-Blank & Multiple Choice

1. One important characteristic of friction ridge patterns is that they _____ between birth and death.
2. The three basic fingerprint patterns are (1) arch, (2) _____, and (3) _____.
3. Fingerprints found at crime scenes or on evidence can be divided into three broad categories (not classifications) based on their appearance and physical makeup: (1) _____, (2) patent (visible), and (3) _____.
4. When a latent fingerprint is compared with a known inked print, and according to the numerical rule, the number of points of comparison required to correspond before a positive identification can be declared is
   a. enough to satisfy the expert latent examiner.
   b. at least eight.
   c. at least twelve.
   d. the pattern and 10 minutiae.
5. Computerized fingerprint search systems match fingerprints by comparing the relative positions of
   a. core and delta.
   b. pattern center and all bifurcations.
   c. all individualizable minutiae.
   d. bifurcations and ridge endings.

Further References

Ashbaugh, D. R. *Quantitative-Qualitative Friction Ridge Analysis: An Introduction to Basic and Advanced Ridgeology.* Boca Raton, FL: CRC Press, 1999.

Champod, C., C. J. Lennard, P. Margot, and M. Stoilovic. *Fingerprints and Other Ridge Skin Impressions.* Boca Raton, FL: CRC Press, 2004.

Federal Bureau of Investigation. *The Science of Fingerprints: Classification and Uses.* Washington, DC: U.S. Department of Justice, 1993.

Gaensslen, R. E., and K. Young. "Fingerprints." In *Forensic Science: An Introduction to Scientific and Investigative Techniques,* 2nd ed., ed. S. James and J. J. Nordby. Boca Raton, FL: CRC Press, 2005.

Lee, H. C., and R. E. Gaensslen. *Advances in Fingerprint Technology.* 2nd ed. Boca Raton, FL: CRC Press, 2001.

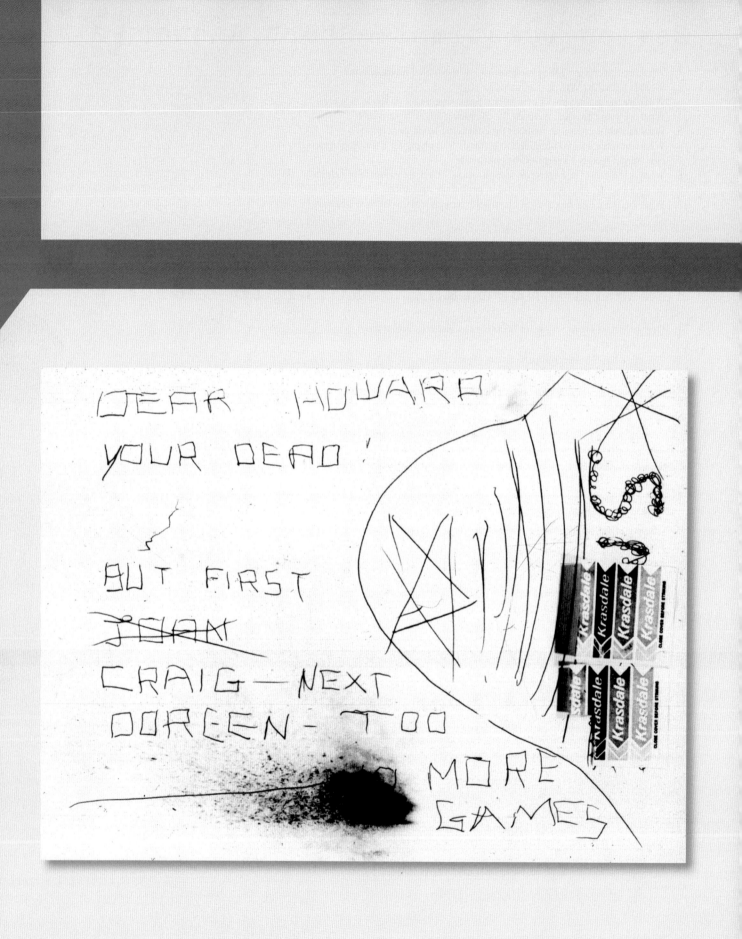

Questioned Document Examination

- The science and technology that underlies handwriting and handwriting comparison

- Class and individual characteristics as applicable to handwriting

- The importance, and proper methods, of collecting known writing samples

- Basic approaches to the comparison of known and evidentiary writings

- The important nonhandwriting examinations performed by document examiners

- The examination of documents produced on typewriters, computer printers, and copy machines

- The examinations used to reconstruct altered documents

- Some techniques for deciphering of charred documents

- Techniques used to look for and read indented writing on a document

- The problem of trying to determine when a document was written

Outline

Learning Objectives

- The wide variety of evidence that can be examined by a questioned document examiner

- The evolution of an individual's handwriting from childhood to adulthood

- The major steps in preparing a document

- Special problems involved in properly collecting and preserving document evidence

chapter

7

Lead Case

Lindbergh Kidnapping

It was called "the crime of the century." In 1927, Charles Lindbergh had become a national hero by being the first to complete a solo flight across the Atlantic Ocean. He had married the beautiful and aristocratic Anna Morrow, and they were perceived as a dream couple. Tragically, only five years later, in 1932, the kidnapping and death of their first child received even more public attention than the solo flight.

On March 1, 1932, the 20-month-old son of the Lindberghs was taken from his second-story nursery at the Lindbergh estate near Hopewell, New Jersey. Beneath the child's window, a three-section handcrafted ladder was found, and a handwritten note had been left. That ransom note, and those that followed, clearly revealed the writer to have difficulty with English and likely to be of German extraction.

A month later a $50,000 ransom, approximately two-thirds of which was in the form of gold certificates (notes), was paid through an intermediary in St. Raymond's Cemetery in New York City. About a year after the ransom was paid, President Roosevelt ordered the turning in of all gold certificates. A list of the serial numbers of the ransom bills had been printed and circulated to banks.

Extract from one of the ransom notes in the Lindbergh kidnapping case.

A little over a month after the ransom was paid, a truck driver came upon the partially decomposed body of a child a short distance off the road about two miles from the Lindbergh estate.

In September of 1934, two-and-a-half years after the kidnapping, the driver of a 1930 Dodge sedan bearing New York plate 4U13-41 gave a New York gas station attendant named Walter Lyle a $10 gold note for 98 cents worth of gasoline. Lyle recorded the plate number on the bill's margin in the event the bank refused to cash it.

The finding of this ransom bill was reported to the authorities by the bank and they determined that New York plate 4UI3-41 was registered to Bruno Richard Hauptmann of 1279 E. 222nd Street in the Bronx. Hauptmann was arrested. A ransom bill was in his wallet, and $14,560 of ransom money was found in his garage.

In January of 1935, Hauptmann was brought to trial in Flemington, New Jersey. After a month-and-a-half trial, Hauptmann was found guilty on February 13, 1935, and sentenced to die for the death of the Lindbergh baby, which occurred during the commission of a theft.

The trial and conviction of Bruno Richard Hauptmann was largely on the basis of scientific evidence, and it created landmarks in the utilization and presentation of scientific evidence. Unfortunately, the enormous public interest in this case created something of a circus atmosphere at the trial.

Questioned document (QD) evidence played a central role in this case. The examination and association of 14 ransom notes was critical to the prosecution. In fact, Hauptmann was heard to say to his counsel: "Dot handwriting is the worstest thing against me."

Although there was considerable important physical evidence— including association of the handmade wooden ladder left at the kidnap scene to Hauptmann's house and tools, examination of cloth and thread from the baby's handmade nightshirt to help identify the decomposed remains, and of course the finding of the ransom money in his home—the association of the ransom notes to Hauptmann was critical. The primary thrust of the defense was that Mr. Hauptmann had an accomplice or had been "framed" by another individual. Thus, the prosecution had the job of proving two things about the 14 ransom notes: first, that they were *all* written by the same individual; and, second, that they were all written by the defendant, Mr. Hauptmann. This was not as simple as it might seem, because, even though the defendant had quite unusual writing, examination of the notes indicated to the experienced QD experts that attempts had been made to disguise that writing.

The highly unusual approach taken by the prosecution was to have all the material examined independently by eight document examiners from across the country. This went against the common wisdom that having more than one examiner would give the opposing party the opportunity to exploit the inevitable subtle differences of approach and reporting to create uncertainty in the mind of the jury. This was indeed the tack the defense team took in cross-examination of the experts. It is a tribute to the highly experienced group of examiners that this defense strategy was not successful.

Another reason for the multiple examiners was because the defense said it had 14 experts who would say the notes were not written by the same person. To counter this testimony, the prosecution chose to have their QD examiners distance themselves from the potential defense witnesses by explaining the difference between a QD examiner and a graphologist. The defense witnesses were graphologists. The following testimony of Albert Osborne, the most well known of the prosecution witnesses, discussed this difference:

> Graphology in America, in this country, and in England is understood as determining from handwriting the character of the writer, as distinguished from the students of handwriting and so forth document examiners, who examine writing for the purpose of determining whether it is genuine or not, that is; the question of forgery and also examining writing for the purpose of determining whether it can be identified as the writing of a certain individual.
>
> There are two classes of handwriting examiners. One class examines writing for the purpose of determining whether it is genuine or not and whether it can be identified. The other class examines handwriting for the purpose of determining whether it indicates the character of the individual who did the writing. And the questions are entirely different. In one case, it is a question of genuineness and the question of identity. The other case is a question of whether the writer is honest, whether the writer would be a good husband or wife; whether the writer likes children and dogs . . . Any kind of question.

And the graphologists go further than that, some of them . . . To determine disease from handwriting . . . Diagnosing disease. The two classes of examiners are entirely different.

This strategy was successful in the end, since the defense chose not to offer its parade of experts to counteract the prosecution examiners. Further, the unanimity and strength of the opinions and the demonstrative evidence presented clearly convinced the jury. The skill of these experienced experts can be seen in the conclusions stated by Mr. Clark Sellers, another of the prosecution's witnesses:

> In examining these documents, I have also kept in mind an important thing . . . And that is the dangers of error: what might lead to error, such as mistaking a natural characteristic for an individual characteristic; such as coming to a conclusion on too few standards or too small an amount of disputed writing.
>
> The character of the writing, the manner in which it was written, have been taken into consideration, having in mind many other things besides those which I have mentioned here. And, I believe this combination of characteristics, some of which have been mentioned, others not mentioned . . . But in order to save time I will make this general statement . . . That a combination of characteristics in Mr. Hauptmann's writing, may just as truly identify him as a combination of scars, moles and birthmarks, or whorls and loops in combination may identify a man by his fingerprints. So convincing to my mind that Mr. Hauptmann wrote each and every one of these ransom notes—*it is, I say, so convincing to my mind, that he might just as well have signed each and every one of them.*

Questioned document examination is an underutilized area of forensic science with a great variety of examinations that can provide useful, practical information. It is impotant to become aware of the numerous examinations that can be done, and the many skills that QD examiners bring to this type of evidence. Questioned document examination can make significant contributions to many investigations and prosecutions, paticularly when a knowledgeable examiner has the appropriate evidence to examine.

Types of Document Evidence

The most well known activities of QD examiners are examination and comparison of handwriting, typewriting, and copier output. Was the document written by this individual or not? Was the document typed on this particular machine or not? Was a particular handout done on a particular copying machine? These are all questions asked frequently of QD examiners. The output from other mechanical printing devices such as rubber stamps, various commercial printing processes, and computer printers also lend themselves to careful examination and comparison.

In addition to the types of examinations just mentioned, many other technical examinations can be conducted, such as looking for erasures, an **alteration,** or the sequence of writing or printing. These may also provide useful information. For example, a QD examiner might be asked: Was the document written and then signed, or was it created over an existing signature? Such timing considerations can have important consequences in an investigation or legal controversy. It is not uncommon to hear of situations where someone alleges: "I signed this piece of paper with one thing on it and all of a sudden my signature now appears on the bottom of a changed document." The QD could be a will, a contract, or some other potentially legally binding agreement.

Document examiners are often asked to **authenticate** the author, the signer, or the contents of a document. The question of whether a document was properly executed can also be an important issue. For example, an individual says that he or she signed a particular contract and when the terms are satisfied, the other party indicates that a different figure from the one specified in the original contract is due. The contract presented is different from the complaining party's copy. Which, if either, is the authentic agreement? The question of whether one of the parties has altered the original contract is an important question and often not easy to answer. The authenticity of a signature is an issue in court frequently, though more commonly in civil than in criminal cases. Although **forgery** is a criminal offense, most cases are about money or power and are usually settled without resort to the criminal law. On the other hand, check forgery (Figure 7.1) or alteration is a very common criminal complaint. That is, many complaints state that their checks came back from the bank and one was not written by them or at least not signed by them. In general, banks do not even look at the signatures until there is a complaint.

In one common scenario, a benefits check is not received on time, so a missing check form is filed with the employer or agency providing the benefits. The payer receives a number of such claims and when the checks (microfilm copies) are received, the payees are asked to come in and check the signature.

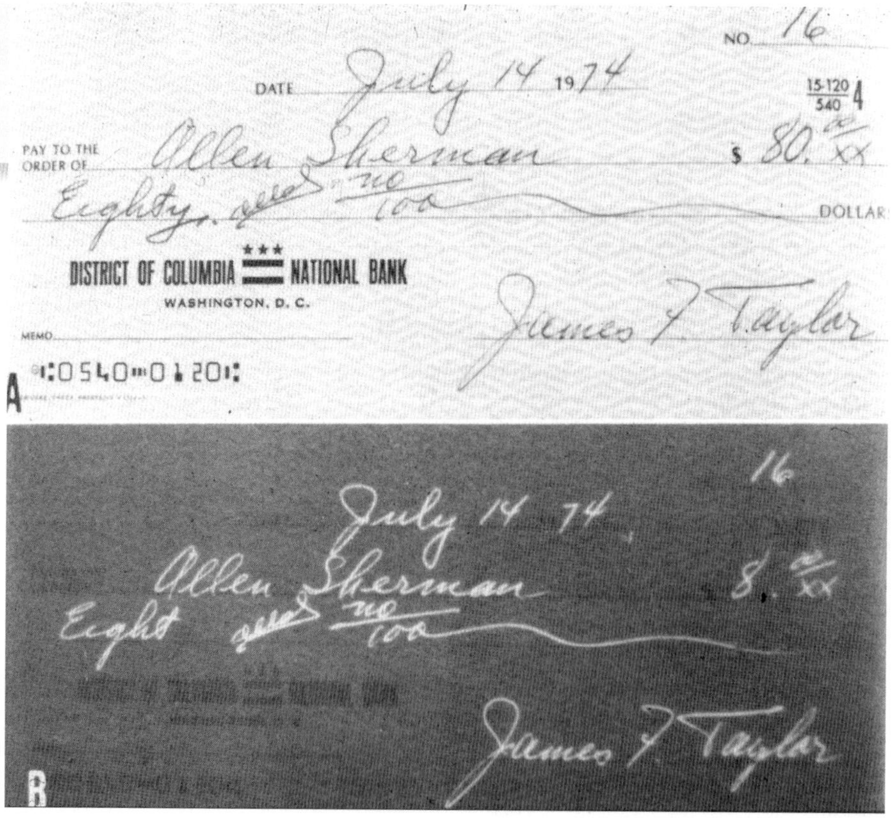

authenticate

To prove that something is real, true, or what it is said (purported) to be.

forgery

To make an illegal copy of something in order to deceive.

Figure 7.1

Check photo in visible light and showing infrared luminescence.

A common variation of the Case Study 7.1 scenario occurs when the individual who claims not to have received the check is suspected of having cashed it and then disguising the signature in order to claim forgery and obtain a replacement check.

Development of Handwriting

A good deal of science and technology underlies the examination and comparison of handwriting. It starts with an individual's basic handwriting style, which initially is determined during early schooling by the copybook (Figure 7.2) from which the person learned to make the different letters. The teacher or a textbook would draw the letters out, and the child would try and follow the example. This process begins with printing and then moves on to **cursive writing** in a later grade. Everyone who attended that school at that time learned the same basic style. Probably everybody in that school district, and maybe most of the school districts in that state, also learned that style. Nonetheless, there are always a number of different handwriting copybooks being used by schools across the country. They have slight variations in style so that different people may have learned slightly different styles.

Because of the persistence of these class features in people's writing, it is often possible to recognize writing as being from a person who went to school in another country. Similarly, document examiners can sometimes analyze writing in alphabets and languages they don't speak or understand. However, would one expect even individuals who went to the same school in the same year to still make their letters exactly the same way 25 years later? For most individuals, writing does not remain static between grammar school and adulthood. As people mature and become more independent, their handwriting changes. Particularly during the teenage years, most individuals experiment with their writing style, and especially with their signatures. This eventually results in a style with which a person is comfortable, and one that is usually quite distinctive. Again, this is particularly true of an individual's signature. Our handwriting evolves with time, but usually the major characteristics are set by the time we finish our formal education.

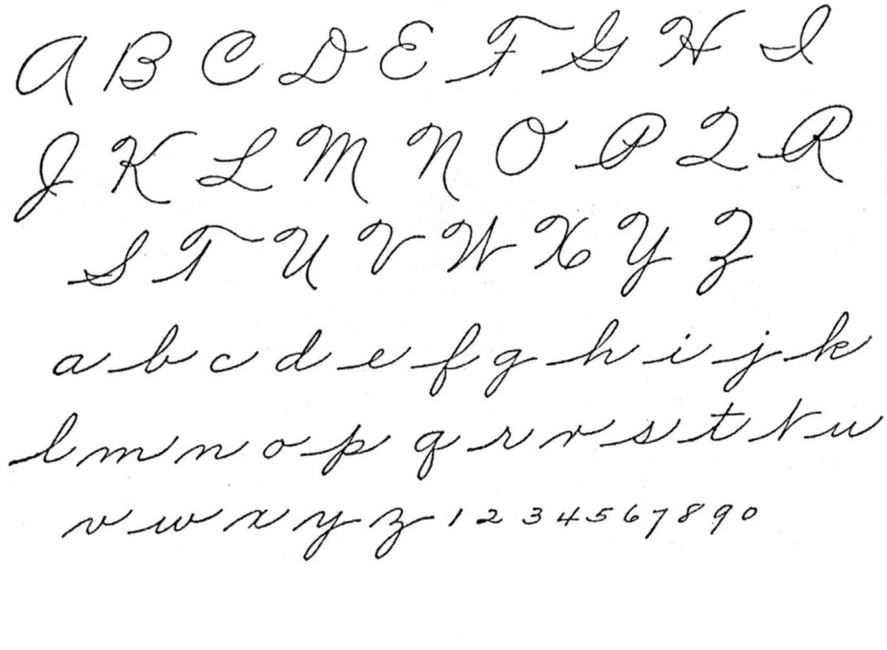

Case Study 7.1

Stolen Checks

Consider the case in which it was discovered that a whole group of checks had gone astray. Whoever had stolen this batch of checks had endorsed the beneficiary's check with the signature Herman Harris. The check was actually made out to H. Harris (Howard). Since the person who stole it didn't know what the H stood for, he or she just picked an "H" name; in this case, it is not a question of a forged signature because the check does not even have the right name. Unfortunately, even though there is no real question of the signature being forged, someone is still going to be out some money that ended up in the thief's pocket.

cursive writing

Writing that is written with rounded letters that are joined together.

Figure 7.2

A page from the Palmer Method copybook used in many American schools.

The important point, from a document examiner's perspective, is that most people develop individual characteristics in their handwriting. By the time people are in the late teens or early twenties, handwriting has largely stabilized. It will continue to evolve slowly with time, but basic characteristics are set for most people at young adulthood. If you were to look at a sample of the handwriting of someone in middle age, you would see that there have been some changes in the way it looks, but careful examination, the way a document examiner looks at writing, would show that there is a great deal of consistency. Because of this drift, it is important when obtaining known control handwriting samples to try to obtain samples from about the same time period as the evidence samples were written.

Other things can affect individuals' handwriting in addition to aging effects. For example, when people are sick or become infirm, their handwriting often deteriorates. This arises in the classic deathbed will situation where someone is holding the testator's hand and he or she is barely writing at all. This often causes challenges to the will. Medical effects can come and go. Someone could have a stroke and the person's handwriting might deteriorate seriously, but it could slowly come back to something like it was before the stroke if the person's recovery is good. Alcohol or some drugs (therapeutic or illicit) also have the potential of influencing the features of a person's handwriting.

In document examination, as in most of forensic science, examiners are usually faced with comparisons between a known control and an evidence sample. A crucial point in these examinations of handwriting is the amount of **normal variation** in an individual's handwriting. The variation within the known writing sample must be significantly less than the variation between samples from different individuals. As discussed, although handwriting tends to stabilize at adulthood, there is some day-to-day handwriting variation, particularly when a person is tired or the conditions are less than ideal. Most students can attest that writing done while seated at a desk at home is different from that done when seated in a classroom in a chair with a small arm on it that is not particularly stable. The key observation is that the variation within an individual's writing caused by minor discomforts is much less than the variation between that individual's writing and that of most other individuals. If that were not the case, experts could not validly compare handwriting.

Writing Process

All aspects of the writing process can yield useful information. We can look at three basic parts associated with the document: the surface for the writing, the **writing instrument,** and the **transfer medium** between the instrument and the surface. The most common surface is a piece of paper. The most common writing instrument is a pen or pencil. The most common transfer media are ink or pencil lead. However, the possible variations are nearly endless. The surface may be a bathroom wall or a subway car. The instrument may be a paintbrush, a crayon, or a spray can. The transfer medium may be paint, chalk, or even blood. A rare exception would be exemplified by ancient writing on clay tablets where a stylus was used to make marks in the soft clay (Figure 7.3). In such a case, there is no transfer medium. Even with mechanical printing such as with a typewriter, computer printer, or other device, there is a surface, a writing instrument, and a transfer medium to make the writing visible. For example, in a thermal printing device the instrument is a hot wire that causes a chemical or physical change (transfer medium) in a coating on the surface of the paper.

Each of the three components can produce important information for a document examiner under the right condition. A document examiner can look at the paper of a questioned document and quickly tell whether it is expensive paper or cheap paper, whether it has a high content of cotton fibers in it, and something about the surface treatment. In addition, with a little more careful examination or testing, an examiner

normal variation

That variation in writing characteristics seen by examination of numerous examples of an individual's writing.

writing instrument

An item used by individuals to mark handwriting motions or mechanical printing onto a surface to prepare a more permanent record.

transfer medium

The material that records markings (handwriting or mechanical printing) on a receiving surface.

Figure 7.3
Clay tablets with impressed symbols.

can tell if the document was produced from mechanically pulped or chemically pulped wood and perhaps a whole variety of other things as well. Paper has many other characteristics that can provide useful information in certain cases, such as the type of surface treatment, as mentioned earlier. When people write on normal paper, they are not actually writing directly on the paper fibers. Paper, even fairly inexpensive paper such as copier paper, has a thin **surface coating (sizing)** on it. That coating is usually a starch or a clay type of material. It is necessary because paper is a mat of interwoven fibers, and the surface of it is a bit rough. The surface treatment smooths that roughness so that the paper provides a nice surface for writing or printing. Every company that produces paper has its own technology for this process. Thus, a paper manufacturer may use different things in its clay, different techniques for applying and bonding this surface finish, and many other possible variations. These variations may help determine whether or not two papers were manufactured by the same company or at the same plant. That information could turn out to be important to an investigation.

surface coating (sizing)
Material placed on the surface of paper to smooth the roughness of the interwoven fibers.

As an example, imagine that a QD expert is examining a five-page document. It is alleged that one of the parties in the dispute about the document slipped in an extra page. Initially the examiner is unable to find much evidence that it has been altered as has been alleged. However, a document examiner looks at many different things, including the paper. Perhaps at execution the parties did not bother to initial each page, as is customary on legal documents to prevent someone from slipping in an extra page. Even if the alteration was done some time later, it could still easily have been typed on the same typewriter, or generated from the same computer printer, but if an additional page was added, although it may look the same, a chemical analysis might show that there are four pages of one kind of paper, and one page of a similar, but distinguishable kind of paper. This could be a convincing piece of evidence in court to back up the claims of an added page.

The type of and exact nature of the writing instrument used can also give investigators useful information in many QD situations. There are, of course, literally hundreds of different brands of ballpoint pens (Figure 7.4). These can be divided into a much smaller number of different mechanical types. There are also many manufacturers of ballpoint pen ink, but far fewer than the number of different brands of pens. Different pen makers may be buying their ink stocks from the same company. Visual examination, with perhaps a little bit of magnification, can easily differentiate many of them. That alone may be sufficient to differentiate pens that have the same color ink

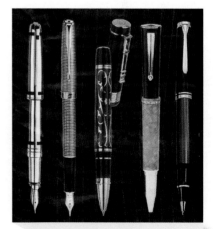

Figure 7.4
Different types of pens, including fountain and several different ballpoint types.

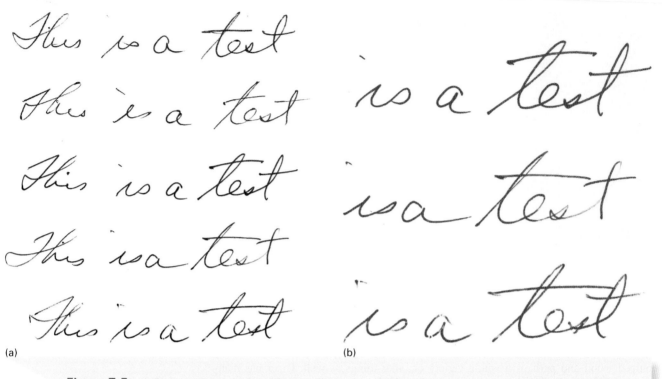

(a) (b)

Figure 7.5 A: Phrase written with five different ballpoint pens. B: Magnified portion of three of the five pens' writing showing differences in line quality.

fountain pen

A pen where the point (nib) is supplied with liquid ink from a refillable container inside the pen.

ink compositions

The mixtures of solvent and dyes or pigments that make up the ink.

but have a different way of delivering the ink. The writing from a ballpoint pen, a razor point, or a nylon tip can look quite different when carefully examined. Similarly, a **fountain pen** produces a different-looking line than any of the preceding types of pen. Examination of the lines produced by an inexpensive ballpoint pen compared with those from a high-quality pen (Figure 7.5) will usually show differences in both line quality and ink application. Further, a mechanical device such as a typewriter, computer printer, copying machine, or printing press produces a characteristic type of printing.

Finally, when the ink, paint, wax, toner, or other transfer medium is examined, it may allow examiners to differentiate the writing that is made with certain types of devices and that produce very similar-appearing writing. Manufacturers of different writing instruments often use different **ink compositions.** Evidential writing may be made using spray paint, a crayon, or a colored pencil, but most commonly it is from a pen of some sort. Today, ballpoint pens are by far the most common writing instrument. Experts can examine the writing from two pens that appear to produce exactly the same color and, by extracting some ink (Figure 7.6) from the writing and analyzing it, determine that the inks have a quite different chemical composition. Inks are made from dyes or pigments that are mixed to produce a particular color; for example, to achieve exactly the right shade of blue, the ink manufacturer may mix a little red, some blue, some black, and maybe a little yellow. Document examiners can remove a tiny sample of ink from the page and chemically separate the color components of the ink. Finding a different mixture of dyes can conclusively prove that two writings were not written with the same pen. Typically, if someone tries to alter a document, he or she will usually try to find a pen with the exact same color ink. There is a good chance that the person did not find the exact same pen, so even if the color matches well, the ink composition may be quite different. In sum, examination of a document surface, writing instrument, and transfer medium can give valuable information in many QD examination contexts and needs to be considered as an integral part of each QD investigation.

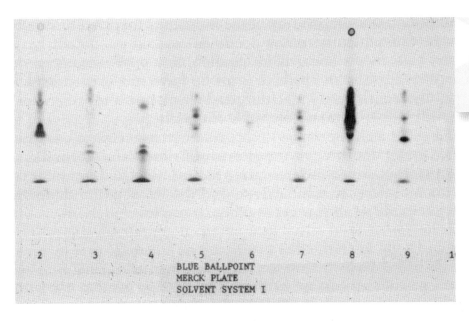

Figure 7.6
Thin-layer chromatographic separation of several ballpoint pen inks.

Recognition, Collection, and Preservation of Document Evidence

A significant reason for the underutilization of handwriting examination is that handwriting examiners must be quite demanding, particularly in the quality and quantity of the known control samples they need. It is essential that the control samples and evidence samples provided be sufficient in amount of writing and be in pristine condition. As a rule, samples must be original writings and not copies. A handwriting examiner is much more concerned with the way the handwriting was written than how it looks. For example, examiners look at where people stop and start their letters, how they connect letters, whether or not they connect letters in some situations and not others, and what are the subtle variations in how they write (see later). All these things can be ascertained from an original writing, but often subtle differences are not evident in a copy. The key "how" information—that is, how a document is written in terms of greater or lesser indentations or variations in inking—is usually on the original. Information easily discerned from an original writing just does not show up on copies. The importance of how a document is written to its examination is illustrated by the fact that part of the initial examination done by a handwriting examiner is to look at the reverse side of the document. An expert often can see more clearly on the back how letters were formed and where the strongest pressure was applied.

Although handwriting examination can provide much important information, other valuable information may be available from a document as well. For example, it is crucial to preserve and protect any fingerprints that might be present. The ability to develop an identifiable fingerprint (Figure 7.7) unambiguously indicates that the individual leaving the fingerprint handled the document. This may identify the writer, or it may bring a third party into the picture. Careful handling and protection of a document may also allow an examiner to find other useful evidence, particularly trace evidence. With this type of evidence, investigators must think about which lab examiner should process it first, because, as mentioned previously, some latent fingerprint development techniques (Chapter 6) have the potential to cause ink to run, for example. Thus, examinations must be done in an order that permits all the potential information to be extracted.

Examination of the handwriting can be very helpful and can allow an examiner to say that a suspect might have forged another person's signature or changed the amount of a check. Finding a fingerprint of an individual where it should not be is often more critical evidence than a handwriting opinion that may have to be qualified

Figure 7.7

Check backs showing fingerprints developed after ninhydrin treatment.

Figure 7.8

Questioned document protected in a plastic sheet protector.

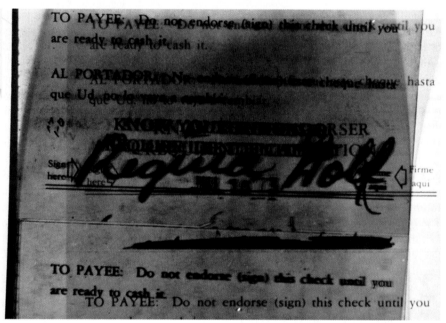

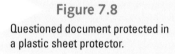

because of lack of sufficient sample or identifiable characteristics. It is important to use all the potential evidence in a document case. Investigators must look at everything that can be of assistance, be it fingerprints, trace evidence, hairs, fibers, or even dust. Unfortunately, there is a tendency to think about a handwritten document as a handwriting case and to forget to make use of all the potential evidence available from the document evidence.

When an investigator obtains a document that may be important to a case, he or she should immediately put it inside of a plastic sheet protector (Figure 7.8) or protect it in some other way. If a person receives a **threatening letter,** an **extortion note,** or a communication claiming credit for a bombing incident, it should not be passed around to everybody in the office. Such behavior, although tempting, can compromise a whole variety of possibly useful evidence. Although almost everyone knows that

threatening letter

A communication usually threatening to harm an individual or individuals if some demand is not met.

extortion note

A communication usually demanding some form of payment to the writer to prevent his/her carrying out a threat.

forensic scientists can dust for fingerprints on a window or water glass, many people do not know that they can develop fingerprints on absorbent materials such as paper with a high degree of success. Therefore, individuals may not be as careful not to leave fingerprints on documents as they would on other surfaces. Forging a document with gloves on is often not practical.

As previously indicated, preserving physical evidence, fingerprints, and trace evidence, in particular, is vital. If you were to visit the document section in most labs and hand an examiner a piece of paper, the document examiner might, out of habit, grasp it between the knuckles of the first and second finger, where there are no friction ridges.

In addition to proper handling, gaining the most information from QD evidence requires submission of sufficient control or known standard writing. This is critical because, as indicated earlier, variation occurs within an individual's writing, due to the time it was written, due to the speed it was written, due to the implement with which it was written, and other factors. If examiners have sufficient known writing, they can determine how much variation is natural and then whether the observed variation might be due to a different writer.

It is also critical that the control writing be reliably attributed to the writer. An examiner, no matter how experienced, needs a good standard exemplar before putting his or her reputation on the line. The expert must say: "In my expert opinion, this letter was written by this particular individual." To do so with confidence, a sufficient quantity and quality of known writing must have been studied, and the examiner must know unequivocally that the sample came from the party in question.

In addition, the examiner must know the source and the circumstances of collection of both evidence and known control samples. He or she must know if the material being compared was written 3 weeks ago or 25 years ago. The examiner will have to make some allowances for differences in writing mechanics due to age. Obtaining known standards that were written about the same time as the questioned materials greatly increases the chances of a successful outcome. Document examiners must often tell the investigator to please find additional standards or more **contemporaneous** standards. A great variety of potential sources of known writing exist, but it takes considerable investigative time and knowledge to ferret them out.

Case Study 7.2

Hitler Diaries Case

Even the best QD examiners can be led astray. A number of years ago the so-called Hitler diaries were published in Germany in *Der Stern* magazine. The documents were reported to be Hitler's diaries up until his death in the bunker where he committed suicide. They came out of East Germany from a particular well-known collector of Hitler memorabilia. He claimed that the source was someone who was actually in the bunker with Hitler. Sold as an exclusive to the influential *Der Stern*, a major magazine in Germany with a large circulation, the writings were made available in portions over a period of four or five years. Before the magazine published these diaries, it took them to several document examiners for authentication. They checked the paper, examined the handwriting, and also verified the style and authenticity of the historical references. One of the document examiners the magazine publisher used was Ordway Hilton, who was one of the most prestigious document examiners in the United States and an expert on handwriting in particular.

It later came out that the diaries were forgeries. The East German dealer was found to have made a living for years forging Hitler papers and selling them anywhere he could. He had obtained old paper that was identical to that used during the Third Reich and the proper inks so that the forgeries could not be detected from the materials used. The dealer was an extremely talented forger, and there was little authentic Hitler writing for comparison. Hilton was very embarrassed by his failure to detect the forgeries, but it turned out that it was not actually his error. When Hilton was asked to authenticate the diaries, he was given some supposedly authentic writing of Hitler's, which he used to judge the authenticity of the diaries. He carried out his examination meticulously, and he reported that the same person who had written the control writings provided had written the diaries. Unfortunately, for his reputation and for *Der Stern*, this same forger had forged the supposedly authentic Hitler writings. This individual had been so successful at forging Hitler memorabilia that they were widely accepted as authentic Hitler writings. The importance of the story is that it illustrates the crucial need for carefully authenticated known writing. Sadly, when Hilton died a few years ago, one of the things that was mentioned in his obituary was that he incorrectly authenticated the Hitler diaries. Ordway Hilton, one of the world's best and most-respected document examiners, was remembered for one of the few instances where he had reached the wrong conclusion.

contemporaneous

Happening or existing in the same period of time.

Handwriting Comparison

The comparison of handwriting is one of the most common questioned document examinatons. It is done in several steps, one of which is determining which writing characteristics are class characteristics and which are individual or nearly individual.

Class and Individual Characteristics

Superimposed on the class characteristics we learned from our copybooks are individual characteristics we have developed as we matured. The combination of class and individual characteristics is often sufficient that a handwriting examiner, with an adequate amount of written material and good known exemplar writing, may say: "In my expert opinion, this writing was done by this person." Not all people develop sufficient character to their handwriting, but the vast majority do. As mentioned earlier, because individuals' writing has normal variation, sufficient evidential writing and sufficient standard writing are critical to successful comparison. The more writing available, the better the chance that the examiner will be able to come to a decision. If an expert has nothing but a single questioned signature, a large number of known control signatures would be needed. With other writings, a much larger sample of writing would be required, because a person's signature is almost always much more distinctive than the person's normal handwriting. If an expert had just three words of normal handwriting, and nothing else, an identification or exclusion would be unlikely, unless the writing showed a highly unusual writing style. On the other hand, if the examiner had a full page of writing and obtained a set of high-quality standard writing written roughly contemporaneously, and hopefully with the same kind of writing instrument, then chances are good that the examiner can make an identification or an exclusion.

As discussed, signatures are particularly distinctive, much more so than other writing. The distinctive nature of signatures (Figure 7.9) arises because people do not have to think about forming each letter of each word when they write. That is, because our brains have been "programmed" over time, we can write largely without conscious thought about how to form each individual letter. The actions are automatic. Once we have developed the "writing circuits" in the brain, through long practice, writing becomes possible with little conscious thought. These brain circuits also account for the comparative uniformity and individuality in a person's writing. Since an individual signs his or her name much more often than performing other writing functions, the "writing circuits" take over more completely and signatures are usually more characteristic than other writing.

Another result of the automatic nature of writing is that it becomes difficult for individuals to **disguise** their writing; and, when trying to write in a way much different from their normal writing, it is difficult to consistently maintain the disguise. Those automatic writing circuits want to take over. The importance of this phenomenon is discussed later.

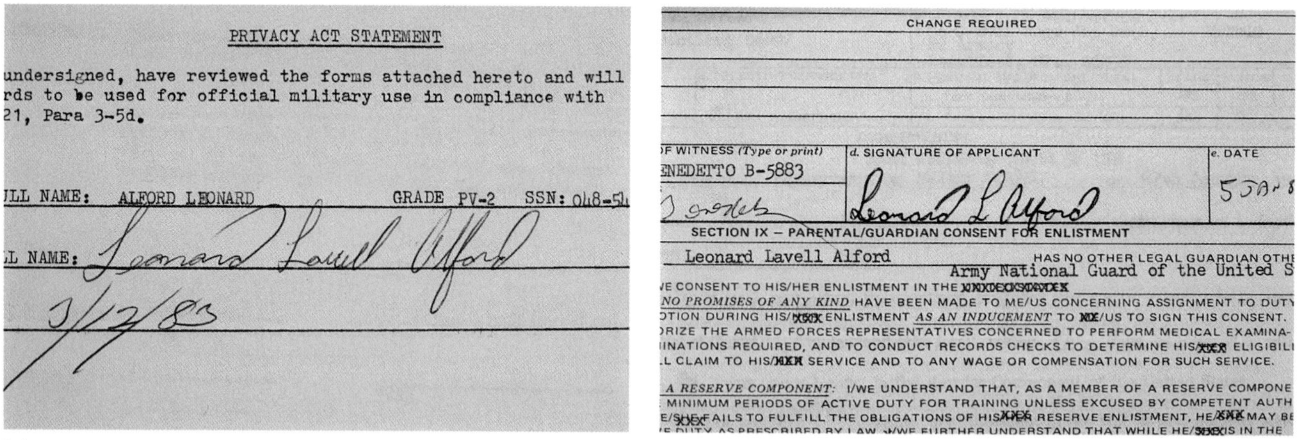

disguise

To give a new appearance in order to hide its true form.

(a)

(b)

Figure 7.9   A: Dated authentic known control signature. B: Questioned signature to be compared with known control signature.

When document examiners look at handwriting, one characteristic they analyze is the **skill level** of the writer. Skill level, which is represented in the smoothness and flow of the writing, is not something that can be measured with precision. Some writers write with a smooth, even flow of letters and words and some write with a very jerky motion, and, of course, there are many levels of skill in between. As in many actions, writing is a function of fine motor control. An experienced examiner can look at how well the letters are formed and the flow of the writing and clearly see the writer's skill level. Skill level is an important characteristic of a writer because people can only write with the fine motor control that they have. Someone with a lower fine motor control level cannot consistently write in smooth, flowing handwriting. Someone with a higher skill level might be better able to write with a "lower skill" appearance. But it is difficult, because the person must write unnaturally. Therefore, skill level, or the level of fine motor control, is an important writing characteristic that can help document examiners determine authenticity.

Other factors are important in the detailed examination of how a document was written. The pictorial and contextual elements such as style, spacing, **grammar,** and spelling are all significant. Some writers tend to cram the letters and/or words together, and others spread their writing out. Some writers have the letters close together with the words well spaced; some have the words close together and the letters well spaced. There are myriad variations. Another important set of features are the mechanical characteristics, such as the formation and slant of the letters, and the ratios of small to tall letters.

Importance of Known Standards

The variability of handwriting both in terms of day-to-day variation and variation caused by other physical changes, as indicated earlier, complicates the handwriting comparison process. A document examiner has the difficult problem of assessing whether the differences between a known sample and evidential writing are due to this variation or to the writing having been done by a different writer. The more comprehensive the set of known standard writings, the better the examiner can define and judge the normal variation level. Further, knowledge of when the evidence writing was supposed to have been written and the availability of standard writing from the same period, or at least within a fairly narrow time range, can further help in defining natural variation. Thus, both an appropriate quantity and a well-documented known writing sample are critical to the success to handwriting comparison. This may be frustrating for the investigator who must usually gather these samples, but failure to do so can often lead to an inconclusive result.

Collected Writings   Handwriting standards fall into two general categories: authenticated, collected writings; and requested (ordered) samples. **Collected writings** are the most useful but often the most difficult to obtain. Investigators get these samples from the subject's life experience and history. They can be letters written to friends, job applications, business papers, school records, loan applications, insurance claims, and myriad other sources. Original writing is highly desirable, and many of the sources can provide only microfilm or imaged copies of the original record. Further, many of the sources may simply not exist for a particular person. The investigator must be persistent and often patient to try to obtain the desired materials. These types of samples can provide an accurate record of an individual's writing and can often contribute important information on how the writing looked in a particular period of interest, or how it changed with time. Further, each sample must be carefully authenticated to ensure that the sample came from the individual in question and not a spouse or someone else with the same name.

Requested (Ordered) Writings   **Requested writings** are those obtained either voluntarily, or through a court order, directly from the individual. Although this might sound ideal, because the investigator can tell the individual exactly what to write, there are at least two problems. First, the individual now knows that he or she is a target of an investigation and may try to distort or disguise the handwriting. Second, this is a

---

skill level

The level of fine motor control displayed in an individual's writing.

grammar

The rules concerning how words are used, change their form, and combine with other words to make sentences.

collected writings

Writing samples obtained from a variety of sources that represent a valid sample of an individual's writing.

requested writings

Writing samples obtained from an individual either voluntarily or as the result of a court order.

Figure 7.10

Individual providing request handwriting sample from dictation.

contemporaneous sample. If the evidence writing was done some time before or if the individual's medical condition has changed, the writing may also have changed, making comparison more complex. To address the first problem, the sample must be taken under carefully controlled conditions. The material should always be dictated, and the dictation should be repeated several times (Figure 7.10). Individuals trying to disguise their writing will tend to lose concentration and the writing on the second or third dictation will tend to drift toward their normal writing habits. Professional document examiners can apply several other tricks in drafting a dictation that will help to provide a more truly characteristic standard. As a result, whenever an investigator applies for a court-ordered sample, he or she should seek assistance from a well-qualified document examiner in drafting and taking the requested or ordered sample.

Dictation is critical because it allows one to gain information on important characteristics such as spelling, page layout, and a variety of other significant aspects of how an individual writes, in addition to the mechanics of their handwriting. If someone is asked to copy a typed or printed exemplar, most of that information is lost. Spelling, word spacing, page layout, and line spacing will all tend to follow that on the template and not necessarily be characteristic of the individual's writing.

Detailed Comparison of How Documents Are Written   Handwriting comparison encompasses many more things than how the writing looks. When comparing an evidentiary document to known handwriting standards, the first area of interest is the appearance of the writing on the page. Such things include how writing is located on the page; line, word, and letter spacing; word usage, spelling, and grammar; margins; whether lines run parallel to the top of the page; and many other appearance characteristics. Not all these things will be appropriate for every document but those that apply must be compared. Obviously, if a standard is a form, line spacing and margins will be of little consequence, but letter spacing, spelling, and many of the other characteristics can be compared. After looking at the general appearance, the examiner is concerned with the more detailed aspects of the writing: how the letters are made (letter forms), where pressure is applied, connections between letters, word and letter spacing, and other subtle characteristics of the writing.

Writing Mechanics

Handwriting comparison is most concerned with how letters are formed individually and into words. A well-trained examiner will look at each letter and how it is made, where it starts and ends, where pressure is heavy, and the general flow of the writing.

Letter and word spacing are important characteristics as well as letter connection within words and marks such as "i" dots and "t" crosses. The size ratios of the large and small letters and between the upper and lower portions of the same letter are also important. Slant of the writing is likewise a useful characteristic. The ability to distinguish between different writers depends on the examiner's ability to fully appreciate the subtle differences in the way writers write. That ability is developed only after careful study of **writing mechanics** and hundreds of hours of practice, usually under the tutelage of a seasoned examiner. As previously mentioned, another characteristic of an individual's writing is the writer's skill level.

Handprinting

It seems that in recent years, with the replacement of the letter by computer e-mail, more people are using **handprinting,** rather than handwriting, when writing is necessary. Much of what has been said about handwriting examination is also true about handprinting. However, the comparison of handprinting is handicapped by the loss of the connecting strokes and several other characteristics useful in handwriting comparison. Handprinting can be successfully compared and identified in many cases if sufficient evidence printing is available and good handprinting knowns are obtained.

Legal Status of Underlying Science

The *Daubert* decision (Chapter 2), which set down new standards for admissibility of scientific and technical evidence into court, has enabled some pattern comparison areas to be challenged—and handwriting is one of those. Interestingly, this is true even though handwriting comparison and identification have been accepted in the courts for about 100 years.

The Daubert issue is not so much whether one "believes" that handwriting can be individualized by document examiners but whether the underlying basis for the examination can be documented and articulated. One federal appeals court determined a few years ago that a "scientific" basis for handwriting comparison had not been appropriately established. By a sort of circular logic, the court allowed the results of the examination as "technical" expertise, since Daubert criteria did not strictly apply unless the examination was intrinsically scientific. The court did note that handwriting identification would not meet the Daubert threshold. Subsequent rulings by the Supreme Court made it clear that the Daubert standards must indeed be applied to "technical" areas. Thus, the issue is not completely resolved. Research has shown that trained document examiners achieve far better accuracy than untrained people or even students who have been taught a little bit about the subject. This work demonstrates that experienced questioned document examiners obtain the correct results. But more research is needed on the levels of intraindividual handwriting variation and on the creation of good measurement models for how handwriting comparison experts do their work. The scientific basis for handwriting examination has become an active area of research because of the legal controversy.

Nonhandwriting Document Examinations

In many types of cases, questioned document examiners can provide a useful service with other than handwriting evidence. Unfortunately, many investigators are unaware of the full range of document examination services and, as a result, the evidence may never be submitted. Documents produced on typewriters, copiers, computer printers, commercial printing, and even rubber stamp impressions can be scientifically examined and compared.

Typewriter and Printer Comparisons

Typewriters, check writers, stamps, computer printers, even commercial printing—all have characteristics that can often yield valuable identification or investigative

writing mechanics
The way an individual writes, particularly letter shapes and connection.

handprinting
Noncursive writing where letters are individually formed and normally not connected.

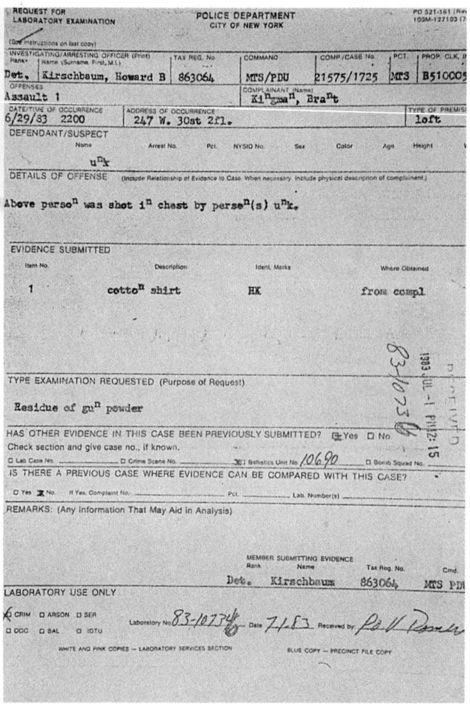

REQUEST FOR LABORATORY EXAMINATION
POLICE DEPARTMENT
CITY OF NEW YORK
PD 521-161
(See instructions on last copy)
INVESTIGATING/ARRESTING OFFICER (Print) Rank Name (Surname, First, M.I.): Det. Kirschbaum, Howard B
TAX REG. No.: 863064
COMMAND: MTS/PDU
COMP./CASE No.: 21575/1725
PCT.: MTS
PROP. CLK.: B510005
OFFENSES: Assault 1
COMPLAINANT (Name): Kingman, Brant
DATE/TIME OF OCCURRENCE: 6/29/83 2200
ADDRESS OF OCCURRENCE: 247 W. 30st 2fl.
TYPE OF PREMISES: loft
DEFENDANT/SUSPECT
Name Arrest No. Pct. NYSID No. Sex Color Age Height
unk
DETAILS OF OFFENSE (Include Relationship of Evidence to Case. When necessary, include physical description of complainant.)
Above parson was shot in chest by persen(s) unk.
EVIDENCE SUBMITTED
Item No. Description Ident. Marks Where Obtained
1 cotton shirt HK from compl
TYPE EXAMINATION REQUESTED (Purpose of Request)
Residue of gun powder
HAS OTHER EVIDENCE IN THIS CASE BEEN PREVIOUSLY SUBMITTED? ☒ Yes ☐ No
Check section and give case no., if known.
☐ Lab Case No. ☐ Crime Scene No. ☒ Ballistics Unit No. 10690 ☐ Bomb Squad No.
IS THERE A PREVIOUS CASE WHERE EVIDENCE CAN BE COMPARED WITH THIS CASE?
☐ Yes ☒ No If Yes, Complaint No. Pct. Lab. Number(s)
REMARKS: (Any Information That May Aid in Analysis)
MEMBER SUBMITTING EVIDENCE
Rank Name Tax Reg. No. Cmd.
Det. Kirschbaum 863064 MTS PDU
LABORATORY USE ONLY
☒ CRIM ☐ ARSON ☐ SER ☐ DOC ☐ BAL ☐ IOTU
Laboratory No. 83-10734 Date 7-1-83 Received by
WHITE AND PINK COPIES — LABORATORY SERVICES SECTION BLUE COPY — PRECINCT FILE COPY
83-10736
1983 JUL -1 PM 12:15

Figure 7.11

Laboratory request form typed on a mechanical typewriter with major misalignment.

information. For many years, typewriters were used to create many documents that came to the attention of document examiners. Although the use of typewriters has certainly dwindled, they were extremely important for a long time, and they can still be important. There are millions of contracts and wills still in existence that were typed on a **typewriter** anywhere from 10 to 50 years ago. Document examiners can gain useful information from examination of typewritten documents, particularly those typed with the older lever machines. These typewriters often developed misalignments or damage to the typefaces (Figure 7.11). The constant mechanical impacts involved in transferring ink from the ribbon to paper produced a continuing strain on the moving parts. Damage, misalignments, and mechanical defects of these older typewriters would be reflected in the typewritten document and could serve as basis for comparison. One key process in the examination of typewritten material involves using an accurately ruled template (Figure 7.12) to examine letter alignment.

typewriter

A machine with keys that are pressed to produce letters and numbers on paper.

The amount of useful information a document examiner can obtain from mechanical printing has decreased significantly as such devices have become more technically advanced and more varied. The evolution away from the lever-type typewriter to the ball element and print wheel typewriter made the document examiner's life much more difficult. The ball element typewriters essentially eliminated the ability to tell anything about the make or model from the type font because the ball elements and print wheels were interchangeable.

With more modern types of mechanical printing devices, useful data can still be obtained. Any printer that is an impact device can develop misalignments and can suffer damage to its typing elements because it has the potentially damaging effect of physical movement. But with laser-type printers and other nonimpact printers, like inkjets, the possibility of mechanical defects is virtually eliminated. Laser printers and most copying machines work by causing a light beam to trace out letters on an electrostatic drum. The toner (transfer medium) is attracted to the drum and then fused onto the paper from the drum. There are no writing elements and little opportunity for damage. Some misalignments are possible, and minor damage to the highly polished drum is not uncommon. With these machines, though, it is very hard to individualize a particular machine. The information available from examination of documents produced on such machines is quite limited, unless they develop some kind of a serious problem or suffer damage not related to their printing function.

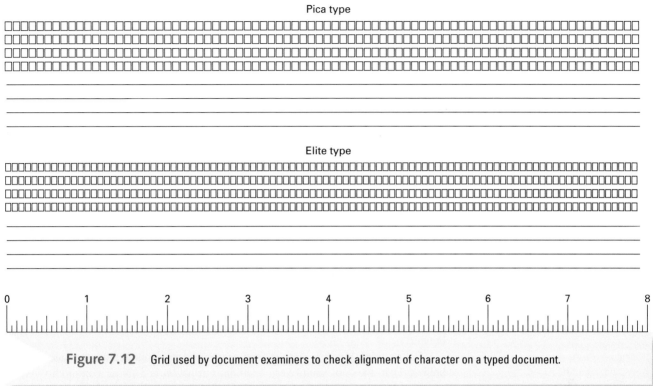

Figure 7.12 Grid used by document examiners to check alignment of character on a typed document.

Copying Machines

Copy machines and the documents they produce can provide some useful investigative information. As indicated earlier, copies of handwritten documents are not usually suitable for handwriting comparison because the important information concerning pressure points, lifts, retraces, and critical information about letter formation is lost. Examiners can develop useful information, however, through analysis of the toner. In a **copying machine** and in laser printers, the toner takes the place of the ink, particularly in copiers using a xerographic or similar process. The toner is attracted to the charged drum and is then transferred to the copy paper and seared onto the paper using heat. Different copier or laser printer manufacturers tend to use different toner formulations. In addition, not only the device manufacturers make toner. Analysis of the toner composition may reveal the manufacturer of the copier, or at least the company who compounded the toner. This can be useful when searching for a machine that might have been used to make a copy and for comparing copies as to source. Experts can often determine the make and the model of the copier used or at least the type of copy process the machine used. There is also the possibility of accidental marks on the drum. On some Xerox copiers, for example, a full revolution of the drum produces three copies, which results in every third page having a mark corresponding to the position of the mark on the drum. The spacing between repeating marks will vary depending on the copier model. When there are a sufficient number of different repeating marks, such marks are potentially individualizing characteristics. Older fax machines used a thermal printing process that could develop some class characteristics, but few individual characteristics. Most modern "plain paper" fax machines use a process similar to laser printers.

copying machine

A machine that makes copies of documents using one of several different duplication processes.

Reconstruction of Document Events

Document examiners provide a wide variety of services other than comparisons. They can help to decipher documents that are not easily read and authenticate that documents have not been altered.

Alterations and Erasures

Document examiners are often asked whether a document is the authentic original or whether it has been altered. Detecting alterations and erasures can be extremely important. For example, if a person has a lottery ticket that is just one digit different from a big winner, the temptation to alter that ticket (Figure 7.13) can be fueled by millions of dollars. If only the three could be changed to an eight, it could be a big winner. It has been tried many times. A person usually would not try this on a 50-million-dollar winner, because the top winners are closely scrutinized. However, very substantial amounts are given out to winners upon presentation of a ticket and with little scrutiny of that ticket.

Most lotteries are now quite sophisticated and have built-in protections such as erasure protection, microprinting that will not copy, or incorporation of a hologram that is difficult to reproduce. Counterfeiting lottery tickets can be as tempting as altering authentic ones. Similarly, with the quality of color copiers and digital scanners, simply making copies of money can produce quite authentic-looking fakes. This is the impetus behind the Treasury Department redesigning the currency to add many new features. We now have off-center presidential portraits, a little line that gives the amount of the bill but is only visible by holding the bill up to a bright light, microprinting that is so small that it is beyond the resolution of copiers, and other security features. Over the years people have found it a challenge to devise new ways to alter documents for their benefit.

Let us think about a simple document such as a contract for the sale of pork bellies. That does not sound very exciting, but bacon is a major commodity. When a person signs a contract for a million pounds of pork bellies, that represents a great deal of money. If the original contact is for a price of $1.16 per pound and the other party who is supplying the pork bellies subtly changes the amount to $1.76 per pound, even that difference is a lot of money. For a million pounds, adding $0.60 per pound is a $600,000 difference. Unfortunately, many people would be tempted to attempt document alteration for $600,000.

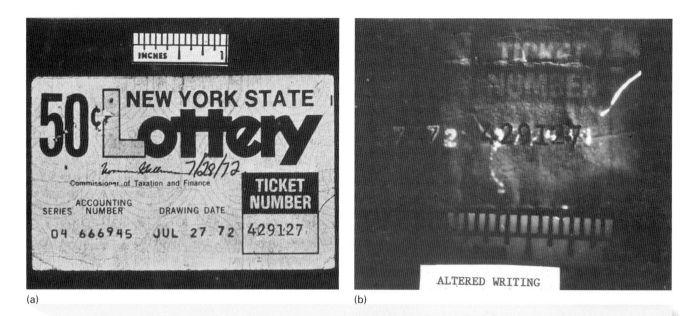

(a)　　　　　　　　　　　　　　　　　　　　(b)

Figure 7.13　A: Lottery ticket as seen under normal illumination. B: Lottery ticket shown in infrared luminescence clearly showing the alteration.

People alter documents in their favor for economic reasons and other reasons as well. One of the simplest ways to determine if a document has been altered is to examine it carefully using good lighting and a stereomicroscope. If this fails to disclose any alterations, several other examinations are possible. For example, photographic techniques may show changes that cannot easily be seen even with magnification. When a person alters a document using an **ink eradicator** fluid, he or she must remove the original writing before replacing it with the desired changes. Thus there are two processes, some sort of erasure and some new writing. In some cases, something only needs to be added, but most often something must be erased so that something else can be added. A good document examiner will look for both, and neither is easy to disguise from a knowledgeable examiner. Alterations are almost always done some time after the original document was executed. It may be years later, or as in our pork belly illustration, it may only be six months or less. Perhaps there has been a sudden change in the market that means a large loss on the original contract. The point is that when the alteration is made, even if a person can do an almost undetectable erasure, whatever must be added often cannot be done with the instrument that was originally used to create the document. It is also rather difficult to achieve perfect alignment if the document is being mechanically printed. If handwritten, obtaining the same or an identical pen that was used when the document was originally created could pose a significant problem.

Individuals can certainly match the color of the ink. They can go to an office supply store and buy 36 different blue pens or 24 black pens and select the one that appears exactly the same color on the document that they wish to alter. In the world of inks, however, having the same color does not necessarily mean the same ink. As discussed earlier, the technology for making virtually all inks involves mixing different **dyes** or **pigments** to get the desired color. Many different combinations of colored dyes and pigments will produce essentially the same color. Forensic scientists can use chemical analysis to look at the mixture of dyes or pigments in a particular ink sample (Figure 7.6). That kind of analysis will often show that inks that look to be the same color have different compositions and therefore must be from different writing instruments.

Although two inks look to be the same color to our eye (i.e., they are in the "visible" part of the **electromagnetic spectrum**), their interaction with other parts of the electromagnetic spectrum may still be quite different. Therefore, an expert might be able to use nonvisible light photography to tell two identical-appearing inks apart. Taking a normal color photograph will show about the same thing that you would see looking through a stereomicroscope. On the other hand, taking a picture with a filter that filters out the visible light, but allows either ultraviolet or infrared light to pass with a special film sensitive to the appropriate light, may allow a forensic scientist to see something that cannot be seen with normal vision—that is, to extend the range of human vision. Since our eyes are only sensitive to a relatively small portion of the spectrum called the "visible" portion. There are many areas of the spectrum our eyes cannot perceive that cameras and film can detect.

Many document examiners now have access to an instrument called a **spectral comparator.** These instruments operate using a specialized video camera and a variety of light sources and filters to make quite a number of nonvisible light examinations and comparisons much simpler and more effective. Examiners can also use mechanical and physical methods to detect alteration. One of the simplest is to look for changes in the paper brought about by the alteration. We mentioned earlier that paper is matted cellulose fibers and it has a thin layer on top of the matted fibers to make the surface smoother and better able to accept the transfer medium (ink). This is normally either glue or clay and is called sizing material. No matter how carefully one tries to erase writing or printing, the process of erasing will disturb that very thin sizing layer and some of that material will be removed. This may not be visible to the naked eye or perhaps even with a microscope, but if the document is examined by backlighting on a **light box,** the erased area will show up. It will show a lighter

---

ink eradicator

A fluid used to decolorize ink on a document to make it invisible.

dye

A deeply colored material that dissolves in a solution or an object to give it a desired color.

pigment

A very finely divided, highly colored material that does not dissolve, but rather is suspended in a solution or dispersed through an object to give it a desired color.

electromagnetic spectrum

The full range of electromagnetic radiation, from low-energy microwaves (transmission of telephone calls) to high-energy gamma rays, including the visible portion to which our eyes are sensitive and X-rays used by doctors to visualize our bones.

spectral comparator

An instrument that has a number of light sources, filters, and a video camera used to examine documents in a way that greatly increases what one can "see" on that document over what our eyes can ordinarily observe.

light box

A box with a very even light source behind a piece of ground or translucent glass or plastic, which is used to backlight an object.

area because some of the opaque sizing material has been removed. The paper fibers will allow more light to penetrate the paper in the erased area than through the area where the glue or clay sizing is undisturbed. Just a simple light box that a person would use to view photographic negatives or slides, or like a doctor would use to view X-rays, is frequently all that is needed.

Experts can also look for alterations mechanically. One of the classic ways that document examiners look for erasures is using a very fine powder such as lycopodium powder (pollen from a plant) or even fingerprint powder. They spread a little bit of the fine powder all over the document that is suspected of having an erasure, shake it around a bit, and then tap it all off. Where the erasure has occurred, the surface coating layer will be disturbed. If the sizing is partially removed, the paper fibers are exposed and a much rougher surface is exposed. The very fine powder is trapped in this roughened fibers surface, and since the powder is usually colored, the disturbed surface is made clearly visible. Usually this technique will work with chemical ink eradicator as well, since the chemical will also affect the sizing layer. Erasing fluids normally works by decolorizing the ink so it can no longer be seen on the document. The ink is still there but no longer visible to the eye. Nonvisible light techniques will often disclose this writing that has been made "invisible."

Charred Documents and Indented Writing

Indented writing and charred documents present a different type of document problem. With **indented writing,** there is no transfer medium, only mechanical indentation in the paper; with a **charred document,** the color of the paper has been changed to black or near black so the ink can no longer be easily seen. Both situations are fairly common. For example, if someone involved in a white-collar crime wants to obscure the paper trail, he or she might take all the files and attempt to burn them. It turns out that paper does not burn as easily as one might think, particularly when a stack of paper consists of many sheets. Although paper burns quite easily when a single sheet or when crumpled-up sheets are ignited, when a person has a stack of paper or a ledger book, it becomes quite difficult to provide sufficient air for rapid combustion. Unless the person keeps stirring and separating the sheets, they will only be charred around the edges. Even if the burning has been more successful, a forensic scientist may recover the charred paper. It will be difficult to read because the writing has become black writing on black paper. The ink residue, however, may still be there. This problem can be solved in several ways through careful examination using transmitted light or using nonvisible light photography to extend our human vision. Recovering the writing on a charred document can be done most easily with a spectral comparator as mentioned earlier. If the original writing absorbs or reflects light outside the visible part of the electromagnetic spectrum and the expert uses the correct combination of film and filters, he or she may make the ink appear as bright on a dark background and thereby visible again (Figure 7.14). The most difficult part is often finding a way to handle the charred sheets of paper without destroying this very delicate material. There are chemicals that can be lightly sprayed on the charred paper to soften it and make it much easier to handle.

Indented writing can also be an important investigative aid in many document cases. Deciphering indented writing has been a favorite device in detective stories. When a person writes on a sheet of paper, particularly if firm pressure is used, the sheet underneath will have an impression of what was written on the sheet above. In a number of both criminal and civil situations, indented writing can provide valuable information. Often, something is written on a piece of paper that's on top of another piece of paper. It could be a pad of paper, a ledger book, or perhaps a multipage document. Another example is provided by sign-in books, which are common for security purposes or used as employee timekeeping devices. These are frequently important in investigations of individuals signing in for someone else or inserting

indented writing

An impression on one or more sheets below the one that a writing instrument was used to produce an image upon.

charred document

A document that has been partially burned or heated until it has turned a very dark color and can no longer easily be read.

Figure 7.14
Fragment of a charred document with the writing contrast enhanced by infrared luminescence.

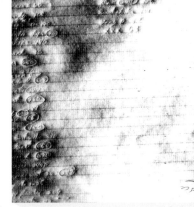

Figure 7.15
Indented writing visualized photographically using low-angle (oblique) lighting.

their name at a much later time, perhaps to provide an alibi or for a variety of other reasons. When a person signs in, an indented image of the signature will appear on the page below in the book. By looking at the indented writing, an examiner can often tell if something was written on the page underneath either before or after the indented writing. Thus something added later will show up as indented over the material on the page underneath.

Indented writing has traditionally been visualized in two different ways. The method that many of us used as children—where we took the pad with the indented writing and used a pencil on its side to very lightly darken the paper—is not used professionally. Where there were indentations, the pencil lead would not darken the indented area and the surface around would be darkened. This produces the appearance of white writing on a dark background. A better method is using **oblique lighting.** Shining light at a very low angle to the paper produces shadows in the indented area, sometimes allowing the indented writing to be read (Figure 7.15). Photography can then be used to make a permanent record of it. This method is analogous to how a person usually tries to see if there might be some indented writing by tilting the page at different angles to the light to make any indentations more visible. Forensic laboratories usually used the low-angle lighting method to visualize indented writing until the development in England some years ago of an electrostatic method.

oblique lighting

Using a bright light at a very low angle (grazing angle) to a document to make indentations on the sheet more visible by shadowing them.

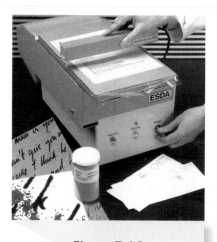

Figure 7.16

ESDA (Electrostatic Document Apparatus) machine used to visualize indented writing.

Figure 7.17

An ESDA instrument with an insert showing some indented writing that was made visible using the ESDA process.

ESDA

Electrostatic Detection Apparatus; an instrument developed in England specifically for making indented writing visible on a clear cover sheet without altering the original document.

platen

A perforated plate used to firmly hold an object using air pressure.

watermark

A mark that is made on some types of paper during its production that can be seen only if it is held against the light.

The development of the **ESDA** machine (ESDA stands for Electrostatic Detection Apparatus) revolutionized the ability to find and document indented writing (Figure 7.16). The ESDA is now the way that most professional document examiners look for indented writing. The ESDA machine has a flat plate, with many closely spaced fine holes, through which air is pulled to create a slight vacuum and thereby hold the paper firmly down on that plate, called a **platen.** An examiner then places a very thin sheet of plastic over the document, and it is held firmly against the paper. An electrostatic charge is put on the sandwich, then a little bit of a very fine powder, which looks a lot like copy machine toner, is dusted over it. The electrostatic charge is concentrated in the areas that were indented in the original document, causing the powder to stick there. The whole platen is then raised up at an angle to allow the excess powder to slide off the plastic cover sheet. The dark-colored powder sticks in the indented areas and makes them highly visible (Figure 7.17). In most cases the indented writing can be clearly read. The results can be photographed to preserve the information, and once the clear plastic is removed the document is unaltered. The process works exceptionally well; in fact, its only disadvantage is that it is almost too sensitive. It is sometimes possible to see indented writing on a pad six or more sheets down using ESDA. This can result in each sheet on that pad having indented writing from the four or five sheets above it. It can be a little confusing trying to determine which indented writing corresponds to which sheet. Nevertheless, investigators should consider examination of documents for indented writing when it seems appropriate.

Age Determination

One of the most troublesome problems in document examination is determination of when a document was written. For example, QD examiners are often asked whether a document was written when it was dated or whether it was forged or altered in some way at a later time. Some approaches can help limit the range of possibilities at times, but as a rule the question cannot be answered reliably. The QD examiner's two most powerful aides in such a determination are context and technology. For example, the document may contain something subtle that refer to an event that didn't occur until sometime shortly after the purported date of the document. Although you might think the forger or alterer would be too careful to make such a mistake, it does happen.

Examination of the composition of the paper, a **watermark** on the paper, and inks used in the document can all on occasion provide useful information to help date a document. Over the years the manufacturing methods to make paper and the raw materials used to make it have evolved. Again, if a document is on paper that was manufactured much earlier or later than the purported date of the document, it suggests that the document is not authentic. Most high-quality paper is watermarked. If you hold such paper up to a bright light, you often see an area that shows a different degree of transparency than the bulk of the paper. It usually appears as a stamp of some sort and results from embossing on the rollers used to make the paper. This watermark normally identifies the company that made the paper and frequently carries information on when it was made and on a number of other characteristics, which can be very important in aging and otherwise identifying the paper. Unfortunately, most inexpensive paper such as copier or school filler paper is not watermarked.

Although an effort has been made to develop reliable methods for dating documents based on the inks used, success has been very limited. Ballpoint pen ink, with which most documents are written today, is made by hundreds of different manufacturers. Further, those who construct the pens and refills tend to treat ink as a commodity and purchase from the lowest bidder, rather than using a consistent supplier. Two federal agencies in the United States and some private examiners collect ink samples from many different manufacturers to maintain a database of ink formulations. The common practice is to determine the combinations of dyes or pigments contained in each ink formulation using chromatographic techniques. As mentioned earlier, there are sizable variations in ink compositions, and as a result examiners can often easily differentiate inks that appear to be the same color in this way. With a document, a sample of the ink is taken by punching out tiny circles of writing from a few letters using a syringe needle. A number of these tiny circles of paper with ink on

Case Study 7.3

Kennedy Letters

A few years ago there was quite a bit of publicity about some John F. Kennedy letters coming onto the market. These letters had come into the possession of an individual whose father had been a lawyer and a friend of President Kennedy. After his father died, the man claimed that while going through his father's papers, he found a cache of letters from Kennedy that his father had saved. One of those letters, which was thought to exist by many, concerned the relationship between President Kennedy and Marilyn Monroe. The letter produced indicated that President Kennedy had an agreement with Marilyn Monroe that he would take care of her mother in her old age, if Marilyn continued her affair with him. This purported affair has been the subject of speculation for many years. At the time a rather well-known investigative reporter named Seymour Hersh was working on a not very favorable biography of John Kennedy. He gained access to this letter and intended to use it to buttress his chapter on President Kennedy and Marilyn Monroe in the book. These Kennedy papers were offered for sale and sold to a group of investors at auction. Before purchasing the papers, they had them authenticated, particularly the signatures, by a dealer in rare and valuable documents, who indicated that, in his opinion, the John F. Kennedy signatures were authentic. The purchase group, at least partially relying on his opinion, agreed to pay 1.6 million dollars for these letters. Shortly after the purchase, they became nervous about their purchase. The papers were then shown to several well-qualified QD examiners. One of them was particularly familiar with typewriters and examination of typewritten documents. He came from a family of several generations of QD examiners and had grown up with typewriter examination. The purchasers brought in the documents, including the Marilyn Monroe letter, asking for his opinion as to authenticity. The story goes that he picked up the Marilyn Monroe letter, looked at it for just a few moments, and said it was a forgery. Their first reaction was, how could he know that from such a cursory examination? He indicated that the letter was typed on an IBM Selectric typewriter that had not been sold until well after the date on the letter. He immediately recognized the model of typewriter used from the type font and other characteristics. This initial opinion was later confirmed using other techniques. The entire group of documents were forgeries and virtually worthless.

Other document examiners who examined the letters agreed that they were forgeries for many other reasons. Even the signatures were not particularly skillful forgeries. The initial finding of an anachronism, the use of a typewriter that was not available until much later than the purported date of the documents, was the most dramatic single piece of incontrovertible evidence. Fortunately for Mr. Hersh, the fraud came to light just before his book was to be published and he was able to rewrite the chapter on the Kennedy/Monroe affair. The seller of the "Kennedy Papers" had created them himself, and he had to pay back whatever he had left of the 1.6 million. In addition, he was convicted of fraud and sent to prison.

them are placed in a small tube and a solvent added to dissolve the ink. This ink solution is then separated into its components using a chromatographic method: thin-layer chromatography (**TLC**) or high-performance liquid chromatography (**HPLC**). The exact same conditions are used as were used on the manufacturers' samples. The pattern of the dyes observed is compared with that found in the ink database to try to determine the ink formulation. These comparisons are again most useful to detect ink formulations that were not developed until after the date on the document. If an examiner can show that the particular ballpoint ink formulation that was used in a document was not manufactured until a number of years after the document was supposed to have been written, the situation is analogous to the Kennedy/Monroe letter (Case Study 7.3). The reasoning does not work in the other direction. An ink formulation in existence before the document was supposed to have been written does not show alteration or forgery.

TLC

Thin-layer chromatography; a separation technique using a plate with a thin layer of an absorbent and capillary action to move a solvent up the plate.

HPLC

High-performance liquid chromatography; a separation technique using high pressure to force a solvent through a tube packed with an absorbent.

Summary

Questioned document examination often involves comparison of handwriting, typewriting, and photocopier output. Erasures, alterations, and other changes are also part of the examination. QD examiners are often asked to authenticate signatures. Forgery is the making of an illegal copy of a signature or document for purposes of deception.

Much of a QD examiner's work involves handwriting. Handwriting has both class and individual characteristics that are conditioned by schooling, by level of education, and by the style an individual ultimately develops. Handwriting comparison involves comparison of questioned writing with known writing. Known writing varies from example to example, and from day to day, in the same individual. But it varies less in the same individual than between individuals. To do a proper comparison, a QD examiner needs multiple examples of a person's known writing, and that writing must resemble (contain the same letters, and be of the same style, etc.) as the questioned writing. Known writing may be "requested" from a person or it may be "collected" from available written documents. A handwriting comparison is based on class and individual characteristics. The more writing an examiner has for comparison, the more information he or she can glean. With adequate writings available for comparison, an examiner can often conclude that a person did or did not write a particular document. There are still unresolved Daubert issues surrounding handwriting comparisons.

Document evidence should be collected carefully and preserved so as to protect not only the writing but also any trace evidence or fingerprints that may be present. The QD examiner must know the circumstances of collection of both the questioned and of the known writing submitted for comparison.

QD examiners also compare typewriting and printing, although typewriting is becoming more and more uncommon. They also compare photocopies to try and determine whether a particular machine might be responsible for a particular copy. Computer printers, copy machines, and fax machines can impart class and individual characteristics upon documents they produce, making comparisons possible.

Alterations and erasures may also be analyzed by QD examiners. Often, such alterations are fraudulent and intended for the economic gain of the perpetrator, such as altering a lottery ticket to appear to have the winning numbers. Inks can be compared to some extent using thin-layer chromatography (TLC) and some other instrumental methods. Inks cannot be individualized, but an ink might be excluded as a possible source of a questioned ink on a document. Some federal agencies maintain extensive ink libraries, with dates of manufacture. If a person were to use an ink first manufactured after the date on a document to alter that document, an examiner could detect that relatively easily. There is no scientific way to tell the age of ink on a document. In addition to ink, comparisons of paper are possible using manufacturer-introduced features of the paper.

Sometimes, QD examiners can discern the writing on charred documents. Although these are very fragile, they are worth submitting for examination. Indented writing can also sometimes be discerned using an ESDA. Instruments that permit viewing of documents under infrared and ultraviolet illumination can also reveal alterations not apparent under visible light.

Key Terms

questioned document (p. 153)
alteration (p. 153)
authenticate (p. 154)
forgery (p. 154)
cursive writing (p. 155)
normal variation (p. 156)
writing instrument (p. 156)
transfer medium (p. 156)
surface coating (sizing) (p. 157)
fountain pen (p. 158)
ink composition (p. 158)
threatening letter (p. 160)
extortion note (p. 160)

contemporaneous (p. 161)
disguise (p. 162)
skill level (p. 163)
grammar (p. 163)
collected writings (p. 163)
requested writings (p. 163)
writing mechanics (p. 165)
handprinting (p. 165)
typewriter (p. 166)
copying machine (p. 167)
ink eradicator (p. 169)
dye (p. 169)
pigment (p. 169)

electromagnetic spectrum (p. 169)
spectral comparator (p. 169)
light box (p. 169)
indented writing (p. 170)
charred document (p. 170)
oblique lighting (p. 171)
ESDA (p. 171)
platen (p. 172)
watermark (p. 172)
TLC (p. 173)
HPLC (p. 173)

Review Questions—Short Answer

1. Discuss how questioned document examiners can provide information useful to many types of investigations.
2. What are the major factors in development of an individual's handwriting?
3. List the two major types of handwriting control samples and their particular advantages and disadvantages.

4. List several important types of examinations that questioned document examiners provide, other than handwriting comparison.
5. What are the main approaches for estimation of when a document may actually have been written?
6. What are the major methods used to decipher indented writing?
7. What are the major methods used to look for erasures on documents?
8. Discuss the environmental factors that can affect the appearance of an individual's handwriting.
9. What types of examinations do document examiners perform on typewritten, computer printed, and copied documents?
10. Discuss differences between handwriting and hand printing and how they can affect the examination of such documents.

Fill-in-the-Blank & Multiple Choice

1. The variation in characteristics in known writing from a single individual is usually _____ (insignificant, less than, more than, equal to) the variation observed between different individuals' writing.
2. The production of a document in the broadest sense required three components, (1) _____, (2) writing instrument and (3) _____, all of which may be examined to produce forensically useful information.
3. A known writing sample _____ (must always, should never, should, must) contain the words and letter combinations present in the questioned document.
4. When collecting document evidence, it is important to carefully protect the document to avoid
   a. loss of trace evidence.
   b. changing handwriting images.
   c. loss of fingerprints.
   d. a and c.
   e. a, b, and c.
5. The success of a questioned document examination is highly dependent on the quality and quantity of _____ (control writing, copies of the evidence, ink used in the writing, fingerprints developed) provided by the investigator submitting the evidence.

Further References

American Society of Questioned Document Examiners Web site, www.asqde.org.

Baden, M. M. "Introduction to Plenary Session on the Lindbergh Kidnapping Revisited: Forensic Sciences Then and Now." *Journal of Forensic Sciences* 28, no. 4 (October 1983): 1035–1037.

Ellen, D. "Scientific Examination of Documents: Methods and Techniques." 2nd Edition, Abington, UK: Taylor Francis Group, 2002.

Haag, L. C. "A Brief Chronology of the Lindbergh Kidnapping." *Journal of Forensic Sciences* 28, no. 4 (October 1983): 1038–1039.

Mnookin, J. L. "Scripting Expertise: The History of Handwriting Identification Evidence and the Judicial Construction of Reliability." 87 Virginia L. Rev. 1723 (2001).

Moenssens, A. A. "Handwriting Identification in the Post-Daubert World." 66 U. of Missouri at Kansas City L. Rev. 251 (1997).

Mokrzycki, G. M. "Advances in Document Examination: The Video Spectral Comparator 2000." *Forensic Science Communications* volume 1 no. 3 (1999).

Osborn, P. A. "Excerpts and Comments on Testimony by the Document Examiners in Regard to *State of New Jersey v. Bruno Richard Hauptmann*." *Journal of Forensic Sciences* 28, no. 4 (October 1983): 1049–1070.

"Questioned Document Examination," www.faculty.ncwc.edu/toconnor/425/425lect05.htm.

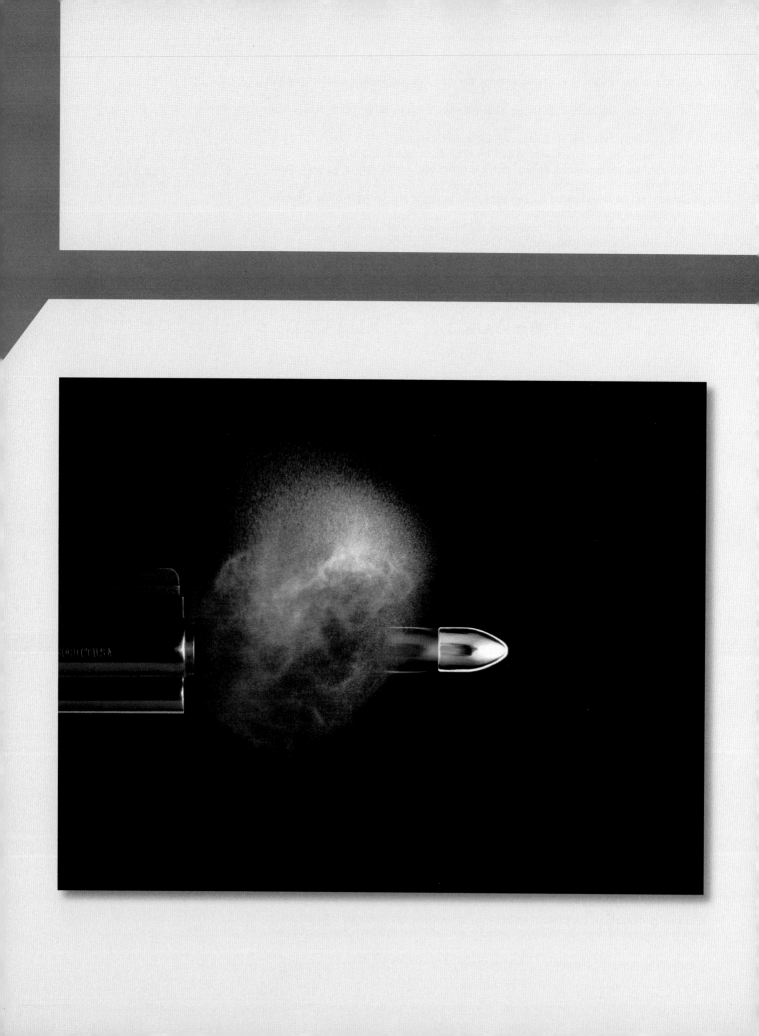

Toolmarks and Firearms

Learning Objectives

- Understand the nature of toolmarks

- The different types of toolmarks

- The importance of looking for trace evidence associated with toolmarks

- The proper ways to collect and preserve toolmarks

- The examination and comparison process

- General nature of firearms

- The function and importance of the cartridge in the operation of a firearm

- The importance of rifling to firearm performance and forensic examination

- The major important types of firearms

- Proper procedures for collecting and preserving firearms and firearms evidence

- Major steps in the examination of a firearm and firearms evidence

- Growing importance of firearms data banks to investigation and prosecution

- Potential utility of examination of even highly damaged firearms evidence

- Uses of firearms evidence in reconstructing shooting incidents

- How and why firearms serial numbers are defaced

- Major techniques for restoring defaced serial numbers

Outline

chapter

Lead Case

.44-Caliber Killer

It began in July of 1976 and gripped the city of New York for over a year. There was a series of random shootings of young people primarily in parked cars in the Lover's Lane type of location. Almost six months elapsed before it was discovered that a serial killer was involved. In New York City each borough is a separate county with its own district attorney and some county government. Because the first incidents occurred in three different boroughs of New York City, the connection was not easily made. There is, however, only one police department and one forensic laboratory for the entire city of New York. Firearms examination was to play an unusually large role in the investigation and solution of this case.

The initial discovery that several shooting incidents in different boroughs were connected was made in the firearms unit of the forensic laboratory. A firearms examiner was looking at the recovered bullet evidence from a recent shooting and remarked that the recovered evidence bullets had been fired from a .44-caliber weapon. He mentioned it only because this was not a commonly encountered caliber. One of his colleagues sitting a few feet away at a comparison microscope mentioned that he, too, had recently encountered some .44-caliber evidence. The older case was found in the file and they were compared. It was soon evident that the bullets had been fired from the same type of weapon, and further examination disclosed that it was the exact same weapon. Further checking of fairly recent cases with .44-caliber evidence disclosed a third shooting in which the exact same weapon had been used. The .44-caliber serial killer investigation was begun when the submitting detectives were notified of the connection between their cases.

The popular press renamed it the "Son of Sam" case a little later when the killer began taunting the police with notes signed "Son of Sam." The shootings continued until August 1978, despite one of the most extensive investigations in NYPD history. By then the toll had risen to six dead and a number of others either permanently disabled or seriously injured—a terrible toll of young lives.

The firearms examiners believed that, because of the somewhat unusual markings on the recovered bullets, it was highly likely that they were fired from a .44-caliber weapon manufactured by Charter Arms Company, specifically its "Bulldog" model. Pictures of this weapon were circulated to the investigators, and it became a significant focus of the investigation.

Because witnesses had seen the killer shooting from a two-handed military stance, investigators theorized that he might be a current or retired law enforcement officer. Files of the weapons possessed by current and past law enforcement officers were searched for any who owned Charter Arms Bulldog revolvers. As a result, hundreds of these weapons were brought in for testing in

A taunting note received during the so called "Son of Sam" series of shootings signed SON OF SAM (backwords) in the bottom left corner.

the firearms unit in hopes of finding the killer. Many samples were sent by nearby law enforcement agencies for comparison as well. The killer was not found, but from examining all those bullets the firearms examiners were even more convinced that the Charter Arms Bulldog was the correct make and model of the weapon.

The case was finally broken when a systematic search of all parking tickets given near the location and during the period of any of the shootings was conducted. The officers checking out a Ford that had received a ticket fairly near the scene of a recent fatal shooting went to Yonkers, a suburban community bordering the Bronx. The Bronx had been the scene of a number of the shootings. The car was parked on the street close to the address of the registered owner. When the investigators approached the car, a gun that resembled a Charter Arms Bulldog was observed in the car. Backup was called, a search warrant for the car and dwelling were applied for, and the vehicle was staked out. David Berkowitz left his apartment and approached his car and was stopped. He offered no resistance and freely admitted he was "Sam." The firearms examiners were relieved to find that the weapon seized from Mr. Berkowitz was indeed a Charter Arms Bulldog, and the test fires it produced were matched to many of the evidence bullets.

As with most high-profile cases there were those who said that Mr. Berkowitz had been set up to take the blame for a more sinister individual. However, in addition to the firearms evidence, Berkowitz had kept extensive notes on his activities that were discovered during the search of his apartment after his arrest. These writings included information that he intended another attack, very shortly, outside New York City on Long Island. These highly incriminating notes, as well as the taunting notes that had been sent to the newspapers and police, were unambiguously tied to Mr. Berkowitz by comparison to known samples of his handprinting. The identification of him as the writer was particularly strong because of the large writing sample available and the individuality of his handprinting.

After the arrest of Mr. Berkowitz, this rather bizarre story unfolded fairly quickly; after being ruled mentally competent to stand trial, Berkowitz pleaded guilty to six charges of murder and was sentenced to 365 years in prison.

Toolmark—Definition

Toolmark and firearms examinations are usually grouped together because for many years the firearms section of most forensic laboratories did the toolmark cases as well, since many of the same skills are involved. Although this is no longer the case in many laboratories, we can still look at bullet and cartridge case comparisons as a subcategory of toolmark examination. **Toolmark** can be defined as a pattern resulting from a harder marking device, that is, the tool, being forced against a softer object.

Most toolmarks of forensic interest are marks left by screwdrivers, pry bars, wire and bolt cutters, and a wide variety of other tools often used to gain forced entry into a dwelling or even a simple cash box. The comparison of bullets and cartridge cases will be covered separately in the firearms section to follow.

Toolmarks are usually either scratches (striations) or impressions made in the surface of the softer medium by a harder tool. These striations are normally the result of the tool moving across the surface leaving behind a pattern of scratches caused by tiny defects in the face or edge of the tool, whereas impressions are formed by forcing the impressing tool into the surface.

Class and Individual Characteristics

Toolmarks can have either class or individual characteristics and sometimes have both. The basic size and shape of the toolmark is certainly a class characteristic and can tell a forensic scientist something about the kind of tool that made the toolmark. For example, the mark left by the nail-puller end of a crowbar (Figure 8.1) would be quite different from that left by the prying end of a screwdriver or perhaps a chisel.

Usually crowbars have a nail-puller on one end and a flat prying surface on the other end. The nail-puller end would leave two parallel rows of stria with a separation similar to the width of the V groove used to grab the nail head. The individual characteristics are usually caused by stria. If a large number of stria are randomly distributed, but reproducible from a particular tool, then it may be possible to individualize the marks left by that tool. That is, an expert may be able to say: "In my opinion, that mark was made by that tool and no other tool."

Residue from Softer Object on Tool

Residue on the evidence tool is evidence that is often overlooked, but potentially quite useful. Where this material is shown to be consistent with the surface that was scratched, the connection of the tool to the marked surface is certainly strengthened. Such residue could be paint, oil, blood, iron, aluminum, or plastic. Although the material is usually left behind in microscopic amounts, and may not be visible to the naked eye, it may still provide a useful connection between the tool and the surface. Therefore, the first step in examination of an evidence tool is to view that tool under a stereomicroscope to see if anything foreign is on the surface of the tool. Anything that is observed can then be removed and compared for possible

toolmark

A marking on a surface caused by the pressing or sliding of a tool into or across the surface.

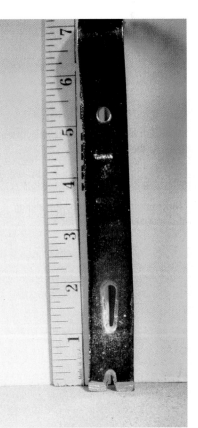

Figure 8.1
Pry bar with nail-puller at one end.

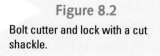

Figure 8.2

Bolt cutter and lock with a cut shackle.

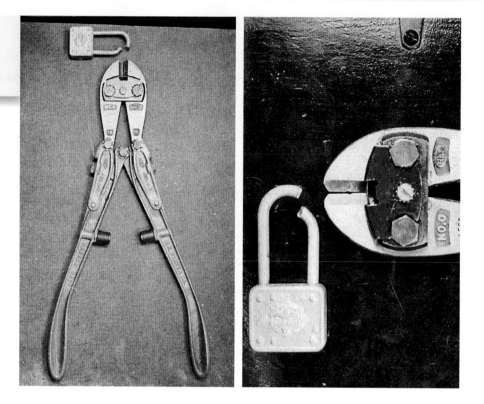

consistencies with the surface on which the toolmark was found. That is why it is so important that a control sample of the softer material from the scene be submitted with the tool, the toolmark, or a cast of the toolmark. Experts can occasionally find material characteristic of the tool left behind in the toolmark as well.

Types of Toolmarks

indented toolmarks

Marks left in a surface by pushing a tool into the surface.

striated toolmarks

Marks left in a surface by the sliding of a tool across that surface.

Toolmarks can be classified into three basic types. There are **indented marks** where the tool was pushed into the surface, **striated marks** where the tool slides across the surface, and toolmarks that are a combination of the two, where the tool is pushed in and then slides across the surface. An indented mark would result when a hammer is struck against a piece of wood to force open a boarded-up window. A common toolmark that is a special case of the striated mark is where a wire cutter or bolt cutter (Figure 8.2) is used to cut through a wire or a lock hasp. This leaves behind striations similar to what one would see from a tool sliding across a surface. As the metal is compressed and forced apart, the jaws of the cutting devise slide across the displaced metal. A combination mark would result when, using a crowbar to break into a house or an apartment, the bar is forced between the door and the frame and then used to pry the door open (Figure 8.3). That would usually leave the combination of an indented mark and a striated mark.

Collection of Toolmarks

When collecting a toolmark at a scene, a mark on anything that can be moved should be protected and then sent for examination. If the toolmark is on a fixed object and can not be moved, it should be photographed both from a distance to allow one to visualize how it might have been made and close-up, with a ruler in the picture, to make the detail visible. A high-resolution cast, using a silicone rubber casting material, should be made after photography (Figure 8.4).

Such silicone casting materials are readily available from dental supply firms or firms specializing in forensic supplies. A good crime scene kit should have silicone casting materials included. If done carefully, such casts can often be successfully

Figure 8.3
Area on door that has been forced and toolmark left behind.

Figure 8.4
Casting the toolmarks on a door using silicone rubber casting material.

compared with control toolmarks made by a suspect tool. If a suspect tool is available at the scene, it should never be fitted into the mark. This could have two very undesirable effects. There is the potential of damaging the mark, and credibility may be lost in comparing any material on the tool to the material of the surface.

Examination and Comparison of Toolmarks

As indicated earlier, the first step in laboratory examination and comparison of tools and toolmarks is a careful visual examination to detect any adhered or associated trace evidence either on the tool or left behind in the toolmark. That is why it is important that whoever collects the tool or makes a casting collect control samples of the surface. If it is a painted area, investigators should take a sample of the paint; if some other material, they should take samples from an area near the mark but not from within the marked area. The next concern is obtaining suitable test impressions in a similar material. Although that sounds quite simple, it is an extremely challenging undertaking. Because the examiner cannot know the exact conditions under which the toolmark was made, trying to reproduce it exactly is by no means trivial. The expert must use the tool at almost exactly the same angle and with the right amount of pressure, or he or she is unlikely to obtain exactly same type of mark. Because the toolmark is caused by imperfections in the marking surface of the tool, the scratches left by a tool moving across a surface at a particular angle may be different if the tool is held at a different angle. Before the expert can even begin to make a

Figure 8.5

Comparison microscope view of the comparison between an evidence toolmark and a control mark made with the suspect tool.

comparison, he or she must make a series of scratches at different angles with differing amounts of force, until a set that resembles the evidence mark is found.

The actual comparison is done under a comparison microscope putting the evidence mark or cast on one side and the control mark on the other (Figure 8.5). This takes a great deal of patience and considerable skill.

The mark must be moved about until all the significant stria (scratches) in the two marks correspond. A fair amount of skill and experience is required to decide how good the correspondence is between the marks. They will never be absolutely identical, so some judgment is required before the examiner can say: "In my opinion, that mark was made by that tool and no other tool." Often it is possible to say that the two marks are consistent in class characteristics and show a number of other similarities and therefore the tool *could* have caused the mark. Forensic scientists can also have the situation where the marks are clearly from different tools (disassociation) or where the results are not sufficiently clear to give an opinion (inconclusive result).

In summary, a toolmark may yield information about what kind of a tool was used, size of the marking portion, any unusual features, some information about the action by which the mark was made, residue consistent with the damaged surface, and in some cases even that a particular tool was responsible for that toolmark.

Firearms Examination—Background

Firearms examination can be one of the busiest and most important sections of a forensic science laboratory. In urban areas, especially large cities, many firearms cases are regularly submitted. Homicide is one of the leading causes of death in the United States overall, with deaths due to firearms injuries in 1999 representing around 1 percent of all deaths. The rate (number per 100,000 of population) of firearms-related deaths declined over the 1990s. The rate is highest among African American males and lowest among White females over that period. In 1999, firearms of some kind were involved in about 65 percent of all homicidal deaths in the United States.

Although in the past firearms examiners were often not educated in science, the training and experience needed to become an expert firearms examiner today is extensive. More entry-level firearms examiners now have four-year college science degrees than ever before.

Before we can discuss the many aspects of firearms examination, you must have a basic appreciation for how firearms work and the vast range of firearms that exist. There are many possible definitions for a firearm and a simple one is as follows: A **firearm** is a device that, using the rapid combustion of an energetic chemical, is

firearm

A device for accelerating a projectile to a high speed and sending it toward a selected target.

designed to accelerate a projectile to a high velocity while directing it toward a target. This is quite general, because a great many objects can be considered firearms in addition to handguns and long guns. Under the law in many states, persons can be charged with possession of firearm for possessing many things that most people do not usually consider guns or even weapons.

A firearm can send a projectile, such as a copper-coated piece of lead, toward a particular target so that when it hits that target, it has some sort of destructive effect on the target. The puncturing of the target by the projectile is not necessarily the main function of a firearm. The main objective may be transferring a large amount of energy and thereby causing enormous trauma. One reason that a firearm can be so deadly is the projectile's ability to transfer this energy to a soft deformable object like a human body, causing critical organs to be severely damaged and resulting in extensive internal bleeding.

The energy that provides the driving force for the projectile is contained in the cartridge. Cartridges came into general use after the Civil War to replace the powder, rag (patch), and ball combination of the muzzle-loading firearm.

In muzzle loaders, a spark ignited the powder, and the expanding gases from the powder forced the ball out of the barrel at a reasonably high speed. Clearly, taking all those pieces and putting them together in one nice convenient package, called a cartridge, was a good idea—no more need to pour powder down the muzzle, tamp down the powder, put in a ball and cloth, and tamp the materials together. Instead a neat little package was designed with the necessary components, which could fire from only the force of a firing pin striking it on the primer. There is a tendency to call the unit (cartridge) a bullet, but the bullet is just one component of a cartridge.

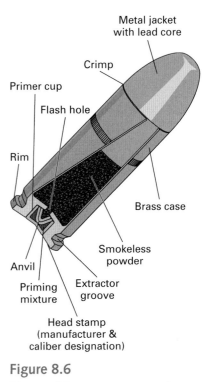

Figure 8.6

Diagram of the component parts of a cartridge.

Firearms Function—the Firing Train

A **cartridge** has four basic components (Figure 8.6). It starts with a case, which is the container of the unit. A handgun or rifle cartridge is usually a cylindrical piece of brass or nickel-plated brass that holds the other three components together. The case is filled with small disks, cylinders, or balls of smokeless powder. **Smokeless powder** is made from cotton that has been treated, very carefully, with nitric and sulfuric acid to make cellulose nitrate. Once ignited, it burns very rapidly and cleanly, producing a great deal of heat and gas. The third component is the **projectile (bullet),** which is put into the case and the case is squeezed down tightly around the bullet to make a tight seal. The bullet is usually made from lead or copper-coated lead. The final component, the **primer,** is very important because it was the key to the development of the cartridge. It takes the form of a little soft metal cup that is part of the case at the end opposite to the bullet. The primer contains a tiny amount of a shock-sensitive material. This little cup has a small hole on the side in contact with the smokeless powder. When the **firing pin** of the firearm hits that cup, it squashes the cup and causes the shock-sensitive chemical in the primer cup to ignite and transfer a spark or a tiny flame through the hole into the powder charge to ignite the powder inside the case. In some .22-caliber cartridges the primer material is in the rim of the cartridge case rather than a separate cup. The burning powder gives off heat and creates gases that develop high pressure inside the case. Because the bullet is swaged into that case, these gases are contained and the pressure rapidly builds up until it forces the bullet out of the case and down the barrel at a high speed. This entire process is sometimes called the "firing train." Thus a cartridge resembles a small explosive device (see Chapter 11), which can direct the explosive energy to drive the projectile down the barrel. The single-unit cartridge provides the powder, containment, and the projectile, which characterized the old muzzle-loading rifles and cannons. Cartridges with their four major components— primer, powder charge, projectile, and case—are the heart of modern firearms. Whether they are tiny for derringer pistols (Figure 8.7) or enormous artillery shells, the basic principle is the same.

---

cartridge

The assembly of a bullet, gunpowder, and primer in a casing that is placed in the chamber of a firearm.

smokeless powder

A nitrocellulose-based explosive or propellant that produces little smoke.

projectile (bullet)

An object that can be fired or launched.

primer

The shock-sensitive portion of the cartridge that provides the initial spark or flame that causes the cartridge to fire.

firing pin

The pin or rod in the firing mechanism of a firearm that strikes the cartridge primer to fire the cartridge.

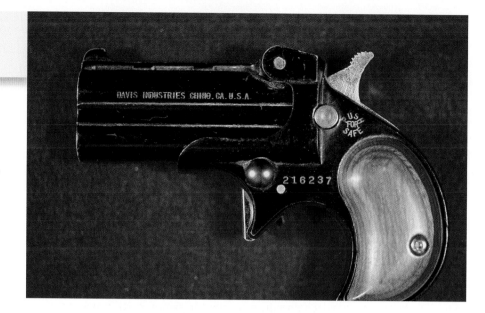

Figure 8.8

Diagram showing the helical groove in the inside of a rifled barrel.

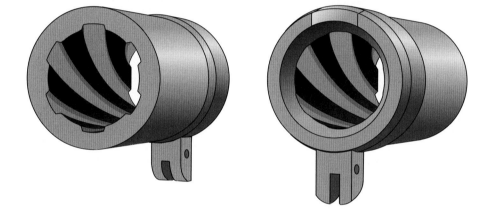

rifling

The helical grooves cut or impressed into the barrel of a handgun or rifle to cause the exiting projective to spin.

grooves

The spiraling depressed areas inside the barrel of a handgun or rifle.

You should not fall into the habit of calling cartridges "bullets." Bullets may do the ultimate damage, but cartridges provide the ultimate power of the firearm. A key aspect of *firearms identification* for the forensic scientist is the fact that modern handguns and rifles have rifled barrel, a feature that enables bullet-to-barrel individualization. When you look down the barrel of a handgun or rifle, you see not a smooth cylindrical surface, but a series of grooves spiraling down the inside of the barrel. These grooves that spiral down the barrel are called **rifling** (Figure 8.8).

Rifling is used because it was discovered many years ago that a spinning projectile proceeds more accurately toward the target. When the projectile enters the barrel, the high areas grip the projectile because the bullet is actually a little larger than the narrowest inside diameter of the barrel. Because the bullet is made of lead, which is fairly soft, it is compressed by the high areas (lands) and actually flows slightly into the **grooves.** As a result, the bullet is forced to follow the helical path of the lands and grooves as it passes down the barrel and out the front of the firearm. Since all this happens almost instantaneously, the effect is that the bullet comes out spinning rapidly. That is the reason for cutting grooves (rifling) in the barrel. A projectile emerging from the barrel with a rapid spin travels a flatter trajectory and flies a truer path toward the target. Before the rifling of barrels, the

Figure 8.9
A homemade firearm of the type made by gangs and usually referred to as a "zip gun."

projectile traveled down the smooth barrel and emerged with no significant spinning motion, and the resulting path would not be as true and therefore as accurate as when the projectile is spinning. One can occasionally encounter a homemade weapon, usually referred to as a zip gun (Figure 8.9), that does not have a rifled barrel, but generally all modern commercially manufactured handguns and rifles have rifled barrels.

The barrels of handguns or rifles are traditionally rifled by gouging the helical grooves in the steel of the barrel using a device called a *broach*. It is a hard steel device that has a series of sharp raised areas (teeth) circling a central shaft and can have as few as 5 or as many as 26 of these cutting surfaces. The helical grooves are cut by pulling this shaft through the tube that is to become the barrel and turning it at the same time. The outside diameter of these teeth is just slightly larger than the inside diameter of the barrel. There are actually several sets of these teeth along the central shaft, each one just thousandths of an inch larger than the one in front of it. Thus each set of teeth gouges a little deeper until the grooves are of the desired depth. Nowadays there are some other techniques to accomplish this as well, but the final result is the same: a series of grooves spiraling down the barrel to engage the bullet as it travels down the barrel and cause it to emerge spinning rapidly. At least partially because of the rifling in the barrel, modern firearms can be highly accurate.

The raised areas between the grooves are called **lands.** The number of lands and grooves in a firearm barrel is a class characteristic of that firearm. The lands and grooves are not necessarily the same width, but there are usually the same number of each. Each barrel manufacturer believes that it uses the ideal rifling and therefore makes the best and most accurate firearm. In addition, the broach can be turned either to the right or to the left. There appears to be no strong advantage of one direction over the other but some manufacturers prefer right **twist** and some manufacturer prefer left twist (Figure 8.10).

For example, Colt, which is one of the large manufacturers of firearms in the United States, uses predominantly left twist, and Smith and Wesson, which is a rival firearms manufacturer, prefers right twist. The number, diameter, and direction of twist of the lands and grooves are class characteristics of a particular firearm. Because their impressions are left behind on the projectile (bullet) they provide the firearms examiner with quite a bit of information about the firearm from which a recovered bullet was fired, without the examiner ever seeing that firearm. The lands on the barrel (high areas) are impressed into the softer bullet, and these indentations are called **land impressions,** and the softer lead flows into the barrel grooves leaving high areas on the bullet called bullet lands. These features do not run parallel to the

lands
The spiraling raised areas between the grooves inside the barrel of a handgun or rifle.

twist
The direction in which the lands and grooves spiral down the inside of a handgun or rifle barrel.

land impressions
The depressed helical grooves in a bullet left by the lands inside the barrel from which it was fired.

Figure 8.10

Two fired bullets, one fired from a right twist rifled barrel and one from a left.

Figure 8.11

Two fired bullets, each showing clear land and groove impressions.

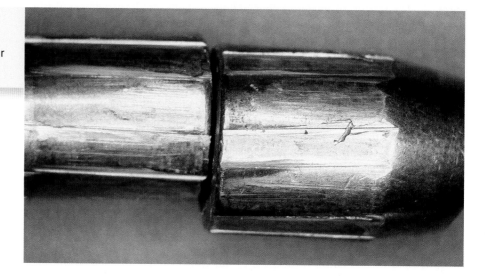

caliber

The inside diameter of a gun barrel, in hundredths of an inch or millimeters.

length of the bullet but appear at an angle (Figure 8.11) because the bullet has been following a helical path through the barrel.

Depending on the shape of the bullet, the land impressions and grooves don't necessarily run the full length of the bullet; with some firearms, the marked area is relatively narrow.

The most important class characteristic used in initial description of a firearm is the inside diameter of the barrel, which is called the **caliber.** It is the distance between two opposing lands and usually measured in hundredths of an inch in the United States and millimeters in the rest of the world. Since the bullet is designed to fit tightly in the barrel, it is also the approximate diameter of the fired bullet. Thus when a handgun or rifle is described as being a "22" (.22-caliber) that means that the inside diameter is 22 hundredths of an inch or a little under a quarter of an inch. The famous U.S. military sidearm is called a "45," which means that bullet diameter is almost one-half of an inch (0.45), and the very common semiautomatic pistol called a "9 millimeter" fires a bullet that is a little over one-third (.354) of an inch (there are 25.4 mm in an inch).

Where the bullet has not been distorted or heavily damaged by its travels after leaving the firearm, it is a simple matter to count, measure, and note the direction of twist of the bullet markings. If the bullet has been deformed by having passed through a victim's body and/or other target, it may become difficult to discern the lands and grooves or whether a deformed piece of lead or copper-coated lead is even a bullet. Determining these class characteristics, however, can turn out to be extremely useful in an investigation, because there are computerized files of information on class characteristics for thousands of different firearms.

For many years this information was collected manually and published in book form. The FBI now maintains a central computerized file, called the General Rifling Characteristic (GRC) file, and most of the forensic laboratories in the United States and many foreign laboratories contribute data on any firearm they encounter that is not already in the file. As a result, experts can enter the caliber, the number of lands and grooves, their widths, and the direction of twist and perform a rapid computer search for firearms that could have fired that bullet. The number of different firearms produced over the years is very large. There are thousands of different makes and models of firearms, some only made for a few years and quite rare, and some produced in enormous numbers over a period of many years. Being able to determine the make and model of a firearm, or at least narrow it to a small number of possible firearms, can be a very useful piece of investigative information.

Most firearms examiners are so familiar with the types of firearms available that they can tell an investigator exactly what a particular firearm looks like, and they probably know where to find a picture of it as well. This can allow an investigator to know what type of firearm to look for even when there were no witnesses to the shooting. Obviously, it is more useful to tell the officer that a bullet was probably fired from a .25-caliber Lorcin and provide a picture of a similar firearm than to say it was a small, shiny-colored semiautomatic pistol.

As mentioned earlier, the inside diameter of the barrel is slightly less than the outside diameter of the bullet, which causes the bullet to be swaged into the grooves. As a result, any imperfections in the lands caused by wear or damage to the broach or other cutting tool, or any nicks or scratches caused by impurities in the steel, will be mirrored in the surface of the fired bullet. These imperfections have been shown to be unique in each barrel and are, therefore, individualizing characteristics. Careful studies have shown on several occasions that if an examiner analyzes bullets fired through two handgun barrels manufactured sequentially using exactly the same broach, the examiner can still distinguish the differences in the markings on the bullets. The fact that such bullet markings, expected to be extremely similar because of the consecutively manufactured barrels, are distinguishable provides strong evidence for the individuality of the striation markings. Therefore, in general, no two gun barrels produce bullets with the exact same markings. Absolutely proving that firearms stria (Figure 8.12) are unique to each weapon is impossible strictly speaking, because it is certainly not possible to compare all existing weapons to one another.

Rifled barrels provide the basis for projectile-to-barrel, and thus projectile-to-firearm, identification. As we shall see, other markings on cartridge cases provide a basis for cartridge case to firearm identification (individualization).

Types of Firearms

One way to classify firearms is to divide them into single-shot firearms, semiautomatic firearms (revolvers are a type of semiautomatic), or automatic firearms. Handguns and rifles are designed to have a single cartridge loaded, fired, and manually ejected (single shot) or have cartridges fed to the chamber in a number of other ways. Many children learn about firearms by having a single-shot .22-caliber rifle as their first firearm. In semiautomatic firearms, the cartridges are fed by some mechanical action from a magazine or tube under the barrel by a spring action, fired

Figure 8.12

Fired bullet with the fine stria running parallel in the land and groove impressions.

semiautomatic

A firearm that fires a projectile each time the trigger is pulled until out of ammunition.

automatic

A firearm that will begin to fire projectiles as soon as the trigger is pulled and continue to fire until the trigger is released or it has run out of ammunition.

rifle

A firearm, usually two or more feet in length, designed to be fired from a shoulder-held position.

magazine

The container for the cartridges in most semiautomatic and automatic firearms.

by pulling the trigger, and then the case is ejected by the action as a new cartridge is fed into the chamber. **Semiautomatic** means, and this is an important distinction from automatic, that the firearm fires one bullet, then reloads a fresh cartridge, each time the trigger is pulled. The trigger must be released and pulled again to fire another bullet. Reloading may be accomplished in several ways, including using the pressure of the exiting gases, spring action, or a mechanical action like a pump or a lever. Semiautomatics (Figure 8.13) are to be distinguished from **automatic** firearms, because the preceding series of steps is repeated when one pulls the trigger and holds it. The automatic firearm will continue firing either until the trigger is released or all the cartridges have been fired.

Many rifles and handguns are designed for semiautomatic operation and, in general, only military firearms are designed for fully automatic operation. The military firearms are usually capable of both semiautomatic and automatic operation. In military firearms, a selector lever allows one to change from semiautomatic to automatic operation. In the United States, it is illegal for anyone who is not in the military or law enforcement to possess an automatic firearm without a special permit. The federal penalty for illegal possession of a fully automatic firearm is a minimum of a $10,000 fine and a year in jail. Infantry troops in the U.S. military are usually provided with firearms such as the M16; the Russians and many others use the AK47; and the Israelis use the Uzi. These are very reliable firearms, which are also sold in many other countries. A civilian version of each of these firearms, which has the selector lever removed, is sold by the manufacturer and often copied by other manufacturers. Therefore, the civilian version will fire only in the semiautomatic mode. It is possible to buy an illegal kit that will convert such firearms from a semiautomatic civilian unit into an automatic firearm. The high incidence of automatic firearms in the movies and as seen on television crime shows, not surprisingly, does not correspond with reality. Most forensic laboratories encounter fully automatic firearms only rarely.

Another way to classify firearms divides them into rifles, handguns, and shotguns. A **rifle** is a firearm that is designed to be fired from the shoulder and normally has a relatively long barrel. As indicated earlier, rifles can be single shot, semiautomatic, or fully automatic. The semiautomatics can have a great variety of different mechanisms for feeding cartridges into the breech for firing. One popular form uses a **magazine,** which is a rectangular device that can hold from 5 to 50 cartridges.

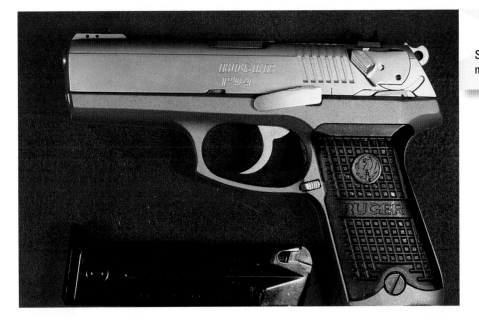

The magazine, which is spring loaded, pushes a cartridge into the breech as the fired case is expelled. It usually slips into the firearm just below the breech in a rifle and into the grip of a handgun. Some rifles have a tube that sits just below the barrel that acts as a magazine.

The advantage of the rifle is that it generally provides a projectile exiting at a high velocity. This is because it can accommodate a larger cartridge with more powder and has a long barrel that contains the gases and allows the bullet to build up speed as it is forced down the barrel. The burning of the powder produces the vast amount of gases that will force the bullet down the barrel, providing energy as long as the projectile is traveling down the barrel. After the bullet exits the barrel and the seal is broken, any additional burning will add nothing to the bullet's speed. The amount of powder and its burning rate are tailored to the type of firearm and the length of the firearm's barrel. The more energy and momentum the bullet has, the farther it can go, the truer it will fly, and the more damage it can do.

The legal definition of a **handgun** is a firearm with a barrel less than a particular length. The statutory length varies from state to state but is usually about 9 or 10 inches. Handguns can be divided into three categories based on their mechanical action. The first type is the single-shot handgun, which is used almost exclusively for target shooting. Because single shot handguns have few moving parts, they can be made with high precision and are very accurate and reliable. The other two types of handguns are revolvers and semiautomatic pistols, which are much more common. **Revolvers** (Figure 8.14) were developed in the mid-19th century and are sometimes referred to as the "guns that won the West."

They have a rotating cylinder that holds anywhere from five to nine cartridges depending on the caliber. Only .22-caliber cartridges are small enough for the cylinder to hold as many as nine cartridges, while most .38-caliber revolvers hold five or six cartridges. When a person pulls the trigger, causing the firearm to fire, a lever turns the cylinder so that a new cartridge is in position to be fired. This mechanism allows the firearm to fire each time the trigger is pulled until all the cartridges in the cylinder are fired. The mechanism is much simpler than a semiautomatic, because the cartridge cases simply stay in the cylinder and are manually extracted later. The concept was developed by Samuel Colt and was the standard for handguns for many years. Because of this simple mechanism, revolvers are generally considered more reliable than semiautomatic firearms. When the trigger is pulled, revolvers fire, and they seldom jam or misfire.

handguns

Firearms, usually a foot or less in length, designed to be held in one or both hands when fired.

revolvers

Handguns that have rotating cylindrical cartridge holders that usually hold five to nine cartridges and allow the weapon to fire semiautomatically until the cartridges are expended.

Figure 8.14
Handgun revolver.

The third type of handgun is the semiautomatic pistol. It is mechanically analogous to the semiautomatic rifle. Cartridges are usually placed in a magazine, which fits into the grip of the firearm and feeds a new cartridge each time the firearm is fired. Normally, a combination of spring action and expelled gases is used to extract and eject the fired case and move the new cartridge into the chamber. The empty cartridge cases are ejected with considerable force to the left or right (depending on the firearm) and are often found at the scene. A hurried exit by the shooter will usually result in at least some of the empty cases being left behind.

Because of their mechanical complexity, it is only in the last 20 or 30 years that semiautomatic handguns have been designed that are considered reliable enough for most police departments. In recent years semiautomatic pistols have become the most popular handgun, because of their superior firing speed and the larger number of cartridges they hold. The magazine holds anywhere from 8 to 10 cartridges. It is now illegal for a handgun to hold more than 10 cartridges. Not many years ago there was no regulation of magazine size, and 15 or 16 cartridges was quite common. Since the law changed such magazines can no longer be imported or manufactured in the United States, but the existing magazines were not outlawed, and they sometimes may still be obtained.

Because cartridge cases are retained in the cylinder, revolvers may produce less forensically useful evidence. The cartridge cases are often not left behind at the shooting scene—unless so many shots are fired that the shooter has to reload. Cartridge cases can have significant value in connecting a firearm to a crime scene. If they are not left at the scene, but taken away in the cylinder, this value is lost. As the popularity of semiautomatic firearms has increased, the occurrence of cartridge cases at shooting scenes has increased and their value as forensic evidence has been realized.

With a semiautomatic pistol or rifle, the cartridge case is ejected with considerable force and usually lands several feet from the shooter. Because of its cylindrical shape, the case can then roll in any direction for a considerable distance. In most settings this can result in the case being difficult to find. As a result, criminals, who are in a hurry to get away, often leave the expended cases, thereby increasing the probability that crime scene personnel will be able to recover them.

There are no truly automatic handguns, although several firearms that are not much larger than a handgun were designed to be very compact automatic military rifles (Figure 8.15).

Figure 8.15   Semiautomatic rifle (carbine) small enough to be handheld and with a large magazine.

As indicated earlier, these cannot be legally sold to people other than those in military or law enforcement, except in semiautomatic form, but semiautomatic models can, under some circumstances, be converted to fire as fully automatic firearms. Generally, rifles and handguns are semiautomatic, even though the media regularly and incorrectly call them "automatic."

Finally, the third type of firearm is the **shotgun.** Shotguns are long guns like rifles, designed to be fired from the shoulder, but they do not generally have rifled barrels. Shotguns, initially designed for hunting birds, shoot a charge of steel or lead pellets. Although lead was the standard for many years, steel pellets must be used in many places to avoid lead pollution of the waters and woods where most hunting is done. If someone is shooting at a bird flying fairly rapidly and at a distance, hitting it with a single projectile is very difficult. On the other hand, if someone sends up a "cloud" of lead shot, some of those pellets are more likely to hit that bird. As soon as the pellets emerge from a shotgun, they begin to spread and anything within the spreading pattern of pellets is going to be hit with a quantity of high-energy pellets. Shotguns are very damaging firearms, particularly at close range.

Shotgun ammunition (**shotgun shells**) can have a small number of fairly sizable pellets or a large number of very small pellets and a whole variety of combinations in between. These pellets are packed into that shotgun cartridge along with a large powder charge and a primer (Figure 8.16 on p. 192) exactly as handgun and rifle cartridges are.

The primary difference is that because shotgun barrels are generally considerably larger in diameter, there is room for more of everything. Even the smallest shotgun has a barrel diameter (bore) larger than the average handgun or rifle. As a result, because of the size of the cartridge, when a shotgun is fired, a great deal of lead (or steel) ermerges with a lot of force behind it. In addition to a variety of different-sized pellet loads, shotgun shells are made with a single **slug.** This

shotgun

A long gun that usually fires a large number of small metal pellets at one time, which is designed to be used for hunting birds and small animals.

shotgun shells

Ammunition that serves the same purpose for a shotgun as a cartridge in a handgun or rifle.

slug

A single projectile used in a shotgun shell instead of pellets, analogous to the bullet in the handgun or rifle cartridge.

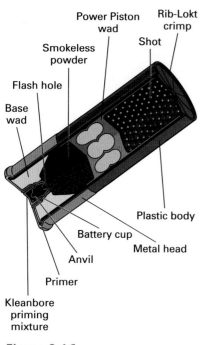

Figure 8.16

Cutaway view of a shotgun shell showing the various components.

slug is the diameter of the shotgun bore and has helical grooves molded into it. Since shotgun barrels are smooth the grooves do not lock in and cause the slug to spin rapidly but are intended to create some spin because of air resistance. Therefore, shotguns are generally not nearly as accurate as a rifle or a handgun, but for relatively short distances or for causing a large amount of destruction, they are extremely effective.

Collection and Preservation of Firearms Evidence

Firearms evidence has great potential forensic utility, and it is particularly important that it be collected with care and properly protected and documented.

Careful Handling of Firearm, Bullets, and Cartridge Cases   Firearms, projectiles (bullets), cartridge cases, and objects that have been in their path must be handled carefully. Each can be of critical value to an investigation. As mentioned earlier, in the United States, a great many crimes are committed using firearms. In addition, accidental shootings, hunting accidents, and a variety of other serious incidents that involve firearms can produce evidence that must be carefully examined. The primary concern in handling and collecting firearms is safety. A firearm must be rendered safe (not able to fire) before collection and packaging. At times, this process will require manipulation to remove a cartridge (live round) from the chamber.

Mark Revolver at Cylinder Position and Mark Recovered Bullets and Cases   When a revolver is collected, the investigator needs to note which cylinder position is lined up with the barrel of the firearm. The cartridge that is lined up with the barrel would be the next one to be fired. The empty cases and live cartridges in the rest of the cylinder will indicate which cartridges were fired and in what order. Investigators often see different brands or types of cartridges in the cylinder of a revolver so this information may be important in reconstructing the events in a shooting incident.

The bullets and cases recovered at the scene must be marked for identification or placed in sealed containers that are properly marked. The evidence should be marked in a place where one is not likely to obscure other relevant markings. For cases, this is on the side and away from the base or just inside the open end; for bullets, it is usually on the base. At one time, the nose was also considered a good place to mark a bullet since the investigator wants to avoid damaging the lands and grooves. It is now recognized, however, that a bullet may pick up material from an object it hits or passes through, which may turn out to be important trace evidence for reconstruction, so it is best not to mark the nose.

Submit Evidence to the Laboratory for Evaluation   Many times, firearms evidence may be collected under circumstances where it would seem to have little forensic value. It may be found property, or there may be little controversy about what happened in a particular incident. Perhaps the firearm belongs to the victim rather than a suspect. Nevertheless, it is important that the firearm or firearms evidence be sent for forensic laboratory examination. The firearm, or the projectiles or cases, may be found to match evidence recovered in another, earlier crime. If the evidence is never submitted for laboratory examination, these important connections will never be made. As will be discussed shortly, the use of information from firearms evidence databases is one of the most rapidly evolving areas of forensic science. Sadly, in some jurisdictions it is not convenient to get such materials to the experts for examination, and even if functional testing is required, the firearm may be test fired at the local training range and not fully examined.

Firearms Evidence Examination and Comparison

Firearms examiners mostly examine firearms, projectiles, and cartridge or shotshell cases. Projectiles and cases are called "fired evidence." They bear marks unique to the firearm that produced them.

Physical Examination of Firearm for Safety and Physical Condition

Firearms examination is a multistep procedure. The first step is a careful physical examination of the firearm for functionality, safety features, and physical condition. Safety issues are extremely important. Firearms must always be handled with respect, and by someone with knowledge of their function, for several reasons. Poorly maintained or abused firearms can explode when being test fired, endangering the examiner and others in the immediate area. On occasion, there can be a bullet that didn't make it out to the end of the barrel for various reasons. Firing a firearm with a bullet lodged in the barrel can cause it to explode in the shooter's hand, causing serious injury. It is also possible that a firearm's integrity was compromised by improper use, or disassembly and improper reassembly. The great amount of energy released by the cartridge explosion can be misdirected to the destruction of the firearm rather than the forcing of the bullet down the barrel and toward the intended target. This may injure the individual who is firing the firearm or those nearby. Therefore, two key parts of the initial physical examination are (1) ensuring that no cartridges are left in the firearm and (2) sighting down the barrel to verify that it is not obstructed by a jammed bullet or other material.

Ordinarily whoever collects the firearm and submits it for examination should remove all cartridges. This may not be quite as simple as it sounds. Someone unfamiliar with a particular firearm (and there are thousands of different ones) could miss a cartridge still in the firearm. Arguably, it may not be necessary to remove cartridges from a revolver, as long as the firearm is safe (hammer not cocked). With semiautomatic firearms, the magazine should be carefully removed and separately packaged. However, removing the magazine from a semiautomatic firearm does *not* remove a round from the chamber. Thus, a live round could inadvertently be left in the chamber of the firearm.

If a firearm has a light **trigger pull** or is dropped, it may discharge. Usually firearms will not fire if dropped, but some may. Further, evidentiary firearms may have had safeties disabled or just not be in proper working order. It is important to carefully address all the safety concerns. The gun is normally dry fired (fired without a cartridge in the chamber) and cycled, if it's a semiautomatic, by pulling back the slide and cycling a cartridge through the firearm without pulling the trigger to ensure that all the different parts are working.

Next, the basic class characteristics, including the caliber, number of lands and grooves, direction of twist, make, model, and serial number are all noted. Interestingly, one of the largest single problems in firearms examination is proper identification of a firearm. Because there are literally thousands of different types of firearms in circulation, this is not a trivial task. Most firearms examiners, who examine a sizable number of firearms in a year, see a few each year that they have never seen before. New firearms are being made all the time, and some old ones just are not very commonly seen. When an officer finds or seizes a firearm, it is his or her responsibility to identify it and locate the serial number. This information is necessary so that the firearm can be checked against the stolen firearms files kept by all states.

Identification is a concern, not only to return the firearm to its rightful owner, but also because it can be important for successful prosecution of an individual charged with theft of the firearm. If any of the descriptive information is not correct,

trigger pull
The amount of force needed to pull (depress) the trigger sufficiently for the firearm to fire.

Figure 8.17   Test firing a handgun into a box of cotton waste to recover expended bullets.

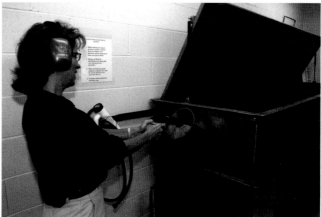

Figure 8.18   Test firing a handgun into a water tank to recover expended bullets.

the search will fail to find the proper firearm. One additional problem is that many firearms have numerous numbers stamped on them and determining which is actually the serial number can be confusing.

Test for Functionality and to Obtain Control Bullets and Cases

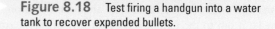

functionality

The ability of a firearm to fire a projectile when the trigger is pulled.

bullet recovery tank

Usually a large horizontal or vertical stainless steel tank filled with water and used to stop the flight and allow recovery of a projectile when a firearm is fired into it.

Another important step in the examination of a firearm is testing for **functionality;** that is, determining whether it can be fired and whether its safety features are functional. Firearms are also test fired to obtain known specimens of bullets and cartridge cases from that firearm. In most states, someone cannot be charged with possession of a deadly weapon unless the weapon has been shown to be functional; that is, when the trigger is pulled, the gun fires. A significant number of firearms received in forensic laboratories are in poor condition, and many will not fire for a variety of reasons. At one time, test firing was done into a long box filled with cotton (Figure 8.17), but it has been shown that water tanks (Figure 8.18) provide a better-quality specimen.

Therefore, in most modern firearms examination facilities, test firing is done into a large bullet recovery water tank. The **bullet recovery tank** is usually six to eight feet long and can be horizontal or vertical. For most handgun cartridges, after a few feet the bullet has lost its energy and settles to the bottom of the tank. Even bullets fired from high-powered rifles will lose their energy in less than eight feet. The bullet is recovered from the bottom of the tank, using a little net that can be raised (bringing the bullet up with it) or with a long stick that has putty on one end so that the bullet will adhere to it.

Normally two or three test fires are taken from each firearm. This allows the examiner to have known bullets to compare with each other in order to ensure that the firearm is marking the bullets in a consistent manner. In addition, known cartridge cases for comparison are also obtained. Although the majority of firearms produce consistent markings on both the bullets and cases, this may not always be the case. Obviously, if control bullets fired under ideal conditions cannot be matched to each other, it will usually not be possible to match evidence bullets to that firearm. A famous example of inconsistent marking is the firearm seized in the shooting of Dr. Martin Luther King. This firearm has been tested, over the years, by at least three different agencies and found not to produce consistent markings. As a result, it is not possible to say that the bullets that killed Dr. King were fired from that gun.

Bullet and Cartridge or Shotshell Case Comparisons— the Comparison Microscope

The comparison of both bullets and cases are done using a **firearms comparison microscope.** Firearms and toolmark comparisons use reflected light with the bullet comparison microscope (Figure 8.19) instead of the transmitted light generally used for transparent or translucent objects, such as hairs and fibers.

The expert must light the bullet or case with strong reflected light. This is usually done with a fiber optic light source. Because the beam from a fiber optic can easily be adjusted to hit the object at almost any angle, the examiner can adjust the light to highlight the fine striations that are used for the comparison.

For a bullet comparison, a firearm examiner is usually examining the fine striations on the interior of the land impressions on the bullet. If the bullet fully occupied the interior of the barrel or bounced around a little, the expert may find useful marking on the raised area that fit into the grooves in the barrel. These striations are formed on the inside of the barrel by the tool used to rifle the barrel. In addition, any imperfections or inclusions in the steel of the barrel may leave markings that can be impressed into the soft lead of the bullet. These are the markings that the examiner tries to match between the known control specimen and evidence bullet using the comparison microscope (Figure 8.20).

As mentioned earlier, the comparison microscope is actually two microscopes connected by an optical bridge. It enables an examiner to look at side-by-side images of known and questioned specimens. The examiner looks for areas of agreement or disagreement between the stria on the two bullets.

Firearms comparison microscopes use relatively low magnification (less than 40X), by comparison to a transmitted light microscope, which is usually in the 40 to 400 times magnification range. There is no single approach to comparing bullets, but generally the examiner searches the test-fired bullet for a somewhat recognizable set of marks and then examines the evidence bullet to try to find a similar set. If the evidence bullet is significantly damaged, the process may be reversed and it is searched first for any clear markings. Once a set of markings is found that appear to match in one land impression, the examiner can now search the subsequent land impressions in sequence to see whether multiple areas of matching stria will be found

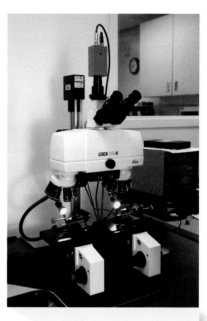

Figure 8.19

A reflected-light comparison microscope used for comparing evidence and known bullet and cartridge case samples.

firearms comparison microscope

Two reflected-light microscopes linked with an optical bridge used for comparison of objects using reflected light.

Figure 8.20

The images of two fired bullets in a comparison microscope showing the agreement of the fine striations in one land impression.

firing pin impression

The impression left by the firing pin on the primer cup portion of a cartridge after it has been struck (fired).

breech face

The surface of a firearm, usually machined, against which the cartridge case is forced by the expanding gases as a result of being fired.

on the control and evidence bullets. This process can require from minutes to hours, depending on the marking clarity of the firearm and the condition of the evidence bullet.

As previously indicated, the popularity of semiautomatic firearms has increased the incidence of finding cartridge cases at shooting scenes, and these too can frequently be individualized to a particular firearm. One key marking is the **firing pin impression** in the metal of the primer.

Firing pins are machined parts and impart their characteristic marks to the primer. In addition, markings on the primer (head stamp) end of a cartridge case can often be associated unambiguously to markings on the **breech face** of a particular firearm (Figure 8.21).

When the bullet is driven out the front of a fired firearm, the cartridge case is forced backward and is pressed up against the breech face with considerable force. The machining marks on the breech face can be transferred to (impressed into) the case head stamp area. Quality handguns and rifles are manufactured by machining and metal working blocks of hard steel. These processes usually leave fine stria on the exposed surface of the breech face. These stria will be impressed into the entire breech face of the case, but the impression of the breech face machining marks are often more clearly impressed in the soft metal of the primer. If a firearms examiner is convinced that these marks are the same on an evidence case as on the known control cases (Figure 8.22) (from the water tank firing), the examiner makes a positive identification.

Simply stated, a positive identification means that the evidence case was fired from the test-fired firearm and no other. An examiner might similarly fail to find matching stria and conclude that the case was not fired from the test-fired firearm. Something important to remember that will be discussed further below in connection with the NIBIN databases is that evidentiary cartridge cases or bullets can be matched to one another—that is, determined to be fired from the same firearm—without having received the suspect firearm itself.

Cases fired from semiautomatic firearms also may have additional markings from the extractor and/or ejector. These are the parts of the firearm that remove the

Figure 8.21

Cartridge case with clearly visible breech face marks and a firing pin impression.

case from the breech of the firearm and eject it from the firearm, so that a fresh cartridge can be loaded from the magazine. Extractor and ejector marks, of course, are not found on cases fired in a revolver. Sometimes theses extractor or ejector markings on the case can provide enough information to allow individualization of the case when compared against test-fired cases from a particular firearm. Sometimes cases fired from a semiautomatic firearm may also show magazine marks. When a person loads the cartridges into the magazine or when they leave the magazine, roughened areas on the magazine may leave characteristic scratches on the cartridge.

Shotshell cases can also have markings that are useful for associating or individualizing a fired shell with a particular shotgun. So, even though the projectiles (pellets or rifled slug) exit through a smooth barrel and thus are not marked, the shell case can acquire firing pin impression, breech face,

Case Study 8.1

CBS Murder Case

The so-called CBS murder case arose when a hired killer executed a victim in the middle of the afternoon on a rooftop parking garage, in New York City, as she approached her car. As he dragged her toward his van and shot her, three employees of CBS observed the struggle. They started toward him to see what was happening, and he turned on them and shot and killed all three and then fled the scene. Eventually the investigation narrowed to Donald Nash as the prime suspect, and he was put under surveillance. When he left the area, he was followed and eventually stopped and arrested, and his van was searched. Two of the most critical pieces of evidence in the CBS murder case were two cartridge cases. An exhaustive search of the defendant's van, which included taking out the seats, disclosed a cartridge case wedged under the driver's seat. When his home was carefully searched, some wooden steps from the backyard into the house were torn up and a cartridge case that had fallen between the two boards of the step was recovered. Although the gun used in the murders was never recovered, the firearms examiner was able to say that these two cases found in different places under the control of the defendant were fired from the same gun as those recovered from the murder site. These results provided the strongest connection between the defendant and the murders.

and potentially extractor and/or ejector marks, just as rifle and pistol cases do.

The firing mechanism of a shotgun is quite analogous to that of a rifle or pistol. The same basic principles govern the operation. When the firearm fires, the pellets go out the front and the shotshell is pushed back against the breech face. When the firing pin hits the primer area, it too leaves a mark. If it's a semiautomatic shotgun, there is a lever that can make marks on the fired and ejected shell case as the new shell is loaded in the breech. Shotgun shells were traditionally largely made of paper, but that has been replaced by plastic. Plastic or paper are not usually useful for preserving markings; however, the breech end of almost all shotgun shells is still brass with a soft metal primer cup and can record marks in exactly the same way as handgun or rifle cases. Therefore, shotgun shells can be individualized to a shotgun just as handgun and rifle cartridge cases can be individualized to a particular firearm.

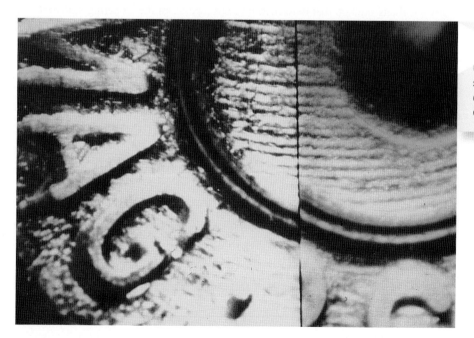

Figure 8.22

Comparison photomicrograph showing the comparison of an evidence and test-fired cartridge case.

Association of Cartridges or Bullets to Firearm or Maker Using Databases

As mentioned earlier, bullets can often be associated with a particular ammunition manufacturer or to possible makers of firearms, even down to a make and model from the class characteristics left on the bullet by the rifling. Often this is true of a recovered cartridge case as well. Frequently the manufacturer's name or a well-known trademark and the caliber are impressed on the base of the case, which makes identification of the ammunition manufacturer quite simple. Even when this is not the case and the markings on the case appear quite obscure, many of these so-called head stamps have been collected in reference books that associate head stamps with the particular manufacturer of that case.

As noted earlier, fired evidence now makes up one of three major evidence databases in forensic laboratories. In Chapter 6, AFIS databases containing fingerprint images were described. In Chapter 10, CODIS databases containing DNA profiles will be discussed. For fired evidence, **NIBIN** (National Integrated Ballistic Identification Network) contains images of bullets and cartridge cases recovered from scenes of crimes or test fired from firearms submitted to the laboratory after seizure by law enforcement. There are regional and national versions of the databases. They have been a very useful tool in law enforcement, since bullets and cartridge cases may now be associated with the same firearm, even though the firearm has not been found. If the evidence comes from a firearm that has been recovered, and test fired, the source of the fired evidence is thereby identified. These databases enable law enforcement to make connections between cases, even from jurisdictions that are far apart, through the bullet or cartridge case evidence. Such case associations can be significant in moving an investigation forward by allowing the investigators on the associated cases to work together and look for possible connections.

NIBIN

The national database primarily of images of cartridge cases used to try to associate evidence cases with test-fired cases from seized weapons or cases collected from shooting incidents where the gun involved is not known.

Comparison of Badly Damaged Projectiles or Cases

It is important to recognize that firearms examiners do not need pristine bullets to make comparisons. Certainly the known control specimen will be in perfect condition, but even a severely deformed evidence bullet can sometimes yield a successful comparison. Such a bullet might not even look like a bullet anymore.

Bullets can be deformed and misshapen by their impact on one or more targets. However, if any area on that deformed piece of lead or on the jacketing still contains even a portion of one of the groove or land impression areas that is intact, it may still be possible to make a successful comparison. Very often a bullet may break into several pieces after hitting something. A piece may still be matched to a particular firearm, by a good examiner, as long as a portion of a land or a groove area still shows its characteristic markings.

Use of Firearms Evidence for Reconstruction

Reconstruction of the events at a shooting scene is often a critical part of an investigation or prosecution.

Recovered Firearm and Fired Evidence in Reconstruction

Important information for reconstruction can come from recovered firearms, recovered bullets or cases, and of course from the location and markings associated with all three. Experts can measure the force needed to pull the trigger, and it is frequently done with a recovered firearm. This is usually done in a simple way using a spring scale or weights, where the examiner observes the amount of pull needed to cause the firearm to fire.

More exotic devices have been made to measure trigger pull, but the principle is the same. Although this is not important in many cases, it may occur that someone charged with a shooting will allege it was an accident. For example, the person may say the gun has an abnormally sensitive trigger or it fired when "I just touched the trigger." If the trigger pull is found to be 8 or 10 pounds, in the normal range, the accidental discharge defense is discredited. An accidental discharge can happen, however, particularly with target-shooting firearms that are often designed or modified to have a very light trigger pull. In the real world, most firearms have fairly substantial trigger pull and will not fire without considerable force being applied to the trigger. Accidental discharge is an important issue in both criminal and civil cases. Could the firearm have fired from being dropped? An individual may say, "We were passing the gun around, nobody had his hand near the trigger, and it went off and my friend was shot." Sadly, such a scenario is frequently offered when children are injured or killed. As indicated, however, virtually all commercial firearms that have not been modified or damaged do not fire unless someone pulls the trigger, and the amount of pressure needed to pull that trigger is not likely to be applied by accident.

Similarly investigators frequently encounter situations where one of the parties claims that a gun was dropped and it fired when it hit the floor. That just does not happen to a properly designed firearm that is in reasonable working order. Quality commercial firearms have had safeties built into them, for many years, so that the only thing that will cause them to fire is pulling the trigger.

There are a number of different safety designs, but they all ensure that the gun will not fire without the trigger being pulled. The firearm could be defective, modified to bypass the **safety,** or cheaply made, but such circumstances are not particularly common. In any case, a firearm can be tested to see if it would fire due to the impact of being dropped.

Another useful piece of information when attempting to reconstruct a shooting incident may be gathered from the recovered bullet or bullets. Careful examination of the bullet, particularly the nose of the bullet, may reveal the presence of blood, cloth, plaster, or other materials that can give information about objects the bullet has encountered in its travels.

Another concern is that a firearm has not been altered. As mentioned earlier, some semiautomatic firearms can be altered to fire in an automatic mode. It is not easy, but it is possible to buy a kit with the necessary plans to convert a firearm to be fully automatic if one has the necessary machinist tools and skill.

Muzzle to Target Distance—Powder Pattern

In some laboratories, firearms examiners do muzzle to target distance determinations as well. As discussed in Chapter 5, this is based on the examination of the **powder pattern** created on the target by materials accompanying the bullet out of the barrel. This pattern is caused by smoke, unburned and partially burned gunpowder, and other residues from inside the gun barrel. This complex mixture of material produces a pattern on a target (Figure 8.23), if it is reasonably close to the firearm, and that pattern can be used to estimate the distance between the muzzle of the firearm and the target.

Both this distance estimate, when possible, and determination of the projectile **trajectory** can be important in developing a reconstruction of a shooting incident. As noted in the earlier chapter, gunshot residue patterns can be produced at measured distances using the same firearm and ammunition. These are then compared to the evidence pattern. Sometimes, chemicals (such as sodium rhodizonate) are used to enhance the visibility of the pattern. As with all reconstruction, though, a pattern match does not prove the exact distance, but it does provide a scientifically defensible estimate.

GSR on Hands—Dermal Nitrate, Lift, Swab, Tape

Another important forensic issue associated with shooting incidents is the deposition of **gunshot residue (GSR)** on the hands of one who fires a firearm, is in close proximity to a firearm when it is fired, or who handles a firearm immediately after firing. GSR is the term used for the very fine particles that are formed during the

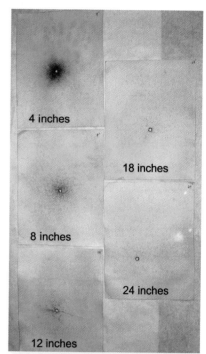

Figure 8.23

Pattern of lead particles deposited from shots into a piece of filter paper at five different distances visualized with sodium rhodizonate.

safety

A component of most firearms that prevents it from firing without the trigger being pulled or that locks the trigger so it cannot be pulled, or to prevent firing even if the trigger is pulled.

powder pattern

A pattern found on an object close to the barrel of a fired weapon caused by small particles of lead, or partially burned gunpowder and carbon smoke that follow the projectile out of the barrel.

trajectory

The path that a projectile takes after it leaves the barrel until it hits an object or falls to the ground.

gunshot residue (GSR)

Materials created by the firing of a firearm that are dispersed by the force of the expanding gases.

firing process, primarily from the ignition of the primer. Besides being blown out the barrel with the projectile, the primer GSR is usually blown back or out of the side of the firearm and often is deposited on the hands of the individual firing the firearm. The definitive determination that someone has recently fired a firearm has been one of the major concerns of forensic science for many years. Unfortunately, this is a particularly difficult problem and has not yet been adequately solved. Finding GSR on someone's hand does not show that the person fired a firearm. Even the unequivocal chemical identification of GSR is not a simple problem.

One of the first attempts to determine if someone had recently fired a firearm was the dermal nitrate test, frequently referred to as the "paraffin test." In this test, a suspect's hand is coated with liquid paraffin wax and the wax is allowed to cool and solidify. The wax cast of the hand is removed and sprayed with a chemical that produces a deep blue color when reacting with nitrates and nitrites. Finding colored spots on the paraffin cast was interpreted as evidence of having recently discharged a firearm. Although the method was used for quite a few years, it has been shown to be unreliable and particularly susceptible to false positive results. False positive results are damaging to the integrity of forensic science because they may make an innocent individual appear guilty. The paraffin test has been discredited since the 1950s, but occasionally even today a police agency will ask for a suspect to be subjected to the paraffin test. The paraffin technique did have one valuable feature: It showed the *distribution* of the residue on the hand, where more current techniques do not. The problem with the test was that the paraffin lifting was not accompanied by definitive chemical tests for GSR.

When a firearm is fired, some very fine particles, primarily lead particles that form from lead vaporized by the heat of the primer explosion, solidify with included barium and/or antimony. Barium and antimony compounds are used in the primer mixture. This fine mist of particles is expelled when the firearm is discharged and will settle on the hands of the shooter or anything else in the immediate vicinity, including the firearm itself. This occurs in both revolvers and semiautomatic pistols, but it can vary greatly in amount depending on the details of design of the firearm and the nature of the ammunition. That is why an individual whose hand is in the immediate vicinity of the firing firearm or who handles the firearm immediately after it is fired may be found to have some of these particles on his or her hands. For many years, forensic scientists have been attempting to develop a reliable method to prove that someone fired a firearm by analyzing material obtained from the person's hands shortly after a shooting.

One technique that has been developed involves very thoroughly swabbing a suspect's hand with a cotton swab dampened with dilute nitric acid. Often four swabs are taken, one from the inside (palm) and one from the back of each hand. The swabs are then analyzed to determine the amount of barium, antimony, and lead present. If an individual fires a firearm while holding it in the right hand, the expert should find a very low level of lead, barium, and antimony on the left hand, and a fairly high level on the right hand. The back of the right hand should have the most GSR since it is normally the most exposed to the cloud of material coming out of the back and side of the firearm.

Such a simple elemental analysis cannot tell if these elements found on the hand came from some form of environmental contaminant or from firing a firearm. Lead is a pretty common environmental contaminant and barium and antimony are not, but both have some industrial applications. Therefore, the argument could always be made that finding elevated lead, antimony, and barium does not prove that someone fired a firearm. Although elemental analysis on hand swabs is not ideal, it has been used for quite a while using several different elemental analytical techniques, two of which are atomic absorption (AA) and neutron activation analysis (NAA). NAA is very rarely used today because it requires a radiation source equivalent to that in a nuclear reactor. Elemental analysis works fairly well with guns that emit a lot of GSR, but many guns do not. More troublesome in many ways is the fact that these particles are not glued to the shooter's hand. They fall on hands and if the potential shooter is arrested immediately and his or her hands are sampled, the examiner may find elevated levels of lead, barium, and antimony. If, however, the suspect is not promptly arrested, he or she leaves the scene and while doing other things those particles are quickly lost from the person's hand. Studies have indicated that within two hours or less, with normal activity, more than half of the particles are lost. Washing the hands or wiping them on clothing or other items will greatly accelerate the loss. Further, if a suspect is rear handcuffed, before sampling or without protecting the hands, then the particles will be lost very rapidly as the hands rub against the individual's back. Three significant problems with elemental analysis for GSR determination are rapid loss of particles, environmental contamination, and highly variable deposit of particles by different firearms.

The most reliable application for elemental analysis for GSR is in suspected suicide cases. Because the suspected shooter is no longer active, the particles will not be as rapidly lost. That is why the medical examiner or the investigators will often place bags over the hands of a shooting victim before removing the body, particularly if it is a potential suicide case. In that way, if there are GSR particles, they are less likely to be lost. If significant lead, barium, and antimony concentrations are found, this will help confirm a suspected, self-inflicted gunshot death.

A more reliable method for detecting GSR particles requires an instrument called the **scanning electron microscope (SEM)**. The SEM is an expensive instrument that requires a highly skilled operator and a considerable investment of time to keep it in good operating condition. Moreover, the SEM must be equipped with a device for identifying chemical elements—the usual one is called an energy-dispersive X-ray analyzer **(SEM-EDX).** If GSR were the only application for this instrument, most forensic laboratories would not find it economically feasible to purchase and maintain one. Large, busy laboratories may be able to find other types of cases where the SEM can be of considerable use and therefore are willing to make the investment. When using a SEM, the sampling of objects for GSR is usually done with an aluminum cylinder that either has a piece of double-sided sticky tape on the top surface or a coating of a sticky material. This aluminum stub is then pressed repeatedly against the area being sampled until the stub seems to have lost all of its stickiness and then some more.

It has been shown that even after it doesn't feel sticky anymore, the stub may still be picking up additional particles. Again, it is best to sample the palms and backs of both hands. The aluminum stub is placed into the SEM and examined under high magnification to see if particles with the characteristic shapes (morphology) of GSR particles are seen. They are quite distinctively shaped and can be fairly easily recognized. These are small particles, which are much too small to be seen with a normal optical microscope. The most difficult and time-consuming aspect is finding them. Since an examiner must work at high magnification, searching the entire surface of the aluminum disk would take days. If there are a great many particles, the expert will find some quickly, but if there are only a few, it may take hours. Computerized searching programs are now available with most SEMs that can identify candidate particles while the operator is off doing something else. That can greatly reduce the time the operator must spend. The enormous advantage that SEMs have is that most include a device that allows scientists to do elemental analysis on individual particles. Therefore, an expert can locate particles that look like GSR and then confirm that they have lead, barium, antimony, or other elements characteristic of GSR. This double identification removes much of the uncertainty caused by the possibility of environmental contamination. Thus, the combination of a visual identification (morphology) with observation of the correct elemental makeup strongly indicates that these particles are GSR particles (Figure 8.24) and largely eliminates confusion from particles from other possible sources.

This does not solve the problem of the particles falling off, however. If someone is arrested two days after the shooting or has washed his or her hands, sampling the

scanning electron microscope (SEM)

A microscope that uses high-energy electrons rather than light for image formation and is capable of very high magnification.

SEM/EDX

A SEM that is equipped with an energy-dispersive X-ray spectrometer, which allows elemental analysis of individual objects seen in the SEM.

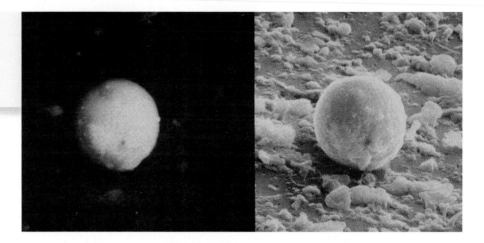

Figure 8.24
A highly magnified image of a GSR particle obtained with a scanning electron microscope (SEM).

person's hands will likely not show any particles. However, if a police officer or detective does arrest a suspect reasonably soon after the incident, there is a real possibility that the sampling will show convincing evidence of contact with a firearm. Many agencies now use the SEM results as a way of indicating a high probability that someone has either fired or handled a firearm. As indicated, this still does not solve the problem of how the particles reached the suspect's hands. If someone has handled a firearm that had recently been fired or was standing right next to whoever fired the firearm, the particles are the same GSR particles. Where circumstances remove that ambiguity, a positive GSR finding can be a very useful piece of investigative information.

Serial Number Restoration

serial number restoration

The attempt to recover a serial number that has been rendered unreadable.

Another important aspect of firearms examination is **serial number restoration.** Firearms manufactured by a legitimate manufacturer are serialized for identification. The manufacturer stamps a unique serial number on the frame of each firearm that identifies that particular firearm. This is done with an automatic machine that has a counter that goes up by one as each frame is stamped. Because all manufacturers must by law keep track of the model and serial number of each firearm they produce, it is the key to identifying a firearm.

Those who come into possession of a firearm illegally or who use a registered firearm to commit a crime would often like to make it impossible to uniquely identify the firearm. There are a number of ways to try to remove or obscure the serial number. The Federal Bureau of Alcohol, Tobacco, and Firearms has the responsibility to keep track of legally manufactured and registered firearms. It has a quite effective system of tracing the movement of firearms from manufacturer to first seller to initial owner. In addition, subsequent sales through licensed firearms dealers are also recorded. If an investigator recovers a firearm at a crime scene or from someone who is not its rightful owner, it is useful to know the previous owner or owners of that firearm. Further, each state keeps records of firearms reported stolen, and a recovered firearm can be checked against those records as well. If someone has come into possession of a firearm illegally, however, or has stolen it from somebody who obtained it illegally, there will be a break in the recorded chain of possession. In addition, many private transactions are often not

Case Study 8.2

Shotgun Killing

Tracing a shotgun provided an important lead in solving a tragic murder case. A young couple and their daughter were returning home from a short trip late in the evening. As their car pulled into their driveway in a quiet residential suburb the headlights picked up an individual standing in the driveway holding a firearm. The exact motivation of the assailant is not known, but it was discovered later that he had forced his way into the home of an elderly couple only a short distance away and robbed them a few days before. Either he was concerned that the driver was going to hit him or he accidentally discharged the shotgun he was holding and killed the husband. In his rush to get away, he left the shotgun behind. The investigators were able to trace the firearm through several owners to a pawnshop in a nearby city. The pawnshop owner was persuaded to disclose to whom he had sold the shotgun, and this led the police to the killer.

Case Study 8.3

Officer Piagentini Shooting

During the civil unrest of the 1960s, a radical group lured two New York City police officers into an ambush using a bogus 911 call and killed them. The killers stole the officers' firearms and made much of their success in striking a blow against their oppressors. Many years later, information was developed that one of the officers' guns had been buried in a field in Mississippi. A team was sent to recover the firearm to confirm the accuracy of the information. A gun was recovered and submitted to the forensic laboratory covered with mud (Figure 8.25A). It was consistent with the type of firearm police carried at the time, but it was so badly rusted that there was no discernible serial number (Figure 8.25B). The firearm was cleaned and acid etched, and it was possible to restore the entire serial number (Figure 8.25C), which proved that this was the firearm carried by the murdered police officer.

Figure 8.25A

A handgun recovered from a field having been buried for many years.

Figure 8.25B

Recovered handgun with soil cleaned off.

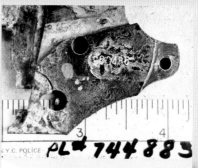

Figure 8.25C

The serial number revealed after acid etching of long buried gun. The serial number indicated that this was the gun taken from murdered NYC police officer Piagentini.

recorded at all, and even if they are, the information is seldom recorded in a way that it can be easily retrieved.

Serial Number Obliteration Methods—Defacing

Because of the importance of serial numbers in proper identification of firearms, and the need for "untraceable" firearms by criminals, many of the firearms that are seized show evidence that someone has tried to remove the serial number. In many cases the serial number is so badly defaced that it is largely gone or impossible to read. The **defacing** (rendering it unreadable) of a serial number on a firearm is a felony in itself in most states. Most firearms examiners develop some skill at serial number restoration. Those who deface serial numbers use a variety of techniques from scratching, to gouging, to even grinding them off. It is not uncommon for as many as 20 percent of the firearms received by a firearms unit to have defaced serial

defacing

Attempting to render a serial number unreadable.

numbers, which can vary in readability from having one or two numbers unreadable to being virtually undetectable. This problem can be addressed in several ways. The easiest and best is if there is a hidden serial number. A number of manufacturers place a second copy of the serial number in a very inconspicuous place. The individual removing the serial number is unlikely to know of this hidden serial number and therefore fails to remove it as well. A knowledgeable firearms examiner will know where to look for the hidden serial number and the problem is solved. Unfortunately, most firearms do not have hidden serial numbers. The approach then must be to try to chemically or physically restore the defaced serial number.

Recovery of Serial Number—Clean, Smooth, Etch

When a serial number is stamped into the frame of a firearm, the pressure of the die that impresses the number deforms the crystal structure of the metal to a considerable depth into the metal. This disruption of the crystal structure goes well below the actual indentations that form the visible serial number. When the crystal structure is deformed, it changes the metal's susceptibility to attack by chemicals.

To take advantage of this fact, the firearms examiner smooths out the area where the serial number was originally stamped using emery cloth or a small hand grinder. If there are gouges or deep scratches, they are also smoothed out, if possible. The examiner then takes one of several **etching** solutions that have been found to work well on the type of metal of which the gun is made. These are generally strongly acidic solutions that will attack the metal and dissolve it slowly. An examiner usually dips a cotton-tipped swab (Q-tip) in the etching solution and paints it on the area where the serial number was stamped. The acid will **preferentially** eat away at the metal where the crystal structure has been deformed, that is, where the numbers were, and the numbers may begin to reappear. This is a tedious process where the area is cleaned, examined, and acid is reapplied until the expert can read some of the numbers. The numbers do not always all come up at once, so an examiner has to go slowly, and if a number becomes visible it must be photographed or recorded. The first numbers that appear may be etched away before some of the other numbers have become visible so the process must be done in steps. If, however, the expert is patient and the individual doing the defacing did not go deep enough, acid etching can reveal the serial number in many cases.

Etching seems to be effective in most laboratories in more than half the cases. Even if an examiner is not able to read all the digits of the serial number, he or she can search the computerized stolen firearms databases with the available information and often determine if the firearm is in the database or narrow it to several possible firearms. For example, an expert may know the make and model and caliber of the firearm from examining it. It may be a .44-caliber Charter Arms Bulldog revolver, and the examiner can read six of the eight digits of the serial number. When the database is searched, only one or two firearms that fit the available data are likely to be found that have been reported stolen. As a result, even the partial serial number restoration will allow the forensic expert to determine if this firearm had been reported stolen.

The same techniques are often used on engine blocks from recovered stolen automobiles, where it is also common to encounter defaced serial numbers. A number of other things are also serialized by stamping a number in metal and can be processed similarly. In the Crafts case (see the Lead Case in Chapter 1), restoration of the serial number on a chain saw recovered from the Lake Zoar reservoir permitted investigators to establish that the suspect had originally purchased the chain saw.

Several other techniques can be used for restoring serial numbers, such as magnetic particles, electrolytic etching, and others. They all are based on the fact that stamping deforms the crystal structure of the metal and thereby changes the way the metal behaves. A majority of forensic laboratories use the simple acid etching technique since it works quite adequately and is simple and inexpensive.

etching

The use of strongly acidic or basic chemicals to dissolve away metal in a controlled manner.

The Firearms and Toolmark Examiner Profession

We have noted in earlier chapters that each major pattern evidence area is specialized, and each has its own professional society, sometimes its own journal, and active peer group organizations that set the practice standards.

The primary professional organization of firearms and toolmarks examiners is the Association of Firearms and Toolmark Examiners (AFTE). Almost all examiners in public agencies and many in private practice belong to AFTE. For years, AFTE published a newsletter, which has now evolved into a peer-reviewed journal. AFTE has its own annual training seminar and has an examiner certification program that was established several years ago.

In recent years, with the evolution of the various Technician and Scientific Working Groups, SWGGUN was formed to examine and recommend standards of practice in the firearms and toolmark field.

Until perhaps a decade ago, most firearms examiners were not necessarily trained or educated in one of the natural sciences. However, that picture is changing. Many laboratories now have the same basic entry requirements for every criminalist—including a natural science degree—whether the person will end up in the firearms, trace evidence, or the DNA section of the lab.

Firearms and toolmark examination, like the other specialized pattern evidence areas (fingerprints, questioned documents), requires extensive training beyond formal education. The initial training for a fully casework-ready firearms and toolmark examiner usually takes about two years. As with all professions, competent forensic examiners make a commitment to lifelong learning and continue to try to improve their skills throughout their professional careers.

Summary

The markings on fired evidence (bullets, cartridge cases) used to individualize them to a particular weapon are examples of toolmarks. Thus, toolmarks is the broader category. Most toolmarks seen in the forensic lab are made by screwdrivers, pry bars, or wire or bolt cutters used by perpetrators to get unauthorized access to a premise. Toolmarks may be striations (the tool slides on a surface) or indented (the tool impresses into a surface). Besides the marking, tools can be examined for trace particles of the target surface to help associate the two.

Toolmarks are collected by photographing them, and collecting the intact object that bears them if possible. Some toolmarks may be cast, and the casts submitted for examination. Investigators should remember to collect specimens of the target surface (the surface or object on which the mark is found). Traces of it could appear on the tool.

Toolmarks, like other individualization pattern evidence, involve comparisons of a questioned with a known mark. Producing known marks with a suspect tool is not a trivial matter, primarily because the tool could have been used in many different ways to produce the questioned mark, such as variations in angle, pressure, distance traveled, and so on. Once a suitable known mark, or set of marks, is produced, the comparison is done under a low-power microscope by carefully comparing all the striation markings or the details of the indentation. An examiner can sometimes conclude that there are sufficient individual characteristics, in addition to the matching class characteristics, to make identification (individualization) rather than just an association.

Firearms work by using an explosive chemical reaction to propel a projectile down a barrel toward a target. The device containing the projectile, gunpowder, and primer is known as a cartridge. There are many types, designed to fit many types of firearms. When the firing pin of the firearm strikes the primer, an explosive reaction is initiated that ultimately forces the projectile down the barrel. Most pistols (handguns) and rifles (shoulder held) have *rifled* barrels. They have been impressed by spiraling grooves particular to the manufacturer and weapon. This rifling imparts spin to the projectile as it travels through the barrel and helps keep its flight trajectory more true. The rifling is a machining process, though, and this machining imparts microstriation markings on the metal that are individual to that barrel. This is the basis of bullet-to-barrel firearms identification. Rifles and pistols are also characterized by the diameter of their barrels, called *caliber*. There are many varieties of pistols and rifles. They may be single shot or semiautomatic. There are fully automatic weapons manufactured for the military, but it is illegal for most civilians to possess them. There are various types of semiautomatic rifles. Pistols may be revolvers or semiautomatics that use a magazine to hold a supply of cartridges. Another type of firearm is the shotgun. It is usually a long-barrel, shoulder-held weapon with a smooth-bore barrel. Shotgun ammunition is loaded with shot of various sizes or can consist of a single "slug."

Safety first is the rule when collecting firearms evidence. After a firearm is rendered safe, it needs to be submitted to the firearms section of the lab as soon as possible. It should be packaged and marked like any other type of evidence. Cartridge cases or fired shotshells are important evidence and need to be collected and marked in a location that will not interfere with examination. A revolver should be marked so the examiner knows which position of the cylinder the hammer was sitting on when the weapon was recovered.

Firearms may be examined for functionality, and the functionality of any safety devices they have should be checked. They may also be examined to determine the force required to pull the trigger. Their serial numbers are then located and recorded. If the firearm is functional, it is fired under controlled conditions to collect a known projectile and/or cartridge case or shotshell casing. Projectiles and cases are usually collected by firing the weapon into a water tank.

Firearms examiners examine two main types of "fired evidence": bullets, and cartridge cases or shotshell cases. These examinations are done with a comparison microscope, which enables the examiner to view questioned and known specimens side by side at the same time. Cartridge and shotshell casings have firing pin impressions, breech face markings, and in the case of semi-automatic weapons, extractor and ejector markings. Bullets fired through rifled barrels have class characteristics, such as the caliber, characteristic number and twist of the lands and grooves, and weight. They also have individualizing striation markings along their longitudinal aspect that are the basis for bullet-to-barrel identifications. Even fragments of bullets can contain sufficient striation markings to enable a comparison. Shot or slugs fired through smooth shotgun barrels have no markings and cannot be compared back to the firearm.

A database of images of fired bullets and cartridge cases called NIBIN is now in use to track the movement of weapons, even if the weapon has not yet been recovered. Semiautomatic weapons often result in scenes having ejected cartridge cases as evidence, and these can be imaged and entered into the database.

Firearms evidence and examinations are used to help reconstruct shooting incidents. Parameters such as trigger pull force and functionality of safeties can be important in these cases. The gunshot residue (GSR) pattern on a target surface can be used to help estimate muzzle to target distance if the pattern is compared with test patterns from the same weapon and ammunition fired at measured distances.

An additional application of GSR analysis is its identification on the hands of a shooter. With many firearms, residue is blown out to the side of the weapon as well as out the barrel. Identifying GSR unequivocally has been challenging. It contains the elements antimony and barium (from the primer) and lead (from the bullet), but GSR is not the only thing that might contain these elements. A sophisticated instrumental method, scanning electron microscopy coupled with energy-dispersive X-ray analysis (SEM-EDX), can provide certain identification of GSR particles. The problem of interpreting how the particles came to be on a person's hands is very real, however. The most that can usually be said is that a hand on which GSR particles have been found was "recently in the vicinity of a fired weapon."

Serial numbers are important in identifying particular firearms. Sometimes, criminals use various techniques to try to destroy or obliterate the numbers. Often, laboratory examiners can use acid etching or other techniques to restore and read the original serial numbers. These restoration techniques can be used on any metal surface (engine block, chain saw, etc.) to restore obliterated numbers.

The Association of Firearms and Toolmark Examiners (AFTE) is the main professional association of firearms examiners. In recent years, a Scientific Working Group (SWG) has been established to create consensus standards and further examine the science underlying firearms and toolmark identification.

Key Terms

toolmark (p. 179)
indented toolmarks (p. 180)
striated toolmarks (p. 180)
firearm (p. 182)
cartridge (p. 183)
smokeless powder (p. 183)
projectile (bullet) (p. 183)
primer (p. 183)
firing pin (p. 183)
rifling (p. 184)
grooves (p. 184)
lands (p. 185)
twist (p. 185)
land impressions (p. 185)

caliber (p. 186)
semiautomatic (p. 188)
automatic (p. 188)
rifle (p. 189)
magazine (p. 189)
handguns (p. 189)
revolvers (p. 189)
shotgun (p. 191)
shotgun shells (p. 191)
slug (p. 191)
trigger pull (p. 193)
functionality (p. 194)
bullet recovery tank (p. 194)
firearms comparison microscope (p. 195)

firing pin impression (p. 196)
breech face (p. 196)
NIBIN (p. 198)
safety (p. 199)
powder pattern (p. 199)
trajectory (p. 199)
gunshot residue (GSR) (p. 200)
scanning electron microscope (SEM) (p. 201)
SEM/EDX (p. 201)
serial number restoration (p. 202)
defacing (p. 203)
etching (p. 204)

Review Questions—Short Answer

1. What role does trace evidence play in the examination of tools and toolmarks?
2. How are toolmarks properly documented, protected, and collected?
3. What is the function and importance of the cartridge in the operation of a firearm?
4. List the three types of handgun and how they differ.
5. What is the process for comparing bullets and firearms evidence to a suspected weapon?
6. What is the role of general rifling characteristics file in the investigation and prosecution of firearms cases?
7. List some of the many ways that firearms evidence may be used in the reconstruction of firearms-related incidents.
8. Discuss the importance and methods for restoration of defaced serial numbers.
9. Discuss the role of NIBIN in investigation of cases involving firearms.
10. Why have cartridge cases become such an important type of firearms evidence in recent years?

Fill-in-the-Blank & Multiple Choice

1. Where possible, the *best* method of submitting an evidentiary toolmark for comparison is to send
   a. a photograph.
   b. the mark itself.
   c. a casting.
   d. a tape lift.
2. The inside diameter of a gun barrel is known as its _____.
3. The four components of a handgun or rifle cartridge are the primer, _____, _____, and case.
4. Handgun and rifle barrels have helical grooves on the interior of their barrels to
   a. improve the accuracy of the weapon.
   b. cause the bullet to spin.
   c. grip the bullet as it enters the barrel.
   d. all of the above.
5. When the serial number on a weapon has been defaced to make it unreadable,
   a. the weapon cannot be properly identified.
   b. the weapon can be identified by other part numbers.
   c. the serial number can often be chemically restored.
   d. the serial number can often be read by using image enhancement.

Further References

Association of Firearms and Toolmarks Examiners Web site, www.afte.org.

FirearmsID.com/new_index.htm.

Heard, B. *Firearms and Ballistics: Handbook of Examining and Interpreting Forensic Evidence.* Chichester, UK: John Wiley & Sons, 1996.

Katterwe, K. "Modern Approaches for the Examination of Toolmarks and Other Surface Marks." *Forensic Science Review* 8, no. 1 (1996): 46–72.

Moenssens, A. A., Starrs, J. E., Henderson, C. E., and Inbau, F. E. "Firearms Identification and Comparative Micrography." In *Scientific Evidence in Civil and Criminal Cases,* ed. A. A Moenssens, F. E. Inbu, J. E. Starrs, and C. E. Henderson. Westbury, New York, Foundation Press, 1995.

Springer, E. "Toolmark Examinations—A Review of Its Development in the Literature." *Journal of Forensic Sciences* 40, no. 6 (1995): 964–968.

Zeichner, A., and N. Levin. "Casework Experience of GSR detection in Israel, on Samples from Hands, Hair, and Clothing Using an Autosearch SEM/EDX System." *Journal of Forensic Sciences* 40, no. 6 (1995): 1082–1085.

Biological Evidence

Biological evidence is one of the major classes of physical evidence. It has become even more important with the development of DNA typing. Now, biological evidence such as blood and semen can be effectively individualized, that is, if a DNA profile from evidence matches the DNA profile from a person (with enough loci included in the profile), it is all but certain that person is the source of the evidence. The "biological evidence" that will be discussed in this chapter includes primarily blood and physiological fluids. It is set apart because its evidentiary value lies in the fact that genetic typing analysis is used to associate it with (or dissociate it from) a particular person or persons. As is often true in forensic science, the category is defined contextually, by the kind of analysis that will define its evidentiary value.

Blood and some other physiological fluids could be "toxicological evidence," for example, if they were to be analyzed for drugs or toxins. Toxicology is discussed separately, with drug chemistry, because its analytical methods are similar or identical to those used for street drugs (Part Five, Chapter 12). Hair is biological too. But its structure and the traditional methods used for its analysis are more closely related to those used for fibers. Moreover, hair is a type of fiber. So, in this book, we group fibers and hairs together (Part Five, Chapter 13). Most of the "biological evidence" we discuss will be human, because that is what is most often encountered in casework. But sometimes the evidence can be from animals. We will talk about species testing in Chapter 9. On rare occasions, genetic analysis has been done on case materials from non-human animal or plant sources.

There are some other kinds of "biological" evidence that have more in common with "trace" evidence (Chapter 13) from an analytical methods and evidentiary viewpoint than with the material in this chapter. Examples are plant materials, like leaves and pollens.

The forensic examination of blood and physiological fluids for the purpose of associating them with or dissociating them from particular persons—the subject of this Part—begins with preliminary examination, documentation, locating biological materials on evidence items, and conducting tests to identify what type of biological material is there. Chapter 9 covers those areas. The next stage is DNA typing, and that is covered in Chapter 10.

Blood and Physiological Fluid Evidence: Evaluation and Initial Examination

- What blood is and some of its different constituents

- How to collect and package biological evidence to best preserve it, and what control and comparison specimens are necessary for biological evidence analysis

- The relationship of certain types of control and comparison specimens to possible evidence contamination, and how contamination may be avoided or controlled

- How forensic scientists do initial examinations of biological evidence

- How blood is identified—presumptive and confirmatory tests

- How different physiological fluids are identified

- How sexual assault cases are investigated, and the role of forensic scientists

- Different types of sexual assault cases, and how the role of the forensic science lab might differ depending on the type of case

- Drug-facilitated sexual assaults ("date-rape" drug cases), and how they are investigated

- The genetic basis for the individuality of blood and body fluids

- The classical (conventional) genetic systems used to type forensic specimens before DNA

Outline

Learning Objectives

- How some terminology associated with forensic biological evidence analysis has changed because of DNA typing

chapter 9

Lead Case

Illinois v. Gary Dotson

In 1977, in a suburb of Chicago, a young woman named Cathleen Crowell reported to police that she had been kidnapped and raped. She was able to identify a man named Gary Dotson as the perpetrator. Key evidence in the case consisted of the victim's panties, which had drainage stains in the crotch area.

At the time this case happened, DNA technology had not yet been applied to forensic cases or biological evidence. The biological evidence testing consisted of identifying semen in the panty drainage stains and ABO blood group analysis. Near the end of the chapter, we present in Case Study 9.1 some sketches showing how powerful DNA analysis is, compared with the conventional blood typing systems, in excluding true nondepositors. To understand the forensic issues in the Dotson case, some explanation of ABO blood group analysis in sexual assault cases is necessary here.

There are four main ABO blood groups: A, B, AB, and O. A person's blood group (or blood type) can be determined from his or her red blood cells, using commercially available antibodies. The antibodies called anti-A react with A receptors on the cells. Those called anti-B react with B receptors. Another test reagent called anti-H reacts with O cells. (The reasons for not calling it anti-O are too technical for this presentation.) Using these antibodies on someone's red cells will tell the analyst the person's blood type. Blood types are genetically determined. Another genetic factor in humans determines whether or not the ABO blood group substances will be present in the person's body fluids, like semen, vaginal secretions, saliva, and so forth. People who have the ABO substances present are called "secretors," and people who don't are called "nonsecretors." Body fluids such as saliva from a person can be tested to see if the person is a secretor. Secretors are about 75 percent of the population. The ABO types in the U.S. White population are distributed approximately as follows: 40 percent, A; 10 percent, B; 45 percent, O; and 5 percent, AB.

In a sexual assault case, if semen is present on a vaginal swab or in drainage stains, it will contain a mixture of male and female secretions. Analysis of this mixture in the evidence stains will show the blood groups of one or both people if they are secretors. The laboratory would then type the people in the case, determine if they are secretors or not, and give an interpretation of the results: that is, whether the blood typing results include or exclude the male, given the evidence and the female.

In the Dotson case, both people were type B and secretors. When the evidence was tested, it showed that semen was present and that blood group substances B and H were present. The following table shows which blood group substances are present in secretor people of the four blood types.

Secretors with blood type	Have in their body fluids
O	H
A	A + H
B	B + H
AB	A + B + H
Nonsecretors	None

The laboratory analysis in sexual assault cases permits an analyst to draw a conclusion as to whether a suspect male should be included or excluded as a possible depositor. Inclusion does not mean that the man is the depositor, only that he is included in a subset of men who could have been depositors. In nonexclusion cases, the analyst can calculate what percentage of the male population is included (in addition to the suspect) using population frequency figures like those previously noted.

The analyst who handled and testified in the Dotson case originally stated that only B secretor males were included as possible depositors. That was wrong. He should have said that B secretor, O secretor, and all nonsecretor men were included. The reason it matters is that he told the original trial jury that only about 7 or 8 percent of men were possible depositors (10% type B × 75% secretors). In reality it was over 66 percent of men (10% type B × 75% secretors + 45% O × 75% secretors + 25% nonsecretors). That is a big enough difference to be misleading to jurors. The lower number made Dotson sound considerably "more implicated" than justified by the data.

Gary Dotson, flanked by his mother and sister, speaking to reporters in May of 1985.

Some two years after the assault, Dotson was convicted by a trial jury and sentenced to a lengthy prison term.

In 1985, the victim stunned the Illinois legal establishment and created a media frenzy when she announced publicly that she had lied in 1977 and at the trial in 1979. Dotson was innocent, she said. She had not been kidnapped nor raped. He should be released.

Lawyers representing Dotson moved to get him released from prison. Getting someone released from prison after he has been convicted by a trial jury is not that simple, however. State prosecutors argued that Crowell could be lying now—how could anyone be sure? Unsuccessful at getting Dotson released, his lawyers asked then Governor Thompson to consider clemency, given the startling recantation by the alleged victim. Governor Thompson was himself an experienced trial lawyer and took the time to hold hearings on the matter. One of the arguments made on Dotson's behalf was that the testimony of the lab analyst at the first trial was extremely misleading, as noted. The only evidence against Dotson was Crowell's testimony that he was the perpetrator, and the semen blood type evidence. The blood group evidence was not very informative when properly interpreted—he was included as a possible depositor along with around 66 percent of White men.

In the late 1980s, DNA technology was starting to find its way into forensic science. The developments are recounted in Chapter 10. At that time, DNA typing was done using a technology called RFLP (restriction fragment length polymorphism) analysis. For purposes of this case, it is enough to note that RFLP analysis required larger quantities of undegraded DNA than current techniques, and that only a few labs could do this testing until the 1990s. One of the outcomes of the clemency hearings before Governor Thompson was an agreement by the parties that the evidence could be sent out for DNA testing. In 1988, the evidence was sent to Alec Jeffreys's lab in Leicester, England, for DNA tests. Dr. Jeffreys was the author of the original forensic DNA typing paper in the scientific journal *Nature*. Unfortunately, there was insufficient undegraded DNA in the evidence specimens, and the testing was inconclusive.

Around this same time, a revolutionary method called the PCR (polymerase chain reaction) was being adapted to forensic DNA typing. PCR and its development are explained in Chapter 10. One important feature of PCR-based DNA analysis is that it requires far less DNA than RFLP, and even degraded DNA in evidence specimens can often be successfully typed. Finally, in 1988, the evidence was sent to Dr. Edward Blake in California for DNA typing of a locus called HLA-DQA1. This typing relied on PCR analysis and, as noted, was often successful on much smaller evidence specimens than the RFLP method. Dr. Blake's testing was successful. Dotson could be excluded as the depositor of the semen on the evidence panties. The DNA type of the semen was, in fact, consistent with that of Crowell's boyfriend at the time of the original complaint. Dotson was finally released.

This case has a few important lessons. First, testing results are not always properly interpreted. The first analyst badly misinterpreted the degree of inclusion of Dotson. Whether providing the trial jury with the correct percentage of included men would have changed the outcome, no one can say for sure. But correct interpretation of an expert's results is an absolute requirement of good forensic science. Second, the case starkly illustrates the limited power of blood typing results to exclude true nondepositors. In this case, and in many others, the suspect could not be excluded, but he was not the real depositor. DNA typing would later prove it. Third, the case shows how much damage can be done, and how large amounts of public resources can be wastefully spent, because of an intentionally false sexual assault accusation. Crowell said she invented the attack as a cover because she thought she had become pregnant by her boyfriend.

How Biological Evidence Analysis Has Changed Because of DNA Typing

The development of DNA typing methods for forensic science laboratories revolutionized the analysis of blood and physiological fluid evidence. It also changed the nature of the biological evidence analyst's work, and the terminology used to describe it. The laboratory work described in this chapter is most often called **forensic biology.** Until the 1980s, when forensic DNA typing was developed, forensic biological evidence analysts relied on blood groups and other so-called genetic markers (like red cell isoenzymes) to help narrow down the number of people who might have deposited blood or body fluid evidence. At that time, a typing match between evidence and a person only indicated that the person *might be* or *could be* the source of the evidence. Blood groups were one of the kinds of "genetic markers" forensic scientists used in the pre-DNA era. Classically, serology is the study of blood groups and blood antibodies. For this reason, forensic biological evidence analysis was often called **forensic serology.** As other inherited factors in addition to blood groups were introduced into forensic labs, the term "forensic biochemistry" also came into use. Now

forensic biology

Today, refers to the preliminary examination of biological evidence in blood transfer and sexual assault cases, much of which will go on to be analyzed for DNA; also sometimes used to refer to subdisciplines like forensic botany.

forensic serology

Refers to the preliminary examination and genetic typing of biological evidence in blood transfer and sexual assault cases before DNA analysis was available.

that DNA typing is the exclusive method of genetic analysis in forensic labs, the non-DNA typing part of forensic biological evidence analysis—the material included in this chapter—is most often called "forensic biology" or "forensic biochemistry."

Nature of Blood

Blood is actually a tissue, like muscle or kidney or liver, but it is liquid. There are many different compounds dissolved in blood, and there are also different types of cells suspended in circulating blood. Blood carries oxygen from the lungs to all the body tissues, and carbon dioxide, a waste product, away from tissues and back to the lungs where it can be exhaled. Blood also carries nutrients, all sorts of chemical signaling molecules (like hormones), and any other ingested substances (like drugs) to bodily tissues and organs. And it carries metabolic waste products from their production sites to other organs for disposal.

Blood circulation is essential for life. Events that cause interruption of circulation, or injuries that cause hemorrhage and accompanying large reductions in blood pressure, can quickly be fatal without major medical intervention.

A tube of blood drawn from a person's vein and allowed to sit undisturbed for a few minutes will form a two-phase, or two-fraction, system (Figure 9.1). The blood will clot, and the lower, dark red fraction (the clot) contains all the **blood cells.**

The upper, straw-yellow colored, watery fraction is called **serum,** and it contains all the dissolved proteins and other compounds. Blood can also be drawn into a special tube that contains an **anticoagulant** (a compound that prevents blood from clotting). After a few minutes, it would look exactly like the other tube—the one that did not contain anticoagulant. Although there is no visible difference between the tubes, the two phases are not the same in both. In the tube with the anticoagulant added, the cells are not clotted. They have merely settled to the bottom. The yellowish, watery upper layer is almost the same as serum, except that it still has all the clotting proteins in it, and is called **plasma.**

The straw-colored serum (plasma) layer contains all the dissolved proteins, including albumin and immunoglobulins (the circulating antibodies). The word *serum* is the basis of the terms *serology* and *forensic serology.* Some of the proteins in the

blood cells

Refers collectively to the red blood cells (erythrocytes) and to all the categories of white blood cells (lymphocytes, monocytes, basophils, neutrophils, and eosinophils).

serum

The straw-colored liquid portion of blood remaining after whole blood has been allowed to clot.

anticoagulant

A chemical substance, such as EDTA or sodium citrate, which, when added to whole blood, prevents it from clotting.

plasma

When treated with anticoagulant, the straw-colored liquid portion of blood after the cells have settled.

Figure 9.1

Diagram of whole blood illustrating the difference in separation when an anticoagulant is present versus when it clots.

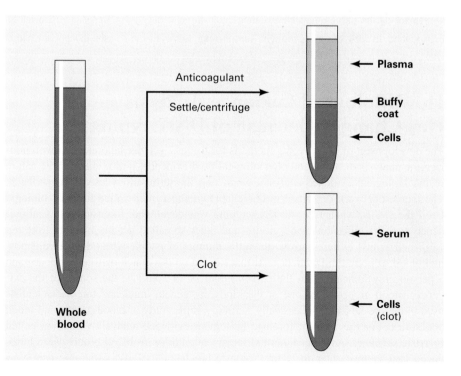

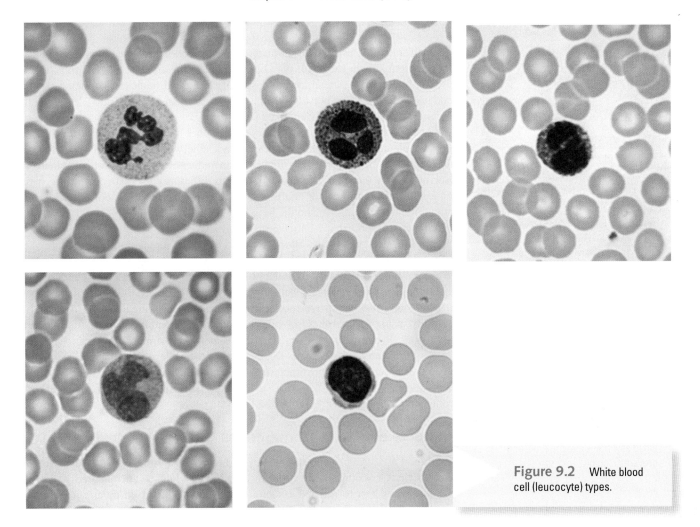

Figure 9.2 White blood cell (leucocyte) types.

serum are specific for a particular species (such as human, cow horse, dog, etc.), and we will be talking about them later in connection with species tests. The cell fraction contains all the cells. DNA comes from the cells. Since DNA is found in the *nucleus* of a cell (see Chapter 10), only cells that have nuclei will have DNA. Most cells do have nuclei, but mature red blood cells do not. They form from precursor cells in the red bone marrow, and the nucleus is lost along the pathway. Therefore, mature red cells have no nuclear DNA. Blood DNA thus comes from the white cells. There are several different types of white cells (see Figure 9.2). Their primary physiological function is fighting infection. Normal human blood contains about 5 million red cells per cubic millimeter (or microliter) of blood—the normal range is a little higher for males, and about 7,000 to 8,000 white cells per cubic millimeter of blood. Human plasma contains about 30–40 mg/mL albumin, the most plentiful blood serum protein, and about 5–6 mg/mL immunoglobulins, the circulating antibodies.

Collection, Preservation, and Packaging of Biological (Including Blood) Evidence

Blood or body fluid evidence specimens are collected, subjected to identification testing, and then to DNA typing. The DNA types are compared with those of known persons. Specimens from known persons are called "known control," or "exemplar" or "reference," specimens. Although investigators and laboratory personnel generally do not actually collect these specimens themselves, they should know how to do it.

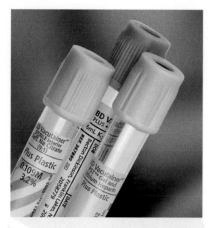

Figure 9.3

A "Vacutainer." A Becton Dickinson & Co. trademarked name for a glass tube that has been evacuated (most of the air removed) at the factory (so as to produce mild negative pressure in the tube). When the inside of the tube is connected to a vein via a hypodermic needle, blood flows into the tube because of the negative pressure. Many Vacutainers contain anticoagulants which immediately mix with the blood as it flows into the tube, and prevents clotting.

Blood or Buccal Swab from Known Person

For a long time, and even today in many places, blood is collected as the reference specimen from known people. It may be collected from suspects, from victims, from consensual partners in sexual assault cases, or from dead bodies in homicide cases. Blood taken from a living person is usually drawn from an arm vein into a Vacutainer, a Becton Dickinson & Co. trademarked name for a glass tube that has been evacuated (most of the air removed) at the factory (to produce mild negative pressure in the tube) (see Figure 9.3). Vacutainer tubes are available with different preservatives or anticoagulants. The color of the stopper is an indicator of which anticoagulant or preservative is in the tube. Blood is drawn into different preservatives because it is intended for different types of analysis or testing. If blood is to be collected from a person for DNA typing, it should be collected in a "purple top" (EDTA [*ethyl-enediaminetetraacetic acid*] anticoagulant) tube. "Blue top" tubes are sometimes used and are also acceptable. Blood for testing in the forensic science lab should not be collected into clot tubes.

It is no longer necessary to collect blood from living persons as a standard for DNA typing. In many places, buccal (cheek) swabbings or light scrapings have replaced blood collection. Sterile collecting devices for the taking of buccal swabbings are readily available, and they provide more than an adequate quantity of cells for DNA typing. In the case of a dead body, the medical examiner may try to collect blood as the reference specimen. Depending on the state of decomposition of the body, blood may still be recoverable in good enough condition for testing. If not, a tissue specimen can be collected as a reference specimen. In cases of advanced decomposition, a bone can be collected.

Biological Evidence from Scenes

Often, blood at a crime scene will be dry or nearly dry by the time it is discovered and collected. Occasionally, fresh or still wet blood might be encountered.

It is always best to seize and submit items having blood on them without any testing or sampling at the scene. The only reason to think about any of the sampling methods discussed next is that the intact item containing the blood or physiological fluid cannot be submitted for some reason—for example, it is too big or cannot be moved. Blood or physiological fluids must be allowed to dry completely before the items on which they are located are handled or packaged.

Fresh or Wet Blood   There are methods for collecting fresh or wet blood, but it is generally advisable now to collect wet blood on a clean, sterile piece of gauze and then allow the blood to dry completely. One exception to this general rule might be blood in snow. In that case, a clean spoonlike utensil should be used to collect the blood specimen with as little surrounding snow as possible into a clean vial.

Dried Blood   Four possible sampling methods can be used for dried blood on items or surfaces that cannot themselves be moved or collected: cutting, swabbing, scraping, and elution (dissolving).

Cutting is obviously applicable only to things that can easily be cut. Investigators should not cut samples from items that can be submitted intact, such as articles of clothing. There may sometimes be bloodstains on items that are judged too large or too cumbersome to submit, such as a large carpet or a clothlike vehicle seat. If cutting is necessary, investigators should cut out a portion of the bloodstained item that is large enough to have unstained areas around the edges—these unstained edges may be required as substratum comparison specimens (discussed later).

Swabbing consists of transferring the blood specimen from its existing surface onto a swab of some kind. With dried blood, the swab must be moistened before use in order to bring about the transfer. Sterile saline solution (made by dissolving

8.5 grams sodium chloride in 1 liter of distilled water), or sterile distilled water itself, can be used to moisten the swab. Using sterile solutions avoids any contamination of the blood specimens with bacteria. Swabs should consist of articles that will dry somewhat easily because the swab with the transferred blood must be thoroughly dry before packaging. Gauze sponges are useful as swabs for blood collection, and they are easily obtainable factory-sterilized. Q-tips or similar cotton swabs are not recommended for swabbing dried bloodstains because the fibers are tightly packed, they are generally not sterile, and they can take a long time to dry completely.

Scraping consists of using a straight- or sharp-edged instrument or object to scrape dried blood or physiological fluid off a surface and onto clean laboratory-weighing or other suitable paper that can then be "druggist" folded. See Chapter 3 for how to make a druggist fold. Scraping has advantages and disadvantages compared with swabbing. The primary advantage is that the investigator does not have to redissolve the blood or body fluid evidence (which is what happens during swabbing), and then redry the material before packaging.

With scraping, the evidentiary material is already dry and stays dry during the collection procedure. The primary disadvantage is that scraping produces small particles that are difficult to contain and handle. Air currents and static electricity can become problem factors with particle or powderlike evidence. If scraping causes some of the surface material to be removed along with the dried blood, as for example would happen with cinder block, then the investigator should scrape some of the surface material into a separate package as a possible substratum comparison specimen. If the particles can be contained and packaged, scraping is preferable to swabbing.

Elution (using a small amount of saline solution or distilled water to dissolve the dried stain) should be considered a last resort, to be used only by investigators who have had some specific training and when there is no reasonable alternative. Swabbing or scraping procedures should be applicable to almost every situation involving dried blood or body fluid stains where the item containing the stains cannot itself be collected.

The most important consideration in preserving blood or physiological evidence is *ensuring that the evidence is thoroughly dry before it is packaged,* and that it is subsequently stored in a cool, dry environment. Moisture and humidity, along with darkness and warmth, are enemies of biological evidence preservation. They promote the growth of bacteria and mold, and putrefaction, which lead to the destruction of biological evidence. Direct sunlight, or any other type of direct illumination that has an ultraviolet component, can have deleterious effects on blood DNA and should be avoided. The molecules that must be intact for any of the tests to work can become degraded to such an extent that forensic testing cannot be done. Although changes in evidence with time can cause problems with some tests, aging alone does not usually preclude DNA typing. Often, the biggest problem with old biological stains is that they become difficult to get back into solution for testing. Extreme heating of evidence can have a similar effect. In dry environments, evidence items can be allowed to air dry before packaging. In humid environments, it may be necessary to move the evidence items to an air-conditioned room to dry them adequately.

Biological evidence must be packaged in paper containers that can breathe, never in airtight containers such as Ziploc plastic bags. There are commercially available paper containers that have plastic "windows." Since investigators ordinarily seal evidence at a scene with evidence tape, and the evidence package is not opened again until it reaches a lab examiner, these "see-through" paper containers are helpful in allowing police and evidence personnel to see what is inside the container. The ability to see what is inside is one of the major advantages of plastic bag packaging, but since plastic restricts airflow and tends to retain moisture, there is considerable risk that the evidence could be ruined in such a container, especially if it was not

Biological Evidence

thoroughly dry when placed in the container. Blood and other biological evidence items should always be packaged in paper containers.

Test Controls, Substratum Comparison Specimens, and Contamination Issues

Controls are a very important part of scientific testing and measurement. They allow scientists to be sure their tests are working properly and that the tests are measuring those things for which they were designed. In some crime scene and evidence collection situations, the investigators must ensure that appropriate control or comparison specimens have been collected along with the evidence itself.

In the case of blood and physiological fluid evidence, it may be important to show that the results obtained came from the evidence itself, and not the substratum (object or material on which the evidence was deposited) or something else. We use the term *substratum* (pl., *substrata*) to designate the surface or object on which evidence is deposited. Some people say "substrate" to indicate the underlying surface. The term *substrate* has other meanings in biochemistry, though, so we use the Latin word for "underlying surface."

There are four different types of control and comparison specimens that might be used in forensic testing of evidence: knowns, alibi knowns, blank, and substratum comparison specimens. They were discussed in Chapter 3. All are important in evidence collection and testing. They are discussed here in the context of biological evidence.

Known (Exemplar or Reference) Controls

known control

A specimen from a known source; it could be known blood, known human blood, known animal blood, or known blood from a particular person; for DNA, it could be a buccal (cheek) swabbing from a known person.

Like many types of forensic tests discussed in this book, biological evidence testing involves comparisons between a questioned (evidentiary) specimen and a known specimen (whose origin is known with certainty). The **known control** (which may also be called the exemplar or the reference) is essential for the comparison. With biological evidence, knowns will be blood, or a buccal (cheek) swabbing, from a person (for comparison with DNA types from evidentiary blood or body fluid specimens).

Alibi (Alternative) Known Control

alibi known control

A specimen obtained from a known source that might be the source of the evidence; usually collected because suspects suggest them (as alibis).

An alibi or alternative known is the same as a known control, but from a different source. Police might suspect, for example, that bloodstains on a suspect's clothing are from an assault victim. The assault victim's blood would therefore be the known control. But the suspect says the bloodstains came from a fight with someone in a bar (and he names the person). Blood from that person would then be an **alibi known control** in the case.

Blank Control

blank control

In many tests, a clean sample containing no specimen, used to ensure that the test is working properly.

A **blank control** refers to a specimen known to be free of the item or substance being tested. Scientists use blank controls as negative controls (generally along with positive controls) to be sure tests and test chemicals are working properly. Generally, investigators do not have to worry about blank controls.

Substratum Comparison Specimens

As mentioned earlier, the term "substratum" refers to the underlying material or surface on which evidence is found or has been deposited. The term "substrate" is sometimes used for the same purpose.

With most blood and physiological fluid evidence, investigators must remember to collect a sample of the substratum separately from the evidence in order to permit the analyst to interpret the scientific tests properly.

Generally, the **substratum comparison specimen** is subjected to the same testing as the evidence (which is on the substratum already) to make sure it is the evidence giving the test result, and not the underlying surface material. As noted in earlier chapters, the substratum comparison specimen has in the past been called a "control." However, it is not a control specimen strictly speaking because control specimens in science have known history and/or composition. The substratum specimen has an unknown history, but is important in the comparison between the known control and questioned evidence specimen. It is properly termed a "comparison specimen," and it can help detect interference in a test coming from the evidence surface.

When intact items that have blood or other biological stains on them are collected, an unstained portion of the item can be used as a substratum comparison specimen. If investigators cannot submit an item with biological stains intact, and they must use one of the sampling methods discussed earlier, then they must take care to collect substratum comparison specimens using the same techniques.

The discussion of substratum comparison specimens brings up the issue of potential **contamination.** Contamination can be an important consideration with crime scene evidence because investigators have no control over evidence items until those items have been recognized, documented, and properly collected. In the biological evidence arena, forensic scientists have to be concerned about the possibility that human biological material that has nothing to do with the case events might get deposited onto, or be admixed with, human biological evidence that is case related. This problem has always existed but is perhaps of greater concern today in some circumstances because DNA typing methods are so sensitive—that is, analysts can generate DNA types from so little specimen.

In theory, evidence might become contaminated in several ways. There could be biological material on an item or surface before the biological *evidence* was ever deposited. Biological material might be deposited onto evidence during scene searching and/or processing activities. Or biological material might be deposited onto evidence during laboratory examinations and/or manipulations. Neither investigators nor forensic scientists have any control over the history or circumstances of evidence prior to its recognition and collection. A major purpose of collecting and testing the substratum comparison specimen—and sometimes alternative known controls—discussed earlier is to check for the possibility of a contaminant. Investigators and scientists do have control over what happens to evidence following its recognition, as well as during their activities at scenes and subsequently.

We emphasize that contamination is not an important issue in many cases—those that have large quantities of biological evidence in comparison with the quantities of any contaminant that might be present, even in theory. There is usually so much biological evidence compared with any contaminant that only the results from the evidence are observed. Only when the quantities of the contaminant start to approach the quantities of the evidence in a mixture does the possibility of contaminant interference become a significant consideration. And even in that circumstance, the analyst would obtain results indicating a mixture. It is also important to emphasize that contamination does not necessarily imply error or accidental or intentional wrongdoing on the part of investigators or scientists.

Thus, even though there can be unavoidable contamination, contamination of evidence by investigators and scientists can be eliminated or minimized. Comparison specimens help forensic scientists detect the presence of contaminants and correctly interpret the results of their tests. Good crime scene and evidence collection practices on the part of investigators, and good laboratory techniques on the part of evidence technicians and scientists, are all designed to prevent contamination of any evidence items.

A number of crime scene and laboratory practices are specifically aimed at avoiding contamination of the evidence specimens. These are discussed in the box "Good Crime Scene and Laboratory Practices."

substratum comparison specimen

A sample of the material or surface on which biological evidence is deposited.

contamination

Refers to unintended, potentially unrecognized, biological material in or on a biological evidence specimen, which could cause difficulty in interpreting the results of some tests under some circumstances.

Good Crime Scene and Laboratory Practices

The "good practices" discussed here are those designed to protect evidence from any contamination by the investigators or scientists, or any other avoidable source, and to protect investigators and scientists from anything harmful in the evidence.

Perhaps the simplest and most basic precaution is protective gloves. Often, latex gloves are used, but some people are allergic to latex. Nitrile gloves may also be used, and they afford some additional protection for investigators and scientists against chemical hazards. Gloves prevent investigators' or scientists' hands from coming into contact with biological evidence that might have some infectious agent present. Viruses that cause AIDS, as well as the hepatitis B and C, and herpes viruses can be present in blood or body fluids. Although there is probably very little risk for someone to contract these viruses from dried biological evidence, the risk may be greater if the biological evidence is still wet. Wearing protective gloves constitutes a normal and widely recommended precaution in handling biological material that is potentially biohazardous.

Gloves also protect the evidence from the evidence handlers—investigators and scientists. Depositing skin cells from the hands or fingerprints is avoided. Evidence handlers should also take precautions to avoid their hair getting into evidence. And they should realize that coughing or sneezing may contaminate evidence.

Sterile solutions and sterile gauze for evidence collection avoid the problem of potential bacterial contamination. Some bacteria may have the ability to destroy biological evidence. They can also contribute unwanted, background DNA. Bacteria are everywhere and probably cannot be completely avoided. As a rule, they do not prevent successful biological evidence analysis. But taking simple precautions to avoid contamination is sensible.

There are strategies to prevent contamination in laboratories as well. Analysts always wear protective gloves. In some DNA laboratories, the DNA profiles of all the employees are kept on file so that the lab can immediately spot contamination of a specimen from a lab person. All DNA analysis relies on PCR (discussed in detail in Chapter 10), which makes large numbers of copies of certain regions of DNA that are important in forensic DNA profiling. The large quantity of copies creates a potential for contamination within the laboratory that must be avoided. Separate rooms in the lab are devoted to pre- and post-PCR activities for these reasons. Many laboratories restrict entry to their DNA units as well to avoid potential problems with contamination by the DNA of visitors.

As we have noted, investigators and scientists must try to avoid contaminating evidence themselves. They have no control over preexisting contamination, however. Furthermore, if the quantity of evidence is very large in comparison to the contaminant, the contaminant will have no effect on the DNA profile. The signal from the evidence DNA will overwhelm the signal from any contaminant. For example, coughing on a large bloodstain is almost certainly not going to change the DNA profile. There is so much bloodstain DNA compared with the small amount that may be deposited from the cough that only the bloodstain profile will be seen.

Initial Examination of and for Biological Evidence

Blood or other physiological fluid stains or residues may be found on almost anything. Part of crime scene processing involves recognizing the presence or possible presence of such evidence, and then properly collecting and preserving the item. Items submitted to the laboratory often have obvious stains on them, but sometimes they do not. Further, an item can have some obvious stains as well as other stains that are subtle and more difficult to find. The initial examination of items by a criminalist in the laboratory is designed to evaluate them for possible evidentiary value. This includes but is not limited to searching for biological stains. With visible stains or with areas where analysts perceive subtle staining or the possibility of staining, preliminary blood (and physiological fluid) tests are used to determine whether there is really anything to examine further. Positive preliminary tests indicate possible presence of blood or body fluids. The item will then be subject to confirmatory tests. Preliminary examiners may cut out or swab stains or areas that are of interest and/or that have given positive preliminary tests. Subsequent examinations are then done on the swabs or cuttings.

Because the first examiner can be the only person in the chain of analysis who actually sees the evidence in context, it is crucial that good lab notes, and sketches or photographs if necessary, be made. Done properly, this strategy allows the evidence (and any results obtained) to be put into proper case context. At this preliminary stage of examination perhaps more so than anywhere else, it is essential to remember that criminalistics involves the evaluation of physical evidence in the context of a case, not just the detailed, serial analysis of submitted items. In large, busy laboratories, there may be considerable division of labor in handling the volume of evidence items. Under those conditions, the role of the initial examining criminalist becomes critical.

To some extent, logic dictates that the search for evidence at a scene, and on items submitted to the laboratory, will be conditioned by the type of case and its circumstances, and the type of evidence. But crime scene investigators and criminalists must always be open to finding something unusual or unexpected. It is also important for both scene investigators and criminalists to be thorough. Getting too focused on or caught up in the obvious may cause an expert to overlook something important. There is considerable truth to the old saying: "One sees mainly what one is looking for."

It may also be noted that presumptive testing can be used to evaluate evidence items at scenes for possible collection, packaging, and submission. Often, these activities are entirely the responsibility of crime scene investigators, but in some places on some occasions, laboratory examiners may go out to provide assistance or advice at scenes. Regardless, the *only* reason to do presumptive testing at a scene is to make a decision about collection and submission of the item. If the item is going to be collected and submitted, there is no point in doing field tests, because the laboratory will do the testing anyway.

Forensic Identification of Blood

Just as identification, individualization, and reconstruction may be seen as the three principal aspects of a criminalistics investigation, they may also be seen as the three main objectives of biological evidence analysis. *Identification* (which can also be called *classification*—see Chapter 1) means showing what the biological evidence is; that is, whether it is blood, semen, and so on. *Individualization* is the DNA typing of biological evidence to try to show that it almost certainly came from a particular individual, or that it did not come from that individual. *Reconstruction* in this context is primarily the interpretation of blood patterns (Chapter 4). It could also involve interpreting physiological fluid stain patterns, such as whether a semen stain seems to have resulted from drainage following intercourse, for example.

Species determination in bloodstains is part of "identification." This chapter, then, discusses the identification aspect of blood and physiological fluids. DNA typing is covered in Chapter 10.

With blood and physiological fluid stains and with several other types of physical evidence, there are two categories of identification tests: presumptive or preliminary, and confirmatory.

A **preliminary test** (or presumptive test) is used for screening specimens that might contain the substance or material. Usually such tests are sensitive, but not necessarily specific for the substance or material. They are also faster and less expensive than confirmatory tests. Nonspecificity means that there may be false positives and false negatives. In a "false positive," other substances or materials give positive results. In a "false negative," the test does not register when the substance or material is present. Ideally, preliminary tests should give a minimum of false negatives. The reason for minimizing false negatives is to maximize the test's utility as a screening tool. If the test gives a low rate of false negatives, specimens that test negative can be assumed to be negative and not to require any further testing. If a screening test does not meet this criterion, it does not serve its primary purpose— which is to avoid having to do confirmatory tests on every specimen.

A **confirmatory test** is generally more complicated, often more expensive, and it requires more analyst time than a preliminary test. A good screening test prevents laboratories from having to do confirmatory testing on every item and thus increases efficiency and evidence throughput. Confirmatory tests must by definition be entirely specific for the substance or material for which they are intended. A positive confirmatory test is interpreted as an unequivocal demonstration that the specimen contains the substance or material. For some types of biological evidence, no confirmatory tests exist. That is, the only tests available are presumptive. Under those circumstances, the most an analyst can ever say is that a specimen "might have" or "could have" the substance present.

preliminary test

A nondefinitive screening test used to give an indication that something might be present (like blood, or a body fluid); positive results indicate the need for further tests.

confirmatory test

A test that, when positive, proves that the material or substance tested for is actually present.

Preliminary or Presumptive Tests for Blood

Preliminary (presumptive) tests for blood have been around for more than a century. Most of them are color tests; that is, there is a distinctive color or color change when the test is positive. The tests in fairly widespread use today include: phenolphthalein (Kastle-Meyer), o-tolidine, tetramethylbenzidine, leucomalachite green, and luminol. All the tests except luminol work on the same principle—they take advantage of the peroxidase-like properties of hemoglobin.

Peroxidases are enzymes that occur widely throughout nature but are especially prevalent in some plants and bacteria. Horseradish is an especially rich source of peroxidase. An enzyme is a protein that can speed up a chemical reaction without being changed in the process. And a peroxidase is an enzyme that specifically catalyzes the reaction:

$$\text{Reduced Dye} + \text{Peroxide} \xrightarrow{\text{peroxidase}} \text{Oxidized Dye} + \text{Water}$$

"Reduced" and "oxidized" are chemical concepts that have to do with a change in chemical structure. The point here is that the reduced and oxidized forms of the dye are different colors. The reaction works as a blood test because hemoglobin acts like a peroxidase enzyme. Luminol under certain conditions and in the presence of peroxide produces light as a reaction product; that is, some of the energy released in the reaction is emitted as light. Substances like luminol that can produce light by undergoing chemical reactions are called *chemiluminescent*.

Presumptive blood tests are routinely used in the laboratory to screen evidence items for the possible presence of blood. The tests may also sometimes be used in the field at crime scenes. They are very sensitive and can give positive results with such small amounts of blood as to be invisible to the naked eye.

These tests can be done directly—by applying the chemicals directly to the specimen—or by a transfer technique. In the latter, which is always recommended over direct testing, a cotton swab (like a Q-tip) is lightly moistened on both its ends using sterile saline or water. One end is used to lightly swab the specimen to be tested, in order to transfer a small quantity of the suspected substance to the swab. The test chemicals are then added, in sequence, to the two ends, and any color changes observed. Adding the chemicals to the second (blank) end of the cotton swab is an example of a employing a *blank control*. Transfer technique minimizes the quantity of evidence needed for the test and avoids adding any external chemicals directly to the evidence.

A two-step test is used. That is, the reduced dye chemical is added first, and any color change is noted. Then the peroxide is added, and any color change observed. The reason for doing the testing this way is to help avoid one category of potential false positive tests—namely, strong oxidants. The reaction that forms the basis of this testing is an oxidation-reduction reaction as noted earlier. If a specimen contained a strong oxidizing agent but no blood, it could cause the chemicals to change color. By applying the reduced dye chemical first, the presence of a strong oxidizing agent would be apparent because the color would change before the peroxide was added. Other things besides oxidants can interfere with the tests. That is why they are presumptive tests. Positive presumptive tests do not prove that blood is present.

It may be noted that luminal is usually used at scenes, not in the laboratory. Further, luminol is usually used to reveal bloodstains or blood patterns that are not apparent to the naked eye because some effort has been made to clean them up. Used in this manner, luminol is typically applied directly to the area thought to contain the blood residue. If blood residue is detected by the luminol becoming chemiluminescent, a photograph can be taken showing the blood patterns. The luminescence reaction must be viewed in darkness, and does not last very long.

Confirmatory Tests for Blood

Confirmatory tests for blood were traditionally **crystal tests** and **immunological tests** using antibodies specific for human hemoglobin. Crystal tests for drug identification are discussed in Chapter 12. Immunological tests are discussed in the following section.

peroxidases

Enzymes that catalyze the oxidation of a dye to form a new compound that is a different color.

crystal tests

Tests in which the formation of characteristic crystals constitutes a positive result.

immunological tests

Tests based on the use of specific antibodies to demonstrate the species or nature of a biological specimen.

There were several crystal tests. The most common were Teichmann's (the hematin halide) and Takayama's (the pyridine hemochromogen) tests. In these tests, chemicals were added to suspected material on microscope slides and, after a suitable waiting period or heating, the slide was examined under a microscope for characteristic crystals. Most forensic laboratories no longer use crystal tests for blood.

The immunological confirmatory test follows the same laboratory protocol as species tests and is thus conveniently done as part of species testing (see the following section). Using antibodies specific for human hemoglobin conveniently combines the confirmatory test for blood and the human species test into a single procedure.

The crystal and immunological confirmatory blood tests might be called *direct* confirmatory tests; that is, they are separate tests dedicated solely to confirming the presence of blood. Most knowledgeable experts would agree that without a positive confirmatory test for blood, an analyst could not say that a specimen contained blood. Today, though, more laboratories are following what might be called an *indirect* confirmatory test procedure. They don't do a separate dedicated confirmatory blood test. Rather, they do species tests and/or DNA typing, and then infer that human blood must be present from positive results in those tests, coupled with the results of the initial presumptive test.

Species Determination

Most dried blood specimens coming into the forensic science laboratory are human, but tests must be done on each specimen to know the **species of origin** for certain. In some types of cases, such as hunting law enforcement or hit-and-runs in suburban or rural areas, investigators may be far more likely to encounter animal blood specimens. The National Fish and Wildlife Forensics Laboratory in Ashland, Oregon, is dedicated exclusively to the identification and sometimes individualization of wildlife specimens in the service of enforcing federal fish and wildlife regulations.

At the beginning of the 20th century, the science of immunology was coming into its own as a medical and scientific discipline, and some of the early workers recognized the potential value of using *immunological* species determination methods in forensic examinations. Until DNA technology was developed, and even today in many laboratories, species of origin tests are done using immunological methods—methods that involve the specific interaction of **antigens** and **antibodies.** Antigens can be thought of as "foreign invaders." The immune systems of animals and humans are designed to keep them safe from viruses, bacteria, and other disease-causing agents. When these agents get into the body, the immune system responds by making specific antibodies to combat the infection. Vaccinations against infectious disease are a way of giving the immune system a "look" at the potential invader, sufficient for it to know how to make specific antibodies should the real infectious agent come along, but the vaccine itself is designed so as not to cause the disease.

Using immunological principles, host animals can be employed to make specific testing serums for the identification of different species. These *antiserums* are commercially available for human and common pet and farm animal species. (Because *antiserum* is treated as a Latin root word, its plural is actually *antisera.*) The test antisera have names that reflect their intended use, such as anti-human serum, anti-dog serum, anti-cow serum, and so on. The most common host animals in which antibodies are made are rabbits and goats. If a rabbit or goat is injected with human serum and a special mixture of chemicals called an *adjuvant,* the animal will begin to make antibodies to all the different proteins in the human serum. Those antibodies will be circulating in the animal's own blood serum. If blood is collected from the animal, and allowed to clot (see the beginning of the chapter), a "serum" layer will form above the clotted cells that can easily be removed. That serum layer contains the antibodies against the human blood proteins and is called an "anti-human" serum. Similarly, hemoglobin from human red blood cells could be used as the antigen (be injected into the host animal with adjuvant) to produce an "anti-human hemoglobin" serum. In this way, it is possible to make specific antisera to any animal's blood, to any protein, or to any mixture

species of origin
The species from which an item of biological evidence originated, such as human, horse, cat, cow, etc.

antigens
Substances, often proteins, that elicit the formation of specific antibodies if injected into an animal of a different species.

antibodies
Substances made by vertebrates in response to a "foreign" molecule, virus, or cell invading the body; specifically directed against the invader and designed to neutralize it and/or rid the body of it.

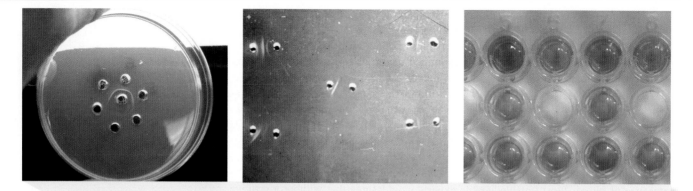

Figure 9.4   Left: Immunoreactions using Ouchterlony method. Here, anti-human serum in the center well reacted with increasingly diluted human serum in the surrounding wells. The white "precipitin" line between two neighboring wells represents a positive test. Center: Immunoreactions using cross-over electrophoresis. Here, small volumes of questioned extract solution and antibody solution are placed in little wells close to one another. Electrophoresis is a process that causes the antigens and antibodies to move together in the gel matrix. The white "precipitin" line between the neighboring wells represents a positive test. Right: Immunoreactions using the ELISA method. ELISA is a general method for studying antigen-antibody reactions. It is often done in a 96-well plate (12 across by 8 down). This is a picture of three rows. Here, extracts from questioned stains can be coated onto the plastic wells of the plate. Next, an antibody solution is added, and after several more steps, the well will show color if the antigen-antibody bond has formed. The positive wells in this ELISA show a blue-green color.

of proteins. The specific antiserum can then be used as a testing chemical to find out whether the corresponding antigen is present in an unknown specimen.

There are several methods for doing immunological species tests, but the most common ones are double immunodiffusion (also called the Ouchterlony method), crossover electrophoresis, and ELISA (*Enzyme-Linked Immunosorbent Assay*). All these methods involve placing extracts of the bloodstain to be analyzed (the antigens in this case) with specific antisera. If the bloodstain contains antigens corresponding to the specificity of the antiserum, a visible result is seen (see Figure 9.4).

Immunological tests involving the Ouchterlony or crossover electrophoresis methods for species were classically called "precipitin" tests, and you may still hear people use that term today. In these tests, the specific species antibodies bind to their homologous antigens and the complex precipitates out. The precipitate is visible in the test gel; hence, the name "precipitin."

As noted earlier in the discussion of confirmatory tests for blood, the use of anti-human hemoglobin in a "species" test provides a confirmatory blood test and a species test all in one. Hemoglobin is specific for blood, and detecting it establishes that blood is present. In recent years, one-step test kits have been commercially available that take advantage of specific antibody binding causing color changes on a small membrane. These have been called "immunochromatographic" tests, and the antibody used is anti-human hemoglobin.

Forensic Identification of Body Fluids

In a forensic case, it is important to identify human physiological fluids in stains, just as it is important to establish that red dried stains are actually blood. The body fluids most commonly encountered in the forensic laboratory are semen, vaginal secretions, saliva, and urine. Sweat, gastric juice, and so on are not regularly seen in evidence specimens.

Although physiological fluid evidence, especially semen evidence, is normally associated with sexual assault cases, physiological fluid evidence might come up in any type of case. DNA typing technology is now sufficiently sensitive that it may be possible to get a profile from a seemingly very small amount of biological evidence. Bits of fingernail, dandruff flakes, the skin cell residues on cigarette butts or filter tips, and shed cheek cells from the dried saliva surrounding bite marks have all been successfully DNA profiled in recent years.

Sexual assault investigations from the particular viewpoint of the forensic scientist and evidence collection protocols and kits are discussed later. In this section, the methods used to identify different human physiological fluid residues are described.

Identification of Semen

Semen, the male reproductive fluid, is a mixture of specialized cells, called *spermatozoa,* and the viscous fluid in which they are suspended, the **seminal plasma.** Many times you will hear the terms **sperm** and semen used interchangeably, but they are not the same, and the distinction is important in forensic biological evidence analysis. Sperm cells are unique to semen, and finding sperm cells with the microscope in a smear made from a stain or a swab proves that semen was present in that specimen (Figure 9.5).

Seminal plasma contains many dissolved substances, enzymes, and other proteins. Most of the seminal plasma comes from the prostate gland, but there are smaller contributions from the bulbourethral (Cowper's) glands. Sperm cells are made in the testes but then stored in the seminal vesicles. When a male ejaculates, the contents of the seminal vesicles (the sperm cells) and of the prostate and Cowper's glands are mixed together to form what we recognize as ejaculated semen. All the substances in semen have biological functions having to do with "liquefying" the semen and "capacitating" the sperm cells (rendering them able to swim), all to assist in fertilization, which is their central biological function.

Sperm cells can be thought of as DNA delivery vehicles. Their function is to find a receptive female egg, attach to its cell membrane, and deliver their DNA to form a fertilized egg or zygote. Mature, fertile males may have from about 15 million to 80 million sperm cells per milliliter of semen.

As with bloodstains, there are preliminary and confirmatory tests for semen stains. Positive preliminary tests show that semen may be present and that additional, confirmatory testing is indicated. That is, the preliminary tests are presumptive. In addition, certain types of light may cause semen stains to fluoresce and can be used as searching aids.

People have known for a long time that semen stains often fluoresce brightly when exposed to ultraviolet (UV) illumination. Fluorescence is the emission of light (often bluish) caused by the excitation of the molecules in a material by higher-energy light

semen

The male reproductive fluid, ejaculated through the penis at male orgasm, and consisting of sperm cells suspended in seminal plasma.

seminal plasma

The fluid in which sperm are suspended in whole semen; consists of fluids contributed primarily by the prostate but also by the Cowper's glands.

sperm

Short for spermatozoon (*pl.* spermatozoa); the male reproductive cell produced in the testes and stored in the seminal vesicles until ejaculated.

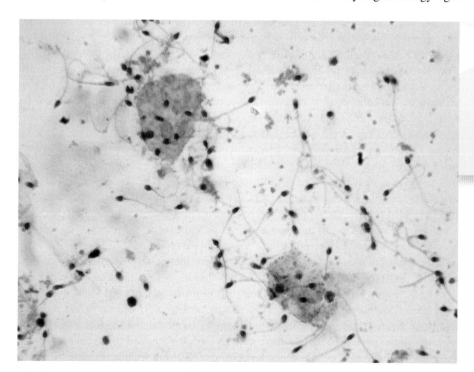

Figure 9.5

Smear of a material containing spermatozoa and epithelial cells viewed under a microscope. The spermatozoa are dyed with Christmas tree stain for better visualization. The epithelial cells are very large compared with the sperm cells.

(see in the Appendix). Accordingly, UV light can be used in examining evidence to help locate stains. Semen stains may also fluoresce under illumination with certain lasers and alternate light sources of the kind that are commonly used in latent fingerprint work (Chapter 6). Using these lights to help find stains is not a "test" for semen. It is merely a finding aid. Just because a stain fluoresces under one of these light sources doesn't necessarily mean it's a seminal stain, just that it should be tested further.

Historically, a number of different preliminary tests for semen have been used in forensic science laboratories. Most of them are no longer used. The only currently important one is called the **acid phosphatase** (sometimes called the "ACP" or "AP") test. Essentially the AP test is a color test and can be done using a cotton swab, the same way that was described for presumptive blood testing, except of course the chemicals are different. Acid phosphatase is an **enzyme** manufactured in the male prostate gland, and semen contains a lot of it. Acid phosphatase is quite robust in dried stains, and the test is generally positive with actual semen stains unless there has been bacterial degradation of the stain or it has been damaged by exposure to heat or some other environmental extreme.

Enzymes, as noted earlier, are nature's catalysts—a **catalyst** can speed up a chemical reaction without itself entering into that reaction or being changed by it. Further, the catalyst is only required in small quantities compared with the compounds actually reacting. Many of the reactions taking place in living cells and tissues that are necessary to maintain life would be too slow if there were nothing to speed them up. The catalysts for all these reactions are enzymes that are proteins. Enzymes are generally very specific for the particular reaction they catalyze. As a result, the reaction can be set up in the laboratory to serve as a "test" for the enzyme in a biological specimen. Enzymes can be useful in forensic science as "identification markers." For example, acid phosphatase is an identification marker for semen. Because other cells and biological materials in the natural world besides semen contain acid phosphatase, the acid phosphatase test is a presumptive, not a confirmatory test.

The oldest *confirmatory* test for semen in dried stains is finding spermatozoa, the male reproductive cell, in a smear made from the dried stain and viewed through a microscope (Figure 9.5). Forensic scientists have known to look for sperm in suspected semen stains as a means of identification since the 1840s, and the procedure is still common today. If sperm is seen, there is no doubt that the specimen came from a semen stain. Histological dyes (compounds that are used to color tissue preparations on microscope slides so the components will contrast with one another and be visible) are often used to "color" the cells during preparation of the smear. In a vaginal swab preparation that contains sperm, a large number of vaginal epithelial cells (cells shed from the tissues lining the inside of the vagina) are also visible along with the sperm cells. A couple of epithelial cells are visible in Figure 9.5. Until fairly recently, finding sperm was the only confirmatory test for semen in a stain. If sperm could not be found, an analyst could not say for sure that the stain was semen. There are several reasons why sperm might not be found in an actual semen stain. A man might be pathologically azoospermic (a medical condition that prevents normal sperm manufacture), or he might have had a vasectomy—a surgical contraceptive procedure that prevents sperm from ever getting into the semen. In addition, sperm may not always be easy to find in some dried stains for various reasons. Recognition of the prostate gland protein, called **p30** by most forensic scientists (and "PSA" for "prostate specific antigen" or **PA** for "prostatic antigen" by most medical people), and development of methods for its detection have solved this problem.

Identifying semen in forensic specimens where there are no sperm cells is an old problem. The protein called p30, PSA, or PA appears to be almost unique to human semen. In recent years, this same protein has taken on a role as a "marker" in the screening of middle-aged men for prostatic cancer. The p30 is made in the prostate, and when prostatic cancer is present, the protein spills out into the bloodstream. Doctors usually call the protein PSA, so testing for it in blood as a means of screening men for prostatic carcinomas is usually called a "PSA test." The lab techniques used by forensic scientists to identify the protein for semen identification, and by clinicians for cancer

acid phosphatase

An enzyme usually found in large quantities in human semen (but also in other tissues and species), used as the basis for a preliminary test for semen.

enzyme

A protein that can speed up a chemical reaction without being consumed by it; an enzyme is a protein catalyst.

catalyst

A substance that speeds up a chemical reaction without being changed or consumed; required in small quantities, because it is not changed by the reaction.

p30

A protein found in high concentrations in human semen and used as the basis for a specific semen identification test; also known as PA.

PA

Short for "prostatic antigen"; a protein found in high concentrations in human semen and used as the basis for a specific semen identification test; also known as p30.

screening, are essentially identical. P30 is identified using immunological methods—similar to those described earlier for species testing. Specific antibodies for p30 are available commercially for use in the various test protocols. Forensic laboratories use several formats, including Ouchterlony double immunodiffusion, certain types of immunoelectrophoresis, ELISA, and the commercial testing strip known as the ABAcard. The ABAcard method is based on a test strip in a kit that has antibodies specific for p30 immobilized on a membrane strip. The color changes in a positive test.

Identification of Vaginal "Secretions," Saliva, and Urine

In sexual assault cases, complainants may be examined in a clinical facility (emergency room or a SANE-SART facility—see later for a discussion of SANE-SART) and vaginal swab specimens taken. These swabs are sent to the forensic laboratory to look for semen and to do DNA typing if indicated. The female cells and other material on a vaginal swab are often called "vaginal secretions" even though everyone understands that the term is not strictly correct. This material consists of shed epithelial cells from the inner lining of the vagina, mucus, and resident bacteria among many other substances. Even though there are occasionally case circumstances where it would be desirable to have a method of identifying this human vaginal material as such, a truly reliable method has never been devised.

Saliva is produced by three pairs of glands, which empty into the mouth cavity. It is a complex fluid containing numerous substances. Biologists have known for a long time that saliva contains a large quantity of the enzyme *amylase*. Amylase helps in the digestion of foods by catalyzing the breakdown of starch, a carbohydrate storage product in plants. There are several different tests for amylase, which can be used on preparations from dried stains to see if saliva might be present. These tests include dyed starch methods (such as the Phadebas assay) and radial enzyme diffusion. Saliva is by no means the only human fluid or material that contains amylase, however, and amylase is also found in many animals and plants. So, while detecting amylase in a stain is indicative, or presumptive, of the presence of saliva, it does not prove it. There is no confirmatory test for saliva. As a result, forensic scientists cannot identify saliva absolutely.

The same thing can be said about urine. Urine contains several substances that are present in fairly large quantity, such as urea and creatinine. But they are not unique to urine, and therefore detecting them in a laboratory test on a questioned stain does not absolutely prove that urine is present.

Forensic Investigation of Sexual Assault Cases

In most jurisdictions, sexual assault case evidence comprises the majority of items submitted to the forensic biology/biochemistry/DNA sections. Table 9.1 shows a

Location	Population	Murder/nonnegligent manslaughter	Rape
Atlanta, Georgia	430,066	114	267
Boise, Idaho	193,864	0	118
Chicago, Illinois	2,886,102	598	1,799
Houston, Texas	2,043,446	272	908
Los Angeles, California	3,864,018	518	1,131
Miami, Florida	385,186	69	102
Hartford, Connecticut	125,109	16	54
New York, New York	8,101,321	570	1,428
Seattle, Washington	575,816	24	145

Table 9.1

Rates of murder and rape in selected U.S. cities in 2004*

*SOURCES: FBI *Uniform Crime Reports* (Preliminary Report for 2004) and Illinois *Uniform Crime Reports* (Chicago numbers are for 2003, the most recent year all data were available.)

SANE-SART Programs

The sexual assault nurse examiner (SANE) specialty is a relatively recent development in most places. The concept started with Dr. Linda Ledray at the Hennepin County Medical Center in Minneapolis over 25 years ago. Both she and Virginia Lynch in Colorado have been prime movers in the development of forensic nursing. Since the 1980s, however, many nurses have received forensic training to become SANEs, and there is at least one very large professional organization in the United States to which many forensic nurses belong (the International Association of Forensic Nurses—see www .forensicnurse.org). Besides their involvement in sexual assaults, forensic nurses are generally trained in forensic evidence collection concepts so that evidence can be recognized and preserved in emergency department settings. Many patients in emergency departments are victims of various types of violence involving knives, firearms, and so on. In the late 1990s, the Office for Victims of Crime of the U.S. Department of Justice's Office of Justice Programs awarded a grant to Dr. Ledray in Minneapolis to put together a guide for the development and operation of a SANE program.

Because one of the major activities of the forensic nurses has been in treating sexual assault complainants, the idea of the sexual assault response/resource team (SART) has come along with the SANE concept. The SART idea originated in California and involved a coordinated response by law enforcement, victim services support, and the clinical/medical aspect (the SANEs). In various parts of the country, SANEs may respond to complainants who appear in emergency departments, there may be separate SANE examination facilities in emergency departments, or in some places there are stand-alone SANE clinics.

SANEs are trained to perform complete clinical workups of sexual assault victims, to document any injuries as necessary, and to collect the evidence using a sexual assault evidence collection kit. Unless there is injury requiring treatment by a physician, the case may be handled without physician involvement. One of the reasons for the success of SANE programs throughout the country is the perception that emergency medicine physicians have not wanted to take the time to document injuries of and collect evidence from sexual assault victims.

Some SANEs may use a device called a *colposcope,* essentially a magnifying device capable of recording images, for examining the inside of the vagina of a sexual assault complainant to document trauma. Some SANEs may also look at slides prepared from the vaginal swab to see if the sperm are still motile (swimming). If they are, it means that the semen deposit is recent—within a few hours.

sexual assault evidence collection kit

Usually packages or boxes, containing numerous containers, tools, and labels, for the collection of clothing and other evidence, including evidence from the body, of sexual assault complainants; designed to allow for proper packaging, labeling, and preservation of sexual assault evidence.

SANEs

Sexual assault nurse examiner.

SART

Sexual assault response team.

sample of crime data from several U.S. cities demonstrating that reported sexual assault cases far exceed murder cases.

Most of the evidence from sexual assaults consists of the items in **sexual assault evidence collection kits** (sometimes called "rape kits") and associated items, such as clothing, bedding, and so on. These kits are described and discussed in more detail later.

Coordination of Effort—SANEs and SARTs

A forensic scientist is one of the parties in a group of different professionals who are involved in the overall investigation and prosecution of sexual assault cases and offenses. Because these cases are of such an intimate and personal nature for victims and are unlike most other cases in a number of respects, they are handled somewhat differently than other cases in many jurisdictions. One of the most significant recent developments in this respect is the expanded role of forensic nurses in these cases. Specially trained forensic nurses may become "sexual assault nurse examiners," or **SANEs.** In that role, they are able to do the medical examination of sexual assault complainants in its entirety, unless a patient is seriously injured and requires emergency medical care. It is also fair to say that the forensic nurses have taken a lead role in prompting many jurisdictions to try to coordinate the overall responses to sexual assault complaints. The coordinated response can take the form of the sexual assault response team, or **SART.** Because of the central role of the forensic nurses in the SART concept, the SANE and SART ideas are inextricably linked.

Initial Investigation

For many years, hospital emergency departments served as the primary medical examination sites for sexual assault complainants, and in many jurisdictions they still do.

Typically, a sexual assault victim contacts the police directly or may first talk to someone else who then contacts police. The police take the complainant's statement and initiate an investigation. Sometimes, the police may find the complainant's allegations insufficient to "found" a case, and no formal investigation will be started. In cases that are pursued, the police may transport the victim to a medical facility for examination or arrange for the transportation. The medical facility is usually an emergency room unless the jurisdiction has a stand-alone SANE-SART facility. There are two primary objectives in taking a sexual assault victim to a medical facility: first, to see to her medical needs; and second, to collect relevant evidence of the assault, generally using a sexual assault evidence collection kit. Many police agencies have guidelines about transporting sexual assault complainants to medical or SANE-SART facilities: Often, if three or more days have elapsed since the alleged assault, and the complainant is not injured, she will not be taken to a medical facility and no sexual assault evidence collection kit will be taken. The reason for these guidelines is that the longer the elapsed time since the assault, the less likely it is to find any useful physical evidence associated with a victim's person that could be connected to a suspect.

The Forensic Scientist's Role

Handling a sexual assault complaint thus involves law enforcement personnel and the doctor or nurse who examines and treats the complainant. If the services are available in a jurisdiction, a victim services agency representative (sometimes these agencies have people specially trained to respond to sexual assaults) can be involved with the complainant. The victim services agency is usually the only one that follows up with sexual assault victims over time. If a sexual assault evidence collection kit is taken, and the victim consents, it goes to the forensic science laboratory for examination. Then, depending on the results and the complainant's continuing desire to go forward with the case, a prosecutor may get involved as a suspect is identified and arrested and as preparations for prosecuting the case move forward. In many jurisdictions, there has been an effort in recent years to try to coordinate the activities of police investigators, medical personnel, forensic scientists, victim services representatives, and prosecutors. These efforts have been very productive in many places in making the community's response to sexual assault more efficient but also more sensitive to complainants' needs.

Forensic scientists' primary involvement is the analysis of the physical evidence from the scene and/or from the complainant's person. Confirming that semen is present helps establish the so-called corpus delicti of the crime (Chapter 2). Similarly, identification of other physiological fluids may be important depending on the individual case circumstances. If semen or another physiological fluid is found, DNA typing is conducted to determine whether the types match a suspect or exclude him. DNA types from some items may match the complainant. Successful DNA typing of the semen essentially positively identifies the semen depositor. Matching a suspect's DNA profile to those of semen recovered from a complainant or her clothing is very important and generally shows that he was the semen depositor. Note that a DNA match is not informative as to whether the sexual contact was consensual or forced.

"Sexual assault" has different legal names in various states. And there are different degrees of it. The most serious form of sexual assault involves sexual intercourse with a woman against her will. To prove the most serious form of the offense in court, it is generally necessary to establish that there was penetration, and that it was against the victim's will. Finding semen on a vaginal swab proves that someone had intercourse with the swab donor. DNA typing can show that a suspect is the semen donor. It can also show that he is excluded—that is, was not the semen depositor.

Medical Examination

As noted, the two main reasons for the medical examination of a sexual assault complainant are, first, to tend to injuries and health matters and, second, to collect evidence. Medical (clinical) evaluation and treatment of sexual assault victims involves taking a history, tending to any physical injuries, and probably testing for pregnancy and exposure to HIV and for other sexually transmitted diseases (syphilis, gonorrhea, chlamydia). Sexual assault victims are understandably concerned about the possibilities of pregnancy or HIV/STD infection as a result of the assault. Testing for these conditions at the time of presentation will not, of course, detect disease or pregnancy that resulted from the assault—it is too early. Follow-up consultation and possibly follow-up care is required. In some places, follow-up on sexual assault complainants is a major problem, because the people just don't come back. Where that is the case, facilities may provide the patient with drugs to treat possible conditions. Treatment of HIV infection is complicated, and HIV testing and treatment cannot be meaningfully done without follow-up. Injuries, such as bruises or contusions that are visible at the time the patient presents, should be documented, since they will inevitably heal, leaving no record of their onetime presence on the victim's person.

Once medical and health concerns have been handled, evidence is collected assuming the complainant/patient is willing to give consent for it. Clothing that has or may have blood or body fluid stains is often collected and should be *separately* packaged. In some protocols, complainants may be asked to stand on a large, clean sheet of paper to disrobe in order that any trace materials will fall onto the paper, which can then be folded back up and packaged. Vaginal, and possibly anal and/or oral swabs may be taken, and smears prepared from them on microscope slides. Head hair may be collected, as may pubic hair combings and cuttings, as known controls. Any dried stains on the person's skin surfaces are collected. Some kits make provision for collecting fingernails or fingernail scrapings. Finally, a "standard" (known control) for DNA typing is required. Traditionally, this specimen has been a tube of blood, but a buccal (cheek cell) swabbing is more than adequate now, and far less intrusive to obtain.

Evidence Collection and Sexual Assault Evidence Collection Kits

Investigators should collect *any* evidence that might be relevant to the investigation of the assault and package it in the normal way (see earlier and in Chapter 3). There may be a tendency for investigators to become so focused on biological and sexual assault evidence collection kit evidence that they neglect to consider other important items, such as fingerprints or other impression patterns, trace materials, and so on.

Sexual assault evidence collection kits ("rape kits") are usually just large boxes or envelopes that contain many smaller evidence containers and instructions for using them (see Figure 9.6). In some jurisdictions, facilities have videos for training clinical and medical personnel in the proper use of kits and their components. Many of the kits have been designed by a coordinating group, consisting of medical, forensic lab, victim services, law enforcement, and prosecutorial personnel.

Figure 9.6

An example of an evidence collection kit used by a hospital for collecting samples from the victim of an alleged sexual assault.

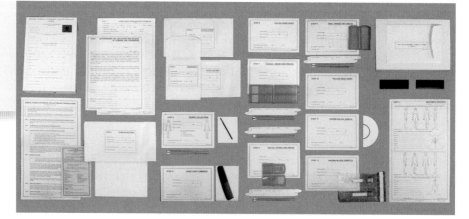

Accordingly, the kits represent a consensus view of what evidence should be collected and how it should be packaged. This may sound pretty trivial, but in some respects it is not. For example, should hairs be collected given the status of hair comparison examination (Chapter 13)? Lab examiners have often been unable to agree on whether exemplar (known) hairs should be cut or pulled. There isn't much point in collecting an item that cannot be reliably examined or that won't be collected in the manner specified by the lab examiner because of other concerns.

In a sexual assault evidence collection kit, there are usually detailed directions for the use of each container. These may be written on the containers themselves, or separately. In addition, there are usually preprinted spaces or lines for information, often on every container in the kit. In many kits we have examined over the years, instructions may be inconsistent or confusing, and in most cases there seem to be far too many repetitious labeling and marking requirements (such as having to record the complainant's name and date of birth on every separate envelope). A lot of these problems can be minimized by careful scrutiny of the kit's design before it is adopted and deployed into the field, and the creative use of preprinted labels and/or bar codes.

It should be noted that every specimen container might not be used in every case. In some jurisdictions, for example, oral (or anal) swabs are not collected unless the complainant reports oral (or anal) sexual contact or responds affirmatively to questions concerning such contact. In other jurisdictions, all the swabs may be collected with the idea that the complainant may be too embarrassed to report oral (or anal) contact even if it did occur. Similarly, if a complainant's pubic hair is shaved off, there would be no pubic hair combings or standards.

Some jurisdictions have designed separate kits for males or have taken steps to make their sexual assault evidence kit usable with either sex. There are two purposes for "male" kits. One is for use with a male sexual assault victim. Not nearly as many males as females report sexual assault, but it does happen. The second purpose is for use with suspects if one is identified, and specimens can legally be taken from him. Typically, specimens that might be taken from a male include penile swabs (especially from a suspect), oral and/or anal swabs from a victim, reference head and pubic hair, and clothing that might have biological stains. A blood specimen or buccal swab is required for a reference DNA profile.

Both the sexual assault evidence collection kits themselves and the instructions have become more complex and sophisticated in recent years as more effort has been put into coordinating the response to sexual assault investigations and giving more careful consideration to what is to be collected. Many jurisdictions (which in this context can often mean a state) have their own kits. State law may now specify the composition of a coordinating group for sexual assault complaint response, and among its responsibilities can be the design and periodic redesign of the sexual assault evidence collection kit. State law may also require hospitals to take and keep sexual assault evidence until law enforcement picks it up or for a proscribed period.

Types of Sexual Assault Cases and Their Investigation

From an investigative and forensic science point of view, there are three types of sexual assault cases. The first two involve adult victims—and consist of those in which the identity of the offender or suspect is unknown (identification cases), and those in which the identity of the offender or suspect is known, but where he claims the sexual relations were consensual (consent cases). The third type of case involves children.

DNA profiling is expected to be informative and helpful in identification cases, but not in consent cases. If the suspect does not deny sexual contact with the complainant, DNA profiling adds nothing to the case. These cases often succeed or fall on the credibility of the parties, since there are rarely other witnesses or other items of physical evidence that can settle the matter. Injuries to a complainant that have been properly documented at the time of the complaint may be helpful in some consent cases.

Cases involving children, especially younger children, are often investigated by specialized child protective services agency personnel. Only occasionally do these cases have physical evidence of the kind normally collected and submitted to forensic science labs, so forensic scientists are rarely involved.

Note that the distinction between "children" and "adults" is a legal one, in the sense that state law defines the age at which a person may consent to sexual relations. A male who has sexual relations with anyone younger than the age of consent, as defined by state law, is guilty of sexual assault under the law—this is often called "statutory rape." These situations can come up with teenagers. Many teenagers are sexually mature before they reach the age of consent. In those circumstances, sexual assault evidence kits may be collected just as they would be for an adult complainant.

It should be noted, too, that the absence of physical evidence does not prove that an assault did not occur. Absence of semen on a vaginal swab could be the result of condom use, failure of a perpetrator to ejaculate, or too much time having elapsed between sexual contact and evidence collection.

Finally, sexual assault complainants must provide a series of consents for different procedures. They must first agree to be transported to an emergency department or SANE-SART facility. Next, they must give consent for medical treatment. Separate consent is often required to take specimens from their person (i.e., to use the sexual assault evidence collection kit), and forward those specimens to a forensic science laboratory. Failure to obtain written consent at any stage of the process effectively ends it. Parents or guardians must give the consent if the victim is younger than the age of consent in that state. And, even if a victim is treated, and a kit taken and sent to the laboratory, she or he may withdraw the complaint or decide not to further press the case at any time.

Drug-Facilitated Sexual Assault—"Date-Rape" Drugs

During the 1990s, a new twist on the sexual assault problem began to emerge. Cases started surfacing where a victim had been drugged—often surreptitiously. Several drugs are commonly encountered in this context: Rohypnol (flunitrazepam) (Figure 9.7), sometimes other benzodiazepines (such as clonazepam), gamma hydroxybutyric acid (GHB) (Figure 9.8), and ketamine. Generally speaking, drugs of the benzodiazepine class are depressants, and different ones are approved for the management

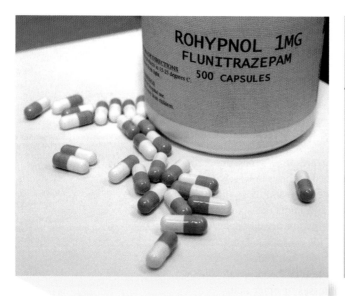

Figure 9.7

Rohypnol.

Figure 9.8

Gamma hydroxybutyric acid (GHB).

of a variety of conditions, from anxiety to sleeplessness. Rohypnol is perhaps the most potent of the class. Although it is available in most of the world, its use and importation are banned in the United States because it was never approved for sale by the FDA and it has became associated with **drug-facilitated sexual assault.** GHB is approved for very limited use as a human drug. Ketamine is a human and veterinary anesthetic.

All these drugs and others have been implicated in sexual assaults. They have in common that they are all depressants, tending to make a person less in control, and they have amnestic effects; that is, the person tends not to remember much about what happened while under the drug's influence. The drugs are frequently used along with alcohol, which tends to make their effects more profound. One of the drugs may be added to an alcoholic drink as a way of getting it into the intended victim. Alcohol itself has long been associated with sexual assaults, in that drinking alcohol is one of the biggest risk factors for sexual assault among teenaged and young adult women. But the association of the previous drugs with sexual assault is relatively new.

One generally thinks of drug-facilitated sexual assault in terms of a victim being surreptitiously drugged by a sexual predator perpetrator. And many cases do happen that way. However, there is also evidence that these drugs are sometimes abused for recreational purposes. Women may thus be sexually assaulted when they are under the influence of a drug they ingested knowingly. This is still drug-facilitated sexual assault.

Drug analysis and forensic toxicology will be discussed in Chapter 12. It is enough to note here that the drug-facilitated sexual assault problem has required that forensic toxicologists become involved in examining evidence from sexual assault complainants (generally urine or hair). It may finally be noted that the full extent of this problem is not yet clear. For various reasons, it is difficult to gather good epidemiological data on the problem.

Blood and Body Fluid Individuality: Traditional (pre-DNA) Approaches

It is the genetic (inherited) characteristics found in cells in both blood and other physiological fluids that are used to try to determine origin—that is, from which person did the blood or body fluid come.

Before DNA typing, blood groups (blood types), red cell isoenzymes, certain plasma (serum) proteins, and hemoglobin variants could be used to partially individualize biological evidence. Since the late 1980s to early 1990s DNA typing is the exclusive method for the individualization of biological evidence. (As mentioned earlier, DNA typing is the subject of the next chapter.)

A brief discussion of the pre-DNA genetic typing characteristics and methods concludes this chapter.

The Classical or Conventional (pre-DNA) Genetic Markers

In the 1990s, DNA typing replaced all genetic analysis that had previously been used for biological evidence. But for most of the 20th century, forensic scientists used **genetic markers** other than DNA to try to individualize blood and body fluid evidence. Today, those pre-DNA systems are often referred to as "classical" or "conventional" genetic markers.

There are five categories of conventional genetic markers: (1) blood groups; (2) isoenzymes; (3) plasma (serum) proteins; (4) hemoglobin variants; and (5) the HLA (human leukocyte antigen) system. Different systems in the first four categories were used in the forensic analysis of biological analysis. The HLA system consists of different "types" on white blood cells or tissues. HLA typing is an important part of tissue matching before a tissue or organ transplant in clinical medicine. HLA typing was also widely used for parentage testing until DNA typing replaced it.

---

drug-facilitated sexual assault

Sexual assault perpetrated on a victim who cannot consent because of mental impairment by a drug or drugs.

genetic markers

Refers to blood groups, isoenzymes, and other substances used to help establish partial individuality (narrow the size of the included group) before DNA typing was available.

Figure 9.9
Karl Landsteiner.

Figure 9.10
Leone Lattes.

The first blood group, the ABO system, was discovered in 1901 by Karl Landsteiner (1868–1943; Figure 9.9). Because ABO typing is so important in the field of blood transfusion, Dr. Landsteiner received the Nobel Prize for Physiology or Medicine in 1930. ABO blood typing was first applied to bloodstains in criminal cases by Dr. Leone Lattes (1887–1954; Figure 9.10) of Turin, Italy, in 1913. From that time until about 1950, many more blood groups were discovered, and some of them were used in the typing of bloodstains in forensic cases.

The isoenzymes and plasma proteins were discovered in the 1940s and 1950s. Isoenzymes are enzymes that occur in multiple molecular forms. That is, there are several potentially different protein molecules that all perform the same enzymatic activity. The differences between the forms is usually very slight. These different forms of the enzyme exist because of genetic variation. The gene (i.e., the DNA) that tells the cell how to make the enzyme has a few different forms, and in turn causes the different enzymes to be made. Which isoenzymes a person has is a direct reflection of his or her DNA sequence in the gene that codes for that enzyme. The plasma proteins are different for the same reasons as the isoenzymes—the DNA segment responsible for making them has a few different forms. And similarly, there are a couple of common variants of the protein hemoglobin, which carries oxygen to all the cells in the body. One of the most widely recognized hemoglobin variants is "sickle." Commonly but not exclusively found in Africans and African Americans, this gene can cause mild anemia problems in people who have one of the genes, but serious illness in persons in whom both hemoglobin beta-chain genes are "sickle." Beginning in the late 1960s, forensic scientists at the then Metropolitan Police Forensic Science Laboratory (currently the Metropolitan Laboratory of the UK Home Office Forensic Science Service) began applying isoenzyme, plasma protein, and hemoglobin variant typing to bloodstains in criminal cases. Use of these genetic marker systems spread quickly to forensic labs in other countries, including the United States.

The analytical methods used for isoenzyme, plasma protein, and hemoglobin typing are called *electrophoresis* and *isoelectric focusing*. These are explained further in the "More on the Science: Electrophoresis and Isoelectric Focusing" box.

How Does Typing Genetic Markers Help "Individualize" a Biological Specimen?

The whole idea behind genetic typing of biological evidence is to be able to tell who the specimen came from. Before DNA typing, a bloodstain or semen stain could never be attributed to only one person just because all the types between the stain and a person matched. The most we could say is that the person was part of a fraction of the population of persons, any of whom could have been the depositor. Of course if the types did not match, we could say absolutely that the person was *not* the depositor. DNA typing works essentially the same way, except that in "match" cases (where the evidence and the person have the same types or profile) the chance that someone other than the person deposited the evidentiary stain is usually very low.

To understand how this whole process works, a little background in *population genetics* is necessary. More is said about genetics and population genetics in Chapter 10. Mendel first worked out the basic rules of inheritance. Mendel's rules apply to individual matings or crosses. In population genetics, we look at how one or several genes behave not in one individual or family but in a whole population.

An important concept in genetics is that of a *gene*. A gene can be thought of in one sense as a region, or segment, of the DNA sequence that tells the cell how to make a particular protein or enzyme. Thus, we can talk about the "gene for hemoglobin" or the "gene for blood type B." Because the chromosomes are paired (one maternal and one paternal), and there is one gene on each chromosome, so

Electrophoresis and Isoelectric Focusing

Electrophoresis is an important tool for separating and analyzing large molecules like proteins and DNA. An electric field is set up in a medium, like a gel made of agarose or polyacrylamide. In the electric field, positively charged molecules will migrate toward the negative pole while negatively charged ones will migrate toward the positive pole. This migration results in the desired separation of the molecules (Figure 9.11). In the pre-DNA era, forensic scientists used electrophoresis to separate isoenzymes, plasma protein, and hemoglobin genetic variants in order to determine their "types." Figure 9.12 shows an example of isoenzyme typing. Electrophoresis is also regularly used in the analysis and typing of DNA.

Another related method, isoelectric focusing, came into use in the 1980s for isoenzyme and serum protein typing. Here, mixtures of special molecules called ampholytes are incorporated into a gel medium and an electric field is applied across it just as in electrophoresis. But the ampholytes cause a pH gradient to form across the gel. Every protein has both positively and negatively charged chemical groupings within it. As pH is changed, the net surface charge changes. For every protein, there is a particular pH at which the positive and negative charges just balance one another. This is called the protein's isoelectric point. In the pH gradient created in an isoelectric focusing gel, proteins move until they reach the pH in the gel corresponding to their isoelectric point, then they stop. As long as the current is on, they are held in place (focused) at their isoelectric point.

Figure 9.11   Diagram illustrating design of a basic electrophoresis apparatus.

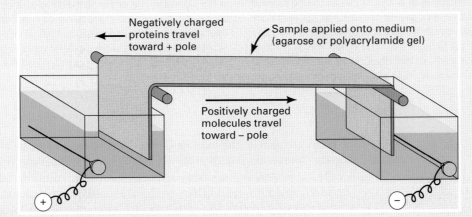

Figure 9.12

Left: A stained electrophoresis gel illustrating the separation of the different forms of the phosphoglucomutase (PGM) enzyme.
Right: A stained electrophoresis gel illustrating the separation of the different forms of the esterase D enzyme.

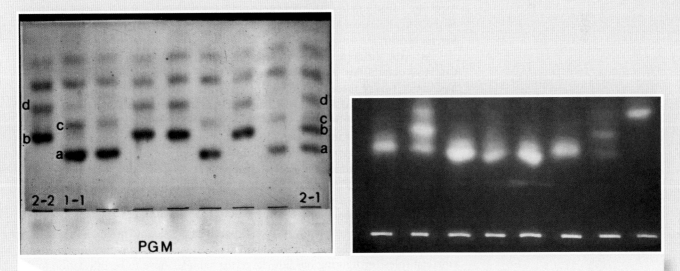

Population Genetics/ Individualization of Evidence

This example illustrates how using population genetics to estimate the frequency of two genetic traits, blood type B and isoenzyme PGM type 2+1+, helps "individualize" a specimen from a person with these two types. Two important concepts in this example are the *independence* of the genetic loci, permitting the use of the *product rule*.

Let's say we find out that the frequency of blood type B in the U.S. White population is about 10 percent. (It turns out that the frequencies of the alleles or types are not always the same in populations of different racial/ethnic groups, so forensic scientists often separate the frequency estimates for the different groups.) Knowing that, we can say that a bloodstain that is type B can only have come from someone in about 10 percent of the population. We have excluded 90 percent of the population as possible depositors. Still, 10 percent of the population is a lot of people. Taking this line of thinking a step further, let's say we find out that the frequency of the isoenzyme PGM type 2+1+ is about 20 percent in the same population for which the frequency of blood type B was 10 percent. Let's also say that we can establish that the inheritance of blood type B and the inheritance of PGM are *independent;* that is, the

inheritance of one of them does not influence the inheritance of the other one. Now, if we knew that a bloodstain was blood type B *and* PGM 2+1+, the combination is expected to be found in only 2 percent of the population ($10\% \times 20\%$). That is, if the loci are independent, the frequencies can be multiplied to get an estimate of the frequency of people who have both types—the product rule. So in this illustration, 98 percent of the population has been excluded as possible depositors. If a person in the case has the same types as were found in the stain, we can say that he or she is *included* as a possible depositor, along with 2 percent of the population. The 2000 U.S. census of population reported that there were 281,421,906 people in the United States. Of those, 12,419,293 lived in Illinois. Within Illinois there were estimated to be 9,125,471 White people. Based on our genetic marker population studies, we could then say that 182,510 (2% of the total) of them are expected to be *both* blood type B and PGM 2+1+. If a person involved in the case is different in blood type or in PGM type from what is found in the bloodstain, he or she is *excluded* as a possible depositor. If we typed more genetic characteristics in the same specimen and they were all independent, the number of people who would be expected to have that same profile of types keeps getting smaller. We will develop this same reasoning for DNA types in the next chapter.

the genes are paired. The location on the DNA sequence (the location on the chromosome) where the sequence for a particular trait or characteristic is determined is called a *gene locus,* or simply a *locus.* "Locus" is Latin for "place." The DNA sequences used for forensic DNA typing are mostly not functional; that is, they do not code for any proteins (see Chapter 10). At any particular locus in one person, there are two genes, one on the maternal chromosome and the other on the paternal chromosome. The genes making up this pair of corresponding genes at a given locus are called *alleles.* Any person could have the alleles at a locus be the same, or the two alleles could be different. The former is called *homozygosity;* the latter, *heterozygosity.*

At many different human genetic loci (*loci* is the plural of *locus*), a person can have quite a few different genes (alleles). Even though any one person only has one or two of them, looking at different individuals in the population reveals that there are several to many possible alleles at the locus. Population genetics looks at how often alleles at some locus occur in a population. For example, a population geneticist might ask: "How many blood type B people are there in the population of the United States?" An answer to that question tells the population geneticist how frequently the gene for blood type B occurs in the population. The way a geneticist discovers the answer to a question like this is by blood typing a lot of people. As a practical matter, it is impossible to type everyone. So, a *sample* of the population is typed; for example, 100 to several hundred people might be typed. The frequency of blood type B in the sample provides an *estimate* of the frequency in the entire population. The science of *statistics* provides mathematical rules for figuring out how large the samples have to be in relation to the level of uncertainty in the resulting measurements. Scientists use statistical methods for a lot of reasons. This is one example. Use of genetic marker frequencies in populations to "individualize" evidence is illustrated in the "More on the Science: Population Genetics/Individualization of Evidence" box.

Case Study 9.1

The Power of DNA versus Conventional Genetic Systems

One of the remarkable, although fully expected, consequences of the widespread availability of DNA typing has been the exclusion of a number of people previously convicted of serious crimes, especially but not exclusively sexual assaults. Sometimes, conventional genetic testing was done but did not exclude the person at the time of the crime and the trial.

From the discussion in this chapter about the individualizing power of the conventional systems, it is clear that they could not even come close to pinning down a particular person as a depositor of blood or semen. In sexual assault cases, the vaginal swabs taken from complainants following the incident contained mixtures of blood group factors and isoenzymes from both the woman and the semen depositor. Analysts had to try to interpret the typing results in terms of the people involved in the case. We will shortly see in Chapter 10 that it is often possible to separate the male and female fractions of DNA in these semen-vaginal mixtures, and this ability is obviously a great help in interpreting the typing results.

In one illustrative case that happened before DNA typing was available, both the complainant and the suspect were type B. They were also both "secretors." Recall the discussion of "secretors" from this chapter's Lead Case, in which the blood types could be detected in the body fluids. The evidence in the case, that is, the vaginal swab on which semen was identified, showed "type B secretor" characteristics. From these results, an analyst could only say that the semen on the swab could have been deposited by a male who was a type B secretor, a type O secretor, or a nonsecretor of any ABO type. That is, approximately two-thirds of White males and three-quarters of Black males could have been depositors. So, even though the suspect was included in the group of possible depositors, the group was very large. The suspect was convicted at trial largely on the strength of the testimony of the complainant in the case. Sometime later, however, DNA typing showed that the semen on the swab could not have come from this particular man.

In another case, a man who was a type O secretor was convicted of sexually assaulting two different women at different times. He could not be excluded as the depositor in either case based on ABO types nor on the PGM isoenzyme types. Several years later, however, the evidence was analyzed using DNA typing, and the man was excluded as the depositor of the semen in either victim.

There are many cases like these in different jurisdictions. The conventional genetic systems just did not have the individualizing power to exclude nondepositors, whereas DNA typing nearly always does have it.

Summary

Biological evidence analysis has been revolutionized by the development of DNA analysis methods. The initial examination of this evidence and identification testing is now most often called "forensic biology." Blood is made up of red cells, white cells, and a liquid fraction called plasma. If the blood is allowed to clot, the liquid fraction is called serum. *Serology* comes from the word *serum,* and "forensic serology" once meant all the initial and identification examinations of blood and body fluids, but also all the blood type and other genetic analysis that was done prior to the availability of DNA.

Known blood specimens from people should be collected in Vacutainers containing the anticoagulant EDTA. It is not necessary to collect blood from people anymore, however. A buccal (cheek) swab is sufficient for DNA typing.

Wet blood at scenes should be collected onto sterile gauze pads and then allowed to dry thoroughly. An exception might be wet blood in snow, which should be collected into a clean vessel, with as little snow as possible, and transported to the lab quickly. Dry bloodstained evidence objects can be collected in a number of ways. The best is to collect the object intact, with no sampling. If that cannot be done, the bloodstain may be cut out, or the dried blood swabbed or scraped from a nonabsorbent surface. Sterile gauze pads and sterile saline or water are recommended for swabbing. Scraped dry blood can be packaged in a druggist fold. Blood and body fluid evidence must always be thoroughly dried before packaging and preserved in paper containers. If investigators swab or scrape dried blood from a surface, a substratum comparison specimen must also be collected in the same manner as the blood. To avoid contamination, investigators should always wear protective gloves when handling biological evidence. They should use sterile gauze pads for swabbing, and sterile water or saline if necessary for any evidence collection step.

There are preliminary (presumptive) tests for blood and confirmatory tests. The blood presumptive tests are "catalytic." They are based on the peroxidase-like activity of heme in blood, and this activity leads to color changes to indicate a positive test. These can be done in the field. Confirmatory tests are done in the laboratory. Today, most confirmatory blood tests are indirect—based on inferences from species and DNA tests. Species tests are generally immunological—based on specific antibodies. Blood serum and hemoglobin can be antigens. As a result, antibodies can be made against them and used in tests. The most common techniques for performing immunological species tests are double immunodiffusion, crossover electrophoresis, or ELISA.

Identification tests for body fluids can also be presumptive or confirmatory. Of the common body fluids seen in forensic labs, only semen can be unequivocally identified. Semen is common evidence in sexual assault cases. It consists of sperm cells and seminal fluid. Sperm cells can be viewed under the microscope to identify semen. Seminal fluid contains a specific protein, called p30, PA, or PSA, that can be used as the basis for an immunological identification test. A presumptive test for semen called "acid phosphatase" can be used to screen evidence. There is no certain way to identify vaginal secretions (to tell the epithelial cells in these secretions from similar cells from other tissues). Saliva is presumptively identified by detecting the enzyme amylase, and urine is presumptive identified by detecting urea and/or creatinine.

The forensic lab has the responsibility for analysis of sexual assault evidence, and thus a key role in sexual assault case investigation. In recent years, the efforts of investigators, clinical personnel, lab examiners, prosecutors, and victim services have been better coordinated through sexual assault response teams, or SARTs. The training and availability of forensic nurses (sexual assault nurse examiners—SANEs) has been a key element in these initiatives. The forensic laboratory receives all the clothing and other external evidence, as well as the evidence from the victim's person, in sexual assault cases. Identification of semen on swabs from a victim or on her clothing help establish an element of the crime. Other evidence, such as hairs or trace materials, may help associate a victim with a suspect or with a scene.

There are three major types of sexual assault cases. With adults, cases may be "identification" cases where the identity of the perpetrator is unknown or "consent" cases where the identity of the perpetrator is not an issue. DNA typing is very important in the former. It is unimportant in the latter. With children, sexual abuse can be of many kinds and may not involve penetration or body fluids deposits. Even in the most egregious cases, though, children do not usually report abuse right away. These cases are usually handled by specially trained investigators.

Alcohol consumption by the parties in sexual assault cases has always been a problem. In recent years, other drugs have also shown up in sexual assault cases. The most common ones, Rohypnol, ketamine, and GHB, act as depressants and their effects are exacerbated by simultaneous alcohol consumption. They are also amnesic, causing victims to remember little about what took place. Forensic toxicologists can find the drugs in urine, or sometimes in hair, provided not too much time has elapsed. Finding the drug, however, does not establish whether it was given clandestinely or ingested voluntarily.

Before DNA analysis was available, forensic scientists used classical or conventional genetic systems to try to individualize blood and body fluids. These systems were blood groups (ABO was the most important one), red cell isoenzymes, serum proteins, and hemoglobin variants. Knowing something about the population genetics of these systems allowed forensic scientists to narrow down the fraction of the population who could have been depositors of biological evidence. This same kind of analysis with DNA types narrows down who could be a potential depositor. The difference is that, with DNA, it can be effectively narrowed down to a single person.

Key Terms

forensic biology (p. 213)
forensic serology (p. 213)
blood cells (p. 214)
serum (p. 214)
anticoagulant (p. 214)
plasma (p. 214)
known control (p. 218)
alibi known control (p. 218)
blank control (p. 218)
substratum comparison specimen
  (p. 219)

contamination (p. 219)
preliminary test (p. 221)
confirmatory test (p. 221)
peroxidases (p. 222)
crystal tests (p. 222)
immunological tests (p. 222)
species of origin (p. 223)
antigens (p. 223)
antibodies (p. 223)
semen (p. 225)
seminal plasma (p. 225)

sperm (p. 225)
acid phosphatase (p. 226)
enzyme (p. 226)
catalyst (p. 226)
p30 (p. 226)
PA (p. 226)
sexual assault evidence collection kit (p. 228)
SANEs (p. 228)
SART (p. 228)
drug-facilitated sexual assault (p. 233)
genetic markers (p. 233)

Review Questions—Short Answer

1. How has biological evidence examination changed because of the availability of DNA typing?
2. What is blood? How is blood evidence collected and preserved?
3. How is blood identified in a questioned stain? What are the presumptive versus the confirmatory tests?
4. How is the species of origin of a dried bloodstain determined?

5. What are the major body fluids besides blood that need to be identified in a forensic lab, and how is this done?
6. How are sexual assault investigations conducted? Who is typically involved?
7. What does the forensic laboratory do in a sexual assault investigation? How do the laboratory findings help resolve the case?
8. What is drug-facilitated sexual assault?
9. What are "genetic markers"? How were they used before DNA was available?
10. How does genetic typing help individualize biological specimens?

Fill-in-the-Blank & Multiple Choice

1. The immunological test known as the "precipitin test" is used in examining unknown bloodstains to determine
   a. ABO blood group.
   b. commonality of origin.
   c. species of origin.
   d. the PGM isoenzyme type.
2. Catalytic tests for the presence of blood in stains (such as the benzidine, o-tolidine, or phenolphthalin tests) are
   a. presumptive tests.
   b. confirmatory tests.
   c. very insensitive.
   d. highly unpredictable.
3. Once blood evidence collected at scenes has air dried thoroughly, it should be packaged in _____ containers.
4. The most unequivocal proof of the presence of semen in an evidence stain from a sexual assault case is furnished by _____.
5. Usually a vasectomized male's semen does not contain any spermatozoa; however, such a stain may still be identified as semen using _____ tests.

Further References

Jones, E. L. "Identification of Semen and Other Body Fluids." In *Forensic Science Handbook,* ed. R. Saferstein, vol. 2, 2nd ed., pp. 330–399. Upper Saddle River, NJ: Prentice Hall, 2005.

Pyrek, K. *Forensic Nursing,* Boca Raton, FL: CRC Press, 2006.

www.sane-sart.com/; Web site operated by the sexual assault resource service, with funding from the U.S. Department of Justice, Office for Victims of Crime.

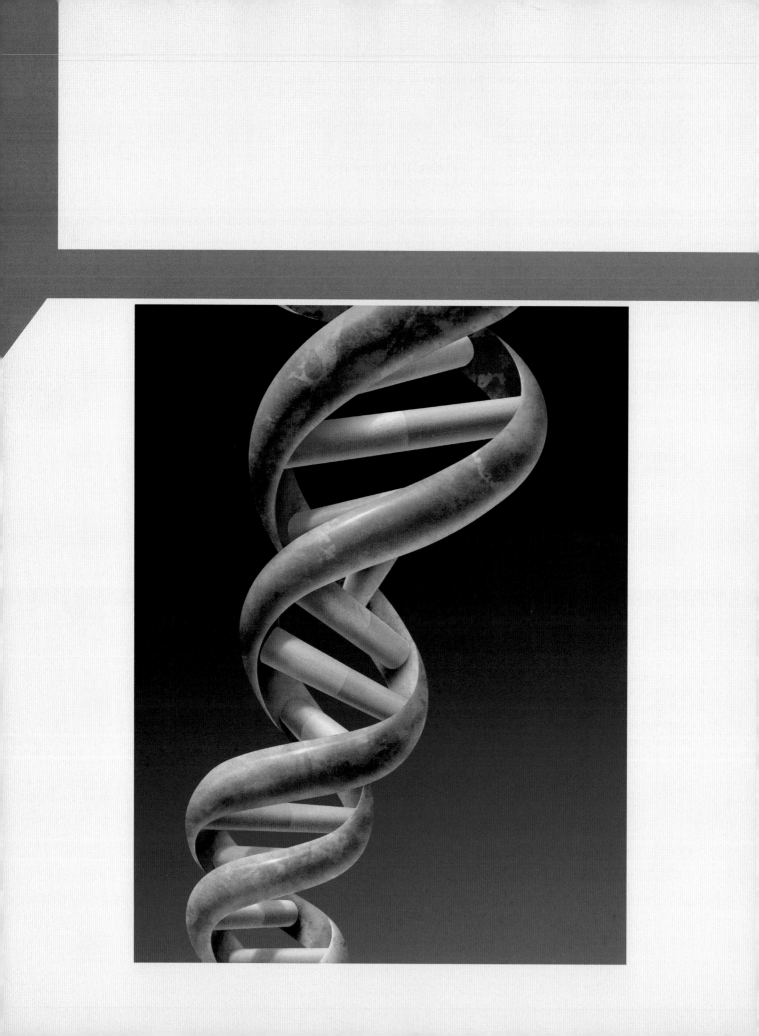

DNA Analysis and Typing

- What DNA is, including its structure and its functions
- The "classical" genetic markers—how forensic scientists partially individualized biological evidence before DNA typing
- How genetic marker typing helps individualize biological evidence—some concepts of population genetics
- Where DNA is found in the body—nuclear and mitochondrial DNA (mtDNA)
- How DNA technologies developed: RFLP, dot-blots, and STRs
- What the polymerase chain reaction is and its importance in biological research and forensic DNA analysis
- Current DNA typing methods, how they work and how DNA typing individualizes biological specimens
- DNA databases and data banks—CODIS
- The forensic applications of DNA typing: criminal, civil, human identification, parentage testing
- Some of the newer DNA technologies: "Y" chromosome and single nucleotide polymorphisms (SNPs)
- The strengths and limitations of DNA technology and how they relate to the media hype and the ultimate potential

Outline

Learning Objectives

- How basic genetics works, and how "genetic markers" work with biological evidence analysis and typing

chapter 10

Lead Case

Security Guard Guilty of Homicide

A week after Dr. Srb, a sociology professor at a community college in Connecticut, died of a heart attack, his widow went by herself to clean out her husband's office. It was a quiet Sunday afternoon. A campus security guard was on patrol, and suddenly gunshots were heard. The guard found a woman's body in the second-floor women's restroom of the social sciences building. She was later identified as the widow of the professor. Police were alerted by a 911 call. Detectives responded to the scene and found Mrs. Srb's partially clad body on the floor of the restroom next to a sink. Her upper body was fully clothed, including a jacket and scarf. Her lower body was exposed, and her skirt and panties were partially pulled down. There were no witnesses and no immediate leads.

When the state police detectives and the forensic laboratory who were contacted to assist in the investigation arrived at the campus crime scene, they carefully studied and documented the scene, and a detailed search was conducted. The following physical evidence was found:

1. A "forensic" light source was used to search the floor, and three spots of apparent fresh semen stains were found.
2. Three bullet wounds were located in the upper back and two bullet wounds in the front of upper body. Autopsy results indicated the victim was shot five times—three times anteriorly and twice posteriorly.
3. Only one spent shell casing was found under the victim's scarf. The suspect must have picked up the other spent shell cases but overlooked the one beneath the scarf.
4. Apparent seminal stains were found on her scarf. These stains were fresh and moist.
5. Hairs were found on her stockings. They were consistent with human Caucasian pubic hairs.
6. Two bullet holes were found on the divider wall of the restroom. Two fired bullets were recovered from the wall.
7. Paper towels were found in the wastebasket in the restroom. These paper towels were wet and appeared to have been recently used.

Detectives interviewed the security guard after they arrived on the scene. The guard provided a statement and indicated he was on patrol outside the social sciences building when he heard several gunshots. He said he rushed into the building, looked on every floor, and found the body in the second-floor women's restroom. He immediately called police and also informed the investigator that he did not carry any weapon. Police searched the building and the guard's office and found no guns.

A search warrant was obtained to search the guard's body, clothing, and vehicle, and to collect known blood and hair samples. The following results were obtained:

1. A gunshot residue test kit was collected from his hands. The test results were negative.
2. Seminal stains were found on the front lower left side of his uniform. These semen stains appeared to be fresh.
3. 9 mm fired cartridge casings were found inside his right boot. The casings were the same brand and caliber as the spent casing found under the victim's scarf.
4. Head and pubic hair samples were collected from the guard. Two pubic hairs found on the victim's stocking had similar microscopic characteristics to the known pubic hair sample from the suspect.
5. A known blood sample was also collected for DNA tests. DNA extracted from the semen stains had the same profile as the known DNA from the suspect. The profile had an extremely low probability of chance duplication.
6. The guard's car had heavy seat covers. After the seat covers were removed, a 9 mm automatic pistol was found under the right front seat.
7. A firearms examiner test fired the weapon and found that the bullets found in Mrs. Srb's body and in the restroom wall were fired from this same gun.
8. Bullet trajectories were reconstructed. These trajectories showed that the victim was first shot twice in the front while she was in standing position. Three additional shots were then fired at close range.

The security guard was arrested and charged with first-degree murder. He subsequently pled guilty and is currently serving a life sentence without the possibility of parole.

DNA analysis and typing for forensic purposes is based on the fact that DNA is the genetic material of all living organisms, including human beings. Through the DNA, that genetic information is passed from generation to generation, from parents to child. This process and its details form the basis of the science of genetics. The rules of inheritance—which are faithfully followed in all sexually reproducing, multicellular organisms—were worked out by an obscure Augustinian monk named Gregor Mendel (1822–1884, Figure 10.1). He lived in a monastery in what was then Brünn, Austria, and is today Brno, Czech Republic. Working with pea plants in the monastery garden by purposely crossing them and observing what happened with specific characteristics in the next generation, Mendel figured out the basic rules of inheritance. He did publish his work, but in a relatively unknown journal. Around 1900, when the science of genetics started to explode, other scientists rediscovered Mendel's experiments. The basic rules of inheritance are often called "Mendelian," as a tribute to Mendel.

Figure 10.1
Gregor Mendel is considered the father of modern genetics.

Genetics, Inheritance, Genetic Markers

Genetics is the science of inheritance—how parents pass their traits and characteristics to their offspring. Inheritance can be extremely simple—where a cell divides to form two identical daughter cells. It can also be more complicated—where human parents form sperm and egg cells, each of which contains half the genetic material of the parent, and these cells recombine at fertilization to form a unique new cell capable of developing into a new individual.

In higher animals, including humans, DNA, the genetic material, is organized into **chromosomes** that are found in the **nucleus** of most cells. Humans have 46 chromosomes. Forty-four of them are paired—that is, there are 22 pairs. The other two are called sex chromosomes, which can be either X or Y. Women have two X chromosomes, and men have one X and one Y. Individuals inherit one member of each of the 22 pairs from their mother and the other member from their father. They also inherit an X chromosome from their mother. The father's sperm may provide either an X chromosome (producing a female) or a Y (producing a male).

When men make sperm or women make eggs, a modified cell division process takes place that randomly sorts the pairs of chromosomes so that each reproductive cell contains 23. At fertilization, the characteristic chromosome number, 46, is restored.

DNA regulates cell activity mostly by specifying exactly how cells make their proteins. Some of the proteins are structural, and others are enzymes. Often, the presence or absence of a particular enzyme, which in turn means that some chemical reaction occurs or does not occur, is the basis for a particular trait or characteristic. Before lab tools were available for the analysis or typing of DNA directly, geneticists and forensic scientists looked at the *products* of DNA function (proteins, enzymes, and other characteristics like blood types) to do genetic analysis and to try to forensically "individualize" biological evidence. The proteins, enzymes, and so on that were used for this purposes were commonly called **genetic markers**—"genetic" because of their being inherited, and "markers" because they could serve as a means of narrowing down the number of people in a population who could be depositors.

Genetic difference among people that enables them to be distinguished is called "genetic polymorphism." It is discussed in more detail later.

chromosomes

Physical carriers of DNA (and thus of inheritance information) from one generation to the next; every species has a specific number of chromosomes.

nucleus

A membrane-enclosed structure within a cell that contains the chromosomes, and therefore, the nuclear DNA.

genetic markers

Molecules, usually proteins, that are attributable to a specific gene; any person can have any two of several different genes at this location on DNA, and that is reflected in the "genetic marker" profile.

DNA—Nature and Functions

DNA was first "discovered" in the 19th century, and by the 1940s it was clear that DNA is the genetic material, the chemical blueprint of life itself. In 1953, James Watson and Francis Crick, in collaboration with Maurice Wilkins and Rosalind Franklin, used X-ray crystallography to figure out the chemical structure of DNA—the double helix.

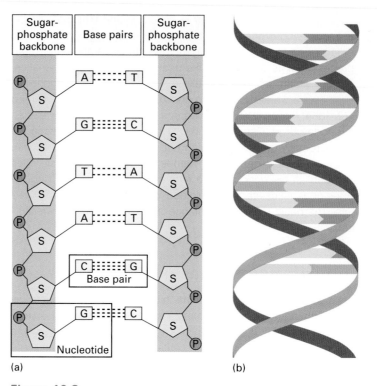

Figure 10.2

A: Diagram of DNA structure. One nucleotide is boxed off. The sugar-phosphate "backbone" of the strands is apparent, along with the bases A, T, C and G. The strands sit next to one another, and the base pairings A-T and C-G are always followed. This structure twists to form form the double helix. Adapted from a drawing at Access Excellence @ the National Health Museum (www.accessexcellence.org/). B: Diagram of DNA structure, emphasizing the double helix structure. The two strands are held together by weak bonds between the paired bases, represented by the "ladder rungs" in the diagram. Adapted from a drawing at Access Excellence @ the National Health Museum (www.accessexcellence.org/).

nucleotide

A molecule that is made up of a nitrogenous base (A, T, C, or G), a ribose sugar component, and phosphate; the building blocks of nucleic acids (DNA and RNA).

DNA is a very large molecule that consists of units called *nucleotides* (Figure 10.2A). The components of a **nucleotide** are an organic base, a five-carbon carbohydrate called ribose, and phosphate. In DNA, the base can be one of four compounds: guanine, cytosine, adenine, and thymine, commonly abbreviated G, C, A, and T. The complete DNA molecule consists of two strands. Each strand is a polymer of nucleotides, each of which can be A, T, C, or G. In the complete, double-stranded DNA, the bases are always paired in a specific way: A is always paired with T, and C is always paired with G. Figure 10.2B shows the double-stranded helical structure.

The base pairing rules establish that wherever there is A in one strand, there will be T in the other strand, and wherever there is C in one strand, there will be G in the other. The two strands are said to be "complementary." This specific base pair bonding holds the two strands of the double helix together. The strands can be separated by heat or under certain chemical conditions. Because of the positioning of the terminal phosphate residues on the two strands, one strand is said to run 5′ to 3′ (5 "prime" to 3 "prime"—these designations refer to numbered positions in the ribose sugar component ring structure), and the other strand runs 3′ to 5′. Because of the base pairing rules, knowing the sequence of one strand dictates the sequence of the complementary strand. Finally, the double-stranded DNA forms a stable helical structure, the now familiar double helix (Figure 10.2B).

It is the **sequence** of bases that is the primary structure of DNA and that makes every DNA unique, thus enabling it to be a chemical repository of information specific to each individual.

The entire complement of DNA in one cell is referred to as the "genome." Human DNA has a total of around 3.5 billion base pairs. Because intact DNA is double stranded, each position is occupied by a base pair, either A-T, T-A, C-G, or G-C. For this reason, it is common to state the length of a strand of DNA in "base pairs" (bp). The sequence is not just a random assortment of base pairs in linear order. The base sequences in the "coding" portions of DNA conform to what is called the "genetic code." The majority of human (and other mammalian) DNA is noncoding, however. DNA scientists have not found any function as yet for this noncoding DNA. Quite a bit of the noncoding DNA has a repeat sequence structure. There are long and short repeated sequences scattered throughout the genome. That is, the same sequence of 100–200 base pairs will be found in hundreds or thousands of different places throughout human DNA. A particular type of repeat sequence structure is very important for forensic DNA typing: tandemly repeated sequences, or tandem repeats. The sequence that is repeated can be as short as two bases (e.g., ATATATATAT . . .) or up to over 100 bases long. In a tandemly repeated sequence region, the repeat structure occurs in a string of "units," set head to tail. In any particular repeat region, there can be several to several hundred tandem repeats.

The two strands of DNA can be separated in the laboratory by heat or certain salt concentrations in solution. During the PCR (polymerase chain reaction), an important process to forensic DNA analysis (see later), strand separation must occur so that the *primers* can anneal to the individual strands. A **primer** is a short single strand of DNA that has a sequence exactly complementary (A for T and C for G) to a short sequence in the larger structure (see later). Separation of the DNA strands is called "melting," or "denaturation." But DNA strands also have to separate in the cell to permit certain functions. During DNA synthesis, one strand is used as a "template" to make a new complementary strand. And during transcription—the process of transcribing the DNA sequence into single stranded RNA—the strands must separate enough to permit synthesis of mRNA (messenger ribonucleic acid) from the coding strand. This mRNA is later used as a template to synthesize proteins.

You may have read or heard about the "Human Genome Project." For most of the 1990s, government and private laboratories worked to determine the complete sequence of human DNA. The project has been completed, and now genetic scientists have to try to figure out the roles and functions for the sequences. As this is accomplished, the possibilities of designing real cures for genetic disorders and of designing drugs for very specific therapeutic tasks are much greater than before.

DNA has two principal functions. One is that it can make accurate copies of itself. This function is essential every time a cell divides, if the daughter cells are to be exact copies of the parent cell. Thus, although humans consist of millions of cells (many of which are constantly being replaced), every one of them has the identical complement of DNA. Every time a cell divides to produce genetically identical daughter cells (a process biologists call **mitosis**), a complete, accurate copy of DNA must be made so that each daughter cell can have one copy. Mitosis is the way single-celled organisms reproduce, and it is the way multicellular organisms grow, develop, and repair damaged cells.

DNA replication is catalyzed by enzymes called **DNA polymerases.** Quite a few different kinds of this enzyme occur in various cells and organisms throughout nature, but, in effect, they all do the same thing. A particular type of DNA polymerase is necessary for the PCR (see later). DNA polymerases catalyze the synthesis of DNA using one of the strands as a template, and "filling in" the complementary bases of the second strand and bonding them together into the complementary strand (Figure 10.3). DNA polymerase will not attach to a single strand of DNA. There

---

sequence

Forms the basis for genetic information; specifies the structure of all the proteins that are made from the DNA template and is the basis of individuality.

primer

A small, single-stranded piece of DNA whose sequence is complementary to the sequence in a long strand of DNA that is to be copied by a DNA polymerase.

mitosis

Cell division, in which a single cell replicates its DNA, then divides allocating to each daughter cell a complete complement of the original DNA.

DNA polymerases

Enzymes that can catalyze the synthesis of double-stranded DNA from another primed strand.

Figure 10.3

Diagram illustrating DNA replication. One strand is used as a template for the synthesis of the complementary strand. Adapted from a drawing at Access Excellence @ the National Health Museum (http://www.accessexcellence.org/).

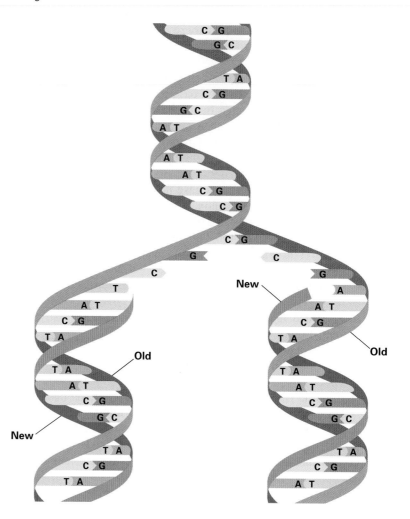

genetic code

The correspondence between the sequence of bases in DNA, taken three at a time, and the amino acids that make up the proteins.

has to be at least a small segment of the complementary strand (the one that is going to be extended by the synthesis) already in place; this little segment may be called a primer. The enzyme attaches to the terminal nucleotide of the incomplete strand and catalyzes the addition of complementary nucleotides one at a time, "sewing up," as it were, the double strand.

The second function is more complicated: DNA, through its chemical structure, controls all cell functions because the DNA base sequence determines the chemical structure of all the proteins. Proteins have structural roles in cells, but their most important function is as *enzymes*. Some years ago, geneticists figured out that DNA can specify protein structure because there is a correspondence between certain DNA base sequences and certain amino acids, the building blocks of proteins. This correspondence is called the **genetic code.** It is thus sometimes said that "DNA codes for proteins."

Proteins are made up of units called "amino acids" that are chemically hooked together in a sequence. There are about 20 naturally occurring amino acids found in proteins. The DNA sequence must therefore be able to specify 20 different amino acids, so that the sequence of bases in DNA will dictate the sequence of amino acids in proteins. Since there are only four bases, the correspondence obviously can't be one to one. If a two-base sequence specified each amino acid, only 16 different ones could be accommodated. So, the fewest bases in a sequence that can "code for" each amino acid, and have enough sequences to be able to do all the amino acids, is three. Since there are 64 different three-base sequences, there is some degeneracy in the code sequences—more than one DNA triplet sequence can code for the same amino acid. As mentioned, this set of triplet sequences that code for amino acids is called the genetic code. Working out the "words" in the genetic code and how the coding takes place is one of the major

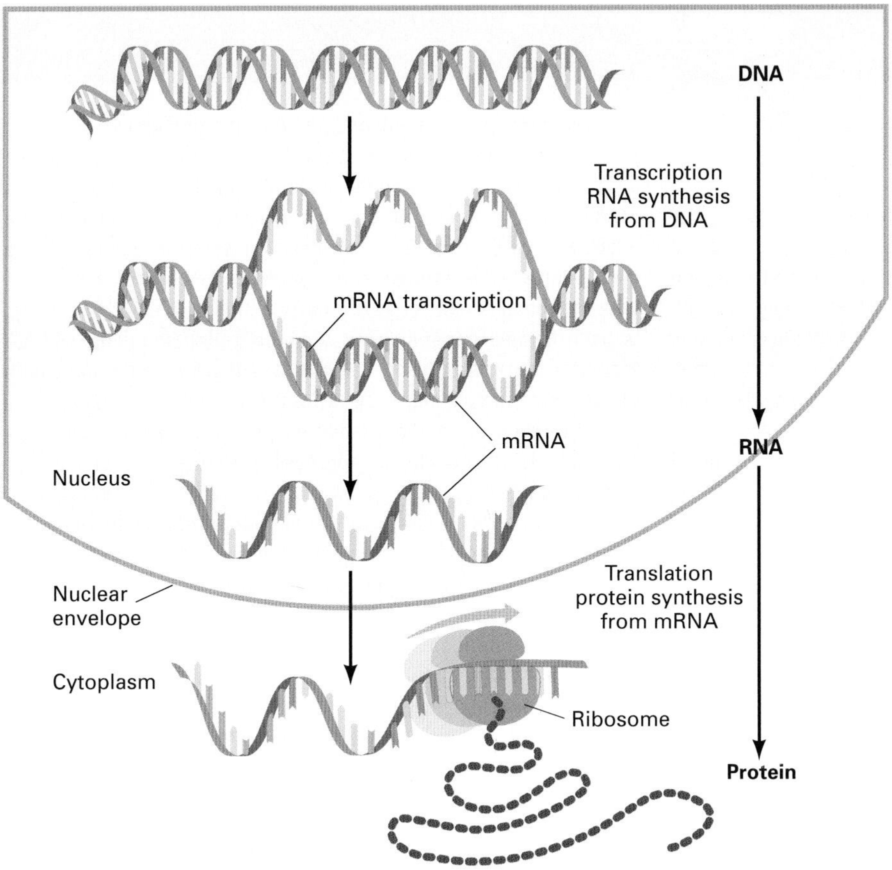

Figure 10.4
Diagram showing DNA specified protein synthesis. Transcription of DNA to mRNA takes place in the nucleus. Translation of mRNA to protein takes place in the cytoplasm. Adapted from a drawing at Access Excellence @ the National Health Museum (http://www.accessexcellence.org/).

milestones of 20th-century molecular biology. DNA does not do the actual coding directly. An intermediary molecule, called messenger RNA (mRNA), is the actual template for protein synthesis. The process of making mRNA from DNA is called **transcription.** The mRNA is single stranded and is a replicate of one strand (the coding strand) of the DNA from which it was made. The process of making protein from mRNA is called **translation.** The process is illustrated in Figure 10.4.

Where DNA Is Found in the Body—Nuclear (Genomic) and Mitochondrial DNA (mtDNA)

Every person starts life as a single cell. As that cell and its progeny divide and differentiate to form the millions of cells that make up different organs and tissues, DNA is faithfully replicated with each cell division. Thus, every cell winds up with a complete copy of DNA. This DNA is always found in the nucleus of the cell and is thus often called **nuclear DNA.** It may also be called **genomic DNA.** Most of the time, when forensic scientists are talking about DNA, it is nuclear DNA. Later we will introduce and describe another kind of DNA in the cell (mitochondrial DNA), which can also be used in forensic cases sometimes.

There are two important practical "exceptions" to the general proposition that every cell in the body has a complete, identical copy of the person's DNA. The first is red blood cells (see Chapter 9). Mature red cells have no nucleus and thus no nuclear DNA. The second exception is the germ cells, spermatozoa and ova (sperm and egg). These cells have undergone a type of cell division that results in their having 23 chromosomes instead of 46. They have one member of each of the 22 pairs and either an X or a Y.

Because most body cells have a copy of DNA, almost any tissue or organ can be used for DNA typing—at least in theory. Isolating DNA from some tissues

transcription

The process by which messenger RNA (mRNA) is synthesized from DNA while preserving the base sequence information.

translation

The process by which a messenger RNA (mRNA) template is used by the cell to assemble proteins based on the genetic code.

nuclear/genomic DNA

The DNA found in the chromosomes in the nucleus of the cell; the terms "nuclear DNA" and "genomic DNA" are synonymous.

Case Study 10.1

Identification of the Unknown Soldier from the Vietnam War

Mitochondrial DNA typing (sometimes called "mitotyping") is the method of choice among DNA typing technologies for the identification of old, highly decomposed, and/or skeletal human remains. The mtDNA is more robust in these specimens, and the laboratory is more likely to obtain results. MtDNA typing is actually sequencing—the analyst determines the sequence of a small segment of the mtDNA. This segment tends to show variation at certain base positions among different individuals.

MtDNA is inherited exclusively from one's mother. Unless a mutation occurs, the sequence of the variable segment in mtDNA passes unchanged from mother to offspring, generation after generation. Mothers pass their mtDNA to their sons, but the sons cannot pass it on to anyone else. Daughters, on the other hand, pass it along to their offspring, and so forth. For this reason, the reference specimen needed to use mtDNA for human identification is one from the suspected person's mother, or another person who would share her sequence (a sibling, maternal aunt, etc.). If the reference and questioned sequences match, a probability of chance duplication can be computed. With mtDNA these probabilities are high in comparison with those obtained from 13-locus nuclear DNA comparisons. That is, a mitotype may

occur in every couple thousand persons in a population. However, the identification of remains is not based on the mitotype alone. There is other circumstantial evidence. In the case of remains of military personnel from theaters of battle, the remains may be associated with a particular airplane, or ship, or location. There may be articles or fragments of clothing or belongings associated with the remains that suggest a certain person. The mtDNA typing is used to help confirm these suspected identifications. MtDNA typing of remains is of no value unless there is some indication of who the person might be. Those clues allow the laboratory to determine who in the suspected person's maternal line may be available to provide an appropriate reference specimen for comparison.

For nearly 80 years, the United States has maintained the Tomb of the Unknowns at Arlington National Cemetery in Arlington, Virginia. It is also sometimes known as the Tomb of the Unknown Soldier. On March 4, 1921, Congress approved the burial of an unidentified American soldier from World War I in the plaza of the new Memorial Amphitheater. The white marble sarcophagus has a flat-faced form and is relieved at the corners and along the sides by neoclassic pilasters, or columns, set into the surface. Sculpted into the east panel, which faces Washington, D.C., are three Greek figures representing Peace, Victory, and Valor. Inscribed on the back of the Tomb are the words:

---

mitochondria (sing., mitochondrion)

Structures that contain a small amount of DNA and are found in the cell, outside the nucleus, responsible for making energy for the cell.

mitochondrial DNA (mtDNA)

The DNA contained in the mitochondria of the cell; inherited only from an individual's mother and passed along a maternal line from generation to generation.

(such as bone) is not as simple as from blood or body fluids. Thus, not every forensic lab routinely does DNA typing from bodily tissues other than blood, semen, or saliva.

In addition to a nucleus, a structure bounded by its own membrane and containing the nuclear DNA within the chromosomes, cells also have structures within them called **mitochondria.** At a simple level, mitochondria can be thought of as the cell's power plants. They have the components and enzymes necessary for cells to make most of their energy. This energy is stored in a chemical form called "adenosine triphosphate" (or ATP) until it is needed. There are hundreds to thousands of mitochondria in every cell. Mitochondria have a small quantity of their own DNA. The "mitochondrial genome," as it is sometimes called, consists of about 16,000 base pairs as opposed to around 3 billion base pairs for nuclear DNA, making it on the order of 10,000 times smaller in size than nuclear DNA.

Mitochondrial DNA (mtDNA) has two regions in its sequence, called "HV1" and "HV2" ("HV" stands for hypervariable region), that show quite a bit of variation between individuals in populations. This variation is not random throughout the sequence but tends to be characteristic of certain base pairs along its length (mtDNA has a universally agreed upon numbering system of its base sequence). Forensic scientists take advantage of this variation in some specific situations, and with certain specific types of evidence. These are developed later in the chapter.

MtDNA also has another feature that makes it different from nuclear DNA—its mode of inheritance. It was noted previously that every person inherits half of his or her nuclear DNA from the father and the other half from the mother. The maternal half is contributed by the nucleus of the egg cell, and the paternal half is contributed by the nucleus of the sperm cell at the time of fertilization. MtDNA is inherited *only* from one's mother, however. There is no paternal contribution to it. Because the sequence of mtDNA is quite stable from generation to generation, a sequence can often be traced through the maternal lineage for many generations.

HERE RESTS IN
HONORED GLORY
AN AMERICAN
SOLDIER
KNOWN BUT TO GOD

The Tomb sarcophagus was placed above the grave of the Unknown Soldier of World War I. Just to the side are the crypts of unknowns from World War II, Korea, and Vietnam. Those three graves are marked with white marble slabs flush with the plaza. For each of the wars, a service member whose identity could not be determined was selected to lie in these crypts.

The unknown soldier of the Vietnam conflict was designated by Medal of Honor recipient U.S. Marine Corps Sergeant Major Allan Jay Kellogg Jr. during a ceremony at Pearl Harbor, Hawaii, May 17, 1984. The Vietnam Unknown was transported aboard the USS *Brewton* to Alameda Naval Base, California. The remains were sent to Travis Air Force Base, California, May 24. The Vietnam Unknown arrived at Andrews Air Force Base, Maryland, the next day. Many Vietnam veterans and President and Mrs. Ronald Reagan visited the Vietnam Unknown in the U.S. Capitol. An Army caisson carried the Vietnam Unknown from the Capitol to the Memorial Amphitheater at Arlington National Cemetery on Memorial Day, May 28, 1984.

Officials had stated that the identity of the Vietnam unknown soldier was likely either Lieutenant Michael J. Blassie or Captain Rodney Strobridge, of the Air Force. The two were shot down on May 11, 1972, near An Loc, about 60 miles north of Saigon, where the remains of the unknown soldier were found. Blassie's wallet and identification gear from his A-37 fighter were found near the remains, leading to speculation that the remains might be those of Blassie. But initial medical tests could not confirm identification.

The Blassie family, convinced that the remains belonged to their relative, pressed the Pentagon for exhumation, which finally took place in May 1998. MtDNA testing at the Armed Forces DNA Identification Laboratory (AFDIL) in Rockville, Maryland, confirmed that the remains in the crypt were those of Lieutenant Blassie. They were handed over to his family for reburial in a cemetery near the family home in St. Louis, Missouri.

The identification was announced by President Bill Clinton himself. These new methods of DNA identification make it likely that other unknowns may be identified in the future. And it is unlikely that any service members from future conflicts will remain unidentified. "It may be that forensic science has reached the point where there will be no other unknowns any more. So we have to look very carefully about where we go from here," then Secretary of Defense William Cohen noted at the time.

www.cnn.com/ALLPOLITICS/1998/07/01/blassie.folo/.

This strictly maternal inheritance has implications for the application of mtDNA typing in human identification cases, to be developed later in the chapter.

Another feature of mtDNA that makes it a good candidate for human identification cases, especially if the DNA must be taken from old, decomposed, or skeletonized remains, is its high copy number.

Each cell has hundreds to thousands of mitochondria, and thus hundreds to thousands of times as much mtDNA as nuclear DNA. The likelihood of isolating a usable mtDNA sequence is greatly increased by the fact that so many copies are present to begin with.

Collection and Preservation of Biological Evidence for DNA Typing

The principles and techniques described in Chapter 9 for collecting, packaging, and preserving biological evidence fully apply here. Biological evidence should be thoroughly dry before packaging—that is the single most important factor in preserving the ability to get DNA types.

Substratum comparison specimens, discussed in Chapter 9, are important when biological evidence is collected for DNA analysis. These specimens will be more important in some circumstances than in others. With large and/or concentrated blood or semen stains, so much DNA will be obtained from the cells in those stains that background biological material will simply not be an issue, because there will be so little of it in comparison to the primary evidence DNA. In the case of smaller, diluted, less concentrated, or trace-type stains, the amount of DNA from the primary evidence might be less. In that case, the comparison specimen is more important, because processing it in parallel with the primary stain helps to establish whether there is or is not "background" DNA that may interfere with or complicate the interpretation of the types in the evidentiary stain DNA.

Compared with the other genetic markers we have described in Chapter 9—those that were used before DNA typing became available—DNA is robust. That doesn't mean you can always get DNA and/or acceptable DNA types from evidence no matter what its history. But it is known from experience that DNA types can sometimes be obtained from evidentiary stains that are old or have been subject to adverse environmental influences. Age and heating tend to make biological stains insoluble, sort of "fixed" to the substratum so that it is very difficult to extract anything from them. Heat tends to mimic aging in that respect. DNA tends to degrade in biological traces or stains that are damp or warm or both. Enzymes called "DNases," which degrade DNA by chemically cutting it into small pieces, can be released during the putrefactive and autolytic (a sort of chemical self-destruction) processes that occur after death. DNases are also present in some bacteria that may infect and grow in biological stains that are not dry. It is important to note, however, that no one can predict in advance whether a biological trace or stain will yield DNA, nor whether it will yield a suitable type or profile. The only way to find that out is to try typing it.

Development and Methods of DNA Analysis

The groundwork for developing DNA typing for forensic casework was laid down by genetic scientists throughout the 1970s and 1980s. Many techniques for manipulating DNA were developed in research labs by molecular biologists. The purpose was to get sequence information (to "map" the human and other organism's genomes), and to learn how genes work. There has been special interest in learning about genes that are directly or indirectly involved in genetic defects or diseases. In the process, much was learned about DNA functionality.

A great majority of human DNA is not "functional"; that is, it does not code for protein structure. In humans, nonfunctional DNA represents about 80 percent of the total. This nonfunctional DNA has been called "anonymous DNA" or "junk DNA," but those characterizations could be premature. It could be that the functions of some of that DNA have just not been discovered yet. Quite a bit of the nonfunctional DNA has repetitive sequence. There are several different types of repetitive-sequence DNA, but almost all forensic applications of DNA typing have exploited what is called "tandemly repeated sequences."

A **tandemly repeated sequence** in DNA is a head-to-tail repeat of the same sequence of bases. Some repeated sequences are as short as two bases, and others may be dozens of bases long. The number of repeats can vary, and it is the *"number of repeats"* that constitutes the polymorphism. People differ in how many repeats of a sequence they have at a particular locus. For this reason, these regions in DNA are called **variable number of tandem repeat (VNTR)** loci.

There have been three "generations" of DNA typing technology. The first was called "RFLP" typing; the second was based on PCR and mainly involved dot-blot techniques; the third is called "STR" typing and is the current method. Before describing the typing methods, however, a discussion on DNA isolation from the biological specimen is in order.

Isolation (Extraction) of DNA

An important aspect of DNA analysis is the isolation, or extraction, of DNA from the biological evidence such as blood, semen, and so on. This process must be done before any of the typing steps, no matter what typing method or system is being used. The most common method for DNA isolation involves digesting the evidentiary material with a broad spectrum proteinase (an enzyme that hydrolyzes and thus breaks down the proteins). This digestion disrupts the cell and nuclear membranes and breaks down the proteins so the DNA can be separated out more readily. Next, organic solvents are used to extract DNA, to separate it from other cell components. Tests are then done to determine how much DNA has been obtained (Figure 10.5A and B).

---

tandemly repeated sequence

A sequence of bases in DNA that is repeated in a head-to-tail fashion several to many times.

variable number of tandem repeat (VNTR)

Different individuals have different numbers of repeat units at many of the locations in DNA that feature tandemly repeated sequences; those different numbers of repeat units are "VNTR."

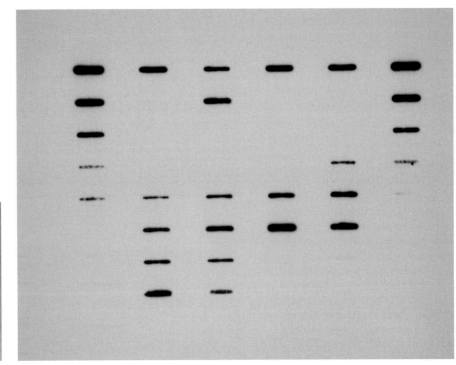

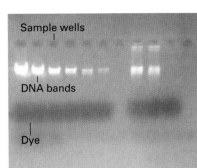

(a)   (b)

Figure 10.5

A: A minigel for assessing DNA quality. This gel, made of agarose, is run in a special electrophoresis chamber. The current causes the DNA to migrate out of the sample wells and down the gel. The dye helps the analyst know how long to leave the current running. The brightness of the DNA band is proportional to the quantity of DNA. B: Quantiblot film for estimation of the amount of human DNA present in samples. DNA specimens are applied via a slot template to a special nylon membrane. The membrane is treated with a special human DNA probe. The probe can emit light. If the membrane is placed together with X-ray film for a time, the emitted light will expose the film. The darkness of a band is proportional to the amount of human DNA. This technique for human DNA quantitation may soon be obsolete, as laboratories switch to a new technique called real-time PCR.

Note that the minigel provides an estimate of the total quantity (and the quality, that is, degree of degradation) of the DNA in the specimen, where the quantiblot provides an estimate of the quantity of human DNA.

A variation of the usual extraction procedure is used for mixtures of sperm cells and vaginal epithelial cells such as are commonly found in vaginal swabs or drainage stains in panties from sexual assault cases. The process is called **differential extraction.** In this variation of the extraction method, the more easily broken epithelial cells have their DNA released without disrupting the sperm cells. When used on a mixture stain, this first fraction is almost exclusively epithelial cell DNA (or female DNA). Then, the sperm cells are broken, and a fraction that is almost exclusively male DNA is obtained. Obviously, the ability to separate the male and female DNA in sexual assault evidence during the DNA extraction is very helpful.

The Beginning—RFLP

In the 1980s, geneticists found a number of VNTR loci in the human genome that could be typed using **restriction fragment length polymorphism (RFLP)** methods. Actually, "RFLP" describes the genetic loci themselves. This typing method, now largely obsolete in forensic science, involved cutting the DNA into smaller pieces with specific enzymes (called "restriction endonucleases"), separating the resulting fragments by electrophoresis, transferring the separated fragments to a nylon membrane by a process known as "Southern blotting," and finally detecting the specific alleles using a radioactively labeled or chemiluminescence-labeled

differential extraction

A process by which an analyst can separately isolate male and female DNA from a mixture of female epithelial cells and male sperm cells, such as might be found in sexual assault evidence.

restriction fragment length polymorphism (RFLP)

The original kind of DNA typing used in forensic science, now obsolete in forensic work.

DNA probe. This process is lengthy, time-consuming, requires a lot of analyst effort, and is not very automatable (Figure 10.6).

In 1985, Sir Alec Jeffreys, a geneticist at the University of Leicester, England, reported in the scientific journal *Nature* that the RFLP DNA typing method was extremely powerful in individualizing people, and further that he had used the techniques to help solve some alleged blood relationship cases in connection with British immigration law (Figure 10.7). Around that same time, there was a double sexual assault-homicide in an English village.

Figure 10.6

The diagram illustrates RFLP by representing each repeat sequence unit as a little box. Two different people have four different chromosomes, and each chromosome has a different number of repeats. When the DNA from this hypothetical area in the DNA sequence is subjected to RFLP, the electrophoresis will cause the different sized fragments to be separated. Bigger ones migrate less distance than smaller ones. A sizing ladder is a special mixture of DNA fragments of known sizes, which analysts use to estimate the sizes of the fragments from the people.

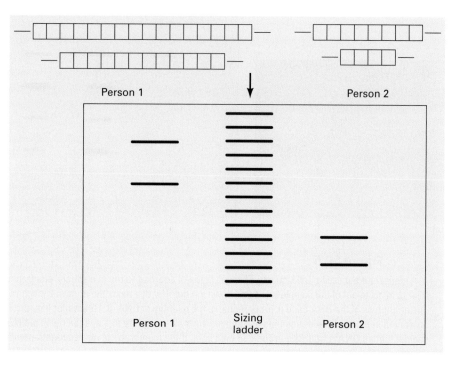

Figure 10.7

In the diagram in Figure 10.6, each person only has two DNA fragments. That is in fact how forensic RFLP typing was done. RFLP could also be done using so-called multilocus probes, and then each person would produce multiple bands that looked sort of like a bar code. Dr. Jeffreys' earliest cases were done using multilocus probes, as shown here.

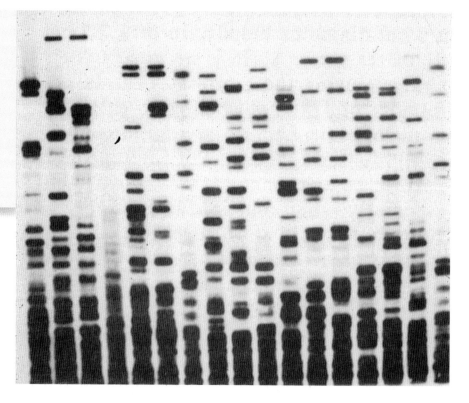

The events surrounding the Narborough case (Case Study 10.2) ignited an explosion in forensic science that has arguably still not completely subsided. In this country and in many other countries, DNA typing methods were rapidly refined in forensic science laboratories and validated for widespread casework use. In the United States, the FBI Laboratory took the lead in this effort because they were to be the main developer of DNA databases (see later), and consistency among labs is important for databasing. The government forensic labs in the United States moved slowly and deliberately in developing, validating, and implementing DNA typing technology in casework. The private laboratories, primarily Lifecodes and Cellmark at that time, moved more quickly, and they did many of the earliest criminal cases (Case Study 10.3).

The Polymerase Chain Reaction (PCR)— The First PCR-Based DNA Typing Methods

While a number of forensic laboratories implemented RFLP DNA typing in casework in the mid to late 1980s, another technology was simultaneously being developed. A technique called the **polymerase chain reaction (PCR)** has revolutionized molecular biology and genetics. It was developed at what was then Cetus Corporation (now Roche Molecular Systems). The stories about the early discovery work with the PCR method are murky, but in 1993, Dr. Kary Mullis (sometimes spelled "Kerry Mullis") shared the Nobel Prize in Chemistry for the discovery.

Briefly, PCR is the copying of a specific, small segment of DNA. Millions of copies of the segment can be made. The specificity of the segment copied is determined by a pair of small single-stranded DNA molecules called "primers." Figure 10.8 illustrates the PCR.

Using PCR as the basis for DNA typing is better for forensic cases and evidence for several reasons. First, PCR methods are many times faster than RFLP ones, and they are automatable. Ultimately, this will help laboratories keep up with casework and databasing demands. Second, PCR methods may work with DNA that is degraded, where RFLP methods typically will not. And third, because the method essentially consists of making multiple copies of segments of DNA, specifically in the case where the segments contain human polymorphisms, PCR is much more sensitive than RFLP; that is, it works with much smaller amounts of DNA (and thus much smaller quantities of evidence). In all these respects, PCR-based methods are better suited to forensic applications than RFLP.

Case Study 10.2

The Narborough Rape Murders—Alec Jeffreys and the First Use of DNA Typing in a Criminal Case

This case, which was the catalyst for the development of DNA typing technologies by many forensic laboratories throughout the world, centered in a village called Narborough, Leicestershire, England. In 1983, a 15-year-old girl was raped and murdered as she was walking home along a country lane. The initial investigation yielded no suspects. Three years later, another young girl turned up dead in Narborough, sexually assaulted and murdered in a similar manner. Police arrested a 17-year-old named Rodney Buckland, a worker in a local mental hospital, who made statements incriminating himself in the second murder, but proclaiming his innocence in the earlier one. Police, certain that Buckland had raped and killed both girls, sent semen samples from the two attacks, along with a blood sample from the suspect, to Leicester University for Dr. Jeffreys to examine with his new RFLP DNA typing method. The DNA analysis confirmed that the same offender had committed both crimes, but it also showed that Buckland could not have been the perpetrator. His incriminating statements were false. Thus, Buckland was the first man ever exonerated by DNA typing. Without it, he might well have gone to jail for life.

Police then began a massive manhunt for the real perpetrator, conducting what would today be called a "biological evidence dragnet." All the sexually mature males in the village were requested to provide reference blood specimens. Most did so—over 5,000 men in all. DNA typing was very new at this point. Forensic science laboratories didn't even do DNA typing as yet. Professor Jeffreys agreed to perform DNA typing in his lab at Leicester. But because this form of DNA typing is so complex and time-consuming, the Home Office forensic science lab first "screened" all the specimens using the conventional genetic marker systems we described earlier. That is, all the men whose specimens allowed them to be excluded as potential semen donors were excluded. The remaining specimens were then DNA typed. In the first round of DNA typing, none of the specimens matched the types of the semen donor. The perpetrator, a 27-year-old named Colin Pitchfork, was ultimately found, arrested, and convicted of the offenses because he had paid someone to give the voluntary blood specimen to the police using his name. He bragged about this while drinking in a pub, was overheard, and turned in. The surrogate admitted to the police what he had done. Pitchfork's DNA types matched those found in the semen recovered from both victims.

The crime writer Joseph Wambaugh describes this interesting case in its entirety in a book called *The Blooding*.

polymerase chain reaction (PCR)

A process used to make many copies of a defined segment of DNA, using a special kind of DNA polymerase that is stable to high temperatures; PCR is now one of the steps in all forensic DNA analysis.

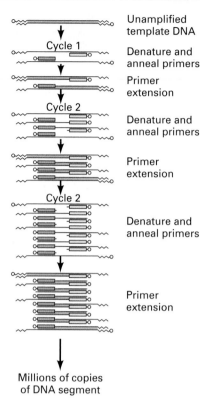

Unamplified
template DNA

Cycle 1

Denature and
anneal primers

Primer
extension

Cycle 2

Denature and
anneal primers

Primer
extension

Cycle 2

Denature and
anneal primers

Primer
extension

Millions of copies
of DNA segment

Figure 10.8

This diagram illustrating the steps in the Polymerase Chain Reaction (PCR) process that allows making enormous numbers of exact copies of a selected portion of DNA and is the basis for much of the modern DNA technology.

minisatellite

Refers to a VNTR region of DNA in which the repeat units are 30 to 50 bases long; the RFLP technique was used to type "minisatellite" regions of DNA.

short tandem repeat (STR)

A VNTR where the repeat unit is short, from two to six bases in length; all the regions used for forensic STR DNA typing have four or five base repeats.

microsatellite

A synonym for STR.

In the late 1980s, scientists at the Cetus Corporation developed a clever typing system for a locus called HLA-DQA1 (originally, it was called HLA-DQ(α) based on the PCR, and a technique called "reverse dot blotting." The first forensic cases using a PCR-based technique in the United States were done using this HLA-DQA1 typing system. In 1986, a case entitled *Pestinikis* arose in Pennsylvania, and was referred to Forensic Science Associates in Emeryville, California. That lab was the first to put the HLA-DQA1 typing system into use in forensic cases (for example in *Illinois* v. *Dotson*, the lead case in Chapter 9). The *Pestinikis* case involved whether tissue specimens in a medical facility belonged to a particular person, and HLA-DQA1 typing allowed the question to be answered. It was the first time that DNA typing had been used in a legal case in the United States. It pre-dated the *Andrews* case (Case 10.3) which represented the first use of DNA in the United States in a criminal matter.

Later, Cetus scientists devised an additional typing system officially called "PM," but widely referred to as "Polymarker" among forensic scientists. The same design was used for PM as had been used for HLA-DQA1. Polymarker actually consisted of five separate genetic loci. Once PM was available, the HLA-DQA1 and PM loci were combined into a typing system having a total of six genetic loci.

For a number of years, the HLA-DQA1 and PM typing systems were the only PCR-based methods available. They were widely used in many laboratories. Some laboratories attempted RFLP typing on specimens first. If there was insufficient DNA or if RFLP did not yield satisfactory results, the PCR-based methods were then used. Other laboratories never developed the ability to do RFLP, and they did PCR-based techniques instead. In the years when the DNA typing options were RFLP or PCR-based reverse dot-blot systems, RFLP was preferable where possible, because it usually provided considerably better discrimination of individuals in the population (individualization), and because only RFLP data were databased (see later).

Current DNA Typing Methods— Short Tandem Repeats (STRs)

From the beginning of forensic DNA typing development, it was recognized that RFLP was too slow and not sufficiently sensitive for widespread forensic casework and database demands. But, at the time, there were no alternatives. As PCR-based methods were developed, it was clear that ideal forensic methods would be based on the PCR, and that they would have to provide a level of individualization as good as or better than the original RFLP methods.

We noted previously that RFLP typing took advantage of several VNTR genetic loci. Several different kinds of VNTR loci can be distinguished based on the size of the repeat unit. The loci used in RFLP typing have the longest repeat units, 50 or more base pairs. They are sometimes called **minisatellites.** Another category of VNTR has a repeat unit length of 15 to 20 base pairs. An example of that one is called D1S80. In the time period when HLA-DQA1 and PM were the primary PCR-based typing systems, Cetus (Roche) also developed and marketed a typing kit based on PCR and D1S80. Some laboratories used this typing kit in conjunction with HLA-DQA1 and PM in their casework. The category of VNTR that forms the basis of current DNA typing methods has repeat units of four or five base pairs. There are hundreds of these loci in the human genome. In the end, 13 loci were chosen, because this number provided a very high level of individualization. These short unit-repeat loci are called **short tandem repeats (STRs.)** They may also be called **microsatellites.** Typing the 13 chosen STR loci provides a high level of individuality in the population, thus minimizing the probability of chance duplicates in the databases.

Several things had to be considered in choosing the STR loci that would be typed using this newer, faster DNA technology. First, a big advantage of DNA typing is that a person's DNA profile can be placed into a database. If that profile shows up in some subsequent situation, the database can be searched and the person found. We will discuss databases in more detail later. But from the beginning, the intention was to have all the forensic labs in the United States participate in entering profiles into the databases and then to be able to later search the databases for unknown profiles. To make this possible, every lab must be typing the same loci, and must be using methods that are reproducible from lab to lab. In other words, a profile generated for a person or specimen in any one lab must be the same as the profile that would be generated in any other lab. For that reason, a set of STR loci had to be universally agreed upon by participating labs.

Another consideration was the degree of individualization that the profile would have in the population. This matter is further discussed later. Briefly though, it should be clear that the more loci that were typed and included in the profile, the fewer the people who would be expected to have that total profile; that is, the greater the individualization. There were also some technical reasons underlying the choice of the 13 STR loci.

Many laboratories in the United States type the STR loci using instruments from Applied Biosystems based on a technique called "capillary electrophoresis." Capillary electrophoresis is just a variant of the electrophoresis process described in Chapter 9. These instruments also use laser light sources to induce fluorescence in the amplified STR

Case Study 10.3

Tommy Lee Andrews—The First DNA Criminal Case in the United States

On May 9, 1986, a young woman in Orlando, Florida, was sexually assaulted in her home by a stranger. Investigation revealed a fingerprint outside her home, leading to the arrest of Tommy Lee Andrews. The victim identified Andrews as her attacker and the fingerprint was identified as his. However, a trial jury was unable to reach a verdict, and the judge had to declare a mistrial. Prosecutors vowed to retry Andrews, who was a suspect in several sexual assaults.

While preparing their case for retrial, they heard about a new form of biological evidence testing—DNA typing. It had been used in the United Kingdom, but not previously in the United States in a criminal proceeding. The state made arrangements for the semen evidence from the case to be analyzed, along with known specimens from the victim and Andrews, using RFLP DNA typing. At the time, no government labs were set up to do the testing, and the evidence was tested by Lifecodes Corporation in New York, one of the early entrants to forensic DNA analysis.

The RFLP pattern of DNA recovered from semen evidence in the victim matched that of Andrews. The victim could be excluded as the source of the pattern. The second trial court admitted the DNA evidence, and the second trial jury heard from a Lifecodes scientist that the odds of the DNA being from someone other than Andrews by chance were 1 in 10 billion. The defendant was convicted and sentenced to long prison terms for sexual assault and robbery.

A Florida appellate court upheld the trial court's decision in admitting DNA in the trial, and the conviction stood.

This trial, in late 1987, was the first time DNA evidence was introduced into a criminal proceeding in the United States.

products and measure it. Software supplied with the computer that controls the instrument analyzes all the data and translates it into STR types (Figure 10.9). See the box "More on the Science: DNA Electrophoresis, Capillary Electrophoresis, and Genetic

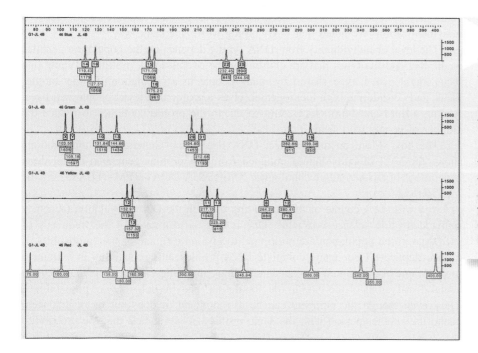

Figure 10.9

This is an example of the results from typing nine of the thirteen possible STR loci used in forensic DNA typing. Another typing kit is used to profile the other four loci. Computer software assigns genotypes to each locus based on its programmed algorithms. The profile also provides gender (XY for males, XX for females). Forensic DNA scientists analyze results like this to reach conclusions about evidence and known control person DNA profiles.

DNA Electrophoresis, Capillary Electrophoresis, and Genetic Analyzers

In Chapter 9 in a "More on the Science" box, we described electrophoresis and isoelectric focusing. Electrophoresis is the separation of charged molecules (proteins or nucleic acids usually) in an electric field. A solution called a "buffer" solution is used to hold the acidity of the solution constant. Scientists measure a property called "pH" to determine acidity, and buffer solutions have constant pH.

In a buffer solution, a protein or nucleic acid molecule has a constant net charge, because its net charge is determined by the acidity of the solution in which it is dissolved. As a result, it will move in a particular direction in an electric field.

Electrophoresis is used all the time in DNA analysis (see Figure 10.3 for example). At pH values around neutrality, DNA is very negatively charged and will migrate toward the + pole in an electrophoresis setup. DNA scientists use electrophoresis to evaluate the quality and the amount of DNA isolated from cells, and to look at the products of the PCR reaction. This kind of electrophoresis is regularly done in gels made from a substance called "agarose."

Many laboratories, as noted, use genetic analyzers from Applied Biosystems for their DNA typing and profiling. These genetic analyzers can also be used for DNA sequencing. They employ a special kind of electrophoresis known as *capillary*

electrophoresis (CE). CE is not different in principle from the other kinds of electrophoresis we have talked about. But CE is done in very finely drawn glass capillary tubes, and the molecules that are being separated (DNA fragments in this case) move in a viscous polymer solution.

The "analyzer" portion of the instrument consists of a laser and a detector system capable of seeing fluoresced light of various wavelengths (see in the Appendix—Scientific Tools of the Trade). In forensic DNA analysis, certain dyes that can be excited by the wavelength of the laser are used to make the PCR primers. Since the primer is incorporated into the PCR product, every molecule has the dye. The capillary electrophoresis separates the molecules on the basis of size to some extent (in addition to the separation based on net charge). Smaller molecules move through faster than larger ones. DNA scientists have control over the size of PCR products because they can position the primers anywhere they want (within certain limits). When a molecule with a dye passes by the laser beam, it is excited, and fluoresces at a characteristic wavelength that is picked up by the detector.

The whole system can be made more efficient by using different dyes on different primer molecules. Now it is possible for molecules, even if they are the same size, to be distinguished by the detector because the fluorescence of each dye used is of a different wavelength. In this way, many STR DNA regions can be analyzed simultaneously.

Analyzers" for further discussion on DNA electrophoresis and genetic analyzers. There are also laboratories that use polyacrylamide gels to separate the amplified STR fragments and determine the types.

The Power of DNA to Individualize Biological Evidence

In chapter 9, we discussed how a combination (i.e., a profile) of the classical (conventional) genetic types could be used to give greater and greater degrees of individualization. We noted that DNA typing works the same way.

The level of individuality from DNA typing depends on the population genetics of the loci and the types that are chosen for the overall DNA profiling. Typing one locus might give a type shared by many people in a population. Typing another locus, and considering both loci together, gives a profile that fewer people will have. Adding a third and fourth locus, and so on, to the profile continues to reduce the number of people who share it.

The box "More on the Science: DNA Population Genetics/Individualization" shows the level of individuality obtained from the profiles generated by all three generations of DNA typing technologies: RFLP, HLA-DQA1—PM—D1S80, and the 13 STR loci.

You will see a couple of things reading through the DNA Population Genetics/ Individualization science box table. One is that the estimates of the frequency of each type in the population are multiplied to give an estimate of the "probability of chance duplicate." For many complete DNA profiles, this probability is extremely low. But one of the common misunderstandings about these numbers is that they are actual distributions of the type in the population. They're not—they're probabilities. Thus, even though the numbers can be astronomical, it does not mean that there cannot be another person with the same profile—it just means that the probability

DNA Population Genetics/ Individualization

As we have noted in the main text, there have been three generations of DNA typing technologies. In the following table are shown the "probabilities of chance duplication" for the RFLP, the HLA-DQA1, PM, and D1S80 loci, and then for the 13 so-called core CODIS STR loci.

The information is presented for Caucasians in U.S. populations, based on population studies that have been done and published in the literature. Similar calculations can be done for other populations and racial/ethnic groups that have been sampled. We present the frequencies as decimal numbers (that is, 0.03 is the same as 3%, etc.). In the final combined profile for each major category, the reciprocal probability of chance match is also given (i.e., 1 out of however many total people).

To give an idea of the range of numbers possible, we present the extreme cases at each end of the spectrum of possibilities—one where a person had the most common type at every locus, and the second where a person had the rarest type at every locus. In real casework, the numbers should always be somewhere in between these two extremes.

Note that in the STR example, a person who had the most common type at every one of the 13 loci would be expected to occur only once in 1.66×10^{11} people. That's a very large number: 166,000,000,000 or 166 billion. Right now, there are about 5×10^9, or 5 billion people on earth. You could say, therefore, that this DNA profile should not occur more than once in the population of earth. Remember, however, that the calculated number is a probability, based on estimates of the population frequencies. Nonetheless, there is discussion among forensic scientists now about stating that a profile like this "originated from the person it matches to a reasonable degree of scientific certainty." For various reasons, many labs do not yet state DNA results in such simple terms. They continue to quote numbers. The FBI Laboratory, however, has adopted a policy that if certain statistical genetic conditions are met, they will testify as to "origin."

DNA population genetics table

Technology	RFLP	
Locus	Most common	Least common
D1S7	0.0127	0.00130
D2S44	0.0257	0.00014
D4S139	0.0459	0.00194
D10S28	0.0139	0.00032
D17S79	0.1207	0.00080
Combined	2.542×10^{-8}	9.039×10^{-17}
Combined: One in	39.3×10^6	1.1×10^{16}

Technology	Dot-Blot and D1S80	
Locus	Most common	Least common
HLA-DQA1	0.1429	0.0070
Five PM*	0.0217	1.3×10^{-6}
D1S80	0.2	0.000001
Combined	0.0006	10^{-16}
Combined: One in	1800	10^{16}

*LDLR, GYPA, HBGG, D7S8, and GC.

Technology	STR	
Locus	Most common	Least common
D3S1358	0.1140	6.05×10^{-6}
VWA	0.1166	2.98×10^{-5}
FGA	0.0655	1.04×10^{-4}
D8S1179	0.0137	1.04×10^{-4}
D21S11	0.0841	6.50×10^{-6}
D18S51	0.0651	4.11×10^{-5}
D5S818	0.2903	6.55×10^{-6}
D13S317	0.1969	1.28×10^{-3}
D7S820	0.1174	6.05×10^{-6}
CSF1PO	0.1954	6.05×10^{-6}
TPOX	0.2762	6.05×10^{-6}
THO1	0.1384	6.05×10^{-6}
D16S539	0.1847	6.15×10^{-6}
Combined	6.027×10^{-12}	3.597×10^{-62}
Combined: One in	1.66×10^{11}	2.78×10^{61}

is low. A second thing to realize is that there are different estimates of probability of chance duplication according to ethnic/racial group. Because the frequencies of types within loci can and do vary in different populations, the different estimates for each of them are commonly given so as not to mislead the courts. Most laboratories can compute probabilities of chance duplication for Caucasians (as in the science box table), African Americans, and certain Hispanic populations. There are also data available for populations such as Native Americans belonging to certain tribes. The main point here is that a defendant whose DNA matches evidence in a case might claim that he is a member of a minority population in which the types observed are more common than in the larger population. It is important to remember that in a forensic case, the race or ethnic group of the actual depositor is not known with certainty. Even in a DNA match case with very low probabilities of chance match, there is still a small chance that another person has the same profile.

Databasing and CODIS

DNA types at individual loci are designated by numbers, letters, or combinations of numbers and letters. A combination of DNA types from one individual (such as a combination of five RFLP locus types, the combination of HLA-DQA1 and PM types, or a combination of 13 STR locus types) is called a "DNA profile." A DNA profile can be written as a set of numbers or numbers and letters. As a result, it is easy with modern computer technology to store DNA profiles in searchable files.

Early in DNA technology development, people realized that from a law enforcement viewpoint, it would be very helpful to store the DNA profiles of convicted offenders in a **database.** Then, if those individuals committed another crime and biological evidence were recovered, they could be readily identified through their DNA profile that was in the file. Since sex offenders typically leave semen behind, having the DNA profiles of convicted sex offenders in a file would help identify one of these individuals if he were to commit another crime after being released from prison. A fairly high rate of recidivism occurs among felons released from prison, and among sex offenders in particular. All the states have now passed legislation enabling storage of DNA profiles from those convicted of felony sex crimes. Many states also collect and store DNA profiles from persons convicted of any felony. There are some variations in the laws of individual states as to which offenders are DNA typed and stored.

Some law enforcement and other public officials have suggested putting criminal suspects in a database. That has not happened in the United States on a broad scale, because of privacy and civil liberties concerns. Recently, however, several states have passed legislation enabling databasing of arrestees and/or suspects. Criminal suspects are put in the database in the United Kingdom. The U.S. DNA database laws are based on a compromise between usefulness to law enforcement and concerns about the protection of individual rights and privacy. Arguments for enlarging the databases rely to a certain extent on the fact that forensic DNA types or profiles are anonymous identifiers—that is, they do not tell you anything about an individual. They can only be used for comparison with a DNA profile generated from a case specimen. Those opposed to enlarging the databases argue that while these "anonymous" DNA sequences have no known function now, a function could be discovered that would then give information about a person. Those same people also argue that once someone's biological specimen or DNA is in the possession of law enforcement, it could be taken out of storage at a later date when the technology might allow the determination of information about someone's appearance or health status from his or her DNA.

There are at least two parts to the forensic DNA profile databases: first, the profiles of convicted offenders; and second, the profiles from biological evidence (usually semen) in unsolved sexual assault cases. The second part is often called the

database

A computer file containing the DNA profiles of convicted offenders, evidence from unsolved cases, or missing persons or their relatives.

"forensic file." There may also be a third file, consisting of genetic information on missing persons. This file can contain the genetic information of the missing person, obtained by typing something known to contain their cells (e.g., a toothbrush), or it may contain parental genetic information that can be helpful in identifying the person or the person's remains. There are also three "levels" of the databases: national, state, and local. The national file is called the **Combined DNA Index System (CODIS)** and is maintained by the FBI Laboratory. Many states and localities have their own databases, called "SDIS" and "LDIS," respectively. This system of interconnected databases enables cross-jurisdiction searches for DNA profiles developed in new cases. You will hear people use the term CODIS for all levels of the databases. The technology allows setting up other databases, such as one containing the DNA profiles of missing persons.

As noted, each state through its own laws controls which convicted offenders are put in the database in that state. Every state allows databasing of offenders convicted of sex crimes. Some states allow databasing of offenders convicted of other felonies as well. State laws also regulate how far back in time the convicted offender databasing program goes, whether juveniles are databased, and whether offenders convicted but placed on probation are databased, among other such matters. Profiles in local files that meet appropriate criteria can be uploaded to state files, and state files meeting appropriate criteria can be uploaded to the national CODIS.

As of mid-2006, there were over 3,139,000 convicted offender profiles in the system, and over 136,000 forensic file profiles. There had been over 32,000 "hits," or matches of case specimen profiles to profiles in the forensic file or in the convicted offender file. Hits to the forensic file help connect cases that police might not otherwise realize were connected. Hits to the convicted offender file tentatively identify the depositor of the biological evidence. The usual procedure is that when a suspect is identified by a database profile match, a court order is requested to obtain a DNA sample from that individual. That sample is then typed for comparison to the evidence sample. This avoids the possibility of an administrative error or sample mix-up in the databasing process causing the wrong individual to be prosecuted.

Case Study 10.4

Developing Suspects Through Database Matches

Several years ago, when DNA profiling was still new, and the data banks were in the process of being built, CODIS "hits" (matches) were something of a novelty. Today, with the technology well established and the data banks much larger, hits are an almost everyday occurrence. A few representative cases will illustrate the point.

There are a couple types of potential CODIS matches. A new, unknown profile is searched against the convicted offender database. A match here putatively identifies the profile, because the offender database profile belongs to a specific individual. We say "putatively" identifies the profile, because the lab does not rely on this "hit" to make the match. A new specimen from the suspected depositor is taken, reprofiled, and compared with the unknown profile. If these are identical, the match is confirmed. We would expect them to be the same, of course, unless some kind of specimen mix-up or labeling failure had occurred. The lab would then calculate the probability of a chance duplication. Another possibility is that the new, unknown profile matches a profile in the forensic file. This links together the two cases from which the profiles came as having the same DNA depositor—but there is no connection as yet to any specific person. Still another possibility is that a new convicted offender profile matches a profile in the forensic file. That connects this offender to a previously unsolved crime.

Case A

In June of 2005, a case in Illinois was solved by a match between a profile in the forensic file and a convicted offender profile. A 2001 sexual assault in Des Plaines, Illinois, was linked to a similar case in Northlake. The suspect's DNA profile matched the crime profiles. He had been added to the database in 2003, following a conviction for driving under the influence. The suspect confessed to the unsolved Des Plaines rape after he was confronted with the DNA evidence.

Case B

A Pennsylvania man pleaded guilty to the rape of two teenagers after his DNA profile, entered into the convicted offender database following a conviction for robbery, matched the semen profiles from the sexual assault cases. Following the CODIS match, witnesses picked the suspect out of a photo array. A new specimen was next obtained, profiled, and matched the male profiles from the sexual assaults.

Case C

In June of 2005, in North Carolina, the SBI Laboratory used a technique called "familial searching" to identify a suspect from CODIS. The lab was searching for the profile of an offender from a case involving the rape and murder of a newspaper editor. The profile was not in CODIS, but another similar one was—one from a person who would have the same parents as the offender being sought. It turned out that the CODIS profile belonged to a convicted offender who had a brother. Police followed the brother and retrieved his discarded cigarette butts for DNA comparison. A match was obtained, and the case was solved.

This case illustrates two points. The first is that there is nothing illegal about the police seizing a discarded item (like a cigarette butt or an empty soda pop can) that contains enough biological material to get a DNA profile. Second, familial searching is still somewhat controversial in the United States, though legal. It is more common in Europe and the United Kingdom.

Combined DNA Index System (CODIS)

A large system of interconnected local, state, and national databases containing DNA profiles; authorized by Congress in 1994 and recently amended to permit databasing of suspects or arrestees provided the latter is legal under applicable state law.

All the states, the U.S. Army Criminal Investigation Laboratory, and the FBI were participating in CODIS as of mid-2006. However, the states are at all different stages of development in their DNA programs. Some states started early and have extensive programs (e.g., Florida, Virginia, and California). Their CODIS databases are typically larger than those in states whose programs are less developed. As of April 2006, the FBI reported that the national CODIS contained over 3,139,000 convicted offender profiles, over 136,000 forensic profiles, and it had had over 32,000 CODIS hits altogether. This information is updated regularly on the FBI Web site at www.fbi.gov/hq/lab/codis/index1.htm. Database matches that have helped solve several cases are described in Case Study 10.4.

CODIS is one of three major databases containing forensic data that are available to law enforcement. The other two were discussed previously. The AFIS databases contain fingerprint images (Chapter 6), and the NIBIN databases contain bullet striation and cartridge case marking images for firearms identification (Chapter 8).

Applications of Forensic DNA Typing

There has been so much hype in the popular media surrounding DNA typing that an uninformed citizen could easily conclude that DNA technology is the solution to every criminal justice problem in the nation. In fact, DNA typing is applicable only in circumstances where biological evidence has been deposited, recovered, and yields DNA that can be typed. It should also be pointed out that even though DNA typing technology has come a long way in terms of automation and specimen throughput, there are still serious backlogs in both casework and in convicted offender database (CODIS) typing in many places. Until these backlogs are cleared up, and there are sufficient resources to keep up with the demands, the promise of forensic DNA typing cannot be fully realized. Two recent reports from the National Institute of Justice documented these persistent backlog problems and made recommendations to provide substantial additional funding to help alleviate them. Further details are described in "More on the Science: DNA Casework and Data Banking Backlogs."

The major applications of forensic DNA typing are criminal cases, civil cases (primarily disputed parentage), and identification of persons when other, easier methods fail or cannot be used, such as in mass disasters (Chapter 6).

Most evidence coming into public forensic science laboratories is from criminal cases. For the DNA section, these will be primarily sexual assault and blood transfer cases. Sexual assault cases outnumber homicide cases in most jurisdictions (see Table 9.1). There are the less frequent saliva or other-than-semen body fluid transfer cases, and situations involving DNA analysis from less usual biological materials like dandruff, fingernail, and so on. Case Studies 10.5 and 10.6 show how DNA typing can include or exclude suspects in criminal matters. Remember that the obverse of the very high degree of individualization provided by the technology is the equally high probability of excluding nondepositors. DNA technology in the criminal case arena has received as much attention for excluding suspects as for including them, especially in some of the cases where individuals were convicted prior to the availability of DNA typing.

It is a good idea to keep in mind, too, that a DNA match establishes a connection between a person and some biological evidence. This connection may be highly incriminating, or it may have an innocent explanation. By the same token, a DNA exclusion shows that a person was not the depositor of evidence tested. Under some circumstances, the exclusion may strongly suggest or almost establish innocence, but in other circumstances it may not. Popular media often say things like "DNA testing proves so-and-so is innocent . . ." or "DNA testing proves so-and-so is guilty . . ." DNA should be thought of as a way of linking or disassociating biological evidence from persons, not as a mechanism for establishing guilt or innocence necessarily.

DNA Casework and Data Banking Backlogs

In March 2003, the National Institute of Justice issued its report to the U.S. attorney general on DNA casework and data banking backlogs. The attorney general had requested the report. The full report is available as document NCJ 199425 from the NIJ.

There were six major recommendations:

1. Improve the DNA analysis capacity of public crime laboratories.
2. Help state and local crime labs eliminate casework backlogs.
3. Eliminate existing convicted offender DNA backlogs.
4. Support training and education for forensic scientists.
5. Provide training and education to police officers, prosecutors, defense attorneys, judges, victim service providers, medical personnel, and other criminal justice personnel.
6. Support DNA research and development.

A substantial appropriation was requested in the president's budget to help address these recommendations and the details contained within them.

In December 2003, a final report to NIJ entitled *National Forensic DNA Study* was published. This document was the final report on Grant No. 2002-LT-BX-K 003 by researchers from Washington State University and Smith, Alling, Lane, P.S. The Executive Summary of Report Findings concludes that the backlog of unsolved rapes and homicides in the United States is massive. Through the data collected from a large, representative sampling of local law enforcement agencies in the United States, the study arrives at the following pertinent estimates:

- The number of rape and homicide cases with possible biological evidence that local law enforcement agencies have not submitted to a laboratory for analysis is over 221,000.
  Homicide cases—52,000 (approximate)
  Rape cases—169,000 (approximate)

- The number of property crime cases with possible biological evidence that local law enforcement agencies have not submitted to a laboratory for analysis is over 264,000.

- The number of unanalyzed DNA cases reported by state and local crime laboratories is more than 57,000.
  State laboratories—34,700 cases (approximate)
  Local laboratories—22,600 cases (approximate)

- Total crime cases with possible biological evidence either still in the possession of local law enforcement, or backlogged at forensic laboratories is over one-half million (542,700).

A significant proportion of law enforcement agencies continue to misunderstand the potential benefits of DNA testing.

While the preceding figures address the first question as to the approximate size of the case backlog, a second question remains regarding how the backlog became so large. The answer to this question is quite complicated, and the phenomenon of a substantial growth in criminal case backlogs involves a variety of factors—some of which are vexing and difficult to manage. However, a series of questions posed to local law enforcement agencies and forensic laboratories revealed several interesting patterns of response that, when considered collectively, begin to provide an accurate picture of how the backlogs tend to develop and why they continue to exist. The following provides some of these responses regarding why cases with DNA evidence have not been submitted to the laboratory:

50.8 percent of responding local law enforcement agencies indicated that forensic DNA was not considered a tool for crime investigations.

31.4 percent responded that no suspect had been identified.

9.2 percent indicated that the prosecution had not requested testing.

10.2 percent responded that a suspect had been identified, but not yet charged.

23.6 percent of responding agencies suggested that DNA evidence from unsolved cases was not submitted for reasons relating to poor funding.

9.4 percent indicated a lack of funding for DNA analysis.

10.4 percent indicated inability of laboratories to produce timely results.

3.8 percent indicated crime laboratory was not processing requests for DNA testing.

Both state and local crime laboratories are overworked, understaffed, and insufficiently funded. Processing times at crime laboratories pose significant delays in many jurisdictions. State laboratories take an average of 23.9 weeks to process an unnamed suspect rape kit, and local laboratories average 30.0 weeks for such tests. The cost for testing these rape kits was estimated at $1,100 per case and does not account for many overhead costs. Both state and local laboratories indicated that personnel needs were among the most significant concerns for their DNA programs. Specifically, most crime laboratories expressed the need for supplemental funding for additional DNA staff; several laboratories indicated that their priority concern was for additional funding to augment current salaries to avoid the loss of skilled personnel to other prospective employers. A strong need was also reported for reagents (chemicals used in DNA analysis) and for technical equipment used for DNA analysis.

Finally, most laboratories also reported that while federal funding has played an important role in assisting with backlogged DNA cases, the proportion of their overall DNA budgets funded through federal sources is minimal. Only 20.5 percent of state crime laboratories receive 50 percent or more of their funding from federal sources; that figure is only 4.5 percent for the local laboratories.

There is additional discussion in the full report on the potential benefits of maximizing DNA analysis in criminal cases.

Case Study 10.5

DNA Inclusions in Criminal Cases

Recently, an Illinois man being held in a June 2003 sexual assault was linked by DNA to an earlier case, from February 2002. This is a case where a DNA profile from the suspect matched the semen from the case under investigation. But when the CODIS forensic file was queried, the profile showed up in the earlier case. This same man is linked to a third sexual assault through a database hit.

If these cases go to trial, an examiner will testify as to the DNA profile matches, and that the probability of a chance duplicate profile in the population is very low, probably less than one in many billion. Since there is no consensual connection between this man and the women, there is no possible innocent explanation for the DNA match.

Today, there are hundreds of cases like this one every week. Many of the cases that reach the DNA section are sexual assaults. As noted in the previous chapter, there are a greater number of sexual assault cases than murder cases. And, as also noted there, DNA profiling is informative (probative) if the perpetrator is a stranger. If the people are acquainted, and the suspect does not deny sexual contact but claims it was consensual, DNA profiling is not very probative.

Similarly, in cases involving blood transfers, DNA profile matches are informative if there is no innocent explanation for the blood evidence. If there is, the profile match carries much less weight in helping prove a person committed a crime.

A project begun at the Cardozo Law School in New York by attorneys Barry Scheck and Peter Neufeld, and known as the "Innocence Project," has worked to use DNA evidence to exclude people who were convicted prior to the availability of DNA analysis. Up to early 2006, the project had established DNA exonerations in almost 175 cases. Cases are screened to ensure that excluding the person convicted as a depositor of the case evidence will essentially establish the individual's innocence. Many of the cases are sexual assaults, and the semen in the evidence was not deposited by the man who was originally convicted. Some states have established their own versions of innocence projects. Further information has been included in the chapter references.

DNA typing is useful in many civil case situations as well. The most prominent of these is **disputed parentage** (usually disputed paternity). In the United States, most public forensic science labs do not do, and have not traditionally done, disputed

disputed parentage

Refers in law and forensic science to a case where there is a question as to whether a person is the true biological father (or mother) of a particular child.

parentage cases. For historical reasons primarily, parentage cases tend to be done by clinical or other labs dedicated to that type of work. Those labs rarely do any criminal casework. Since maternity is rarely in doubt, most parentage cases involve doubtful paternity. The cases usually arise when a mother seeks support payments for her child, and the accused man denies paternity. The cases may also arise through the intervention of the Aid to Families with Dependent Children program in a state.

Case Study 10.6

DNA Exclusions in Criminal Cases

As we have noted in the main text, DNA is as valuable as an exclusionary tool as it is as an inclusionary one. The lead case in Chapter 9 (Dotson) is a DNA exclusion case. Two other cases in this box illustrate the exclusionary value of DNA. One involves an exclusion in an active criminal case. The other involves a postconviction exclusion.

Case A: Exclusion of a Suspect in an Active Criminal Case

In June of 2005, a little girl named Riley Fox was reported missing in Joliet, Illinois. She had been in her home with her brother and father. Her mother was in Chicago taking part in a charity walk. The father, Kevin Fox, told police he had gone to a street festival the night before. He said he had left the two children in the care of their grandparents, and, after picking them up around midnight, he had put them to bed. In the morning, the front door to the home was open, but Kevin Fox said he did not know whether his daughter had opened it and wandered off.

Hundreds of volunteers helped search for the child, and her body was found later in Forked Creek, 4 miles from the family's home.

An autopsy determined that Riley Fox had been drowned. She had also been sexually assaulted. Suspicion fell on the father, and he was questioned and eventually arrested after the police reported that he had given them a confession. Mr. Fox's defense attorney later alleged that the confession had been obtained after lengthy questioning and improper suggestions of what would happen next. The police denied the allegations.

Kevin Fox was held in jail, unable to make bail, for eight months. No DNA testing was immediately done on the vaginal swab taken from Riley Fox. The state police laboratory personnel indicated that they were never given a chance to do the testing before the specimen was sent to the FBI Laboratory. The FBI Laboratory scientists indicated that the prosecutors had told them to stop testing once the confession was obtained. Mr. Fox's defense counsel challenged the state police lab explanation, and she pressed to have the specimen tested at a private lab. This testing excluded Kevin Fox as the source of the semen and effectively established his innocence and the falsity of the confession he had given. There was considerable discussion and finger-pointing about why it had taken such a long time to do the tests and obtain the results. The DNA profile from the swab did not

The states have an interest in trying to determine the paternity of children and enforcing court orders for support, because this can result in savings to the maternal and child welfare program budgets. In a typical case, a mother, child, and putative father are tested. The lab examines the alleles inherited by the child. Then, knowing which ones of those were contributed by the mother, the lab expert looks to see if the putative father could have contributed all the paternal alleles. Exclusion shows that the putative father is not the biological father. Failure to exclude all but proves that the putative father is the biological father because the probability of a chance duplicate in the population is remote. In addition, remember that the burden of proof in civil proceedings is lower than in criminal cases—preponderance of evidence versus beyond a reasonable doubt (Chapter 2).

Once in a while, an unusual case arises where a sexual assault results in pregnancy. In those circumstances, parentage testing can be used to help support a criminal charge against a defendant. Case Study 10.7 illustrates this application.

The third major application of forensic DNA typing is identification of decedents in criminal cases or mass disaster situations when the traditional identification methods (viewing, fingerprints, dental records) cannot be used for whatever reason. With human remains that are fairly recent, nuclear DNA typing may be used for identification. There are two ways this might be done. First, the DNA profile of the remains might be directly compared with that of some reference specimen, such as the suspected person's used toothbrush or a tissue biopsy specimen retained in a pathology lab. Second, parentage testing methods can be used if parents or descendants of the putative decedent are available to provide specimens. With skeletal and/or older remains, mtDNA is the method of choice for identification because it is more robust in the older materials. The Armed Forces DNA Identification Lab (AFDIL) in Rockville, Maryland, has extensive experience using mtDNA typing to identify the remains of U.S. military personnel recovered from war zones, sometimes decades after death (see Case Study 10.1 earlier). It should be noted that DNA typing is the most complicated and costly of all human identification methods and should be considered a last resort. Further, DNA typing for this purpose is not useful unless you already have a putative or suspected

match any convicted offender profiles, nor did it match any profiles in the forensic file. The case is still open and not solved. This case illustrates a DNA exclusion in an active criminal case. Because of the severity of the crime, because it was committed against a child, and because the suspect was the victim's father, the importance of the DNA testing in this case is difficult to overstate.

Case B: Postconviction Exclusion of Ronald Jones

On March 10, 1985, a 28-year-old woman was raped and murdered in an abandoned motel on the South Side of Chicago. Seven months later, Chicago police detectives obtained a signed confession to the crime from Ronald Jones. He was 34 years old at the time, an alcoholic, and lived in the neighborhood where the crime had occurred.

Jones would later claim that he signed the confession because he had been beaten by the detectives. The detectives claimed the confession was voluntary. The confession stated that the victim was a prostitute, when in fact she had no history of prostitution. It went on to say that Jones had agreed to engage in sex for money with the victim, but that she was killed in a subsequent dispute over payment. No physical evidence linked Jones to the scene or to the victim. The confession stated that he had ejaculated, but the

state had contended there was an insufficient quantity of semen for testing. The confession was held admissible Jones's trial in 1989. He was convicted by the trial jury and sentenced to death. The Illinois appellate defender eventually convinced the Illinois Supreme Court to permit DNA testing on the semen recovered from the victim at the time of the crime. The testing was performed in 1997 and showed that Jones could not have been the semen depositor. For a time, prosecutors considered retrying Jones on the murder charge (now decoupled from the sexual assault because of the DNA exclusion), but eventually, in 1999, all the charges against him were dropped, and he was freed.

The Jones case is an example of several hundred cases around the country in which postconviction DNA testing has excluded the convict of being the source of semen or blood associated with the original crime. Around a dozen of the cases in Illinois involved men who were, like Jones, awaiting execution. Then-Illinois governor George Ryan placed a moratorium on executions when these cases began to surface, and he eventually commuted the sentences of all the inmates on death row to life imprisonment just before he left office.

Case Study 10.7

Parentage Testing in Support of Criminal Sexual Assault

A number of years ago investigators from the state Special Prosecutor for Nursing Homes came to a local laboratory for help in a particularly troubling case. They were investigating a sexual assault on a young woman who had been in a coma for nearly 10 years and was discovered to be pregnant during a routine physical examination. Through some interviews, they had developed a possible suspect who had worked at the nursing home at about the right time, and who had been seen leaving the victim's room several times when there was no reason for him to be there.

The investigators felt that they did not have enough evidence to obtain a search warrant to obtain a DNA sample from the suspect. The family of the victim was quite cooperative and allowed a sample of tissue from the fetus to be obtained. This was in the early days of forensic DNA, but some limited work had been done on obtaining DNA from stamps and envelopes and amplifying it using PCR. It was suggested that if they could track down a mailing from the suspect that could be authenticated as being from him, it might provide a partial DNA profile. This was done, and when the possibility of paternity was explored he was included as a possible father. This information along with the other circumstantial evidence was taken to a judge who then issued a search warrant to obtain a blood sample from the suspect.

The victim's parents elected to allow the pregnancy to run to term and when the baby was born, samples of its genetic material were taken. A full paternity trio (mother, child, and possible father) was run, and the suspect was found to be included and the father with a high degree of probability. He was convicted and sentenced to a long term in prison.

identity. The suspected identity enables collection of appropriate reference specimens for comparison. It is remotely possible that a DNA profile from one of these cases could be in a database, but it isn't very likely. In the past decade, DNA typing methods have been used extensively to help identify victims in several air crashes. The most overwhelming application of this kind thus far has been the attempted identifications of all the remains recovered from the World Trade Center terrorist attacks. Many identifications have been made, but the work is slow going because there are so many specimens, because there was not a completely accurate or complete list of all the victims, and there are likely to be many victims for whom no reference specimen is available.

It may be noted that mtDNA is possible in hair shafts. Forensic hair examination and comparison is discussed in Chapter 13. The important points in the DNA typing context are, first, that hair *roots* are made up of cells, and nuclear DNA can be typed if enough of it can be extracted. The hair shaft does not contain any nuclear DNA, but mtDNA typing is possible.

Most operational forensic science labs that have biology/DNA sections can perform nuclear (STR) DNA typing in routine blood and physiological fluid evidence specimens. Some of them may be reluctant to tackle unusual specimens, such as a bone or tissue. However, most forensic labs will send out to a specialized lab any specimens they don't feel they can readily handle in-house. The majority of forensic labs are not equipped to do mtDNA typing. It is done in a relatively small number of specialized public and private laboratories, and it is not a routine method in forensic laboratories.

Newer DNA Technologies

New DNA typing methods are continually being developed. Some may only ever be used in a few specialized labs, or they may become more widely practiced as time goes along.

We noted at the beginning of the chapter that human cells other than sperm and egg have 46 chromosomes. Forty-four of them are paired. The remaining two are called the sex chromosomes. Males are XY and females are XX. In sexual assault case evidence, which is typically a mixture of male and female cells, the only current method for "separating" male and female contributions to the mixture is differential extraction (see earlier). This procedure does not always achieve the desired separation. Further, it only works if the male contribution is in the form of sperm cells. In a mixture of female and male epithelial cells, the DNA will be a mixture. In Chapter 9, we mentioned that men can be azoospermic—have no sperm cells because of medical conditions or vasectomy. Such men do have epithelial cells in semen. And in those cases, a mixture of male and female epithelial cells occurs in semen-vaginal mixtures. In such mixtures, the typing results are more complicated and harder to interpret than results from specimens originating from one person. There are a number of polymorphic genetic loci on the Y chromosome that can be typed. A few laboratories are now able to type Y chromosome loci. The advantage here is that only male cells in a mixture have Y chromosomes. Thus, the DNA types are, by definition, those of the male contributor. Y typing procedures may come into more widespread use.

Now that the human genome has been completely sequenced, a great deal has been learned about DNA variability in the human population. One kind of variability is called the "single nucleotide polymorphism" (or SNP, sometimes pronounced as "snip"). This is the same kind of variability we described in mtDNA— one person differs from another at a particular location in DNA by one base. One person might have C while another has G. There are thousands of SNPs in the human genome. Some number of them could be selected and used to essentially individualize biological evidence, just as STRs are now. Changing from STRs to SNPs would be a sea change in forensic DNA technology. Every analysis would require sequencing. New equipment would have to be obtained and installed in hundreds of forensic labs. SNP typing techniques would require dozens of validation studies to ensure their utility for evidence analysis. Population studies would have to be done to determine the different SNP frequencies so meaningful probabilities of chance match could be calculated. And, perhaps the biggest obstacle, all the databases would have to be redone. Every biological specimen that had been profiled for a database would have to be reanalyzed to get the SNP profile. Forensic DNA typing may eventually be done by SNP analysis, but right now it does not appear to offer any advantage over current technology sufficient to justify the effort and cost of making a change.

It is worth mentioning here, too, that forensic DNA analysis is not always restricted to humans. Animals and plants also have DNA, and efforts are under way to try and exploit the value of plant and animal DNA in forensic cases.

As the genomes of animals are sequenced, and the individualizing segments of DNA identified, laboratories will be able to use technology very similar to what we have described for people to individualize animals, like dogs or cats, for example, if an appropriate specimen is available for testing.

The DNA sequences of plants are likewise being studied. It will take time to work out the sequences of many species, but already there is interest in trying to see whether seized marijuana or cocaine, for example, can be DNA profiled to provide information about where the specimens came from. It might be that plant contaminants in these specimens, such as pollen or bits of leaf material, could also help in this respect. This information can be helpful to investigators who try to track the movements of shipments of illegal drugs.

DNA profiling also has a role to play in the efforts to detect and thwart bioterrorists. The DNA of many infectious disease agents (viruses, bacteria, etc.) has been sequenced, making it possible to detect these agents fairly quickly and unequivocally. Technologies are in the works to quickly take air samples, filter out any bioparticulates, and determine what they are. These techniques can help investigators detect potential bioterrorist threats. Ideally, they would be detected before deployment, but even if it were after the fact, it would help police, military, and emergency service response personnel know what precautions were necessary, and possibly how to contain the agent.

Strengths, Limitations, Promise, Hype

DNA technology is the most revolutionary tool to become available to forensic scientists, perhaps in the whole history of the profession, since fingerprints. For the first time, biological specimens can be effectively individualized—shown to come from one person. Equally important, DNA typing will almost certainly exclude someone who did not deposit a biological specimen. DNA can be typed from many different kinds of biological evidence, making it a more versatile tool in criminal investigations other than blood transfer and sexual assault cases. And the ability to database profiles and search for them at a subsequent time is revolutionary. These data banks represent another large file (besides fingerprints) that can be used to identify specific persons.

There are, however, limitations to the technology. First, many crime scenes or criminal situations do not yield any biological evidence. In those cases, DNA is not useful. And, in many criminal cases where there is biological evidence, there can be a perfectly innocent explanation for the transfer.

Although DNA technology is comparatively straightforward in many cases, complications can arise. Mixtures of DNA from two or more individuals, for example, can become difficult to sort out in terms of depositors. DNA typing from very small quantities of biological materials (like dandruff flakes, partial fingerprints, or one hair root) is of questionable reliability at present. This type of specimen is often called "low copy number." Interpreting the results from typing low copy number specimens is probably not ready for courtroom use as yet.

As we have said, the technology is revolutionary and exciting. And the media have made the most of it—not only in straight news reporting but in popular entertainment programs. The tendency by TV and radio to try to reduce everything to 15-second sound bites, and by all media to oversimplify scientific stories to the point where they are no longer even correct, have not helped the public really understand DNA typing.

One big problem that has received some, but perhaps not enough, attention in the public media is backlogs. Many labs have become overwhelmed with a combination of case materials submitted for DNA typing on the one hand, and specimens from convicted offenders to be typed and entered into CODIS on the other. In many places, there are both casework and CODIS backlogs. None of this is helpful in realizing the full promise of DNA technology. More recently, the federal government has put considerable resources in the hands of the states to help alleviate the backlogs. But it is going to take time.

As backlogs are diminished, we can look forward to a time when cases will be worked quickly and efficiently. In addition, as more and more individual profiles are added to the databases, CODIS hits (matches between database profiles and a specimen profile) will become even more frequent and routine than they are now.

Summary

Inheritance (genetics) is at the heart of DNA analysis and its forensic use in individualizing biological evidence. Human beings have 22 pairs of chromosomes plus their two sex chromosomes in the nucleus of every cell. Chromosomes are the physical units that are passed to the next generation. Male sperm and female eggs contain only one member of each of the chromosome pairs plus one sex chromosome—always X in the egg. When the egg is fertilized, the complete number of chromosomes is restored, and the individual who develops from the fertilized egg has half the genetic material of his/her mother and half the genetic material of his/her father.

DNA is a huge molecule made of units called nucleotides. The nucleotides are abbreviated A, T, C, and G, and the sequence of them in someone's DNA determines the person's individuality. DNA is double stranded. The strands are held together because the nucleotides pair. A pairs with T, and G pairs with C. The double strand has the configuration of a double helix. To make copies of DNA, that is, for DNA to be replicated, the strands must be separated to allow replicating enzymes to gain access to a strand. DNA is replicated by the strands separating, then a new strand being synthesized according to the base-pairing rules. Wherever there is A, the new strand has T and conversely, and wherever there is C, the new strand has G and conversely. Enzymes that perform this DNA replication are called DNA polymerases.

Some regions of DNA are called "coding." Those regions have a sequence that specifies indirectly the sequence of amino acids in a protein. Three bases can specify an amino acid, and all the combinations of three bases are known as the genetic code. In this way, DNA regulates cell function.

DNA is found in the nucleus of every cell in the body. Red blood cells have no DNA because they have no nuclei. The DNA in the nucleus is called "nuclear" DNA. There are membrane-bound structures in cells called mitochondria, which are responsible for producing energy for the cell. Mitochondria have a small amount of DNA, known as mitochondrial DNA. Nuclear DNA is inherited equally from both parents. However, mtDNA is inherited only from one's mother. Two regions of mtDNA vary in sequence in the population and can be used to help individualize biological materials. MtDNA is most often used in identifying skeletal remains, or soft tissue remains in cases of mass disasters. There are many mitochondria in cells, so the DNA in them is present in multiple copy numbers. This is advantageous for forensic work because even if there is limited specimen available, there may be sufficient DNA.

Preservation and packaging of biological evidence for DNA analysis follows the guidelines and principles developed in the previous chapter.

Forensic nuclear DNA analysis takes advantage of the fact that most of the DNA in our cells is not coding DNA. There is a substantial quantity of DNA that has no known function. Much of it is repeat-sequence DNA. Forensic DNA typing takes advantage of a kind of repeat-sequence DNA known as tandem repeats. Tandem repeats are head-to-tail repeats of sequence segments. But the number of repeats is variable among people. This is called variable number of tandem repeat (VNTR) polymorphism. Many people even have different numbers of repeats on their maternal and paternal chromosomes.

Before typing, DNA must be isolated from cells or biological evidence. It must also be quantitated to determine how much total DNA and how much human DNA was obtained. A variant isolation technique, called "differential extraction" allows analysts to isolate "female" (epithelial cell) and "male" (sperm) fractions from mixtures.

There have been three generations of forensic DNA typing. The original method was called restriction fragment length polymorphism (RFLP) typing. It relied on digesting DNA into fragments, separating the fragments, immobilizing them on a nylon membrane, and using single-stranded DNA "probes" to estimate the number of VNTR at several regions. This was the DNA typing method used by Dr. Alec Jeffreys in his original publications. It was used for several years in the United Sates before PCR-based methods were adopted.

Polymerase chain reaction (PCR)-based methods are now used exclusively for forensic DNA analysis. Using PCR, a strand of DNA containing a VNTR region can be copied many times using a special thermostable DNA polymerase and specific primers, and cycling the DNA through temperature changes. For a few years in the late 1980s and early 1990s, PCR-based DNA typing methods called "reverse dot-blot" were used. They had all the advantages of PCR—the ability to work with small quantities of starting material and starting material that was degraded. The dot-blot methods did not type VNTR regions, however, and were nowhere near as individualizing as today's technology. All forensic DNA typing today employs PCR, but the regions are short tandemly repeated sequences (four or five bases). These are called STRs. Thirteen STR regions are used to profile a person's DNA, and that is a sufficient number to effectively individualize. As with the classical systems, genotype frequencies can be multiplied if the DNA regions are independently inherited. The ability to use 13 such regions leads to very small probabilities of chance duplication in the population.

DNA profiles can be saved in computer files and searched for at a later time. The national database of DNA profiles is called CODIS, which contains DNA profiles of offenders convicted of certain specified crimes. Every state now has laws permitting DNA databasing of convicted offenders. States vary as to which crime convictions trigger DNA data banking. CODIS also contains a "forensic" file. This is a file of DNA profiles from evidence in unsolved cases. Finding case-matching profiles in the forensic file connects the cases to a common perpetrator even though he has not been identified or caught. CODIS also contains some DNA profiles from objects belonging to missing persons or from relatives of missing persons. There are local data banks, state data banks, and a national data bank making up the overall CODIS. Recently, there has been some discussion of extending data banking to criminal suspects.

DNA is powerful technology and it can help in identifying suspects and solving a variety of cases that involve biological evidence. However, many laboratories have significant backlogs, and those have to be cleared up before the full promise of DNA technology can be realized.

DNA is just as powerfully exclusionary of nondepositors as it is inclusionary of true depositors. DNA typing has helped undo some serious miscarriages of justice in cases that occurred before the technology was available.

Key Terms

chromosomes (p. 243)
nucleus (p. 243)
genetic markers (p. 243)
nucleotide (p. 244)
sequence (p. 245)
primer (p. 245)
mitosis (p. 245)
DNA polymerases (p. 245)
genetic code (p. 246)
transcription (p. 247)
translation (p. 247)

nuclear/genomic DNA (p. 247)
mitochondria (sing., mitochondrion) (p. 248)
mitochondrial DNA (mtDNA) (p. 248)
tandemly repeated sequence (p. 250)
variable number of tandem repeat (VNTR) (p. 250)
differential extraction (p. 251)
restriction fragment length polymorphism (RFLP) (p. 251)
polymerase chain reaction (PCR) (p. 253)

minisatellites (p. 254)
short tandem repeat (STR) (p. 254)
microsatellite (p. 254)
database (p. 258)
Combined DNA Indexing System (CODIS) (p. 259)
disputed parentage (p. 262)

Review Questions—Short Answer

1. Describe chromosomal inheritance in humans.
2. Describe the structure of DNA.
3. What is the "genetic code"?
4. Where do you find DNA in the body? What is the forensic usefulness of the different types of DNA?
5. How do you collect and preserve biological evidence for DNA analysis?
6. What is RFLP DNA typing and how does it work?
7. What is PCR? How does it work? What are its advantages for forensic work?
8. What are STRs? How does STR DNA typing work?
9. What is CODIS? How does DNA databasing work?
10. Describe how DNA typing works in blood transfer cases; in sexual assault cases; in human remains identification cases.

Fill-in-the-Blank & Multiple Choice

1. The first widely used method of forensic DNA typing is called restriction fragment length polymorphism (RFLP) analysis. The individuality detected in this type of DNA analysis, as it is used by forensic labs, is due to

    a. differences in coding (functional) genes.

    b. variable numbers of tandemly repeated sequences in different people.

    c. slight differences in hemoglobin sequences detected by allele specific oligonucleotide probes.

    d. all of the above.

2. An individual inherits 23 _____ from each biological parent.

3. No two individuals, except for identical twins, can be expected to have exactly the same combination of

    a. blood types.

    b. serum groups.

    c. nuclear DNA markers.

    d. mitochondrial DNA markers.

4. The advantage of PCR-based methods is that they work well with both _____ DNA and require _____ amounts of DNA.

5. All state DNA data banks are currently authorized to collect samples for DNA databasing from

    a. every child born in the state.

    b. every male between 15 and 30 years old in the state.

    c. all individuals convicted of specified crimes in the state.

    d. all individuals arrested for specified crimes in the state.

Further References

Breeze, R., Budowle, B., and Schutzer, S., *Microbial Forensics,* Burlington, MA: Elsevier Inc., 2005.

Cardozo Law School (Yeshiva University, New York) Innocence Project Web site:www .innocenceproject.org. (The Innocence Project was started by attorneys Barry Scheck and Peter Neufeld.)

Connors, E., N. Miller, T. Lundregan, and T. McEwen. *Convicted by Juries, Exonerated by Science: Case Studies in the Use of DNA Evidence to Establish Innocence After Trial.* Research Report, National Institute of Justice, NCJ 161258, June 1996.

Coyle, H.M., Forensic botany: principles and applications to criminal casework, Boca Raton, FL: CRC Press, 2005.

Kobilinsky, L. "Deoxyribonucleic Acid Structure and Function—A Review." In *Forensic Science Handbook,* ed. R. Saferstein, vol. 3, pp. 287–357. Englewood Cliffs, NJ: Prentice Hall, 1993.

Northwestern University, Chicago, IL: Law School Innocence Project, Chicago, IL,www.law .northwestern.edu/wrongfulconvictions/; Medill School of Journalism Innocence Project, www.medill.northwestern.edu/specialprograms/innocence/.

Rudin, N., and K. Inman. *An Introduction to Forensic DNA Analysis.* 2nd ed. Boca Raton, FL: CRC Press, 2001.

Shaler, R. C. "Modern Forensic Biology." In *Forensic Science Handbook,* ed. R. Saferstein, vol. 1, 2nd ed., pp. 525–613. Upper Saddle River, NJ: Prentice Hall, 2002.

Westphal, S.P., DNA profiles link dope to its source, *New Scientist* Print Edition, June 9, 2006.

Chemical and Materials Evidence

The first two chapters in Part Five ("Arson and Explosives," and "Drugs, Drug Analysis, and Forensic Toxicology") concern evidence that requires primarily chemical methods for analysis, and for which individualization is not usually a consideration. The primary goals of analysis with these types of evidence is identification (classification) and in some cases quantitation.

The third chapter in this part ("Materials Evidence") has to do with a large and diverse group of materials that can be evidence in various situations. This category of evidence is often called "trace evidence." The term "trace" comes from the idea that it is often encountered in small quantities. These often very small quantities can still be useful evidence. That is undoubtedly true in many cases, but just as often these items are present in larger than trace quantities. Accordingly, we think that "materials evidence" is a better description and choose to use that term instead.

The most commonly encountered categories of materials evidence are fibers, hairs, glass, paint, and soil. But any of a variety of materials—metal, plastic, oils and greases, cosmetics, and so on—belong to this group. This evidence is generally examined using chemical methods, but it is also particularly amenable to examination with microscopical methods. It is virtually never possible, with methods available today, to individualize materials evidence, but individualization can be thought of as an ultimate goal.

Both hairs and toxicological specimens are "biological." You might remember that, in the introduction to Part Four, we talked about why toxicology was considered along with drug evidence, and why hairs and fibers are considered together. Drug chemistry and toxicology share common analytical methods. Both are dedicated to identifying drugs—the former in seized specimens, the latter in biological fluids. Similarly, hairs are really a type of fiber. The methods used to look at and compare them are similar, as are the conclusions that can be drawn from the analysis. So hairs share more in common with fibers than with blood and body fluids, just as toxicology shares more with drug chemistry.

It is also worth mentioning here that we included gunshot residue (GSR) with the firearms chapter (Chapter 8) because it is so intimately associated with firearms, even though GSR is, in a sense, materials evidence and perhaps, in another sense, a residue similar to arson accelerant or explosives residues. The methods used to characterize GSR are essentially those of materials evidence.

Arson and Explosives

Learning Objectives

- The science underlying combustion (fire)
- Commonly encountered fuels
- Importance of pyrolysis in the combustion of solid fuels
- Useful investigative information available from careful examination of a fire scene
- Primary reasons for individuals setting arson fires
- Proper examination and processing of materials collected in the investigation of suspicious fires
- The most commonly encountered ignitable liquids used as accelerants in arson fires
- Laboratory analysis process for evidence from suspicious fires
- The science underlying an explosion
- Commonly used explosive materials
- Necessary components of an explosive device
- Processing and sampling of an explosion scene
- Laboratory analysis of explosive devices and residues
- Different approaches to examination of exploded and unexploded devices
- How explosives are identified from the analysis of explosive residues

Outline

chapter

11

Lead Case

The Unabomber

For 17 years the FBI had been investigating a series of bombings in the case the agency called "Unabom." On a very chilly day in April in a remote area of Montana there were over 100 agents surrounding a tiny 10- by 12-foot cabin. When a local forest service officer hailed the inhabitant of the cabin, a rather disheveled Ted Kaczynski stepped out and agents served a search warrant and entered the cabin. Within a short time word was radioed to the agent in charge of the massive investigation that the contents of the cabin clearly indicated that they had the correct man. Thus ended one of the longest and most frustrating investigations in the history of the FBI.

However, the difficult job of proving beyond a reasonable doubt, in a court of law, that Kaczynski was guilty of this series of bombings was in many ways just beginning. This reclusive bomber had been extremely careful to minimize the clues that law enforcement could use to find him or prove that he was the bomber. For all those years he had resisted the temptation to preach his cause, thereby making the tracing of this lone bomber almost impossible.

The story started on May 25, 1978, at Northwestern University, where a security guard was injured when opening a package. In total there were 16 bombings over the course of 17 years that resulted in three deaths and quite a number of serious injuries. In 1995 the bomber finally broke his silence with the publication of his manifesto in the *New York Times* and the *Washington Post.* This strange and rambling document concerning the evils of modern industrial society was published partially because the mysterious bomber promised to stop the series of bombings if they would publish the tract. This publication caused David Kaczynski to reluctantly come forward and indicate to the authorities that his reclusive brother, who lived in a small cabin in Montana, might well be the author. This was the first real break in the case and led directly to the arrest of Dr. Theodore Kaczynski as the prime "Unabomber" suspect.

Forensic science had already played an important role in the difficult investigation by clearly establishing that these 16 bombings were all the work of the same individual. Kaczynski had been careful to use as little traceable material as possible in his devices and to remove markings from any commercial parts used. After all, he was an individual of great intellect with a Ph.D. in mathematics; he had a short career as a college professor before becoming so estranged

Theodore Kaczynski, suspected of being the Unabomber, is escorted by federal law enforcement officers in April of 1996.

from society that, with his brother's financial help, he bought the tiny cabin in which he lived in seclusion and fashioned his bombs.

The initial role of forensic science and physical evidence was to convince the FBI that one individual was responsible for the construction of a continuing series of bombs. This belief was based on unmistakable similarities in the construction of the bombs sent to individuals with no obvious connection to one another and over an extended period of time. Just three of the many characteristics that led to this conclusion were similarly constructed electrical fusing systems, highly unusual loop switches, and the fact that all but one of the bombs were enclosed in handmade wooden enclosures. In addition, the bomber used end caps held in by retaining pins to seal the pipes containing the explosive material; this was a system virtually unique to the Unabomber's bombs. Although the series of bombs showed evolving sophistication of construction and increasing emphasis on causing serious damage and injury, the careful examination of materials recovered after each explosion showed these consistent and very unusual characteristics. In addition, each of the devices after the first two was found to have a small metal plate with the letters "FC" stamped into it. Many additional highly technical characteristics also strongly indicated a common source for this series of devices.

Once Dr. Kaczynski was identified and in custody, there remained the problem of proving in court that he was indeed the Unabomber. The fact that he was a recluse and a highly intelligent individual made this task much more difficult. There were no witnesses to any of the incidents since he either left the packages or sent them through the mail. In fact, the famous Unabomber image that was circulated for years was based on a description given by one individual who had seen someone walking away from an area shortly before a bomb went off. Again the burden would fall on examination of physical evidence. Fortunately, Kaczynski's tiny cabin proved to be a treasure trove of evidence that could be used to link him to the series of bombings.

The listing of items removed from that cabin, which had no running water or electricity, runs to about 700 items and included all the necessary materials to construct explosive devices, including some of the highly unusual items already mentioned, such as his unusual electrical fusing systems, loop switches, and many kinds of wood for construction of the boxes. In addition, there were clearly labeled and neatly stored samples of many different chemicals associated with homemade explosives, including the ones used in his devices. He had all the necessary tools, pipes cut to the size he used in his bombs, and many other important linkages to his style of improvised explosive device. Further, the investigators found a completed device and another partially completed one. Other important items of physical evidence included numerous handwritten notebooks with meticulous descriptions of his experiments to develop his style of device and constant efforts to improve the devices. Several typewriters were also found that could be linked to his manifesto and some of the mailing labels, portions of which had been recovered after most of the explosions. He had notes that listed the individuals to whom he had sent bombs and other individuals who appeared to be under consideration as possible recipients of future devices.

There was much legal maneuvering but a jury was picked and pretrial motions were all filed, when, just before testimony was to start, Dr. Kaczynski's motion to defend himself was denied and he decided to plead guilty in exchange for an agreement that he would not receive the death penalty but would spend the rest of his life in prison with no chance of parole.

Sources: D. Johnston, "Success Took Seventeen Years," *New York Times,* May 5, 1998; www.crimelibrary.com/terrorists_spies/terrorists/kaczynski/1.html; Affidavit of Assistant Special Agent in Charge Terry D. Turchie, U.S. District of Montana, www.courttv.com/archive/casefiles/unabomber/documents/affidavit.html, and The Unabomber case, www.unabombertrial.com/archive/1998/01298.07.html.

Section 1: Fire and Arson

Understanding some of the basic chemistry and physics of fire is important to understanding the most effective ways to investigate suspicious fires. Therefore, a look at the nature of combustion is a good starting point.

The Combustion Reaction—Flaming Combustion and Glowing Combustion

To a chemist, **combustion** is simply a rapid oxidation reaction—the combination of oxygen, usually from air, with carbon from some sort of carbonaceous fuel. When oxygen and a carbon source combine with each other to form carbon dioxide and water, the resulting chemical reaction gives off heat. Chemical reactions that give off heat are called **exothermic** reactions, and the combustion reaction is highly exothermic. When the reaction is complete, all the hydrogen in the fuel is converted to water (H_2O) and all the carbon is converted to carbon dioxide (CO_2). When you "flick your Bic," you see a flame caused by butane lighter fuel reacting with oxygen from the air to form carbon dioxide and water. In real fires the reaction is not always complete, but the vast majority of the fuel is converted to carbon dioxide and water. Where combustion is not complete, an important product is carbon monoxide. Because fires seldom have ideal conditions, carbon monoxide poisoning is a frequent cause of death at fire scenes.

Necessary Components for Combustion— Fuel, Oxygen, and Ignition

Like most chemical reactions, oxidation requires something to get it started. Once the reaction begins, under most conditions, it gives off enough heat to keep itself going. Three common mnemonic devices can be used to help remember the requirements for a successful fire (oxidation reaction): the fire triangle, the fire tetradehron, and the fire pentagon (Figure 11.1). The fire triangle shows diagrammatically that you need fuel, usually something that has carbon in it; oxygen, normally air; and heat to get a fire started. The fire tetrahedron has four sides, and adds an additional chemical factor: free radical reactions, or chain reaction. The fire pentagon is a little more complete description of what is needed to have *sustained* combustion, that is, a fire. Three of the five sides of the pentagon are identical to those in the triangle: fuel, oxygen, and heat; a fourth is identical to the fourth side of the tetrahedron: free radical reactions. In addition, the pentagon represents an additional component: ignition, something to get the combustion started, and a sustainable chain reaction. This

combustion

The combination of a fuel with oxygen to produce highly oxidized products and heat.

exothermic

Giving off heat, usually applied to a chemical reaction.

Figure 11.1

Mnemonic devices used to remember the factors and conditions required for sustained combustion: fire triangle, fire tetrahedron, and fire pentagon.

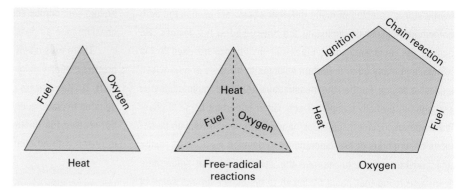

is the chemist's way of saying there is nothing present to keep the heat produced from sustaining the chemical reaction. Certain materials can interrupt the combustion reaction, either by reducing the heat or the chain reaction necessary to maintain the fire. These materials are good candidates for preventing or extinguishing fires. The most common and obvious one is water. Water is capable of "absorbing" considerable heat. It helps extinguish a fire by removing the heat necessary for the sustained reaction. Other chemicals that interrupt the chain reaction are used to make fire-retardant materials (e.g., fabrics for children's sleepwear or upholstery in airplanes) or may be used in chemical fire extinguishers.

The two major types of combustion are flaming combustion and glowing combustion. An important feature of **flaming combustion** is the need to have both the fuel and the oxygen in the gas phase. This is not intuitively obvious because a person can put a match to a piece of paper (a solid, and clearly not in the gas phase) and see a flame almost immediately. Nonetheless, to have flaming combustion, the general rule is that both the fuel and the oxygen must be in the vapor phase. For sufficient heat to be produced to sustain the rate of combustion, the fuel and the oxygen have to interact with each other rapidly, and they can do so only at a high enough rate when they are both in the vapor phase. Since the reaction is using the oxygen from the air, which is already the vapor phase, the issue is getting the fuel to be a vapor. A spark and/or heat is required to get the fuel into the vapor phase. As will be discussed later, one of the other roles for heat is breaking down most solid fuels to produce products that are vapors or can be easily vaporized. Most common solid fuels (wood, wax, paper) can either be readily vaporized or can be broken down by heat to produce materials that are readily vaporized.

There are a few solid fuels that cannot be easily vaporized. Charcoal is a common example. That is why charcoal lighter fluid or an electrical heater is needed to get a charcoal fire started. Although the charcoal will burn and give off a great deal of heat once started, flames are typically not visible (once the lighter fluid burns off). The charcoal is still burning and it will eventually be completely consumed—transformed from carbonaceous material to carbon dioxide, water, and a little bit of ash. What is occurring here is called **glowing combustion** (Figure 11.2), where the fuel is a solid, and the oxygen is in the vapor phase. The combustion reaction is not rapid enough to produce a flame, although it is rapid enough to sustain itself and give off sufficient heat to cook food. Glowing combustion is too slow for an arson fire but is fine for cooking and may be important in accidental fires. A lit cigarette dropped into a couch cushion, for example, may smolder for a long time to build up enough heat and transform enough of the cushion material to provide fuel in the vapor phase before it changes over to flaming combustion.

flaming combustion

When oxygen and fuel are both in the gaseous state, the combustion reaction is rapid, producing light as well as heat (flame) at a high rate.

glowing combustion

When oxygen is in the gaseous state but the fuel is not, the combustion reaction is slowed, producing heat but little light.

Nature of Fuels—Gaseous, Liquid, and Solid

The three states of matter are solid, liquid, and gas. Common fuels can be classified into one of these three groups.

Figure 11.2
A campfire with both glowing combustion and flaming combustion.

Common Gaseous Fuels   As indicated in the preceding, both fuel and oxygen must be in the gaseous phase to support flaming combustion. Certain fuels are already in the gaseous phase, and therefore immediately suitable for flaming combustion. The most dangerous of these is hydrogen. Hydrogen not only burns readily and with a very hot flame, but is easily ignited.

On the other hand, hydrogen is the cleanest possible fuel, because the product of its combustion is only water. There is considerable interest in developing ways to use hydrogen as a clean fuel for automobiles. One difficulty is developing safe ways to store and transport hydrogen.

A much more common gaseous fuel is natural gas. Natural gas is used for home heating and cooking in much of the United States and in many industrial applications as well. Where it is readily available, it is usually the fuel of choice. Natural gas is primarily methane, CH_4, which is a gas at room temperature and which burns very cleanly. Similarly propane, another room-temperature gas, is widely used as fuel where natural gas is not readily available. Propane is supplied from tanks to provide readily transportable fuel for hand torches, lanterns, camp stoves, and many other items.

Common Liquid Fuels   Liquid fuels are even more common. Gasoline may be the most well known fuel for transportation vehicles. Many millions of gallons of gasoline are consumed by the automobiles, buses, and trucks that move us and our goods from point to point. Although gasoline is a liquid fuel, some of it is in the gas phase, even at room temperature (as is obvious because we can smell it). Thus, gasoline is a liquid fuel that is easily vaporized and burns quite readily. Fuel oil, on the other hand, also has a strong odor, but at room temperature very little is in the gas phase. In fact, a flaming match can be extinguished if plunged into fuel oil. It is an excellent fuel, however, because once it starts burning, the heat produced easily vaporizes sufficient additional fuel to sustain the fire.

Another common liquid fuel is ethyl alcohol (ethanol). In flaming desserts such as bananas Foster or crêpe suzette, or any other flambé dish, the flame is from the ethanol contained in an alcoholic beverage. Any alcoholic beverage with over 40 percent alcohol, if warmed, will produce enough ethanol vapor to be readily ignited and provide the pretty blue flame associated with a flaming dish

Figure 11.3

A flaming (or flambé) dessert dish. The flames are produced using ethanol from an alcoholic beverage as the fuel. Once the alcohol burns off, the flames will go out.

(Figure 11.3). The ethanol quickly burns off, leaving behind that nice flavor associated with the beverage. Kerosene is another very common liquid fuel that falls between gasoline and fuel oil in terms of vapor above the liquid. It is the fuel of jet engines and lanterns and often camp stoves.

Common Solid Fuels—Pyrolyzable and Nonpyrolyzable There are also many very common solid fuels. Although wood has become a more popular fuel in recent years (wood stoves are quite common in rural areas), it is not usually thought of as a heating fuel. Coal is actually a much more widely used solid fuel, particularly in industrial and commercial heating. Coal is derived from vegetable matter that has been under high pressure and at high temperature deep in the earth for millions of years. During that time, it has been largely converted to carbon, but it does contain other residues from its plant beginnings. It is an excellent fuel that has been used for centuries. Many polymeric materials such as plastics will also burn, but they are not usually used as commercial fuels. Unfortunately, because some plastics produce carbon monoxide, hydrogen cyanide, or other toxic gases when they burn, the combustion of plastics can kill people in accidental fires. Most commercial fuels burn largely to carbon dioxide and water, which are not toxic. Finally, a common solid fuel is charcoal. Charcoal is perhaps best known as the fuel for grilling food in the backyard. It is not hard to light, and it produces that nice smoky taste so desirable to many. Charcoal is wood that has been very slowly heated and burned in an oxygen deficient atmosphere, until it is essentially pure carbon. That is why charcoal will not vaporize and will only burn slowly at its surface, producing a nice even heat for a long time, but not producing a flame. The flames we see on the barbecue grill are from fats and oils dripping from the food and then vaporized and ignited by the hot charcoal.

Characteristics of Fuels—Measures of Combustibility

Fuels are characterized by certain features related to their combustibility. Appreciation of these properties can help in the investigation of suspicious fires.

Flash Point and Fire Point

Two of the most common measures of combustibility are flash point and fire point (Table 11.1). **Flash point** is the lowest temperature at which a liquid produces enough vapor to be ignited by a small flame. This was originally done in an open-cup flash-point tester. The flash-point tester has a little cup in which the flammable liquid is placed so that it can be slowly heated and a small flame can be swung over the cup. The cup is heated and tested with the flame until it ignites; the lowest temperature that produces ignition is the flash point. Flash point is a very important characteristic of a fuel because it indicates the temperature below which it is safe to handle the fuel with little danger of accidental ignition. Simply, if a fuel has a very low flash point, then it vaporizes easily and must be handled with great care; and if it has a high flash point, it is not very easy to light and is safer to handle.

flash point

The temperature at which a fuel in the presence of oxygen in air has sufficient material in the gaseous phase to be ignited by a small flame or other source of ignition.

Table 11.1
Properties of representative fuels in order of increasing boiling point

Material or fuel	Flash point, °F	Boiling point, °F	Flammable range, %	Ignition temperature, °F
Hydrogen	very low	−423	4.1–74	1075
Carbon monoxide	very low	−313	12–75	1290
Methane	very low	−258	5.5–14	1200
Ethylene (ethene)	very low	−155	3–34	1010
Ethane	very low	−126	3.2–12.5	986
Acetylene (ethyne)	very low	−119	2.5–80	635
n-Propane	very low	−44	2.4–9.5	874
n-Butane	−216	31	1.6–6.5	806
Ethyl ether (diethyl ether)	−49	94	1.8–~50	355
n-Pentane	−40	97	1.4–8.0	588
Petroleum ether (benzine)	−40	95–175*	1.4–5.9	475
Gasoline	−50	102–230*	1.3–~6	495
Acetone	−4	134	2.2–13	1000
Methyl alcohol (methanol)	54	148	6–36.5	880
n-Hexane	−7	156	1.2–6.9	477
Ethyl alcohol (ethanol)	48	173	3.3–19	800
Methylethyl ketone (2-butanone)	35	175	1.8–11.5	960
Benzene	50	176	1.4–8	1075
Isopropanol (2-propanol)	53	180	2–12	852
n-Heptane	30	209	1.1–6.7	~450
Toluene	50	231	1.3–7	1025
Butyl alcohol (n-butanol)	97	243	1.5–11	695
n-Octane	56	258	0.9–~6	450
Cellosolve (2-ethoxyethanol)	111	275	2.6–16	460
Naphtha (Stoddard solvent)	100–110	300–400*	1.–~6	450
Kerosene	110–185	300–600*	1.2–~6	490
Ethylene glycol	232	388	3.2–?	775

*Liquids that are complex mixtures have a boiling range rather than a boiling point. In addition, mixtures from different sources are often not the same composition. Thus, differences in both boiling range and flash point can be expected with such mixtures.

NOTE: The data in this table were taken from several sources. These include *The Merck Index,* Merck and Co., Rahway, NJ; the *Handbook of Chemistry and Physics,* Chemical Rubber Co., Cleveland, Ohio; and "Properties of Flammable Liquids, Gases and Solids," *Loss Prevention Bulletin* No. 36-10, Factory Mutual Engineering Division, Boston, 1950. These figures should be taken as approximations. The various sources did not always agree on the exact values, although agreement on the boiling points of pure compounds was good. Most of the flash-point figures are "closed-cup" values. Others were not specified. Closed-cup values are always somewhat lower than open-cup values.

fire point

The temperature at which a fuel in the presence of air will ignite without an external source of ignition.

flammable range

The range of concentrations of a fuel in air that will support combustion.

Of course, room-temperature gaseous fuels have flash points below room temperature. The **fire point** is the temperature at which there is enough heat to cause combustion even in the absence of a source of ignition.

Notice how flash points roughly parallel boiling points. The correlation is particularly good with chemical compounds within a single class. Generally, deviations from a good correlation are caused by differences in other combustion properties. This is particularly true of the influence of the lower flammable limit. The correlation does not extend to ignition temperature. In fact, within the same family of compounds a negative correlation is seen.

Flammable Range   Another useful measurement used to characterize fuels is the flammable range (Table 11.1). **Flammable range** is a measure of the percentage of the fuel that, when mixed with air, is needed to sustain combustion. For sustained combustion, the correct ratio or amounts of fuel and oxygen must be present for the chemical reaction of combustion to be self-sustaining. If there is too much or too little of either fuel or oxygen, conditions are not ideal, and combustion will not be sustained. Each fuel has a particular range of fuel-to-air ratios that will sustain combustion. Hydrogen is particularly dangerous because it has such a wide flammable range, from 4 percent to 74 percent, much wider than almost any other fuel. This makes hydrogen a particularly serious fire threat. On the other hand, gasoline, which we think of as very flammable, is only flammable in the 1 percent to 6 percent range. If you have significantly more than 6 percent of gasoline vapor mixed with air, it will not burn. Most common liquid fuels have a similar flammable range, in the 2 percent to 10 percent range.

Relative Vapor Density   Since carbon dioxide is heavier than air, it will tend to settle and push the air away from areas near the floor (see the box "More on the Science: Relative Vapor Density"). If there is limited ventilation, the carbon dioxide will displace the needed oxygen (in the air) and slow the burning process. That is why carbon dioxide fire extinguishers are effective. If the carbon dioxide is directed to an area of active burning, it tends to keep the oxygen away and slows down or even extinguishes the fire.

Several other important consequences can result from vapor density effects. People lying on the floor or ground in an area where there is or has been a sizable fire can be suffocated by the carbon dioxide, because the oxygen they need to breathe has been displaced by carbon dioxide.

Pyrolysis of Solid Fuels   Solid fuels are as important as liquid or gaseous fuels, but their combustion is more complex because they have to be converted into more volatile (gaseous) material before they can take part in flaming combustion. Everyone has seen wood burning, but we all know that wood does not vaporize readily. Gasoline or alcohol spilled onto a surface will evaporate in a short time even at normal room temperature, but solid materials like a log or some sawdust on the same surface will not. Yet, everyone has seen the glow of a campfire, or a wood fire in a fireplace (Figure 11.2), or more tragically, a wood frame house being violently consumed by fire. However, if you looks closely at a wood fire, you will see that the fire is actually burning just a little bit above the surface of the wood. The flames do not touch the wood but are actually an eighth or quarter of an inch above it. The reason solid fuels can be burned is that once the ignition has taken place, there is **pyrolysis.**

Pyrolysis is a process by which solid materials are decomposed by heat. When a solid fuel is heated sufficiently, it starts to break apart and form smaller molecules that are vaporizable, and it will then support flaming combustion. As the combustion continues, the heat produced will then pyrolyze more of the solid fuel to sustain the combustion process.

With a solid fuel like wood, enough heat must be produced to drive out the resinous materials, which are volatile enough to vaporize and burn, in turn

pyrolysis

The process whereby a material with little vapor pressure is broken down by heat, usually in the absence of oxygen, to produce flammable products with significant vapor pressure.

Relative Vapor Density

Another important property of both fuels and combustion products is called the relative vapor density. A rule in chemistry says that one mole of a chemical compound, which is an amount equal to its molecular weight expressed in grams, will occupy a volume of 22.4 liters at standard temperature and pressure. In other words, when one vaporizes water, which has a molecular weight of 18, a little over one-half a shot glass (18 grams) will produce 22.4 liters of gas (steam) at about room temperature at approximately atmospheric pressure. That is roughly a volume the size of a 5-gallon can. Whatever the material, the molecular weight of it in grams it will occupy 22.4 liters. Thus, if a fuel has a molecular weight of 400, there will be 400 grams of that fuel in about 5 gallons of vaporized fuel. Therefore, the higher the molecular weight of a material, the more of that material will be needed to occupy 22.4 liters when in the gas phase. Air is about 79 percent nitrogen and 21 percent oxygen and has small amounts of several other gases. Nitrogen has a molecular weight of 28, oxygen has a molecular weight of 32, so you could estimate the molecular weight of the gaseous mixture called air at about 29. If you have a mixture of gases like air that has an average molecular weight of 29, then 29 grams of it too will occupy 22.4 liters. The net result is that most materials when vaporized are much heavier than air, and a few are lighter. The important fact about vapor density is that any vapor composed of a material that has a molecular weight higher than 29 will tend to settle, because it is heavier than air. It will tend to push down on the air, forcing the air up. Any vapor composed of material that has a molecular weight less than 29 will tend to rise. So hydrogen, which has a molecular weight of 2, is very much lighter than air and it would rapidly rise. On the other hand, carbon dioxide, which is the combustion product of almost all carbon-based fuels, has a molecular weight of 44.

producing enough heat to begin breaking down the wood structure to produce more volatile material. Thus, pyrolysis is what makes possible the burning of wood, plastics, cloth, and other solid fuels. As long as there is adequate fuel and oxygen, the fire will continue to grow in intensity. That is why people who start fires with the intention of burning buildings (which are mainly solid) use **accelerants.** The accelerants will vaporize to get the fire going. Once the fire is going strongly, it will produce enough heat to make the building materials and furnishings viable fuels. More will be said about accelerants later in this chapter.

accelerants

Flammable liquids or solids that may have been used to start or sustain a suspicious fire.

Investigating Suspicious Fires— Arsonists' Motives

The forensic aspects of investigating suspicious fires include a consideration of motive as well as investigating and physically processing the scene. All fires should be investigated, and consideration given to the possibility that they could have been intentionally started. A primary goal of fire investigation is determination of cause. Where there is any doubt as to what might have caused a fire, a careful investigation of all the circumstances should be made to determine if it might have been intentionally set. There are four motives for most arson fires. These are economic, revenge, intimidation, and extortion.

Economic Motives

Investing in property can be a viable way to make money. A person can invest in property hoping that it will increase in value and then sell the property later at a profit. Investment property can be rented to produce a nice return on investment. Sometimes, the desired profits do not materialize. Tenants may seriously damage the property, or the areas surrounding the property may deteriorate, and the property becomes unrentable.

Various fraudulent schemes can be used to make fire insurance collection a profitable option when real estate investments have a negative return. In these schemes, buildings are purchased for almost nothing and the prices inflated by the buildings being sold back and forth between dummy companies set up just to carry out these sales. Finally, the building is burned to collect the artificially inflated insurance value. Owners or people fronting for them in the sales rarely actually burned the building themselves. They would hire a "torch," a professional arsonist, to do it for a fee. Since the actual arsonist has no connection with the financial scheme or building, investigation of such schemes is quite difficult. Unfortunately, although these arsons are planned as economic crimes, and the buildings typically are empty or efforts are made to get the tenants out of the building rapidly when the fire is discovered, things do not always go as planned, and people are sometimes killed in the fires. In addition, the fire makes the tenants homeless.

Arson fires are a criminal activity that is very difficult to effectively police. It is not easy to prove that someone committed arson. In most jurisdictions, the percentage of arson cases where those involved are arrested, convicted, and sent to jail is low. It is important to keep in mind that it is usually easier to establish that a fire was set than it is to establish a good case for who set it.

Revenge, Vandalism, Intimidation, and Other Motives

Another common cause for arson fires is simply revenge. Frequently, boyfriend/ girlfriend disputes erupt, and the individual who feels wronged decides to teach the other party a lesson by setting fire to the place where he or she lives. Also in this category is the devastating situation where someone is ejected from a dance or after-hours club and returns with a flammable liquid to teach the offending club (Figure 11.4) a lesson. Often, many individuals are injured or killed in the ensuing panic. Other major causes for arson fires are vandalism, or intimidation, either for economic or personal reasons; for example, to burn out the undesirable neighbor or to teach the small businessman a lesson for refusing to pay for protection.

Less commonly, arson fires may be set purely for the thrill. Some disturbed individuals may derive a thrill, even a sexual thrill, from setting and then watching a fire. Photographing the crowd of onlookers at a fire scene can be helpful to investigators since such arsonists often need to watch the fire. Fires are also sometimes set to cover up other crimes, such as burglaries or even murders. It can be difficult to tell whether a person who died in a fire was a victim of the fire or the victim of another crime the arsonist was trying to cover up.

Figure 11.4

Happy Land Social Club fire, Bronx, New York, 1990. This fire was deliberately set by Julio Gonzalez, using gasoline as the accelerant. His attempt to get back at a love interest who had jilted him resulted in 87 deaths.

Investigation of Fire Scenes

Fires are investigated to determine the cause of the fire and its origin. Burn patterns can be helpful, but must be interpreted with caution.

Burn Patterns

It has been long recognized that fires burn upward. Although not especially startling, this knowledge is an important factor in trying to figure out how a fire started. Most fires depend on solid fuel once they get started, and solid fuels burn because they can be pyrolyzed into gases needed to sustain the fire, as discussed previously. Since heat travels upward, the pyrolysis occurs in materials above the area where the combustion is producing the necessary heat. In a fire that originated where someone poured gasoline as an accelerant into a fairly small area and ignited it, the resulting fire, if allowed to burn unobstructed, will produce a **burn pattern** that looks like an upside-down cone—this "inverted-cone" pattern is more obvious if the fire has walls or vertical surfaces to climb.

The inverted-cone pattern is a strong indication that the **point of origin** lies at the point of the cone. There are several other fire burn patterns that can help in tracing the pathway of a fire and reconstructing its course. They include melted materials (such as a plastic can), alligatoring, concrete spalling, and even smoke stains and smoke color. The initial objectives of a fire investigation are determining the cause and origin of the fire.

> **burn pattern**
> The pattern of charring and burning left after a fire has been extinguished that may give insight into how the fire developed.

> **point of origin**
> The location or locations where a fire started.

Search for Point or Points of Origin

Identifying the point or points of origin is one of the main objectives of a fire investigation. In the case of the inverted cone, an investigator usually sees the burn pattern as a "V" pattern on a flat wall. Although not always seen, the pattern strongly suggests a point of origin. Multiple points of origin strongly suggest but do not alone prove that a fire was intentionally set. Determination of the point or points of origin is critical to the initial investigation of possible causes of the fire.

Search for Causes

An important purpose of the scene investigation is determining the cause of the fire, including searching for any possible accidental cause. If the cause of the fire is accidental, the point of origin gives one a place to look for the accident that caused that fire. For example, if it was an electrical short circuit, the primary point of origin will be somewhere near a fuse or breaker box, or near electrical wiring. If the accidental cause was somebody cooking pork chops and splattering hot oil that started the fire, the point of origin will be near the stove. Investigators should look for failures of a household electrical appliance, careless smoking, and other possible accidental causes. Interestingly, the toaster is the household appliance that is submitted most often to fire insurance laboratories for examination as the possible cause of a fire. Determination of the cause of a fire is basically a reconstruction. If a thorough examination of the scene is done and all appropriate evidence is collected and analyzed, the chance of a successful reconstruction is greatly improved.

Recovery of Ignitable Liquid Residues from Suspicious Fire Scenes

Reasons for Finding Ignitable Liquid Residues

Even when a fire produces significant damage, debris recovered from the area where the fire started often contains trace residues of an **ignitable liquid,** if one was used as an accelerant. It seems illogical, because you might expect all the

> **ignitable liquids**
> Liquid materials that can be ignited in the presence of air.

accelerant to be burned up. Common accelerants, like gasoline, kerosene, and other petroleum products, are volatile and flammable. Nonetheless, they are usually not completely consumed, because the accelerants soak down while the fire burns up. Gravity and capillary action will cause the accelerant to soak into the area below where it is spread, and the heat from the fire will rise and intensify the fire above where it starts. Modern methods used for finding traces of ignitable liquid are very sensitive, and this makes the search for residues successful more often than might be expected. The longer fires burn and the hotter they are, the more likely volatile ignitable liquids will be vaporized or burned and thus not detectable in debris. Often in rural areas, where a fire may have burned for hours before it was discovered and destruction is complete, finding any trace of ignitable liquid is unlikely.

Notice that the terms "ignitable liquid" and "accelerant" are not completely interchangeable. An ignitable liquid can be used as a fire or arson accelerant. When the laboratory scientist examines debris and finds traces of an ignitable liquid, the expert does not know whether these traces are part of the scene background or whether they may have been used as an accelerant. For this reason, fire debris analysts speak of detecting "ignitable liquid" residues, not "arson accelerant" residues. For many years, laboratories did talk about "arson accelerant" or "accelerant" residues in fire debris, but this terminology issue was recently resolved in *NFPA 921,* a standard and widely accepted reference on fire investigation.

Search for Places to Collect Debris— Sniffers and Arson Dogs

Searches for residual ignitable liquid may be aided by the fact that as the fire burns, pyrolysis converts some of the solid fuels to carbon. Such material may act as activated carbon, which is an effective adsorbent for ignitable liquid vapors in the immediate area and can help prevent their being vaporized and burned. Any unburned ignitable liquid will most likely be found at or near the point or points of origin. That is a major reason that attempting to locate the point or points of origin of the fire is so important. A point of origin is the most logical place for fire debris evidence collection. Fire investigators use burn patterns to assist in locating points of origin, but it may be difficult to see where that fire actually started.

There are instruments that will detect abnormally high amounts of ignitable liquid vapor at a particular location, suggesting that the location may be a good place to collect debris samples. These devices are often referred to as **sniffers.** Well-designed sniffers are most sensitive to hydrocarbon vapors and do not respond as strongly to carbon dioxide. Otherwise, pockets of carbon dioxide remaining from the fire could mislead the investigators. Many jurisdictions use "arson" dogs (Figure 11.5) to aid in locating areas for debris collection. Since certain dogs have a particularly fine sense of smell, they can be trained to use that superb sense of smell to sniff out areas where the odor of common accelerants is detectable. This is similar to the well-known use of dogs as trackers, and to detect drugs or explosive devices. Areas that the dog indicates are sampled, and the debris is sent to the laboratory for examination. Although arson dogs have a good success rate, they aren't always right and may hit on a vapor that laboratory analysis cannot confirm as an ignitable liquid residue.

Collection of Debris Samples and Proper Packaging

Collection of debris requires insight into the fire process and is helped by the techniques described earlier. Areas an investigator thinks might be a point of origin or a location where ignitable liquid was poured should be sampled and the material sent to a laboratory for analysis. One key to successful analysis of debris or of discarded empty containers for the presence of ignitable liquid is proper

sniffers

Mechanical devices that detect gases in the atmosphere other than the normal nitrogen and oxygen and that are used to look for traces of flammable liquid after a fire has been extinguished.

Figure 11.5

An arson dog at work searching for indications of residual ignitable liquid residue at a fire scene.

packaging. Poor packaging was a serious problem for many years. Possible arson accelerants or fire debris that may contain such residues can present special packaging problems. Common accelerants are primarily hydrocarbons, and liquid forms of them will dissolve in many materials typically used for evidence packaging. A more serious possible problem is evaporation of the residues. Fire debris that may contain ignitable liquid residues must be packaged in airtight containers. One versatile and effective container for fire-related specimens is a clean metal paint can (Figure 11.6). They are essentially unbreakable and nonpermeable to any ignitable liquid residues. Plastic bags are not a good choice since residues can be lost by evaporation through the plastic. There are some special double-layer plastic bags designed to retain possible ignitable liquid vapors, but they are still subject to puncture by sharp edges in the debris, which would then allow the residues to escape. Some forensic laboratories provide suitable paint cans to agencies whose samples they analyze. Of course, the cans must be tightly sealed once the evidence has been placed inside them.

Collection of Samples Other Than Debris

Empty cans or containers that contained ignitable liquids at or near the fire scene are important because there is always some vapor in the container, and often there is a small amount of liquid. Usually, a sufficient specimen can be recovered to permit identification of what was in the can. Empty or nearly empty cans (Figure 11.7) that can be associated with a suspect or a suspect's vehicle can be very helpful to the investigation. Investigators should look for ignition devices or devices used to delay the ignition to allow the arsonist to flee before the fire starts. Such devices can be as simple as a candle or as complex as a remote radio-controlled detonator.

Collection of Other Physical Evidence

Once fire debris that may contain ignitable liquid residues has been packaged, investigators should turn their attention to the recognition and collection of other physical evidence. Evidence such as fingerprints, footprints, toolmarks, blood, or

Figure 11.6

A sealed one gallon paint can containing debris from a fire scene. The contents can be examined for ignitable liquid residues that could have been used as accelerant.

Figure 11.7

Cans recovered from near a fire scene. They will be screened for residual flammable liquid.

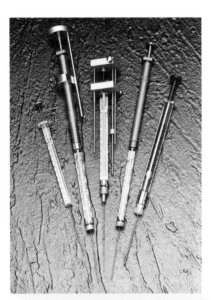

Figure 11.8

Typical microliter syringes used for injecting samples in gas chromatographs. Syringe on the right is a gas-tight syringe with Teflon seal for injecting gaseous samples.

anything else that might be of value to the investigation should not be overlooked because of the preoccupation with collection of debris to search for possible accelerant.

Remember that ignitable liquid residue evidence is useful in establishing that the fire was arson, but it is seldom helpful in identifying the arsonist. On the other hand, an arsonist may leave fingerprints on a can or other item, footwear impressions, even blood if glass is broken. Those types of evidence could prove to be valuable. Recovered timing or ignition devices can sometimes provide a "signature" of an arsonist.

Laboratory Analysis of Debris and Other Samples— Recovery of Ignitable Liquid Residues

Laboratory analysis of debris and other fire-related evidence is a significant part of the work of virtually every forensic laboratory. After the initial examination and description of the evidence, one must prepare the samples for analysis.

Preparation of Liquid Samples

Preparing liquid samples is relatively easy. The sample is drawn into a special syringe (Figure 11.8), which is used to inject it into a gas chromatograph. (See the "More on the Science: Chromatography and Gas Chromatography" box.)

Four Primary Techniques for Preparation of Debris Samples

Most of the time, forensic laboratories receive burnt debris, soggy carpeting, or a variety of other things that may contain accelerant. If there is an ignitable liquid residue present, it is usually in trace amounts and mixed with the debris. There are four commonly used methods of processing such material to try to separate or concentrate any ignitable liquid from the debris. Since fires are usually extinguished with large volumes of water, the ignitable liquid residue may be washed away. It is fortunate that the most commonly used accelerants are not soluble in water. Although they may still be mechanically removed by the flow of the water, if they are absorbed into debris, the water will not extract them efficiently.

Heated Headspace   The simplest of the four techniques is called **heated headspace.** Consider the scenario where the laboratory receives a metal paint can with debris collected from the scene at a possible point of origin of the fire. The examiner will usually briefly lift the lid and take a little sniff. If there is a strong odor of gasoline or other recognizable ignitable liquid, then probably the best technique is heated headspace. It is not the most sensitive technique but it is simple, avoids introduction of contaminants, and works well where there is adequate amounts of accelerant present. If, however, only a burnt odor is detected, then one of the other techniques may be best. Another reason for taking a quick look into the sealed can is to make sure there are no ignition devices present that could cause the closed can to explode when it is heated.

The paint can lid is punctured with a nail, and the small hole is covered with a piece of tape. The can is then placed in an oven set at a temperature that will vaporize any ignitable liquid residue but not create enough steam to pop the lid of the can. Seventy or eighty degrees Celsius will usually work well. After allowing an hour or more for the contents to thoroughly equilibrate, the can is removed from the oven and the airspace above the debris quickly sampled. The higher the vapor pressure of the material, the more will be in the gas phase, and since most accelerants have fairly high vapor pressures, there will often be a significant amount in the gas phase. Sampling is done simply by inserting the needle of a gas-tight syringe into the can through the hole and drawing a small sample of the vapor into the syringe. This vapor sample is injected immediately into the gas chromatograph.

Heated headspace is a very simple technique with little chance for contamination. Nothing is added to the sample, and handling is kept to a minimum. The weakness of the technique is that it is not good for trace amounts of ignitable liquid residues or for high boiling or mixtures of ignitable liquids.

Steam Distillation   **Steam distillation** is an older technique that works quite well, but it is no longer popular because it is time-consuming and there is a real possibility for contamination. In this technique the debris is placed in a large flask and then either water or ethylene glycol is added. The flask is attached to a distillation apparatus and brought to a boil. The vapors that are distilled from the debris are passed through a condenser, and the resulting condensate is collected in a specially designed trap. Any volatile ignitable liquid that is in the debris will mix with the boiling solvent, be vaporized and carried with it into the condenser, and, when cooled, reenter the liquid phase and drip into the trap. If there is hydrocarbon ignitable liquid residue in the condensate with the water or ethylene glycol, it will separate into a second, discernible liquid phase. This second layer can be removed and subjected to gas chromatography.

Carbon Strip or Tube Absorption   **Carbon strip or tube absorption** is now the technique most used by forensic laboratories. The active component of the absorption strip or tube is activated charcoal (Figure 11.9) which is a very high surface area carbon material that strongly absorbs hydrocarbon vapors that come in contact with it. Charcoal absorption strips (Figure 11.10) were developed for the badges that people who work in chemical plants wear to determine any exposure

heated headspace

A technique for processing debris from a suspicious fire in which the debris is warmed in a closed container and then a sample of the vapors above the debris is removed for analysis.

steam distillation

A technique for processing debris from a suspicious fire where the debris is mixed with water in a large flask and the mixture heated until a sizable portion of the water has boiled and been condensed; the condensate is examined for accelerant.

carbon strip or tube absorption

A technique for processing debris from a suspicious fire where the vapors above the debris are absorbed on activated carbon and then washed off with a solvent for analysis.

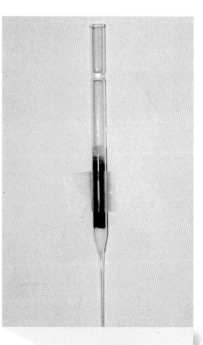

Figure 11.9

A Pasteur pipette containing activated carbon used to absorb flammable material vapors.

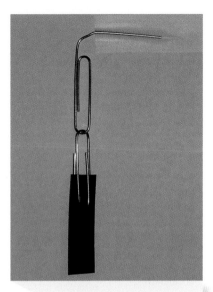

Figure 11.10

An activated carbon strip used for recovering flammable material from debris samples.

to chemicals in the workplace atmosphere. It was discovered that a piece of one of those strips could be used to sample hydrocarbon and other chemical vapors from the headspace over a can of debris from a fire. The ignitable liquid residue isolation technique involves suspending a small absorption strip with its thin coating of activated carbon in a can of debris and heating the can as with the heated headspace technique. During heating, the residues are vaporized and absorbed onto the charcoal strip. The strip is then removed and any absorbed hydrocarbon (ignitable liquid) residue washed off using a volatile solvent such as diethyl ether, carbon disulfide, or pentane. The wash can then be analyzed directly, or gently concentrated by evaporation of the volatile solvent. This technique has proven to be efficient and sensitive for detecting any residual ignitable liquid in arson debris. There are some newer variations on the basic technique, such as the use of solid-phase microextraction fibers, but the basic principle is the same.

Because of the sensitivity of the absorption methods, one must be particularly concerned with avoiding contamination. The strips must be handled carefully, and exposing the strips to the atmosphere in a laboratory where arson evidence is stored has to be avoided.

Solvent Wash   Solvent wash is the fourth common technique for recovering possible accelerant material from fire debris evidence. Solvent wash works better for higher boiling ignitable liquids that cannot be easily vaporized, and for extracting ignitable liquid residue from larger pieces of debris. A low boiling solvent, which can be gently evaporated to concentrate any residue extracted, is used. The items to be treated are placed in a clean container and the extraction solvent added. The solvent is swirled around the debris (Figures 11.11a and b) and allowed to make contact for some time. Until recently, fluorochlorocarbon solvents (Freons) that were available as

Figure 11.11A

Debris submitted from a fire scene being washed with a low boiling solvent to recover any traces of ignitable liquid material left on the debris.

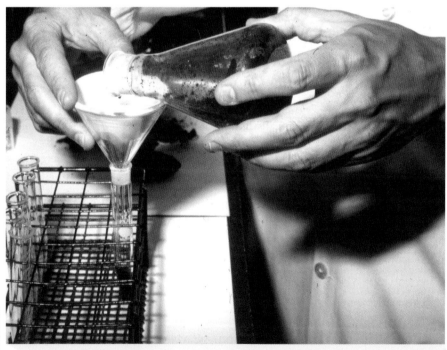

Figure 11.11B

Separating the debris from the washing solvent so that the solvent can be concentrated to analyze for residual ignitable liquid material.

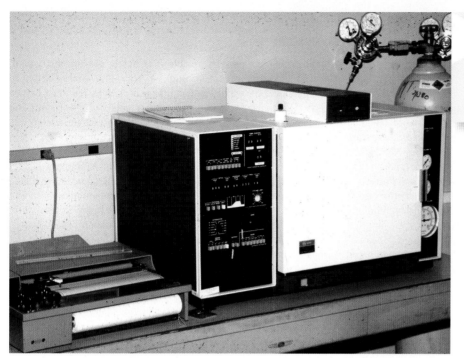

Figure 11.12
A gas chromatographic instrument, the instrument most commonly used in analysis of debris recovered from fire scenes for flammable materials.

refrigeration liquids, were used. Unfortunately, because of concerns about their effect on the atmospheric ozone layer, they are no longer readily available. They were ideal because they were very volatile and could never be mistaken for ignitable liquids since they are not flammable.

There are several solvents available that can be used in place of the Freons. This is a more macro technique than the adsorption tube or the strip and can be used with larger quantities of evidence. After the solvent wash, most of the solvent is removed to concentrate any ignitable liquid residue present, and then analyzed as with any of the other techniques.

Laboratory Examination of Prepared Debris Samples

Once any potential accelerant present in the debris is isolated and/or concentrated by one of the preceding techniques, it must be analyzed to determine if an ignitable liquid residue is present. Chromatography, and particularly gas chromatography (GC) (Figure 11.12), is a technique that uses the partition between a mobile and stationary phase to separate mixtures of chemical compounds (see the box "More on Science: Chromatography and Gas Chromatography"). Since most of the common accelerants are complex mixtures of many compounds, this is an ideal way of analyzing them.

Gas Chromatography   Gas chromatography is the technique of choice in searching for ignitable liquid residues in debris from suspicious fires. Forensic laboratories use it for examination of materials from suspicious fires and for a great variety of other analyses as well.

The concentrated solution of a possible accelerant isolated from the debris is injected into the column and the clock is started. If you have some gasoline residue in that sample, you will see many peaks on a display, one for each different chemical in the gasoline. Because there are over 200 different chemical compounds in gasoline, you obtain a very complex pattern of the emerging peaks

Chromatography and Gas Chromatography

Chromatography is a name given to certain chemical separation methods. The word itself comes from a Greek word meaning "color," because the procedure was originally used to separate colored pigments from plants.

There are several different kinds of chromatography: paper, thin-layer, gas (once called "gas-liquid"), and high-performance liquid. Paper chromatography is a thing of the past. The others are typically abbreviated TLC, GC, and HPLC. Chromatography brings about separation of substances based on their differing affinity for one or the other of the chromatographic "phases." In TLC, for example, there is a solid phase and a mobile liquid phase. A plate, coated with a solid layer of adsorbent, is placed vertically into a tank so that it just contacts a liquid (the mobile phase). By capillary action, the liquid "climbs up" the solid phase. Substances that have been placed on and absorbed into the solid phase ahead of time may have greater affinity for the liquid phase as it moves and be carried along with it. Or they may have more affinity for the solid phase and move more slowly. Because different substances have differing affinities for the phases, they are separated.

In GC, the mobile phase is a gas (helium). The "liquid" phase is a liquefied high-molecular-weight waxy adsorbent that coats the inside of a long column. The substances the analyst wants to separate are heated to high temperatures, causing them to vaporize. The vapors then pass onto the column and are carried along by the gas. The more affinity the substances have for the liquid phase, the more slowly they travel. Over the years, chemists have designed many different liquid phases and discovered many different instrument conditions for separating a variety of different compounds.

The gas chromatograph allows complex mixtures, such as concentrated fire residue sample, to be separated into its many components. The sample is injected into the instrument, vaporized, and swept through a very fine glass, or more commonly a pure silica column (Figure 11.15 by the inert carrier gas. The carrier gas is usually either helium or hydrogen. The flowing gas moves the sample through the column, which has a thin coating of a high boiling liquid on the walls. The thin layer of the liquid on the walls causes the components of the sample to be partitioned between the liquid (stationary phase) and the flowing gas (mobile phase). This partitioning is a dynamic process in which the different chemical compounds dissolve in the liquid coating and then are revaporized many thousands of times during their passage through the column. The different components are moved along through the column while in the gas phase, but they are stationary when dissolved in the liquid phase. Since each different chemical compound has a slightly different tendency to move from the gas to the liquid phase, they take different amounts of time to pass through the column. The more time a compound spends in the liquid layer, the less time it is moving and the longer it will take to make the trip through the column. Conversely, the more time a compound spends in the gas phase, the sooner it will emerge. The net result is that even very similar chemical compounds with only a slight difference in their partitioning between the mobile and stationary phase will take slightly different amounts of time to pass through the column. Any slight differences in their boiling points or their attraction to the stationary phase will cause them to emerge at different times. At the end of the column a detector tells the operator when something other than the carrier gas is emerging from the column. Accordingly, the length of time each component of a mixture takes to traverse the column can be measured accurately. In addition, the sizes of the peaks produced by the detector are proportional to the quantity of the component represented by that peak in the mixture.

Figure 11.15 **A Schematic Diagram of a Typical Gas Chromatograph.**

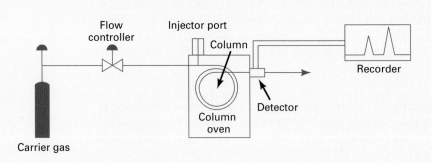

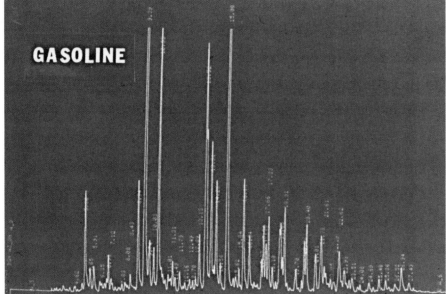

Figure 11.14
A gas chromatogram of a known gasoline standard.

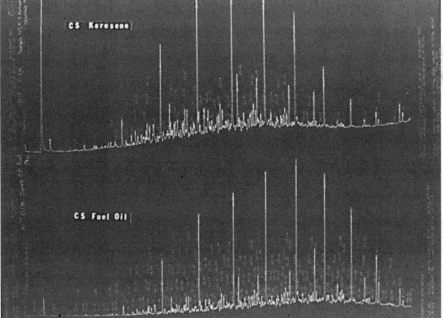

Figure 11.15
Gas chromatograms of kerosene and fuel oil standards.

(Figure 11.14). Some components are major components and will have large peaks, and some are minor components and will produce only tiny peaks. The gas chromatograph is designed to allow the scientist to carefully control conditions so that each run with the same specimen is reproducible. These data are usually collected in a computer and can be examined to compare results from different samples. The pattern of when the peaks emerge, and their relative sizes, is characteristic of the mixture of materials injected.

Accelerant Classification by Pattern Recognition—Importance of Reference Collections
Every time one injects gasoline, even different brands of gasoline, the same general pattern of peaks is observed in the GC. Different ignitable liquid compounds will generally produce very different patterns. An analyst can develop a library of known standards with examples of all the things that anyone might use as an accelerant. Specimens of any material that might be used as an accelerant, such as kerosene, fuel oil (Figure 11.15), paint thinner, lacquer thinner, lantern fuel, and many more,

are obtained from vendors, then injected into a GC, and the chromatograms obtained under exactly the same conditions, to build the library.

The problem with fire debris extracts is that many of the most volatile components of an accelerant tend to be lost and will not be seen. GC patterns from residues of hydrocarbon mixtures like gasoline, kerosene, or paint thinner from fire debris do not look exactly the same as GC patterns from the pure hydrocarbon liquids (Figure 11.16). Thus, although chromatograms from fire debris can be compared with those of liquid accelerants to get some idea of what the accelerant was, GC is not and should not be considered an ignitable liquid identification technique. An analyst may be able to tell from the chromatogram that a low-, medium-, or high-boiling hydrocarbon was present (i.e., a potential accelerant), but generally will not know its identity with certainty. Petroleum-based accelerants are usually divided into nine classes as shown in Table 11.2.

Figure 11.16

Gas chromatograms of highly evaporated gasoline.

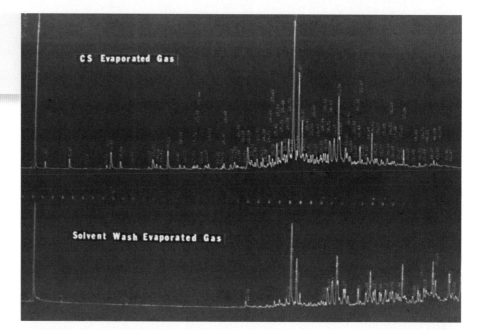

Table 11.2

Classification of ignitable liquids according to current ASTM standards

Category	Examples
Gasoline	Most of the compounds are in the C_4–C_{12} range
Petroleum distillates	Some cigarette lighter fluids, charcoal starters, paint thinners, dry cleaning fluids, and jet fuels; kerosene; diesel fuel
Isoparaffinic products	Aviation gas, specialty solvents, some charcoal lighters
Aromatic products	Some paint and varnish removers, xylenes, toluene-based products, some automotive parts cleaners and industrial cleaning solvents
Naphthenic paraffinic products	Cyclohexane-based products, some lamp oils
n-Alkanes products	Pentane, hexane, heptane, some candle oils
De-aromatized distillates	Some camping fuels, charcoal starters, paint thinners, charcoal starters; odorless kerosene
Oxygenated solvents	Alcohols, ketones, some lacquer thinners, fuel additives, surface preparation solvents, lacquer thinners, industrial solvents
Others—miscellaneous	Single-component products, some blended products, some enamel reducers; turpentine products, various specialty products

*All the categories except gasoline may be divided roughly into "light," "medium," and "heavy," according to boiling points.

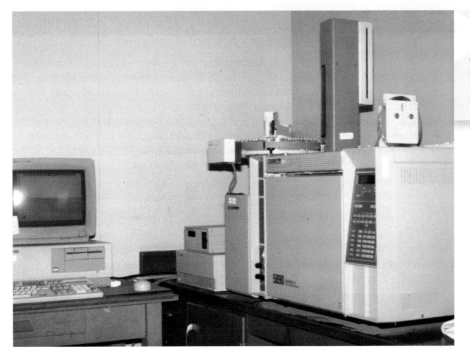

Figure 11.17

A gas chromatograph/mass spectrometer instrument used to help analyze complex samples that pattern recognition fails to identify.

Identification of Individual Components, Identification of Ignitable Liquid, and Indirect Identification   Most forensic laboratories now have an instrument called a gas chromatograph/mass spectrometer (Figure 11.17), GC/MS for short, which allows the identification of each individual peak in a gas chromatogram. The mass spectrometer is used as a sophisticated detector for the gas chromatograph. As each material comes to the end of the column in the gas chromatograph, it is passed directly into the mass spectrometer. As each compound enters the mass spectrometer, it is bombarded with high-energy electrons and as a result breaks into many fragments. The mass spectrometer measures the size of these fragments and plots them out as a graph (mass spectrum). Because virtually every different chemical compound will show its own characteristic pattern in this graph (mass spectrum), it is possible to identify that chemical entity from its characteristic mass spectrum. (See the box "More on Science: Gas Chromatography—Mass Spectrometry" and the Appendix: Scientific Tools of the Trade.) Once a particular chemical compound is identified, a chemist can say whether or not it is flammable and perhaps whether it is known to be a component of any commonly encountered ignitable liquid.

As we noted earlier, when a potential accelerant compound or chemical component is identified in fire debris, it is termed "ignitable liquid" residue. The laboratory does not identify the residue as "accelerant," because even though the compound is a potential accelerant, the chemical identification does not demonstrate why the compound was present at the scene nor that it was used as an accelerant. This is an important point for fire investigators to understand. It is now recommended by the International Association of Arson Investigators and others that the laboratory identify ignitable liquid residues in fire debris according to the categories in Table 11.2.

Although the primary emphasis in analysis of debris from suspicious fires is looking for traces of possible arson accelerants that may remain, experts can sometimes obtain indirect evidence of the presence of an ignitable liquid even if none of the organic components remain. Sometimes, inorganic chemicals are used in petroleum products, particularly gasoline, to improve its properties as an automotive fuel. Because these materials are not volatile, they will be left behind after the organic

Gas Chromatography—Mass Spectrometry

The combination of the gas chromatograph and mass spectrometers is a marriage made in heaven. The gas chromatograph vaporizes the components of a mixture, separates the mixture into its individual components, and feeds each component, one at a time, into the mass spectrometer. The mass spectrometer produces a pattern for identification that usually allows each component to be chemically identified. This combination of separation of a mixture into its individual components (GC) and the ability to then unambiguously identify each of these components (MS) using one very versatile instrument has become one of the most useful scientific tools in a forensic laboratory. Not only is it important in arson and explosive analysis but is one of the chief tools of the drug chemist and the toxicologist as well.

components have all evaporated or been destroyed. For many years, gasoline manufacturers used tetraethyl lead and some other very similar compounds as gasoline additives. More recently, manganese compounds have been used as gasoline additives. Detection of such materials in debris can be an indicator that gasoline was once present.

Comparison Samples In Chapter 3, we discussed different control and comparison specimens that were necessary for the comparison of various types of evidence. These were knowns, alibi knowns, blanks, and substratum comparison specimens.

Until recently, books on fire and arson investigation advised investigators to try and collect unburned areas of carpeting, flooring, and so on to serve as "controls" for the burned debris when the lab looked for ignitable liquid residues. The reason for this advice was that certain natural and synthetic materials contained volatile compounds that produced GC peaks when released from the substrata by heating or extraction techniques. Fire investigators are still advised to collect unburned or unaffected areas of burned objects if they can; sometimes no such area is available. As noted in earlier chapters, these specimens are not, however, to be considered "controls." Arson investigators correctly realized that a control specimen is one with a completely known history. Specimens from fire scenes, even though unburned, are still unknowns in terms of any possible ignitable liquid residue content. Accordingly, they are to be called "comparison samples." We have applied this same correct terminology to these specimens in the context of other categories of evidence, as noted in Chapters 2, 3, and 9.

Although these intrinsic volatile compounds in certain materials are usually not a source of confusion in an ignitable liquid residue analysis, the **comparison sample** can sometimes be helpful in interpreting the results of an analysis.

comparison specimen

A separate specimen taken of a material for comparison purposes; in fire investigations, a sample of surface or substratum on which ignitable liquid residue might be present.

Examination of the Other Criminalistics Evidence Collected

In processing the scene of a suspicious fire, identification of a possible accelerant is very important in making the determination of whether a particular suspicious fire was the result of arson. However, it is particularly important to remember that identification of a possible accelerant is not usually, by itself, very helpful in identifying the arsonist. A competent fire scene processing must include the search for all other types of physical evidence (Figure 11.18) such as bloodstains, fingerprints, toolmarks, and many other useful items of physical evidence. Such evidence can be critical in the investigation of the incident, and in the identification and prosecution of an offender.

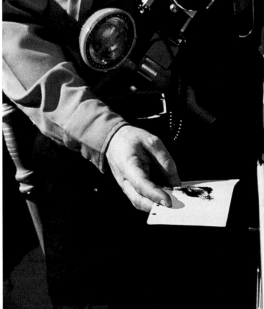

Figure 11.18
Fingerprinting evidence at an arson scene.

Figure 11.19
A large commercial building destroyed by the force of an explosion.

Section 2: Explosives and Explosion Incidents

One thinks of explosives-related crimes as acts of terrorism or major destructive events that make the nightly news on television (Figure 11.19). There are, however, many additional incidents involving explosives or explosions that are more localized, such as a pipe bomb placed under a car, injury of an individual transporting an **explosive** device, or bombings as an extortion device. Both the Bureau of Alcohol, Tobacco, Firearms and Explosives (ATF) and the Federal Bureau of Investigation (FBI) in the United States Department of Justice have considerable resources that can be dispatched to explosion scenes or in response to possible

explosive

A chemical material that undergoes a very rapid chemical reaction on being heated, struck, or otherwise energized with production of large volumes of gas.

acts of terrorism. They also assist state and local law enforcement agencies on request. As a result, both the ATF and the FBI have specialized equipment for processing explosion scenes and analyzing a wide variety of explosion-related evidence. However, the less spectacular incidents are usually the responsibility of state and local law enforcement agencies and forensic laboratories. Large local jurisdictions and most states have bomb squads to handle such incidents and ensure that any suspicious object is examined and safely disposed of, if necessary. These units are trained to carefully process explosion scenes and collect any potential evidence for analysis by the appropriate forensic laboratory.

Characteristics of Explosives and Explosions

As with arson and fires, some understanding of explosives and of the explosion process is necessary to fully appreciate the forensic aspects of explosive incidents, their investigation, and how the related evidence is handled in the laboratory. An explosion is a very rapid chemical reaction that produces heat and gaseous products. A great deal of heat and gaseous product can be produced by a relatively small quantity of explosive material. This brief definition really does not give one much insight into what is happening in an explosion, so we will explain in more detail in the following sections.

Exothermic

The single most important characteristic of explosions is the production of a great deal of heat. A small amount of energy is required to get an explosion reaction started, but, once started, it produces heat in large quantities and in a much shorter period of time than even rapid combustion. Although some explosions are really a special type of combustion, they are much more rapid and produce enormous amounts of heat very quickly.

Molecular Fragmentation to Produce Gaseous Products

Almost equally important to the process is molecular fragmentation. Larger molecules (with many atoms bonded together), which are usually solids and are typically not very volatile, are violently broken apart, in a fraction of a second, into many smaller molecules that tend to vaporize (become gaseous molecules). Nitrogen, carbon dioxide, water vapor, and nitrogen oxides are typical of the gaseous products produced in an explosion. In an explosion, a small volume of solid material is instantaneously transformed into an enormous amount of gaseous material that must obey the laws of chemistry and therefore occupy many times the volume.

Since this happens in a fraction of a second during an explosion, those molecules are bumping against one another very rapidly trying to obey the gas laws. In addition, heating a gas causes the molecules to move more rapidly and therefore want to expand further (refer back to the box "More on the Science: Relative Vapor Density"). Thus an explosion produces a double effect: the increase in the number of molecules that itself causes expansion, and the heating effect that causes additional expansion. The solid, which occupies a small volume, is converted almost instantaneously into an enormous number of gas molecules occupying a much greater volume, and at a very high temperature.

Rapid Expansion

shock wave

A region of sufficiently high pressure traveling through a gas at a high velocity that can cause physical damage to objects it encounters.

The rapidly expanding gases from the explosion are retarded by the air surrounding the explosive mass. The air will be compressed by the explosive gases pushing on it rapidly, resulting in a **shock wave.** The shock wave is the result of gases from the explosive and surrounding air molecules crowded together in the rush to expand, and it takes on the character of a physical force that pushes things out of its way violently. This shock wave is what causes much of the damage associated with an

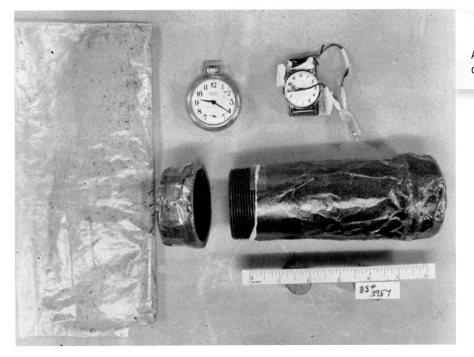

Figure 11.20
A pipe bomb that failed to explode, disassembled to show all the parts.

explosion. It is not generally the heat, but the shock wave, that causes such violent destruction. The expanding gases are transformed into a tremendous force that can break windows, knock down trees, and fragment almost anything in its path. However, a shock wave's awesome power also can be harnessed to do useful work, such as mine raw materials, prepare building sites, and flatten unwanted structures.

Containment

"Low explosives" are explosives that burn rapidly but do not **detonate;** as we shall discuss in the following, there must be **containment** to have an explosive event. "High explosives," on the other hand, will detonate even without containment. With low explosives, such as smokeless powder, fireworks, or certain chemical mixtures, a person can cause detonation and increase the force produced by trying to contain the products of the rapid reaction. A low explosive might be enclosed in a piece of pipe (Figure 11.20), for example, then the material ignited with a fuse, blasting cap, or other source of ignition. As the explosive material fragments and is heated by the energy released by the reaction, the gases produced try to expand violently. Pressure builds, and the pipe is burst, releasing the gases and propelling broken pipe fragments in all directions. The released gases also form a shock wave that can damage anything in its immediate path. Generally, the stronger the container, the stronger the force necessary to rupture it. Thus, when the stronger container does rupture, the potential damage is increased.

detonate
Causing an explosive material to release energy in the form of an explosion.

containment
Confining a rapid, exothermic reaction within a sturdy container until it develops sufficient force (pressure) to shatter the container.

The Three Major Classes of Explosives

As noted briefly above, there are several categories of explosives. The explosives in the different categories have somewhat different properties.

Low Explosives

Low explosives are materials that burn rapidly and will explode only when contained. Some sort of ignition is needed, such as a fuse or spark, to cause them to start decomposing. This decomposition reaction is a very rapid reaction that results in the explosive molecules being converted into much smaller gaseous molecules. The most

low explosives
Materials that will burn rapidly, but not detonate, unless contained.

Figure 11.21
Different-shaped grains of smokeless powder.

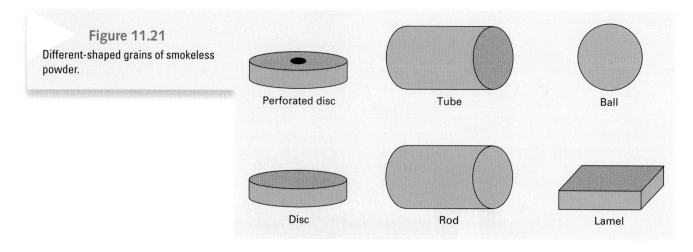

Perforated disc　　　　Tube　　　　Ball

Disc　　　　Rod　　　　Lamel

Figure 11.22
Small pyrotechnic device (firecracker) cut open to show its construction.

common low explosives are smokeless gunpowder (Figure 11.21), which is nitrocellulose, and black powder. Black powder is a mixture of charcoal, sulfur, and sodium nitrate or potassium nitrate. Also in this group are most fireworks. The technical name for fireworks is pyrotechnics, and they are made from chemical mixtures of a number of different highly energetic inorganic salts, usually nitrates and perchlorates.

Fireworks are a large group of low explosives. At one time the only fireworks commonly available were the so-called Chinese firecrackers and cherry bombs (small round devices, about the size of a cherry, painted red). They had a wick and, when ignited, produced a loud bang. In recent years, the most popular firecrackers have been M80s and super M80s (Figure 11.22), and even more powerful cousins. M80s are cylindrical in shape, about three-quarters of an inch in diameter with a wick in the center. They produce a perceptible shock wave and are much louder than the old Chinese firecrackers. If you were to cut one open, you would see they contain only a rather small amount of pyrotechnic mix but many, many layers of tightly wound heavy paper for containment. The reason for their higher power lies more in the containment (Figure 11.22) than in the nature of the explosive mixture.

Primary High Explosives

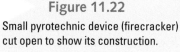

primary high explosives

Explosive material that is caused to explode fairly readily by physical shock, electrical spark, or other disturbances.

The second class of explosives is **primary high explosives.** These are the most treacherous explosive materials and are used as primers or detonators. They are not usually the explosive material that does the major work or damage but are used to cause that material to explode. Primary high explosives are sensitive to many possible disturbances. An electrical spark, intense heat, mechanical force, and many other disturbances will cause these materials to explode. The most well known primary high explosive is nitroglycerine. It has become widely used because a chemist named Alfred Nobel discovered a simple way to convert it from a primary high explosive to a secondary high explosive (see the next section) that allowed it to be used to do useful work. Nitroglycerine is an oily liquid that explodes violently for a variety of reasons, with potentially deadly effects. It was used as a primary high explosive at one time, but its unpredictability made it too dangerous to handle safely.

The most common primary high explosives are mercury fulminate and lead stybnate, which are used in firearms cartridges as the shock-sensitive priming material (Chapter 8), and in blasting caps. In a firearm, when the firing pin strikes the primer in the head end of the cartridge or shell, it causes a tiny amount of the shock-sensitive primary high explosive inside to explode. This produces a flash of intense heat and a little flame or spark, which then ignites the smokeless powder in the cartridge and "fires" the weapon. The gunpowder burns very rapidly, producing rapidly expanding gases that are contained by the combination of the bullet and the cartridge case. Thus, the cartridge is essentially a small explosive device. When containment is breached, the gases propel the bullet from the firearm at very high speed.

Secondary High Explosives

Secondary high explosives can be fairly safely handled, but with the proper inducement, they will explode with great force. The primary distinction between these and low explosives is that high explosives do not have to be contained to explode. Once sufficient initiation is provided, they will explode violently. Containment may be used to intensify or direct the explosion but is not necessary for it to occur. Depending on the circumstances and the explosive, the "inducement" (often referred to as "initiation") can take many forms. The most common are an electrical spark, a small flame (from a fuse), intense heat, or a sharp blow. Some common military examples are TNT (trinitrotoluene), the active ingredient in military dynamite; PETN, the material used in detcord; and RDX and HMX, which are explosive components of common military explosives usually referred to as "plastic explosives."

Detcord is a thin cord that can be wrapped around an object and when detonated explodes with sufficient force to shatter or cut whatever it envelops, such as door handles, fence posts, bridge supports, and so on. RDX and HMX are military explosives that are the primary components of the so-called plastic explosives, or "plastique." They are secondary high explosives that have been mixed with other materials to make them into a puttylike material that can be easily formed into any shape. The explosive material can then be molded into or around anything one wants to destroy. With the placement of a detonator in it, and a timer or remote trigger to set off the blast, the combination can destroy bridges, buildings, or other military targets.

Secondary high explosives are also important in civilian applications, such as major construction projects, mining, and road building. The most common secondary high explosives used commercially are different types of dynamite (Figure 11.23) based on nitroglycerin and its derivatives, ammonium nitrate, and water gel explosives based on monomethylamine nitrate. With knowledge and care, these materials can be safely handled, and their potential energy harnessed to do useful work. This was not always the situation. It was Alfred Nobel who made the major breakthrough that allowed the safe use of high explosives to become practical. As indicated, nitroglycerine is a very sensitive explosive that can explode with little warning and with devastating effect. Nobel worked for years to develop a way to stabilize nitroglycerine so it could be handled safely and its power harnessed. He found that

secondary high explosive

Explosive material that can be safely handled but will explode violently when subjected to an electrical spark or small flame.

Figure 11.23

Fused sticks of dynamite.

Explosives versus Combustion Fuels

A major difference between most explosives and materials that just burn very rapidly is that the explosives do not require oxygen from the air. They have the oxygen necessary for their destructive reaction as part of the explosive molecule. When things burn, the speed at which they burn is governed by how quickly the fuel can combine with the necessary oxygen. Thus, with explosives it is an internal reaction with the molecules fragmenting or rearranging themselves into products that are small gaseous molecules. This may be thermal decomposition or oxidation, but it can occur more rapidly, since all the necessary components are already built into the explosive chemical. All that is required is something to start the explosive reaction; for example, the detonation of a small amount of primary high explosive.

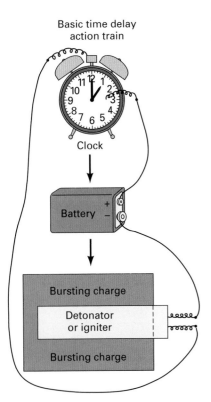

Basic time delay action train

Clock

Battery

Bursting charge

Detonator or igniter

Bursting charge

Figure 11.24

Diagram of the basic components of an explosive device including simple timer, battery, and detonator.

explosive train

The combination of components that are put together to form an explosive device.

nitroglycerine, when absorbed on a high-surface-area solid, such as diatomaceous earth or later even sawdust, became a material that could be safely handled, but when detonated with a blasting cap or fuse still carried the enormous explosive force of the nitroglycerine. The stabilized nitroglycerine, wrapped in waxy paper and with a fuse inserted, became dynamite. Dynamite could be safely moved, handled, stored for considerable periods, and even dropped. It made modern mining, quarrying, and major road and other construction projects possible. Nobel had thus taken a primary high explosive and converted it to a secondary high explosive. It became such a useful material that the Nobel Company became enormously successful. It is still the largest manufacturer of explosives in the world. The success of his company made Alfred Nobel enormously wealthy. Some of this wealth was used to fund the well-known "Nobel" prizes in perpetuity.

Another material used as a commercial secondary high explosive is ammonium nitrate. Anyone who has ever been in a chicken coop knows of the strong ammonia smell that arises from the slow decomposition of the ammonium nitrate in the animal droppings. Ammonium nitrate mixed with fuel oil (home heating oil) is called ANFO and has been used as a military explosive for many years. Ammonium nitrate is the explosive that was used in the bombing of the Oklahoma City Federal Building.

Currently, the most widely used explosive, particularly for mining, is called a water gel explosive and has at its main ingredient monomethylamine nitrate. This compound is chemically similar to ammonium nitrate, but it can be mixed with water to make a gelatinous material, then poured into a hole drilled in rock or coal and detonated. The resulting explosion breaks thousands of tons of the desired material, which is then collected with enormous front-end loaders. This is a very rapid and efficient method of mining.

Secondary high explosives are the materials that provide the majority of the energy and are therefore the major constituent in most explosions. They work in combination with very small amounts of primary high explosive that are used to initiate the explosion. See "More on the Science: Explosives versus Combustion Fuels."

The Explosive Train or Device

The **explosive train** is the term used to refer to the combination of components necessary for a successful explosion. In many cases, the explosive train might be simply called a bomb (Figure 11.24). Every bomb has an explosive train, but not every explosive train is a bomb. An explosive device or explosive train has three primary components, and sometimes a fourth component is added. There is an igniter, primer or detonator, main charge, and sometimes containment.

The first component is an *igniter*. Its primary function is to get the explosive event started. A number of things can serve as igniters, such as a fuse that when lit burns until the flame reaches either a primary or secondary high explosive, in which it will then initiate an explosion. A spark or a delayed spark can also be an igniter. In old western movies someone always had a box with a T-shaped handle on top, which was connected by a long wire to a great deal of dynamite or to powder kegs. When the handle was pushed, an electrical connection would be made, and a spark would initiate the explosion. The delayed spark is quite common nowadays. It consists simply of a small timer that can be set to provide the spark after a preset amount of time. Often, at least in the movies, a digital counter allows one the drama of counting down to the initiation of the explosion.

The second component of the explosive train is the *primer*, or *detonator*. A blasting cap is one of the most common detonators. It is most often a little cylinder with a small amount of primary high explosive and two wire leads. The spark (igniter) travels down the wires and sets off primary high explosive, which in turn is in contact with a much larger amount of secondary high explosive. There are other ways to prime or detonate the main charge, but most involve a small amount of easily exploded material used to set off the main charge.

The third component is the *main charge*. This is a sizable quantity of a low explosive or secondary high explosive that will provide the main source of energy for the explosion. It can be dynamite, ammonium nitrate, or even black or smoke-less powder. The main charge may also include a booster. A booster is a material that is not itself an explosive, but which, when involved with an explosive, will significantly increase the amount of energy released by the explosion. For example, dynamite frequently has sodium nitrate added to it to intensify the explosion. Similarly, in the ANFO material mentioned earlier, the fuel oil is not an explosive but intensifies the ammonium nitrate explosion. These are the three primary components of an explosive train.

In some cases the fourth component of the explosive train is *containment (confinement)*. Particularly when the main charge is a low explosive, there must be containment for an explosion to occur. Even when a secondary high explosive is used as the main charge, the force released can be intensified or directed by using proper containment. Confinement is most often provided by a container to hold the components of the explosive train. Containment is most common in homemade devices, and also in certain military explosives where maximizing the damage, often in a particular direction, is desired. Containment can be provided in many ways. The container can be a piece of iron pipe, like in a "pipe bomb" as mentioned earlier, or it can be provided by tightly wound cardboard as in the small firecracker called the M80. Confinement can be provided by any device that will retain the gases generated by the explosion until the pressure builds to a high level, then ruptures, allowing the sudden release of the gases. When the containment is breached, there is a very rapid release of the confined gases, producing an intense shock wave and thereby a much more potent explosion than if there were no containment.

The Role of the Scene Investigator

When a device has exploded and caused damage or injury, the scene must be evaluated so that the maximum amount of useful information can be gathered. The investigator is faced with a complex mixture of materials recovered at the scene, most of which are from the scene and not the device. The first step is to try to sort through all this material to recover any portions of the device and **explosive residues** that have survived. Careful visual and microscopical examination of debris can yield a great deal of information.

The first step in this process is sifting. Much of this process is usually done by bomb investigators at the scene or in a designated area set up adjacent to the scene. For example, in a major explosion at an airport, the investigators are typically given a large section of a hangar for several months to sort through the debris. All the collected debris is first examined by eye, and larger pieces that do not appear to have been at the center of the explosion are removed by hand. Next the

explosive residues

Materials that can be found on debris from an explosive incident that may contain trace amounts of the unchanged explosive or chemical reaction products produced by the explosive reaction.

screening process is begun. The debris is first passed through a screen with fairly large holes, and material that does not pass through is examined and put aside if it looks relevant. The material that passed through the first screen is then sifted again, with a smaller-mesh screen. The process is continued with smaller and smaller size sifting devices. At each stage, investigators look for pieces that might be parts of the device, or that could have been used to contain or transport it. Items are collected that show evidence of proximity to the seat of the explosion; such as heavily deformed pieces of metal or contorted debris items. This is a tedious and time-consuming process but it is quite surprising how much potential evidence material survives even a devastating explosion. Once the debris has been culled to find the most promising pieces, they are sent to the laboratory for more detailed examination, such as chemical identification of the explosive residues, and examination of the recovered parts of the device.

Laboratory Analysis of Explosives and Explosive Residues

Unfortunately, most explosion-derived evidence is received after an explosion, and, as we shall see later, analysis is a complex process. However, because bombs intended to explode sometimes fail to do so or are seized before they can be exploded, an unexploded device may be submitted.

Examination of the Unexploded Device

Forensic laboratories receive unexploded devices for three common reasons. First, a bomber may be intercepted before the device is placed or detonated. Second, there may be a defect in the way the device was constructed, and it fails to explode, and third, the detonation may not be properly executed, and there is no explosion. For example, the wick may fall out of a Molotov cocktail when it is thrown and before it ignites, or a component of the electrical circuit could have broken (see Figure 11.20 on page 297) during transport, so the circuit is not complete when the detonating switch is closed.

Render Safe   With an unexploded device, there is the immediate problem of rendering it safe. This can be a significant problem, particularly if an amateur or poorly trained individual made it. These devices can be extremely dangerous, and often the safest option is to remove them to a remote area and detonate them. This practice results in the loss of considerable information about how the device was constructed, but the lives of bomb experts or the public are not jeopardized.

Description of Device Components   When an unexploded device is received, it should be described in considerable detail. This type of information can be of great importance, particularly when there have been a series of possibly related explosions. Successfully making explosive devices and living to tell about it is not a trivial exercise. As a result, most bomb makers develop a scheme that seems to work for them and continue to use that scheme. In many cases, explosive devices carry almost a "signature" that can be compared, and it will usually indicate if different devices have been made by the same bomb maker or perhaps one of his or her "students." For this reason, a careful description of each of the components used, and how they are connected to make the explosive train, is critical. Sometimes, if a good understanding of the bomb maker's method has been developed from unexploded devices, the person's work may still be recognizable even when present only as debris from an explosion that has occurred (see later).

Chemical Identification of the Explosive   In addition to the way the device is constructed, the actual nature of the explosive used is an important characteristic of a bomb maker or a group of bomb makers. Such people generally have access to a particular type of explosive or will favor a particular combination of ingredients in a homemade explosive. These features help not only to point out similar construction, but also can sometimes provide investigative leads. Identification of the explosive in an unexploded device is much simpler than trying to determine what it was from traces left behind after the explosion. If the device uses a commercial or stolen military explosive, there will often be markings on the wrapper that can be traced to when it was made and often where it was distributed after manufacture. Even in a pyrotechnic mixture, the exact nature of the chemicals used can often give useful information about where they were obtained. Perhaps the most common low explosive used in bomb making is smokeless powder. It is available from a number of commercial sources to sportsmen who reload their own cartridges. Although different brands of smokeless powder are chemically similar, each manufacturer has preferred shapes that they make for certain applications, or to distinguish themselves from their competitors. Careful examination of smokeless powder under a stereomicroscope can often be as useful as chemical analysis in distinguishing different types and different manufacturers. Further, each manufacturer uses certain additives that may allow identification of the manufacturer.

Examination of the Exploded Device and Associated Debris

There are several steps involved in the examination of explosive debris, pieces of the recovered exploded device, and explosives residues.

Microscopical Examination and Picking   Microscopical examination and picking are important steps in selecting materials of interest for further examination. If a pipe bomb was involved, the forensic investigator will often find a portion of the pipe cap with a threaded portion of the pipe still inside. Small specks of the explosive may have been trapped, thereby protected from the heat of the explosion, and therefore can be recovered. The same might be true of homemade pyrotechnics or other low explosives. Sometimes, even small traces of dynamite may survive the explosion. As noted earlier, these unexploded materials are much more easily identified than trace explosive residues recovered from washings (see next section). Even if no unexploded dynamite is recovered; pieces of the wrapper might be present. The wrapper is often blown apart into small pieces, but unless consumed by fire, they may survive. Such a piece of wrapper may have a portion of a serial number or other marking on it, enabling investigators to trace the origin and distribution of the material. Tiny pieces of wire, parts of batteries, timing devices, and myriad other items can survive the explosion and provide information about the nature of the device, and sometimes important investigative leads, or even evidence that can be used in a subsequent prosecution.

Use of Washings of Selected Debris   Where the information from microscopic examination and picking is insufficient to determine the nature of explosive or leaves doubt about its nature, the next step would normally be washings. Unfortunately, particularly with high explosives, lack of visible residues is frequently the case. Here, pieces of debris, selected by appearance or screening tests, are washed with a small volume of an organic solvent, such as acetone, to collect any traces of unburned or partially burned residue from the explosive charge. These samples do not have to have been part of the device itself, but could be material on which the device was resting, or could have been in the immediate path of the hot gases produced. The solvent wash solution is then concentrated and subjected to a variety of screening tests to see if any residual explosive might be present. Any washings that show positive screening reactions (Table 11.3) are then examined more closely using more sensitive and specific instrumental examinations. As with blood (Chapter 9) and illicit drugs (Chapter 12), there are preliminary screening (presumptive) as well as

Table 11.3 Common chemical spot tests for explosives*

Substance to be tested for	Test reagents				
	Cupric tetrapyridine	Diphenylamine	Griess Reagent	J Acid	Alcoholic KOH
Chlorate	NR	Blue to blue / black	NR	Orange / brown	NR
Perchlorate	Purple, ppt	NR	NR	NR	NR
Nitrate	NR	Blue to blue / black	Pink to red	Orange / brown	NR
Nitrite	Green	Blue / black	Red to yellow	Orange / brown	NR
Nitrocellulose	NR	Blue / black	Pink	Orange / brown	NR
Nitroglycerine	NR	Blue to blue / black	Pink to red	Orange / brown	NR
TNT	NR	NR	NR	NR	Red / violet
RDX	NR	NR	Pink to red	Orange / brown	NR
PETN	NR	Blue	Pink to red	Orange / brown	NR
Tetryl	NR	Blue	Pink to red	Yellow to Orange/ brown	Red

NR no reaction.

Ppt precipitate.

*Expanded From R.G. Parker et al., *Journal of Forensic Sciences,* 1975; Vol. 20, pp. 133–140.

confirmatory tests for explosives and residues. Table 11.3 is a summary of chemical screening tests. A second set of washings may be taken, especially where it is suspected that an inorganic explosive such as ammonium nitrate or a pyrotechnic mixture may have been used, since they are usually not recovered efficiently with the acetone washings. The second washing is usually done with water. It is not easy to concentrate a water wash without destroying the residues, and the washing also tends to be contaminated by salts and other materials from the explosion scene. In cold climates, road salt from ice melting is ubiquitous; near the coast there is salt from ocean spray; and calcium sulfate from plaster will be present in large quantities at a scene in virtually any building. Even in the face of the difficulties caused by such contaminants, many laboratories can sometimes successfully characterize the type of explosive used from such washings.

Purification or Separation of Explosive Residues from Washings

With washings, it is usually necessary to try to separate the explosive residue from other contaminants from the scene that were carried along through the washing step. A number of different types of chromatography can be used to obtain a sample sufficiently free of interfering materials to enable unambiguous identification by instrumental methods. Preliminary screening tests (which are usually color tests) can be helpful in deciding what materials should be examined further and what fraction from the chromatography may contain the sought-after explosive residues. The Greiss test and the diphenylamine test are useful in looking for nitrate and nitrite residues. If these are not present, one with a few exceptions does not have explosive residues, since even organic explosives produce nitrate when they explode.

Thin-layer chromatography is the simplest and most rapid separation technique frequently used with explosives and explosive residues. An analyst obtains characteristic spots on the developed thin-layer plates that can be tentatively identified as nitroglycerine, TNT, or the most common organic explosives. Although the TLC results do not provide a rigorous identification, they provide a strong indication, and the identity of the specimen can then be confirmed with other techniques. Other chromatographic techniques can be used with difficult samples and can provide an even stronger indication of the identity of the material. Not every laboratory will use every technique, but GC, HPLC, ion chromatography, and capillary electrophoresis are all used to some extent in dealing with the complex mixtures produced by explosions. There are even special detectors used with HPLC that are particularly suited for chromatography of explosive residues. They are designed to detect primarily the types of materials characteristic of explosives and not most extraneous contaminants.

Chemical Identification of the Residues   Isolation of even minuscule amounts of the unchanged explosive will usually allow rapid identification using modern instrumentation. Organic explosives such as TNT or most military explosives can be identified using infrared spectroscopy or GC/MS. These are instruments available in virtually every forensic laboratory. Other more specialized instruments may be available in laboratories that are specifically equipped for explosive residue analysis. Residues from inorganic explosives are examined using infrared spectroscopy, X-ray diffraction or fluorescence, or several other specialized techniques. GC/MS is particularly useful for reasonably volatile organic residues. Unfortunately, many explosive materials are not sufficiently stable to survive a trip through the GC/MS. If one can obtain crystalline material by picking it out, or after purification of material from washings, X-ray diffraction can provide a chemical identification. Many other instrumental techniques can be used depending on the nature of the explosive and the quality and quantity of the material available.

Examination of the Device or Debris for Other Physical Evidence

Explosive devices are a combination of many objects and materials assembled in a particular way. Careful examination of the type of wire, how the timing devices have been designed to make the timing circuit, or the nature of the pipe or other containment used, and how it was cut or modified, can provide valuable investigative information. Tool marks, fingerprints, how wire was stripped of its insulation, and dozens of other analyses make up the rest of the examination and produce results often as useful as the analysis and identification of the explosive residues. Even when fairly common everyday items are used to construct the device, a salesperson may remember an individual who came in and bought 36 cheap watches. That might turn out to be an important investigative lead, particularly if watches or parts of watches are recovered and are serialized or have other identification of the manufacturer (Figure 11.25).

Figure 11.25
An inexpensive watch with battery and flashbulb with necessary simple circuitry to convert it to a timer designed to ignite an incendiary device.

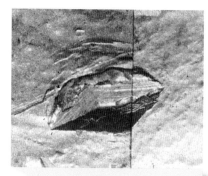

Figure 11.26

A comparison image of pits in a control pipe and a pipe recovered from an explosion scene showing the tool marks made by a pipe vise in each pipe, indicating that both pipes were held in the same vise.

The discovery of a workshop where bombs are being or have been constructed can provide a wealth of information that might allow an expert to associate related bombings and aid in prosecution of the workers in the bomb factory by tying them to specific explosive incidents. The usual way of discovering a workshop is when something goes wrong, resulting in an explosion and/or fire. In one case, a workshop where pipe bombs were being made was discovered in this way. A pipe vise is usually used for cutting and treading, or even handling pipe in other ways. This is a special type of vise that is designed with jaws to grip the round pipe and hold it steady. When these vises squeeze down on that pipe, they make indentations in the pipe (Figure 11.26). These marks are a type of tool mark, and pipe vises often develop a characteristic set of marks. As a result, the marks on a pipe can sometimes be used to say that the pipe was gripped in that particular vise. When the workshop was discovered with its pipe vise, it was possible to associate pipe debris from several explosive scenes with that particular pipe vise and thereby with that workshop and the group that ran it.

Whenever someone performs an antisocial act fairly successfully, many others, who did not think of it or could not have done it, claim credit for it. The false claimants who take credit or confess usually know only what has been reported in the news. It is very important to have detailed knowledge that is not given to the press, to help sort out the false claimants. The careful examination of physical evidence allows investigators to sort out bogus claims of responsibility from those of the individual or group responsible.

Summary

Section 1: Fire and Arson

Fire is a form of combustion. Combustion, in turn, is a reaction chemists call oxidation. Usually, a carbon-containing fuel undergoes a rapid reaction with oxygen, forming oxidized fuel products and generating heat and light. Complete oxidation of carbon fuel produces carbon dioxide and water. If oxidation is incomplete, a dangerous, very toxic gas called carbon monoxide can be formed. Certain conditions are necessary for sustained combustion. The "fire triangle" (fuel, oxygen, heat), "fire tetrahedron" (fuel, oxygen, heat, chain reaction) and the "fire pentagon" (fuel, oxygen, heat, chain reaction, and ignition) are used as mnemonics to remember the conditions. Fire suppression techniques try to eliminate one of these conditions. Water can absorb considerable heat. Chemical fire retardants can interfere with the chain reaction (free radical) aspect of the fire. *Flaming* combustion requires that both fuel and oxygen be in the vapor phase. Oxygen is in the vapor phase under most conditions already. So, heat must be sufficient for liquid fuel to be volatilized or solid fuel to be pyrolyzed, in the presence of oxygen, to sustain flaming combustion. *Glowing* combustion takes place at the surface of a solid, nonpyrolyzable solid fuel (like charcoal).

Fuels may be gaseous, liquid, or solid. Common gaseous fuels are hydrogen, natural gas, and propane. There are many possible liquid fuels, but gasoline, kerosene, and ethyl alcohol are common ones. Solid fuels, such as wood, charcoal, and coal, may be pyrolyzable or nonpyrolyzable. The former can support flaming combustion.

The *flash point* of a liquid fuel is the lowest temperature at which there is sufficient vapor to be ignited by a small spark. The *fire point* is the temperature at which there is enough heat to cause combustion, even in the absence of an ignition source. Fuels also have a *flammable range*. This is the range of fuel-to-air ratios over which combustion is sustainable. The *relative vapor density* of a fuel is a function of its molecular weight. Some fuels will sink in air while others will rise. This parameter may be important in a fire investigation. Pyrolysis is the process by which heat causes the volatilization of solid fuel to the vapor state.

Arsonists usually have one of several motives. Economic gain is a common one. Revenge, vandalism, thrill, and trying to cover up another crime are also common motives.

Two major objectives of fire scene investigations are finding the origin and the cause of the fire. Fire patterns can help in fire scene investigations. The classical "inverted-cone" pattern in an indoor fire suggests a point of origin near the point of the cone. Other patterns, such as alligatoring, concrete spalling, and smoke stains, can help fire investigators reconstruct the progress of a fire. Natural causes of a fire, including malfunctions in the electrical system or in electric appliances, accidents involving stoves or heating appliances, gas leaks, careless smoking, and others are usually considered first. If no natural cause emerges, the possibility of arson must be considered. If a fire's cause is suspicious, investigators will search for ignitable liquid residues that might have been used as accelerants. Laboratory methods are sufficiently sensitive today that traces of ignitable liquid residue can often be detected even after a big fire. The distinction between "ignitable liquid" and "accelerant" is important. An ignitable liquid can be and might have been used as an accelerant. But finding ignitable liquid traces in fire debris does not necessarily prove that. The ignitable liquid residue could be from a source unrelated to the cause of the fire. Investigators may use chemical sniffers or specially trained dogs to locate areas likely to have ignitable liquid residue in the fire debris. Debris suspected of containing such residue should be packaged in a sealed paint can—to prevent any further evaporation—and the can then labeled as any other evidence container. Investigators should always look for ignitable liquid containers and for any ignition devices as well. In addition, they should look for other physical evidence, especially of the kinds that may be able to help link a person to the scene. Even laboratory identification of ignitable liquid residue along with other corroborating evidence of arson merely establishes that a crime has been committed, but gets investigators no closer to identifying a suspect.

In the forensic science laboratory, fire debris is generally solid material of some kind and may be soaked with water. Debris is processed to isolate and concentrate the ignitable liquids in one of four ways: heated headspace, steam distillation, carbon strip adsorption, and solvent wash. In the rare situation where the suspected ignitable liquid evidence is liquid, the specimen can be analyzed without further preparation. The method of choice for ignitable liquid analysis is gas chromatography, often coupled to a mass spectrometer (GC/MS). GC can separate the numerous components present in many common ignitable liquids, generating chromatograms that can then be compared to standards. A gas chromatogram alone, however, cannot be used to identify a multicomponent ignitable liquid (like gasoline or charcoal lighter). Using GC along with MS, unequivocal identifications may be possible. In Chapter 3, we talked about control and comparison specimens that are often necessary to make a forensic comparison meaningful. One of these was a substratum comparison specimen. Fire investigators must collect specimens of unburned, unstained materials near those suspected of containing ignitable liquids as comparison specimens.

Section 2: Explosives and Explosion Incidents

An explosion is a rapid chemical (oxidative) reaction that produces enormous heat and molecular fragmentation. Gases are produced very rapidly and they expand, producing a shock wave, and heat.

There are low explosives, and primary and secondary high explosives. Low explosives burn rapidly, but do not explode unless contained. Smokeless gunpowder, black powder, and fireworks are common examples of low explosives. Primary high explosives are the most dangerous type. They do not require containment to detonate. They are generally used as primers or detonators of secondary high explosives. An electrical spark or mechanical disturbance can trigger these materials to detonate. Nitroglycerine is a common example. Mercury fulminate and lead stybnate are commonly used as primers for firearms cartridges. Secondary high explosives are generally safe to handle. Once detonated, however, they cause considerable damage. Containment may be used to "direct" the explosion, but containment is not necessary for detonation. Examples include TNT, PETN, RDX, and HMX. RDX and HMX are components of "plastic" explosives, which are moldable like putty. These

are primarily military weapons, but applications can be found for them in construction, mining, or road building. Alfred Nobel (of Nobel Prize fame) invented dynamite, a stabilized (and thus handleable) form of nitroglycerine. Ammonium nitrate is also a common commercial secondary high explosive. It was used in the Oklahoma City Federal Building bombing.

The *explosive train* or *explosive device* describes the combination of components necessary for a successful explosion. These are igniter, primer or detonator, and main charge. Sometimes, there is also containment. The igniter can be a fuse or a sparking device. The primer or detonator is often a small quantity of primary explosive, which, when triggered to explode, in turn triggers detonation of the main charge. A blasting cap is a common detonator. The main charge is a substantial quantity of low explosive or secondary high explosive that will provide the primary energy source of the blast. It may contain a "booster." The booster is not itself an explosive, but it can greatly increase the quantity of energy released when combined with an explosive. Sometimes, containment is a component. It is essential if the main charge is a low explosive.

Explosion scene investigation involves tediously processing the debris from the explosion scene to try to recover portions of the explosive device and explosive residues. The debris is often sifted through smaller and smaller mesh screening devices, and suspected bits of material are recovered. Items that show evidence of proximity to the seat of the explosion (e.g., heavy deformation) are collected. These are sent to the forensic science laboratory for further examination.

The laboratory has to be prepared to receive explosion debris, but also unexploded devices. Judgments about detonating such devices as a matter of safety are probably best left to bomb experts. The rule should be: safety first. An unexploded device, if it can be safely examined, can contain considerable information specific to its maker. There may be information on wrappers about the explosive. This information might help narrow down the source. Smokeless powder, a common ingredient in explosive devices, has several morphological forms distinguishable microscopically. Explosion debris, especially elements of the device itself, is searched for small traces of unexploded explosive. This is much easier to identify than having to draw inferences from explosive residues. Bits of wire, batteries, or other components should be sought. These examinations are done microscopically at fairly low powers.

The next step in lab examination is usually doing solvent washings. Items for washing are selected based on their likelihood of having some residue. Those that are positive in screening (presumptive) tests can be examined more thoroughly using instrumental methods. Water washings may also be taken, especially if inorganic (like ammonium nitrate) explosives are suspected. It is difficult to concentrate these washings for analysis, however. Washings can be analyzed by chromatographic methods (TLC and HPLC are most common) to look at the different components. Isolation of even tiny quantities of the explosives themselves generally permits instrumental identification using FTIR or GC/MS.

The laboratory examination should also focus on other aspects of the debris and device. Explosive devices are usually hand assembled. Every component has potential information. Tape might be cut or torn a certain way, or even have a latent fingerprint on it. Tool marks on stripped wire should not be overlooked. The ignition device may be identifiable and traceable. No possible source of information should be overlooked that could help link the device to a particular person.

Key Terms

combustion (p. 275)
exothermic (p. 275)
flaming combustion (p. 276)
glowing combustion (p. 276)
flash point (p. 279)
fire point (p. 280)
flammable range (p. 280)
pyrolysis (p. 280)
accelerants (p. 281)

burn pattern (p. 283)
point of origin (p. 283)
ignitable liquid (p. 283)
sniffers (p. 284)
heated headspace (p. 287)
steam distillation (p. 287)
carbon strip or tube absorption (p. 287)
comparison specimen (p. 294)
explosive (p. 295)

shock wave (p. 296)
detonate (p. 297)
containment (p. 297)
low explosives (p. 297)
primary high explosives (p. 298)
secondary high explosives (p. 299)
explosive train (p. 300)
explosive residues (p. 301)

Review Questions—Short Answer

1. Discuss the importance of pyrolysis in the combustion of solid fuels.
2. What role can the careful processing of a fire scene play in the investigation of the incident?
3. What aids are available to the fire investigator for selecting evidence to be sent to the laboratory?
4. How is evidence collected from a fire scene processed in a forensic laboratory?
5. What are the major objectives of a fire scene investigation?
6. Discuss what is happening when an explosive device detonates and why it can cause so much damage.
7. What are the similarities and differences in the processing of a fire scene and an explosive incident scene?
8. What are the differences in a laboratory's approach to examining materials from an incident where the device failed to explode and one where the device exploded?
9. Briefly describe how a pistol or rifle cartridge can be looked at as a simple explosive device.
10. Give some examples of low explosives and some examples of high explosives.

Fill-in-the-Blank & Multiple Choice

1. A low explosive becomes explosive and most dangerous only when its decomposition is _____.

2. For a liquid fuel the lowest temperature at which sufficient volatilization occurs to produce an ignitable vapor at the surface is called the
   a. boiling point.
   b. flash point.
   c. explosion point.
   d. relative vapor density.

3. Most solid fuels are able to support flaming combustion only because _____ converts them to volatile materials.

4. A fuel will only achieve sufficient reaction rate with oxygen from the air to produce flaming combustion when it is in the _____ state.

5. The most sensitive and reliable instrument for detecting and characterizing flammable residues in debris from a suspicious fire is the _____.

Further References

Beveridge, A. D. "Development in the Detection and Identification of Explosive Residues." *Forensic Science Review* 4 (1992): 17–49.

Beveridge, A. Ed., *Forensic Investigation of Explosions,* London, Taylor & Francis.

Bertsch, W., and Q. Ren. "Contemporary Sample Preparation Methods for the Detection of Ignitable Liquids in Suspected Arson Cases." *Forensic Science Review* 11 (1999): 141.

DeHaan, J. D. *Kirk's Fire Investigation.* 5th ed. Englewood Cliffs, NJ: Prentice Hall, 2002, 638 pp.

"Forensic Science Committee Position on Comparison Samples." *Fire and Arson Investigator* vol. 41 (no.2) 50–51 (1990).

Fultz, M. L., and J. D. DeHaan. "Gas Chromatography in Arson and Explosives Analysis." In *Gas Chromatography in Forensic Science,* ed. Ian Tebbett, 109. Chichester, England: Ellis Horwood Ltd., Chapter 5, 1992 Prentice-Hall, 1999.

Lentini, J. J. *Scientific Protocols for Fire Investigation.* Boca Raton, FL: CRC Press, 2005.

National Fire Protection Association. *NFPA 921: Guide for Fire and Explosion Investigations.* Item # 92104. Quincy, MA: NFPA, 2004.

Newman, R., M. W. Gilbert, and K. Lothridge. *GC-MS Guide to Ignitable Liquids.* Boca Raton, FL: CRC Press, 1997.

Stauffer, E., and J. Lentini. "ASTM Standards for Fire Debris Analysis: A Review." *Forensic Science International* 132 (2002): 63–67.

Drugs and Drug Analysis and Forensic Toxicology

Learning Objectives

- Why a substance is called a drug

- The nature of drug dependency and its two major forms

- The impact of drug abuse on society and how society reacts

- Each of the major classes of abused drugs, with examples

- The rationale behind the controlled substances laws

- Processing of suspected controlled substance samples through the crime lab

- The major analytical steps from initial physical description to unambiguous identification

- The important distinction between qualitative and quantitative analysis

- The analysis of body fluid and tissue samples for drugs and poisons (forensic toxicology)

- The critical role of alcohol and drugs in impaired driving cases

Outline

chapter 12

Lead Case

Bufotenine Poisonings

Four men died in New York City after they ate a purported aphrodisiac sold at New York shops during a little over a two-year period. The substance was supposed to be rubbed on the genitals, but it was not labeled and when the victims ate it, they began to vomit and have erratic heartbeats. In addition, at least two other deaths in major cities were eventually attributed to this material, and it seems likely that it may have been involved in other deaths where the connection to this unusual material was not made. The story of what happened was eventually pieced together by the federal Centers for Disease Control from information developed by several law enforcement and health agencies, and the material was banned from import as a result.

During this period a dark brown resinous substance that was sold in grocery stores and tobacco shops under such names as Stone, Lodestone, and Black Stone was also being submitted to the New York City Police Department forensic laboratory. In most cases, the packaging lacked labels listing ingredients or directions for use. The initial recorded deaths occurred in New York City, but the material was also available elsewhere around the country.

These odd-looking little dark brown resinous cubes were submitted as suspected hallucinogenic substances or were thought to be hashish. Initial tests indicated they might contain low concentrations (small amounts) of a hallucinogen called "psilocin" most commonly encountered in so-called magic mushrooms. These mushrooms of the genus *Psilocybe* have been used by native peoples in religious ceremonies for centuries and by drug abusers, particularly in the 1960s, and even today as hallucinogens. More careful analysis disclosed that this component was actually not psilocin but a material called "bufotenine." Bufotenine is chemically very similar to psilocin and is what chemists call an isomer of psilocin. That means that it has the same chemical composition, but the individual atoms in the molecule are arranged slightly differently.

Although this material is a strong hallucinogen, it is not typically very toxic and it was therefore unlikely to have caused the deaths of the individuals who used the material. Nevertheless, its identification was an important clue in unraveling the puzzle of this odd material and the unexplained deaths. For centuries, native peoples as part of their religious ceremonies have used natural hallucinogens. That bufotenine is of natural origin, and not synthetic like LSD and phencyclidine, was important in trying to determine what these odd-looking cubes were.

Bufotenine is most commonly found in three different types of natural materials. Its most common source is in the seeds of plants of the *Anadenanthera* genus, and it is also found in certain mushrooms and in the skin toxins exuded by some toads. It was important in

Small block of brown resinous material which caused several deaths when taken internally rather than topically. Photo courtesy Reddy Chamakura, N.Y.C.P.D. laboratory.

tracing this material and understanding its properties to discover from which of these sources the dark brown resinous cubes arose. A visit to the New York Botanical Gardens to consult with and have the material examined by their curator of mycology (study of mushrooms) quickly eliminated mushrooms as the source. Enough was known about the complex chemical constitution of the plant extracts and toad toxins to distinguish material from these two sources based on careful chemical analysis. This analysis determined that this resinous material originated from the toad toxin rather than the plant seeds. This was consistent with the fact that Chinese herbal medicine used this material in treatment of low sexual potency, whereas the mushroom and plant-derived materials were more commonly used as snuffs or extracts to induce hallucinations. One of the folk uses of these cubes involved topically applying it to the penis to prolong sexual prowess. Unfortunately, several purchasers thought that the material was to be taken orally and this resulted in vomiting, convulsions, and, as indicated earlier, several deaths.

In addition to the bufotenine these cubes were founds to have significant amounts of materials called "bufadienolides." These are the most toxic component of the black resinous material. Bufadienolides are very potent cardio active steroids that cause heart arrhythmias. This means that they act to cause the heart to beat irregularly, which can be fatal. In toads, these very toxic compounds protect them from predators. This property is consistent with the observation that several of the victims had irregular heartbeat and convulsions before they died.

The 1994 Dietary Supplement Health and Education Act (DSHEA) creates a presumption that dietary supplements are safe, which thereby removes them from FDA regulation. This places the burden on the FDA to show that they are dangerous. By proving that these odd-looking brown cubes contained known drug materials that were seriously threatening to human health, they could be brought out from the protection of DSHEA and placed under the regulatory control of the FDA as drugs. The FDA then banned the cubes from importation. Although there is a toad that is found in the southwestern United States that produces similar skin toxins, which have been abused as hallucinogens, the dark brown cubes known to have been available in New York and several other large U.S. cities appear to have been of Chinese origin. For all practical purposes, the importation ban stopped their flow into the United States as Chinese herbal remedies.

Sources: "Legal 'Love Drug' Eyed in Deaths of Three Men," *New York Post,* January 18, 1995 ; "Cops Declare War on Head-Shop 'Love Drug'," *New York Post,* February 20, 1995; "U.S. Says 4 Died in New York Eating an Alleged Aphrodisiac," *New York Times,* November 25, 1995; "Deaths Associated with a Purported Aphrodisiac—New York City February 1993–May 1995," *Morbidity and Mortality Weekly Report* 44 no. 46 (1995): 863; and R. P. Chamakura, "Bufotenine—A Hallucinogen in Ancient Snuff Powders of South America and a Drug of Abuse on the Streets of New York City," *Forensic Science Review* 6 (1994): 1–18.

Nature of Drugs and Drug Abuse

Drugs and drug analysis form a particularly important forensic topic since a significant portion of all the scientists who work in forensic laboratories are employed in drug-related analyses. The drug analysis section is the largest section in the majority of forensic laboratories in the United States. Interestingly, the Canadians and the British have traditionally given drug analysis responsibility to health department laboratories, perhaps because neither the Canadians nor the British have the same level of controlled substance abuse that we have in the United States.

Working Definition of a Drug

What is a good working definition of a drug? Because of the importance of drugs in our society it would seem trivial to come up with a good definition of a drug, but it is not. A good starting point is a very broad statement such as: A drug is any substance that produces physiological or psychological change. Such a definition may be necessary because the term *drug* means different things to different people.

Someone who is an expert in physiology might like the above definition. It covers all the possibilities that one might encounter. However, for law enforcement purposes it would be much too broad to be useful. Under that definition, almost everything one touches can be thought of as producing *some* physiological or psychological effect on the body. The real question is how strong an effect and how soon after it is taken. Medical science is currently trying to deal with the problems of substances that produce effects only many years after exposure, that is, showing an extended induction or incubation period. In the context of drug abuse and the regulation of controlled substances, such substances are not a concern. For example, is a substance like cholesterol a drug? Much medical research indicates that it does have some physiological effect on the body. Certainly some people, after having above-normal concentrations of it in their systems for an extended period of time, develop heart conditions.

One of the few things in the world that virtually no one considers a drug is water. However, there is a condition where people drink enormous quantities of water, gallons and gallons every day. Although water is generally good for you, these people destroy their electrolyte balance and become quite sick and can die if not treated.

These examples suggest that the definition should be modified by adding two conditions. One, which is not very controversial, is that to be a drug the substance must have its effect within a relatively short period of time after ingestion, within minutes or at most hours. The second important proviso involves dosage. Almost everything will have an effect on the body if the dose is large enough. Conversely, with a few exceptions, few substances have much effect if the dose is very low. Thus, a **drug** is a substance that produces a **physiological** or **psychological** effect that is significant, occurs within a reasonable time after dosing, and results from an easily ingested dose. With these added provisions, the overly broad definition becomes much more realistic.

drug

A drug is a substance that produces a physiological or psychological affect that is significant, occurs within a reasonable time after dosing and results from an easily ingested dose.

physiological

Relating to or arising from the functioning of living organism.

psychological

Relating to or arising from the mind or emotions.

Nature of Drug Dependence

dependence

When an individual becomes so strongly attached to a drug that the individual either becomes physically sick or mentally disoriented when its use is discontinued.

Drug **dependence** is the primary reason drug interdiction is a major law enforcement problem in the United States. It is also the reason drug chemistry (controlled substance identification) is such a large part of forensic science laboratory efforts. Law enforcement spends an enormous amount of its resources dealing with many aspects of illegal drugs such as their distribution and the many secondary effects they have on society.

Drug abuse and drug dependence are important concepts. Although specialists might quibble, the terms *dependence* and *addiction* can be used almost interchangeably for law enforcement purposes. If people did not become addicted to or dependent upon certain drugs, society would not be so deeply involved in drug enforcement. The fact that some people who take drugs are no longer productive members of society drives the need to try to control availability of such substances. It is well known that the most abused drug in the Western world is alcohol. People have been abusing alcohol since before recorded history. Alcohol and drug abuse have enormous effects on our society in many ways. The potential of individuals who abuse substances is reduced. Their families are often affected. Considerable productivity in the workplace is lost every year. Substance abuse is frequently involved in other crimes, such as murder, manslaughter, and sexual assault. It is also involved in a very high percentage of serious highway accidents that result in injury and death. The concept of dependence is often subdivided into the categories: physiological dependence and psychological dependence.

Physiological Dependence   *Physiological dependence* occurs when one takes a substance, usually in increasing dosages because the body seems to require increasing dosages to get the *same* effect. When one stops taking the drug, many unpleasant symptoms occur. One may become sick to one's stomach, have terrible headaches, experience shakes, sweat profusely, or even go into convulsions. Thus, if a drug on which a person is physiologically dependent is withheld, the body reacts. Many adults are probably at least mildly physiologically dependent upon (addicted to) caffeine. Many of us take most of our liquids in the form of coffee, tea, or carbonated beverages. Almost all have caffeine in them, as do many other things we ingest. Most individuals who carefully avoided caffeine for a day would almost certainly have a headache before the end of that day, because a common physiological effect of caffeine withdrawal is headache. Physiological dependence is fairly easy to understand at a practical level since the withdrawal symptoms are quite tangible. Dependency on heroin or morphine is the prototype with which everyone is familiar. The movies and literature are rife with heroin withdrawal: the sweats, nausea, cramps, and a variety of other unpleasant physical symptoms. Alcoholics become dependent on having a sizable dosage of alcohol every single day. If they stop or are in the process of trying to break the dependence, they can go into violent fits called delirium tremens (DTs).

Psychological Dependence   *Psychological dependence* can be just as strong an effect as physiological dependence. The tremendous increase in the abuse of cocaine in the last 20 years of the 20th century has changed the way many experts think about psychological dependence. Abusing cocaine for even a short period of time and then stopping does not usually cause physical illness. Often, however, a person does develop what is usually called an "uncontrollable craving" for the drug. That craving is more than a wish to continue taking the drug; it is a desperate need to continue. People who are dependent on cocaine will do awful things to themselves and others to provide themselves with cocaine. Psychological dependencies are every bit as difficult to break as physiological dependencies. This brief description is a bit of an oversimplification, since physiological dependency certainly has a psychological component and psychological dependence has a physical component as well. Moreover, the detailed mechanisms of substance dependence are complex and remain somewhat unclear.

Drugs and Society—Controlled Substances

Drugs generally have become extremely important in treating and preventing disease and illness. Many drugs are available only by prescription—a physician must order them for the patient. Prescription drugs are generally designed for specific conditions and with specific directions about how they are to be used and proscribed in dosages appropriate to the desired action. In addition, many drugs are also available "over the counter"; that is, no prescription is required.

Access to drugs is regulated by the federal Controlled Substances Act and state acts in all 50 states. Under these laws, drugs are placed on various "schedules" (lists), depending on the extent to which they are to be regulated. Some drugs are highly addictive and have no recognized or approved medical use in the United States. They are the most highly regulated, and mere possession of them, unless prescribed by a physician, is a violation of the law. The Drug Enforcement Administration of the U.S. Department of Justice administers the Controlled Substances Act. In this chapter, we discuss drugs that are subject to abuse. A few of these have no recognized therapeutic use. However, many of them do. Forensic science laboratories get involved in this area because a drug or substance has been, or can be, abused. Substance abuse affects the abuser directly, but also affects his or her family, and can very well affect the greater society. Some abused substances are not ordinarily thought of as "drugs." Alcohol is the best example. And, although society and the law do not treat it as a drug, it certainly fits the definition of a drug discussed earlier.

Society through its laws tries to control the abuse of drugs. There is generally a relationship between the degree of regulation of a substance and the amount of harm its abuse is perceived to cause in society. Drug dependence is a serious problem and not tolerated in most segments of our society. The extent of society's acceptance of an addictive drug depends to some extent on the extent to which the abuser is functional in spite of the drug abuse. A drug-abusing physician, for example, may go along for years as long as the problem does not obviously affect the care and treatment of patients. The doctor likely has the funds to buy the drugs and does not have to resort to committing crimes to get them. On the other hand, a drug abuser who has to commit robberies to finance a drug habit is having an obvious negative effect on others and if apprehended is more likely to be prosecuted.

There is a high tolerance for those dependent on alcohol. Alcohol has been a legal drug in the United States (except for one short period) throughout its history. The fact is, however, that alcohol abuse costs society an enormous amount in various ways—traffic accidents, broken families, crime, lost productivity, and so on. By comparison, society has almost no tolerance for people who use, or become dependent on, cocaine. It is illegal to possess the drug, and selling it carries even greater penalties.

Society's attitude toward a particular drug can change over time. An interesting case is tobacco. Tobacco is a "drug" under our definition but is not treated as a drug under the law. It has been a major positive factor in the U.S. economy since colonial days. It was not only tolerated but revered, even though its users develop a strong dependence. In the past few decades, however, society's attitude toward tobacco has undergone a major change, primarily because the long-term health effects of chronic smoking have finally made a clear impression on the public consciousness. Although it is still legal, attitudes toward its use have changed significantly. Whereas smoking was widely advertised and encouraged (at least it wasn't discouraged) a few decades ago, it is now broadly discouraged in every venue of popular culture.

Major Classes of Abused Drugs

The important drugs of abuse can be divided into six basic categories, the first four based on their physiological action.

> *Narcotic Drugs*—The narcotic drugs (with recognized medical use) are taken primarily to dull pain. Analgesic is a better name, but law enforcement

Figure 12.1

Poppy pods being harvested for opium by being slit to allow the thick sap to flow out of the pod to be collected later when it had solidified.

tends to refer to drugs such as heroin and others related to morphine as "narcotics." Heroin has no recognized medical use in the United States.

Stimulants—The stimulants are a group of drugs, including the amphetamines and cocaine, that are used to increase an individual's mental and physical energy level.

Hallucinogens—This broad group of substances changes a person's mental state. They primarily affect perceptions of oneself and of environmental stimuli. Most hallucinogens have no recognized medical use.

Depressants, Hypnotics, and Tranquilizers—This group of substances tends to dull our senses. In most ways, their effects are the opposite of stimulants. Many are used to reduce anxiety or to help induce sleep. These three different types of drugs are treated together since their abuse is similar and many have actions that are somewhat similar. Depressants, hypnotics, and tranquilizers have different medical uses, but abusers tend to use them almost interchangeably, often in combination with alcohol.

Club Drugs—This is not a physiological or pharmacological category, but a loose grouping of substances abused primarily by young people in an effort to enhance their enjoyment of music, dancing, and partying. We treat them as a separate group because of their recent rapid growth into a major drug abuse category. Most of them are in fact depressants, some with amnesic effects (i.e., a person under their influence has no memory of what took place). Some are also associated with "drug-facilitated" sexual assault.

Performance-Enhancing Drugs—Although the first four categories of drugs have been abused for many years or even centuries, performance-enhancing drugs are relatively recent additions to the controlled substances lists. These are materials such as anabolic steroids, stimulants, or painkillers that are taken primarily by athletes to give them an advantage over their competitors by building muscle or endurance or by enhancing other important performance factors. Their control is primarily the result of the dangers to young athletes that arise from taking them without medical supervision, and for purposes far different from their approved medical use.

The preceding categories are designated with drug abuse in mind. We have not attempted to categorize all drugs, and particularly not those primarily used for medicinal purposes, but seldom abused. These categories include many of the drugs that tend to develop dependency in abusers and therefore have been the subject of drug legislation.

Opiates or Narcotic Drugs

narcotic

A drug found as a natural constituent of the opium poppy or a derivative thereof.

analgesics

Drugs used to reduce or eliminate a patient's perception of pain.

Narcotic drugs, more properly known as **analgesics,** are used medically as painkillers and are abused as euphorients. They allow one to better tolerate pain and are beneficial particularly for those experiencing severe pain from a variety of conditions or the last stages of many illnesses. These are also called narcotics or opiates for historical reasons. Morphine is one of the oldest and most effective painkillers. Morphine is the primary active drug in opium. Opium is the dried sap from the opium poppy plant, which produces a small red flower. The seeds from the plant are used on rolls, bagels, and in Danish pastry. If you scored the pod (Figure 12.1) with a sharp instrument just before the poppy blooms, gooey material oozes out. This material can be scraped from the pod, dried, and processed to make opium. Opium can be smoked directly, as it has been for centuries in the Orient, or it can be chemically processed to isolate pure morphine.

About 30 to 35 percent of the dry weight of opium is actually morphine, and it is the largest single drug component in opium. There are many other chemical compounds in opium and many of them have drug activity. All these compounds, and many others that can be made from them, are referred to as *opiates,* because of their origin in opium. Morphine has been abused for centuries because it has the ability to make users fall into a drugged sleep with accompanying feelings of extreme well-being and blissfulness. This property makes the opiates both physically and psychologically addictive drugs. The desirable feelings coupled with the classic need for larger and larger doses to obtain the desired effect make dependence rapid and strong. Further, the severe physiological withdrawal symptoms also reinforce the dependency.

Morphine's strong dependence-producing side effect has caused scientists to search for other drugs that are as effective as painkillers, but not as addictive. Interestingly, one of the many attempts to find a nonaddicting form of morphine produced a fine painkiller by chemically adding acetate groups (combining form of acetic acid) to morphine; the drug produced was called heroin. Heroin, which is now the most abused opiate (Figure 12.2) and is not approved for medical use in the United States, was actually developed by a pharmaceutical company in its search for a nonaddicting form of morphine. Heroin is at least as addictive as morphine, possibly more so.

Codeine is the second most plentiful chemical component of opium. It is a prescription drug that is both a strong painkiller and a good cough suppressant. It is not quite as effective a painkiller as morphine, but also not as addicting. If one looks at the chemical structures, codeine is very similar to morphine. Heroin specimens coming into a forensic lab usually contain a small amount

of codeine (or an acetylated form of codeine). Codeine itself is a controlled substance. There are quite a number of drugs that are made by chemical modification of morphine. Chemists take morphine or some of the other components of opium and chemically modify them to produce painkillers with slightly different properties. In recent years, one of these morphine derivatives, oxycodone, has become a major drug abuse problem under the trade name of Oxycontin. It has become a popular substitute for heroin in communities where heroin has not traditionally been readily available.

There are also a variety of totally synthetic painkillers, including mepiridine (Darvon), pethidine (Demerol), fentanyl, and many more. They are available by prescription and are sometimes abused as well.

Stimulants

Stimulants are taken to make one feel more energetic or strong, or to help keep one awake. Truck drivers may use them to drive for extended periods without falling asleep at the wheel. College students or businesspeople may take stimulants to allow them to study or work for extended periods. One problem with the use of stimulants is that, when the effect wears off, the user "crashes," that is, goes from a higher-than-normal energy level to a lower-than-normal energy level. The most widely used stimulant, as mentioned earlier, is caffeine. However, many people abuse more potent stimulants, such as amphetamine-type drugs or cocaine.

Amphetamine and methamphetamine were used medically for many years for dieting, narcolepsy (tendency to fall asleep at inappropriate times), and several other conditions. Since methamphetamine became heavily abused, and had very limited medical use, it was taken off the market. Although it is no longer produced commercially, it is now the drug most commonly produced in clandestine (illegal) laboratories. Although it is not quite as potent a stimulant as cocaine, its effects last for several

---

Case Study 12.1

Drug Abuse Dangers

A rather sad story illustrates the dangers of abuse of synthetic painkillers. Some years ago, a serious problem broke out on the West Coast. A number of heroin addicts were showing up in emergency rooms unconscious and dying soon thereafter. The cause of death was not immediately obvious, because when blood and urine samples were analyzed, little or no heroin or its metabolites (see toxicology section that follows) were found. Thus, they did not seem to be simple overdose victims. When a rash of addict deaths occurs, it is common for the police to come into possession of samples of the drug the addicts were taking. No heroin or other commonly abused drug was found in these samples, either. The word on the street was that something called "China White" was supposed to be the new "hot shot"; that is, a very strong heroin. Initial analysis again showed only cutting agents and no commonly encountered drug of abuse. Upon a more involved and careful analysis, analysts discovered that an extremely potent synthetic analgesic, which had never been sold commercially, was present in these samples in very small amounts. It was closely related to a drug called fentanyl, which is also a very potent analgesic used in hospitals. Because this drug is about 3,000 times as potent as morphine, the amount in samples called China White was too small to detect with the routine analytical procedures used at the time in forensic laboratories. Although present in barely detectible amounts, it was still enough to be fatal to the drug abusers. It seems likely that someone with knowledge of painkiller chemistry synthesized a batch of it and was able to sell it. It was somehow distributed as China White and, because of its extreme potency, caused several hundred deaths. Subsequently there were several other outbreaks, but the originator was never found. Several individuals who synthesized similar drugs were arrested.

Figure 12.2

A typical glassine bag of street heroin.

hours per dosing rather than perhaps 30 minutes as with cocaine. Methamphetamine is widely distributed and widely available (Figure 12.3).

Cocaine has been the "star" of abused stimulant drugs for the last 20 or 30 years. During this period, it grew from a curiosity to the drug of choice for many drug abusers (Figure 12.4).

Cocaine is a very powerful stimulant and is enormously psychologically addicting. The abuse of cocaine has caused literally hundreds of thousands of people to destroy their lives. It has victimized rich and poor alike. Cocaine hydrochloride, the way cocaine was sold on the street for years, is usually inhaled through the nose. Cocaine in its free base form is called "crack." Crack cocaine can be easily vaporized by heat in a pipe and then is inhaled into the lungs. Inhalation of these vapors delivers cocaine to the bloodstream very quickly and efficiently. This action produces a very quick high, which is intense and became the experience of choice for many stimulant drug abusers. Crack cocaine is marketed in small doses that are sold cheaply on the street. However, since the intense high is short-lived, repeated doses are the rule. Cocaine powder is generally marketed in larger units and tends to be used by drug abusers who have more ready money.

Hallucinogens

hallucinogens

Drugs taken to cause a significantly altered mental state, often including hallucinations.

Hallucinogens have been used for centuries to affect one's perceptions. One of the oldest and the most widely used is marijuana. It has been used in the Middle East

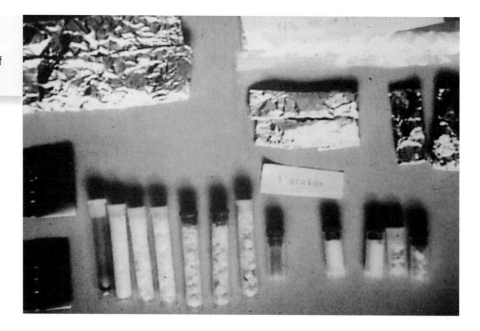

Figure 12.5
Marijuana cigarettes typical of those sold at the retail level.

for probably thousands of years. No one knows exactly when it was discovered that the leaves of the hemp plant, the stem of which was used for making rope, would also made one feel a little bit woozy and a little strange when smoked or ingested with foods. Many people think these sensations are pleasant. People have smoked, chewed, "brewed" marijuana in teas, and taken it in a variety of other ways. The leaves of the hemp plant (the marijuana plant—*Cannabis sativa*—Figure 12.5) have a coating of a resinous material. It is this resinous material that contains the physiologically active ingredients, which are called "cannabinoids." The most well known and most important of the cannabinoids is tetrahydrocannabinol, or THC. Much of the marijuana purchased on the street today is a totally different product than it was 20 years ago. The breeding stock has now been improved to produce more resin and thus more THC. Premium grades of marijuana now have THC content in the 6 to 7 percent range, two or three times more active ingredient than seen in material a number of years ago. Because marijuana is more potent now, it has become a more dangerous drug.

Another form of marijuana is called "hashish"; it was traditionally a more potent form of marijuana. Originally, hashish was made by going down the rows of growing marijuana plants, when they flower, with a large piece of leather on the harvester's arms and hitting the tops of the plants. The sticky stuff and the flowers, particularly, would stick to the leather. When the leather was well covered, the material sticking to it was scraped off. These scrapings were then collected and compressed to make the hashish. This material was considered a more potent form because it had more resin than the leafy material. Normal marijuana has a lot of plant material and a little bit of resin. As noted, plant breeding practices have changed the nature of much marijuana and, as a result, hashish made from "unimproved" marijuana may have a lower THC content than premium marijuana.

A third form of marijuana is called "hash oil." It is made by taking a large quantity of marijuana plant material, placing it into a large vessel, and "cooking" it with alcohol or some other solvent. Hash oil processors often use gasoline or kerosene. In this way the resin, which is very soluble in solvents like gasoline and kerosene, is dissolved off the plant material. The solid material is removed and the solvent is then evaporated down (concentrated) until it is a thick oily material, which is almost pure resin and has very little vegetable matter in it. This process produces a concentrate, which can be more easily smuggled, and which can also be used to increase the potency of marijuana plant material. Smuggling small bottles of a highly concentrated hallucinogen is much easier than large bales of marijuana plant material.

Figure 12.6

Some of the many forms of LSD encountered in crime laboratories.

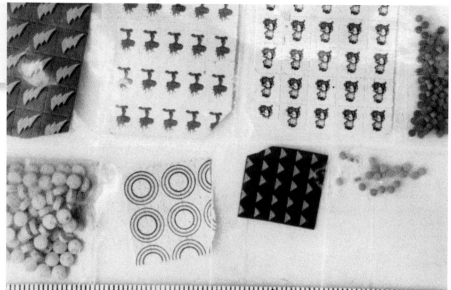

Concentrated hash oil can be reconstituted by mixing it with tobacco or other vegetable material, which makes even a small volume of it valuable.

LSD is probably the most potent and the best known of the true hallucinogens. The great guru of LSD in this country, Timothy Leary, had been a professor at Harvard who advocated the "mind-expanding" nature of the LSD experience in the 1960s. LSD is short for lysergic acid diethylamide, its chemical name. It is an extremely potent hallucinogen. Very minute doses (Figure 12.6) of it cause long and often frightening hallucinations. Obviously, some find the experience satisfying since it has been abused since it was first synthesized.

Unfortunately, many people have done serious harm to themselves under the influence of LSD. It is said to cause visual hallucinations, brilliant colors, and the perception that one is very wise, or in touch with a supreme being. The normal LSD dosage is 30–50 micrograms (millionths of a gram), which is a thousand times less than that required for most other drugs to produce a physiological effect. One of its greatest dangers is that children sometimes are attracted to the dosage forms and cannot tolerate the dosage taken by abusers. Another danger of LSD is that some people will continue to have hallucinogenic episodes even long after they stop taking the drug. Recurring and/or delayed hallucinations can occur even after a single use of this drug.

Phencyclidine, usually known as "PCP" or "angel dust," is another hallucinogen that was extremely popular for a while. It is a drug that is fairly simple to make, so the vast majority of it is made in clandestine laboratories. The term *laboratory* is actually not very accurate since the clandestine "laboratory" is often someone's bathroom, garage, or barn. It is fairly easy to find out how to make PCP from inexpensive starting chemicals. Unfortunately, safety is often not a concern in these operations. Even if the people involved in the activities know better, they ignore safety factors. Many times, clandestine laboratories are discovered because the operators blow themselves up or cause a fire. PCP has decreased in popularity, because the hallucinations are frequently not very pleasant and because it tends to make people aggressive. There was a period when PCP was the number one drug of abuse, particularly on the West Coast. It was even more popular than cocaine or heroin, in some areas. Clandestine drug laboratories pose potentially extreme chemical and explosion hazards for investigators. The Drug Enforcement Administration (DEA) and many forensic laboratories have "clan lab" teams trained to safely disassemble these makeshift laboratories in a safe manner.

A number of naturally occurring hallucinogens have been used by native people for centuries, usually as part of religious rituals. For example, peyote is the bud of a particular kind of cactus (Figure 12.7). It contains as the main active ingredient a hallucinogen called "mescaline." In fact, it is legal to use peyote as part of the ritual of the Native American Church. It is a controlled substance under any other circumstances. One of the disadvantages of peyote is that it is not pleasant to take. It is said to be extremely bitter and unpleasant tasting. Users report that it makes people feel like they are having an out-of-body experience and are closer to their God, which is a common thread among plant hallucinogens abuse. The plants or parts of them were discovered, like LSD, to cause people to have feelings of being very wise or closer to their supreme being.

So-called magic mushrooms were also popular hallucinogens in the 1960s and are still being abused. These are mushrooms of the genus *Psilocybe* (Figure 12.8). The two major active components are psilocin and psilocybin. It is possible to buy spores through the mail. These can be placed in humus or some similar growth medium, placed in a dark damp place, and psilocybe mushrooms may emerge. The spores themselves are not illegal because they don't contain any psilocin or psilocybin, which are the controlled materials in the mature mushroom.

A number of other synthetic hallucinogens were also popular in the 1960s and early 1970s. They had abbreviated names like MDA, DOM, STP, and DMT. Interestingly, one of the most heavily abused drugs in the current "club drug" scene, which will be discussed later, is a close relative of MDA known as MDMA, or "Ecstasy."

Depressants, Hypnotics, and Tranquilizers

Alcohol, alone and in combination with other depressants, is certainly the most common and widely used depressant drug. It is the most abused drug in the Western world. Almost everyone knows something about the effects of alcohol.

Abuse of depressants usually results in a mental and physical state similar to alcohol-induced intoxication. Barbiturates are compounds that were widely used as sleeping pills. For many years, the barbiturates were the sleeping products of choice. They are still prescribed for several different functions and used in hospitals. The many slight variations on the basic barbiturate structure allow tailoring the drug to a desired effect. There are fast-, slow-, and intermediate-acting barbiturates. Phenobarbital, given in small dosages, is also used to control seizures in epileptics and others subject to seizures. It is considered a slow-acting barbiturate, because it takes significantly longer than the rapid-acting barbiturates to induce sleep. Barbiturates are not currently abused extensively in the United States, but they were a major problem in the past and contributed to the death of several famous people, including Marilyn Monroe. They are highly physiologically addictive and can produce extremely unpleasant withdrawal symptoms and even death when usage is abruptly stopped.

Similarly, methaqualone, developed as a nonaddictive sleep medication to replace barbiturates, was popular for a while but has largely disappeared from the "abuse" scene. The abuse was so heavy that two different companies that manufactured it stopped making it, largely because of diversion of the drug from legal trade to the illegal market and the resulting pressure from the DEA and other law enforcement agencies.

Tranquilizers are drugs designed to relieve anxiety. Valium, which was one of the first and most popular tranquilizers, was the most prescribed drug in the United States for a number of years. It may have been overprescribed, taken by some people to be "fashionable," rather than for sound medical reasons. Valium belongs to a class of drugs called "benzodiazepines." Benzodiazepines (Figure 12.9) are not only useful as tranquilizers but have largely replaced the barbiturates as sleep aids as well. Rohypnol, a benzodiazepine that has never been approved for sale in the United States, has become one of the major drugs of abuse in the "club drug" scene. Under street names such as "roofies," it is popular at raves and at after-hours clubs. The Rohypnol available at such gatherings is illegally imported from other countries where it is a legal prescription drug.

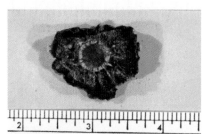

PEYOTE BUTTON

POLICE LABORATORY, N. Y. C.
P. L. No.
DATE

Figure 12.7

A Dried Peyote Button.
This is a portion of the peyote cactus that contains hallucinogenic materials used in native American religious rites and abused by those seeking the hallucinogenic experience.

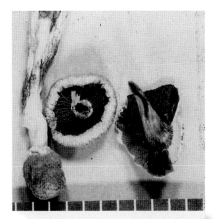

Figure 12.8
Psilocybe mushrooms that contain the hallucinogens psilocin or psilocybin.

Chemical and Materials Evidence

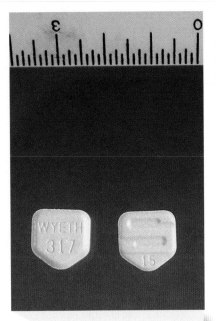

Figure 12.9

Oxazepam tablets, which are among the many benzodiazepines (tranquilizers) that are frequently abused.

club drugs

Any of a group of drugs whose primary abuse is associated with marathon youthful dance parties.

rave

A dance party, usually lasting all night, that tends to be characterized by stroboscopic light effects, loud music, and high human density and attended ordinarily by youthful participants.

licit

Not prohibited by law.

illicit

Proscribed by law (illegal).

Club Drugs

Club drugs are separately discussed because they have become a major area of concern for law enforcement, and thus for many forensic labs in the United States. The DEA puts out a monthly publication called *Microgram Bulletin* that goes to all law enforcement agencies active in drug enforcement, including all the forensic laboratories in the United States. It is a means of rapid communication and, in addition to technical articles, contains reports from laboratories all over the world concerning new and unusual specimens they have encountered. Recent issues of *Microgram* suggest that different forms of MDMA (Ecstasy) (Figure 12.10) have become a major problem.

The effects of MDMA, particularly at the dosages taken by abusers, are not yet fully understood. It was originally called the "love drug." The first reported uses were by psychotherapists, who felt that it made their patients more open to social interaction; hence the name love drug. MDMA was never approved by the FDA and cannot be prescribed or sold legally in the United States. As a result, it is not a drug that is always of pharmaceutical quality. The material sold on the illegal market is either synthesized legally for sale outside the United States, but with no U.S. FDA oversight, or is prepared in clandestine laboratories. MDMA stands for *methylenedioxymethamphetamine*.

Two other popular drugs in the club and **rave** environment are GHB (gamma hydroxybutyrate) and ketamine. Both can be synthesized in clandestine laboratories or diverted from legal production sources. Control of GHB abuse is complicated by the existence of a similar chemical GBL (gamma-butyrolactone), which the body can convert to GHB. GBL is actually sold as an industrial solvent for cleaning floors and has never been directly investigated as a drug, although it has powerful effects on the body, because of its rapid conversion to GHB. These drugs are abused primarily as hypnotics or depressants, often in combination with alcohol. The final member of this group, ketamine (Figure 12.11), has been around for over 30 years.

The primary medical use of ketamine is as an anesthetic and an animal tranquilizer. Since the **licit** use of ketamine is primarily by veterinarians, much of the ketamine on the **illicit** market is stolen from veterinarians. Few if any clandestine ketamine laboratories have been encountered. It was also used on humans for a number of years, particularly in emergency surgery situations. Anterograde amnesia, loss of memory while under its influence, is one of the side effects that reduced its

Figure 12.10 A variety of MDMA tablets of the type often abused at dance parties and most commonly referred to as "Ecstasy."

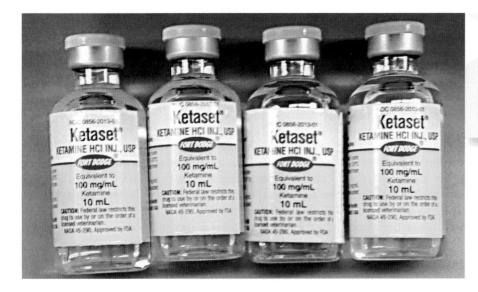

general utility. The other side effect, hallucinogenic episodes, is one reason for its abuse. The memory loss aspect is an advantage for surgery performed under less than ideal conditions on seriously injured patients. For example, ketamine was a popular anesthetic with medics in field hospitals during the Vietnam War. It tends to be a tranquilizer or hypnotic drug when given in low doses, whereas larger doses cause unconsciousness with partial or full memory loss.

Rohypnol, GHB, and ketamine along with some other substances have been implicated in cases of **drug-facilitated sexual assault** within the past decade or so. For that reason, they are sometimes called "date-rape" drugs. In some cases, unsuspecting victims are given these substances clandestinely by perpetrators (or by someone else, like a bartender, at the behest of a perpetrator). In other cases, perpetrators exploit victims who are abusing the substances voluntarily. The tranquillizing effects of these substances tend to make a potential victim more compliant and less able to resist, while the amnesic effects prevent her (victims are usually but not always women) from remembering what happened. In any event, it is clear that persons under the influence of these substances are unable to give informed consent for sexual relations. Thus, anyone who has sexual relations with someone incapacitated in this way is guilty of rape.

One of the major problems with drugs of abuse in general and with club drugs in particular, is that they are not used in proper dosages as would be prescribed by a physician. Any drug can become dangerous if the dosage is too high. Thus, overdoses are likely, and a number of deaths have occurred because of these drugs. Research on the prevalence of these drugs is difficult, and although there is a lot of anecdotal information around, it is not clear just how common they are. These club drugs were briefly discussed in Chapter 9 in connection with sexual assault.

Athletic Performance Enhancers

Athletic performance enhancement drugs are a relatively new phenomenon in the drug abuse context. They have not been of concern to law enforcement until recently, although they have been of some concern to those who regulate athletic competition, both amateur and professional, for much longer. The first drugs controlled because of their use by athletes, particularly young athletes, were **anabolic** steroids. These drugs are used to rapidly build muscle in conjunction with vigorous physical training. The concern of the regulators is that, as with most abused drugs, the abusers use much larger doses than have been shown to be safe, and as a result can suffer serious side effects. Further, because many of the young athletes are still growing, they are more susceptible to the serious side effects.

Again, as with most abused drugs, drug dealers often sell the materials under incorrect names, and mislabeling is rampant. Most abused anabolic steroids

drug-facilitated sexual assault
A sexual encounter where one party, the victim, has been rendered unable to resist or voluntarily participate by ingestion of a drug, often in combination with alcohol.

anabolic
Promotes cell growth and division, resulting in growth of muscle tissue and sometimes bone size and strength.

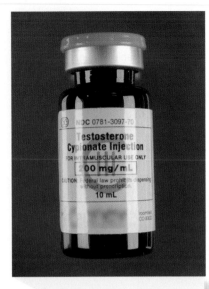

Figure 12.12

Testosterone injectable solution of the type often abused by athletes to enhance muscle growth.

controlled substance

A drug that is named in either federal or state controlled substances statues as illegal to possess except when prescribed by a physician.

(Figure 12.12) are produced by pharmaceutical manufacturers but are frequently produced for foreign sale, and either not approved for usage in the United States or brought into the country illegally.

The substances can be mislabeled as to what the drug actually is, as well as to the amount in a single dose. This problem is compounded by the fact that "proper" dosage for the muscle-building function is not known, and, as with club drug abusers, athletes sometimes take massive dosages recommended by fellow abusers with no knowledge of possible side effects.

As law enforcement and athletic organizations have tried to control the abuse of existing substances, new drugs have been introduced, or abusers have tried different drugs with supposed anabolic properties. Human growth hormone and a few other nonsteroidal materials have gained a reputation as having muscle-building properties. The information in circulation on the Internet or in some athletic magazines is seldom based on well-designed research studies. Athletes desperate to gain a competitive edge or to perform when injured also abuse stimulants and painkillers.

Controlled Substance Laws

Controlled substance laws are extremely complex and can be more a reflection of the political climate when they are passed than of pharmacology or law enforcement needs. The federal scheduling of controlled substances is based on well-researched findings of pharmaceutical professions. It is important to understand that the scheduling determines what substances are controlled but does not determine the severity of the penalties imposed for possession or sale.

Because trafficking in drugs of abuse almost always involves interstate commerce, there is often dual jurisdiction, both state and federal. Since many drugs of abuse are illegally imported into the country, the federal government can have jurisdiction in most drug cases. Even so, the majority of drug enforcement activity is at the state and local level.

The federal government has created five controlled substances "schedules." These are based on two primary concerns: abuse potential and medical value. Schedule I contains drugs that have no current medical use and have a high potential for abuse. For example, drugs like heroin and LSD have no current medical use, plus a high potential for abuse, so they are on Schedule I. Schedule II contains drugs that have high abuse potential, but have some current medical use. Cocaine, for example, certainly has high abuse potential, but since cocaine has a currently approved clinical use as an anesthetic in eye surgery, it is on Schedule II. Morphine is also on Schedule II because it is still a widely used painkiller and has considerable medical use in spite of its very high abuse potential. Schedule III is for drugs that have some abuse potential, but less than those on Schedules I and II, and also have current medical use. Anabolic steroids, which have been controlled only in recent years, are on Schedule III. They have now become a significant area of activity in many forensic labs because of growing abuse, particularly among the young athletes. Codeine also falls in Schedule III. It is not quite as addictive as morphine or heroin and has considerable medical use. Schedule IV is for drugs with low abuse potential and considerable medical use, which describes most tranquilizers and many diet drugs. Schedule V drugs are what are called "exempt preparations." They are usually drug preparations that contain at least one ingredient that is listed on one of the higher schedules, but it is present in a relatively small amount and in combination with much larger amounts of other noncontrolled ingredients. A number of cough syrup preparations, which contain a small amount of codeine, dextromethorphan, and two or three other drugs in flavored syrup are in Schedule V. They have a very low abuse potential because of the small amount of the controlled drug and general utility to the public.

Perhaps the most controversial thing in the federal scheduling laws is the placement of marijuana in Schedule I. Placement of marijuana on federal Schedule I is a result of the idea that marijuana is a "gateway" drug; that is, that its use leads to the use of more dangerous and/or more addictive drugs in many people. There is some basis for this belief, but there is also considerable evidence that many people use marijuana casually without ill effects. Chronic or heavy use of marijuana is known to have undesirable health effects.

Many states have moved marijuana to a lower schedule and decriminalized possession of small amounts. In New York and California, for instance, possession of small amounts of marijuana is a violation penalized by a fine and is not considered a criminal offense. In addition, medical necessity laws have recently been passed in several western states. They allow possession of marijuana for medical reasons if prescribed by a physician. This clearly conflicts with the federal scheduling, and these laws are strongly opposed by federal drug enforcement authorities. The medical community is somewhat divided on this issue, with some doctors sympathetic to the fact that marijuana is medically useful in alleviating nausea caused by chemotherapy, glaucoma, and a few other conditions. Other doctors feel that there are other drugs more effective for these applications and there is no medical necessity for marijuana as a therapeutic agent. Interestingly, the primary active ingredient in marijuana, THC, is available in capsule form by prescription. This conflict will undoubtedly eventually be resolved by Congress or by the United States Supreme Court.

Analysis of Controlled Substances in the Forensic Laboratory

As with some types of evidence already discussed, such as gunshot residue (Chapter 8) and blood and physiological fluids (Chapter 9), the laboratory identification of controlled substances uses screening tests followed by more reliable confirmation tests. The screening tests are designed to be quick, easy to perform, and to allow for screening many specimens in a short time. Confirmatory tests are typically more complicated and time-consuming.

Screening Tests

An important adjunct to drug enforcement is the utilization of drug screening tests. These are "presumptive" tests. Positive results indicate possible, but not certain presence of drugs. Most of these tests are simple and based on color changes and are thus easy to use outside a laboratory. Nowadays screening tests are usually found in the form of little packets (Figure 12.13) called drug test kits.

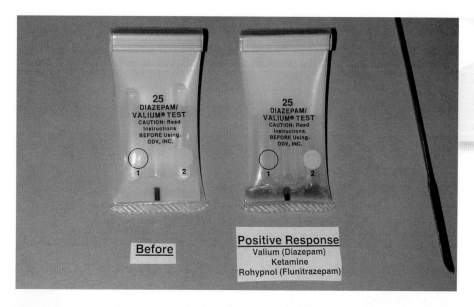

Figure 12.13

A test kit of the type used by officers to test suspected controlled substances on the street. This kit is for the commonly abused tranquilizer Diazepam.

The packet has some small tubes and a sealed ampoule of a chemical test reagent. One places a small amount of the suspected drug in one tube from the kit, breaks an ampoule, adds the reagent, mixes, and looks for a certain color. The kits are designed in several different ways, with some having several steps, but the result is a quick and relatively simple set of operations that give a fairly reliable indication of the probable presence of the target controlled substance or substances. These screening kits were designed for use by law enforcement officers who, after a short training program, can perform the tests quite successfully. Their importance comes from the requirement for probable cause when making a drug possession arrest. An officer can see someone who appears to be dealing drugs and want to make an arrest. In many states, more than just the officer's experience that the incident looks like a drug deal is required. Using a test kit to show that it is likely that there is a controlled drug in the material seized adds another reason to believe it is a drug deal. These field tests or screening tests are very similar to the initial screening tests used in the forensic laboratories. They are not a substitute for laboratory analysis! Prosecution for possession of a controlled substance requires that the material be submitted to a forensic laboratory, and an examiner qualified to testify as an expert verifies the identity of the material.

Perhaps the most commonly used screening kit at the present time is the Scott test for cocaine. It is not totally specific for cocaine, since there are some related drugs and other substances that give a positive test.

Another important screening test is the Duquenois-Levine test for marijuana (*Cannabis sativa*). It is a two-part test that works well to distinguish marijuana from other vegetable material. It has been reported that some herbs and spices also give the same color with the test, and therefore it is not absolutely specific. However, this particular test for marijuana is quite specific if the drug analyst knows exactly what the color should look like.

The Marquis screening test is an interesting test that has been around for many years. The chemical reagent for the Marquis contains formaldehyde and concentrated sulfuric acid—potentially dangerous substances. The test reacts with almost all the opiate drugs. It gives a variety of reds or purples depending on which drug is present. It also reacts with amphetamines to give an orange to brown color. As a result, an analyst can screen for both amphetamines and opiates with the same test.

The last of the very common screening tests is the Van Erk test, useful for many hallucinogenic drugs. It not nearly as specific as the screening tests just discussed.

When seized materials come into a forensic laboratory, the first step is usually testing with screening tests. These tests are similar, but not identical, to those used in the field by police. The laboratory chemist screens the alleged drug substances to decide which specimens require confirmation with more accurate methods. One of the problems with commercial screening test packets is dependence on the officer to add the proper amount of sample. Chemists with more experience and understanding of the process can better judge the amount to use and judge the significance of the color. Therefore, the repetition of the screening test in the laboratory is not at all redundant.

Isolation and Separation

purification

The physical or chemical process whereby a substance is separated from other accompanying substances or impurities to obtain the pure chemical substance.

diluents

Materials that are added to a drug to add bulk and thereby make it easier to handle.

Each laboratory may follow a slightly different set of detailed steps in controlled substance identification, even though the general analytical scheme forensic laboratories use is very similar. The steps might include viewing a small portion of the exhibit under a microscope to more closely examine what is present. This microscopic examination gives the examiner some idea of whether there are several different materials present. A **purification** step to separate the controlled substance from the other materials present usually follows the microscopic examination. Liquid/liquid extraction is one of the simplest separation methods and, with proper choice of solvents, the drug component or components can frequently be separated from most inert **diluents.** Gas chromatography, high-performance liquid chromatography, and several other chromatographic techniques are also commonly used (see the box "More on the Science: Chemical Separations"). One of the most useful

Chemical Separations

The simplest chemical separation technique is called "extraction." For example, imagine a scenario where an analyst has a mixture of two or more drugs in a body fluid sample and wants to largely remove one of those drugs into a different solution to help identify it. The mixed drug solution is shaken with an immiscible solvent, that is, a solvent that will form a separate layer when mixed with the first solution (Figure 12.14).

A common example of the principle is oil and vinegar salad dressing, where the oil and vinegar layers can be shaken together to form what appears to be one phase, but upon standing will always separate back to two layers.

The immiscible solvent is selected such that much more of one of the drugs will move into the solvent when they are shaken together. Thus when the mixture separates, the second solvent will have more of the desired drug and little of the other drug or drugs. The layers are then separated, a fresh portion of the immiscible solvent is added, and the process is repeated. The separated solvent layers can be combined, and thereby much of the desired drug is separated from the other drug or drugs. As a result it can be more efficiently analyzed.

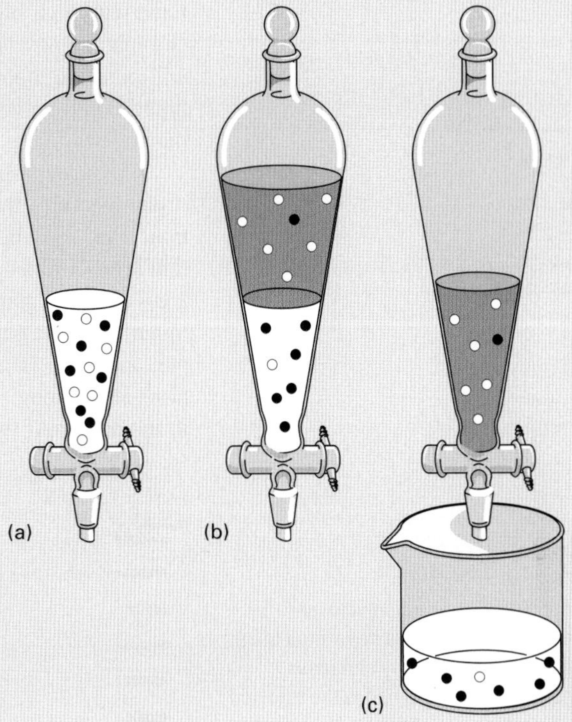

(a) (b)

(c)

Figure 12.14 This illustrates the process called "liquid/liquid extraction" where substances can be separared by shaking with two immiscible liquids, where one of the compounds is preferentially moved to one of the liquids. In that way, when the liquids are separated, the separated compound can be isolated.

things about a screening test is that it does not require an extraction (isolation) step before use. Screening tests generally are effective on the kind of mixtures usually encountered in "street" drug samples.

Microcrystal Tests

A type of confirmatory test that works well on "street" drug samples directly (no separation or purification necessary) is the microcrystal test. It is useful for rapid yet reliable identification of many drugs and was widely used for many years before some of the more sophisticated spectroscopic (see later) techniques became available. The microcrystal test is performed simply by taking a small amount of the street drug sample, placing it on a microscope slide, and adding a drop of a chemical reagent that is known to give crystals of a particular shape (Figure 12.15) with the suspected drug component. The shape (morphology) of the crystals formed is characteristic for that particular drug combined with the chemical reagent used to form them. Chemists can be trained to recognize these crystals as a way of identifying many drugs.

Crystal tests have fallen out of favor as spectrometric confirmatory techniques have become available, but they are still used in many laboratories as rapid confirmatory tests. One of the problems in laboratory drug identification is the way controlled substance laws are written and interpreted. If a lab receives a seizure of 50 identical envelopes containing white powder, the examiner may not just take two or three envelopes randomly and analyze them; the courts often require analysis of a sample from each of the 50 envelopes. A big advantage of crystal tests, and the reason they are still used in many crime laboratories, is that they are rapid and, in conjunction with other tests, specific. Thus, multiple specimens can be processed rapidly and simultaneously.

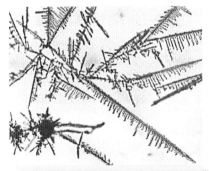

Figure 12.15

Microcrystals formed when a material containing cocaine is mixed with a dilute solution of Gold Chloride on a microscope slide and viewed at about 100X in a compound microscope. The characteristic shape of these crystals is highly indicative of the presence of cocaine in the material.

Chromatography (Separations)

All forms of **chromatography** are actually separation techniques. (See the "More on Science: Chromatography and Gas Chromatography" box in Chapter 11.) Thin-layer or gas chromatography can be used to separate the components of a specimen that contains a mixture of compounds. Originally devised to work on paper, the technique was later extended to thin layers of silica gel or cellulose, and to columns lined with high boiling liquids designed to aid in particular chemical separations. All chromatography is based on the principle that the chemical components of a mixture will partition themselves between the phases of a two-phase system (just like in the liquid/liquid solvent extraction method described earlier). If one of these phases is moving while the other is stationary, physical separations can be achieved.

Chromatographic techniques can also provide a method of tentative identification if one measures the time that a drug takes to emerges from the instrument after injection, the so-called retention time, or the distance that a drug travels on a thin-layer chromatography plate. For example, a known heroin sample is injected into a gas chromatograph under carefully controlled conditions. The heroin always takes 8.3 minutes to emerge under these conditions. Now, if one injects a suspected heroin sample, and there is a significant amount of that sample that emerges at 8.3 minutes, it provides a strong suspicion that the specimen contains heroin, though it does not prove it. In addition, if two additional materials emerge at 7.5 and 7.7 minutes (Figure 12.16)

Figure 12.16

A mixture of six common over-the-counter drugs is separated using gas chromatography and mass spectroscopy. Top half is the total ion chromatogram of the six-drug mixture and the bottom half is the mass spectrum of Dextromethorpham, the peak at about 11 minutes.

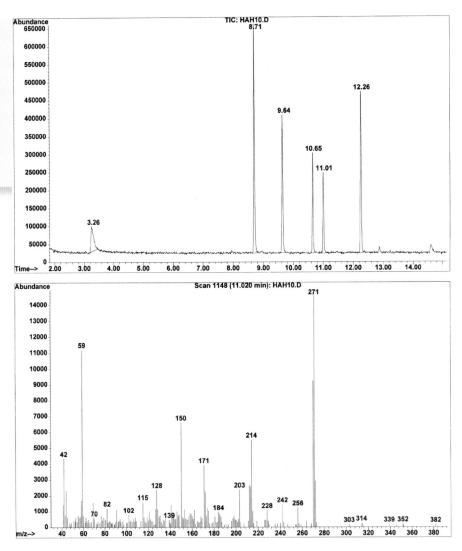

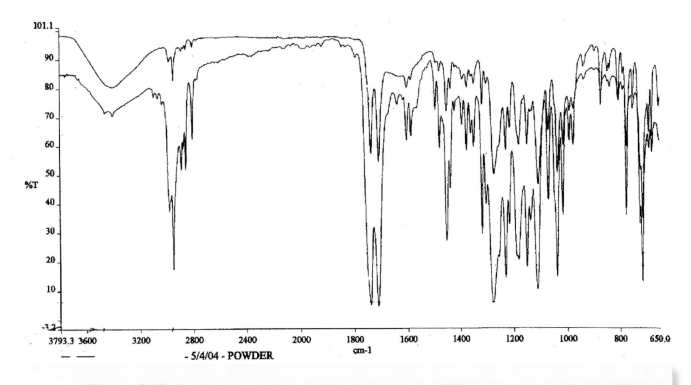

Figure 12.17   The infrared spectrum obtained from cocaine base (crack). The upper trace is a small amount of known cocaine base standard.

and street heroin virtually always shows these same two peaks, there are now three different peaks observed that indicate heroin. Thus, although chromatography is not an identification technique as such (it is a separation technique), it can be used in connection with other information (Figure 12.16) to assist an examiner in identifying controlled substances.

Spectroscopy/Spectrometry

Spectroscopy (also called "spectrometry"), either **mass spectroscopy** or **infrared spectroscopy,** provides a complex pattern (spectrum) (Figure 12.17) that is characteristic of a particular drug and is different from that obtained from other drugs. If we have a mixture of several drugs or a drug and several diluents, the spectrum produced from the mixture would not be identifiable because we cannot say which peak belongs to which component of the mixture. Therefore, spectroscopic identifications work best when the sample examined is a relatively pure material. Infrared and mass spectrometry are excellent ways to identify drugs, particularly when combined with a chromatographic technique to separate and isolate the individual pure components.

Although chromatographic techniques can, as noted, give indications of the identity of controlled substances, the identifications must generally be confirmed by mass spectroscopy or by infrared spectroscopy For some time, instruments have been available that combine **gas chromatography** with mass spectroscopy or with infrared spectroscopy. Such instruments—and the combination of techniques they perform—are typically called GC-MS or GC-IR (Figure 12.18). These may also be called "hyphenated techniques."

The so-called hyphenated techniques use a single instrument that combines chromatographic separation with a highly specific spectral identification technique. Gas chromatography, for example, is combined with either mass spectrometry or infrared spectroscopy to allow separation of the drug mixture into its pure

spectroscopy

The interaction of electromagnetic radiation with a chemical to give a pattern characteristic of that material's interaction with the radiation.

mass spectroscopy

A technique for identification of materials by bombarding them, while in the gas phase, with a high-energy species (usually electrons) and causing them to fragment into ions whose mass is determined by a mass sorting device.

infrared spectroscopy

The use of the measurement of the absorption of infrared radiation by a substance to characterize that substance.

gas chromatography

A chromatographic technique where the mixture is to be separated is vaporized and the separation occurs during partition between the gas and a solid or liquid absorbent.

Figure 12.18

Typical gas chromatograph/mass spectrometer with auto-sampler tower. This is the most used instrument in the controlled substances analysis section of most crime laboratories.

components in one part of the instrument and then passing of each component, one at a time, to the identification part of the instrument for identification. High-performance liquid chromatographs can also be combined with mass spectrometers (LC-MS). These instruments provide a characteristic retention time from the chromatographic portion of the instrument along with an unambiguous spectrum that allows for identification from the other part. There are known standard spectra to compare with those obtained from case specimens. This combination of a chromatographic retention time and a spectrum provides a much stronger identification than either alone.

Qualitative versus Quantitative Analysis

The examination of a street drug specimen and identification of a particular controlled substance in it enables one to say that this material contains a particular controlled substance. The analyst is *not* saying that the specimen contains nothing else, nor is he or she saying *how much* of that sample is made up of that controlled substance. That is a *qualitative* analysis. Qualitative analysis means determining whether something is there or is not there. To charge someone with possession of a controlled substance under most drug laws, a qualitative identification is all that is necessary. The drug law makes it illegal to possess *any* of the material. The legal term is "aggregate weight based law." If a brick of compressed powder weighing a pound has been seized, and that powder contains cocaine, the defendant will be charged with possession of a pound of material containing cocaine.

The concept of quantitative analysis becomes important when a drug law is written in such a way that the severity of the charge varies with the actual amount of the controlled substance possessed. In such cases, a *quantitative* analysis is required. Depending on the law, it may be necessary to establish not only that the seized one-pound brick contains cocaine, methamphetamine, or heroin, for example, but also that such-and-such percentage of the total is the controlled drug. Qualitative analysis says the substance is there and what it is, and quantitative analysis says how much of it is in the specimen. In most cases, forensic labs do not have to perform a quantitative analysis, since most drug laws are aggregate weight laws. Because it takes about 10 times as much effort to do a quantitative analysis as it does to do a qualitative analysis, quantitative analysis is normally done only when legally required or for intelligence purposes.

Forensic Toxicology— Antimortem and Postmortem

A toxicologist analyzing body fluid or tissue samples has a significantly different task than does a crime laboratory chemist analyzing a street drug sample. As we will see, however, most of the analytical techniques used are the same. For the drug chemist, the sample is submitted in a form such as an envelope of white powder, a collection of tablets or capsules, crude-looking cigarettes, or a large seizure that may fill a suitcase or a large carton. The chemist can usually see it, touch it, weigh it, and easily take a small sample to analyze. Toxicologists have a much more difficult problem. They receive blood, urine, or body tissues. The sample may be only 5 to 10 milliliters (normally a tube of blood taken from a person at a doctor's office contains about 5 milliliters of blood), and in most cases is only a small fraction of the total amount in the donor. There are usually only milligram quantities of drug distributed throughout the whole body fluid and organ system. For a solid pure drug, a milligram is about the amount that would easily fit on the end of a flat toothpick. Thus, the toxicology specimen provides only an extremely small amount of the drug material for analysis. Not only is the drug in very low concentration, there are many other biological materials in the sample. The toxicologist must, therefore, be able to analyze for small amounts of drugs, but must also be able to isolate them from the complex biological matrix. In contrast to the drug chemist, toxicologists generally need quantitative information as well. They must know how much of a drug is in a person's body fluids to determine if that amount is consistent with a therapeutic dose (an amount prescribed by a doctor to be taken) or an amount consistent with an abuse dosage taken by a drug abuser or an amount sufficient to cause death.

An important function of the forensic toxicologist, perhaps the most important, is to aid others in understanding the effects of the substances found in the individual. For example, was it likely that the drugs or poisons found caused impairment, loss of normal reason, unconsciousness, or even death? This information can have many legal ramifications.

It is convenient to divide toxicology into two major areas. Samples from living individuals (antemortem) and samples collected after death, usually from an autopsy (postmortem).

Forensic Toxicology on Samples from the Living

Many forensic toxicology laboratories analyze specimens from living persons as well as postmortem samples. Any analysis of drugs or toxins from the body for regulatory or law enforcement purposes can be considered forensic toxicology.

A number of laws and rules are in force having to do with the workplace use of drugs. In some occupations, such as police, airplane pilots, and so forth, drugs of abuse are absolutely forbidden. These rules are enforced by random drug testing of the persons affected. Those specimens (usually urine) are sent to forensic toxicology laboratories for analysis. These labs must generally meet high testing and quality-control standards set by the National Institute for Drug Abuse (NIDA), which regulates them.

The examination of samples from persons involved in serious accidents or suspected of operating a motor vehicle while impaired by alcohol or drugs is such an important forensic toxicology activity that it is treated separately later.

In addition, forensic toxicology laboratories may now test for the presence of certain drugs in victims of sexual assault who believe they may have been drugged, as an adjunct to the assault.

Postmortem Toxicology

Although scientists have been engaged in toxicology for many years, it was not until the 1960s that modern analytical instrumentation made it possible to routinely identify most drugs in most body fluid samples. The availability of gas chromatography and the gas chromatograph/mass spectrometry advanced toxicology enormously.

As we have noted earlier in Chapter 1, a medical examiner is responsible for determining the cause and manner of sudden, suspicious, or unattended deaths. In fulfilling that responsibility, the medical examiner must consider the possibility that poisons or drugs caused or contributed to the death. Postmortem toxicology is done primarily to assist the medical examiner in that duty. Larger medical examiners' offices have toxicology laboratories associated with them. In jurisdictions that have coroners, forensic science laboratories often provide toxicology services. A medical examiner can usually do an autopsy in a few hours, but the toxicological examinations will often take much longer. A medical examiner or coroner generally does not make a final determination as to cause of death, except in the most obvious cases, until the toxicology examinations are complete. Not only is there typically very little drug or poison in the body fluid samples, there is also an enormous variety of drugs and poisons that might be encountered. The toxicologist's work is further complicated by the fact that very few drugs go through the human body intact. The natural process called "metabolism" is the way that the body processes and eliminates foreign substances. The body adds or removes chemical entities to convert the foreign substance (drug) into something that can be more rapidly excreted. Therefore, the toxicologist must look not only for the drug itself, but also for the metabolites—the compounds into which the body can convert the drug. This situation makes the analytical problems more complicated. Many drugs and poisons are quickly metabolized, so none of the unchanged drug or poison is present in the body fluids tested, and conclusions are then based solely on characteristic metabolites found.

Classes of Poisons

The presence of a poison or poisons in someone's body fluids or tissues can be critical to many law enforcement and public health investigations. We can divide poisons into three basic groups: (1) inorganic poisons; (2) organic poisons; and (3) biological toxins.

Some examples of inorganic poisons are metals like arsenic, beryllium, or cadmium and cyanide or hydrogen sulfide. Some examples of organic poisons are the classic plant poisons, the alkaloids such as strychnine, coniine, and curare as well as digitalis, belladonna, and many others. The biological toxins can have many sources, such as venoms from snakes or spiders, biological toxin that comes from microorganisms such as botulism from foods, bacteria that cause red tides, and many others. These toxins are chemicals produced as byproducts of the growth of the bacteria and can be extremely toxic to humans.

Interestingly, it is a fish that produces a material called "tetradotoxin," one of the most toxic materials known to man. That fish is a great delicacy in Japan, but it can only be safely eaten if a little gland that contains the tetradotoxin is completely removed. Chefs must be licensed in Japan as qualified to perform this task. Nonetheless, a few people die every year from the toxin. An interesting point about tetradotoxin, which has a very complex chemical structure, is that there is a salamander that lives on the other side of the earth from Japan that makes exactly the same toxin.

It is rather ironic that although many people think rather simplistically that "chemicals" are unhealthy or evil and that all "natural" things are wholesome, the most highly poisonous things on earth are "natural" biological toxins.

Alcohol and Drugs and Driving

The analysis of blood, breath or urine for alcohol has been a major function of forensic laboratories for much of their history.

Driving While Impaired by Alcohol

In many ways alcohol is one of the easiest substances for toxicologists to find in body fluids. It is the only drug frequently analyzed that is present in such large quantities in body fluids. A person has to take a large amount to obtain the desired effect—gram rather than the milligram doses characteristic of most other drugs.

If an individual drinks several 12 oz. beers (each is about 4 percent alcohol, which provides roughly 15 grams of ethyl alcohol per beer) or several shots of liquor (one ounce of 80-proof liquor has about 12 grams of alcohol per shot), close to 30 grams of alcohol are being ingested. That is about a thousand times as much material as the normal dose, or even an abuse dose, of most other drugs. This high dose causes the alcohol to be present in easily detectable quantities—for a considerable time after the ingestion.

Alcohol is metabolized and excreted from the body fairly rapidly; however, not nearly as rapidly as it can be taken in when one is actively drinking. As a result, the drinker's level of impairment will increase for a period even after he or she stops drinking as the alcohol in the stomach is absorbed and then begins to decline. The length of time required after cessation of drinking for the level of impairment to return to below the legal limit can be from an hour or two to more than 10 hours for someone who has been drinking heavily.

Alcohol's effects on people have been well studied over a long time, and there is a good correlation between the amount of alcohol in a person's *system* and the level of impairment of judgment and motor skills. For that reason, state legislatures defined a level of alcohol content at or above which a person would be considered impaired for purposes of operating a motor vehicle. For many years, a driver had to have at least 0.10 percent (i.e., 0.10% percent, weight to volume, or 100 mg per 100 mL blood) alcohol in his or her blood in most states in the United States to be considered intoxicated. In recent years, most states have lowered the legal limit of blood alcohol concentration to 0.08 percent.

Another reason alcohol is easier to analyze than some other substances is that it is volatile. That means it passes readily into vapor from liquid, especially if warmed. That property allows the alcohol to be fairly easily separated from almost everything else in the body fluid. Other drugs and almost all other materials found in body fluid samples are not nearly as volatile. Thus, the separation problems mentioned earlier that make analysis of body fluid samples for most drugs so challenging are not as challenging for alcohol analysis. As a result, analysis of blood or other body fluid samples for alcohol in impaired driving cases can be done in laboratories not equipped to do other, more complex toxicology analyses.

As mentioned, postmortem toxicology is the analysis of drugs and poisons in body fluids to assist in determining the cause (and manner) of death. Determining the presence of small amounts of drugs or poisons may be critical to this determination. Although a fatal dose of alcohol is rare, cases where alcohol has contributed to a death are quite common. Alcohol is a factor in an extremely high percentage of fatal automobile accidents. In incidents of particular automobile accidents where an individual is not killed, but alcohol involvement is suspected, a specimen will often be sent to a local forensic laboratory. There are also cases in which a clinical laboratory in a hospital does an alcohol analysis on an accident victim.

The analyses necessary for impaired driving enforcement are quite important because in many large forensic laboratories, particularly those serving the State Highway Patrol, they make up the largest single class of evidence submitted to that laboratory. Caseloads can reach into the hundreds per week. Impaired driving enforcement cases are unusual in that they reach the trial stage more frequently than many other types of cases. Even though they are usually violations of a state law, where the penalty is likely to be a fine or perhaps loss of driving privileges for a time, they are often vigorously litigated. An important reason for this is that many people consider that the ability to drive is closely tied to their ability to get to work

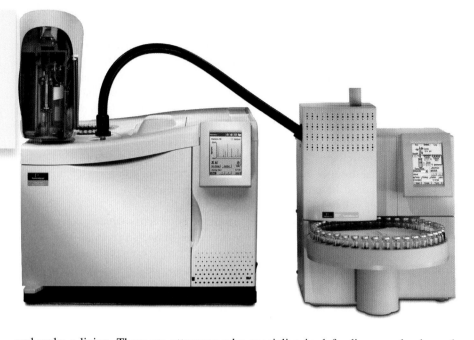

Figure 12.19

A gas chromatograph with a heated headspace sampler of the type used by many laboratories for determining the concentration of alcohol in blood samples from individuals suspected of driving while impaired.

under the influence

Acting while significant quantities of a drug are in an individual's system.

and make a living. There are attorneys who specialize in defending people charged with driving **under the influence** of alcohol. Therefore, the laboratory analysis in blood alcohol cases may be put under particularly strong scrutiny.

There are many methods to perform alcohol determinations. In the field, the Breathalyzer, Intoxalyzer, or another field instrument are used. This type of test is administered by a police officer trained to do so. The suspect is asked to blow into the instrument that allows most of the person's breath to pass through it but captures a known volume of that breath that comes from deep in the lungs. That known volume is then bubbled through a chemical solution capable of converting it to a compound the instrument can detect, or the alcohol in it is physically measured in one of several ways. The techniques are simple, yet quite reliable. There is an established correlation between breath alcohol level and blood alcohol level. As a result, the instrument can convert breath readings to blood alcohol levels (which is how the prohibited amounts are defined in the laws).

In the laboratory, it is generally blood that is subjected to alcohol determination. Such analyses are usually done using gas chromatography. Gas chromatography techniques (Figure 12.19) can quite accurately determine the quantity of alcohol present in a blood specimen. A number of checks and balances are built into the analysis to ensure the concentrations are accurate. The obvious issue with blood alcohol testing is that it requires taking blood from a suspect. While this does happen regularly, it is worth noting that taking blood from someone for alcohol testing is surrounded with complex legal search and seizure rules.

The situation with field test instruments is not as uniform. There are quite a number of different breath test instruments that use a variety of different analytical techniques, including some portable gas chromatographs. The National Highway Traffic Safety Administration (NHTSA) tests and approves instruments for breath testing. When the instruments are properly maintained and calibrated, and used by properly trained individuals, they produce reliable results. Because of the difficulties of administering such testing programs, they are more often challenged in court. There is a third class of instruments, which is used for screening only. In fact, individuals can buy low-cost breath test instruments to test themselves after drinking to see if their alcohol level is within legal limits before driving.

Other Drugs and Driving

driving while impaired

Operating a motor vehicle while one's judgment or physical capabilities are reduced by alcohol or drugs.

All states have laws against **driving while impaired** by drugs besides alcohol. In most states, these laws are used when a driver is observed to be driving erratically and preliminary tests indicate no alcohol or a low alcohol level. The observation of poor driving practice, rather than blood levels of the drug, is used as the primary gauge of the level of impairment. Although a charge of driving while impaired by drugs is primarily supported by the behavioral observations, a laboratory analysis showing a "significant level" of a drug, usually a controlled substance, is almost always required for such a charge to be successfully prosecuted.

Driving while impaired by drugs cases are more complex because prohibited levels for each drug have not been developed and placed into state law, as with alcohol. The problem here is the way the body metabolizes and excretes different drugs. Some drugs or their metabolites may be present in tissue or fluids for a long time after ingestion, and a long time after the physiological effects are no longer present. Thus, unlike with alcohol, there is no necessary correlation between body fluid levels and levels of impairment that would affect the operation of a motor vehicle. This situation makes it almost impossible to define by law levels of different drugs at or above which a person would be considered impaired, which leads to a lack of uniformity across the states as to what might constitute a "significant level" of a particular drug.

Summary

The majority of analysts working in forensic science laboratories in the United States are engaged in the analysis of drugs, because the majority of cases reaching the lab are illegal possession of controlled substance cases.

A drug is a substance that produces a physiological or psychological effect on the body that is significant, that occurs within a reasonable time after dosing, and that results from an easily ingested dose. Drug dependence and drug abuse are major problems in American society. The most abused drug is ethyl alcohol. Drugs can cause physiological or psychological dependence in users. Access to many drugs is controlled by the federal Controlled Substances Act, administered by the U.S. Drug Enforcement Administration within the Department of Justice, and by state laws. Drugs are placed onto "schedules" according to their recognized therapeutic utility and potential for abuse. Some commonly abused drugs have no recognized medical use, but others do. The drug laws are a reflection of society's views on particular drugs at particular times, and they can change.

The major classes of drugs of abuse are narcotic drugs; stimulants; hallucinogens; depressants, hypnotics, and tranquillizers; club drugs; and performance-enhancing drugs.

The narcotic drugs are called opiates because many of them contain major components originating from opium. The opium poppy produces a sap that can be processed to yield opium, of which morphine is a major component. Morphine can be chemically modified to produce heroin, the most abused opiate drug. Other drugs in this class are codeine and oxycodone. These drugs are very effective painkillers. They also produce euphoria and are extremely addictive.

The stimulants produce wakefulness and a sense of being energetic or strong. Amphetamine and methamphetamine had limited medical uses, but methamphetamine is no longer approved for use because of its potential for abuse. Cocaine is the best-known drug in this class. Cocaine salt (powder) is usually inhaled, while the base (crack cocaine) is usually smoked. Crack cocaine is cheaper by the dose than cocaine salt. Cocaine is extremely psychologically addictive.

The hallucinogens have been used by people for centuries. These drugs affect perception. Marijuana, and a variant of it called hashish, are among the oldest-known hallucinogens. LSD is a potent hallucinogen that was a popular drug of abuse in the 1960s. Phencyclidine (PCP, angel dust) was also popular for a time. These substances are very dangerous because the hallucinations may reoccur after drug use has ceased. PCP abusers tend to be aggressive, and violence often results as well. There are also some naturally occurring substances, such as peyote and psilocybe mushrooms, that are hallucinogenic. A hallucinogen that is currently commonly abused is MDMA (Ecstasy).

Depressants tend to induce relaxation or sleep. Alcohol is by far the most widely used depressant. For a time, barbiturates were the next most widely encountered depressants, but they have been supplanted by the benzodiazepines (e.g., Valium). Rohypnol, an infamous club drug, is a member of this class. GHB (and its relative GBL) as well as ketamine are also found in the rave and club drug environment. They have depressant effects on users, especially when combined with alcohol, and tend to prevent users from remembering events. Rohypnol, GHB, and ketamine all have reputations as "date-rape" drugs.

Athletic performance-enhancing drugs are comparatively new to the drug abuse scene. They have always been of concern to regulators of athletic events, but more recently, their use has spilled over into the amateur athlete population, especially younger people. The drugs are often mislabeled or can come from places where their synthesis is not monitored or regulated. They are seldom used under a physician's care. As a result, they can cause great harm to adolescent users.

Drug regulation is based on controlled substances schedules. Schedule I substances have great potential for abuse and no recognized therapeutic uses, whereas Schedule V substances have recognized medical uses and are considered to have low abuse potential. Sometimes, scheduling of a substance reflects political views more than pharmacology. Marijuana, for example, is on Schedule I. It is hotly debated whether marijuana is a "gateway" drug; that is, whether marijuana users will "graduate" to using more dangerous drugs of abuse. Some people, including some physicians, think marijuana should be available to help relieve pain and suffering in certain patients. State and federal laws can clash in these matters.

Laboratory examination of controlled substances and other drugs is designed to identify them. There are presumptive (screening) tests and confirmatory tests. The screening tests can be used in the field, but the field tests are not substitutes for laboratory confirmation of a drug's identity. The Scott test for cocaine, the Duquenois-Levine tests for marijuana, and the van Erk test for hallucinogens are examples of screening tests. The laboratory also uses screening tests for drugs and controlled substances to decide which specimens require further testing. Specimens might be viewed microscopically to see if there is evidence of multiple components. They may also be subjected to solvent extraction or chromatography to isolate the components of a mixture for further analysis. Crystal tests are confirmatory tests for many controlled substances. They are not as widely used as they once were but have the advantage that no purification of the street drug is necessary for their use. Liquid and gas chromatography may be used to see how many components are present in a street specimen. These are separation techniques. Spectroscopic techniques, primarily mass spectroscopy and infrared spectrometry, are the principal methods of confirmation. Both gas chromatograhs and liquid chromatographs can be interfaced with mass spectrometers to produce LC-MS or GC-MS instruments that can do the separation and spectroscopic analysis all on a single platform. It is sometimes necessary to perform quantitative analyses on controlled substance specimens. Laws may be written such that there is variation in the degree of offense with the quantity of substance possessed. Accordingly, an analyst may need to show that a certain minimum quantity of the controlled substance is present in the specimen.

Forensic toxicology is an identifiably separate discipline from forensic drug chemistry, even though some of the analytical techniques are the same. Toxicologists ordinarily receive blood, urine, or other body fluids or tissues as specimens and have to analyze them for toxic or controlled substances or drugs. In toxicology, the substance must first be isolated from its biological matrix, then identified, but also quantitated. The quantity found determines the concentration of the substance in the body. Finally, toxicologists are qualified to *interpret* the effects of different concentrations of drugs on the body, and on behavior. Toxicologists receive specimens from living persons as well as from decedents.

Both laws and regulations govern the use of drugs under certain circumstances. Driving under the influence of alcohol or of drugs is prohibited, for example. In many professions, including airline pilots, public safety, military, and others, drug use is strictly prohibited. Specimens may be taken from persons in these professions at random and sent to toxicology laboratories for analysis. Standards are established for this testing. Someone testing positive for prohibited drugs under one of these programs can lose his or her job.

Postmortem toxicology helps coroners and medical examiners decide the cause and manner of death. Toxins or drugs can cause a death, but they may also contribute to a death. Many drugs are quickly metabolized in the body, forming new compounds different from the parent. Toxicologists must have methods to detect metabolites as well as parent compounds, and they must understand the metabolism of drugs and the speed with which it occurs in the body.

Poisons may be inorganic (like arsenic or cyanide), organic (like strychnine or digitalis), or biological (like botulinin toxin).

Testing specimens from drivers for alcohol or drugs is a common task in the toxicology laboratory. Because the effects of alcohol on motor skills and attentiveness have been well studied, the law sets a limit for the amount of alcohol a person can have in his or her system while operating a vehicle. For years, the limit was 0.1 percent weight-to-volume, but most states have now lowered it to 0.08 percent, or 80 mg/100mL blood. Some laboratories devote considerable resources to blood and breath alcohol analysis. Several types of "breathalyzer" instruments, designed for use by law enforcement personnel, are approved by the NHTSA. Laboratories may be involved in training officers in the use of these instruments and/or in their calibration. They convert a breath alcohol measurement to a blood alcohol equivalent value. Under some conditions, blood may be drawn from a person suspected of driving under the influence, but there are significant search and seizure laws surrounding these blood draws. DUI cases are among the most vigorously litigated of all criminal cases. Laboratories may test drivers' blood for drugs, too, to help determine if the person was driving under the influence of a drug other than alcohol. With drugs other than alcohol, it has not been possible to come to an agreement on some specific blood concentration, above which the law defines a person as DUI. The lab must find a significant amount of drug in a person's system, and an arresting officer must have administered various behavioral tests. Driving under the influence of drugs is harder to enforce than driving under the influence of alcohol.

Key Terms

Review Questions—Short Answer

1. Give a general definition of what makes a chemical a drug.
2. List and give a few examples from each of the major categories of abused drugs.
3. Outline the scheme used by most forensic laboratories for the examination of a sample suspected of containing a controlled substance.
4. What are qualitative and quantitative analysis and when is each important in the analysis of controlled substances?
5. Why is the examination of body fluid samples by a forensic toxicologist more complex than the identification of street drugs in a forensic laboratory?
6. Why is the determination of alcohol and drugs in samples from an impaired driving case so important to the case?
7. What are the general criteria used to decide on which federal schedule a drug is to be placed?
8. Discuss the role of separation techniques in accurate identification of controlled substances.
9. Discuss the major forms of drug dependence.
10. Why has the development of the so-called "Hyphenated Techniques" made drug identification much more reliable?

Fill-in-the-Blank & Multiple Choice

1. The two most commonly abused stimulant drugs are cocaine and _____.
2. The development of _____ dependence on a drug is shown by withdrawal symptoms such as convulsions when the user stops taking the drug.
3. Forensic Toxicology is a specialty that deals primarily with the identification of drugs and poisons in _____ samples.
4. Name three drugs that are commonly abused as part of the club drug scene. (associated with youth oriented music and dance clubs)
5. The most common sequence of steps in the identification of suspected controlled substances evidence is:

   a. AA/NAA, Microcrystal test, color test, quantitative analysis

   b. Color test, crystal test, GC/MS

   c. FT/IR, separation, GC/MS, color test

   d. Color test, FT/IR, separation, GC

Further References

Baker, P. B., and G. F. Phillips. "The Forensic Analysis of Drugs of Abuse." *The Analyst* 8 (1983): 777.

Bradley, D. "Tracking Cocaine to Its Roots." *Today's Chemist at Work,* May 2002.

Cole, M. D. *The Analysis of Controlled Substances.* New York: John Wiley, 2002.

Cole, M. D., and B. Caddy. *The Analysis of Drugs of Abuse: An Instruction Manual.* London, England: Ellis Horwood Ltd., 1996.

Drug Enforcement Administration Web site, www.dea.gov.

"Drug Fighter Turn to Rising Tide of Prescription Abuse." *New York Times,* March 18, 2004.

"Drugs and Chemicals of Concern: Oxycodone," www.deadiversion.usdoj.gov/drugs_concern/summary.html.

Gomm, P. J., I. J. Humphreys, and N. A. Armstrong. "Physical Methods for the Comparison of Illicitly Produced Tablets." *Journal of the Forensic Science Society* 283 (1976).

LeBeau, M. A., and A. Mozayani. *Drug Facilitated Sexual Assault: A Forensic Handbook.* New York: Academic Press, 2001.

Moffat, A. C. "Drugs of Abuse." *Science & Justice* 40 (2000): 89–92.

National Institutes of Drug Abuse (NIDA) Web site, www.nida.nih.gov.

"SWGDRUG Methods & Reports Subcommittee: Minimum Recommended Analytical Scheme for Forensic Drug Identification," users.erols.com/scitechz/twgm&r.html.

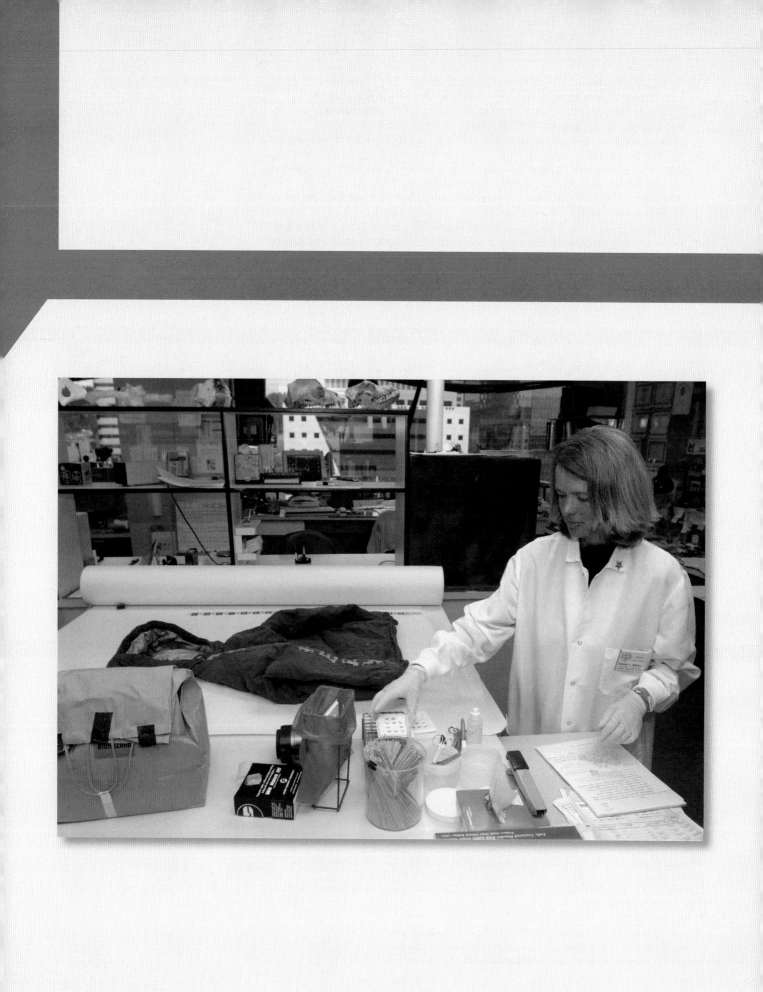

Materials Evidence

- The process of examination of materials evidence
- The major techniques for collecting materials evidence
- Five more important types of materials evidence
- The range of fibers encountered as evidence
- The structure and growth of human and animal hair
- The proper collection of hair control standards
- The laboratory examination and comparison of fiber and hair evidence
- The nature of paint and the importance of architectural and automotive paint evidence
- The collection of proper paint control standards
- The laboratory analysis and comparison of forensic paint evidence
- The nature of glass and its manufacture
- The proper collection of glass evidence
- The laboratory analysis and comparison of forensic glass evidence
- The composition of soil
- The common forensic occurrences of soil evidence
- The proper collection of soil evidence
- The laboratory analysis and comparison of forensic soil evidence

Outline

Learning Objectives

- Materials evidence is used primarily for indicating possible connections
- The nature of and difference between transfer and trace evidence
- The most common sources of materials evidence
- The major categories of materials evidence

chapter 13

Lead Case

Illinois v. Cecil Sutherland

Facts

At 9 A.M. on July 2, 1987, an oil field worker discovered the nude body of a 10-year-old girl approximately 100 feet from an oil lease access road in rural Illinois. Her body was lying on its stomach covered with dirt. There were shoeprints on her back and several hairs were found stuck in her rectal area. In addition, a large open wound on the right side of her neck exposed her spinal cord area, and a pool of blood next to the head indicated that the murderer had killed her where she lay.

The victim's clothes—shirt, shorts, underpants—and shoes and socks were found strewn along the oil lease road. Within 17 feet from the body, automobile tire impressions were found. Near the tire impressions, a shoeprint impression similar in design to the shoeprint on the body was found. Plaster casts of the tire and shoeprint impressions were made.

An autopsy was performed and indicated that a 14.5-centimeter wound that ran from the middle of the throat to behind the right ear lobe cut through the neck muscles, severed the carotid artery and jugular vein, and cut into the cartilage between the neck and vertebrae. The victim's right eye was hemorrhaged and there was a small abrasion near her left eyebrow. Her ear was torn off the skin at the base of the ear and both her lips were lacerated from being compressed against the underlying teeth. There were also linear abrasions to the outer lips of the vagina, which indicated that force had been applied to the back, pressing the vagina against the ground. Examination for internal injuries uncovered three hemorrhages inside the skull, a fractured rib, and a torn liver. There was also evidence of tearing of the rectal mucosa.

From the foregoing, it was deduced that the victim was strangled to unconsciousness or death and anally penetrated, her throat was slit, and she was stepped on. The time of death was estimated as between 9:30 and 11 P.M. on July 1, 1987.

The Evidence

The plaster casts of the tire print impressions made at the scene of the crime were examined and it was reported that the tire impressions left at the scene were consistent in all class characteristics with only two models of tires manufactured in North America, the Cooper "Falls Persuader" and the Cooper "Dean Polaris."

Several months later, the police at Glacier National Park in Montana called the county sheriff's office in Illinois regarding Cecil Sutherland's abandoned car, a 1977 Plymouth Fury. At the time of the murder, Sutherland had been living in Illinois, quite close to the murder scene. It was determined that the car in question had a Cooper Falls Persuader tire on the right front wheel. Inked impressions of the right front wheel of Sutherland's car were taken.

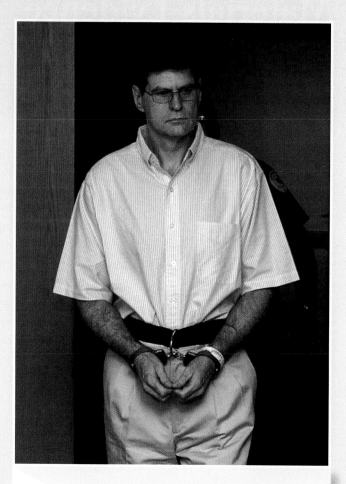

Cecil Sutherland on his way back to jail after the first day of testimony in his trial on May 3, 2004, for the murder of 10-year-old Amy Schulz in Belleville, Illinois, 17 years earlier.

The plaster casts of the tire impression at the scene were compared with the inked impression of the tire from Sutherland's car and it was concluded that they corresponded with Sutherland's tire and could have been made by that tire. The examiner could not positively exclude all other tires due to the lack of comparative individual characteristics, such as nicks, cuts, or gouges.

The forensic hair examiner microscopically compared the two pubic hairs recovered from the victim's rectal area with Sutherland's pubic hair as well as with pubic hairs from members of the victim's family and those from 24 other possible suspects in the case. He concluded that the pubic hairs found on the victim did not originate from her family or the 24 suspects, but "could have originated" from Sutherland.

The hair examiner also examined the approximately 34 dog hairs found on the victim's clothing and concluded that the hairs were consistent with and could have originated from Sutherland's black Labrador retriever. He further found that the dog hairs on the victim's clothes were dissimilar to her family's three dogs, her grandparents' dog, and three neighbors' dogs. Numerous dog hairs found in Sutherland's car were found to be consistent with the hairs from the black Labrador.

The victim's clothing was examined for the presence of foreign fibers. A total of 29 gold fibers were found on the victim's socks, shoes, underwear, shorts, and shirt. It was concluded that all but one of the gold fibers found "could have originated" from the defendant's auto carpet, but the examiner could not state that the fibers originated from Sutherland's auto carpet to the exclusion of all other auto carpets. It was determined that the one remaining gold fiber found could have originated from the upholstery of Sutherland's car.

Twelve cotton and four polyester fibers found on the front passenger side floor of the defendant's car were compared with cotton and polyester fibers from the victim's shirt. These fibers from the car displayed the same size, shape, and color as the fibers from the shirt and it was concluded that they could have originated from the shirt. Furthermore, three polyester fibers found on the front passenger seat and floor of the defendant's car were compared with the fibers from the victim's shorts and found to be consistent in diameter, color, shape, and optical properties. They could, therefore, have originated from the shorts.

A forensic expert for the defense agreed with the State's expert's conclusions on all the comparison evidence except as to the comparison of the cotton fibers found in the defendant's car to the victim's shirt. He did not agree that the cotton fibers were consistent, as he noticed some differences in size and color.

The victim had last been seen alive at approximately 9:10 in the evening of July 1, 1987, while walking alone in the town of Kell, Illinois. The defendant's sister-in-law testified that on the evening of July 1, 1987, the defendant was visiting his brother and her at their home. She testified that on the night of the murder, the defendant left her home at approximately 8 to 8:30. It was established that the distance from Kell to the crime site was 12.1 miles and took 14 minutes to drive.

The jury found the defendant guilty of aggravated kidnapping, aggravated criminal sexual assault, and three counts of murder.

The jury found the defendant eligible for the death penalty under the felony murder aggravating factor, and subsequently returned a verdict of death. The verdict was upheld on appeal by the Illinois Supreme Court, which found that some overstatements by the prosecution were not sufficient to affect the verdict in the face of the overwhelming physical evidence.

The saga did not end here, however. Because a number of cases of prosecutorial misconduct and/or extremely poor quality defense representation were found to have resulted in several serious miscarriages in justice, the governor suspended the death penalty in the state. The next governor established a large fund to provide adequate defense for those charged with capital crimes.

A new appeal by the defendant in this case again reached the Illinois Supreme Court and this time the case was sent back for retrial. The court cited the failures of the defense at the trial to present possible mitigating evidence that might have reduced the weight of the footprint and tire track evidence and, more important, the defense's failure to bring out the fact that the victim's grandfather, at whose house she was before her disappearance, was a convicted sex offender.

The case was retried, almost eighteen years after the crime, and although the weakening of the footprint and tire track evidence and the grandfather's record were presented, the second trial resulted in a second guilty verdict. In the intervening years DNA and particularly mitochondrial DNA on hair shaft became possible. Reanalysis of the dog hairs and, more important, a hair found in the victim's rectum using DNA technology supported the original hair examiner's conclusions. The dog hairs from the victim's clothing were found to be consistent with the dog hair from the defendant's truck and inconsistent with that of dogs owned by the victim's family. The hair from the victim's rectum was consistent with the defendant and inconsistent with the grandfather as a possible source.

The defendant is again on death row primarily because of the large number of items of materials evidence that, when taken together, convinced two juries of the defendant's guilt.

Sources: The People of The State of Illinois, Appellee v. Cecil Sutherland, Appellant; 155 Ill.2d. 1; 610 N.E.2d 1; December 4, 1992; The People of The State of Illinois, Appellee v. Cecil Sutherland, Appellant; 194 Ill.2d. 289; 742 N.E.2d. 306; November 16, 2000; "Convicted Killer Seeks Execution," St. Louis Post-Dispatch, June 15, 2004, Five Star Late Lift Edition.

Introduction to Materials Evidence

The types of evidence discussed in this chapter—paint chips, glass fragments, hair, fibers, soil, and many other materials—are often grouped under the term **trace evidence.** For this category of evidence, microscopy is probably the single, most important method for its examination and comparison. These materials have been called "trace evidence" by forensic scientists to suggest that the transfer of very small quantities can be detected, and that associations (or dissociations) can be

trace evidence

Physical evidence, potentially small in size, that is usually used to make connections between suspect and victim, suspect or victim and crime scene, or suspect or victim and an instrumentality.

inferred from these transfers. In actuality, our methods cannot always detect the transfer of very small quantities of materials. Further, these materials are often present in larger quantities in evidence specimens. Thus, although the term "trace evidence" will persist, it is preferable to refer to this category of evidence as **materials evidence.**

materials evidence

Physical evidence, either trace or transfer, that is usually chemically or microscopically analyzed and used to make connections.

transfer evidence

Physical evidence that is transferred between objects as the result of contact.

Transfer of Materials Evidence Is Used to Establish or Disprove Connections

Materials evidence is important when it is transferred. This simple fact gives rise to the concept and the term **transfer evidence.** Materials evidence is not the only type of physical evidence that takes on meaning when it is transferred. You could say the same thing about blood or semen evidence, but we don't usually call those "transfer evidence" even though they really are. The transfer of a material provides evidence that the source and the target have been in contact or close association.

Transfer evidence thus arises by objects coming into contact, which can be violent, or close association. For example, fibers can be transferred from one person's sweater to another person's clothing, head hairs may be shed and "stick" to another person's clothing, or soil particles can be transferred from someone's yard to a person's shoes.

The concept of transfer evidence dates back a century. Edmond Locard was a scientist who started one of the earliest forensic laboratories in the world in France. Dr. Locard enunciated the idea that when two objects come in contact there is a mutual exchange of material across the contact boundary. This notion was adopted as a basic concept in forensic science and is called the "Locard exchange principle." It is not unexpected that forcing two objects into contact would result in a transfer of material from one onto the other, and/or vice versa. This transfer could be of very small quantities of material or of a larger amount, visible to the unaided eye. For example, the transferred material could be a blond head hair 8 inches long or a hair fragment too small to be seen without magnification. Thus, transfer evidence can be hairs, fibers, paint chips, or myriad other things. Paul Kirk, who many consider to be the father of forensic science in the United States, expressed a similar idea somewhat differently by saying that criminals leave evidence behind at crime scenes and take evidence with them when they leave. Both great forensic scientists clearly saw the potential evidentiary value of these often inconspicuous exchanges of materials.

Both Locard's and Kirk's concepts are sound in principle, but it is important to remember that even though something may be transferred or left behind does not mean that the transferred material can be found or detected by our scientific methods. The material transferred may be too tiny or there may be too little of it, or it may not cling long enough to be discovered. Transferred contact materials may well be lost shortly thereafter, and, in fact, that is what happens with many materials. They do not stick but rather end up on the floor or on the ground nearby. Further, transfer evidence may not be discovered for a variety of other reasons. Nevertheless, careful examination of items thought to have come in contact still has a good chance of providing useful physical evidence.

We will see later in the chapter that most materials evidence cannot be individualized in the true sense. It is not scientifically possible to show that two fibers, two hairs, two soil specimens, or two tiny glass fragments had a common origin. The best that can be said when the materials match in all the properties compared is that they "could have had a common origin." Materials evidence that appears consistent in a case is, therefore, circumstantial. On the other hand, if there are significant differences between specimens, it can be stated unequivocally that they did not have a common origin. Thus, materials evidence, when transferred, can suggest connections (but not prove them) and can often prove that evidence and a known control sample do not have a common source.

Materials Evidence Can Be Transferred or Deposited

As indicated, contact transfers can be on a micro or macro scale. A transfer might involve tiny specks of broken fiber, too small to be visible to the unaided eye, or an 8-inch long hair, a visible piece of fabric, a chip of paint, or a tiny piece of glass. Particularly on coarsely woven clothing, even a fairly sizable piece of material may become trapped in the weave of a sweater, for example, and be carried around for a while.

Materials evidence does not have to involve contact transfer. Things that fall out of the sky may be useful evidence. Materials such as pollen, muzzle blast from a gun, oil dripping from a crankcase, and many other examples, represent the transfer of materials without direct contact and can provide useful information. One common example of materials evidence found on an object that does not involve contact is dust. In an urban area, there is considerable particulate matter in the air, and even in rural areas particulate matter is suspended in the air. This suspended material is only temporarily suspended, however. Sooner or later it will fall, and some will land on objects that might become forensically significant. For example, we mentioned in the chapter on controlled substances that an analyst might be able to geographically locate the source of a marijuana brick by examining pollen and plant residues that fell on it. Material falling on the leaves while they were growing is going to be characteristic of where it was grown. The material deposited will certainly be different in Australia than, for example, in Nigeria.

Clothing and Vehicles Are the Most Common Sources of Materials Evidence

In almost all forensic laboratories, the two most common sources of transferred materials evidence are clothing and vehicles. It is standard operating procedure in most jurisdictions to collect clothing from victims when a violent crime occurs, whether it was a homicide, a sexual assault, or a mugging. In all these situations, there is a potential for contact. If a suspect is arrested either immediately or even sometime later, the clothing from the suspect is also collected. Such items are usually the starting point for the examination for materials evidence. Similarly, should a vehicle be involved, it is the starting point of the search for transferred materials evidence. Sexual assault can occur in a car, bodies can be transported in the trunk of a car, hit-and-run incidents involve cars, and there are many more possible ways vehicles can be involved in cases. Materials evidence will often be transferred between the victim and interior, trunk, or even exterior of a vehicle. For example, the carpeting in the trunk of an automobile is one of the most common sources of fiber evidence. Transporting a body in the trunk of a car to a remote location for disposal is not uncommon. During its stay in the trunk, a body has been resting on the carpeting, and carpet fibers can be transferred onto its surface. Although this is just one of many possible scenarios, the evidence vaults of most forensic laboratories contain many paper bags full of clothing and other items to be searched for materials evidence. In addition, you would usually find several evidence bags with material collected from vehicles. In fact, if the laboratory has a forensic garage, which many laboratories now do have, several vehicles could be waiting for "processing" for materials evidence.

An important part of processing a crime scene, or of being an effective investigator, is the ability to *recognize* what might turn out to be useful evidence. This task is particularly difficult when dealing with potential materials evidence that has been transferred. Recognizing that a bullet is likely to be important evidence at a shooting scene, or that a glass containing some residue at a possible suicide scene might be valuable evidence, is not particularly subtle. However, recognizing what may prove useful out of the enormous variety of materials evidence can be quite difficult. What kinds of things could be useful materials evidence? It would be nice to have a complete list, but the list would be so long it would not be helpful. Actually, almost anything could turn out to be useful as materials evidence under a particular set of circumstances. Some of the more common sorts of things that have proven to be useful as transferred materials in the past are discussed in the following sections. It is worth reemphasizing, though, that any material might be important as materials evidence in a particular case. The best crime scene investigators are able to distinguish items of evidentiary value from items and things that are just part of the background.

Collection Methods for Materials Evidence

Various methods of collecting evidence were first mentioned in Chapter 3. Most of these techniques are applicable to materials evidence.

Collection Without Sampling

When materials evidence is found on surfaces and objects (substrata) at scenes, it is best to carefully package the entire item or object without disturbing the materials evidence, if possible. If the item or object is immovable, scene personnel must collect the materials using one of several techniques. Some of these methods are also used in the laboratory to remove materials evidence from its substratum. Investigators who must remove materials from items at a scene should take care to record the original position/location of the evidence.

mechanical dislocation

The scraping or shaking of an item of physical evidence over a clean surface to dislodge any trace evidence clinging to the surface.

Techniques for collection of materials evidence include picking off the material with forceps, tape lifting, **mechanical dislocation** of surface materials (shaking or scraping), and vacuuming. Small bits of materials evidence should be packaged in druggist folds. A druggist fold is easy to make from any piece of paper. If laboratory weighing paper is available, it is very useful for this purpose because it is relatively nonabsorbent and nonsticky.

Scraping or shaking should be done in the laboratory in most cases. An exception might be in clinics seeing and treating sexual assault complainants. As we noted in Chapter 9, complainants may be asked to disrobe while standing on a clean, white piece of paper that can later be folded up so as to contain any trace materials that may have fallen from the clothing surfaces.

Vacuuming consists of using a vacuum device equipped with a special clean collection hose and a readily changeable filter to capture all the debris and materials. Vacuuming is a field (scene) procedure, not a laboratory technique, for materials evidence collection. Furthermore, it should be considered only as a last resort. The reason vacuuming is less desirable is that it picks up materials indiscriminately. Material deposited on the surface or deep in the nap will be collected—and the probability is high that most of it is background, not evidence. Examination of vacuum sweepings in the laboratory is very time-consuming, and potentially not a productive use of examiner time.

As noted, some of the collection techniques used at scenes are also used in the laboratory. They are discussed next.

Use of Forceps—Always the First Approach in the Lab

The first technique used in the lab in the collection of transferred materials evidence from a wide variety of objects is picking it off the underlying substratum. The use of good lighting is essential, and a fine forceps or a probe is used to examine the surface of the object and pick off any foreign material observed. This works very well if the material is large enough and/or contrasts sufficiently with the surface to be readily visible. Further, it provides a sample of the material of interest that is largely free of extraneous material and fibers from the substratum garment or object. Its limitation is that it depends on the visibility of the material under the light in use. In addition, the object bearing the materials evidence must be amenable to being properly lighted and placed under magnification.

Mechanical Dislocation— Shaking or Scraping of Surface Material

The limitations of picking off materials mean that other, less specific but more efficient techniques may have to be used. For example, clothing can be hung up, a clean piece of paper placed under it, and mechanical agitation technique used to cause the trace evidence to fall onto the paper. The clothing object might be shaken, or scraped vigorously with a spatula, to cause foreign materials to fall from the surface of the object and onto the paper. The material that falls on the paper is collected into a small pile and then transferred to a labeled container for storage before examination. Each piece of clothing would be treated similarly. These collected materials must then be put through a preliminary examination to decide whether materials are present that might be of evidentiary value. The collected sample is examined under the stereomicroscope, and using a fine forceps or probe, the analyst would try to pick out all the hairs, fibers, paint chips, seeds, or any other recognizable items present. Each of the different types of materials would then be further subdivided. Using a stereomicroscope with good lighting, forensic examiners can often recognize hairs from different people, or from different parts of the body. Similarly, fibers can be sorted, not only on the basis of color but also on general appearance. The different hairs or fibers observed would be separated and compared to known control samples of someone's hair or clothing to determine which appear to be similar or different and thereby might be excluded or included. Much additional examination would be needed to associate items to a specific possible source. The preliminary examination, just using a stereomicroscope without going into more complex examinations, can be of great value in determining how useful the evidence is going to be in a particular case. The initial stereomicroscopic examination is particularly valuable because the examiner can often quickly identify and disregard certain things that are not going to be valuable, and, therefore, be able to concentrate on those items that might turn out to be most useful. Later we will cover some of the ways in which such evidence is actually compared.

Tape Lifts—Sticky but Not Too Sticky

A third useful technique for collecting transfer evidence, the **tape lift,** utilizes adhesive tape. The object to be sampled is placed on a flat surface, and the relevant part of the surface of the object is covered with a piece of sticky tape. When the tape is removed, any loose materials on that surface will be removed with the tape. The tape is then placed on a clear backing sheet to protect any material gathered. It is important that the tape be sticky, but not too sticky, because the desire is to remove material adhering to the surface without removing too much of the surface itself. This is the most time-consuming trace collection method, but also the most efficient at collecting any material of interest. The pieces of tape are then examined using a stereomicroscope, and any material of potential interest is marked on the clear plastic backing. The examiner can then go back and carefully cut through the tape at the places marked and, by dissolving the adhesive with a minuscule drop of solvent, recover the trace of interest. As noted, in circumstances where objects bearing materials evidence cannot be collected intact, tape lifting can be used by trained investigators to collect material evidence at scenes.

tape lift

The use of clear sticky tape to remove trace evidence from the surface of a piece of physical evidence.

Laboratory Examination of Trace and Transfer Evidence

Laboratory methods for the examination of materials evidence may be broadly divided into initial or preliminary examinations, methods involving microscopy, and instrumental methods.

Chemical Microscopy

As discussed in Chapter 1, the microscope is probably the single most important instrument used in forensic science. The compound (biological) microscope is commonly used in two special ways in the examination of materials evidence, particularly trace materials evidence. Chemical microscopy allows an expert to carry out chemical reactions on a microscope slide, usually in a tiny drop of liquid, and observe the results using the microscope. The importance of microcrystal reactions in identification of controlled substances was mentioned in Chapter 12. Similar results can be obtained with many other types of materials using chemical microscopy. These identifications can be obtained on extremely small amounts of materials evidence.

A wide variety of inorganic materials is composed of a combination of a *cation* (positively charged) and an *anion* (negatively charged) parts. The most common example is table salt, which most people know is chemically sodium chloride. You can dissolve salt in a drop of water and add a chemical that reacts with the sodium ion and produce crystals with a characteristic shape. Similarly, using a different chemical, the chloride ion will produce characteristic crystals as well. In this way, a person knowledgeable in microchemical reactions with a supply of the necessary crystal-forming chemicals can identify many trace materials encountered as evidence (Figure 13.1).

Figure 13.1

An example of using micro-chemistry on drop of liquid on a microscope slide. The shape (morphology) of the crystals formed with this reagent indicate that the liquid contained calcium ions.

Initial Physical Examination—Stereomicroscope, Hand Lens

The preliminary examination of trace and transfer evidence is usually quite similar for all the different types. After the initial examination for evaluation of possible evidentiary value, the more detailed examination must be tailored to the specific type of evidence. Examination first starts with simple visual observation and separation of the sample into its different components, often using a stereomicroscope.

Microscopy

As noted earlier in the chapter, microscopes are the singularly most important instruments for examining most types of materials evidence. There are several different types of microscopes and of microscopy. These are discussed in the Appendix: Scientific Tools of the Trade.

Analysts can use biological stains to make biological materials more easily recognized. Many quick and easy tests can be done on the tiniest particle, which may help identify the kind of material of which that particle is made (see later). Another simple technique that can help identify certain particles is the use of a magnet. If an examiner has a number of particles on a microscope slide with a thin glass cover and waves a magnet closely over the slide while observing it under the microscope, any iron or other magnetic particles will move; the analyst can then separate the ones that are magnetic from those that are nonmagnetic.

Chemical Microscopy   In addition to simple visual examination, chemical microscopy can often give useful information. Small particles that an examiner cannot visually identify can often be identified by using some simple chemical tests. Is a particle a piece of plaster, a bit of a broken tooth, a speck of white paint, or a particle of sugar? Such particles can be placed on a microscope slide and a tiny drop of a chemical reagent added, which will allow the scientist to quickly test for a particular chemical or class of chemicals.

Polarized Light Microscopy A second very useful adaptation of the compound microscope is polarized light microscopy. This is done with a slightly modified compound microscope that can control the plane of oscillation of the light passing through the sample and also passing from the sample through the optics to the viewer's eye. The physics of this process are beyond the scope of this text, but they allow a knowledgeable scientist to make many different optical measurements and observations on crystalline materials. This will often allow chemical identification of such crystals. The technique, requiring only a single or a few tiny crystals of a material, can be quite helpful in examining materials evidence. Using polarized light microscopy to identify the particular minerals found in a soil sample, for example, can often aid in comparing soil samples. A skilled microscopist can identify many common materials and quite a few not so common materials very quickly even on minute samples. This is a skill that requires considerable patience and extensive experience to develop, but it is very valuable and keeps on improving with added experience.

Instrumental Comparison and Identification— Micro FTIR and SEM/EDX

The most important development for the analysis of materials evidence since the development of the microscope itself was the perfection of the microscope attachment for a Fourier transform infrared spectrometer. This device is usually referred to as a micro FTIR (Figure 13.2) for short. The availability of such instruments in the early 1980s was a very important addition to the methods available for analysis of trace evidence. Infrared (IR) spectroscopy has been an excellent way of identifying chemicals and many more complex materials for a long time (see Chapter 12). The major limitation of IR spectroscopy was that an expert had to have a fairly pure chemical and a reasonable amount of that material to successfully identify it. In addition, the sample preparation required was time-consuming. With the micro FTIR, the analyst has a special microscope connected to an IR spectrometer, and all the time-consuming sampling and need for larger quantities of sample disappears. The scientist places a tiny amount of a sample on a special microscope slide (transparent

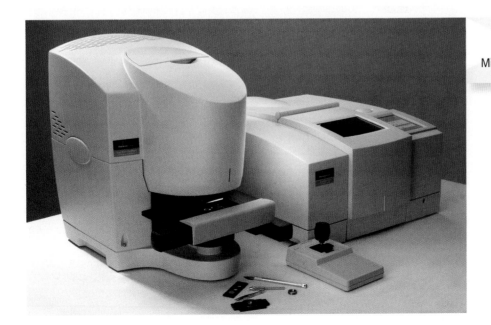

Figure 13.2
Micro FTIR instrument.

to IR light) and finds the item or crystal he or she wants to identify in the microscope field; using a diaphragm, like on a camera, to close down on just the particular object of interest, the expert can obtain a spectrum in a minute or two. Scientists can now take a paint chip that can barely be seen, or a fiber that is equally small, and obtain an IR spectrum in a matter of minutes.

Infrared spectrometry (and its more sophisticated variant, FTIR) has been called "chemical fingerprinting." This terminology means that a pure compound could be identified through its IR spectrum (see appendix: Scientific Tools of the Trade). There are large libraries of spectra available for this purpose. Many of the materials that come into forensic labs for analysis are not, however, pure chemical compounds. Take a chip of paint, or fingernail polish, or a particle of cosmetic powder as examples. All of them are mixtures, not pure compounds. But an examiner can still obtain an IR spectrum. That spectrum will be more complex than one of a pure compound, because it represents a sort of "mixed" spectrum containing features of all the compounds present in proportion to their relative abundances. So what good is it? The IR spectrum from a paint chip by itself may indeed not be very useful from a forensic standpoint. But FTIR is an excellent *comparison* tool. As we will discuss in the next section, most materials evidence examinations, like many other forensic examinations, consist of comparisons between a "questioned" (evidentiary) item and a "known control." If the IR spectrum of a questioned paint chip very closely matches that of a suspected source, then the examiner can form a real conclusion—that the potential source *could be* the actual source. Similarly, if they did not match, an examiner could conclude that the evidence did not come from the suspected source.

Another powerful instrument occasionally useful for trace evidence analysis is the scanning electron microscope (Figure 13.3) (usually abbreviated SEM). This very powerful microscope has the capability of not only visualizing very small samples like a normal light microscope, but with much higher magnification than with a light microscope. But, in addition, when it is equipped with a special analyzer known as an energy-dispersive X-ray analyzer (EDX), the elemental composition of the specimen can be determined. The combination is known as a SEM/EDX instrument. It is a complex and very expensive piece of equipment. It has been quite useful for certain specific analyses, such as gunshot residue identification (Chapter 8). The instrument can also be used for the identification and comparison of other particles and biological materials such as pollen. There was an example in Case Study 4.2 of

Figure 13.3
Scanning electron microscope.

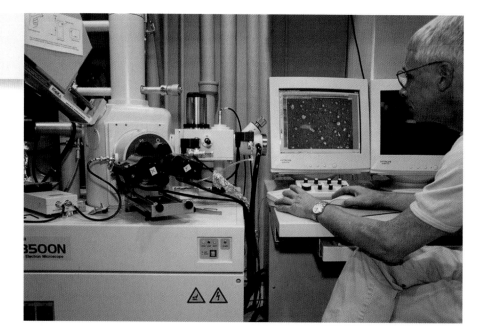

using SEM to identify diatoms. Knowing the elemental composition of a chemical material will often help in determining what the material may be. Because the instrument has limited applicability to forensic evidence, many laboratories have not acquired one, because it cannot be justified as cost-effective.

Materials Evidence Comparisons— Individualization, Inclusion, and Exclusion

Before discussing several specific, regularly encountered categories of materials evidence, it is important to reemphasize (Chapter 1) the concepts of individualization and association in connection with transferred materials evidence.

As we have noted, materials evidence has potential value when transferred because its presence on the target surface or object can indicate contact with the source surface or object. Once in a while, the objective of an examination might be to identify what the material is. But most of the time, the objective is comparison between an evidentiary specimen and a known control. Investigators are nearly always responsible for providing the lab with the known control for comparison. Could this red fiber have come from the victim's red sweater? Could the soil on the suspect's shoes have come from the scene? Could the paint smear on the hit-and-run victim's bicycle have come from the suspect's vehicle? Could the head hair on the victim's coat have come from the suspect? All these are relevant forensic questions. And trying to answer them requires a comparison—a comparison between the evidence specimen and a known control.

An important point about materials evidence: It generally *cannot* be individualized. This fact means that the preceding questions cannot be answered definitively, unless the answer is no. If questioned and known control specimens match in every property and aspect compared, the most the examiner can say is that the "questioned specimen could have come from the suspected source." Another way of saying the same thing is that the "questioned specimen could not be excluded as having come from the suspected source." Criminalists sometimes refer to this process as "partial individualization." Many items in a class of materials can be excluded, but the questioned specimen still cannot be attributed exclusively to the known. A questioned red nylon fiber with certain microscopic properties can match the known fiber, for example. Here, the source of the questioned fiber must be one with red nylon fibers having those same properties. All other fibers can be excluded as a potential source. But the analyst cannot say that the questioned fiber came from this particular known, because there are still many potential sources. However, if properties do not match, then an examiner can say definitively that the "questioned specimen did not come from the suspected source." For this reason, materials evidence is sometimes said to have primarily **exclusionary value.** Exclusion is the only definitive result from a comparison of a known control and a questioned specimen.

Some Common Types of Materials Evidence

Immediately following are examples of the most commonly encountered types of materials evidence. Although these categories are the most common, they are by no means the only types of materials that will be encountered as evidence. At scenes, evidence is not found with a little sign that says it is evidence. Collecting everything is not a viable solution, because the critical trace evidence might be obscured in the enormous amounts of submitted material. As we have noted, what really distinguishes a quality investigator or crime scene specialist is the ability to *recognize* what may turn out to be useful evidence. This skill requires a systematic, scientific approach to the scene and the case, along with a realistic appreciation of the value of various types of evidence. Investigators need to understand what information the lab can provide based on an analysis or comparison of different types of evidence.

exclusionary value
When physical evidence is of a type that cannot be individualized, but only associated, it may have significant value by excluding the possibility of a common source, and exclusion is an absolute conclusion.

How significant is the evidence? Is the information that can be provided by the piece of evidence relevant to the case? Investigators must also be familiar with various control and comparison specimens (Chapter 3) that are required in order to make laboratory analysis or comparison possible.

Fibers

natural fibers

A fibrous material composed of a material found in nature either in plants or animals.

synthetic fibers

A fibrous material composed of material that does not occur in nature, but rather is man-made.

Fibers, both natural and synthetic, are common pieces of evidence. Many **natural fibers** such as cotton, wool, and silk, are used in clothing, while others, such as jute, manila, and hemp are used in cordage and ropes. If an investigator finds cordage fibers on a victim's body or the person's clothing, it might indicate that the victim was tied up. Those fibers could be very useful in identifying what type of rope was used to immobilize the victim. **Synthetic fibers** now have become major components of many types of clothing and many other things as well. Draperies, bedding, and carpeting, to name just a few, now are largely composed of synthetic fibers. Hair, both human and animal, is also an important type of fiber-type evidence. The basic physical structure of human and animal hair is very similar. Hairs are shed from both humans and other animals as part of the natural growth cycle. People who are in and out of houses where people have pets often walk away with samples of shed animal hair on their clothing and shoes. These shed hairs are everywhere, and even if not readily visible, microscopical examination can quickly disclose the presence of these pet hairs. In fact, it can be difficult not to walk away with pet hair.

Biological Materials

In the Part Four introduction, we noted that "biological" is a complicated modifier in the forensic evidence context. Often, it refers to human blood and body fluid evidence that can be subjected to genetic testing to establish individuality. But, there are "biological" items that are classified differently for forensic purposes. Blood or urine collected for toxicological analysis is an example. Other examples are the items discussed in this section. They are biological, but fall into the "materials evidence" category because the methods used to examine them, and the information that can be derived from the examinations, approximates other materials evidence more than it does human blood or physiological fluids deposited at scenes.

One example of a biological material is pollen. Information that may be available from examination of pollen is whether an object was left outside at a particular time of year or how long it was left out. Pollen falls out of the air at particular times of the year depending on the life cycle of the plant that released it. Those who have hay fever are acutely aware of the life cycle of goldenrod or whatever plant pollen to which they are sensitive. Because pollen is biological and has very characteristic shapes, it can be recognized as pollen and associated with a particular plant source. Other examples are plant residues and feathers. Feathers can be rather interesting evidence in some circumstances, because in cold climates many people wear down coats. Down coats are supposed to be stuffed with duck down (feathers). "Supposed to" is the operative phrase, because unless a person buys a down coat from a highly reputable source, the stuffing is frequently not actually duck down. The stuffing is either totally or partially chicken feathers. Since there are many more chickens than ducks sold at the grocery store, chicken feathers are much less expensive. When someone wearing a down coat is stabbed, feathers will fly everywhere. Under such circumstances, identification of the type of feathers transferred to a suspect's clothing could turn out to be a very useful piece of evidence.

Wood and Paper

An additional category of biological evidence is wood and paper. Paper is made from highly processed wood, and both are composed largely of cellulose fibers. Most other natural fibers are made of cellulose as well, but they can easily be

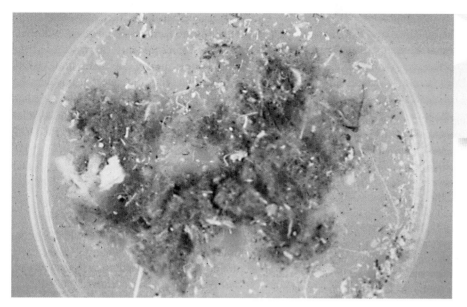

Figure 13.4
Typical complex mixture containing hairs, fibers, and other materials to be sorted using a stereomicroscope so that individual items can be categorized or identified.

differentiated, because nature makes things that have interesting and identifiable shapes. In virtually every household, no matter how well kept, it is likely that careful examination will disclose a few little balls of fluff underneath a bed or hiding in an inaccessible corner. There are several names for these little dust balls, such as "dust bunnies" or "woolies" (Figure 13.4), depending on what part of the country you come from. They are made of intertwined fibers and hairs. Interestingly, one of the main components in these bundles is wood fiber. There are no trees in most homes so why are there so many wood fibers? The simple reason is that wood fibers are used to make paper and in every home there are many different types of paper, for example, facial quality tissues, toilet tissues, and paper towels. Tiny cellulosic fibers become abraded off these products and accumulate to help form dust and dust bunnies. Usually, they are not very useful as evidence because they are so common. However, sometimes if something a little more unusual is mixed into the bundles, someone who burglarizes a house, or is otherwise in it uninvited, may come away with, or occasionally leave behind, a minute dust bundle that can be useful evidence.

Building Materials

A wide variety of building materials under some circumstances can provide useful evidence. Because glass breaks easily and comes in many varieties, it can be useful materials evidence. Should a criminal gain entry to a building or room by breaking through a wall, the investigator will likely find plaster dust all over that individual's clothes and shoes. If a person commits a homicide near a highway, for instance, and moves the body, examination for trace evidence may disclose tiny pieces of rubber. As an individual drives down the road, the car tires go around and around, and tiny pieces of rubber are dislodged. They are being thrown up in the air and eventually settle near the road. As a result, fine tire rubber particles can be fairly useful pieces of evidence to indicate that an object was at one time on the ground near a road or highway.

Many types of foam-based materials are used as building materials, in furniture, and as insulation. Foam rubber is familiar to everyone, but much more common now is polyurethane foam. It is the material that is most often used in pillows and cushions, especially the seats of automobiles and furniture pillows. There have been many cases where tiny specks of polyurethane foam have proven to be useful as transfer evidence. Nearly everyone has seen an old couch or a

Case Study 13.1

Transferred Foamed Material Associates a Suspect with Murder Victims

There was a multiple murder case on Long Island several years ago where the bodies were dumped in dumpsters. After considerable investigative effort, the detectives developed a strong suspect. Interestingly, examination of the bodies and clothing of the victims showed that one type of materials evidence found on several of the victims was a particular kind of yellow powder that, when observed microscopically, was clearly foamed material. The investigators went to a suspect's apartment to interview him. He and his brother had a successful business and were making a good living, but he was living in a filthy cluttered apartment. The furnishings were old and decrepit. One particularly decrepit chair was clearly his favorite chair. That chair was leaking fine dust from several places, and there was powdered foam all over the floor near that chair. This observation alone reinforced the idea for the investigators that they probably had the correct individual. They obtained a search warrant for the apartment, and subsequent analysis showed that this was exactly the same type of yellow powdered foam found on the bodies, and it was useful in linking the victims to this particular apartment.

very used automobile that "leaks" little bits of fine yellowish powder. When an analyst examines this "powder" with a microscope, he or she may find visible tiny bubbles that indicate the powder is a foam, probably polyurethane foam. When a chair seat begins to leak this fine powder through seams in the fabric, anybody who sits in that chair will leave with some of that powdered foam on his or her clothing.

Metallic Residues

Because metal is used so widely in building and manufacturing, many forensically important metallic traces are encountered, from lead residue left behind by a bullet, to rust, to magnesium residue from a flare used to start a fire. When someone forces open a door with a pry bar, the Locard exchange principle says that some of that pry bar metal is left on the door frame, and some of the metal door frame material is transferred to the pry bar, thus an exchange of traces. If an examiner finds residue of the door frame on a tool, it may be possible to determine the composition of that metal. Steel is mostly iron, but also has chromium in it and easily detectible amounts of four or five other elements. Besides steel most other metals have small amounts of other metallic elements added during manufacture to give them desirable properties. It is possible, for example, to compare the elemental composition of a piece of material recovered from a tool that gouged it out of a cash box to a control sample taken from that cash box and have a pretty good indication of whether or not the cash box *could* have been the source of the tiny trace of metal found on a particular tool.

Paint and Other Coatings

Most forensic laboratories would list paint as one of the three or four most commonly encountered types of materials evidence, probably right after the top two, hairs and fibers. The types of paint used to color and protect buildings are different from those used on automobiles and other vehicles. Automotive paint is often encountered not only as tiny paint chips on the clothing of a hit-and-run victim, but also as the result of an automobile having hit a building, rural mailbox, wall, tree, or other stationary object, including another vehicle. Architectural paint is encountered in breaking and entering cases, on burglars' tools, on shoes, and may even be picked up from recently painted surfaces. Specialty paints from tools, boats, truck beds, and a variety of other sources are also encountered. Red paint may be occasionally mistaken for blood, prior to testing.

Cosmetics and Beauty Products

Figure 13.5

A residue of lipstick left on a drinking glass that can be examined for both color and chemical composition.

Although cosmetics and beauty products are not a frequent type of evidence for most forensic laboratories, there are cases where a lipstick stain left behind, on a glass, for example, may prove to be a useful piece of evidence. Experts can both analyze the composition and match the color of a lipstick stain (Figure 13.5) to a known control sample from a suspect or victim. The variation in color alone is enormous. A visit to a large department store can quickly convince one that the variety of lipstick shades available exceeds even that of automobile colors. Similarly nail polish can be chipped off at a violent scene; again, the variety of colors is enormous. Keep in mind that color and even composition of these materials are class characteristics, and matching class characteristics does not mean individualization, but it can indicate or eliminate possible common origin. There was analysis of nail polish in the Crafts case, the lead case presented in Chapter 1.

Soil and Dust

Soil evidence can be recovered from shoes or from muddy footprints left behind on doors, casts of impressions taken at a scene, and many additional sources. Automobiles, too, can provide an excellent source for soil evidence. When an individual drives off the road, perhaps to dump a body out in the woods, the automobile will begin to pick up soil or debris characteristic of that particular area as soon as it leaves the pavement. Perhaps someone drives down to a lake to throw a body into the lake. The vehicle may leave tire tracks at the edge of the lake, and probably take a good bit of that soil away on the tires or in the wheel wells. If you look inside the wheel wells on any automobile that has been driven off paved roads even for a short distance, you usually find soil that has been thrown from the tire onto the inside of the wheel well. If a sample of that dirt were dislodged, and examined for its layers of soil, you might find a "history" of the different soils through which the vehicle has driven. There is a lot of potential for soil as useful forensic evidence, but because it is difficult to examine and requires considerable special expertise, many laboratories do not extensively examine soil evidence.

A subcategory of soil is dust, and some experts specialize in examining dust. Dust is very much a part of our environment. It can often tell quite a lot about where any item that has collected that dust has been. Dust is nothing more than fine particles that fall out of the air. Anything left undisturbed either in or out of doors will soon have a coating of dust on it. An item left exposed to the air for a while will collect a history of what has been falling from the air for the period it was exposed. There may be a considerable amount of information in that dust for a person who knows how to interpret it, so a dust sample may prove to be a useful piece of evidence. Every area has dust characteristic of that particular area. It may be due to pollen from the local plants, fly ash from industrial furnaces, or just airborne soil. The variety of things settling out of the air, particularly in highly populated areas, is enormous and ever changing as well. Therefore, it may be useful in determining where something was lying, or if it has recently been moved, as well as many other things.

Discussion of Major Categories of Materials Evidence

As indicated, the five most commonly encountered types of materials evidence are fibers, hair, paint, soil, and glass. For this reason, it is useful to discuss each one in more detail. One thing all have in common is the importance of microscopical examination, particularly using the comparison microscope. The comparison microscope is critical for careful comparison of microscopic or near microscopic evidence objects for both color and morphology. The type of comparison microscope used for materials evidence uses transmitted light to look through the objects, rather than the reflected light used for bullet and cartridge case comparisons. (See the discussion of microscopes and microscopy in the Appendix: Scientific Tools of the Trade.)

Fibers

Probably the most common kind of materials evidence encountered in forensic laboratories is fibers. Because fibers are so widely used in commerce, and because they are easily broken and they tend to stick to things, they are very commonly transferred during contact. They are light and will catch on rough surfaces of garments and many other things. A nylon jacket that is very smooth will seldom retain fibers (lint), whereas a flannel shirt, a sweater, or a wool jacket will have fibers tangled in the weave and thereby retained on its surface. Such retention of fibers can provide forensically important information in many situations.

Fibers are usually divided into two major groups, natural fibers and synthetic or manufactured fibers. About 60 years ago, it would have been only one group, the natural fibers. Development of manufactured fibers really became important with the need to find a substitute for silk for making parachutes during World War II.

Natural Fibers   Natural fibers can be subdivided as in the game of 20 questions: Is it animal, vegetable, or mineral? All animal fibers are protein, all vegetable fibers are cellulose, and mineral fibers are not very common and seldom of forensic interest (with the possible exception of asbestos). Yet there are dozens of different natural fibers.

There are really only two mineral fibers of forensic significance: asbestos and mineral wool fibers. Asbestos is an unusual mineral that has a naturally fibrous structure as it is mined from the earth. It was used for many years as insulation and in many other applications. Because it is essentially rock, it is nonflammable, which is an important advantage for an insulation material. Before its ban in certain applications, asbestos was used in fire safes to protect the papers in the safe from even prolonged fire outside the safe. For that reason, it could be encountered when safe burglars were forced to drill or use explosives to blow a safe. They invariably disturbed the layer of insulation between the inner and outer wall of the safe and released asbestos fibers into the surroundings including onto themselves. There are a number of different forms of asbestos, and several tend to produce fibers that are so small and light that they can remain suspended in air for extended periods. Prolonged inhalation of such asbestos fibers can cause asbestosis, which is an eventually fatal disease of the lungs. Because of this danger, asbestos is no longer used in any application where it might be released into the atmosphere. Although a great deal of asbestos is still around, it is slowly being removed, covered up, or disposed of in one way or another. Forensic microscopists and materials analysts who perform work for civil cases or regulatory enforcement matters may still do asbestos cases.

Mineral wool is a material made by melting glassy minerals and forcing them through a fine die in close analogy to the regenerated fibers discussed later. Its uses are quite analogous to asbestos and primarily of interest forensically because of its use as safe insulation.

Different varieties of vegetable fibers, because they are primarily cellulose, cannot be easily differentiated by chemical analysis. Because they are natural and formed in plants by biological processes, they have complex three-dimensional shapes (morphology). They can usually be recognized by careful microscopical examination, and the morphology is often more easily observed in the microscope if the fibers are stained with a biological stain that preferentially colors a particular component of the fiber. Therefore, vegetable fibers are usually identified in the forensic laboratory by a combination of visual and microscopical examinations. These days, cotton is the most important natural fiber, and linen is also a popular vegetable fiber. In the laboratory, analysts encounter a great variety of cotton fibers (Figure 13.6) in many different cases. Unfortunately, undyed white cotton is often not of much use forensically, because so many things, from undergarments to bed sheets, are made out of white cotton. Dyed cottons, although still very common, can be more useful forensically because of the many colors and types of dyes used. Manila, hemp, and jute are coarse natural plant fibers that can be used in fabrics, but they are much more commonly encountered in packaging twine, rope and door mats, or in the padding used under carpeting.

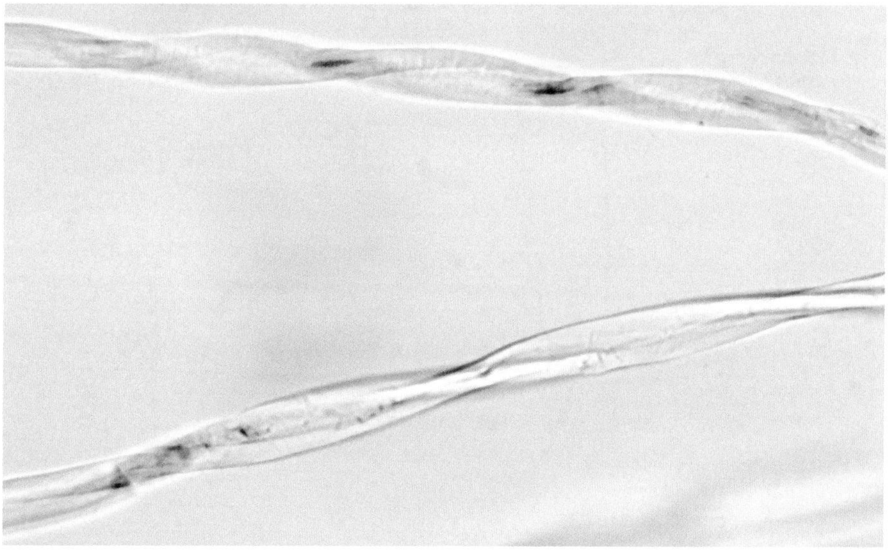

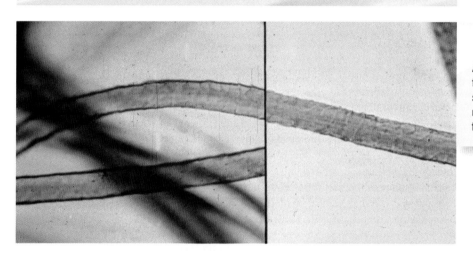

Figure 13.6

A photomicrograph of a cotton fiber. Notice the very characteristic twisted structure often used to recognize cotton.

Figure 13.7

A photomicrograph of a blue wool fiber. Notice the very characteristic scaly appearance of wool used to recognize wool and most other animal fibers.

The most important animal fibers are wool (Figure 13.7) and similar animal hair materials. Wool, of course, comes primarily from sheep, but it also comes from goats and llamas and a number of other related animals, such as alpacas. All these animals have fine hair that can be shaved off the animal, then spun into thread and used to make fabrics. An expert can usually easily tell whether a fiber is a vegetable fiber or an animal fiber just by looking at it. Animal fibers, which are essentially hairs (see later), have an outer layer of scales that overlap like shingles on a roof to form a protective layer. This structure is often visible to the unaided eye or under slight magnification. Animal fibers are spun to make thread before being woven into cloth, and each thread has the strength of many strands; therefore, the resulting cloth is very durable. Although cotton is currently the most popular fiber for clothing, wool is still very important and a premium fiber for many applications such as pants and sport jackets, sweaters, blankets, and coats.

Many animal hair products are not spun and woven into fabrics but are used as the animal used them—as fur coats. "Fur" is the term used when the animal hair is not removed from the pelt and is still embedded in the animal's skin. Coats made from seal, mink, beaver, and a variety of other animal pelts have been popular for centuries. Natural fur coats are both warm and very durable. There have been periods of time when it is not "politically correct" to own or wear fur coats, but many such garments are in use. Animal hair is used in other products as well. Rabbit hair is used as the soft inner lining in gloves and is woven with other natural and synthetic fibers into mixed fabrics.

Figure 13.8

A photomicrograph of a silk fiber. Notice striations and other structure in the fiber characteristic of natural fibers.

The most unusual animal fiber is one of the oldest and most widely used in high-quality fabrics. Silk (Figure 13.8) is definitely an animal fiber, but it's not an animal hair—rather, it is the unraveled cocoon of a silkworm caterpillar. Silkworm caterpillars spin cocoons during the part of their life cycle where they are transforming themselves into a butterfly (biologists call it the "pupa stage"). Silk is made by unraveling those cocoons. The cocoons are gathered and boiled before being unraveled into silk thread. The silk thread is not formed like a hair, but rather is exuded from a little organ called a "spinneret" in the abdomen of the silkworm. Silk is more like a spiderweb than hair and does not have a scale pattern like the other animal fibers. Silk has been made into excellent fabrics for thousands of years in the Orient. The use of silk had been moderated by its high price in the Western world. However, with the recent increased entry of China into world markets, the availability of silk has increased and its price has dropped. Silk has many excellent properties and is highly prized for clothing, undergarments, and a variety of other applications.

regenerated fibers

Fibers made by dissolving cellulose-based material and forcing it through fine holes into a solution that causes it to immediately solidify, thereby transforming a natural vegetable material into a man-made fiber.

Synthetic Fibers   An important fact about synthetic (man-made), manufactured, and some natural fibers is that, chemically, they are all *polymers*. Polymers are compounds made of repeating units. The repeating units may be the same, or there may be several different ones. See the box "More on the Science: Polymers."

Synthetic and manufactured fibers, which became generally available primarily after World War II, have come to dominate the fiber business. We can divide man-made fibers into two basic categories: one small, but historically important category, referred to as *regenerated* fibers; and the now much more important category of *synthetic* fibers (Figure 13.9). **Regenerated fibers** were the first man-made fibers. Rayon was developed as a synthetic version of vegetable fibers like cotton or manila. Rayon, like the vegetable fibers, is cellulose. The key step in the manufacture of regenerated fibers was devising a way to dissolve a source of cellulose, like sawdust or cotton waste. This is not an easy thing to do, since cellulose is not soluble in many things that do not destroy it. Several

Case Study 13.2

Unusual Combination of Fibers Provide Key Evidence

Pink dyed rabbit hair, in a mixture with acrylic, played an important part in a murder case a number of years ago. When last seen, the victim was wearing a very fluffy sweater with that unusual combination of fibers. Finding traces of those fibers in a suspect's house cast serious doubt on his denials of having any contact with the victim after she dropped off her car for some service. He was eventually arrested, and fiber evidence played a prominent role in his trial and subsequent conviction for murder.

Polymers

Polymers are both nature's and humans' construction materials. They are chemically built up of large numbers of repeating units called "monomers." A polymer may be composed of up to hundreds of thousands of monomer units, as with the common plastic called "polyethylene." Polymers may also be more complex, such as the natural polymers we call proteins that are also made of repeating units. Here the units (monomers) are chemically similar, but not necessarily identical repeating units, called "amino acids."

Cellulose, the construction material of the vegetable world, is made up of repeating units of simple sugar molecules. Forensic science's most-talked-about polymer is DNA, which is made of repeating nucleotide units, that have phosphate ester groups and organic bases attached to the sugar backbone (Chapter 10). It is the sequence of the four different organic bases that make up the genetic code.

These repeating units can be visualized as links in a chain. Different polymers are composed of different types of links. Further, the chains can be of different length and can be lined up parallel or can be mixed together randomly or tangled. This means that the same polymer (type of link) can have different physical properties depending on chain length or arrangement. A polymer material made up of many polymer strands (chains) can sometimes be modified after its initial formation by chemically causing different polymer strands (chains) to have points of attachment. This process is called "cross-linking" and is very important in adding strength or rigidity to polymeric materials. When a paint film "cures" on the painted surface, it becomes stronger because of the cross-linking of chains caused by reaction with oxygen in the air.

Humans imitated nature in developing synthetic polymer materials using a very wide variety of building blocks (links). We call most of these materials plastics; man-made polymers include synthetic fibers, synthetic rubber, and a great many other simple or very complex polymers. The very common polymer polyethylene terphthalate, usually referred to as polyester, is used in many forms, from clothing fibers to soda bottles to engineering polymers used to make many other useful objects.

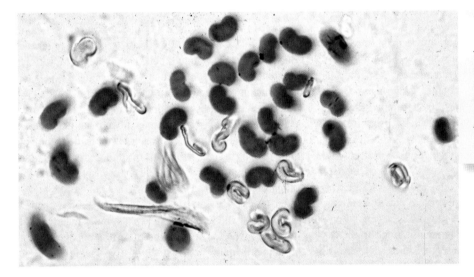

Figure 13.9

Two different types of fibers, one natural and one synthetic, shown in cross section. The synthetic fibers (deep blue) have a consistent bean-shaped cross section, whereas the natural fibers have varied cross sections.

different rather ingenious processes were developed to accomplish the task. Once the cellulose is in solution, it can be forced through a die, which is usually a piece of steel with many tiny holes, into a different chemical solution that immediately causes the cellulose to deposit from the solution as a solid "fiber." In this way, many long, thin fibers are formed, and they can be recovered and dried to form the final manufactured fiber. This process is used for rayon and acetate fiber production. Fibers are produced having the diameter of the holes in the die. Rayon and acetate fibers are called regenerated fibers because the starting material is a natural cellulose source. The regenerated fibers are based on cellulose but processed in a way to produce a fiber different from any natural fiber. A variation on the solution process for producing man-made fibers is a melt process. A starting material for a fiber that can be melted more easily than dissolved is heated above its melting point, and then the liquid material is forced through fine holes in a die and rapidly cooled it as it emerges from the die, causing it to instantly solidify into the desired fibers.

Although rayon found a solid market in tire cord, the real impetus behind the development of synthetic fibers was World War II, and the control of silk production at that time by the Japanese. The importance of aviation to the war effort and the fact that early parachutes were made from silk made it critical that some substitute for silk be found. Silk was the only material available that was strong enough and light enough to make a canopy large enough to support the weight of a pilot and compact enough to be carried in a pouch on the fliers' backs when they bailed out of an airplane. When Japan came into World War II and quickly took control of the Far East, silk became unavailable in the West, prompting an urgent search for an alternative material.

A chemist named Caruthers, who worked at Dupont, led a team that developed a polymer they called nylon. Nylon proved to be a material with many important properties quite similar to silk. You can think of nylon as imitation silk. It is chemically similar, and very light in weight for its strength. As a result, the United States was able to manufacture parachutes for our pilots using this new synthetic fiber.

When synthetic polymers are extruded through dies to form filaments, they have a relatively uniform diameter and a smooth surface—in contrast to most natural fibers, which have complex morphology (shape) and uneven diameter. This is one of the major differences between natural fibers and synthetic fibers. Again, as mentioned, silk was the one exception to this rule of thumb, appearing more like a synthetic fiber than a natural one.

Modern technology has allowed synthetic fibers to have more complex cross sections, because, when making the extrusion dies, instead of simply drilling round holes, manufacturers can now use a laser to create very thin holes of any desired shape. As a result, there are fibers manufactured that have a square, pentagonal, or even cloverleaf-shaped cross sections. They still do not have the complex morphology that we see in the natural fibers, which helps forensic scientists to differentiate natural from man-made fibers. Over the years since World War II, a great variety of other synthetic fibers have become available. Because these different fibers are made from various synthetic polymers, they can be differentiated using chemical and physical tests—in stark contrast to the natural fibers, all of which are formed from either cellulose (vegetable) or protein (animal) and can best be differentiated using their differing morphology.

Each of the different types of synthetic polymers used in fiber manufacture has been optimized for particular applications. For example, polyester has become the major synthetic fiber in the world economy. It has a great variety of desirable properties, and it is used in an enormous variety of applications. It is relatively inexpensive to make, is quite strong, has a fairly high melting point, and is easily processed. At one time, men's suits were made from pure polyester (and it was once fashionable to make fun of men who wore such suits), but a mixture of wool and polyester makes a popular material that is much more desirable. Nylon replaced rayon in tire cord, because it is much stronger, and, of course, nylon became the standard for women's stockings (replacing silk).

Polyolefins (polyethylene and polypropylene) are the low-price leaders of the commercial fibers, but they are best known as the fiber of Astroturf, or more mundanely, as that of indoor/outdoor carpeting. Polyethylene fibers are inexpensive not only because of low raw material cost, but also because polyethylene is used for so many other nonfiber applications. It is well suited to applications where its resistance to bacterial action and water are advantageous, and its low melting point is not a problem. Acrylics are important fibers that are used in clothing, particularly sweaters and blankets. In fact, consumers are hard-pressed to find a blanket that is not made from acrylic fibers these days. Such blankets are bulky and light and fluffy, which gives them their insulating power and thereby their warmth. Many other types of synthetic polymers find use as fibers. One interesting one is spandex, a stretchy fiber that is used for many types of form-fitting clothing such as bicycle shorts, gym outfits, and some jeans, to give them a little stretchiness.

Another rather important fiber, particularly to law enforcement, is polyamide, which is a rather expensive fiber but an extremely strong one. It is used to make bulletproof vests for law enforcement officers. Better known by its brand name, Kevlar, it is widely used for applications where strength is absolutely critical. People who are avid sailboat racers, and want to have the "racer's edge," purchase Kevlar sails.

Another specialty synthetic fiber is fiberglass, which is made by forcing molten glass through a die. At one time, it was used for curtains and some kinds of fabrics but is not as common now in fabric-type applications. It also is not used in clothing because of the obvious scratchiness problem, but it is used particularly in draperies. Fiberglass is strong, chemically resistant, and rejects dirt fairly well. One of the largest applications for glass fiber is as insulation. The attics of most homes are insulated from the main floors with glass fiber, and it is often used in the walls as well. In addition, enormous amounts of glass fiber are manufactured to be incorporated into fiberglass objects. The glass fibers are woven into cloth and used to make a whole range of very durable composite materials generally called fiberglass. These items are made by combining a fiberglass cloth with a liquid polymer resin that sets to a hard, strong plastic material. Frequently many layers of cloth and resin are used to build up the final fiberglass structure. It is found in furniture, car bodies, boats, and myriad other products. When these materials wear down or are broken, glass fibers can be released and occasionally become evidence.

Known Standards Successful laboratory examination of materials evidence, including fibers, depends upon the collection of proper control samples. Questioned (or evidentiary) fibers must be compared with known controls, and those controls must normally be obtained by investigators and submitted to the laboratory. Most examiners agree that an adequate reference sample must take into consideration the various types of fibers, including different colors at the fiber source. Also, where fibers have been exposed to sunlight for extended periods, the color may fade or otherwise change. This possibility needs to be considered in collection of standards. Because modern laboratory fiber analysis techniques require only minuscule amounts of fiber, only a small amount of control sample need usually be taken.

Laboratory Examination of Fibers The initial laboratory examination of fibers, because of their generally small size, is usually microscopical examination, regardless of whether they are natural or synthetic fibers, but this is particularly true of natural fibers, which are usually identified almost exclusively from their morphology. Natural fibers tend to have complex and distinctive internal and external structures. Each different type of natural fiber has its own characteristic appearance. This applies to all of the vegetable fibers such as cotton, linen, ramie, manila, sisal, and most of the animal-derived fibers such as wool, rabbit, mohair, and cashmere. The prime exception is silk, which has little structure and may look more like a man-made fiber than an animal-derived fiber. Because all these fibers are cellular in origin they are built up from many millions of units and thereby have complex structures. Most of the animal fibers are actually hairs and have scale patterns and medullas in addition to the cortex (see next section). In fact, in animal hair the medulla is a particularly important feature, because it usually makes up a much larger portion of the hair than with human hair and often shows interesting and complex structure. In addition, plant and animal fibers often have natural color and even show things like banding patterns, highly variable diameters, and quite variable cross sections. Because of their complex morphology, natural fibers may not absorb dyes evenly and this, too, can be a useful property to observe.

Synthetic fibers provide much less information when viewed in the microscope. The main reason is that most artificial fibers are formed by being forced through a die. As a result they have a uniform diameter and cross section. The diameter is determined by the size of the hole in the die and the cross section by the shape of the hole in the die. In addition to this diameter and cross section, the key property of man-made fibers is the color, because of the enormous variety of colors that are now produced. Unlike hairs, the color in synthetic fibers is, as a rule, fairly uniformly distributed throughout the fiber. In fact, when a fiber shows a nonuniform color, it is an important property for comparison because it is not common. This consistent color distribution makes the comparison of two fibers on a comparison microscope much easier. Thus, a fiber from a crime scene and a control fiber from the carpeting

Figure 13.10

A synthetic fiber with tiny specks of titanium dioxide (delusterant) added to reduce the shininess of the fiber.

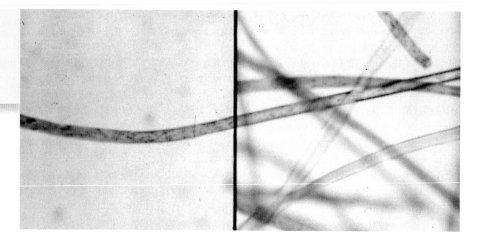

in a suspect's vehicle can be reliably compared in terms of color and diameter. Because Western society is very consumer oriented, and people are concerned about having their possessions look just right, the fiber industry has created an enormous variety of colors. There are hundreds of different dyes, dye combinations, and pigments that are used to produce those colors. This adds a major dimension to the comparison of man-made fibers, which would otherwise be largely restricted to chemical analysis to determine the type of polymer, as we shall discuss shortly.

Another important property of synthetic fibers is their shininess, more accurately called luster. The first artificial fibers, the regenerated fibers rayon and acetate, tended to be rather shiny, and fabrics made from them took on a consumer perception of being cheap, even though shininess of silk always had a luxury connotation. Therefore, manufacturers of synthetic fibers sought to control this shininess. It was discovered that addition of the basic white pigment titanium dioxide to the fiber added depth to the color and reduced the shininess. As a result, many synthetic fibers now have varying amounts of titanium dioxide added. This is referred to as a **delusterant,** and when delustered fibers are viewed microscopically (Figure 13.10), they appear to have many dark specks distributed throughout the fiber. The delusterant appears dark when viewed with transmitted light and white when viewed in reflected light. The appearance is somewhat similar to the pigment granules observed in hair but the delusterant appears black rather than brown or red. These specks of delusterant provide another characteristic in comparing synthetic fibers. The amount of delusterant, and the way it is distributed within the fiber, is a characteristic of a particular type of fiber. The delusterant may be evenly distributed, clumpy, or perhaps more pronounced around the outside portion of the fiber.

Size and cross section are key fiber characteristics. The diameter of a fiber is easily measured under the microscope. Observing fibers next to each other in the field of a comparison microscope also allows the analyst to compare the relative diameter of the fibers. If, as in the first man-made fibers, the cross section were always round, there would not be much information in the cross section. Modern technology allows manufacturers to make dies with holes of virtually any shape. As mentioned earlier, fibers are now seen with cross sections that are oval, square, pentagonal, clover-shaped (Figure 13.11), and many other variations. The various shapes (Figure 13.12) give the fibers different physical properties and thus are often favored for particular applications. As a result, the cross section of a fiber has become a useful characteristic for examination and comparison of synthetic fibers.

Several **optical properties** can also be used in the comparison of synthetic fibers. Fiber examiners have several ways of measuring the refractive index of a fiber. The *refractive index* (discussed later in the glass section) is defined as the ratio of the speed at which light passes through a vacuum versus the speed at which light passes through the fiber. The speed of light through a fiber depends on which direction it is

delusterant

An opaque pigment (usually white) that is added to man-made fibers to reduce their shininess.

optical properties

The way a material interacts with light, such as refractive index and dispersion.

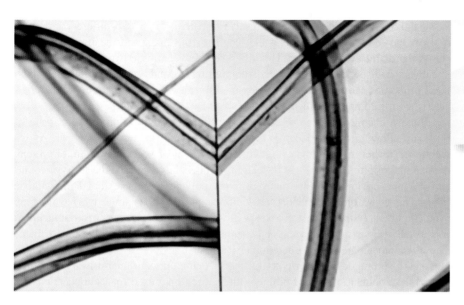

Figure 13.11
Nylon fiber typical of those used in carpeting with trilobal cross section. The trilobal cross section shows up as a channel up the center of the fiber when observed in the microscope.

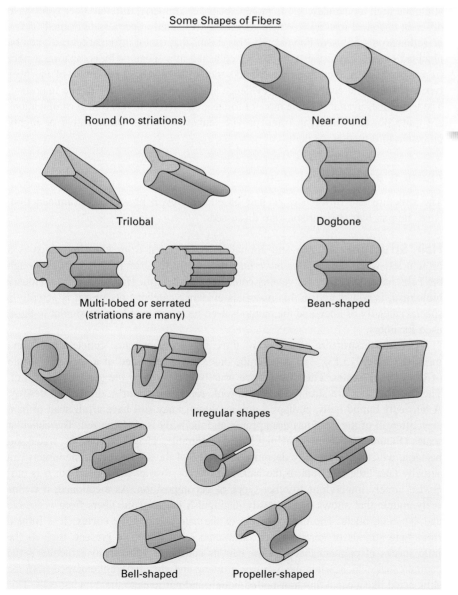

Figure 13.12
Because synthetic fibers are made by being forced through fine holes in dies, they can be formed with any cross-section shape that a laser can make in the die.

passing through the fiber, and as a result most fibers have two different refractive indices: the refractive index along the length of the fiber, and the refractive index across the diameter of the fiber. The difference between these two refractive indexes is called the dispersion of the fiber. Although this sounds rather complicated, both these properties can be fairly easily measured for most fibers and are important characteristics for comparison of fibers.

Finally, chemical properties can be useful in the identification or comparison of fibers by allowing one to identify the type of polymer in a synthetic fiber. As we mentioned earlier, natural fibers are either cellulose, if of vegetable origin, or protein, if of animal origin. Development of man-made fibers has exercised the skills of countless polymer chemists so that many different polymer types are found in synthetic fibers. This gives forensic scientists an additional property to examine when comparing synthetic fibers. Using either infrared spectroscopy or **pyrolysis gas chromatography,** it is usually possible to determine the chemical composition of even the tiniest fibers. These techniques are used to determine if a fiber is nylon, rayon, acrylic, olefin, or any one of several dozen other types of fibers. Again, our consumer-driven society has caused development of myriad different fibers, each optimized for its application. For example, polyolefin-type fibers melt at a lower temperature than most other fibers so they would not be used in applications where heat is a problem, whereas nylon melts at a quite high temperature but is more expensive. Similarly, different fiber types have different chemical reactivity. Where chemically resistant properties are desired, Tyvex or Teflon would be used. Forensically, this means that useful information can often be obtained by looking at the type of fiber collected at a scene or by comparing a fiber from a scene to a fiber from a suspected source. Both the identification of the fiber type and the direct comparison of evidence and control fibers can be quite important. The techniques available in the modern forensic laboratory to make such examinations are quite powerful and can often provide either important investigative or highly probative information, or both.

Human and Animal Hair

The structure and differences in hair based on growth phases are examined first. Next, human hair comparisons are discussed.

Hair Structure   Human and animal hair is formed from **keratin,** which is a protein left when the *cellular material* produced in the hair follicle dies. Although the cells have died, the hair retains considerable strength. Hair, although obviously biological, is considered in this materials evidence category because it is actually a special category of fiber, and the methods used for examining hair are similar to those used for fibers.

Hair has a structure consisting of three major components: cuticle, cortex, and medulla (Figure 13.13). The **cuticle,** the outer layer, is formed of a very thin sheath of overlapping scales. These scales are usually compared to the shingles on a roof. They overlap and are strong and waterproof. As a result, hair is difficult to destroy. A hurriedly buried body, perhaps a murder victim, may still have a full head of hair, even after all of the flesh has disappeared and the body is skeletonized. The cuticular scales (Figure 13.14) are what make hair so durable. They keep out the water and bacteria, which fairly quickly decompose the rest of the soft tissue. Some insects can actually take little bites out of the hair, and thereby disrupt the cuticle, but it is otherwise largely impervious to other types of decomposition. As mentioned, it is this scaly cuticle that allows one to easily distinguish hair and fur fibers from vegetable and synthetic fibers. The major portion of the hair is called the **cortex.** It is formed from long strands of keratin. There are some other materials present, such as the little specks of pigment that give the hair its color. The third major structure is the central canal, which, when the hair was growing and alive before it emerged from the skin, acted like a canal that transported liquids and nutrients to the growing cells. This

pyrolysis gas chromatography

A separation technique where a nonvolatile material can be chromatographed by flash heating it in an inert atmosphere to break it into more volatile decomposition products.

keratin

Fibrous, tough, and insoluble protein that forms the hard but nonmineralized structures such as hair, fingernails, and toenails.

cuticle

The impervious outer layer of cells that protects hair.

cortex

The primary structure of the hair shaft.

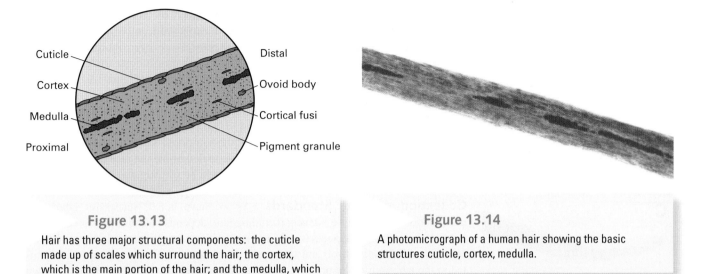

Figure 13.13

Hair has three major structural components: the cuticle made up of scales which surround the hair; the cortex, which is the main portion of the hair; and the medulla, which is a central air channel that is in the middle of the hair.

Figure 13.14

A photomicrograph of a human hair showing the basic structures cuticle, cortex, medulla.

area in the center of the hair is called the **medulla** and is usually an air-filled channel that goes up the middle of the hair. If you look at a hair through a microscope, (Figure 13.13) the medulla usually appears as dark line going up the center of the hair.

The color we see in hair is derived from a pigment called **melanin.** Hair can be from light blond to almost black, and this gradation of color is caused by varying amounts and distribution of this pigment. Those whose hair appears in the reddish shades have a different form of melanin, and the amount and distribution determine the shade.

Growth Phases   Hair does not grow continuously, but rather passes through three different growth phases (Figure 13.15). The longest is called the **anagen phase,** which is the active growth phase. When hair is in the anagen phase, new cells are being produced in the hair follicle in the skin and are pushing the older cells out, which lengthens the hair. The second phase is the **catagen phase,** where the hair follicle stops making new cells and hair growth stops. During the catagen phase, which is relatively short, the little bulb of live cells in the follicle begins to shrink and dry up, destroying the hair's attachment to the scalp, and allowing it to fall out. The third phase is the **telogen phase,** which is a resting period. After a resting period, which is quite variable depending on the part of the body and the individual, the hair follicle again enters the anagen (growth) phase and a new hair starts to grow. The forensic significance of the cycle is that, at any given moment, a certain percentage of a person's hairs is ready to fall out (telogen phase). Everyone sheds many hairs every day. Further, because telogen hairs are about to fall out, even slight pressure will remove them. As a result, a struggle or other strenuous activity is likely to cause telogen hairs to be shed. These hairs may become important evidence, particularly if transferred between a victim and an attacker.

An understanding of the growth phases, and what the root end looks like during the three phases, allows an analyst to determine, in many cases, whether a hair was forcibly removed or just fell out as part of the normal cycle. If someone is hit in the head with a hammer, or hairs are pulled out during a violent altercation, the hairs have a bulb of live tissue clinging to the root end. Thus, a hair examiner can often look at an evidence hair and determine whether it was forcibly removed or whether it fell out as part of the normal hair life cycle. This life cycle is also the underlying reason that there are often many loose hairs that an intruder may carry away from a scene on his or her clothing, shoes, or body.

medulla

A canal that runs up the center of the cortex of a hair and is usually air filled in forensic samples.

melanin

A natural brown pigment that gives most hair its color.

anagen phase

The active growth phase of the hair follicle.

catagen phase

The hair follicle phase in which hair growth stops.

telogen phase

The third growth phase of the hair follicle, which is a resting period.

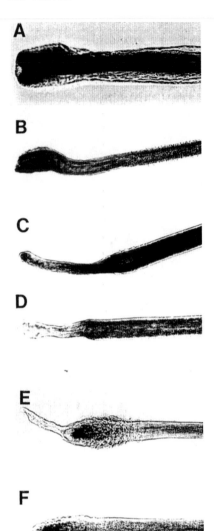

Racial Characteristics of Human Hair

Each of the three "major" races (Caucasoid, Negroid, Mongoloid) generally have significantly different-looking hair, especially head hair. Because these differences are even more apparent by microscopical examination, it is often possible for a hair examiner to "guesstimate" the race of individual who was the source of a particular hair (Figure 13.16). We say "guesstimate," because there are many children of mixed-race couples, and because there has been considerable mixing of the races over the centuries. Thus, the "racial" characteristics of the hair may not be consistent with the appearance of the hair donor. A hair examiner might offer a guesstimate of the hair donor's race to investigators, but most hair examiners would not claim to be able to determine the race of a donor from his or her hairs. However, even a guesstimate could be investigatively useful.

Collection of Hair Standards

As we have noted, successful laboratory examination of materials evidence, including hair, depends on the collection of proper control samples. Questioned (or evidentiary) hair must be compared with known controls, and those controls must normally be obtained by investigators and submitted to the laboratory. The proper collection of a control sample of hair from a known persons is critical to the success of hair comparison. Several factors should be kept in mind when collecting known control hair. Hair examiners often ask that known control hairs be plucked (pulled), not cut. Examiners want to be able to examine the entire length of the hair, including the root. The detailed structure of the root end of the hair can vary significantly in different individuals. Further, the length of a hair can only be determined if the full hair from root to tip is present. Note, however, that hair analysts do not universally agree on whether known control hairs must be plucked or whether they can be cut close to the scalp. In addition, there is not uniform agreement on how many hairs are required to constitute a usable known control specimen. Most examiners agree that an "adequate sample" is necessary, that is, hairs from different

Figure 13.15

This series shows the stages by which a hair progresses from the growth stage (A) with a large live root to the final released stage where only a rounded club remains of the root tissue (F).

Figure 13.16   Although a great deal of genetic mixing occurs among the three races of humans, each has some significant differences in the appearance of hair. The three hairs pictured are from individuals with primarily Caucasian, Negroid, or Mongoloid hair characteristics.

parts of the scalp, in sufficient number to show the full range of variation between different hairs in an individual head. Another factor is that known control hairs must be taken from the same part of the body as the questioned hairs. Most of the time, hairs in question will be from the head. But pubic or other body hairs can be evidence in some cases. In most sexual assault cases, it is necessary to look for transferred pubic hairs, usually by combing, and to collect known control pubic hairs from sexual assault complainants (see Chapter 9).

Laboratory Examination of Hair Evidence   Hair examinations can be broadly divided into two categories. The traditional method, microscopical comparison of hair morphology, is widely regarded by experts as valuable primarily as an exclusionary tool. As we noted previously about materials evidence in general, hair cannot be individualized by microscopical morphological comparison. Even hair samples that are microscopically consistent can be said only to potentially be from the same source. If a questioned hair is sufficiently different from the known standard, the examiner can say it did not come from the source of the standards. That is what is meant by saying hair comparison has primarily exclusionary value. In the past few years, cases have surfaced where examiners testified to greater certainty of hair individualization than most experts think the science can support.

The other category of hair comparison is DNA analysis (see in Chapter 10). Most forensic DNA analysis involves nuclear DNA, as noted in the earlier chapter. With hair, nuclear DNA is found only in the root sheath cells, and the root sheath is present only if the hair was pulled out of the scalp or skin. Shed hairs have no root sheath and therefore no nuclear DNA. However, there is mitochondrial DNA present in the hair shaft. As explained in Chapter 10, mtDNA does not individualize as nuclear DNA does. The majority of evidentiary hairs are telogen (shed) and not amenable to nuclear DNA analysis. If present in sufficient quantity, they may be amenable to mtDNA typing. Anagen hairs—again if present in adequate quantity and if properly recognized, collected, and preserved—may be suitable for nuclear DNA profiling.

Most examinations begin with a microscopical inspection. Hairs are usually examined using a transmitted light (compound) microscope. Although most hairs do not look transparent, they will allow sufficient light to pass through them if brightly illuminated. Placed on a glass slide on the stage of a microscope, and with appropriate illumination, an analyst can actually see into the structure of the hair. Although the hair shaft is translucent, sometimes very heavily pigmented hairs, particularly very dark Mongoloid-type hair, may not let much light pass through and are difficult to examine microscopically. This problem may be overcome with a very bright microscope light source. Interestingly, hairs that have no pigment granules appear nearly transparent with transmitted light under the microscope but appear white to our eyes under normal (reflected light) illumination. It is the pigment granules that give hair its color. Hairs can range from blond to black in color by having differing amounts of the same pigment. Only red hair has a different pigment. Usually, even in very dark hairs, the root and tips ends are thinner and allow more light to pass; thus, they can be observed more easily.

Because most evidentiary hairs are telogen, microscopical examination for morphology is still an important part of many laboratory methods. It is just not possible at present to think about doing mtDNA typing on every submitted hair. At present, there are just not enough forensic resources.

Hair examiners usually examine up to 30 or 40 different characteristics when doing a full microscopical hair comparison. Color again provides a useful point of comparison, but there are a great many other important characteristics such as pigment distribution, the appearance of the medulla, a variety of structures in the cortex and tip characteristics (Figures 13.17 and 13.18). The area where the hair is emerging from the skin, the root to shaft interface, has a number of important

Figure 13.17

Comparison micrograph of two human hair samples with closely corresponding microscopic hair characteristics.

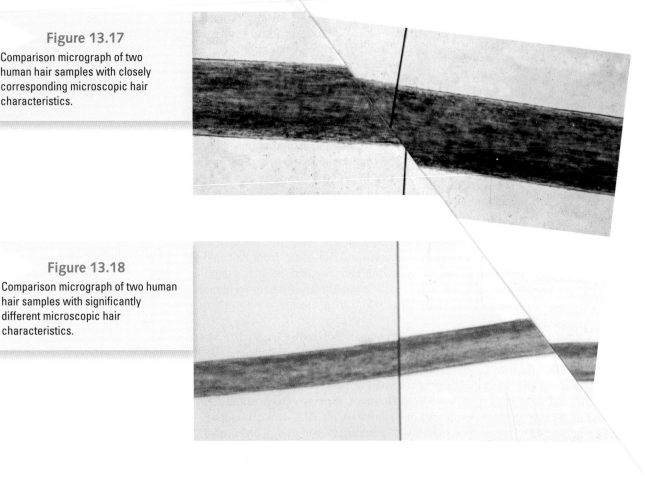

Figure 13.18

Comparison micrograph of two human hair samples with significantly different microscopic hair characteristics.

characteristics commonly included in hairs comparisons. Examiners can generally tell whether a hair was pulled or cut, and whether certain cosmetic treatments have been applied to it, such as bleaching or dyeing.

It should again be noted that hair cannot be individualized by microscopical morphological comparison, no matter how many features the examiner compares and finds consistent. If the evidentiary hair is consistent in its observed properties to a known control specimen, it could have come from that person. If it differs sufficiently from the known control specimen, then it could not have come from the person. However, the combination of both microscopic consistency and a consistent mtDNA profile greatly elevates the evidentiary value of hair comparison. However, it must be understood that even this combination of microscopical consistency and matching mtDNA sequences does not provide individualization.

Microscopical Examination of Animal Hair   Animal hair examination in forensic laboratories is usually primarily to differentiate human and animal hair, and to determine what type of animal an evidence hair could have come from. There are some good reference collections of hair from many different types of animals available. Some laboratories have developed their own, even more extensive collections. Although more detailed comparison between evidence and control hairs from a particular animal can be done, such comparisons are usually restricted to color comparison and consistency of major features. It is usually possible to exclude an animal as a possible source, but strong conclusions that a particular evidence hair came from a particular animal based on microscopic characteristics are unlikely. Some work has been done attempting to use DNA technology to make more positive association, but such work is highly specialized and not yet fully validated.

Paint

Paint has the dual function of protection and beautification. In the United States it seems that virtually every surface, both vertical and horizontal, is painted. This is not necessarily a bad thing from a forensic point of view, since paint can provide useful transfer evidence.

On the basis of composition and application, paint can be divided into two major categories: **architectural paints,** used to paint commercial buildings, bridges, houses, and a variety of other structures; and **automotive paints,** used for cars, trucks, and other vehicles. There are dozens of other types of paint as well, but forensically architectural and automotive paints are the most important because they are the most commonly encountered. It is useful to discuss them separately because they are quite different in composition and easily distinguished.

Architectural Paint

The variety of paints used for both interior and exterior painting of buildings is staggering. Walking through the paint displays in a large home improvement store will quickly convince you of this proposition. Most paints have four basic components: *binder,* to hold it to the surface; *coloring agent; fillers and additives;* and a *carrier solvent,* to allow it to be applied easily. The combinations of ingredients used in these four basic components are large, and they make different paints distinguishable, and therefore make analysis of evidentiary paint worth the effort (Figure 13.19).

Architectural paint can become evidence, for example, in the form of paint chips transferred to a pry bar during a break-in, chips on the floor being picked up by an intruder, and from smears of still damp paint from a fence.

With architectural paint on the outside surfaces of houses, commercial buildings, bridges, and many other applications, weathering can loosen paint and cause it flake or bubble. Such loose paint must be removed to prepare the surface for repainting. This puts paint chips into the nearby environment.

If there are several layers of paint, the **layer structure** may add weight to the value of a comparison over and above the color and type of paint. Particularly in an older home, or building that has been repainted many times, the layer structure can become nearly unique. Those who restore historic buildings often look at paint chip cross sections to discover what original or early paint colors were used.

Automotive Paint

Automotive paints are useful not only because there are many different compositional varieties, but also because of the variety of colors. An astonishing number of colors of automotive paint can be found on cars driving around

architectural paints

Paint that is used on houses, buildings, and other structures.

automotive paints

Paints that are used primarily on automobiles, trucks, and other motor vehicles.

layer structure

Where multiple layers of paint have been applied, a paint chip will show the number, color, and thickness of the layers.

Figure 13.19

A multilayer paint chip of the type encountered in architectural (home) paint cases.

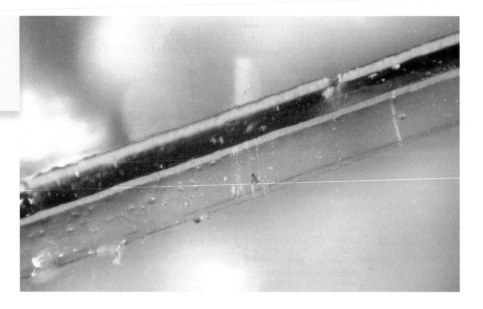

Figure 13.20

A multilayer paint chip of the type encountered in automotive paint cases.

the United States. A number of years ago, the National Bureau of Standards (now National Institute of Standards and Technology) began collecting samples of all the automotive paints used on American-made automobiles. Each year they added to the collection all the new paints used that year. They collected samples of each paint and painted small metal squares. Each square had a code on the back that identified the make and model of vehicles on which it had been used. Most laboratories had these reference sets and arranged them by color; as the collection grew, it became clear how many shades there were of each color. Toward the end of the nearly 20-year existence of the collection, there were more than a dozen pages (20 paint squares per page) of just shades of white. This was a handy little volume when paint chips from a hit-and-run case were examined, because the lab could often give an investigator a list of the makes and models of cars on which that particular shade had been used. This information was often an aid in their investigation. Unfortunately, the collection was too expensive to maintain and was discontinued a number of years ago, although several large investigative agencies continue to collect reference paint information.

One important fact about the painting of automobiles and usually trucks that makes paint chips from them particularly useful is that the paint is always multilayered (Figure 13.20). Generally, there is a prime coat to protect the metal from rusting, then on top of the prime coat, at least one color coat. Often, the color coat has metallic flecks added to it or a separate metallic coat is added. Then usually another layer is applied, which is clear and designed to make the sheen on the car appear deeper. That means that when a paint examiner receives a chip of automotive paint from a case, at least three different kinds of paint and usually three different colors on a single paint chip can be identified. The net result is that there is a great deal of often quite useful information in that tiny chip of automobile paint. Of course, if an automobile has been damaged and touched up or repainted, usually over the original paint, it has two or three more layers of paint. It is not uncommon to find a paint chip from a hit-and-run case that has five or more distinct layers of paint. In fact, even a new car often has more than three layers, at least in certain areas, because a surprisingly high percentage all new cars have been damaged in transit and retouched before the car is delivered to its "first" owner.

Collection of Known Control Paint Samples   As we have discussed, most paint examinations are, like other materials examinations, comparisons. Having an adequate and representative control sample with which to compare the evidence material is critical. With both architectural and automotive paints, known control samples should be taken in the immediate area where the evidence material is thought to have arisen.

The sample should be taken close to that point, but not directly from the suspected area. The reason for this procedure, as will be mentioned again shortly, is that on occasion, a physical fit match between a paint chip and the area from which it came is possible (Figure 13.21). Nothing should be done in collecting a known control that might destroy that possibility. Further, control samples should include all the layers of paint in the area of interest. Even if the evidence sample appears to be a smear involving only the top layer, traces of other layers may be present. Another important reason for taking the control sample close to the area of damage is the possibility that retouching has changed the number of layers in that immediate area. Because of the sensitivity of modern analytical techniques, the control sample does not have to be large. Quality of the control sample (location and completeness) is more critical than quantity.

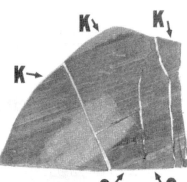

Figure 13.21

A jigsaw match between several sizable paint pieces, indicating that they were at one time a portion of the same painted surface.

Forensic Analysis of Paint Samples

The first step in examining paint evidence is usually a simple visual examination, frequently using a stereomicroscope to see surface details and color. The examiner should observe inclusions and scratches as well as the sheen and other visual characteristics. Next, the color and the cross section for the layer structure should be examined under appropriate illumination. A razor blade can be used to make a clean cut through a paint chip if necessary, and then the cut piece turned onto its side to look at the layer sequence and any inclusions in the paint. In addition, the analyst can occasionally physically fit a paint chip into the area from which it came. As indicated in Chapter 5, a direct physical match may well produce an individualization. Since examinations based on other characteristics and features produce only associations (inclusions) or exclusions, the prospect of a physical match is highly desirable when possible.

The single most important examination is the careful comparison of the color between the evidence sample and the known control sample (Figure 13.22). This comparison is done using a comparison microscope that allows the paint samples to be viewed simultaneously, adjacent to each other in the microscope field of view, using carefully controlled lighting. The human eye can perceive even subtle differences in the shade of colors. There are certainly cases where the chemical analysis is needed to differentiate paints that have virtually identical colors, but in the vast majority of cases if the well-trained human eye indicates that two chips appear identical, further testing will not contradict that conclusion. There are also microscopes equipped with **visible spectrometers,** similar to the microscopes equipped with FTIR spectrometers discussed earlier. Spectrophotometers (Figure 13.23) can produce a visible spectrum

visible spectrometers

Devices for examining a sample and determining its ability to absorb or reflect electromagnetic radiation in the visible portion of the spectrum.

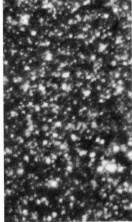

Figure 13.22

An evidence automotive paint chip from a truck compared for color similarity with a known sample of paint from a large collection of automotive paint samples.

Figure 13.23

A spectrophotometer, an instrument for measuring ultraviolet or visible light spectra of solutions.

of the specimen. Because color is a function of the absorption, reflection, and transmission of different wavelengths of visible light, the visible spectrum trace provides an analytical record of the "color." These instruments can be used to compare known and questioned specimens to see if the visible spectra are truly identical. They can confirm the visual examination, or sometimes "see" differences too subtle for the human eye. Many forensic laboratories have invested in such instrumentation to add further weight to their visual conclusions.

Paint evidence usually arrives in the forensic laboratory in one of three forms, and it most often arrives riding on another object. It may be in the form of tiny fragments or chips of paint resulting from a forceful shattering of a paint film. This is the common result of a hit-and-run case where paint fragments are found on the victim's clothes or at the scene of the impact. Evidence also may arrive as a paint spatter or transfer from liquid paint or from drying paint. Finally, and most difficult to work with, is evidence that is a smear (Figure 13.24). **Paint smears** result from a painted surface moving across another object. A common and rather sad example is a smear on the bicycle of a youngster who has been hit a glancing blow by an automobile. There will often be paint from the automobile smeared on the area of the bicycle that was hit, and there can also be paint from the bicycle smeared on the portion of the automobile that hit it. Paint smears are very challenging evidence to examine because of the very small amount of paint transferred and the mixing of the top layers of the two painted objects. It is often not possible to remove the smear, so the examiner must work with the material in place. That makes the instrumental identification of the paint type much more difficult. As indicated earlier, the existence of multiple layers can add considerable weight to matches when they are found.

The basic type of polymer in the paint can be estimated fairly quickly using solubility or spot color tests. These may be considered preliminary classification tests. If more specific identification of the film former is needed, or if additional comparison is to be done, chemical analysis is necessary. Such analysis is complicated by the fact that many paint samples are multiple layered. To make the information useful, chemical data must be obtained for each of the layers. This process can be attempted by "peeling off" individual layers using a scalpel or razor blade with a steady hand. With a multi-layer chip an analyst can sometimes gather data on the top layer, scrape that layer away, and then look at the next layer, and so on. The instrument of choice for identification

paint smears

A very thin film of paint transferred to another surface as the result of glancing contact.

Figure 13.24

An infrared spectrum obtained on a small chip of red paint using a diamond ATR-based infrared spectrometer showing it to be an acrylic-based paint.

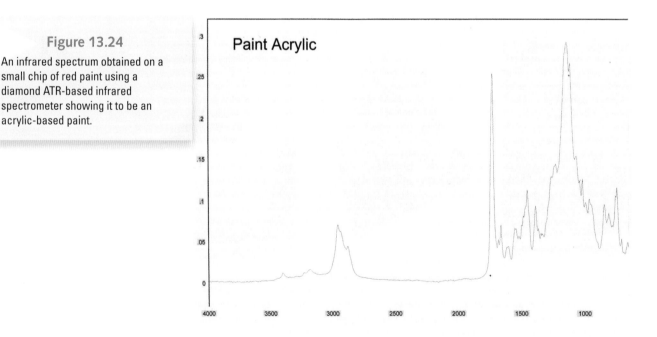

of the film-forming polymer is the IR spectrometer. The last 10 years have seen some important improvements in these instruments. The newest ones can look at a very thin surface layer and obtain high-quality data using an **attenuated total reflectance (ATR)** (Figure 13.24) or a **diffuse reflectance infrared Fourier transform spectroscopy (DRIFTS)** accessory. There are also microscope sampling devices for IR spectrometers that allow analysts to locate a microscopically small area and obtain an IR spectrum. With such a device, a chip can be turned on its side, the microscope focused on each layer, one at a time, and a spectrum collected to identify that layer. In that way, multi-layer paint chips provide the chemical composition of each layer, as well as their color. In some cases, these techniques can allow determination of the chemical nature of the organic or inorganic pigments used to color the paint as well as the binder type.

Other instrumental analysis techniques can highlight subtle differences in the chemical composition of the polymer that the IR spectrometer cannot see. Further, an expert can use other techniques to look at the elemental composition of the inorganic pigments in the paint, even though the pigment makes up only a small percentage of the paint layer.

Glass

Glass is another familiar material that can be important evidence. A scientist's definition of glass is that it is a melted mix oxide that does not crystallize on cooling. The most common types of glass have three primary chemical components: silicon dioxide, sodium carbonate, and calcium oxide. In common language that means it is largely sand, with a little lime (calcium oxide) and some washing soda (sodium carbonate) added in. If the sand is heated until it melts and then is allowed to cool down, it will become solid again, look opaque, and appear as combined sand grains. If, on the other hand, the correct amount of soda ash and lime are added to the melt, it will now not crystallize when it cools and the resulting material will be solid and have a glassy appearance. This process was discovered, probably by accident, in ancient times. When you look out a window, it is not obvious that the material was once sand. To a chemist, glass is not a crystalline solid but a "supercooled liquid." That means it has a structure more like a liquid than a crystalline solid, even though it is quite solid. It is this structure that allows light to pass directly through it rather than be diverted by crystal boundaries.

Types of Glass   Although we now think of glass primarily as a material for making windows, many useful and decorative things were made of glass before people discovered how to make relatively flat sheets to use for windows. One important early use of glass was to make a wide variety of bottles and containers. Many different kinds of glass have been developed for different applications. The most common type is **soda lime glass,** a very inexpensive form of glass made mostly of sand, with a little soda (sodium carbonate) and some lime (calcium oxide). All three starting materials are readily available and inexpensive. Sand is one of the least expensive starting materials in the chemical industry. Almost all window glass is soda lime glass, as is most bottle glass. Specialty bottles such as perfume bottles, or crystal pieces, which will be mentioned shortly, are made from quite different glass formulations.

A second important type of glass is low modulus glass. It is formulated so that when it is either heated or cooled, it does not shrink or expand significantly. One problem with soda lime glass is that if you heat it or cool it too rapidly, it wants to either expand or shrink, which causes internal strain that may cause it to shatter. For example, pouring boiling water into a drinking glass too quickly may cause it to shatter. Folk wisdom said that a person should always put a spoon in the glass before pouring boiling water into it, because the metal spoon helps to dissipate the heat. Low modulus glass was developed to solve that problem—it allows glass containers to be placed directly on a heating device like a stove or hot plate. Silex and Mr. Coffee carafes would not be possible without low modulus glass. Scientists

---

attenuated total reflectance (ATR)

An infrared sampling technique that depends on passing an IR beam through a crystal in a way that a small portion of the beam emerges from the crystal and can interact with a sample in intimate contact with the crystal.

diffuse reflectance infrared Fourier transform spectroscopy (DRIFTS)

An infrared sampling technique where the sample is ground to a fine powder and mixed with a nonabsorbing powder and the spectrum is obtained by collecting IR radiation that is diffused by the mixture.

soda lime glass

The most common type of glass including window glass and bottle glass that has as its major ingredients sand, soda (sodium carbonate), and lime (calcium oxide).

discovered that adding just the right amount of borax, another fairly inexpensive mineral, to the glass formulation greatly reduces the material's tendency to change size upon heating or cooling, which allows a whole range of new uses.

The beautiful material we call "crystal" is a special form of glass, which is much clearer and appears more brilliant than normal glass. It is made from starting materials that are specially purified and has small amounts of a number of additional materials, such as lead, added. Each manufacturer of crystal has its own formulation and manufacturing process. In most cases, these are carefully guarded trade secrets. Famous manufacturers such as Steuben in the United States, Waterford in Ireland, and Lalique in France, command high prices for the beauty and artistry of their products.

Optical glasses are also highly specialized glasses that have been developed to have very specific optical properties. They are used to manufacture lenses for eyeglasses, cameras, telescopes, microscopes, and many other specialized devices. The chemical composition of optical glasses is often quite different from that of most other glasses. When you look through window glass, it appears quite clear. However, if you look at window glass carefully, you will see a bit of a tint. Most window glass has a bit of a red, blue, or a green tint to it, caused by the impurities that were present in the sand that was used to manufacture it. For letting light into our houses and buildings, absolute clarity is not critical. For optical applications, the ability to pass as much light as possible, and at all wavelengths equally (be colorless), is much more important.

Manufacture of Window Glass

The manufacturing process for flat glass, for many years, involved heating the proper mixture of sand and other minerals in a huge cauldron made of a ceramic material. This mixture is heated until it melts, at about 1100–1200 degrees centigrade, and is then poured out so it will flow down a runway as it cools. As it is cooling it is passed through a series of rollers, the separation of which slowly decreases until the mixture is thinned out to the desired thickness. It has nearly completely cooled when it reaches the end of the line of rollers, where it is polished and cut into large sheets. The glass picks up tiny scratches and imperfections from the rolling process so that it must be polished with a fine polishing material to smooth it and make it more transparent. The polishing step was a very expensive step in the glassmaking process. Glass is relatively inexpensive because the starting materials are very inexpensive, so most of the cost comes from the energy needed to melt them and the time and energy necessary to polish the glass.

float glass process

The most common modern manufacturing process for making flat glass by floating the molten glass on a pool of tin while it cools.

Virtually all of the flat glass in the world is now made using the **float glass process,** but for only about the past 50 years. Many older buildings still have window glass that was made before the float glass process was developed. As a result, there is still quite a bit of glass in the environment that was made by the old roller glass process, which can add to the utility of forensic glass examination.

One reason glass can be important as evidence is because it is used for so many different purposes, and therefore there are an enormous number of different kinds of glass produced. In addition to all the flat glass, there are bottles, drinking glasses, pitchers, bowls, optical glasses, and many other items. Second, in addition to the many varieties of glass and the large amount produced each year, when glass is not treated with proper respect, it breaks or shatters, producing numerous pieces of potential evidence. When a violent confrontation of some sort occurs, if there is glass around, it is very likely to end up in pieces. There are many different types of glass, and even subtle differences can have forensic value in determining whether two pieces of glass could have the same or a different source. Automobile accidents contribute more than their share of broken glass. Windshield glass is a special type of glass—laminated safety glass, designed to hold together upon being broken to lessen injuries from flying glass. Automobile side window glass is tempered saftey glass, designed to resist breakage and to disintegrate into small pieces when it does break to minimize injury. Thus the windshield and side window glass are different types of glass, as are the headlight glass, the mirror glass, and the glass in lightbulbs. For example, materials evidence from a hit-and-run case may include broken headlight glass, windshield glass, side window glass, mirror glass, and even optical glass (from someone's eyeglasses).

Collection of Glass Evidence   As noted earlier, materials evidence cannot be individualized using microscopical, chemical, or instrumental techniques. This is as true of glass as of other materials. However, because glass fractures randomly, physical fit matches are sometimes possible between glass fragments. Physical fit matches are often individualizations (Figure 13.25)—such a fit proves that the pieces were originally part of the same structure. This fact is an important consideration in discussing glass fragment collection. Further, a fingerprint on a piece of glass can identify the person who left the print. In a hit-and-run case, if the side view mirror is broken, pieces collected at the scene may be jigsaw matched to any mirror fragments remaining in the frame on the damaged car. Jigsaw fit matches of such evidence are a real possibility. Further, glass is a wonderful substratum for fingerprints. Fingerprints can often be developed readily on glass surfaces (Chapter 6). Both physical fit matches, and the possible presence of fingerprints, must be considered first when collecting glass evidence. Among other things, these considerations mean that larger pieces should be carefully collected and cushioned against breakage during transport. Investigators should always wear latex or other protective gloves when handling this evidence (and all evidence for that matter).

A second important concern in collection of glass evidence is prevention of loss from clothing or other surfaces. Tiny glass chips that are on clothing or other objects can easily be lost if the objects are not properly handled and protected. When glass is broken, often little shreds of it are propelled backward and land on the clothing of the person doing the breaking. Under a microscope an examiner can find those tiny pieces, pick them out, and compare them to control samples from a scene. These tiny pieces can easily be lost, unless the object on which they sit is handled gently and properly packaged. Any evidence with the potential of containing glass fragments should be carefully wrapped in paper and put in a bag. Another important concern is to prevent contamination or further breakage. Evidence should be handled with forceps or gloves. If there are sizable pieces of glass, which have the possibility of being jigsaw matched, they should be protected from further breakage. Chipped edges or further breakage will lower the probability of making a jigsaw match.

Laboratory Examination of Glass   The examination of glass evidence is usually a three-step process. An initial observation and measurement of the glass is the simplest but often the most critical step. It involves looking at properties such as color, thickness, surface characteristics, and the shape and size of the pieces. Although we think of glass as being clear, placing it on a white surface under proper illumination usually reveals subtle shades of color. Only fine crystal or optical glasses are likely to be almost colorless. Multiple pieces of glass from an incident can be quickly sorted using color. Similarly, thickness is an important property of flat glass. An expert can measure the thickness if any of the pieces are large enough. If two pieces of glass were broken out of the same larger piece of flat glass, they will have the same thickness. Surface characteristics such as pebbling, surface grinding, or imperfections caused by being exposed to the elements for 10 or 20 years can be helpful in examining glass evidence. With window glass, determining "inside" and "outside" may be important and is usually possible because of the differences in exposure of the two sides to different environments. Once the initial observations are completed, the physical properties of the glass may be examined. An important optical property of glass, the fact that light passes through it, is the basis for much of its utility. One of the important physical properties of glass is its **refractive index (RI).**

As mentioned earlier, RI is defined as the speed of light as it passes through a vacuum divided by the speed of light in the glass. Scientists can measure this ratio for any transparent material, and it is a useful property for distinguishing different

Figure 13.25
Large pieces of broken glass fitted back into window frame to prove common origin.

refractive index (RI)

The refractive index of a substance is the ratio of the speed at which light passes through a vacuum to the speed that light passes through the substance.

kinds of glass. It is affected by both the chemical composition and the density of the glass. There are several simple ways to measure RI, even on very small glass chips. It is often the first optical property measured because it is a good way to determine that two glasses could not have had the same origin since their RIs are significantly different. If, on the other hand, their RIs are very close, then they could have come from the same source.

A second important physical property is density. An analyst usually measures the density of a glass chip using liquids of known density. Placing a little chip of glass into a liquid and observing whether it floats, sinks, or is just suspended (is floating in the liquid and not on top of the liquid) can reveal the density. When an object (like a glass fragment) is placed in a liquid of greater density than itself, it floats; when placed in a liquid of less density than itself, it sinks; and when in a liquid of the same density, it is suspended. Examiners can adjust the density of the liquid by mixing a heavy liquid and a light liquid in different proportions until the glass is suspended, which means the liquid and glass have the same density. The density of the liquid is then determined, and the density of the glass chip is known. Since, again, different kinds of glass have different densities, this becomes another characteristic to help determine if two glass samples could have had the same origin. Many glasses have the property of giving off visible light when illuminated with ultraviolet light, called "fluorescence". When illuminated with UV light, the glass may give off a colored glow (fluoresce) when observed in the dark. Fluorescence is another useful physical property of glass that can be used in comparing glass samples. It is useful not only because some glasses fluoresce and some do not, but also because it is the way to determine which was the "tin side" of float glass. Because of the trace amounts of tin left on the tin side, the tin side of the float glass fluoresces more strongly than the air side. Sometimes when trying to jigsaw match pieces of a glass knowing which side is up can greatly assist in putting the pieces together correctly. Fluorescence is not limited to float glass. Many other kinds of glass also show fluorescence.

In a crime laboratory proficiency test a number of years ago, laboratories were sent three small pieces of glass. The labs' task was to determine whether any of the three pieces had a common origin. Two of the pieces of glass matched each other very closely in refractive index, density, and even chemical composition. One, however, fluoresced strongly and the other did not. Some laboratories indicated possible common origin because they failed to check for fluorescence. A lab could have immediately eliminated common origin of those two pieces, and saved many hours of additional analysis, by spending the relatively short time required to observe the two pieces with ultraviolet illumination and look for fluorescence. This anecdote illustrates another important point as well, one that we have tried to emphasize. When questioned and known control specimens of materials evidence are compared, and found to be substantially the same *in the properties compared,* they *may have* had a common origin. Other ways of saying this same thing are as follows: They are consistent with having had a common origin; or the possibility of common origin cannot be excluded. Note how important the words *in the properties compared* are in the proficiency testing story. Labs that did not compare fluorescence, and thus said that the specimens could not be excluded (could have had a common origin), were not wrong. Their conclusion was correct based on the properties they compared. With any "match" result in materials evidence, it is always true that comparison of another property could result in exclusion. This is one reason materials evidence comparisons are difficult to evaluate—there is no basis for knowing whether one more measurement might produce an elimination or further strengthen the association.

The major elements present in glass and their relative concentrations are usually the result of materials added to provide desired properties. Therefore, it is often possible to determine the type of glass an evidentiary sample falls into, if a database of major elemental composition of many different types of glass is available.

Element	Glass from victim's auto	Glass from suspect #1 auto	Glass from suspect #2 auto
Mg (%)	2.15 ± 0.03	2.16 ± 0.03	2.28 ± 0.02
Ca (%)	5.93 ± 0.06	5.97 ± 0.02	6.00 ± 0.06
Na (%)	11.7 ± 0.8	11.9 ± 1.7	9.1 ± 0.9
Al (ppm)	531 ± 12	528 ± 15	558 ± 18
Fe (ppm)	3690 ± 30	3710 ± 30	3320 ± 50
Sr (ppm)	32.5 ± 0.2	32.2 ± 0.2	43.4 ± 0.1
Mn (ppm)	14.4 ± 1	13.9 ± 0.8	11.3 ± 1.2
Ba (ppm)	17.9 ± 1.3	18.1 ± 1.1	15.2 ± 0.5
Ti (ppm)	97 ± 5	107 ± 8	99 ± 3

Table 13.1

Use of minor and trace elemental composition of glass fragments to connect them to a particular broken automobile window

The major elements in glass are usually silicon with some calcium, some sodium, and a little iron or other elements added to tailor properties as discussed previously. If an analyst looks very carefully, there are trace amounts of many other elements. This is because glass is made from sand, and sand, being formed from naturally occurring minerals, will have traces of other elements. More important, where the sand comes from will determine its trace element composition. Since sand is cheap to mine, but expensive to ship because it is heavy, companies who manufacture glass tend to use sand from nearby sources. Therefore, glass manufactured in different places will have different trace element composition (Table 13.1). Even glass manufactured in the same place but of different types will have different trace element compositions due to different proportions of sand and other materials used in the glassmaking process. Further, as sand is mined its trace element composition may change depending on where in the sand deposit it was found. An examiner can determine elemental composition, measuring as many as 15 different elements, and be able to use that information to determine if two glass samples have a similar or different distribution of trace elements. Determining the elemental composition profile of glass specimens is time-consuming and requires specialized instrumentation. Specimens that do not have similar elemental compositions can be distinguished even where other physical properties are consistent.

Soil

Soil can be encountered under a wide variety of circumstances that can make it useful evidence in a criminal or civil case. In fact, soil evidence would be much more widely used as evidence if more forensic laboratories were proficient in analyzing it. Analysis and comparison of soil evidence can be a complex and time-consuming problem. As an example of the utility of soil evidence, someone might leave behind footwear impressions in a flowerbed or some other area at or near a crime scene. This is clearly a contact process, where, as Locard postulated, there is likely to be an exchange of material between the shoe or boot and the ground. That is a formal way of saying: "you step in the mud, your shoes get muddy." Muddy shoes or tires provide potential soil evidence (see Figure 13.26). Cases often arrive at the forensic laboratory where the question is: Could a particular shoe have made a footwear impression found at the crime scene? Examination of the pattern of the impression may disclose that it is not sufficiently clear to allow it to be compared to the suspected shoe. There is, however, sufficient soil on the submitted shoe for a comparison to be made with a known control sample from the scene (see Figure 13.27). Unfortunately, it can happen that no known control soil evidence was collected for comparison, because the investigator submitting the evidence knew about the potential value of shoe print pattern evidence but did not realize the potential value of the soil on that shoe. Similarly,

Figure 13.26

Partial sneaker print in soil. Such an indentation provides the possibility of a pattern comparison with a sneaker (Chapter 5), but also the possibility of a soil comparison between soil in the vicinity of the print and soil clinging to a sneaker suspected of having made the impression.

soil on the tires or in the wheel well of an automobile may be compared to that found at a location where a body was dumped.

Cases have arisen where someone is missing but the investigators cannot find the body. There is a suspect, and a soil sample is obtained from the suspect's car. The investigators ask for assistance from a local agricultural station. The soil expert examines the soil and, based on extensive knowledge of local soil types, may suggest an area to search. Even if it is a fairly large possible area, it may focus the search and significantly aid the investigator's ability to locate the body.

Soil evidence provides a challenge for forensic laboratories because the composition of soil is so highly variable. Soil is generally composed of the physical, chemical, and biological weathering of the uppermost layer of the exposed rock, plus decomposed biological material and miscellaneous material that falls from the sky, including, in many places, man-made materials. It is certainly a complicated material. Forensically, this complexity can be useful. It means that soil from different places is likely to be different. Anyone who has dug in a backyard and a flowerbed and in adjacent woods knows that the soil usually looks different in the three places, even if they are not far from one another. These differences have potential forensic utility but may not be easy to exploit because of the difficulties of soil analysis. There are, however, some relatively simple examinations of soil evidence that can yield useful information.

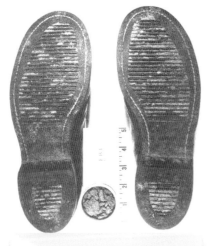

Figure 13.27

Soil clinging to the bottom of a shoe suitable for comparison to soil from a crime scene.

Major Components of Soil   We can look at soil as having three primary components. There are biologically derived materials, mineral (rock-derived) materials, and in many places, material associated with human activity. The biological components are bacteria and products from the decomposition of plant and animal residues. If you take a walk in the woods, you are walking on dead plant and animal residue. The breakdown of this material into soil is aided by bacterial and insect activity. In more common terms, it rots and becomes the organic portion of the soil. We also have mineral residues broken from surface rock by weathering (in the north, freeze-thaw cycles) and the abrasive action of water. Fine pieces of rock are washed down in the rain and are eventually deposited as part of the soil. Anybody who has lived on an active farm also knows that natural actions bring rocks to the surface, grinding off small portions along the way, and exposing them to the surface erosion just mentioned. These soil minerals can be quite varied in soils because they depend on the kind of rocks characteristic of a particular area.

The third component, which can be particularly informative, is the component due to human activity. Many types of man-made residues can become incorporated into soil. They are most important in soil from areas near sizable human population. A simple example would be paint chips. Examination of a sample of soil from the Adirondack State Park in upstate New York, or some other fairly remote area, would not likely disclose any paint chips. On the other hand, were a detective to investigate a burglary and soil from a flowerbed along the side of the house is the sample of interest, finding paint chips would be quite likely. Every three or four years most homes need an exterior painting. The first job, before the actual painting, is to scrape off any paint that is not on the surface tightly. All those flakes of paint fall to the ground along the side of the house and frequently become incorporated into the soil. Another common synthetic component of many soils is rubber. Why would you find rubber in soil? As automobiles move down the road the tires go around and very tiny pieces of rubber are worn away and thrown into the air and some settle in the soil near the road. The millions of tires running down the highways in the United States produce many tons of rubber that can get incorporated into soil, sometimes quite a distance from the road. Another significant man-made component of soil is fly ash. Industrial plants and utilities usually have a prominent smokestack to disperse the gases and solid residue from the burning process. What people call smoke is actually tiny particles of unburned or partially burned fuel expelled in great quantities as a by-product of the combustion process. The purpose of the smokestack is to disperse these particles into the wind and spread them over a large area. However, the particles that go up in the air from the stack eventually fall down. That material, when it returns to earth, becomes part of the dust in a home and it becomes incorporated into the soil almost everywhere else.

Examples of Investigative Value of Soil Analysis

Forensic scientists may be able to provide useful information from the examination and comparison of soil samples. Two examples can provide some insight into this process. Perhaps someone is assaulted. The person is knocked down to the ground and then dragged a distance and thrown in the back of a car. The body is taken 25 miles away and dumped along the side of a narrow dirt road in a remote area. Say that there is soil on the victim's clothing from being dragged along the ground. Examination of that soil can quickly reveal that the soil on the clothing is not the same type of soil as that from where the body was found. One might be an urban or suburban type of soil and the other a soil characteristic of a wooded area. This apparently simple bit of information, that the two soils are different, is useful to the investigation—it says that the assault did not occur where the body was found. If information is developed concerning where the crime might have occurred, soil samples from that location can be taken and compared with the soil found on the victim's clothing. If they are found to be consistent, it is a corroborative piece of evidence for the information developed about the possible site of the crime.

The second example is soil from shoes or boots. Shoes can provide soil samples that may be important in connecting a suspect to a particular crime scene. Let us say someone steps in the flowerbed to break a window to gain entry to a house to burglarize it. The crime scene investigators find a shoe impression and photograph it and prepare a dental stone cast. This evidence is submitted to the forensic laboratory so that it may be compared against material from shoes of a suspect, when one is developed. Properly trained crime scene investigators know that they should not clean the cast, but rather submit it with all the dirt clinging to it. By submitting the

Case Study 13.3

Inclusion Particles in Soil Help Reconstruct the Location of a Homicide

An interesting application of soil evidence occurred in upstate New York a few years ago. An elderly lady, who lived alone, took a walk almost every day on a path that ran alongside some seldom used railroad tracks near her home. She suddenly disappeared and her friends and family feared that she had been murdered. Her body was found a number of miles away in some woods. One of her neighbors, who knew her habit of walking along the tracks, became a suspect. If she had been murdered while out for her walk, this would have fit with other information the investigator had on the suspect. When the victim's clothing was examined, quite a bit of soil was recovered, which, on further examination, did not appear to be from the location where she was found. Microscopical examination of the soil showed many tiny hard black particles. They did not appear like anything commonly encountered in soil samples. Consultation of *The Particle Atlas,* a reference book for forensic materials analysts that contains hundreds of pictures of different kinds of microscopic particles that have been encountered over the years, revealed almost a whole page showing a variety of similar shiny black pieces. These particles turned out to be coal. The soil along railroad tracks that were in use by coal-fired locomotives for many years contains tiny particles of coal. Even if it has been 50 years since coal-burning trains ran up and down that track, there will still be residual coal particles. It turned out to be an important investigative lead that this victim's clothing had picked up soil from the path along the railroad tracks. It indicated that she was attacked on her walk, struggled, and was knocked down, and the body was then moved by the attacker to divert suspicion. The soil analysis, and finding the coal particles, played a key role in the investigation by helping to show where the crime had probably taken place.

dirt-laden cast, the laboratory examiner not only has an impression of the shoe, but also a soil sample from the area of interest in that flowerbed (see Chapter 5). In fact, it is the best possible soil sample for any soil found on the shoes of the individual who left the print in the flowerbed. When a suspect is developed, his or her shoes can be compared to the pattern. But also, if the shoes are muddy or have some small clumps of soil trapped in a patterned sole, that soil can be collected and compared with the soil that was taken from the cast. If the comparison shows consistency, these soil samples are associative pieces of evidence, and the combination of this association with that of the pattern match is considerably more compelling than either one alone. Soil could also help in the case where a body may have been buried, dug up, and then reburied.

Automobiles can be another important source of soil evidence. Driving along a paved highway will not usually produce soil evidence on the vehicle. However, driving on a dirt road or anyplace off-road may provide a significant amount of soil evidence. People who are trying to conceal a body will not usually want to dump it right along the side of the highway. They will search for a little road going up into the woods so that the body will not be found too quickly. If that road has mud or soft dirt, some of it will be picked up in the tread or on the sidewalls of the tires. As the tires go around, they will often fling soil or mud onto the inside of the tire well. If wet spots occur anywhere along the route, their presence will wet the tires and/or the dirt and contribute to the formation of dirt layers that mirror the soil along the pathway. A chunk of dirt from the inside of the tire well can have layers of soil that may give a "history" in soil of any off-road driving that a car has done.

Collection of Soil Evidence The collection and preservation of soil evidence is not trivial, especially collection of appropriate known control samples. If the soil is on a movable object, it should be left undisturbed and the intact object submitted for analysis. As we have noted, submission of intact items bearing materials evidence is the best method of collecting materials evidence. If the soil evidence is adhering to a footwear impression cast, as mentioned earlier, the cast should be submitted with clinging soil because removing it may result in the loss of useful information. Further, there may be layers of soil, and removing the soil would destroy the layer information. The object should be wrapped carefully or placed in a paper bag. If the soil dries and some falls off, it will still be present in the wrapping material. If the soil evidence is not on an object, than the soil should be placed in a plastic or glass vial, or other similar container and protected as discussed. Finally, and essential to any subsequent comparison, crime scene investigators must collect known control samples from the suspected origin and areas around it. If they have an area where the crime may have been committed, they should sample that area and also take soil samples from four or five surrounding areas, about 20 to 50 feet away, depending on how uniform the surrounding area appears. A simple way would be to take samples about 20 feet from the suspected point of origin at the compass points, north, south, east, and west. This practice makes sense if the potential for soil variability is not obvious, such as in woods or on covered ground. It makes no sense if the soil is all the same, such as in a uniformly plowed field or on a beach. If the evidence soil is consistent with the soil at the suspected location, it can be a useful piece of information. But if the control samples taken from areas around that location prove to be inconsistent, that makes the observation of consistency between evidence and control sample more useful. Having several different known control samples can show there is detectable variation of soil types even within a relatively small area. This information adds to the value of a comparison in a case where the questioned and known control soil samples appear consistent.

Laboratory Examination of Soil   Because soil can be so enormously variable and the experience of most laboratory examiners with soil analysis is quite limited, there is little standardization of procedure for soil analysis. The first step is almost always simple physical observation and examination of the soil.

Prior to any examination, the sample must be properly prepared. It should be dried, gently broken up, and any stones or large pieces of extraneous material removed and put aside. Those larger pieces may provide some useful information, but they would interfere with the preparation of the soil. The purpose of the initial preparation is to achieve homogeneity of the specimen insofar as possible. One technique for obtaining a homogenous sample is called "coning and quartering" (see insert below). The origin of this technique is not clear, but it has been used in both analytical and pharmaceutical chemistry applications to homogenize a particulate specimen, so that any portion removed for analysis will be identical to any other portion.

In many cases, simple visual inspection of the texture and general appearance of the soil is all that is required. If an analyst looks at the evidence sample and the known control sample(s) and they are a different color or texture, the scientist knows they did not come from the same location. You may think of soil as simply brown, but there are actually hundreds of different shades of brown, from nearly yellow to nearly black. Careful observation of the color (see Figure 13.28) under proper lighting conditions frequently can unambiguously distinguish properly prepared soil samples in a few minutes. Proper preparation is important, particularly with respect to moisture content, because the color and general appearance of soil is very dependent on how wet it is. Soil may have to be dried by placing it in a warm oven overnight or until its color has stabilized.

Another simple examination that can very often include or exclude a soil sample from further consideration in a comparison is simple microscopical examination for miscellaneous inclusions. As already noted, an examiner might see items that are not natural components of soil, such as coal, paint, rubber, or one of hundreds of items indicative of nearby human activity. An expert can also quickly examine the sample to determine the texture of the soil. It may be very uniform, very fine, with lots of clumps, or it may appear to have quite a high content of organic residues. Even if the color is consistent between two samples, if the texture is significantly different, they are very unlikely to be from a common source.

If the preceding examinations on evidence and known control samples indicate they are similar, further analysis is required to attempt to distinguish them. One of the common things that can be done by many forensic laboratories is **particle size distribution.**

particle size distribution

A quantitative estimation of the percentages of particles that fall into defined size ranges in a soil sample.

Coning and quartering is the process where a representative subsample of a fairly large sample that consists of a mixture can be obtained. After the material has been generally mixed, the sample is piled into a cone shape with a flattened top, and the cone is divided into quarters. Two opposite quarters are discarded, and the remaining quarters are mixed together to form a second cone. The process is repeated until the desired sample size is reached. The process is based on techniques originally developed in the pharmaceutical industry to ensure the homogeneity of solid dosage forms prior to packaging.

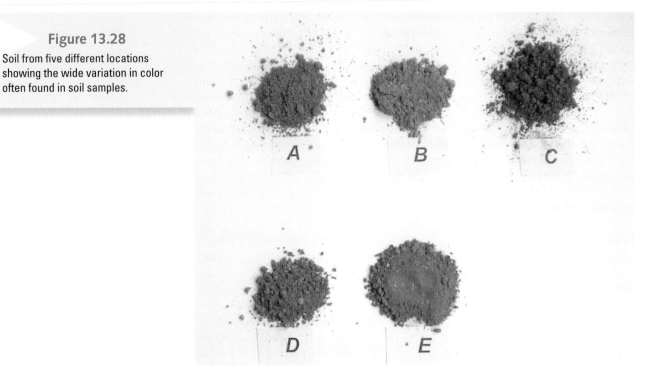

Figure 13.28
Soil from five different locations showing the wide variation in color often found in soil samples.

Dried, homogenized soil is placed into a stack of sieves with different size holes, ranging from coarse to fine. The soil is placed into the top sieve and then allowed to distribute itself through the series of sieves as the whole stack is shaken. By using a standard set of sieves, an examiner can separate a soil into different fractions based on the size of the particles. The soil distributes itself with the largest particles staying on top, the slightly smaller particles falling to the second sieve, and so on, with the finest (clay fraction) passing all the sieves. The sieves have been preweighed, and the analyst then weighs each one again after the shaking step, and calculates the percentage of the soil in each fraction. In a random selection of different soils, a very different distribution of the particle sizes is observed. Thus, if two samples show very similar particle size distributions, it is an indication of possible common origin.

Another technique for examining soil samples is called "density gradient." One creates a density gradient in a glass tube by mixing liquids of high and low density and allowing the mixture to equilibrate over hours to days. Once equilibrated, the bottom of the column will correspond to the densest liquid and the top to the less dense one. Density will vary linearly along the length of the column. When a small soil sample is introduced into the tube and allowed to distribute itself, the heavy particles tend to settle toward the bottom of the tube and the lighter particles fall only to the level that matches their density. A few may even float on the top. Little patches of material are usually observed along the length of the tube, and the distribution of these patches of material is used to compare soil samples. There are a number of additional instrumental approaches that include measuring the acidity or alkalinity of the soil, the elemental composition, and finally comparing the different minerals present in the soil.

Some effort has been made over the years to try and exploit the biological materials in soil specimens as a means of comparing them. Recently, with the surge in interest in novel DNA profiling techniques, a few laboratories have investigated the possibility of discriminating soils. There is still work left to be done with these techniques, but they will likely be developed further. The idea is based on using differences in DNA to profile the soil bacterial content.

Summary

Materials evidence has often been called "trace" evidence. The term "trace" is undesirable because, on one hand, traces may be too small to be detected, and on the other, there may be much more than trace quantities of the material present in case evidence. Microscopy is the single, most important technique used for examination and comparison of evidence in this category. This category of evidence is important when it is transferred. Detecting the transfer can help associate or dissociate things or persons. The "Locard exchange principle," attributed to French forensic scientist Edmond Locard, states that entities coming into contact will mutually exchange some material. This idea is theoretically sound, but it does not mean forensic scientists can always *detect* the results of these exchanges. Materials evidence generally cannot be fully individualized; that is, questioned and known specimens of materials cannot be determined to have had a common origin.

Materials evidence can be deposited or transferred, and this may occur on a macro or on a micro scale. Clothing and vehicles are common sources of materials evidence. Recognizing materials evidence at a scene is an important skill.

Several methods are available for collecting and preserving materials evidence from crime scenes. The best and preferred method is to collect the intact item that bears the trace, package it, and submit it. If this cannot be done, because the item is immovable or for some other reason, there are several alternatives. These include: picking off materials evidence with forceps; tape lifts; mechanical dislocation, such as shaking or scraping; and vacuuming. Use of forceps is a commonly used as the first technique in the laboratory, but may also be used with care in the field. Tape lifting is a good, if tedious, technique in the field. Investigators should remember to sample and collect *substratum* control specimens if necessary, using the same sampling techniques. Shaking or scraping are efficient ways of getting materials away from substrata, but the technique is indiscriminate—all materials will shake off and may or may not be related to the investigation. This technique should only be used in the laboratory. Sexual assault complainants are sometimes asked to disrobe while standing on a large, clean piece of paper. This practice protects and saves all the materials evidence from the clothing if it is needed later for examination. Vacuuming is a last-resort materials evidence collection technique and should be used in the laboratory or under the direction of laboratory personnel. It is difficult for an examiner to discriminate relevant materials from irrelevant background materials in vacuum sweepings. Almost all types of materials evidence can be packaged in paper druggist folds.

Laboratory examination of materials evidence begins with the stereomicroscope or a hand lens. Different types of materials are noted and separated. Next, compound microscopy, chemical microscopy, and polarized light microscopy are likely to be employed. Microscopes equipped with FTIR are also available and permit the determination of an IR spectrum from microscopic specimens with essentially no specimen preparation, and nondestructively. A scanning electron microscope (SEM) can also be useful for certain types of materials evidence.

Materials evidence analysis almost always consists of comparison between known (or alibi known) and questioned specimens. If there is an unexplained difference, the questioned specimen cannot have come from the known (exclusion). If the two match in every property compared, the examiner cannot say they had a common origin. He or she can say they "could have" had a common origin, or that the "known cannot be excluded as a possible source" of the questioned specimen. In a match case, the questioned specimen has been *partially* individualized, because lots of similar items can be excluded as sources. But materials evidence cannot be fully individualized. This class of evidence is sometimes said to have "primarily exclusionary value."

Major categories of materials evidence include fibers and hairs, certain biological materials (such as pollen or feathers), wood and paper, building materials, metallic residues, paints and coatings, cosmetics, and soils and dusts.

Fibers are common materials evidence. There are natural and artificial fibers. Natural fibers can be mineral, such as asbestos or mineral wool. They can be vegetable (cotton, linen, manila, hemp, jute), or animal (mainly hairs, wool, or silk). Many fibers are artificial or synthesized. Some are modified from natural fibers (rayon, mercerized cotton), but most are synthesized. Synthetic fibers are polymers. The first commercially successful artificial fiber was nylon. There are also many products made from polyethylene, polypropylene, acrylics, polyamide, and fiberglass fibers.

Many natural fibers can be identified by their microscopic morphology. Manufactured fibers do not yield as much information from their morphology alone, but contain dyes and delusterants that can help in their comparison. Size and cross section are important properties. And refractive index and dispersion are optical properties typically determined for manufactured fibers. Chemical properties can also be determined, by pyrolysis GC or by FTIR. Comparison polarized light microscopes can be used to compare fibers side by side in the same way bullets or cartridge cases are compared side by side in a reflected light comparison microscope.

Hairs can be thought of as a type of fiber, and hair comparisons are done microscopically, much like fiber comparisons. Hair consists of an outer layer that is made up of cuticular scales, a cortex, and an inner medula that is a central air-filled canal. The pigment in hair is melanin, and its density and distribution vary widely. Human hair has three growth phases anagen, catagen and telogen. In the anagen phase, it is actively growing. An anagen hair must be pulled from the scalp. In the telogen phase, it falls out or is shed easily. Anagen hairs have roots; telogen hairs do not. Telogen hairs are the most common as evidence. There are microscopically discernible differences in the head hair of Caucasian, Negro, and Mongoloid peoples. But a "guesstimate" of the race of a person based on examining head hair could be wrong, because the "races" are now so mixed and blended in human populations.

Head hair can be of more than one color or type. There is typically less variation in pubic or other body hair. For hair comparisons, therefore, a sample of known hairs is required for comparison. Hair examiners do not agree on the number required, but it should be a representative sample. Many examiners also prefer "plucked" standards, but some will examine cut standards. Many sexual assault evidence collection kits make provisions for collecting head and pubic hair standards from complainants and suspects, and pubic combings from complainants. Hairs are examined and compared microscopically to determine whether the knowns can be excluded as a source of the questioned specimens. If they cannot, then the hairs "could have had a common origin." Some older cases have recently surfaced where examiners made hair comparison sound more definitive than it is in terms of including a specific person. There is also now the possibility of DNA typing in hair. If the hairs are anagen, with roots present, DNA typing is comparatively straightforward, because nuclear DNA can be profiled. In telogen hairs, however, there are no nucleated cells, and DNA analysis is limited to mitochondrial DNA typing. Mitotyping is far less individualizing than nuclear DNA profiling. Hair examiners can almost always identify the species of nonhuman animal hair. But animal hairs cannot be attributed to a particular animal.

Paint is an important category of materials evidence. It can consist of architectural or automotive paint. Large files of known automotive paints are available. Paint consists of binder, colorant, fillers and additives, and carrier solvent. Paint specimens can be multilayered, and this feature is helpful in comparing questioned and known samples. Known controls should be taken as close to the apparent source of the questioned specimen as possible, so as to have the same layer structure and environmental exposure history. With paint chips, an examiner can consider the possibility of a physical fit match. The initial examination of paint is done with a stereomicroscope to get an idea of layer structure, color, sheen, and so on. Color is evaluated visually, but it can be evaluated instrumentally if the lab has a visible spectrophotometer-equipped microscope. Paint evidence may come in as chips, spatter, or smears. Smears are the most difficult to examine, but they are seen often in vehicle-to-vehicle collision transfers. Besides color, the basic paint polymer can usually be determined. Instruments that can help in paint comparisons are attenuated total reflectance and diffuse reflectance IR, and microscope accessories for FTIR instruments. Other instruments can be used to examine inorganic components of paints.

Glass is another class of materials evidence. Glass is "solid," but it is not crystalline. Its molecular structure is more similar to liquids, and it is often called a "supercooled" liquid. Glass is primarily silicon dioxide (sand). Other components are added to give the glass desired properties.

Many types of glass fracture randomly. Thus, physical fit matches should be considered when dealing with glass evidence. Only a physical fit match can provide an individualization with glass evidence. Investigators should consider evidence like fingerprints on fragments of glass as well. Laboratory comparisons take advantage of color, thickness, surface characteristics, and of density and refractive index. Sometimes, "outside" and "inside" surfaces can be identified. Fluorescence can help determine different intrinsic properties of some glasses, and it can also be used to determine the "tin" side of float glass. Automobile windshield glass has special properties that can be helpful in reconstructions, as discussed in a previous chapter.

Soil is another type of materials evidence. It is common on the undersides or lower aspects of vehicles, and on footwear. Note that casting a footwear impression in dirt automatically results in collecting a soil specimen, because soil will stick to the hardened dental stone. Soil is a difficult specimen for forensic comparison because its composition is so variable. While this can be useful, there are also situations in which there are few differences between samples from an area (such as on a beach). Soil is a combination of biologically derived material, mineral-derived material, and accidental materials from human activity in the area. The mineral content can be analyzed by polarized light microscopy, and the combination of accidental materials may be informative as well. Soil specimens are typically dried thoroughly, then "coned and quartered" to render them homogeneous before sampling. Soils may be compared as to color, miscellaneous inclusions, particle size distribution, or density gradients. Some progress has been made in recent years in attempting to use DNA technology to obtain the profile of the biological component of soil. It is important that known control soil specimens be properly collected. This means that representative samples be collected from several feet to several yards, at all four compass points, from the suspected point of origin of the questioned sample. This strategy helps ensure that variation in soil composition in an area will be properly accounted for in the comparison.

Key Terms

trace evidence (p. 341)
materials evidence (p. 342)
transfer evidence (p. 342)
mechanical dislocation (p. 344)
tape lift (p. 345)
exclusionary value (p. 349)
natural fibers (p. 350)
synthetic fibers (p. 350)
regenerated fibers (p. 356)
delusterant (p. 360)
optical properties (p. 360)

pyrolysis gas chromatography (p. 362)
keratin (p. 362)
cuticle (p. 362)
cortex (p. 362)
medulla (p. 363)
melanin (p. 363)
anagen phase (p. 363)
catagen phase (p. 363)
telogen phase (p. 363)
architectural paints (p. 367)
automotive paints (p. 367)

layer structure (p. 367)
visible spectrometers (p. 369)
paint smears (p. 370)
attenuated total reflectance (ATR) (p. 371)
diffuse reflectance infrared Fourier
    transform spectroscopy (DRIFTS)
    (p. 371)
soda lime glass (p. 371)
float glass process (p. 372)
refractive index (RI) (p. 373)
particle size distribution (p. 379)

Review Questions—Short Answer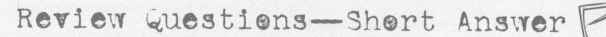

1. What are the differences and similarities between transfer and trace materials evidence?
2. List and give examples of the major techniques used by investigators and in forensic laboratories to collect materials evidence.

3. Name some things that could be considered materials evidence.
4. Why do fibers have such importance in the materials evidence class?
5. What are the major types of fibers that can become evidence?
6. Why does an analyst need large control samples for successful hair comparison and how should these control samples be collected?
7. What types of incidents are likely to produce forensically important paint evidence?
8. Briefly discuss the nature of glass and why it is so often important forensic evidence.
9. What are the major components of soil?
10. Discuss the proper collection of soil evidence and the importance of proper control samples.

Fill-in-the-Blank & Multiple Choice

1. The Locard exchange principle concerns evidence resulting from physical _____ between objects.
2. The laboratory device most commonly used in the *search for* trace and transfer evidence is the _____.
3. The preferred method for submitting an object that may have trace evidence adhered to it is
   a. submission of the object without prior removal.
   b. submission of the object and the removed trace material.
   c. in a clean metal paint can.
   d. in a clean plastic bag.
4. Soil samples can be _____ by careful determination and comparison of the particle size distribution of the questioned and known samples.
5. Hair forcibly removed from the body
   a. is known as telogen hair.
   b. has cellular material adhering to its root, and may be analyzed for nuclear DNA.
   c. is much more common as evidence than hair that just falls out of the skin.
   d. is analyzed primarily with an instrument known as the FTIR.

Further References

Caddy, B., ed. *Forensic Examination of Glass and Paint.* London, England: Taylor & Francis, 2001.

D'Andrea, F., F. Francoise, and R. Coquoz. "Preliminary Experiments on the Transfer of Animal Hair During Simulated Criminal Behavior." *Journal of Forensic Sciences* 43 (1998): 1257–58.

Deedrick, D. W. "Hairs, Fibers, Crime, and Evidence." *Forensic Science Communications* 2 (2000). Available at FBI Web site: www.fbi.gov/hq/lab/fsc/current/descript.htm.

Deedrick, D., and S. Koch. "Microscopy of Hair Part 1: A Practical Guide and Manual for Human Hairs." *Forensic Science Communications* 6, no. 1 (2004).

"Microscopy of Hair Part 2: A Practical Guide and Manual for Animal Hairs." *Forensic Science Communications* 6, no. 3 (2004).

Demmelmeyer, H. "Forensic Investigation of Soil and Vegetable Materials." *Forensic Science Review* 7 (1995): 120.

"Forensic Fiber Examination Guidelines." Scientific Working Group on Materials Analysis, *Forensic Science Communications,* April 1999, available at FBI Web site: www.fbi.gov/hq/lab/fsc/current/descript.htm.

"Forensic Paint Analysis and Comparison Guidelines." Scientific Working Group on Materials Analysis, *Forensic Science Communications* 1 (1999).

Houck, M. M., ed. *Mute Witness: Trace Evidence Analysis.* New York: Academic Press, 2001.

Houck, M. M., and B. Budowle. "Correlation of Microscopic and Mitochondrial DNA Hair Comparisons." *Journal of Forensic Sciences* 47 (2002): 964–967.

"The Ingredients of Paint and Their Impact on Paint Properties." Accessed at www.paintquality.com/ under specifiers.

Junger, E. P. "Assessing the Unique Characteristics of Close-Proximity Soil Samples: Just How Useful Is Soil Evidence?" *Journal of Forensic Sciences* 41 (1996): 27–34.

Keto, R. A. "Analysis and Comparison of Bullet Leads by Inductively-Coupled Plasma Mass Spectrometry." *Journal of Forensic Sciences* 44 (1999): 1020–1026.

Lesney, Mark. "Eyeing the Glass Past." *Today's Chemist at Work* (February 2004): 55–56.

Ogle R. R. Jr., and M. J. Fox. *Atlas of Human Hair: Microscopic Characteristics.* Boca Raton, FL: CRC Press, 1998.

Palenik, S. and Palenik, C. "Microscopy and Microchemistry of Physical Evidence." In *Forensic Science Handbook,* 2nd ed., ed. R. Saferstein, chap. 4. pp. 175–230, Upper Saddle River, NJ: Prentice Hall, 2005.

Robertson, J., ed. *Forensic Examination of Fibres.* 2nd ed. London, England: Taylor & Francis, 1999.

The Forensic Examination of Hair. London, England: Taylor & Francis, 1999.

"Weighing Bullet Lead Evidence." National Research Council Monograph, 2004.

Scientific Tools of the Trade: Methods of Forensic Science

As we have noted, forensic science is science in service of the law, with the emphasis on *science*. All sciences make use of various methods and techniques, some of which involve sophisticated analytical instruments. Throughout the book, various methods and instruments are discussed in the context of particular evidence types and their analysis and comparison. Here, we introduce and briefly discuss a few basic scientific concepts, terms, methods, and instruments that are extensively used in forensic science laboratories. Many of them are methods that come from analytical chemistry.

Forensic science and criminalistics tend to borrow techniques and methods from the basic sciences, like biology, chemistry, physics, geology, and so on, and adapt them if necessary to be applicable to resolving forensic questions. Basic sciences are not, for the most part, directed toward forensic questions. Chemists, for example, are seldom asked to find ways to individualize materials like body fluid stains or bullets to a firearm. So forensic science uses the techniques of the basic sciences to serve its purposes.

In this appendix, we discuss some fundamental science and chemistry concepts, methods, and techniques that are regularly encountered in forensic laboratory practice. Scientists tend to use and talk about these concepts as second nature. Many of them are not second nature to nonscientists, however. Scientists use the metric system for measurements, but the metric system is not used in everyday life in the United States, so it is also introduced here. We discuss and refer to the material in this appendix at appropriate points in the main text of the book chapters.

Physical Properties and States of Matter

Physical properties of matter are properties that are intrinsic. They do not depend on any actual or potential chemical reaction. They are also generally independent of quantity. Some examples are density, temperature, melting point, and boiling point. Often, the first step in looking at physical evidence is physical examination.

Mass may be thought of roughly as the quantity of a substance. It is often confused with weight. Although they are not identical, scientists do weigh things to determine their masses. Mass is usually expressed in grams in the metric system, and in pounds or ounces in the English system.

Density is the mass of a material per unit volume. Denser liquids or gases will sink if placed in less dense ones. A cork floats on water because it is less dense. A lead weight sinks in water because it is more dense.

Temperature is a measure of how much thermal energy an object has, which we commonly think of as how cold, warm, or hot it is. The two main temperature scales in use are the Fahrenheit scale, used throughout the United States, and the Celsius scale, used almost everywhere else. A conventional freezer operates at about $-20°C$ or $0°F$. Water freezes at $0°C$ or $32°F$. Water boils at $100°C$ or $212°F$. Normal human body temperature is about $37°C$ or $98°F$. The melting and boiling point temperatures of a substance are characteristic and may sometimes help in identifying the substance. The "°" is a universal symbol for degrees of temperature.

There are three main states of matter: solid, liquid, and gaseous. The state of a substance is temperature dependent. If we heat water, it will boil and turn to steam. If we cool it, it will freeze and become ice. Other substances behave the same way. There are some other states of matter too, such as supercritical fluids, but they will not be of concern in this book.

Structure of Matter—Atoms and Molecules

Chemistry is in many ways the study of matter at the level of atoms and molecules. There are 92 naturally occurring *elements* that make up all of matter. An element is the most fundamental unit in chemistry. *Atoms* are the units of elements. Atoms in turn are made up of protons, neutrons, electrons, and other elementary particles. A neutral atom has the same number of protons as electrons. Protons are positively charged, and electrons are negatively charged. An atom having equal numbers of them is electrically neutral. Atoms can gain or lose electrons, causing them to have a net positive or net negative charge. Charged atoms are called *ions*. Positively charged atoms are *cations;* negatively charged atoms are *anions*.

Elements can be systematically arranged on a chart known as the *periodic table* (Figure A.1). Different elements are characterized by atoms having different numbers of protons and neutrons. These numbers contribute to and are related to each element's atomic weight, which is shown on the periodic table.

Atoms can combine to form *molecules*. A molecule is the unit of a *compound*. Thus, atoms of elements combine to form molecules of a compound. Compounds can be very simple, such as the combination of two chlorine atoms to form a chlorine gas molecule. They can also be very complex, such as a molecule of DNA consisting of hundreds of thousands of carbon, hydrogen, oxygen, nitrogen, and phosphorus atoms. A compound's *molecular weight* is the sum of the atomic weights of all the atoms making up that compound. Molecular weight is a useful physical property for

Figure A.1
Periodic Table of the Elements.

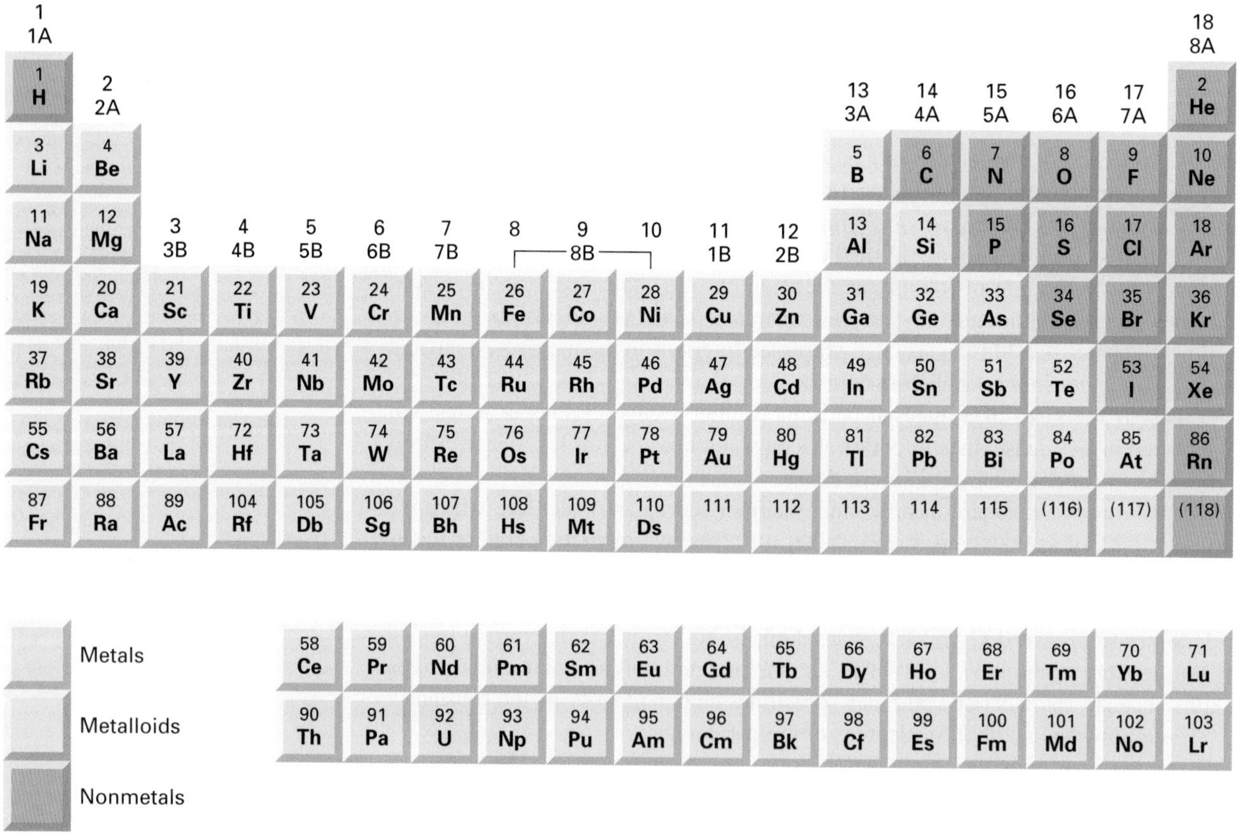

identification of compounds. For instance, the molecular weight of any compound in grams is called one *mole* of that compound. One mole of any compound always contains the same number of molecules. This allows chemists to calculate how much of a compound is needed to combine with a given amount of another compound in a chemical reaction.

Most of chemistry has to do with the transformations of compounds through chemical reactions. Compounds A and B react to form Compound C, or maybe Compound C and Compound D. These *chemical reactions* are balanced in terms of the atoms involved, and they may also require energy or release energy.

The most important element in the world is probably carbon (symbolized by C). Carbon can combine with itself, and with oxygen, nitrogen, sulfur, and other elements, to form a bewildering number of different compounds. The study of the compounds of carbon is called *organic* chemistry. Biochemistry, the study of the chemistry of the molecules that make up living things, is a subfield of organic chemistry.

Metric System

Scientists use the metric system for measurement. So does everyone in Europe and much of the rest of the world. But in the United States, the English (or engineering) measurement system has persisted. In Figure A.2, a few metric-English equivalencies are given. The basic units of metric system measurement are the *gram* (for mass), the *liter* (for volume) and the *meter* (for length). Prefixes are attached to these basic unit names to designate multiples or fractions of them. All the prefixes designate an

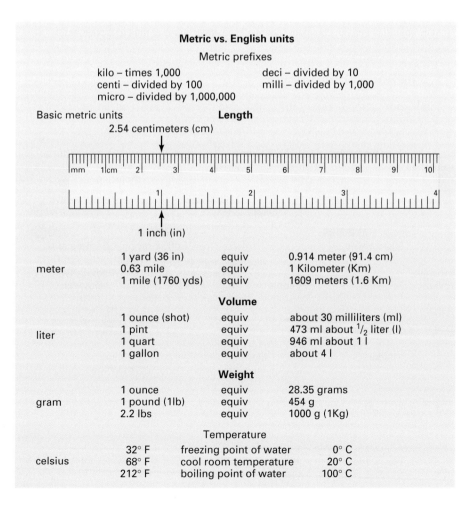

Figure A.2

Some common equivalents between units in the Metric and English systems of weights and measures.

amount that is a multiple or fraction by a factor of 10. For instance, *kilo-* means 1,000, *centi-* means 1/100, *milli-* means 1/1000, *micro-* (often indicated by the Greek letter µ) means 1/1,000,000.

Light, the Electromagnetic Spectrum, and Color

Another physical property is color, and it results from the interaction of the material with the light that it is hitting it and how the light it reflects interacts with the light sensors in our eyes. Light—the light that we see is called the visible spectrum—is part of a much larger spectrum of different wavelengths called the *electromagnetic spectrum* (Figure A.3). The different forms of electromagnetic energy along that energy spectrum are distinguished by their wavelength. At the very short wavelength end (high energy) are cosmic rays, gamma rays, and X-rays. Toward the center are infrared light, visible light, and ultraviolet light. And at the long end are radio, microwave, and television waves (low energy).

The perception of color, and many of the instrumental methods used in forensic science, rely on measurements of light's interactions with substances and materials. When electromagnetic radiation strikes a substance, three things can happen: It can be reflected; it can be transmitted; or it can be absorbed. Essentially, *reflected* means bounced (as with reflection in a mirror). There is no effect on the substance. *Transmitted* means the radiation passes through the substance unchanged. *Absorbed* means that the molecules of the substance absorb energy from the radiation and

Figure A.3

An illustration of the full range of the electromagnetic spectrum and the commonly encountered applications of the electromagnetic radiation.

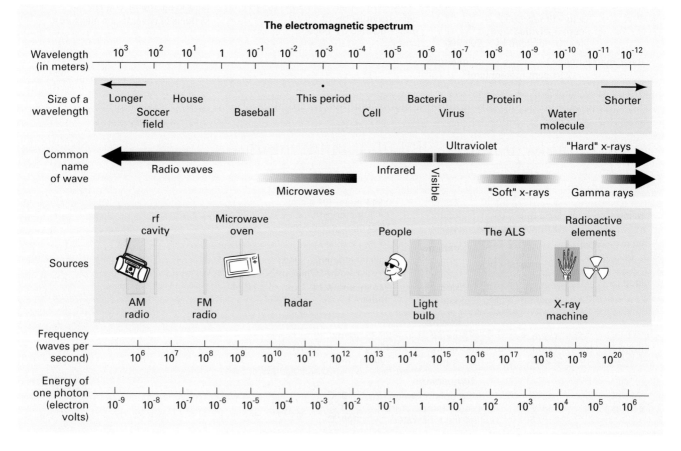

undergo changes as a result. The differential absorption of electromagnetic radiation is the basis of all spectrometric and some spectroscopic methods (see later). Sometimes, when a substance absorbs electromagnetic radiation, the molecules can go into an excited state briefly, and then relax. This relaxation can take the form of emission of radiation of a longer wavelength (sometimes visible light). This phenomenon is called *fluorescence,* and we refer to it often in the main text. Usually, ultraviolet light (which is of shorter wavelength than visible) is impinged onto a specimen. If the specimen absorbs radiation and is excited, upon relaxation it may emit bluish or other colors of visible light (fluorescence).

In the visible light portion of the spectrum—the part we see with our eyes— visible light consists of a mixture of many wavelengths, which we see as different colors. Mixed together, they appear white. A mnemonic for remembering the colors in the visible spectrum is "ROY G. BIV." Red Orange Yellow Green Blue Indigo and Violet is the order of the colors, from long to short wavelength visible light. Something looks green to our eye because the green wavelength light is reflected by that object. The rest of the light might be absorbed or transmitted.

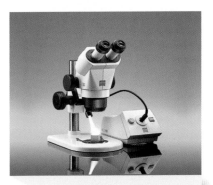

Figure A.4
A stereomicroscope that allows three dimensional views at moderate magnification, also called a dissecting microscope.

Microscopy and Microscopical Methods

Because much physical evidence is microscopic or near microscopic, forensic scientists make use of microscopes in many ways, including for finding, separating, and examining evidence. Forensic scientists primarily use four different types of microscopes, each for a different type of activity. The four discussed in the following are the stereomicroscope, compound microscope, comparison microscope, and the scanning electron microscop. Note: We use the term "microscopic" to mean small—small enough to require a microscope for viewing clearly. We use the term "microscopical" to mean "of, or having to do with, microscopes." Thus, a forensic scientist uses microscopical methods to examine microscopic dust particles.

The stereomicroscope (Figure A.4) actually has two separate optical paths, one for each eye of the viewer. In that way it gives the viewer a three-dimensional view of objects in the field of view that allows the examiner, with a steady hand, to touch, grasp, and move objects while viewing them. These are also called "dissecting microscopes," because biologists use them to carefully observe objects while they are being taken apart, that is, dissected. These microscopes are designed for relatively low magnification and a long working distance. "Working distance" is the distance between the objective lens of the microscope and the object being viewed. This is critical so that a probe, forceps, or scalpel can be manipulated without the lens being in the way. Thus material collected from a hit-and-run scene can be sorted into different piles of paint chips, sand, or broken glass. The magnification range of a stereomicroscope can be from life size to as much as 60 times life size. It is the product of the magnification of the eyepiece and the objective. The objective lens is the one closer to the object. More expensive stereomicroscopes have a zoom objective, which allows continuous magnification change usually between 0.7 and 3.5 times (some have an even larger zoom range). With a 10 times eyepiece lens, this produces a magnification range of 7 to 35 times, which is quite adequate for most forensic applications. The most important forensic application of the stereomicroscope is searching for evidence, for example, clothing for foreign hairs or fibers, and initial examination of potential evidence to gain information about what it might be.

The compound microscope (Figure A.5) is also known as the "biological microscope." It is the most widely used type of microscope, combining an eyepiece lens with one or more different objective lenses to provide a wide range of magnification. The objective lens is usually on a rotating turret and must be quite close to the sample to provide proper focus. As with the stereomicroscope, the total magnification is the product of the magnification of the eyepiece and the objective lens. For example, a 10-power eyepiece is often combined with a 4-power objective to provide a total

Figure A.5
A compound microscope.

magnification of 40 times. One can usually rotate the objective turret to a 10-power objective and obtain a magnification of 100, and so on. The compound microscope is usually used in the range of magnification of about 40 times to about 1,000 times. Unlike the stereomicroscope, it has a single optical path, even when provided with binocular viewing, and produces a flat field with a very small depth of focus. Its optical design provides a very short working distance, particularly at high magnification.

Most compound microscopes used forensically are designed for transmitted light applications. The object to be viewed is usually placed on a transparent glass microscope slide, and the light is passed through the sample. This process, of course, works best with very thin items that will allow enough light to pass for observation. Hairs, fibers, small paint chips, and most small crystals are suitable for transmitted light examination. As we will discuss in the following, items like bullets, cartridge cases, and toolmarks can be best examined using reflected light and usually are examined at lower magnification than that customary with a compound microscope.

The comparison microscope (Figure A.6) is one particularly useful for forensic applications. It is designed to optimize the examiner's ability to make careful comparisons on a microscopic scale. It is actually just two compound microscopes joined together by an optical bridge. Using some simple controls on the optical bridge, the examiner can look into the optical bridge and view either what is on the left or right microscope or can split the field of view to allow viewing both simultaneously. Thus, the examiner can place a control hair from the victim on the right microscope and bring a particular area of that hair into focus. A corresponding portion of an evidence hair from the suspect's clothing can be located in the view of the left microscope, and then the two can be brought into the field of view together, each on its half of the split field of view, to allow precise comparison. The transmitted light comparison microscope is particularly useful for small items of materials evidence (Chapter 13).

For bullets or cartridge cases (Chapter 8) or other opaque objects, a different type of comparison microscope is used. It works the same way, by linking two

Figure A.6

A transmitted light comparison microscope.

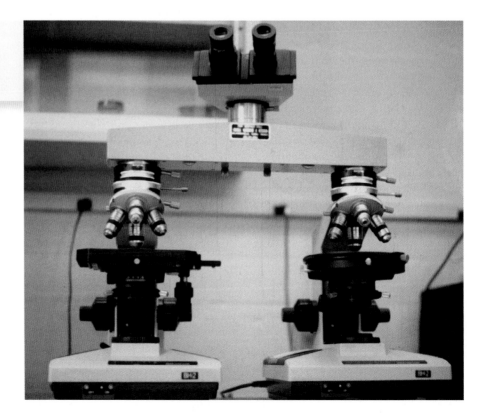

microscopes with an optical bridge, but is used with microscopes designed to use light reflected from the object being observed rather than light passing through the object. For the observation of bullets, examiners mount them with sticky wax to a holder that can be rotated in all three dimensions; the bullets are usually lighted with fiber optic light cables to allow highlighting or shadowing of the particular areas of interest. Reflected light comparison microscopes usually also have other stages to hold other types of samples. The areas of interest are selected by observing the objects on each microscope independently and then closely comparing them using the split field.

The scanning electron microscope (SEM) (Figure A.7) uses a focused beam of electrons, instead of visible light to image objects. It is a much more complex and expensive instrument and is used for special applications. It has magnification capabilities much greater than an optical microscope, being capable of magnification from only a few times to several hundred thousand times. Its other advantage is its ability to perform elemental analysis on the objects it is magnifying. This is done with an accessory called an EDX, for energy dispersive X-ray spectrometer, that is included with many SEMs. The disadvantage is that it requires that the objects to be observed are in a high vacuum chamber. Therefore, there is no working distance since the objects must be in a sealed chamber. One important forensic application is visualization of gunshot residue particles collected from the hands of a person suspected of firing a weapon (Chapter 8). Because the SEM can allow visualization of the rather characteristic appearance of such particles and has the ability to determine that they contain the characteristic elements of barium, antimony, or lead, the reliability of their identification is raised to a much higher level. The SEM has application to many other types of materials (trace) evidence as well.

Computers and Computer Programs

As computer technology has overwhelmed society in the past several decades, it has also become an essential feature of scientific instruments and laboratory practice.

Every major analytical instrument is now interfaced with a computer, and the instrument makers typically design proprietary software to go with it. The instrument is controlled by the software, which also captures the instrument's output signals and translates them into usable formats, like gas chromatograms or mass spectra. Since chromatograms and spectra can be represented fairly easily by a series of numbers, large libraries have been built. And, since computers are fast at comparing numbers, these libraries can be searched quickly and efficiently to see if the spectrum of the specimen being run is in the library. This type of search helps analytical chemists enormously in their work and speeds up identification of compounds.

Since digital imaging is rapidly becoming commonplace in forensic science, the ability to use computer imaging programs to clarify and improve contrast has been put to good use. Ever more sophisticated computer algorithms can be used to improve the value of digital images in many ways. This technology can be applied to all areas of forensic science and is particularly useful with pattern evidence (Chapter 5).

As mentioned briefly in Chapter 1, the use of computerized databases has truly revolutionized the role of forensic science in the criminal justice system. The availability of these databases and their growing contents has made physical evidence and its forensic examination much more investigatively useful. This trend is likely to continue and further move forensic science from a mostly reactive role (did we arrest the right individual?) to the proactive role of being a partner with the investigator in solving the case.

There are also computer programs designed to manage laboratory operations, inventories, and so forth. And so-called LIMSs (laboratory information management systems) are big, integrated systems for managing a laboratory's entire operation, from evidence accession, through analysis, evidence storage, evidence return, and report writing. These systems bring savings in the high costs of keeping track of the vast amounts of information generated by modern forensic laboratories.

Biological Methods

A number of methods in biological sciences are employed in the examination of biological evidence. Probably the most prominent and worthy of mention are enzymatic assays, histochemical staining, and DNA manipulation. Enzymes are nature's catalysts—catalysts speed up a chemical reaction without entering into it. All the enzymes are proteins, and we discuss more about them in Chapter 9. Some methods involve trying to find an enzyme in a specimen, while others involve using enzymes to look for some other component of it.

Histochemical staining is regularly employed when cells are to be examined under a compound microscope. The stains are organic compounds that can differentially color various components of cells and make it easier to see and study them microscopically. One stain commonly used in the forensic lab, for instance, is called "Christmas tree." It makes sperm cells have red heads, green midpieces, and blue tails. This staining makes it easier for examiners to locate sperm cells in smears of vaginal swabs from sexual assault complainants. This is discussed further in Chapter 9 as well. Another potential type of biological evidence comes from plants (see Chapter 13). Although botanical traces will typically be examined in a manner similar to other trace/materials, histological staining could play a role in that analysis.

In Chapter 10, we describe how DNA can be isolated and manipulated so that it can be typed for forensic purposes.

Chromatography and Chromatographic Methods

Chromatography is a name given to certain chemical separation methods. The word itself comes from a Greek word meaning "color," because the procedure was originally used to separate colored pigments from plants. Of the many different kinds of chromatography the most important in forensic analysis are thin-layer chromatography, gas (once called "gas-liquid") chromatography, and high-performance liquid chromatography, typically abbreviated TLC, GC, and HPLC.

Chromatography brings about separation of substances based on their differing affinity for one or the other of the chromatographic "phases," that is, the partitioning of individual materials in a mixture between a moving and a stationary phase. In TLC, for example, there is a stationary solid phase and a mobile liquid phase. A plate, coated with a solid layer of adsorbent, is placed vertically into a tank so that it just contacts a liquid (the mobile phase). By capillary action, the liquid "climbs up" the solid phase. Substances that have been placed on and absorbed by the solid phase ahead of time ("spotted" onto the TLC plate) may have greater affinity for the liquid phase as it moves, and thus be carried along with it. Or they may have more affinity for the solid phase and move more slowly. Because different substances have differing affinities for the phases, they are separated.

In GC, the mobile phase is a gas (often helium). The "liquid" phase is a high molecular weight liquid absorbent that coats the inside of a long column. The substances the analyst wants to separate are heated to a high enough temperature for them to vaporize. The vapors then pass onto the column and are carried along by the gas. Over the years, chemists have designed many different liquid phases and made use of different instrument conditions (mostly related to temperature and flow) for separating a great variety of compounds.

The gas chromatograph allows complex mixtures, such as a concentrated fire debris residue sample, to be separated into its many components. The sample is injected into the instrument, vaporized, and swept through a very fine glass, or more commonly a pure silica, column by the inert carrier gas. The carrier gas is usually either helium or hydrogen. The flowing gas moves the sample through the column, which has a thin coating of a high boiling liquid on the walls. The thin layer of the liquid on the walls causes the components of the sample to be partitioned between the liquid (stationary phase) and the flowing gas (mobile phase). This partitioning is a dynamic process in which the different chemical compounds dissolve in the liquid coating and then are revaporized many thousands of times during their passage through the column. The different components are moved along through the column while in the gas phase, but they are stationary when dissolved in the liquid phase. Since each different chemical compound has a slightly different tendency to move from the gas to the liquid phase, each takes a different amount of time to pass through the column. The more time a compound spends in the liquid layer, the less time it is moving and the longer it will take to make the trip through the column. Conversely, the more time a compound spends in the gas phase, the sooner it will emerge. The net result is that even very similar chemical compounds with only a slight difference in their partitioning between the mobile and stationary phase will take slightly different amounts of time to pass through the column. Any slight differences in their boiling points or their attraction to the stationary phase will cause them to emerge at different times. At the end of the column, a detector tells the operator when something other than the carrier gas is emerging from the column. Accordingly, the length of time each component of a mixture takes to traverse the column can be measured accurately. In addition, the sizes of the peaks produced by the detector are proportional to the quantity of the component represented by that peak in the mixture.

High-performance liquid chromatography is the favored technique for the separation of compounds that cannot be easily vaporized or that break down on vaporization.

In HPLC, the mobile phase is a liquid solvent or solvent mixture, and the stationary phase is a finely divided solid usually with a surface coating that interacts with the compounds to be separated. Again, as the mixture dissolved in the liquid phase passes through the column, its components are partitioned between the mobile and stationary phases, and the time for their passage through the column is governed by the relative time in each phase.

Spectroscopy and Spectroscopic Methods

Spectrometric methods of analysis are all based on measuring the wavelengths of light that are absorbed, transmitted, or reflected by a specimen. All the different wavelengths of the electromagnetic spectrum (EMS) have been exploited in designing analytical instruments. As mentioned earlier, the EMS spans a wide range of wavelengths (energies) ranging from very short wavelength gamma rays to very long wavelength communications wavelengths. The key to using the EMS is tuning in on a particular group of wavelengths with a specific detector. We all carry such a detector for the visible portion of the EMS in the back of our eyeballs, and many carry a detector for the microwave portion of the EMS in our pockets in the form of a cell phone.

We can understand a great deal about spectroscopy by looking at a general picture of a spectrometer. Such instruments, although available in hundreds of specific types, virtually all have five common components (Figure A.8). They have a source of the desired electromagnetic radiation, a sample holder, a sorting device for the region of the EMS being used, a detector sensitive to that region, and a recorder to collect and display the information obtained.

Earlier we discussed scanning electron microscopy and energy-dispersive X-ray analysis in connection with the identification of gunshot residue, for example. Some of the most widely used analytical instruments rely on the infrared (infrared spectrometer), visible (visible spectrophotometer), and UV (ultraviolet spectrophotometer) portions of the EMS. For purposes of this book, you can think of IR (or its more sophisticated relative FTIR) as a method of chemical "fingerprinting" of pure substances. IR and FTIR (Figure A.9) are used in the analysis of drugs, toxins, and many materials comparisons. Visible spectrometry is, if you will, an analytical method for determining color. And UV spectrometry uses the UV wavelength range for detection and often quantitative analysis of drugs and many other primarily organic compounds. Some additional types of spectroscopy are atomic absorption (AA) and inductively coupled plasma (ICP), which can be

Figure A.8

The major components of a generic spectrometer.

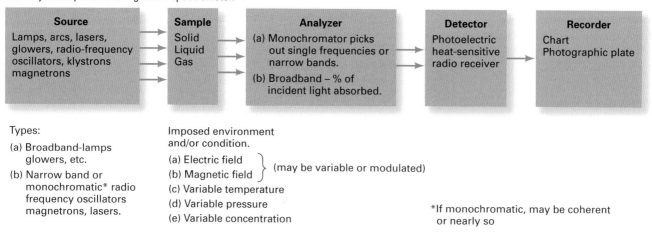

Source	Sample	Analyzer	Detector	Recorder
Lamps, arcs, lasers, glowers, radio-frequency oscillators, klystrons magnetrons	Solid Liquid Gas	(a) Monochromator picks out single frequencies or narrow bands. (b) Broadband – % of incident light absorbed.	Photoelectric heat-sensitive radio receiver	Chart Photographic plate

Types:

(a) Broadband-lamps glowers, etc.

(b) Narrow band or monochromatic* radio frequency oscillators magnetrons, lasers.

Imposed environment and/or condition.

(a) Electric field
(b) Magnetic field ⎬ (may be variable or modulated)
(c) Variable temperature
(d) Variable pressure
(e) Variable concentration

*If monochromatic, may be coherent or nearly so

used to identify which elements are present in a substance, and mass spectroscopy. Mass spectroscopy is probably the single most important analytical tool in the forensic chemist's arsenal.

In a mass spectrometer, although the EMS is not involved, the basic portions of the generalized spectrometer are present. The molecules in a specimen are first ionized by bombardment with electrons and they usually break into ionized smaller fragments. The ions formed are specific to a given compound. The sorting device in a mass spectrometer sorts on the basis of mass (actually mass to charge ratio) of the fragments rather than wavelength. The detector then counts the ions of each mass that reach it. A display of the relative number of ions at each mass produced by each compounds is usually unique to that compound and therefore allows identification of the compound. The mass spectrum of a compound is usually unique and allows most compounds to be unequivocally identified quickly and reliably. It is sometimes said that mass spectrometry, particularly when coupled with a gas chromatograph (see next section), is the "gold standard" for drug and toxicological compound identification.

Hyphenated Methods

One of the most significant advances in analytical instrumentation was developing the ability to interface chromatographs (for their separation ability) with mass spectrometers (for their chemical identification ability). These instruments (and the associated techniques) are sometimes called "hyphenated techniques." Gas chromatograph/mass spectrometry (GC-MS) (Figure A.10) is very commonly used for drug and toxin identification, and generally for the identification of a great variety of organic compounds.

The weakness of the mass spectrometer and most other spectroscopic techniques is the need for pure single component samples. In the real world (forensic science is as real as it gets), samples are usually mixtures, sometimes quite complex mixtures. The combination of a chromatographic technique to separate a mixture into its individual components and feed them one at a time to the spectrometer is ideal. Thus the spectrometer acts as a very specific detector for the chromatograph. A gas

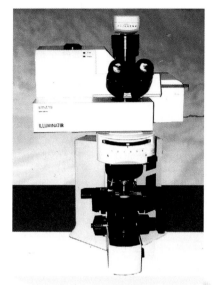

Figure A.9

A Fourier-transform infrared spectrometer mounted on a microscope. An infrared spectrum can be quickly and nondestructively obtained from a microscopic specimen with this instrument.

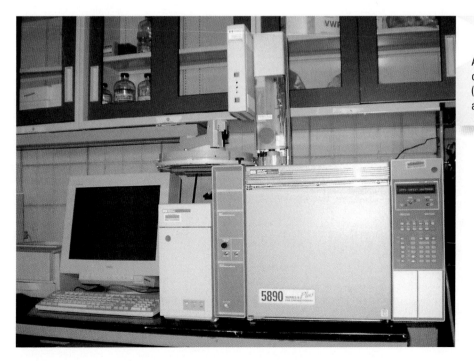

Figure A.10

A popular model of a gas chromatograph/mass spectrometer (GC-MS) with an auto sampler attachment.

chromatograph can be interfaced with either a mass spectrometer or an infrared spectrometer.

Sometimes, a mixture will not survive a trip through a gas chromatograph because it decomposes when being vaporized or is changed by passage through the gas chromatographic column. For such cases, a liquid chromatograph interfaced with a mass spectrometer (LC-MS) can be used to identify the components of the mixture. This allows a mass spectrometer to be used with samples that would otherwise not be suitable for mass spectral analysis.

A

accelerants Flammable liquids or solids that may have been used to start or sustain a suspicious fire.

accreditation Recognition by a body or organization external to a lab that inspection and evaluation of the laboratory have determined that its work meets high professional, predefined standards.

ACE-V method An acronym that stands for analysis, comparison, evaluation, verification, which are the four steps in the analysis and comparison of a latent print impression with a known.

acid phosphatase An enzyme usually found in large quantities in human semen (but also in other tissues and species), used as the basis for a preliminary test for semen.

AFISs Automated Fingerprint Identification Systems; several AFISs are commercially available for the imaging, storage, and rapid retrieval of single fingerprints; national system maintained by the FBI is called IAFIS (for Integrated AFIS).

alibi An innocent explanation of events used by a person accused or suspected of a crime.

alibi known control A specimen obtained from a known source that might be the source of the evidence; usually collected because suspects suggest it (for an alibis).

alteration A change in the physical appearance or meaning of something, often only slight.

alternate light source A high-intensity white light source filtered to emit only a limited range of wavelengths of visible light.

anabolic Promotes cell growth and division, resulting in growth of muscle tissue and sometimes bone size and strength.

anagen phase The active growth phase of the hair follicle.

analgesics Drugs used to reduce or eliminate a patient's perception of pain.

angle of incidence The angle at which a blood droplet impacts a surface, measured with respect to an imaginary line perpendicular to that surface.

antemortem Occurring before death.

anthropometry (bertillonage) A system of bodily measurements devised by Alphonse Bertillon for personal identification of persons with criminal histories; eventually supplanted by fingerprints.

antibodies Substances made by vertebrates in response to a "foreign" molecule, virus, or cell invading the body; specifically directed against the invader and designed to neutralize it and/or rid the body of it.

anticoagulant A chemical substance, such as EDTA or sodium citrate, which, when added to whole blood, prevents it from clotting.

antigens Substances, often proteins, that elicit the formation of specific antibodies if injected into an animal of a different species.

architectural paints Paint that is used on houses, buildings, and other structures.

attenuated total reflectance (ATR) An infrared sampling technique that depends on passing an IR beam through a crystal in a way that a small portion of the beam emerges from the crystal and can interact with a sample in intimate contact with the crystal.

authenticate To prove that something is real, true, or what it is said (purported) to be.

automatic A firearm that will begin to fire projectiles as soon as the trigger is pulled and continue to fire until the trigger is released or it has run out of ammunition.

automotive paints Paints that are used primarily on automobiles, trucks, and other motor vehicles.

B

ballistics The science of projectiles in flight; ballistics is not firearms identification.

basic fingerprint patterns: arches, loops, and whorls The basic overall fingerprint patterns; variations and subcategories occur within these major classes.

biometrics Use of measurements or portions of complex patterns from the human body to build a database that can then be used to "verify" the "identity" of person within that database.

blank control In many tests, a clean sample containing no specimen, used to ensure that the test is working properly.

blood cells Refers collectively to the red blood cells (erythrocytes) and to all the categories of white blood cells (lymphocytes, monocytes, basophils, neutrophils, and eosinophils).

blood spatter pattern A pattern of dried blood on a surface resulting from an event that caused blood to exit the body and/or be broken into particles and distributed by force.

breech face The surface of a firearm, usually machined, against which the cartridge case is forced by the expanding gases as a result of being fired.

bullet recovery tank Usually a large horizontal or vertical stainless steel tank filled with water and used to stop the flight and allow recovery of a projectile when a firearm is fired into it.

burn pattern The pattern of charring and burning left after a fire has been extinguished that may give insight into how the fire developed.

C

caliber The inside diameter of a gun barrel, in hundredths of an inch or millimeters.

camera An analog or digital device equipped with a lens and capable of recording images on film or an electronic storage medium.

carbon strip or tube absorption A technique for processing debris from a suspicious fire where the vapors above the debris are absorbed on activated carbon and then washed off with a solvent for analysis.

cartridge The assembly of a bullet, gunpowder, and primer in a casing that is placed in the chamber of a firearm.

catagen phase The hair follicle phase in which hair growth stops.

catalyst A substance that speeds up a chemical reaction without being changed or consumed; required in small quantities, because it is not changed by the reaction.

certification The determination by an appropriate organization, after an application that includes qualifications, experience, and an examination, that an individual meets a high level of skill in the area of expertise in which he or she works.

charred documents A document that has been partially burned or heated until it has turned a very dark color and can no longer easily be read.

chromatography A process that separates a mixture of different chemicals into its individual components, often for the purpose of analysis.

chromosomes Physical carriers of DNA (and thus of inheritance information) from one generation to the next; every species has a specific number of chromosomes.

class characteristics Characteristics that define a class or category of items or objects but are not alone sufficient to define individuality; often an intentional result of manufacturing; examples include shoe size and pattern, tire tread pattern and width, first-level fingerprint pattern, and bullet caliber.

classification (identification) To place things into groups according to their basic characteristics.

classification system A method of organizing large files of 10-print cards according to the features of the fingerprints; in the United States, a modified Henry system of classification was used.

club drugs Any of a group of drugs whose primary abuse is associated with marathon youthful dance parties.

CODIS, AFIS, and NIBIN The acronyms given to databases of DNA profiles, fingerprints, and firearms evidence images, respectively, maintained for investigative purposes and used to search evidence patterns against previously existing patterns.

cold case An investigation that has become inactive for a period of time, for a variety of reasons, although the case has not yet been solved.

collected writings Writing samples obtained from a variety of sources that represent a valid sample of an individual's writing.

Combined DNA Index System (CODIS) A large system of interconnected local, state, and national databases containing DNA profiles; authorized by Congress in 1994 and recently amended to permit databasing of suspects or arrestees provided the latter is legal under applicable state law.

combustion The combination of a fuel with oxygen to produce highly oxidized products and heat.

comparison specimen A separate specimen taken of a material for comparison purposes; in fire investigations, a sample of surface or substratum on which ignitable liquid residue might be present.

confirmatory test A test that, when positive, proves that the material or substance tested for is actually present.

containment Confining a rapid, exothermic reaction within a sturdy container until it develops sufficient force (pressure) to shatter the container.

contamination Refers to unintended, potentially unrecognized, biological material in or on a biological evidence specimen, which could cause difficulty in interpreting the results of some tests under some circumstances.

contemporaneous Happening or existing in the same period of time.

control specimens Separate specimens included in a test protocol to ensure that the test is performing properly.

controlled experiments Experiments carefully designed to test one variable of a hypothesis.

controlled substance A drug that is named in either federal or state controlled substances statues as illegal to possess except when prescribed by a physician.

controls In general, required to ensure that a laboratory test is working properly or to permit a proper comparison; the major types important in forensic investigations are blank, known, and alibi known.

copying machine A machine that makes copies of documents using one of several different duplication processes.

coroner An elected official whose responsibility is to look into suspicious or unattended deaths.

corpus delicti Latin term for the facts necessary to prove a particular crime.

cortex The primary structure of the hair shaft.

crime scene photography Technically proper photography of a crime scene for purposes of complete documentation.

crime scene security Limiting and controlling access to a crime scene and maintaining records of who was present.

criminal profiling Application of psychology and of knowledge developed from past similar offenses and offenders to help create a hypothetical picture of an offender in an unsolved case.

criminalistics The recognition, classification (identification), individualization, and evaluation of physical evidence using the methods of science.

cross-projection sketch Sketch of a three-dimensional room or structure in two dimensions, by "collapsing" the walls and ceiling flat in the sketch.

crystal tests Tests in which the formation of characteristic crystals constitutes a positive result.

cursive writing Writing that is written with rounded letters that are joined together.

cuticle The impervious outer layer of cells that protects hair.

D

database A computer file containing the DNA profiles of convicted offenders, evidence from unsolved cases, or missing persons or their relatives.

Daubert standard A broad set of criteria laid out by the U.S. Supreme Court opinion in the *Daubert* case for the admissibility of scientific evidence, with the judge as the "gatekeeper" responsible for applying those criteria.

defacing Attempting to render a serial number unreadable.

delusterant An opaque pigment (usually white) that is added to man-made fibers to reduce their shininess.

dependence When an individual becomes so strongly attached to a drug that the individual either becomes physically sick or mentally disoriented when its use is discontinued.

deposit Material that is laid down or left behind by a physical process.

depth of field A photographic term describing the distance behind and in front of the subject that is in focus; inversely related to lens opening.

detonate Causing an explosive material to release energy in the form of an explosion.

development (enhancement, visualization) Physical or chemical treatment or special illumination, or a combination of both, that enhance the visibility of ridge detail of a latent fingerprint impression sufficiently to enable comparison.

differential extraction A process by which an analyst can separately isolate male and female DNA from a mixture of female epithelial cells and male sperm cells, such as might be found in sexual assault evidence.

diffuse reflectance infrared Fourier transform spectroscopy (DRIFTS) An infrared sampling technique where the sample is ground to a fine powder and mixed with a nonabsorbing powder and the spectrum is obtained by collecting IR radiation that is diffused by the mixture.

diluents Materials that are added to a drug to add bulk and thereby make it easier to handle.

direct physical match A jigsaw fit match of pieces of a randomly fractured solid object that shows the pieces were originally part of the same item.

disguise To give a new appearance in order to hide its true form.

disputed parentage Refers in law and forensic science to a case where there is a question as to whether a person is the true biological father (or mother) of a particular child.

DNA polymerases Enzymes that can catalyze the synthesis of double-stranded DNA from another primed strand.

documentation Creation of a detailed, complete record of a crime scene, including notes, sketches, photographs, and possibly audio- or videotape.

driving while impaired Operating a motor vehicle while one's judgment or physical capabilities are reduced by alcohol or drugs.

drug A drug is a substance that produces a physiological or psychological affect that is significant, occurs within a reasonable time after dosing and results from an easily ingested dose.

drug-facilitated sexual assault A sexual encounter where one party, the victim, has been rendered unable to resist or voluntarily participate by ingestion of a drug, often in combination with alcohol.

drug-facilitated sexual assault Sexual assault perpetrated on a victim who cannot consent because of mental impairment by a drug or drugs.

duty to preserve An obligation imposed by courts on law enforcement agencies and personnel to preserve certain audio and video recordings for a specified length of time.

dye A deeply colored material that dissolves in a solution or an object to give it a desired color.

dye stains Chemicals that stain cyanoacrylate polymer and can thus be used to further enhance the visibility of Super Glue–developed latent prints; some of the chemicals require the use of alternate light or laser illumination.

E

electromagnetic spectrum The full range of electromagnetic radiation, from low-energy microwaves (transmission of telephone calls) to high-energy gamma rays, including the visible portion to which our eyes are sensitive and X-rays used by doctors to visualize our bones.

elimination fingerprints A ten-print set of inked (or live-scanned) fingerprints from everyone who enters the secure crime scene area.

entomology The branch of zoology that deals with insects.

enzyme A protein that can speed up a chemical reaction without being consumed by it; an enzyme is a protein catalyst.

ESDA Electrostatic Detection Apparatus; an instrument developed in England specifically for making indented writing visible on a clear cover sheet without altering the original document.

etching The use of strongly acidic or basic chemicals to dissolve away metal in a controlled manner.

evidence collection and preservation The actual seizing and packaging of physical evidence items for submission to a forensic science laboratory in a manner that ensures integrity of the evidence, and/or documenting scene patterns that cannot be physically collected.

evidence collection techniques Methods used to collect evidence when the intact item or item containing the evidence cannot be seized; usually includes using forceps or tape lifts at scenes; shaking, scraping, and vacuuming may be done in the laboratory or as last resorts.

evidence recognition Determination of which physical evidence items and/or patterns are relevant to the case as opposed to being part of the scene background.

exclusion A conclusion that a known and a questioned specimen do not match and could not have had a common origin.

exclusion A demonstration that two objects do not have a connection, relationship, or association.

exclusionary value When physical evidence is of a type that cannot be individualized, but only associated, it may have significant value by excluding the possibility of a common source, and exclusion is an absolute conclusion.

exothermic Giving off heat, usually applied to a chemical reaction.

expert witness An individual who by training, knowledge, or experience is a specialist in a subject and therefore is qualified to give opinion testimony in legal settings.

explosive A chemical material that undergoes a very rapid chemical reaction on being heated, struck, or otherwise energized with production of large volumes of gas.

explosive residues Materials that can be found on debris from an explosive incident that may contain trace amounts of the unchanged explosive or chemical reaction products produced by the explosive reaction.

explosive train The combination of components that are put together to form an explosive device.

extortion note A communication usually demanding some form of payment to the writer to prevent his/her carrying out a threat.

F

fire point The temperature at which a fuel in the presence of air will ignite without an external source of ignition.

firearm A device for accelerating a projectile to a high speed and sending it toward a selected target.

firearms comparison microscope Two reflected-light microscopes linked with an optical bridge used for comparison of objects using reflected light.

firing pin The pin or rod in the firing mechanism of a firearm that strikes the cartridge primer to fire the cartridge.

firing pin impression The impression left by the firing pin on the primer cup portion of a cartridge after it has been struck (fired).

first responder The first police officer or investigator to arrive at and witness a crime scene, often a uniformed patrol officer.

flaming combustion When oxygen and fuel are both in the gaseous state, the combustion reaction is rapid, producing light as well as heat (flame) at a high rate.

flammable range The range of concentrations of a fuel in air that will support combustion.

flash point The temperature at which a fuel in the presence of oxygen in air has sufficient material in the gaseous phase to be ignited by a small flame or other source of ignition.

float glass process The most common modern manufacturing process for making flat glass by floating the molten glass on a pool of tin while it cools.

forensic Having to do with the law.

forensic biology Today, refers to the preliminary examination of biological evidence in blood transfer and sexual assault cases, much of which will go on to be analyzed for DNA; also sometimes used to refer to subdisciplines like forensic botany.

forensic science Science applied to legal problems.

forensic serology Refers to the preliminary examination and genetic typing of biological evidence in blood transfer and sexual assault cases before DNA analysis was available.

forensics The art of argumentative discourse, debate.

forgery To make an illegal copy of something in order to deceive.

fountain pen A pen where the point (nib) is supplied with liquid ink from a refillable container inside the pen.

friction ridge skin The skin on the fingertips, palms of hands, and soles of feet, characterized by patterns of hills and valleys.

Frye rule The basic standard enunciated by the U.S. Supreme Court in 1929 for admissibility of new scientific or technical evidence, which placed emphasis on general acceptance in the appropriate scientific community.

f-stop/lens opening A selectable parameter on a camera that defines the amount of light entering the lens.

functionality The ability of a firearm to fire a projectile when the trigger is pulled.

G

gas chromatography A chromatographic technique where the mixture to be separated is vaporized and the separation occurs during partition between the gas and a solid or liquid absorbent.

genetic code The correspondence between the sequence of bases in DNA, taken three at a time, and the amino acids that make up the proteins.

genetic markers Refers to blood groups, isoenzymes, and other substances used to help establish partial individuality (narrow the size of the included group) before DNA typing was available.

glowing combustion When oxygen is in the gaseous state but the fuel is not, the combustion reaction is slowed, producing heat but little light.

grammar The rules concerning how words are used, change their form, and combine with other words to make sentences.

grooves The spiraling depressed areas inside the barrel of a handgun or rifle.

gunshot residue (GSR) Materials created by the firing of a firearm that are dispersed by the force of the expanding gases.

H

hallucinogens Drugs taken to cause a significantly altered mental state, often including hallucinations.

handguns Firearms, usually a foot or less in length, designed to be held in one or both hands when fired.

handprinting Noncursive writing where letters are individually formed and normally not connected.

heated headspace A technique for processing debris from a suspicious fire in which the debris is warmed in a closed container and then a sample of the vapors above the debris is removed for analysis.

high-velocity blood pattern A pattern caused by blood spattering in all possible directions from extreme force, such as might happen with a gunshot or explosion; many of the droplet stains are very small (aerosol spray size) and often more numerous than in a medium-velocity pattern.

HPLC High-performance liquid chromatography; a separation technique using high pressure to force a solvent through a tube packed with an absorbent.

hypothesis An as yet unproven attempt to develop an explanation for an observation or series of related observations.

I

ignitable liquids Liquid materials that can be ignited in the presence of air.

illicit Proscribed by law (illegal).

immunological tests Tests based on the use of specific antibodies to demonstrate the species or nature of a biological specimen.

impressions Negative imprints or indentations of an object.

imprint A mark (pattern) that is essentially two-dimensional left by an object on a hard receiving surface through contact with another object; an imprint has very little depth.

inconclusive A conclusion by an examiner that a comparison of known and questioned specimens permits neither an identification nor an exclusion.

indentation A three-dimensional mark (pattern) left in a deformable object through contact with another object.

indented marks Marks left in a surface by pushing a tool into the surface.

indented writing When writing on the top sheet of a stack or pad, impressions of that writing are impressed into the sheets below.

indirect physical match A secondary physical match between soft, pliable objects, such as torn fabric, between pieces of a randomly fractured object with some pieces missing, or between cross sections of a broken wooden object.

individual characteristics Accidental (unintentional) characteristics resulting from wear or random markings on items during manufacture; a sufficient number of matching individual characteristics between a known and questioned specimen can permit an examiner to make an individualization.

individualization Demonstration that an object is unique, even among members of the same class, or that two separate objects were at one time a single object (had a common source or origin).

individualization patterns Pattern evidence that can potentially uniquely associate the pattern with the item or author responsible for it; fingerprints, handwriting, bullet striations, and footwear and tire impressions are examples.

infrared spectroscopy The use of the measurement of the absorption of infrared radiation by a substance to characterize that substance.

ink compositions The mixtures of solvent and dyes or pigments that make up the ink.

ink eradicator A fluid used to decolorize ink on a document to make it invisible.

insufficient detail for comparison A conclusion by an examiner that a questioned specimen lacks enough class and/or individual characteristics to do a proper comparison with knowns.

iodine fuming A latent print development technique in which solid iodine is sublimed to iodine vapor, which can then deposit on the ridge patterns of a latent print impression, especially on porous surfaces.

K

keratin Fibrous, tough, and insoluble protein that forms the hard but nonmineralized structures such as hair, fingernails, and toenails.

known control A specimen from a known source; it could be known blood, known human blood, known animal blood, or known blood from a particular person; for DNA, it could be a buccal (cheek) swabbing from a known person.

L

land impressions The depressed helical grooves in a bullet left by the lands inside the barrel from which it was fired.

lands The spiraling raised areas between the grooves inside the barrel of a handgun or rifle.

laser A special light source that emits light that is of a single wavelength (monochromatic light) and, further, vibrates in a single plane; extremely efficient at exciting chemicals that absorb its wavelength, and can then fluoresce or phosphoresce as the molecules relax.

latent print A fingerprint impression that requires development or special illumination to reveal the ridge detail in sufficient detail for comparison.

layer structure Where multiple layers of paint have been applied, a paint chip will show the number, color, and thickness of the layers.

lens An optical component of a camera that focuses light onto the recording medium (film or digital recorder); "standard" lenses with a 50 mm focal length provide a "normal eyeball" view of the subject, "wide angle" lenses provide more peripheral views, and "telephoto" lenses provide closer but narrower views.

level I , level II, and level III detail Terms used to describe the overall fingerprint pattern, such as loop, whorl, arch (level I), the minutiae (level II), and pore numbers, locations and relationships, and the shape and size of ridge features (level III).

licit Not prohibited by law.

light box A box with a very even light source behind a piece of ground or translucent glass or plastic, which is used to backlight an object.

linkage A connection, relationship, or association between objects and/or persons.

Locard Exchange Principle States that when two objects come into contact, there is a mutual exchange of material between the objects across the contact boundary.

low explosives Materials that will burn rapidly, but not detonate, unless contained.

low-velocity blood pattern A pattern caused by blood falling onto a surface, influenced only by the force of gravity.

M

magazine The container for the cartridges in most semiautomatic firearms.

magnetic brush technique A variant of powder dusting that uses a magnet and magnetic particles instead of a brush and powder.

mass spectroscopy A technique for identification of materials by bombarding them, while in the gas phase, with a high-energy species (usually electrons) and causing them to fragment into ions whose mass is determined by a mass sorting device

materials evidence Physical evidence, either trace or transfer, that is usually chemically or microscopically analyzed and used to make connections.

mechanical dislocation The scraping or shaking of an item of physical evidence over a clean surface to dislodge any trace evidence clinging to the surface.

medical examiner A medical doctor, usually a forensic pathologist, whose responsibility is to determine the cause and manner of suspicious or unattended deaths.

medicolegal A reference to forensic or legal medicine; in the past, the term could encompass many activities that would be called "criminalistics" today.

medium-velocity blood pattern A pattern caused by blood spattering in all possible directions from moderate force; many of the droplet stains are smaller than low-velocity pattern droplets and more numerous.

medulla A canal that runs up the center of the cortex of a hair and is usually air filled in forensic samples.

melanin A natural brown pigment that gives most hair its color.

microsatellite A synonym for STR.

minisatellite Refers to a VNTR region of DNA in which the repeat units are 30 to 50 bases long; the RFLP technique was used to type "minisatellite" regions of DNA.

minutiae Features of the friction ridge skin pattern on fingertips that make the overall pattern individual; ending ridges, bifurcations, and dots are the primary minutiae.

mitochondria (sing., mitochondrion) Structures that contain a small amount of DNA and are found in the cell, outside the nucleus, responsible for making energy for the cell.

mitochondrial DNA (mtDNA) The DNA contained in the mitochondria of the cell; inherited only from an individual's mother and passed along a maternal line from generation to generation.

mitosis Cell division, in which a single cell replicates its DNA, then divides allocating to each daughter cell a complete complement of the original DNA.

modus operandi (MO) The habits of a criminal; actions a criminal repeats in different crimes that may help investigators recognize that the same person was responsible.

N

narcotic A drug found as a natural constituent of the opium poppy or a derivative thereof.

natural fibers A fibrous material composed of a material found in nature either in plants or animals.

natural law A generally accepted explanation of a phenomenon or a series of phenomena so thoroughly tested that it is regarded as highly reliable.

NIBIN The national database primarily of images of cartridge cases used to try to associate evidence cases with test-fired cases from seized weapons or cases collected from shooting incidents where the gun involved is not known.

ninhydrin A chemical for latent print impression enhancement especially on porous surfaces; postninhydrin treatments can further increase the value of this method.

normal variation That variation in writing characteristics seen by examination of numerous examples of an individual's writing.

notes Written or audiotaped records for documenting a crime scene that contain information such as initial conditions, names and contact information for witnesses, license plate numbers of vehicles in the vicinity, and that may be constructed to include scene security logs, photo logs, and evidence logs.

nuclear/genomic DNA The DNA found in the chromosomes in the nucleus of the cell; the terms "nuclear DNA" and "genomic DNA" are synonymous.

nucleotide A molecule that is made up of a nitrogenous base (A, T, C, or G), a ribose sugar component, and phosphate; the building blocks of nucleic acids (DNA and RNA).

nucleus A membrane-enclosed structure within a cell that contains the chromosomes, and therefore, the nuclear DNA.

O

oblique lighting Using a bright light at a very low angle (grazing angle) to a document to make indentations on the sheet more visible by shadowing them.

odontology The study of the physiology, anatomy, and pathology of teeth.

optical properties The way a material interacts with light, such as refractive index and dispersion.

P

p30 A protein found in high concentrations in human semen and used as the basis for a specific semen identification test; also known as PA.

PA Short for "prostatic antigen"; a protein found in high concentrations in human semen and used as the basis for a specific semen identification test; also known as p30.

paint smears A very thin film of paint transferred to another surface as the result of glancing contact.

particle size distribution A quantitative estimation of the percentages of particles that fall into defined size ranges in a soil sample.

pathology The medical specialty that deals with disease and the bodily changes caused by disease.

peroxidases Enzymes that catalyze the oxidation of a dye to form a new compound that is a different color.

physical anthropology The study of human evolution, as revealed by the skeleton or by evolutionary patterns in DNA.

physical developer A special silver-based solution for enhancing latent print impressions by reacting with the fatty (lipid) components; a chemical method.

physical matches Matches between or among pieces of a randomly fractured, torn, or cut objects that might show that the pieces were originally part of the same item.

physiological Relating to or arising from the functioning of living organism.

pigment A very finely divided, highly colored material that does not dissolve, but rather is suspended in a solution or dispersed through an object to give it a desired color.

plasma When treated with anticoagulant, the straw-colored liquid portion of blood after the cells have settled.

plastic (impression) print A three-dimensional fingerprint indentation in a soft receiving surface, such as tar, margarine, or Silly Putty.

platen A perforated plate used to firmly hold an object using air pressure.

plea bargaining A negotiation between a defendant and his attorney on one side, and the prosecutor on the other, in which the defendant agrees to plead "guilty" or "no contest" to some crime, in return for reduction of the severity of the charges or a lighter sentence recommendation.

point of origin The location or locations where a fire started.

polymerase chain reaction (PCR) A process used to make many copies of a defined segment of DNA, using a special kind of DNA polymerase that is stable to high temperatures; PCR is now one of the steps in all forensic DNA analysis.

positive identification In the pattern evidence context and fields, identification means individualization; "making the identification" means the examiner is concluding the known and the questioned items had a common origin.

postmortem Occurring after death.

powder dusting An old but tried-and-true method for visualizing fingerprints on nonporous surfaces.

powder pattern A pattern found on an object close to the barrel of a fired weapon caused by small particles of lead, or partially burned gunpowder and carbon smoke that follow the projectile out of the barrel.

preliminary test A nondefinitive screening test used to give an indication that something might be present (like blood, or a body fluid); positive results indicate the need for further tests.

primary high explosives Explosive material that is caused to explode fairly readily by physical shock, electrical spark, or other disturbances.

primer A small, single-stranded piece of DNA whose sequence is complementary to the sequence in a long strand of DNA that is to be copied by a DNA polymerase.

primer The shock-sensitive portion of the cartridge that provides the initial spark or flame that causes the cartridge to fire.

probable cause Sufficient reason based on known facts to believe a crime has been committed or that certain property is connected with a crime.

projectile (bullet) An object that can be fired or launched.

psychiatry The branch of medicine concerning the diagnosis, treatment, and prevention of mental illness.

psychological Relating to or arising from the mind or emotions.

psychology The scientific study of the mind and behavior of humans.

purification The physical or chemical process whereby a substance is separated from other accompanying substances or impurities to obtain the pure chemical substance.

pyrolysis The process whereby a material with little vapor pressure is broken down by heat, usually in the absence of oxygen, to produce flammable products with significant vapor pressure.

pyrolysis gas chromatography A separation technique where a nonvolatile material can be chromatographed by flash heating it in an inert atmosphere to break it into more volatile decomposition products.

Q

questioned document Any means of communication that is suspect, entirely or in part, as to authenticity or origin.

questioned specimen A piece of potential evidentiary material that will be examined and may be compared to a control specimen.

R

radial fracture lines Fracture lines in glass that appear to radiate outward from the center of the point of force.

rave A dance party, usually lasting all night, that tends to be characterized by stroboscopic light effects, loud music, and high human density and attended ordinarily by youthful participants.

recognition To know something because one has seen, heard, or experienced it before.

reconstruction Formulation of a "best theory" of a set of events in a case based on consideration of all the available evidence and information.

reconstruction The process of putting together the evidence available with the objective of understanding the nature and sequence of events that created it.

reconstruction patterns Pattern evidence that is principally useful to help reconstruct past events; blood spatter, glass fractures, fire burn, and track and trail patterns are examples.

reenactment A hypothetical rendition of a set of events at a crime scene partially based on a reconstruction theory, but with all the "blanks" filled in to make a smooth, continuous story.

refractive index (RI) The refractive index of a substance is the ratio of the speed at which light passes through a vacuum to the speed that light passes through the substance.

regenerated fibers Fibers made by dissolving cellulose-based material and forcing it through fine holes into a solution that causes it to immediately solidify, thereby transforming a natural vegetable material into a man-made fiber.

requested writings Writing samples obtained from an individual either voluntarily or as the result of a court order.

restriction fragment length polymorphism (RFLP) The original kind of DNA typing used in forensic science, now obsolete in forensic work.

revolvers Handguns that have rotating cylindrical cartridge holders that usually hold five to nine cartridges and allow the weapon to fire semiautomatically until the cartridges are expended.

rifle A firearm, usually two or more feet in length, designed to be fired from a shoulder-held position.

rifling The helical grooves cut or impressed into the barrel of a handgun or rifle to cause the exiting projective to spin.

S

safety A component of most firearms that prevents it from firing without the trigger being pulled or that locks the trigger so it cannot be pulled, or to prevent firing even if the trigger is pulled.

SANEs Sexual assault nurse examiner.

SART Sexual assault response team.

scanning electron microscope (SEM) A microscope that uses high-energy electrons rather than light for image formation and is capable of very high magnification.

scene search A detailed, systematic search of a crime scene with the objective of noting every condition and every relevant item of physical evidence.

scene survey A preliminary walk-through and look at the overall scene to try to establish the type of scene, note any transient physical evidence, and get a first impression of the relevant physical evidence.

scientific method The multistep method by which scientists approach problems, formulate them for experimental inquiry, and validate their conclusions.

secondary high explosive Explosive material that can be safely handled but will explode violently when subjected to an electrical spark or small flame.

SEM/EDX   A SEM that is equipped with an energy-dispersive X-ray spectrometer, which allows elemental analysis of individual objects seen in the SEM.

semen   The male reproductive fluid, ejaculated through the penis at male orgasm, and consisting of sperm cells suspended in seminal plasma.

semiautomatic   A firearm that fires a projectile each time the trigger is pulled until out of ammunition.

seminal plasma   The fluid in which sperm are suspended in whole semen; consists of fluids contributed primarily by the prostate but also by the Cowper's glands.

sequence   Forms the basis for genetic information; specifies the structure of all the proteins that are made from the DNA template and is the basis of individuality.

serial number restoration   The attempt to recover a serial number that has been rendered unreadable.

serum   The straw-colored liquid portion of blood remaining after whole blood has been allowed to clot.

sexual assault evidence collection kits   Usually packages or boxes, containing numerous containers, tools, and labels, for the collection of clothing and other evidence, including evidence from the body, of sexual assault complainants; designed to allow for proper packaging, labeling, and preservation of sexual assault evidence.

shape and form   Refers to the ability of the human mind to recognize individual characteristics in complex shapes or forms, such as a human face; handwriting and morphological hair comparisons are examples.

shock wave   A region of sufficiently high pressure traveling through a gas at a high velocity that it can cause physical damage to objects it encounters.

short tandem repeat (STR)   A VNTR where the repeat unit is short, from two to six bases in length; all the regions used for forensic STR DNA typing have four or five base repeats.

shotgun   A long gun that usually fires a large number of small metal pellets at one time, which is designed to be used for hunting birds and small animals.

shotgun shells   Ammunition that serves the same purpose for a shotgun as a cartridge in a handgun or rifle.

sketches   Drawings of scenes with measurements or to scale, depicting the correct spatial relationships between scene fixed points and evidence items.

skill level   The level of fine motor control displayed in an individual's writing.

slug   A single projectile used in a shotgun shell instead of pellets, analogous to the bullet in the handgun or rifle cartridge.

small particle reagent (SPR)   A formulation of small inorganic particles in special suspension that can be applied to latent print impressions to enhance the visibility of ridge pattern features; can be useful with weathered latents, especially those that have been exposed to moisture.

smokeless powder   A nitrocellulose-based explosive or propellant that produces little smoke.

sniffers   Mechanical devices that detect gases in the atmosphere other than the normal nitrogen and oxygen and that are used to look for traces of flammable liquid after a fire has been extinguished.

soda lime glass   The most common type of glass including window glass and bottle glass that has as its major ingredients sand, soda (sodium carbonate), and lime (calcium oxide).

species of origin   The species from which an item of biological evidence originated, such as human, horse, cat, cow, etc.

spectral comparator   An instrument that has a number of light sources, filters, and a video camera used to examine documents in a way that greatly increases what one can "see" on that document over what our eyes can ordinarily observe.

spectroscopy   The interaction of electromagnetic radiation with a chemical to give a pattern characteristic of that material's interaction with the radiation.

sperm   Short for spermatozoon (*pl.* spermatozoa); the male reproductive cell produced in the testes and stored in the seminal vesicles until ejaculated.

steam distillation   A technique for processing debris from a suspicious fire where the debris is mixed with water in a large flask and the mixture heated until a sizable portion of the water has boiled and been condensed; the condensate is examined for accelerant.

stimulants   Drugs taken to produce feelings of high energy and to suppress the desire to sleep.

striated marks   Marks left in a surface by the sliding of a tool across that surface.

striation   A number of parallel or nearly parallel lines or scratches on a surface inscribed by another object passing over that surface.

substratum comparison specimen   A sample of the material or surface on which biological evidence is deposited.

suitability for comparison   A latent print impression that has sufficient ridge detail for an examiner to determine it to be suitable for comparison with known print impressions.

Super Glue (cyanoacrylate)   An adhesive material that polymerizes (the chemicals in it react to form a solid matrix) in place when applied to surfaces; Super Glue vapors, produced by heating it, interact with latent fingerprint residue and produce the solid matrix polymer on the ridges.

surface coating (sizing)   Material placed on the surface of paper to smooth the roughness of the interwoven fibers.

synthetic fibers   A fibrous material composed of material that does not occur in nature, but rather is man-made.

T

tandemly repeated sequence   A sequence of bases in DNA that is repeated in a head-to-tail fashion several to many times.

tangential fracture lines   Fracture lines in glass that appear to encircle, or form a polyhedron, around the point of force.

tape lift   The use of clear sticky tape to remove trace evidence from the surface of a piece of physical evidence.

telogen phase   The third growth phase of the hair follicle, which is a resting period.

theory   A plausible explanation of a phenomenon or a series of phenomena that has gained some general acceptance; a well-tested hypothesis.

threatening letter   A communication usually threatening to harm an individual or individuals if some demand is not met.

TLC   Thin-layer chromatography; a separation technique using a plate with a thin layer of an absorbent and capillary action to move a solvent up the plate.

toolmark   A marking on a surface caused by the pressing or sliding of a tool into or across the surface.

toxicology   The medical study of the chemistry, effects, and treatment of poisonous substances and drug action and detection in the body.

trace evidence   Physical evidence, potentially small in size, that is usually used to make connections between suspect and victim, suspect or victim and crime scene, or suspect or victim and an instrumentality.

trajectory   The flight path from muzzle to target of a projectile fired by a firearm.

trajectory   The path that a projectile takes after it leaves the barrel until it hits an object or falls to the ground.

transcription   The process by which messenger RNA (mRNA) is synthesized from DNA while preserving the base sequence information.

transfer evidence Physical evidence that is transferred between objects as the result of contact.

transfer medium The material that records markings (handwriting or mechanical printing) on a receiving surface.

translation The process by which a messenger RNA (mRNA) template is used by the cell to assemble proteins based on the genetic code.

trier of fact The person or persons charged with critically evaluating the facts as presented in a legal case. The judge or the jury.

trigger pull The amount of force needed to pull (depress) the trigger sufficiently for the firearm to fire.

TWG and SWG Working groups made up of highly experienced individuals with technical or scientific expertise in a particular subject, who meet to develop standard procedures to be used in their area of expertise.

twist The direction in which the lands and grooves spiral down the inside of a handgun or rifle barrel.

typewriter A machine with keys that are pressed to produce letters and numbers on paper.

U

under the influence Acting while significant quantities of a drug are in an individual's system.

V

variable number of tandem repeat (VNTR) Different individuals have different numbers of repeat units at many of the locations in DNA that feature tandemly repeated sequences; those different numbers of repeat units are "VNTR".

videography The use of a video recording device, in this context, to document a crime scene.

visible (patent) print A fingerprint impression that is visible with no enhancement or any special illumination.

visible spectrometers Devices for examining a sample and determining its ability to absorb or reflect electromagnetic radiation in the visible portion of the spectrum.

W

watermark A mark that is made on some types of paper during its production that can be seen only if it is back-lighted.

working hypothesis An initial theory about what may have happened in a case based on observation of the crime scene; properly formulated, can generate predictions about physical evidence that are testable during the investigation, laboratory, and medicolegal stages of analysis.

wound ballistics A subset of forensic pathology that examines the wounds and wound patterns made by various projectiles.

writing instrument An item used by individuals to mark handwriting motions or mechanical printing on to a surface to prepare a more permanent record.

writing mechanics The way an individual writes, particularly letter shapes and connections.

All images are courtesy of the authors unless otherwise noted below.

Page vii second from top: Vicki Cronis/AP/Wide World Photos; middle: Christopher J. Morris/Corbis; page vii fourth from top: Paul Kizzle/AP/Wide World Photos; page viii bottom: Vicki Cronis/AP/Wide World Photos; page ix: Christopher J. Morris/Corbis; page xi: Bebeto Matthews/AP/Wide World Photos; page 4 left: Bob Lucky, Jr./AP/Wide World Photos; page 13 right: Agence Roger-Viollet/The Image Works; page 24 top left: Agilent; page 26: Richard Megna/ Fundamental Photos; page 30: Vicki Cronis/AP/Wide World Photos; page 32: The New York Daily News; page 53: J. Scott Applewhite/ AP/Wide World Photos; page 58: Christopher J. Morris/Corbis; page 60: Reprinted with permission, copyright The Lakeville Journal Company, LLC, 2006. Photo by Robert Estabrook; page 84: Paul Kizzle/AP/Wide World Photos; page 86: William Ing; page 124: Anne Cusack/AP/Wide World Photos; page 137: Courtesy of Sirchie Finger Print Laboratories, Inc.; page 152: Bettmann/Corbis; page 164: DCA Productions/Taxi/Getty Images; page 176: Al Francekevich/Corbis; page 178: Bettmann/Corbis; page 194 top right and page 195 top: Mikael Karlsson/Arresting Images; page 210: Elise Amendola/AP/ Wide World Photos; page 212: AP/Wide World Photos; page 215 all: Carolina Biological Supply Company/Phototake; page 216: Courtesy, Becton Dickinson & Company; page 230: Courtesy, TriTech; page 232 left: Merja Ojala/AFP/Getty Images; page 232 right: Fabian Bimmer/ AP/Wide World Photos; page 240: Bodell Communications, Inc./ Phototake; page 272: Bebeto Matthews/AP/Wide World Photos; page 274: Seanna O'Sullivan/Corbis Sygma; page 278: Kevin Summers/ Photographer's Choice/Getty Images; page 282: Bettmann/CORBIS; page 285: Elise Amendola/AP/Wide World Photos; page 295 bottom: Eric Draper/AP/Wide World Photos; page 310: SuperStock, Inc./SuperStock; page 334: Courtesy of PerkinElmer Life Analytical Sciences, Shelton, CT 06484; page 338: Greg Wahl-Stephens/AP/ Wide World Photos; page 340: Charles Rex Arbogast/AP/Wide World Photos; page 347: Courtesy of PerkinElmer Life Analytical Sciences, Shelton, CT 06484; page 348: Visuals Unlimited/Corbis; page 352: Ciarin Griffin/Stockbyte Platinum/Getty Images; page 389: Courtesy of Carl Zeiss Microimaging, Inc.; page 389: BSIP/Phototake; page 391: Jean Claude Revy - ISM/Phototake.

Note: Definitions of terms appear on pages indicated by bold type. Figures or tables are indicated by italic type.